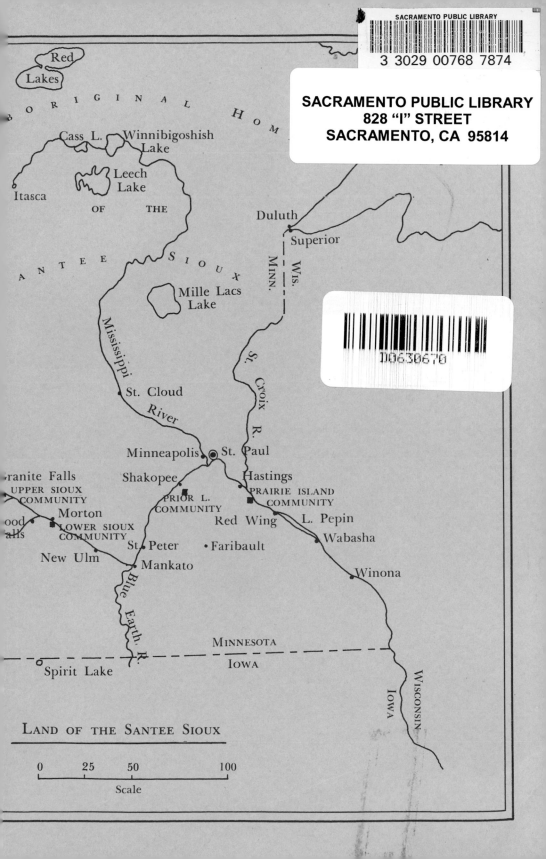

Red
Lakes

B O R I G I N A L   H O M

Cass L.   Winnibigoshish
Lake

Leech
Lake

Itasca

OF   THE

Duluth

Superior

A N T E E   S I O U X

MINN.   WIS.

Mille Lacs
Lake

Mississippi

St. Croix R.

St. Cloud

River

Minneapolis   St. Paul

ranite Falls   Shakopee   Hastings
UPPER SIOUX   PRAIRIE ISLAND
COMMUNITY   COMMUNITY
                   PRIOR L.
ood   Morton   COMMUNITY
alls   LOWER SIOUX   Red Wing   L. Pepin
          COMMUNITY
          St. Peter   • Faribault   Wabasha
New Ulm   Mankato

Blue Earth R.   Winona

MINNESOTA

IOWA

Spirit Lake

IOWA   WISCONSIN

LAND OF THE SANTEE SIOUX

0   25   50   100

Scale

HISTORY OF THE
SANTEE SIOUX

History of the
Santee Sioux

United States Indian Policy on Trial

by

ROY W. MEYER

UNIVERSITY OF NEBRASKA PRESS · LINCOLN

Publishers on the Plains

UNP

Manufactured in the United States of America

To Betty

Preface

WHEN WHITE Americans began penetrating the homeland of the Sioux Indians, they found those people divided into seven subtribes. Along the Mississippi and the lower Minnesota rivers were the villages of the Mdewakantons; inland, hunting mainly along the upper Cannon River, the Blue Earth, and west to the Des Moines, were the Wahpekutes; on both sides of the Minnesota and in the vicinity of the lakes that today separate Minnesota and South Dakota were the Sissetons and Wahpetons; between there and the Missouri roamed the Yanktons and Yanktonais, who spoke a dialect slightly different from that of the four eastern subtribes; and west of the Missouri were the Tetons, accounting for more than half the Sioux population and divided into seven bands, some of them large enough to be considered subtribes. To the Yanktons and Yanktonais, the people living east of them were the Issati, or Santees.

Until the middle of the nineteenth century, most white contacts were with the Santees, and especially with the Mdewakantons, whose permanent villages along the great rivers became well known to travelers visiting the upper Mississippi region. It was these people who fought the whites in the great Sioux Uprising of 1862. Hence it is not surprising that the literature about the Santee Sioux is voluminous for the period up to the 1860's. After the uprising, however, and the expulsion of the Santee Sioux from Minnesota, the attention of historians was diverted to the more spectacular Teton Sioux—the Oglalas, the Hunkpapas, the Brulés, and the rest, with their leaders Crazy Horse, Sitting Bull, Red Cloud, Gall, and Spotted Tail. Thus we have the excellent books of George E. Hyde, Robert Utley's *The Last Days of the Sioux Nation*, Royal B. Hassrick's *The Sioux: Life and Customs of a Warrior Society*, James C. Olson's *Red Cloud and the Sioux Problem*, and a wealth of other writings.

Contrary to what this shift in historical emphasis might suggest, the Santee Sioux did not disappear after 1862. They merely exchanged their old homes in Minnesota for new and less satisfactory ones beyond the western boundaries of that state, and there they endured the dreary

vii

monotony of reservation life for the rest of the nineteenth century and on into the twentieth. Although their history after 1862 contains less drama and excitement than the earlier period, when painters, authors, and just plain tourists sought the upper Mississippi and recorded what they found, it does not deserve the oblivion into which it has been allowed to fall. If for no other reason, it is a story that needs to be told for the light it can shed on our Indian policy in the past century. The Santees were in some respects quite different from their brethren on the Great Plains, and at the time of their expulsion from Minnesota they had traveled much farther on the road toward acculturation than had those western Sioux when the latter were first induced to gather near agencies in 1869. The story of the Santees during the last thirty years of the nineteenth century therefore contrasts sharply with that of the Tetons in the same period.

The first six chapters of this book deal with the Santee Sioux as subtribes, or bands, with emphasis on the Mdewakantons, since the information on them is relatively more copious than on the other three. From 1863 on, however, the reservation rather than the tribal division became the functional unit in relations between the United States government and the Santees, and so they are discussed reservation by reservation. Those of the Mdewakantons and Wahpekutes—the lower Sioux—who surrendered or were captured wound up on the Santee Reservation in Nebraska, from which a few courageous souls later fled, some to the valley of the Big Sioux River near Flandreau, South Dakota, others to their old homes in Minnesota. The Sissetons and Wahpetons, known as the upper Sioux, were placed on the Sisseton Reservation in northeastern South Dakota and on the Devils Lake Reservation in North Dakota. A few Sioux remained in Minnesota and became the nucleus of the colonies that formed as people from the Santee Reservation returned.

Not all the Santee Sioux who fled Minnesota in 1862 are accounted for in the foregoing list of reservations and settlements, however. Some joined the western Sioux and were absorbed by them; others settled on what became the Fort Peck Reservation in Montana and ultimately disappeared into the population of Tetons, Yanktons, and Assiniboins; still others crossed the Canadian border and never returned, their descendants today remaining on small reserves in Manitoba and Saskatchewan. None of these groups were numerous, and none receive more than passing mention in this book. A more numerous body to which this book gives only casual treatment consists of those Santees who have left their reservations in comparatively recent years and found homes in towns and cities, either as members of expatriate Indian colonies or as a nearly indistinguishable part of the general population. Although studies of such migrated Indians are extremely valuable, it would be difficult and not very helpful to segregate the Sioux from other Indians who have taken the great plunge. Consequently, their history, in so far as it can be said to have any independent existence, is left to other investigators.

Two points need to be made, lest this book be accused of failing to do certain things which it does not attempt to do. In the first place, it is history, not ethnology. Although some treatment of a group's culture cannot be avoided when the group written about is culturally different from that of the author and the reader, such ventures outside the proper realm of the historian are distinctly subordinated here. The observations and opinions of early white visitors to the Santee Sioux are cited where they seem appropriate, but no attempt at culture reconstruction or sociological analysis of the present culture of the Santee Sioux is made.

This leads to a second point. Despite the obvious advantages of a book about Indians written from the "inside," this one is quite frankly written from the "outside." History is based largely on written records, and most of the records from which the history of the Santee Sioux must be reconstructed were kept by white men. The chief sources used in the preparation of this book were government documents, both published and manuscript; contemporary newspapers; books and articles, both primary and secondary; and the private papers of missionaries and others who worked with the Indians. Interviews have been of value in straightening out some perplexing details in the recent history of the Santee groups, but I have made no attempt to "correct" the received version of events in the nineteenth century by recourse to oral traditions as expressed by present-day Indians.

Every book ought to be equipped with a few operating instructions to enable the reader to derive the maximum benefit from it with the least amount of effort. A few matters of terminology and spelling may call for explanation. Though it is well known by now that the Sioux are really the Dakotas, the long adherence by the government to the former name has led to its almost universal acceptance, even by the people it designates. I have therefore thought it best to use the familiar name, and to reserve "Dakota" for the language, although there are reputable books that speak of the "Sioux" language, and many anthropologists use "Dakota" exclusively for both the tribe and the language.

The spelling of familiar Dakota names usually follows the most widely used form. Thus the spellings "Wabasha" and "Shakopee" are used, though they are not particularly accurate renditions of the original pronunciation. An exception to the rule is the name of the band led by a succession of chiefs called Little Crow. In order to approximate more nearly the correct pronunciation, I have elected to spell it "Kapozha" rather than the more usual "Kaposia" or the less familiar "Kapoja." Names which are too unfamiliar to have any established spelling are given as they (or their component parts) are spelled in the Riggs grammar and dictionary, published in 1852. Following the precedent not only of such historians as George Hyde and James C. Olson, but of anthropologists like E. Adamson Hoebel, I have used the customary English plurals for the names of Indian tribes and subtribes.

Down through the years the department of government charged with the management of Indian affairs has functioned under two slightly varying names. It was originally established in 1824 as the Bureau of Indian Affairs, and that is the title it officially bears today. For most of its history, however, it was generally known as the Office of Indian Affairs. The two names are here used interchangeably. The term "Indian Service" is occasionally used, with much the same significance.

Acknowledgments are due many people for their help in the making of this book. My thanks go first to the personnel of the National Archives, especially Miss Jane F. Smith, Director of the Social and Economic Branch, Office of Civil Archives, who helped me track down several elusive items. Assistance also came from the staffs of the state historical societies of Minnesota, Nebraska, South Dakota, and North Dakota. Several county officials, particularly registers of deeds and welfare officers, have made valuable contributions. Mr. Edwin D. Bronner, Curator of the Quaker Collection at Haverford College, provided me with copies of unpublished manuscripts containing information on certain Indian agents who were members of the Society of Friends. The maps were drawn by Mr. Richard W. Piepenburg, Mankato State College geography student.

Any detectable bias in favor of the Bureau of Indian Affairs may be due to the unfailing and even enthusiastic co-operation I have received from Bureau officials, notably agency superintendents, who have given their time to answering my questions about the present condition of the various Santee groups. Miss Evelyn Robeson, Records Officer at the Bureau's Central Office in Washington, aided me in the use of current records. My thanks go also to the many members of the Indian communities, tribal council officers and others, who have provided me with another vantage point from which to view the Santee Sioux of today.

Finally, my heaviest debt is owed to the American Association for State and Local History, from which I received a grant-in-aid in 1963 for this project.

ROY W. MEYER

Contents

List of Illustrations and Maps

History of the Santee Sioux

CHAPTER 1

The European Meets the Sioux

ONE OF THE great historic confrontations between European man and the American Indian occurred in the early spring of 1660. The scene was a "rendezvous" in what is now northwestern Wisconsin or, possibly, eastern Minnesota. The principals were, on the one hand, two French explorers, Pierre Esprit Radisson and Médard Chouart, Sieur des Groseilliers; and on the other, the chiefs and braves of the Santee Sioux. Radisson and Groseilliers had arrived the previous fall at Chequamegon Bay on Lake Superior, and then traveled inland to an Indian village, probably on Lac Court Oreille, near modern Hayward, Wisconsin. After spending a miserable winter of near-starvation, surrounded by a multitude of Indians, many of whom did starve, the explorers revived somewhat with the approach of spring and better hunting.[1]

When conditions had begun to improve, the Frenchmen were visited by eight ambassadors from the Sioux, each with two wives laden with wild rice, corn, and other grains. The food, offered to the hungry party, was welcome, but, as Radisson remarks somewhat ungraciously, would have been more so "if they had brought it a month or two before" (p. 207). Anticipating the ceremonies at the Feast of the Dead a

[1] Pierre Esprit Radisson, *Voyages of Peter Esprit Radisson*, ed. by Gideon Scull (New York: Peter Smith, 1943), pp. 201–206.

short time later, these emissaries greased the visitors' feet and legs and replaced their clothing with buffalo and beaver robes; then they wept copiously and smoked the calumet with the strangers. Radisson's description of the calumet leaves no doubt that it was the catlinite pipe that became so familiar to later explorers. Of red stone, as big as a fist and as long as a hand, it had a reed five feet long and as thick as a man's thumb. Tied to it was a cluster of eagle tail feathers, painted in several colors and arranged so as to open like a fan. Feathers of ducks and other birds were also attached to it. The Frenchmen, who enjoyed the status of "demi-gods," could not resist showing their superiority to their guests. Since the Indians, at the end of the smoking ceremony, had thrown tobacco into the fire, the whites decided to dispose of some gunpowder in the same fashion, to show how much more powerful their "tobacco" was. Unfortunately, it "had more strenght [*sic*] then we thought," and the Indians scattered "without any further delay" and without looking for the door. When Radisson and Groseilliers had, with some difficulty, calmed the Indians' fears enough to resume the council, they feasted for eight days (pp. 207–209).

The meeting just described was only a prelude to the real confrontation, the Feast of the Dead, which took place a few days later at a previously arranged site. Among the eighteen nations that assembled, easily the most spectacular were the Sioux. They first sent an advance guard of thirty young men, who were followed the next day by the main body. In preparations for the distinguished company, the snow was cleared away from the area where the tipis would be erected, and boughs of trees were laid on the ground. The Indians arrived "with an incredible pomp," their feathers as prominent as jewels in an assemblage of European royalty. First came the young warriors, their faces painted several colors, their hair burned off except for a tuft, which was ornamented with "some small pearles or some Turkey [turquoise?] stones . . ." (pp. 209–211). This tuft was made to stand erect by saturating it with bear's grease mixed with reddish earth. The warriors were dressed in light deerskin robes, "stokens" (leggings) embroidered with porcupine quills, moccasins decorated with a piece of buffalo hide that trailed more than a foot and a half behind them, and white robes made of painted beaver skins. Their weapons were "swords" and knives a foot and a half long, hatchets "very ingeniously done," wooden clubs, and bows and arrows; apparently they also carried some kind of shield "uppon which weare represented all manner of figures, according to their knowledge, as of the sun and moone, of terrestriall beasts, about its feathers very artificaly painted" (pp. 211–212). After the braves came the elders, "with great gravitie and modestie," wearing buffalo robes that swept the ground. Each one carried a calumet and a medicine pouch. Unlike the young braves, their faces were not painted, but their hair was dressed in the same fashion. Behind them came the women loaded with the tipis, which they erected in less than half an hour (pp. 212–213).

At the first council the Sioux chiefs offered presents to the French, under whose protection they expressly placed themselves. They further solicited a visit from these powerful strangers, "having by their means destroyed their Ennemyes abroad & neere." So eager were the Indians to receive the French ("being wee kept them alive by our marchandises," Radisson says) that they claimed to have cut down trees, built bridges, and otherwise paved the way to their villages. The speech was concluded with a request for firearms—a thunder, as the Indians expressed it (pp. 213–214).

Allowing for the hyperbole commonly found in Indian oratory and for some exaggeration by Radisson when he recalled the episode several years later, the speech suggests at least two facts about the relationship between the Sioux and the Europeans. In the first place, the Indians were evidently already to some degree dependent on European goods, obtained presumably through intermediaries. It is clear also, despite the naive terror shown by the ambassadors at the exploding gunpowder, that they were sufficiently familiar with firearms to know their value and to wish to obtain them. The only enemies they mentioned by name, the Crees, had probably already received firearms and used them in wars against the Sioux.

Besides these diplomatic negotiations, the Feast of the Dead included much reciprocal gift-giving, at which the Frenchmen showed a sure instinct for the Indian love of ritual, and, of course, feasting, with wild rice the principal dish. To demonstrate their capability of defending the Sioux, the explorers shot off their "artillery"—twelve guns. Having got good results earlier, they repeated their stunt of throwing powder into the fire—with what effect Radisson does not say (pp. 215–217).

According to Radisson, he later made two trips, one to the Crees on a peacemaking mission, accompanied by about fifty Sioux, and another to the "nation of the beefe," or prairie Sioux, in fulfillment of a promise made at the Feast of the Dead (pp. 217–220). The first of these was probably no more effectual than many later efforts by Europeans to stop intertribal warfare, though Radisson apparently imagined that the ostentation of friendship—dances and games joined in by both tribes—meant that peace had been established. No doubt the two enemies had a good opportunity to size each other up in anticipation of the next attack by one tribe or the other. Radisson's account of the second expedition is so circumstantial, despite his claim to have lived among the prairie Sioux for six weeks, that doubt has been cast on the validity of the whole story. Nearly all of what he says about the manners and customs of these people could have been taken from the Jesuit *Relations* or obtained at second hand elsewhere.

Whatever the source of Radisson's information, the record he left is invaluable as an early description of the Sioux. His biographer says of his account of the Feast of the Dead that "probably there is nowhere any better account than here of Indian customs before the natives had been influenced by white men's ways and goods."[2] Besides what he actually saw, Radisson reported, accurately, what he heard about such characteristic activities as harvesting wild rice: "Two takes a boat and two sticks, by which they gett the eare downe and gett the corne out of it. Their boat being full, they bring it to a fitt place to dry it, and that is their food for the most part of the winter, and doe dress it thus: for each man a handfull of that they putt in the pott, that swells so much that it can suffice a man." The prairie Sioux, he said, were polygamous, and unmarried girls had "all maner of freedome, but are forced to marry when they come to the age." Once married, they were expected to remain faithful; adultery was punished by cutting off the nose and sometimes the crown of the head.[3]

Along with much that has to be dismissed as fabulous, Radisson provides a body of ethnological information from which inferences may be made. Possessed of a sense of humor and not so hopelessly blinded by his own ethnocentrism as some later observers were, he saw the Sioux as human beings whose customs were strange to him but who were people with whom he could establish a man-to-man relationship. We can only speculate as to what the Sioux thought of the strangers with the formidable weapons. Though probably not so awed as Radisson thought, they undoubtedly recognized the technological superiority of the European weapons and tools and quite likely saw their visitors as a new resource to exploit. If such exploitation required flattery and even abasement, they were willing to pay that price. Once the first shock had

    [2] Grace Lee Nute, *Caesars of the Wilderness* (New York: D. Appleton-Century Co., 1943), p. 64.
    [3] Radisson, *Voyages of Peter Esprit Radisson*, pp. 215–220.

worn off, they were probably more amused than angered by the exploding gunpowder trick and were willing to humor the white men if it pleased them to play it a second time. After all, the practical jokes of the Sioux, as reported by later observers, were neither subtle nor kindly.

The Sioux did not break suddenly upon the world of European knowledge at that momentous conclave in the spring of 1660. Their name, at least, had been known for two decades. The Jesuit *Relation* of 1640 includes it among the names collected by Jean Nicolet on his visit to the Winnebagos at Green Bay a few years earlier. The earliest spelling, recorded there, was "Naduesiu," a variant of the Algonquian "Nadouess-iw": a diminutive of snakes, adders, and, by extension, enemies, the term applied to them by the Chippewas. This was shortened by the French later in the century to "Scioux" and then to "Sioux."[4]

As the Jesuits extended their missionary activities westward, more rumors about the Sioux came from the vast forested wilderness. They were reported to till the soil and harvest corn and tobacco. Because of their constant wars with the Crees and other tribes, the Sioux were said to have larger villages in a better state of defense than those of the Hurons, who were well known to the missionaries. The language differed from those of the various Algonquian tribes and from the Iroquoian dialect spoken by the Hurons.[5]

The reports brought back by Radisson and Groseilliers were incorporated into the *Relation* of 1659–1660. Their diplomatic negotiations were seen as opening the way for missionary activity among the Sioux, a prospect that called for additional information about them. As more reports filtered through to the missionaries, a picture, not entirely consistent, of the Sioux began to emerge. They were a warlike nation, it was agreed, although they had "no other arms . . . than the bow and the club." Father Claude Allouez, who visited the Lake Superior region late in 1665, reported that their agriculture was limited to tobacco and that they lived mostly on a kind of "marsh rye" which they harvested toward the close of summer in the small lakes that dotted their country. They lived in "cabins" which were not "covered with bark, but with Deerskins, carefully dressed, and sewed together with such skill that the cold does not enter."[6]

[4] Reuben Gold Thwaites, ed., *The Jesuit Relations and Allied Documents* (New York: Pageant Book Co., 1959), XVIII, 231, 233.

[5] *Ibid.*, XXIII, 225, 227.

[6] *Ibid.*, XLVI, 69; L, 279; LI, 53.

The famous missionary-explorer Father Jacques Marquette contributed to the emerging picture of the Sioux by calling them "the Iroquois of this country . . . but less perfidious than they, and who never attack until they have been attacked. . . ." This early view of the Sioux as morally superior to the Iroquois and Algonquins occurs as a persistent theme in the writings of the Jesuits. They were said to far exceed the other tribes in magnanimity, "being often content with the glory of winning a victory, and sending back free and uninjured the prisoners taken by them in battle."[7] Such sweeping generalizations about particular tribes are frequently encountered in the writings of early travelers, and there is a temptation to dismiss them as gross oversimplifications. Yet this favorable picture of the Sioux occurs so frequently, and is expressed independently by so many observers, that one wonders if there was not something to it.

The first white men to visit the Santee Sioux in their principal center near Mille Lacs Lake were Daniel Greysolon, Sieur du Luth, and Father Louis Hennepin, a Recollet missionary. Du Luth, who planted the French flag in the Sioux village of Izatys on July 2, 1679, left only a brief, soldierly statement of his achievement; but Hennepin wrote extensively—and, one suspects, imaginatively—of his experiences among the Sioux.[8] Taken prisoner by a war party on the Mississippi in April, 1680, Hennepin and his two companions were conducted to Izatys, held there about three months, and then taken back down the great river to the mouth of the St. Croix, where Du Luth met them and obtained their release. Despite his intermittent anxiety over his fate, Hennepin took advantage of what was really an unexcelled opportunity to study the Sioux customs, language, religion, and whole way of life, and left for posterity a description of these people as they were in essentially their aboriginal state. His account has much the same value as the writings of Captain John Smith about the Virginia Indians. Both men were shrewd observers, both necessarily interpreted what they saw in terms of their own culture, and neither was entirely veracious when an opportunity to glorify self came along.

The picture Hennepin gives of the Sioux shows them to have been dependent almost wholly on hunting, fishing, and wild-rice gathering. Arriving at their village in the lean season, the white men were fed scanty rations; "a little wild rice or some smoked fish eggs which they

7 *Ibid.*, LIV, 191; LV, 171.

8 Appendix to Louis Hennepin, *A Description of Louisiana*, ed. by John Gilmary Shea (New York: John Gilmary Shea, 1880), pp. 374–375.

[the Indians] cooked in water in earthen pots" was offered them only five or six times a week. On the way up the river, and again on the return trip, the warriors hunted buffalo, driving them off the bluffs and into the river, where they could more easily be killed. On one of these hunts Hennepin encountered the institution of the "soldiers' lodge"— the tribal police force whose duty it was to maintain order and punish any hunters who pushed ahead of the main body. When he saw the tipis of such offenders pulled down and their meat confiscated, he thought at first that they were enemies, but a self-appointed mentor explained to him the need for rigid discipline on the hunt.[9] More than a century and a half later, Henry Hastings Sibley, on a hunt with the Indians, was to be threatened with much the same punishment for a similar offense.

Although he does not positively say so, Hennepin implies that the Sioux were nonagricultural. During his stay at their village, he planted some tobacco and vegetable seeds that he had brought with him; but upon his return in August with Du Luth, he found that the Indians, though professing an interest in the experiment, refused to use the products.[10]

Some of Hennepin's observations merely confirm those of earlier sources. Like Radisson, he noted the favorite Sioux trick of weeping; Aquipaguetin, the chief of the party that took him prisoner, wept copiously in hopes of inducing his companions to consent to killing the white men. Upon arriving at Izatys, where a friendlier chief, Ouasicoudé, took charge of them, their feet and legs were greased in the manner described by Radisson. Earlier observers had commented on the Sioux enthusiasm for dancing. Hennepin had plenty of opportunities to verify the report, for on the way up the Mississippi the young braves danced until midnight every night. Once, when Aquipaguetin had killed a fat bear, he held a feast, after which all the warriors danced:

[9] Marion E. Cross, ed., *Father Louis Hennepin's Description of Louisiana* (Minneapolis: University of Minnesota Press, 1938), pp. 101–102, 108, 118.

[10] *Ibid.*, pp. 108, 124. Lloyd A. Wilford, who excavated mounds in the Mille Lacs area in 1941, identifies Hennepin's Sioux with the late Woodland culture, which is characterized by a very limited agriculture, sometimes confined to tobacco. Although there is no historical record that the Sioux built mounds, Wilford credits them with building the mounds near Mille Lacs Lake. These mounds contained no mortuary offerings or other objects of human manufacture except for debris found on village sites. See Wilford, "The Prehistoric Indians of Minnesota," *Minnesota History*, XXV (June 1944), 153–157; and "The Prehistoric Indians of Minnesota: The Mille Lacs Aspect," *Minnesota History*, XXV (December 1944), 329–341.

Their faces and bodies were smeared with paint, each warrior being painted with the symbol of some animal appropriate to his family or selected by his own fancy. Some had their hair short, full of bear grease, and decorated with red and white feathers. Others sprinkled their heads with the down of birds, which clung to the grease. They all danced with their hands on their hips, striking the soles of their feet upon the ground so hard that they left footprints.[11]

Hennepin confirmed the earlier characterization of the Sioux as morally superior to the other tribes familiar to the French. They were equal in bravery to the Iroquois, he said, adding that "they also make all the surrounding tribes tremble even though they have only the bow and arrow. These Indians run faster than the Iroquois but they are not so brutal and do not eat the flesh of their enemies, being content to burn them" (p. 165). There is some doubt as to whether the Sioux did, in fact, burn their enemies; at this stage of their history they are usually not charged with torturing captives. Father Joseph Marest, who visited them in 1687 and 1689, reported that they "did not wreak on their prisoners those horrors which disgrace most of the other nations on this continent. . . ."[12]

To a greater extent than is true of Radisson's rather straightforward account, Hennepin's story is marred by the intrusion of the author's ego. One is inclined to be repelled by Hennepin's evident satisfaction at the death of a child soon after he had baptized it and to be suspicious of a man who claimed, during the reign of Louis XIV, that "Louis" was the Dakota word for "sun." Yet Hennepin is probably truthful in claiming to have earned the Indians' good will by curing some of their ailments, and he clearly learned something of their language. *Manza Ouckange*, the Indians' term for firearms, is too close to *maza wakan*—mysterious (i.e., powerful) metal—to be mere coincidence. He did not begin to understand his hosts' religion, but he noted that Aquipaguetin carried with him the bones of an important dead relative wrapped in dressed skins decorated with red and black porcupine quills.[13]

With all his self-importance and his inevitable ethnocentrism, Hennepin is still one of the most valuable sources of information on the early Sioux. It was to be some time before another European would take the trouble to describe their manners in as much detail. There

[11] Cross, *Description of Louisiana*, pp. 97, 99–101, 107, 111.

[12] Pierre F. X. Charlevoix, *History and General Description of New France*, trans. by John Gilmary Shea (New York: John Gilmary Shea, 1866–1872), III, 32–33.

[13] Cross, *Description of Louisiana*, pp. 98, 100–101, 109, 112–113.

were, however, others who had the opportunity. The French contact opened by Du Luth was maintained intermittently for the rest of the period of French dominion in the lakes region, and the Sioux were repeatedly visited by traders, missionaries, and military men pursuing their respective occupations. One of the traders, Nicholas Perrot, who also served as commandant in the upper Mississippi region, in 1686 established a fort on the east shore of Lake Pepin and on May 8, 1689, proclaimed French sovereignty over the entire area occupied by the Sioux. Although much of his information was obtained at second hand, it has considerable value. He told, for example, about the friction that developed between the Sioux and a group of Hurons and Ottawas who fled west to escape the Iroquois and settled about 1656 on Isle Pelée, in the Mississippi (supposed to be Prairie Island, above Red Wing). The Sioux received them hospitably and even behaved obsequiously in the hope of getting hatchets, knives, and other European goods from them. Mistaking their manner for a sign of weakness, the intruders treated the Sioux contemptuously, with the result that the latter rose up and drove the eastern Indians out of their country.[14]

Another anecdote told by Perrot is that of the Huron war party that attempted to penetrate to the heart of the Sioux country and met disaster there. Perrot describes the country as "nothing but lakes and marshes, full of wild oats; these are separated from one another by narrow tongues of land, which extend from one lake to another not more than thirty of forty paces at most, and sometimes five or six, or a little more." Living in small villages of five or six families, near enough together to be able to help one another if attacked, the Sioux were able to assemble three thousand warriors to oppose a hundred Hurons, who became lost in the marshes. Unable to find the attackers but knowing they were in the wild-rice beds, the Sioux stretched the nets they used to catch beaver across the narrow tongues of land and attached trade bells to them. When the Hurons tried to crawl out of their refuge, they set the bells to ringing and were promptly captured. In keeping with Sioux notions of humanity, some of the prisoners were shot to death (not tortured) by young boys, and the rest, after witnessing the slaughter, were sent home.[15]

[14] Emma Helen Blair, ed., *The Indian Tribes of the Upper Mississippi Valley and Region of the Great Lakes* (Cleveland: Arthur H. Clark Co., 1911), I, 159–164; Newton H. Winchell, *The Aborigines of Minnesota* (St. Paul: Pioneer Co., 1911), p. 526.

[15] Blair, *Indian Tribes of the Upper Mississippi*, I, 166–168, 170. These events are supposed to have occurred about 1662 or 1663.

By the late seventeenth century the Sioux were being caught up in the power struggle between France and England for control of North America. One of the instruments of French policy was Pierre Charles Le Sueur, who had been present at Perrot's proclamation. In 1695 he established a fort on Prairie Island in the Mississippi, and in July of that year escorted a Sioux chief, Tioscaté, and a Chippewa chief, Chingouabé, to a conference at Montreal. Tioscaté, described as "the first of his nation who has seen Canada," showed by his behavior that a Sioux was not at all inhibited by alien surroundings from putting on a good show. Charlevoix, the historian of New France, describes the performance:

> While de Frontenac [the governor] was giving orders to the Indians who had accompanied him, a Siou chief approached him with a very sad air, laid his hands on his knees, and with streaming eyes, begged him to take pity on him; that all the other nations had their Father, and that he alone was like a forsaken child. He then spread out a beaver skin on which he arranged twenty-two arrows, and taking them one after another, he named for each a village of his nation and asked the general to take them all under his protection.[16]

Whatever the results of this appeal were (and Charlevoix implies that there were none), Tioscaté did not live to tell the folks back home of what he had seen in the metropolis of New France. Still in Montreal, he fell ill the following winter and died after thirty-three days of suffering.[17]

In 1700 Le Sueur returned to the Sioux country and established a fort, called Fort L'Huillier, a few miles above the mouth of the Blue Earth River, where he believed there was a large deposit of copper. Nothing came of the mining enterprise, but Le Sueur left a record of his winter among the Sioux that sheds some light on their condition and tribal organization at the beginning of the eighteenth century.

Hennepin had attempted to list the subdivisions of the Sioux nation and had come up with some names recognizable as those of certain of the historic subtribes. His "Tinthonha or men of the prairie" are clearly the Tetons, who had evidently already left their marsh-and-forest home and become nomadic buffalo hunters. The "Oudebathon" are probably the Wahpetons, and the "Chongaskethon" somewhat less certainly the Sissetons. The people Hennepin called "Issati" prob-

---

[16] "The French Regime in Wisconsin, 1634–1727," *Wisconsin Historical Collections*, XVI (1902), 177–178 (excerpt from La Harpe, *Journal Historique de l'établissement des Français à la Louisiane*); Charlevoix, *History of New France*, IV, 272.
[17] "The French Regime in Wisconsin, 1634–1727," p. 178.

ably included the Mdewakantons and perhaps the Wahpekutes. His other names are not readily identifiable with the historic groups. Le Sueur brought somewhat more order to this classification, though he also introduced some new and unrecognizable names. His most important contribution was to divide the nation into "Scioux of the West," in whose country the fort was built, and "Scioux of the East," (i.e., east of the Mississippi), with whom he wished to trade. The latter included not only Hennepin's Oudebathons and Chongaskethons, but also a group called the "Mendeouacantons"—obviously the Mdewakantons. Not much is said about the respective locations of these subtribes, but there is a suggestion that one group was already living around the mouth of the Minnesota River.[18]

Le Sueur gives no indication that any of the Sioux in the year 1700 depended on agriculture. In fact, one of his objectives was to reduce intertribal warfare, which was injurious to French trade, by making farmers out of the Indians. Believing, as he said, that it was "not possible to subdue the Scioux or to hinder them from going to war, unless it be by inducing them to cultivate the ground," he proposed that they form a sedentary village around the fort.[19] This earliest of many efforts to transform the Sioux into farmers was, like most of its successors, a total failure. Though the Indians apparently agreed to Le Sueur's proposal as the only means of obtaining French goods, on which he represented them as being heavily dependent, before they could have fulfilled their promise, Le Sueur had left the region (in the spring of 1701); and about a year later the garrison that stayed behind abandoned the fort in the face of attacks by the Foxes and Mascoutens.[20]

Despite their growing dependence on European goods, the Sioux appear less often in French records in the first half of the eighteenth

[18] Cross, *Description of Louisiana*, p. 92; "Le Sueur, The Explorer of the Minnesota River," *Minnesota Historical Collections*, I (1850–1856), 208, 268–271. Early in the twentieth century Newton H. Winchell tried to reconstruct the aboriginal geography of Minnesota and prepared a map, based on history and tradition, to show the distribution of the Sioux in Hennepin's day. Winchell placed the Mdewakantons in the Mille Lacs area and to the east, the Wahpetons north and west of Mille Lacs Lake, the Sissetons north of Cass and Winnibigoshish lakes, the Yanktons in two groups, one between Leech Lake and the Red River, the other in the Pipestone area, and the Tetons around Big Stone Lake and Lake Traverse. No attempt was made to show the locations of the Wahpekutes or the Yanktonais. See Winchell, *Aborigines of Minnesota*, p. 68.

[19] "Le Sueur, The Explorer of the Minnesota River," p. 273.

[20] *Ibid.*, pp. 273–274; Edward D. Neill, "Relation of M. Penicaut," *Minnesota Historical Collections*, III (1870–1880), 10–11.

century than in the last forty years of the seventeenth. To the extent that they were taken notice of at all, they were seen as mere pawns in the imperial designs of the French government. As early as 1701, D'Iberville, governor of Louisiana and Le Sueur's brother-in-law, wrote a memorial on the Mississippi valley in which he set forth his theories on the management of Indian affairs. He saw the Sioux as essentially useless to the French if they stayed in their own country, and proposed resettling them on the Missouri River, where they would be more accessible from the lower Mississippi and less accessible to the traders of the Hudson's Bay Company. He opposed giving presents to the Indians; instead, he said, "When they come to us, it will be necessary to bring them in subjection, make them no presents, and *compel* them to do what we wish, *as if they were Frenchmen.*"[21] Although D'Iberville's scheme of resettling the Sioux was not carried out during the French period, doubtless the kind of cold-blooded calculation it manifested was present in the policies that were actually followed by the French.

The period was one of intensified intertribal warfare, and such hostile nations as the Foxes kept the normal trade routes unsafe if not absolutely closed. In order to dominate the western trade, the French needed to establish and maintain a fortified post in the Sioux country. Perrot had built at least two short-lived forts late in the seventeenth century, and in 1727 Fort Beauharnois was erected on the west shore of Lake Pepin, near the present town of Frontenac, Minnesota. The Foxes made this post untenable, however, and it was evacuated within a couple of years, to be rebuilt later and finally abandoned again during the French and Indian War.[22]

French contacts with the Sioux during the first half of the eighteenth century were extensive enough to permit a few more observations concerning their culture and the first passably accurate estimate of their numbers. Le Sueur had estimated the Sioux population at 4,000 families—a mere guess based upon unknown information. In 1736 a census, said to have reflected the opinion of voyageurs, credited them with 2,300 men, or roughly 8,000 to 10,000 people. The vast majority of them were classified as Sioux of the prairies, which here probably included all but the Mdewakantons.[23] Both Pierre Boucher, the com-

[21] Quoted in Edward D. Neill, *The History of Minnesota* (Philadelphia: J. B. Lippincott and Co., 1858), p. 174.

[22] Louise Phelps Kellogg, "Fort Beauharnois," *Minnesota History*, VIII (September 1927), 243–244; "The French Regime in Wisconsin, 1727–1748," *Wisconsin Historical Collections*, XVII (1906), 7–9, 22–26, 264.

[23] "The French Regime in Wisconsin, 1727–1748," pp. 247–248.

mandant at the first Fort Beauharnois, and a priest who accompanied him, Father Michel Guignas, testified to the intelligence, courage, and physical prowess of the Sioux, but they also noted a propensity toward thievery, a characteristic frequently mentioned in the early nineteenth century. Suggestive of a change taking place in their methods of hunting and waging war is Boucher's statement that "although they have had firearms but a short time, they can use them perfectly well."[24]

So far as the Santee Sioux were concerned, the most important event of the eighteenth century was their expulsion by the Chippewas from their traditional homes around Mille Lacs Lake. Such scanty evidence as there is suggests that the wars between these tribes did not begin until after the visit by Tioscaté and Chingouabé to Montreal in 1695. Chippewa tradition, as recorded by William W. Warren, attributes the outbreak of hostilities to private quarrels, but it is more likely that the Chippewas, moving westward along the south shore of Lake Superior and armed with firearms obtained through trade, developed expansionist ambitions similar to those displayed earlier by the Hurons and Ottawas. Being far more numerous than those eastern tribes and probably better armed, the Chippewas succeeded where the others had failed. The Sioux had been gradually moving out onto the prairies since before Hennepin's visit and very likely had only a few small bands left in their old territory. The population estimate made in 1736 indicated only three hundred men belonging to the Sioux of the lakes. Later missionaries were to claim that the attraction of traders operating around the junction of the Mississippi and Minnesota rivers was as important a motive as Chippewa pressure in causing the remnants of the Sioux to abandon their old haunts.[25]

Whatever the underlying causes, the Sioux did leave the Mille Lacs area, and their departure was at least hastened by their defeat in the three-day battle of Kathio (a misreading of "Izatys" on a manuscript), which is supposed to have taken place about 1750. Warren provides the only detailed account of the battle, and the traditions on which his story is based contain so many discrepancies of fact that one hesitates to accept any of it. According to Warren, the Sioux lived in three earthlodge villages, of which the second and largest was captured by the stratagem of throwing bags of gunpowder through the smoke holes of the lodges. The siege tactics employed by the Chippewas on this

[24] *Ibid.*, pp. 27–28, 56–57.
[25] William W. Warren, "History of the Ojibway Nation," *Minnesota Historical Collections*, V (1885), 157–159; Neill, *History of Minnesota*, p. 206.

occasion are so unlike the usual pattern of Indian warfare as to have given rise to the theory that French strategy and possibly French soldiers were involved.[26]

Though much remains obscure about the battle of Kathio, its effects were of immense significance to the Santee Sioux. The battle is the most readily identifiable event in the process by which they were transformed from a typical tribe of the Eastern Woodlands culture to a people at least on the margin of the Plains Indian culture, to which the western Sioux became thoroughgoing converts. In the years that followed, other traditional Sioux villages on Sandy, Cass, Winnibigoshish, Leech, and Red lakes were taken by the Chippewas. Although the Sioux made at least one serious attempt to recover their lost territories in 1768, the failure of the campaign apparently discouraged them from repeating it. After this, as Doane Robinson says, they accepted the finality of the Chippewa conquest, and their attacks became mere raiding expeditions, designed to provide scalps and military experience in keeping with Sioux tradition.[27]

Expulsion from their northern homes deprived the Sioux of none of the arrogance they had begun to display earlier in the century. Late in the French and Indian War a party of twelve braves appeared before the British commander at Green Bay, Lieutenant James Gorrell, who had been sent to take over the French forts in that region. They told Gorrell that "if ever the Chippewas or any other Indians wished to obstruct the passage of the traders coming up, to send them word, and they would come and put them off from the face of the earth, as all Indians were their slaves or dogs." Gorrell was much impressed by what he saw and heard of the Sioux and wrote:

> It is certainly the greatest nation of Indians ever yet found. Not above two thousand of them were ever armed with fire-arms, the rest depending entirely on bows and arrows and darts, which they use with more skill than any other Indian nation in North America. They can shoot the wildest and largest beasts in the woods, at seventy or one hundred yards distance. They are remarkable for their dancing; the other nations take the fashion from them. It is said they keep regular guards in their chief town or metropolis, relieving once in twenty-four hours, and are always alert.[28]

How much of his admiration derived from an objective evaluation of

[26] Warren, "History of the Ojibway Nation," pp. 159–161.
[27] *Ibid.*, pp. 176–178, 183, 185, 222–231; Doane Robinson, *A History of the Dakota or Sioux Indians* (Minneapolis: Ross and Haines, 1956), p. 67.
[28] "Lieut. James Gorrell's Journal," *Wisconsin Historical Collections*, I (1855), 36–37.

the merits of the Sioux and how much from their own boasts is not apparent.

After the war, British replaced French explorers, and the Sioux were exposed to contacts with a different European power. The first English explorer to leave a record of his adventures was Captain Jonathan Carver, who, after service in the war, undertook an expedition with the authorization of his immediate superior, Major Robert Rogers, though without any official sanction from higher authority. He entered the Sioux country late in 1766, after a trip from Mackinac along the Fox-Wisconsin route and up the Mississippi. He first examined the region around St. Anthony Falls and above that point, and then, late in November, began ascending the St. Peter's, or Minnesota, River. After wintering with a band of prairie Sioux (possibly Wahpetons) and learning their language "perfectly," he headed down the river in the spring, stopping near the mouth to harangue the Indians, and then continued his explorations outside the region dominated by the Sioux.[29]

The mendacity of which Hennepin and others have been accused is particularly noteworthy in Carver, and renders almost everything he says at least suspect. A large section of his account of his travels, concerned with the customs and manners of the Indians, was plagiarized from earlier sources, some of which were themselves fabricated in large part; and, like Hennepin, Carver usually fails to distinguish one tribe from another. Even the story of his travels is of questionable veracity, particularly his claim to have gone two hundred miles up the Minnesota. Peter Pond, who made the trip less than a decade later, thought Carver had ascended the river only about fourteen miles.[30] Likewise, his claim to having been made a chief of the Sioux may be seriously questioned, as may many other details in his account, such as his finding the Minnesota open at a season when the Mississippi was already obstructed by ice. Still, if used with due caution, Carver's narrative may provide some accurate information on the condition of the Sioux between the French and Indian War and the American Revolution.

Carver divided the "Naudowessies," as he called them, into the "River Bands" and the "Prairie Bands." The former, whom he found living along the St. Croix, consisted of the Nehogatawonahs, the

[29] Jonathan Carver, *Three Years Travels Through the Interior Parts of North America* (Philadelphia: Key and Simpson, 1796), pp. 37–54; William W. Folwell, *A History of Minnesota*, I (St. Paul: Minnesota Historical Society, 1956), pp. 53–58.

[30] "The British Regime in Wisconsin—1760–1800," *Wisconsin Historical Collections*, XVIII (1908), 340.

Mawtawbauntowahs, and the Shahsweentowahs—names that bear little resemblance to those of bands elsewhere reported, although the second may have been the Mdewakantons and the third possibly the Sissetons. The Sioux of the plains comprised the Wawpeentowahs (Wahpetons), the Tintons (Tetons), the Afrahcootahs (perhaps the Wahpekutes), the Mawhaws (Omahas), the Schians (Cheyennes), the Chianese, the Chongousceton, and the Waddapawjestin. The Assiniboins had constituted a twelfth band but had separated from the rest at some remote time in the past. The total manpower of the Sioux (including presumably the Omahas and Cheyennes) was given by Carver as two thousand warriors, of whom only four hundred belonged to the river bands.[31]

Whether from his reading or from his experiences, Carver assembled quite a collection of miscellaneous facts about the Sioux and other Indians. His observations on their material culture are probably more reliable than those on their religion and social organization. He described both their skin tents and their bark huts, the latter apparently similar to those of the Algonquian peoples. Although long in contact with European traders, they still made household vessels of a black clay or stone and bowls and dishes of the knotty excrescences of maple or other wood. He noted especially the daggers used by the Sioux, made originally of flint or bone but now of iron. He described them as ten inches long and three inches broad at the handle and remarked that they were worn only by the principal chiefs. Like other tribes in this part of the country, the Sioux now had trade knives and steels to strike fire with. Carver of course noticed the catlinite pipes and, like other explorers, erroneously located the place of origin of the material in a mountain high on the so-called Marble River, a branch of the Minnesota. He was surprised to find the inland tribes wearing sea shells as ornaments, and he thought it worthy of remark that their moccasins were decorated with pieces of brass or tin attached to leather strings an inch long, which made "a cheerful tinkling noise either when they walk or dance."[32]

Carver's observations on the customs and manners of the Sioux contain little new information, despite his avowed purpose of rectifying earlier accounts, which he said had been based on tribes already strongly influenced by European culture. Nor do his remarks on the Dakota language prove very useful. He did compile a vocabulary of the

[31] Carver, *Three Years Travels*, pp. 37, 50.
[32] *Ibid.*, pp. 63–64, 145–150.

"Naudowessie" language containing many words that resemble those in later Dakota lexicons. *Tatanka* (bison) he records as *tawtongo*; *tanka* (great or big) appears as *tongo*; *maza* (iron) is *muzah*; and his *wakon*, recorded earlier by Hennepin, is an alternative spelling of the word that usually appears as *wakan*.[33] Every European heard the Indian languages in his own way, and recorded them in the orthography familiar to him; Carver's recording of Dakota is accurate enough to exonerate him from the charge of imposture in this respect, however much he may have exaggerated his own command of the language.

It is fortunate that the next English-speaking visitor to the Sioux who kept a journal of his adventures did not try to compile a vocabulary, for his spelling was too bizarre to afford much indication of how a word was supposed to be pronounced. This was Peter Pond, who made a trading expedition into the Sioux country in 1773–1775. Despite extensive travels and a variety of adventures, Pond looked upon all he saw with the unwearied interest of a novice, noting all manner of detail about the countryside and its white and red inhabitants. He and two other traders set out in October from Prairie du Chien for the St. Peter's River. Shrewd businessmen, they took a practical view of the Sioux and "went on Sloley to Leat the Nottawaseas Git Into the Plain that we Mite not be trubeld with them for Creadit as thay are Bad Pay Marsters."[34] Most of the trading took place from January onward and yielded Pond a good profit after he learned from a competing Frenchman to attract trade by leaving a few trinkets around for the Indians to steal. It was not an exciting winter—"Well thare was not Eney thing Extrodnerey Hapend Dureing the Winter," he says—and not until the following winter did his contacts with the Sioux become close enough to impel him to describe them in detail.[35]

Instead of staying at the post he had established the previous year, Pond, at the request of the Indians, followed the river about two hundred miles upstream and set up shop among a band of Yanktons. Upon arriving, he was accorded the standard reception. After his goods had been hauled up from the river, the calumet was passed around and pointed toward the four cardinal points, up, and down; then Pond's shoes were taken off and moccasins substituted, and he was carried on a blanket to the encampment, where he was subjected to the customary weeping ritual, though apparently without tears. An old man fed him

[33] *Ibid.*, pp. 288–292.
[34] "The British Regime in Wisconsin," p. 339.
[35] *Ibid.*, p. 340.

three spoonfuls of a soup concocted of corn meal and meat boiled in three brass kettles in the middle of the lodge. After this he was given a bark dish and a buffalo-horn spoon and invited to fall to. Not knowing that he would receive the same hospitality at two more lodges, he ate "Hartey" of the brew. After the third round, the trading began, under the stern surveillance of the chiefs, who saw to it that the proceeding went on in an orderly manner. Pond's narrative breaks off at the approach of spring, 1775, before his departure from the Indian country. Although he does not greatly enlarge our knowledge of the Santee Sioux on the eve of the American Revolution, he does mention that those living near the mouth of the Minnesota River "Rase Plentey of Corn for thare one [own] Concumtion," indicating that the agricultural tradition had not perished with the exodus from the Mille Lacs region, or else had been revived in the new location.[36]

The spring when Pond left his improvised trading post saw the battles of Lexington and Concord. Soon the Indians of the Northwest were involved in another of the white man's wars. The loyalty, or at least the benevolent neutrality, of the Sioux and their neighbors was sought by both sides, but the British had the odds in their favor. Perhaps some of the Indians realized that the British government had tried since 1763 to prevent occupation by white settlers of the Indian country west of the Appalachians, and that the colonials had negated those efforts by pouring across the mountains. More likely, the British simply had a better-organized Indian policy and administrators with greater experience, and were in a position to do more for the Indians than the colonials could.

Among the allies the British attracted to their flag were the Sioux, under the leadership of Wabasha, a Mdewakanton chief who seems to have exerted wide influence. His name, spelled "Ouabachas" by the French, appears as early as 1740, when he and another chief met the French commandant at Lake Pepin, Paul Marin, on the Rock River, in present-day Illinois, and apologized for killing some Ottawas. Although he seems to have been implicated in the murder of a Frenchman in the Illinois country in 1736, twenty years later he went to Montreal to offer himself as a vicarious sacrifice for a tribesman who had killed an English trader and then escaped while being taken there for punishment.[37]

[36] *Ibid.*, pp. 350, 352.
[37] "The French Regime in Wisconsin, 1727–1748," pp. 323, 402, 420; Neill, *History of Minnesota*, pp. 225–228; Winchell, *Aborigines of Minnesota*, pp. 540–541.

This was the man who now firmly allied himself with the British and who earned their respect by his behavior during the war. Lieutenant-Governor Patrick Sinclair was struck by the military prowess of the Sioux, whom he described as "a warlike people undebauched, under the authority of a chief named Wabasha of very singular & uncommon abilities, who can raise 200 men with ease, accustomed to all the attention and obedience required by discipline."[38] When Wabasha visited Mackinac in July 1779, he was accorded a special artillery salute, in which live ammunition was used in order to accustom the Indians to large firearms. Some Choctaws, Chickasaws, and Chippewas were present, "and great was their astonishment when they beheld balls discharged from the cannons of the fort flying over the canoes, and the Dahkotah braves lifting their paddles as if to strike them, and crying out, 'Taya! taya!'"[39] Colonel Arent Schuyler de Peyster, who had an unfortunate penchant for writing extemporaneous verse, commemorated the occasion with a piece of wretched doggerel that purported to be a tribute to Wabasha:

> Hail to the chief! who his buffalo's back straddles,
>> When in his own country, far, far, from this fort;
> Whose brave young canoe-men, here hold up their paddles,
>> In hopes, that the whizzing balls, may give them sport.
>> Hail to great Wapashaw!
>> He comes, beat drums, the Scioux chief comes.
>
> They now strain their nerves till the canoe runs bounding,
>> As swift as the Solen goose skims o'er the wave,
> While on the lake's border, a guard is surrounding
>> A space, where to land the Scioux so brave.
>>> Hail! to great Wapashaw!
>>> Soldiers! your triggers draw!
>> Guard! wave the colours, and give him the drum.
>>> Choctaw and Chickasaw,
>>> Whoop for great Wapashaw;
> Raise the portcullis, the King's friend is come.[40]

Despite this comic-opera touch, Wabasha's potential contribution to the war was taken seriously by the British. Although the Sioux played

[38] "Papers from the Canadian Archives, 1778–1783," *Wisconsin Historical Collections,* XI (1888), 145.
[39] Neill, *History of Minnesota,* p. 228.
[40] *Ibid.,* p. 229.

a less important role than expected, they took some part in the war along the central Mississippi and earned warm praise from a British officer, Lieutenant Charles F. Phillips, who wrote that

> General Wabasha was well contented with his commission & believe me his Warriours are nothing inferior to regular Troops in regard to Discipline in their own way, it being their first & principle care to examine their arms in the morning, by drawing & drying their Powder and always fresh loaded at Sun Sett—[41]

Wabasha's British loyalties, to which the commission he held was a testimonial, did not prevent him from accepting the outcome of the war with equanimity. When the end of the war was announced to the Indians at Prairie du Chien in 1783, Wabasha replied with what Newton H. Winchell calls "some ambiguous words":

> My father, I am content that the great chiefs on the other side of the greatest lake are for making peace. . . . My English father, you give us pleasure to have come upon our ground; our heart is joyful and content. It is you give us light. We will be quiet.[42]

Except for the reports of explorers and isolated comments by military officers, our picture of the Santee Sioux at the end of the eighteenth century must be based to a considerable extent on conjecture. After a century and a half of European contact, their material culture had been markedly altered. Steel weapons and tools had largely replaced those of bone and stone which the early explorers had found them using. They still made many household utensils of wood and bark, however. They had almost certainly given up the manufacture of pottery, since Peter Pond found even the rather remote Yanktons using brass kettles in 1774; and the use of skins had partially given way to European cloth and the trader's blanket. Dependent though the Indians had become on materials of European manufacture for their everyday life, their religion and social organization were largely unchanged at the end of the eighteenth century. Descriptions of their customs and manners dating from the fourth and fifth decades of the nineteenth century bear a remarkable similarity to those by eighteenth- and even seventeenth-century observers.

The geographical location and political organization of the Santee

[41] "Papers from the Canadian Archives, 1767–1814," *Wisconsin Historical Collections,* XII (1892), 49.

[42] Winchell, *Aborigines of Minnesota,* p. 542.

bands were at this time gradually emerging from the state of flux that had characterized them since the expulsion from Mille Lacs and were settling into the pattern they retained until the beginning of the reservation period. It is not possible to reconstruct the successive settlements of the migrating Sioux with precise accuracy, but some reasonably sound conjectures may be offered. After leaving the northern lake area, the various Santee bands moved southward. Very likely the Sissetons and Wahpetons went first, moving into the Minnesota valley and onto the plains, where they adopted some features of the material culture of the true plains tribes that had preceded them westward.

After the battle of Kathio those who had remained in the old homelands fled south. The Wahpekutes, who may have split off after the expulsion, became nomadic, with no permanent villages; but the Mdewakantons continued their village life in the new surroundings. Although it has been claimed that they lived for a time in a single village near the mouth of the Minnesota, the numbers ascribed to them later make it seem improbable that this arrangement lasted long. More likely, they soon scattered to a number of sites, which they may have occupied only temporarily at first, and which did not become permanent villages until about 1800 or later. It is said that there were no villages on the Mississippi below the mouth of the St. Croix until after 1783.[43] Sometime between then and 1805, Wabasha's band moved down the great river to a point near the mouth of the Upper Iowa River. It was probably about this time that the Khemnichan, or Red Wing, band moved down the river to the site of the present city named for their chief. When the Wabasha band moved, a portion of the village remained and formed the nucleus of a new band. This was the pattern followed earlier and later: a subchief might take a few of his followers and establish a new village, or the principal chief might leave without taking all the members of his band along. In this way the historic villages of the Mdewakanton Sioux were formed.

In attempting to picture the Santee Sioux in 1800, we should envision them as nomadic hunters much of the year. Although the Mdewakantons and some of the Sissetons and Wahpetons had permanent villages of bark houses, they lived there only during part of the spring and summer, when they were planting or harvesting their meager corn

---

[43] Neill, *History of Minnesota*, p. 231; "Memoir of the Sioux," trans. by John H. Ames and ed. by Edward D. Neill, *Macalester College Contributions*, First Series, No. 10 (1890), p. 226.

crops. Once the corn was planted, they had to spend most of their time searching for food to tide them over until harvest. They fished in nearby lakes and streams; hunted deer or waterfowl when there were any to be had; and gathered berries, plums, and a variety of roots and tubers, such as the wild turnip, the *mdo* (which resembled the sweet potato), and the *psincha* and *psinchincha*, which were found at the bottom of shallow lakes.[44]

When the corn was ready to eat, the greater part of it was boiled and consumed immediately. Some was allowed to ripen, dried and shelled, and stored underground in bark barrels for use in the winter. When the corn had been harvested, the Indians left their villages, most of the men to take part in the fall muskrat hunt, the women and some of the men to gather wild rice. In October the deer hunt began, the most important hunt of the year. Assembling their household goods and their skin tipis, the entire population left their villages for a three-month search for deer and any other game, such as elk or bear, that they could find. Hampered by their impedimenta and by the meat they obtained, they moved only short distances and remained camped in one spot for several days or weeks. A strict division of labor was followed: the men did the hunting, and the women did nearly all the other work.

If the hunt was successful, in January the band returned to their village or settled down in a sheltered spot and lived comfortably for a couple of months off the venison they had killed, supplemented by whatever corn they had preserved from the previous summer's crop. About the beginning of March the men set out on the spring muskrat hunt, which was more important than the fall hunt because the fur was better then. The animals were trapped, shot, or speared, and while the weather was cold the flesh was eaten. The women meanwhile tapped maple trees and boiled down the sap for sugar. With the band's return from these missions, the yearly cycle began once more.

[44] Samuel W. Pond, "The Dakotas or Sioux in Minnesota as They Were in 1834," *Minnesota Historical Collections*, XII (1905–1908), 342–346 and *passim*. The picture of life among the Sioux given in the following paragraphs is drawn principally from this source, whose 183 pages provide the most detailed and probably most reliable description that we have of the Sioux in the early nineteenth century. Largely free of the ethnocentrism that one might expect, it attempts to show the Sioux as he really was, a human being neither better nor worse than the European at a similar stage of his cultural development. Except for somewhat greater dependence on the fur traders, the condition of the Sioux in 1834 was probably not significantly changed from what it had been at the end of the eighteenth century. Some information has also been drawn from Edward D. Neill, "Dakota Land and Dakota Life," *Minnesota Historical Collections*, I (1850–1856), 205–240.

There were, of course, variations in this cycle, particularly among the more westerly Sissetons and Wahpetons, who participated in the annual buffalo hunt on the prairies. Some of the skins and robes obtained on those hunts were traded to the semisedentary bands for goods received in payment for furs. Even the western bands, however, came east to the Big Woods to hunt deer. It is evident from the pattern of life followed by the Santee Sioux that theirs was still essentially a woodland culture. They hunted deer and other timber game, they depended partly on fishing, they gathered wild rice, they still used the canoe (though by 1800 their canoes were made of hollowed-out logs rather than birchbark, as in Hennepin's day), and horses were owned by only a minority of families, at least among the Mdewakantons. The transition to the plains culture that had been accomplished by the Tetons, Yanktons, and Yanktonais was only begun among the Santees.

Nevertheless, changes had taken place in Santee society since Hennepin's day. The four eastern bands had made a successful adjustment to their new surroundings, which they had in considerable measure chosen for themselves. Though their life was no doubt a "perpetual, unceasing struggle for existence," as Samuel W. Pond described it,[45] it had always been so. The influence of white culture was evident mainly in the form of tools, weapons, and utensils, which contributed to greater proficiency in hunting and to an improved standard of living. If white contact had also made the Santees more dependent on the trade system, the integrity of their culture was largely intact. They had no notion that they were on the verge of enormously increased white contact, which would produce massive changes in their way of life and ultimately shatter their whole culture.

[45] Pond, "The Dakotas or Sioux . . . in 1834," p. 373.

CHAPTER 2

The Americans Move In

OFFICIAL RELATIONS between the Santee Sioux and the United States government began with the expedition of Lieutenant Zebulon M. Pike to the upper Mississippi in 1805–1806. Expressed in general terms, Pike's mission was to establish United States sovereignty over the territory, where British traders continued to operate much as they had before the Revolution. Recognizing that control over the area would not be achieved without a military presence, the government planned to establish military posts in the upper valley. Pike was to obtain cessions of land from the Indians to be used for this purpose. In addition, he was to lay the groundwork for a series of "factories," or government-operated trading posts which would furnish the Indians with their needs at lower cost than the commercial traders. Finally, Pike was to make peace between the Sioux and the Chippewas, a formidable task at which he proved no more successful than Du Luth, Le Sueur, or Carver, each of whom had in turn tried to end the incessant warfare between the tribes.[1]

On his way up the Mississippi in the fall of 1805, the young officer stopped at the mouth of the Upper Iowa River for a council with Wabasha, son of the "great Wapashaw" so much admired by the

[1] William W. Folwell, *A History of Minnesota*, I (St. Paul: Minnesota Historical Society, 1956), p. 91.

British during the Revolution, and near the mouth of the Cannon River for a similar conference with Tatankamani, the Red Wing chief, described by Pike as the second war chief of the nation. The most important council, however, was held September 23 at a village about nine miles up the Minnesota River from the future site of Fort Snelling.[2] Because this conference produced the first treaty between the United States and the Sioux Indians, it has considerable historical importance, despite certain irregularities about the manner in which the treaty was made and in its subsequent history.

Pike constructed from his sails a bower or shade which only the high contracting parties were permitted to enter. At noon the council began with a speech by Pike in which he stated the purposes of his expedition and requested the cession of two vaguely described tracts of land, one at the mouth of the St. Croix, the other at the junction of the Minnesota and the Mississippi. Seven "chiefs" (probably not all were so recognized) were present, of whom only two signed the treaty, and they with much reluctance, for they thought their word of honor should be enough. Looked at objectively, the treaty was such as to give them good reason for hesitation, if they comprehended at all what they were doing. They ceded about 100,000 acres, according to Pike's estimate, valued by him at $200,000, but no specific sum was named in the treaty as compensation. They received $200 worth of presents and some liquor on the spot; and when the Senate later approved the treaty, the blank left by Pike was filled in with the figure of $2,000—far short of even Pike's modest estimate of the value of the land ceded.[3] Indians were often defrauded in treaties, but rarely did any group allow themselves to be so grossly imposed upon as the signatories to this treaty were.

Who were the men with whom this agreement was negotiated? Most of them have been identified. Of the two signers, one was Little Crow, chief of the Kapozha band, whose village was then located on the east bank of the Mississippi, fourteen miles below the mouth of the Minnesota; the other was Way Ago Enagee, elsewhere referred to by Pike as "Le Fils de Pinchow." Though the identification is not positive, the latter was probably the son of a French trader whom Lieutenant Gorrell called "Pennenshaw" but who is usually known as Pinichon. Some writers make him chief of the remnant left behind when Wabasha and most of his band migrated down the Mississippi. He is also identified as

[2] Elliott Coues, ed., *The Expeditions of Zebulon Montgomery Pike* (New York: Francis P. Harper, 1895), I, 43–48, 66–68, 82.
[3] *Ibid.*, pp. 83–84.

the father of the later chief Good Road. Those who were present but did not sign were "Le Boeuf que Marche" (Walking Buffalo, or Tatan-kamani), "Le Demi Douzen" (Six, or Shakopee), "Le Original Leve" (correctly spelled "L'Orignal Levé," Rising Moose, usually identified with Tamaha, a member of the Red Wing band), and two men of whom nothing can be said with certainty, "Le Grand Partisan" and "Le Beccasse."[4]

Identification of these men is not merely an exercise in ingenuity. Since the treaty made with them was taken by the United States as representing the will of the Sioux nation, one may have a legitimate curiosity to determine what proportion of that people were actually represented. The seven "chiefs" who counciled with Pike were evidently all Mdewakantons. They may have represented three of the four villages or bands into which that subtribe seems then to have been divided, but the two actual signers cannot have represented more than two villages. If those two villages contained half the population credited by Pike to the Mdewakantons (2,105), they had about 525 inhabitants each. It was highhanded, to say the least, for two chiefs, speaking for slightly more than a thousand people, to cede a portion of valuable land (if they knew what they were doing) in the name of the entire Sioux nation, which Pike considered to have a total population of 21,675.[5] And for the United States government, which certainly did know what it was doing, to take this purported cession at face value, as it did when the Senate ratified the treaty, was disingenuous, if not downright dishonest.

After a winter among the Chippewas and the English traders, Pike returned to the Sioux in April, 1806. He immediately called another council, mainly to convey to the Sioux the results of his efforts to induce the Chippewas to make peace with their traditional enemies. About forty chiefs of the Sissetons, Wahpetons, and Mdewakantons were pres-

[4] *Ibid.*, pp. 86–89 n. Coues' identifications are based on those provided by Thomas Foster in an earlier edition of Pike's *Expeditions*, found in *Minnesota Historical Collections*, I (1850–1856), 312–313. There is a possibility that "Le Beccasse" or "Le Boucasse" was a Wahpekute, better known under the traditional name of Wah-kan-tah-pay and living in 1825 about five miles below the later site of Le Sueur. See Foster, p. 312. William J. Snelling includes a story about the trader Pinichon in his *Tales of the Northwest* (1830), a collection which, though published as fiction, is probably as reliable a source of fact as most of the early travel narratives.

[5] Coues, *Expeditions of Zebulon M. Pike*, I, 346. Coues devotes some seven pages of notes to pointing out the deficiencies in the treaty. His objections are summarized in Folwell, *A History of Minnesota*, I, 94.

ent, in addition to more than five hundred tribesmen who had gathered for the festivities. Although handicapped by incompetent interpreters and the opposition of a few of the Indians to any reconciliation with the Chippewas, Pike managed to communicate the essential parts of his message. His mission completed, he started on his way downriver, stopping briefly at Kapozha and at the villages of Tatankamani and Wabasha.[6]

How much was accomplished by Pike toward gaining the allegiance of the Sioux is questionable. As will be seen, nearly all of them fought on the British side in the War of 1812, and Pike's visit does not seem to have had much of a deterrent effect on the activities of the English traders. But the voyage did add to the sum of geographical information on the upper Mississippi and to our knowledge of the Sioux in 1805–1806. Besides the three Mdewakanton villages on the Mississippi, there was the one on the Minnesota at which the grand council was held. The "Minowa Kantongs," as Pike called them, were described as the only Sioux who used canoes, built log huts, or cultivated vegetables. Of the last, Pike was not certain, for although they were said to raise a small amount of corn and beans, he saw none of either on his visit. Wild rice, which they used for bread, was available in sufficient quantities to last them all winter, supplemented by the animals they could kill. They were by now well supplied with firearms, but this fact did not entitle them to any superior position in the eyes of the other bands.[7]

The Wahpekutes, who impressed Pike as the "most stupid and inactive of all the Sioux," were said to be a band of vagabonds recruited from the refugees of the other bands, expelled for their misdeeds. They numbered only about 270 and roamed widely, with some tendency to concentrate around the headwaters of the Des Moines River. The Wahpetons, who numbered 1,060, had their base on the lower Minnesota River but hunted widely. The Sissetons, some 1,110 strong, were situated on the upper Minnesota, as far up as Big Stone Lake.[8] The center of trade for all these bands was Michilimackinac, except for the Wahpekutes, who traded principally at Prairie du Chien. Pike estimated the value of the Indians' annual consumption of merchandise at $13,500 for the Mdewakantons, $12,500 for the Sissetons, $6,000 for the Wahpetons, and $2,000 for the Wahpekutes. Their annual return in peltries was given as 230, 160, 115, and 50 packs, respectively, for the four

[6] Coues, *Expeditions of Zebulon M. Pike*, I, 197–206.

[7] *Ibid.*, pp. 342, 344.

[8] *Ibid.*, pp. 344, 346–347.

bands.[9] This sort of statistical information was, of course, designed to be used by those in charge of establishing the government factories.

Pike was a soldier, and although he saw fit to publish the journal of his expedition, he wasted few words on the culture of the Indians he saw. Aside from his accounts of a dance at Wabasha's village and a lacrosse game at Prairie du Chien, some remarks on a scaffold burial he saw near Kapozha, and a few scattered observations on the ritual of holding councils, he told little about the customs or manners of the Sioux. In the performance of his duties he collected the kind of information he deemed would be of most value to his superiors. If this is less exciting reading than Carver's narrative, it has the advantage of being trustworthy, within the limits imposed by the brevity of Pike's stay in the Sioux country. And the expedition is itself an important milestone in the history of the eastern Sioux.

When the War of 1812 broke out, the Sioux, like the other Indians of the Northwest, rallied to the British side with a near-unanimity that showed the inefficacy of Pike's attempt to establish American sovereignty over these tribes. The reasons were much the same as those which governed their actions in the Revolution: the British held the trump cards and played them better. One of the most active instruments of British policy was a trader named Robert Dickson, who, even before the formal declaration of war, held a conference of some 300 Indians belonging to various tribes to sound them out and to show them the advantages of adherence to the British. Wabasha and Little Crow, among others, made speeches in which they reported that "they had been amused for some time by bad birds, but that they lived by the English traders and would adhere to the English."[10] Dickson arrived about July 1, 1812, at Mackinac with a force of about 130 Sioux, Winnebagos, and Menominees who played a part in the swift capture of that American outpost. At the beginning of 1813 he was appointed agent and superintendent for the Indians west of the Mississippi, and the next June he brought a force of over 600 warriors, including 97 Sioux, to Mackinac.[11]

It should not be supposed that the Sioux, who rarely held to one purpose very long in their own wars, remained unswervingly committed to the British cause in the sense that regular troops, subject to military dis-

---

[9] *Ibid.*, pp. 346–347.

[10] Ernest Alexander Cruikshank, "Robert Dickson, the Indian Trader," *Wisconsin Historical Collections*, XII (1892), 140.

[11] *Ibid.*, pp. 141–142, 146.

cipline, would have done. When an opportunity to wage war on the Chippewas came along, there were always parties of warriors ready to disregard the wishes of their chiefs and to allow themselves to be diverted from the campaigns for which those chiefs had promised their services. This was especially true toward the end of the war. During the winter of 1813–1814 the Sioux and Chippewas were fighting, and it was reported that many western Indians had gone over to the Americans. Although Doane Robinson says that Wabasha's loyalty was called into question and that the other Mdewakanton chiefs stuck by their alliance, contemporaneous documents convey the impression that the Red Wing chief, Tatankamani, was the main source of anxiety to the British.[12]

Toward the end of the war at least one renegade band seems to have deserted the British completely. This was a group called the Gens de la Feuille Tiré, or Fire-Leaf band, who had supposedly withdrawn from Wabasha's band. (Actually they were Wahpekutes and are so designated by Pike.) The trader Joseph Rolette had contracted to supply provisions to the British garrison at Fort McKay (Prairie du Chien); and when he found himself unable to fulfill the terms of his contract, he entered into unauthorized dealings with this band. When two of his men were killed by members of the Fire-Leaf band, which "had been publickly declared Americans," the incident was blown into a *cause célèbre* and ultimately led to a court-martial for Rolette and execution for an Indian found guilty of the murders.[13]

[12] *Ibid.*, p. 150; "Dickson and Grignon Papers—1812–1815," *Wisconsin Historical Collections*, XI (1888), 276, 286; Doane Robinson, *A History of the Dakota or Sioux Indians* (Minneapolis: Ross and Haines, 1956), pp. 87–88. Louis Grignon wrote Dickson in October, 1813, that "the Sioux have exhibited great discontent, particularly the son of L'elle rouge [L'Aile Rouge, or Red Wing], but I think from the speech of Petit Corbeaux, who I believe is the best disposed, that the least may be expected. L'elle rouge is for whipping the Sauteaux [Chippewas]." And the following January, Dickson wrote from Lake Winnebago that "the Sioux have behaved like the villains as they are, they must soon suffer for their villainy," adding that "the Ail Rouge is at the bottom of this & got the Sauteux killed on purpose to prevent any Siouxs coming this way." The genealogy of the Red Wings presents more than the usual number of problems, but Tatankamani appears to be the son of Whoo-pa-doo-ta or Hoo-pa-hoo-sha, the original Red Wing, who took part in the conspiracy of Pontiac. He may have been born about 1759, and he died in 1829. His successor, Wacouta, is probably not the "young Red Wing" described as a beggar by Forsyth. Wacouta is variously referred to as the son, the stepson, and the nephew of Tatankamani, and one story has it that his mother was the daughter of an English trader. See *History of Goodhue County* (Red Wing: Wood, Alley and Co., 1878), pp. 414–415.

[13] "The Bulger Papers," *Wisconsin Historical Collections*, XIII (1895), 23, 36–37, 47, 49, 50–51. Rolette was cleared by the court-martial.

When news of the Treaty of Ghent reached the upper Mississippi in the spring of 1815, the British found themselves in an embarrassing position, for they had made numerous promises to the Indians which the terms now agreed upon made it impossible for them to fulfill. In the last months of the war, the British authorities had tried to impress upon the Indians that the war was now being fought exclusively for their benefit, all other causes for hostilities between England and the Americans having been settled. When the war's end left the western country and Indian relations there on much the same footing as before, some of the Indians felt that they had been sold out by their quondam allies and benefactors. Some of this feeling of betrayal appears in speeches made at the great conference of western Indians called by the British in 1816 on Drummond Island. Although the minutes of the council, as reported by Doane Robinson, have Wabasha and Little Crow protesting only mildly over the separate peace made by the British, the Indians' recollections in later years represent the two chiefs as spurning the British presents and accusing the givers of betrayal. Little Crow is supposed to have said:

> After we have fought for you, endured many hardships, lost some of our people, and awakened the vengeance of our powerful neighbours, you make a peace for yourselves and leave us to obtain such terms as we can! You no longer need our services, and offer us these goods as a compensation for having deserted us. But no! We will not take them; we hold them and yourselves in equal contempt![14]

The termination of the "second war of independence" left the United States in a somewhat improved position with regard to Indian affairs, a posture which the government took advantage of by negotiating a series of "peace and friendship" treaties with the various Indian tribes that had served the British during the war. Two such treaties were made with the eastern Sioux bands at Portage des Sioux, on the Mississippi above St. Louis, in the summer of 1815. Both dated July 19, they were signed by chiefs and headmen of the "Sioux of the Lakes" and the "Sioux of St. Peter's River," respectively. Their content is identical, consisting largely of pledges of friendship to the United

14 Edward D. Neill, *The History of Minnesota* (Philadelphia: J. B. Lippincott and Co., 1858), pp. 292–293; Robinson, *History of the Dakota*, pp. 98–99. See also Thomas L. McKenney and James Hall, *The Indian Tribes of North America*, ed. by Frederick Webb Hodge (Edinburgh: J. Grant, 1933), I, 126, which may be Robinson's ultimate source.

States on the one hand and what amounted to acts of oblivion regarding past behavior on the other. A name recognizable as that of Tatanka-mani appears on the first, but those of Little Crow, Wabasha, and Shakopee are all conspicuously missing; apparently the latter chiefs had not entirely reconciled themselves to the new order.[15]

Although Pike's treaty with the Sioux had been ratified by the Senate in 1808, no further action had ever been taken, either to establish a fort on the upper river or to pay the Indians the $2,000 the Senate saw fit to offer them. The experience of the late war, however, had demonstrated the hazards incurred by the failure to bring the Indians of that region under the effective control and supervision of the United States. In 1816, therefore, plans were formulated by the War Department for a system of military posts in the remote northwestern country, and the following year Major Stephen H. Long was sent up the river in a six-oared skiff to investigate further the sites purchased by Pike more than a decade earlier.

Long's journal, like Pike's, is more useful for the information it gives about the locations of the Sioux villages than for what it reveals about their culture. After meeting a small war party on the Mississippi above Prairie du Chien, Long reached Wabasha's village on July 12. It was now situated on the Prairie aux Ailes, the later site of the city of Winona, and was almost deserted at the time of Long's visit, the chief and most of his people being absent on a hunting expedition. Here the party took on a passenger, a loquacious subchief named Wazzacoota (cf. Hennepin's Ouasicoudé) who regaled them with stories, including the tale of the maiden who leaped from a cliff rather than marry a man not of her choice.[16] Already current in Pike's day, this legend later acquired its definitive form in William J. Snelling's *Tales of the Northwest* (1830).

Long also visited the Red Wing band, at that time divided into two villages, one at the site above Lake Pepin, the other, probably temporary, at Sandy Point, where Fort Beauharnois had once stood. Farther upstream his party passed Little Crow's village, comprising

[15] Charles J. Kappler, comp. and ed., *Indian Affairs, Laws and Treaties*, II (Washington: Government Printing Office, 1904), 113, 114. Another treaty was negotiated June 1, 1816, with "eight bands of the Siouxs, composing the three tribes called the Siouxs of the Leaf, the Siouxs of the Broad Leaf, and the Siouxs who shoot in the Pine Tops." Red Wing ("Tatangamarnee") signed this treaty also. See Kappler, *Indian Affairs*, II, 128–129.

[16] "Up the Mississippi in a Six-Oared Skiff in 1817," *Minnesota Historical Collections*, II (1889), 22–25.

fourteen cabins, and across from it a burying ground containing two scaffolds in an enclosure. Long was not displeased to find this village temporarily deserted, for its inhabitants were said to be the most notorious beggars among the Sioux of the Mississippi. He noted that one cabin had loopholes and was so situated as to bring the opposite bank within musket shot, from which he concluded that Little Crow was a sort of robber baron.[17]

Long did not go up the Minnesota and only remarked that there were three considerable villages up that river, nor did he give much information on the villages he did visit. Interestingly, in view of the role played by the Sioux in the recent war, wherever Long stopped the Indians raised an American flag to show their loyalty. The fact that Wabasha's village had changed location since 1805 is also of some interest. Since the bark-covered cabins had to be replaced fairly often, it is not surprising that new ones were occasionally erected on a new site. In time, and especially after the Sioux had come more immediately under the surveillance of the United States government, the Mdewakanton bands settled more or less permanently at the locations where the Pond brothers found them in 1834.

The information collected by Major Long was added to that gathered by Pike, and the peninsula between the Mississippi and the Minnesota was finally selected as the site of the new military post on the upper river. In the summer of 1819 Major Thomas Forsyth, an experienced Indian agent, was sent up from St. Louis with provisions for the fort soon to be erected and with about $2,000 worth of goods for the Indians, who were somewhat tardily to be paid for the cessions made to Pike. From Prairie du Chien he accompanied Lieutenant Colonel Henry Leavenworth, who was to establish the fort. On his way up the river and at the conferences held with the various bands, Forsyth had extensive opportunities to observe the Sioux; and he, like his predecessors, recorded his discoveries and impressions in a journal.[18]

Forsyth noted that the habit of begging had become firmly entrenched by this time. The younger Red Wing met him at Prairie du Chien and issued a piteous appeal for goods to assuage his grief over the loss of one of his men to the Chippewas. When this importunate beggar left, he was followed by his father, whose mission was much the same. Forsyth decided to make what use he could of the old chief, however, by

[17] *Ibid.*, pp. 26–27, 30–31.
[18] Thomas Forsyth, "Journal of a Voyage from St. Louis to the Falls of St. Anthony, in 1819," *Wisconsin Historical Collections*, VI (1872), 188–189.

quizzing him about the notorious Carver grant, a large cession of lands in present-day Wisconsin and Minnesota which two Sioux chiefs had supposedly made to Carver. The chief said he remembered hearing his father say that certain lands east of the Mississippi had been given to an Englishman but had no recollection of the transaction himself. Since he seemed reluctant to say more on the subject, Forsyth did not press him for further information (pp. 197–199).

On August 10, two days after leaving Prairie du Chien, Forsyth's party stopped briefly with "the Bourgne, or One-Eyed Sioux," whose village was said to be on the Upper Iowa River and who had "placed themselves on the banks of the Mississippi to be in readiness to receive anything we might have to give them." Forsyth says he gave them a little powder and "milk," i.e., whiskey, "they agreeing with me that it was better to give the blankets, etc., to the Indians above, as they were most in want" (pp. 201–202). The subchief whose heirarchy of values led him to rate whiskey above blankets was none other than L'Orignal Levé, also known as Tamaha, one of the two of his nation who had served on the American side in the War of 1812. According to fairly reliable sources, he was sent by General William Clark on a mission to the Missouri River Sioux and upon his return to Prairie du Chien was imprisoned by Dickson, who was unable to extract any information from him and finally released him. A story more on the fringes of legend has it that when the British set fire to Fort McKay after evacuating it in 1815, Tamaha rushed into the flames and rescued an American flag and an American medal (p. 201 n.). He lived until 1860 and is said to have been a familiar figure to early settlers in the Wabasha vicinity.

Upon reaching Wabasha's village, Forsyth delivered the first in a series of speeches explaining the benefits to the Indians of having a fort at the proposed site. It would be a place for them to trade as well as a place where they might have blacksmithing done. Their enemies would not dare attack them in the vicinity of the fort, and they must of course observe similar restraint in respect to the Chippewas. He asked the Indians to guarantee freedom of passage on the river to American vessels and warned them not to be led astray by the "bad birds" from the north—an indication that the influence of British traders was still great. Like Long, he praised Wabasha, and he also had good things to say about Little Crow, whom he found "a steady, generous and independent Indian; [who] acknowledged the sale of the land at the mouth of the St. Peter's river to the United States, and said he had been looking every year since the sale for the troops to build a fort, and was happy now to see us all, as the Sioux would now have their Father with them" (pp. 202–204, 217).

Forsyth conferred with several other chiefs in the performance of his mission. On August 24, while his party was in the vicinity of Kapozha, men whom he called Pinichon and White Bustard arrived with their followers; and the next day "Six" (Shakopee), Arrow, and Killiew joined them. All were from up the Minnesota; White Bustard's village was four miles upstream, Pinichon's two miles above that, Shakopee's thirty miles up, and Arrow's and Killiew's fifty-four and sixty miles up, respectively (pp. 205–206). Thus Forsyth, unlike Long, had dealings with the Wahpetons and Sissetons and probably with the Wahpekutes, as well as with the Mdewakantons. He told these chiefs the same things he had told Wabasha and doled out goods to them, giving preference to those nearest the fort soon to be built. The only one he singled out in his journal is Shakopee, whom he did not like. He wrote: "I by no means liked the countenance of Mr. Six, nor did I like his talk; I gave them the remainder of my goods, yet the Six wanted more. . . . I found on inquiring that Mr. Six is a good-for-nothing fellow, and rather gives bad counsel to his young men than otherwise" (p. 206).

Forsyth's general opinion of the Sioux was not high. He noted that early travelers, such as Hennepin, had praised their hospitality, generosity, and freedom from guile, but he found them "much altered" by 1819. He attributed their degeneration entirely to "their too great intercourse with those whom we call civilized people. . . ." Whatever they may have been, the Sioux were now "actually a poor, indolent, beggarly drunken set of Indians and cowards." He saw nothing of the "genuine Indian" in them, none of the independence and "enterprising character as hunters or warriors" that had been associated with the race (pp. 212–213). Considering that Henry H. Sibley and Samuel W. Pond dated the beginning of the decline among the Sioux from 1837, when they began receiving annuities, it is noteworthy that Forsyth thought the process already under way nearly two decades earlier. It is only fair to point out, however, that Forsyth saw the countryside through which he passed as "a mountainous, broken, rocky and sterile country, not fit for either man or beast to live in," which he wondered why Carver would want to buy (p. 211). Perhaps his view of the Indians was as wide of the mark as his estimate of the rich valley of the upper Mississippi.

Forsyth had opinions also on two matters of importance to his government: the influence of the British traders and the relations between the

Sioux and the Chippewas. He attributed the greater success of the British to the superiority of their goods and to their more careful selection of agents. Before a man was appointed agent, he was expected to be familiar with at least one Indian language, and hence it was to be presumed that he would know something of the Indians themselves. Although all the goods sold to the Indians were of British manufacture, the Americans, intent on making money, dealt in only the cheaper and inferior quality goods. Forsyth thought that our relations with the Indians would benefit by the application of the golden rule in treating with them, and he advocated a return to William Penn's policy of honest dealing with the Indians. As to intertribal warfare, he began with the supposition that it was bad but was persuaded by Little Crow's reasoning that for the Sioux, at least, it afforded more benefits than a treaty of peace would bring. At a cost of one or two men a year, the chief said, the Sioux were able to hold their hunting grounds east of the Mississippi, whereas peace between the tribes would permit the Chippewas to extend their domain clear down to the east bank of the river (pp. 213–214).

The establishment of a military post at the mouth of the Minnesota in the late summer of 1819 was an event of great significance to the Indians living in that vicinity. At first called Fort St. Anthony, the post was renamed Fort Snelling in 1825 in honor of the man who became its commander in 1820, Colonel Josiah Snelling.[19] Although its garrison was small in the early years, its situation, on the bluffs overlooking the junction of the two rivers, made it virtually impregnable to Indian assault, had any been attempted. To the Indians the most important personality associated with Fort Snelling was not its commandant but the United States Indian agent who made it his headquarters. Commanding officers came and went, but for nearly twenty years Indian affairs in the upper Mississippi region were conducted by one man, Major Lawrence Taliaferro. From his arrival, probably in the early summer of 1820, to his resignation at the end of 1839, he represented the Great Father in Washington to the Sioux people.

Taliaferro was a strong personality, possessed in ample measure of the qualities of firmness and integrity—William Watts Folwell calls him "incorruptible." His view of the Indian question was enlightened for his day, and he unquestionably discharged his duties with fidelity and forcefulness. At the same time, it is impossible, in reading his voluminous

[19] Marcus Hansen, *Old Fort Snelling* (Minneapolis: Ross and Haines, 1958), pp. 29–30.

papers—he was a compulsive letter-writer and journal-keeper—to avoid being struck by his colossal egotism, amounting at times to a messiah complex. He saw himself as fighting, singlehandedly, a twenty-year war against the "malefic" designs of the fur traders, who were out to exploit the Indians and defraud the government. His dependence on the military post (he had no council house in which to meet the Indians until 1823, no dwelling for himself until 1828) increased his sense of insecurity and loneliness. Nor were his relations with the military always the most harmonious. Before taking up his post, he had been instructed by Secretary of War John C. Calhoun that "it is of the first importance that, at such remote posts, there should be a perfect understanding between the Officers, civil and military, stationed there to give energy and effect to their operations."[20] But there were clashes almost from the first. Despite these handicaps and a constitutional weakness that obliged him to spend many of his winters away from his post, however, he discharged his duties so well that he was reappointed to the St. Peter's Agency under every administration from James Monroe's to Martin Van Buren's.

Taliaferro's aims were essentially those of his government: to gain and hold recognition by the Indians of United States sovereignty over the country they occupied, to protect the Indians from the baneful influence of the fur traders, to stop intertribal warfare, and to conduct his charges along the road toward civilization. The last of these is best dealt with in the next chapter, for it was only with the advent of missionaries that much was accomplished toward civilizing the Sioux, but the other objectives occupied Taliaferro throughout his long term of service.

The outcome of the War of 1812 had not induced the Indians automatically to shift their allegiance from England to the United States. Many of the fur traders, especially those in the employ of the American Fur Company, were British in sympathies, even though required by a law passed in 1816 to be American citizens. To wean the Indians away from their British ties, Taliaferro encouraged remote bands to visit the

[20] Clarence E. Carter, comp. and ed., *The Territorial Papers of the United States*, XV (Washington: Government Printing Office, 1951), 577. The following statement, made in an autobiographical sketch written at the age of seventy, is characteristic of Taliaferro: "In the midst of many perplexities, single-handed and alone, the Agent was consoled by many testimonials of well-done, good and faithful servant." See "Auto-Biography of Maj. Lawrence Taliaferro," *Minnesota Historical Collections*, VI (1894), 212. Similar remarks are found throughout his correspondence and his journals, particularly in his later, bitterer years.

agency and to hold councils there, at which he would collect all the British medals and flags he could, substitute equivalent symbols of American sovereignty, and also distribute a great number of useful articles such as axes, awls, beads, blankets, combs, shotguns, hats, hoes, knives, plumes, needles, and shifts—much the same sort of goods as the traders were dispensing in exchange for the Indians' valuable furs. In addition, he sometimes gave the chiefs powder, lead, tobacco, and even whiskey, though he was aware of the dangers involved in giving liquor to Indians. For the first two or three years of Taliaferro's tenure as agent, such gift-giving cost the government at least $1,200 annually, over and above ordinary aid furnished to the needy. Later it was greatly reduced. The distribution of provisions does not at this time appear to have been necessary, since game was still to be found, but in later years flour, beef, and other food became important items on the agent's list.[21]

The occasion for the giving out of presents was normally a council, which might be either a spontaneous visit to the agency by a band from the hinterland or a formal conference called by the agent, perhaps to adjudicate a difference between Indians of the same band or between separate tribes. A council was an extremely formal occasion, made even more so by the need to conduct all business through an interpreter. There is no evidence that Taliaferro learned enough of the Dakota language to converse fluently with the Indians in that tongue. His interpreter during almost his entire term of service was Scott Campbell, the mixed-blood son of the trader Colin Campbell. Young Campbell had spent his childhood among the Indians and was discovered by Lewis and Clark on their trip up the Missouri in 1805. Sent into white society to be educated, he acquired a good command of English and was thus qualified, by education at least, for the interpreter's job that he held for so many years. Whether he was qualified by temperament for his sensitive job may be questioned. The Reverend Samuel W. Pond, whose acquaintance with Campbell began in 1834, thought him inclined to soften harsh statements in interpreting them and even to distort or suppress unpleasant remarks so as to avoid ill feeling.[22] In his later years Campbell's tendency toward intemperance

21 "Auto-Biography of Maj. Lawrence Taliaferro," pp. 200, 205; Taliaferro Journal, June 2 and 7, and September 4, 1821; June 3, 1829; undated entries, MS., Minnesota Historical Society.

22 Samuel W. Pond, "The Dakotas or Sioux in Minnesota as They Were in 1834," *Minnesota Historical Collections*, XII (1905–1908), 339–341. Campbell must have taken

got the better of him and was finally responsible for his discharge by Taliaferro's successor.

Taliaferro did not deceive himself about the success of his efforts to win the allegiance of the Indians. As late as 1827 he wrote to his superior, General William Clark, Superintendent of Indian Affairs at St. Louis, that in the event of war between the two countries, every tribe under his jurisdiction would take the British side. Although he thought he had made a good impression on the Indians, he confessed, "I have not the slightest confidence in any professions of friendship or attachment which they may demonstrate either in regard to the United States or myself individually."[23] Fortunately, no British-American war broke out, and the loyalties of the Sioux were never put to the test.

Among Taliaferro's most difficult tasks, which neither he nor any of his successors ever really accomplished, was to effect a lasting peace between the Sioux and the Chippewas. Although in his first seven years he brought the tribes together at ten councils, the age-old enmity seems to have been only temporarily quenched each time, to break forth with renewed fury before many months had passed. He did what he could to keep his Indians from being reminded of the feud. Once when a couple of Sioux chiefs visited the agency, they noticed a pipe hanging on the wall and remarked that the hair on it had been taken from a Sisseton killed by the Chippewas the previous summer. Taliaferro promptly removed the object, saying that no such pipe would be allowed in the council room.[24]

Having convinced himself that peace could be achieved by setting up a geographical line of separation between the two tribes, in 1823 he proposed that they should both send delegates to Washington to negotiate

the interpreter's job quite early in Taliaferro's term, and he seems to have enjoyed the confidence of the agent—so much so that during one of Taliaferro's winter furloughs, the commanding officer at Fort Snelling, nominally in charge of the agency, complained that Taliaferro was circumventing the proper chain of command by sending instructions directly to Campbell.

[23] Lawrence Taliaferro to Superintendent William Clark, October 7, 1827, NARS, RG 75, LR, St. Peter's Agency. All National Archives material cited in this book is from Record Group 75. Microfilm copies have been used for correspondence up to 1881. Letters Received from the St. Peter's Agency, Santee Sioux Agency, Flandreau Special Agency, Minnesota Superintendency, and Northern Superintendency, as well as all Letters Sent (all on microfilm) are in the possession of the Mankato State College library; other microfilm correspondence is in the possession of the author. Unless the agency is specified, the St. Peter's Agency is meant.

[24] Abstract of Councils Between Chippewas and Sioux, accompanying Taliaferro to Clark, May 25, 1829, NARS, RG 75, LR; Taliaferro Journal, September 20, 1821.

a settlement and draw up a line. The following year he took a party of Sioux, Chippewas, and Menominees on the first of a series of trips to Washington, one purpose of which was to give them a chance to see something of the white man's strength and numbers. Traders at Prairie du Chien frightened some members of the party into dropping out there, and another took flight when the steamboat was on the Ohio River; but the rest made the trip and returned by way of New York and the Great Lakes. Although no treaty was signed, the groundwork was laid for a great intertribal council at Prairie du Chien the next year.[25]

The first Prairie du Chien conference was a spectacular performance, whatever may be said of its consequences. Great numbers of Indians from the Sioux, Chippewa, Menominee, Winnebago, Sac and Fox, Iowa, Potawatomi, and Ottawa tribes assembled early in August, to be wined and dined by officials of the United States government and (it was hoped) to negotiate a general settlement that would put an end to the intertribal wars that were costing them so many of their best men and interfering with the orderly management of Indian affairs by the government. Taliaferro has left a graphic picture of the theatrical entry of his 385 Sioux and Chippewas:

> There was a halt before entering the town, at the "Painted Rock," where, after attending to their toilet and appointment of soldiers to dress the columns of boats, the grand entry was made with drums beating, many flags flying, with incessant discharges of small arms. All Prairie du Chien was drawn out, with other delegations already arrived, to witness the display and landing of this ferocious looking body of true savages.[26]

Although liquor was liberally dispensed, not all of it found its way down the throats of the Indians. To counter the charge that they were niggardly in comparison with the British, the American officials, it is said, hauled out two kegs of whiskey, broke them open, and poured the contents out onto the ground. According to an account attributed to William J. Snelling, son of Colonel Josiah Snelling, the Indians were much offended by this waste. One chief, identified only as "old

[25] Taliaferro Journal, July 1823; "Auto-Biography of Maj. Lawrence Taliaferro," pp. 203–205. The proposal was evidently made at a council held in June, for the Long expedition which paused briefly at Wabasha's village late that month found the chief looking forward to the trip. See William H. Keating, *Narrative of an Expedition to the Sources of St. Peter's River* (Minneapolis: Ross and Haines, 1959), p. 282.

[26] "Auto-Biography of Maj. Lawrence Taliaferro," p. 206.

Wakhpakootay," is supposed to have remarked with real grief, "There was enough to have kept me drunk all the days of my life."[27]

At the council speeches were made by spokesmen of the various tribes, proclaiming their distaste for war and their fervent hope that peace would be established for all time. Wabasha and Tatankamani, Little Crow and Shakopee all offered their contributions toward the general sense of well-being and fellowship. The naive notion that a mere arbitrary line set up at such a conference would be honored by the tribes concerned seems to have been accepted without question by the American officials who called the council. Some of the Indians tried to warn them that aboriginal concepts of land ownership were different. Caramonee, a Winnebago chief, stated the customs of his race:

> The lands I claim are mine and the nations here know it is not only claimed by us but by our Brothers the Sacs and Foxes, Menominees, Iowas, Mahas, and Sioux. They have held it in common. It would be difficult to divide it. It belongs as much to one as the other. . . . My Fathers I did not know that any of my relations had any particular lands. It is true everyone owns his own lodge and the ground he may cultivate. I had thought the Rivers were the common property of all Red Skins and not used exclusively by any particular nation.[28]

Despite such words of caution, a dividing line was designated between the lands of the Sac and Fox tribe and those of the Sioux, running across northern Iowa, and another drawn on the map to separate the Sioux from the Chippewas. The latter began on the Mississippi in present southwestern Wisconsin, at the mouth of the Black River, crossed the Chippewa and the St. Croix well upstream, and continued on across what is now central Minnesota to the Red River of the North, opposite the mouth of the Goose River.[29]

Although the great council at Prairie du Chien began festively for the Indians, it ended tragically for some of them. Several of Taliaferro's delegation died on their way home, supposedly from drinking a concoction of whiskey and sugar that had been served them. A rumor

[27] [William J. Snelling], "Running the Gauntlet," *Minnesota Historical Collections*, I (1850–1856), 361–362. The same story is told, with minor differences in detail, in another account supposed to have been written by Snelling, "Early Days at Prairie du Chien," *Wisconsin Historical Collections*, V (1868), 124.

[28] "Journal of Proceedings at Prairie du Chien," August 6, 8, and 9, 1825 (photostatic copy in Minnesota Historical Society).

[29] Kappler, *Indian Affairs*, II, 250–251.

spread that the white men had deliberately tried to poison them. Although scouting this report, the younger Snelling predicted that many of the Sioux would continue to believe it for the rest of their lives.[30] He might have guessed that they would pass it on to their children, and the ugly rumor would survive as oral tradition among the Santee Sioux for well over a century after the treaty. In the 1960's elderly people were still telling this story, sometimes confusing it with the treatment given the men imprisoned at Davenport after the Uprising of 1862, and speaking of it as if it were something that had happened in their own lifetimes.

The treaty was also a failure in the larger sense that it did not accomplish what it was intended to. The Sioux-Chippewa line was not surveyed until 1835, and then the Indians (supposedly the Chippewas) pulled up the stakes as soon as they were planted. In any case, no respect was paid to the line by either side when it suited their interest to cross it. There may have been some temporary reduction in the number of raids made by one tribe on the other, but within a year or two hostilities were in full swing again. In the summer of 1827 a small group of Sioux treacherously attacked a party of visiting Chippewas almost under the walls of Fort Snelling. Regarding this act as flagrant disregard of the American flag, the commandant seized several hostages and held them until the culprits were delivered up. The latter were then turned over to the Chippewas, who forced them to "run the gauntlet," a form of punishment tantamount to death. From this time on, raids and counterraids were the dominant feature of relations between the two tribes.[31]

The story of the Santee Sioux in the 1820's is not entirely one of warfare with the Chippewas. In the discharge of his responsibilities, Taliaferro felt obliged to battle constantly with the traders, not only those whom he considered agents of the British but the whole fraternity, whose most serious offense was the sale of whiskey to the Indians. Early in 1822 he charged that the Lac qui Parle trader, Joseph Renville,

[30] Taliaferro Journal, August 23 and September 19, 1825; [Snelling?], "Early Days at Prairie du Chien," p. 124.

[31] Taliaferro to Clark, September 2, 1835, NARS, RG 75, LR; Taliaferro Journal, June 1, 1827; [Snelling], "Running the Gauntlet," pp. 362, 365–370; Charlotte O. Van Cleve, "A Reminiscence of Ft. Snelling," *Minnesota Historical Collections*, III (1870–1880), 79–81; Ann Adams, "Early Days at Red River Settlement and Fort Snelling," *Minnesota Historical Collections*, VI (1894), 109–110. See also Colonel Josiah Snelling to Henry Atkinson, May 31, 1827, in Carter, *Territorial Papers*, XI (Washington: Government Printing Office, 1943), 1082–1083.

besides flying the British flag just prior to 1822, had been selling liquor. In fact, Taliaferro recorded in his journal that "*ardent spirits* compose his principal article of his trade." He found Renville and his Columbia Fur Company less offensive, however, than the agents of the American Fur Company, whom he characterized as "men of *mean* principles and low origin—consequently are jealous—evil disposed and great vagabonds." [32] His especial bête noire was Joseph Rolette—"this *beast of the Creation*," as he once called him—the company's agent at Prairie du Chien, with whom he carried on a running feud during nearly his entire period as agent. He alleged that Rolette, related to Wabasha by marriage, had that chief under his influence and was responsible, through his sale of liquor to the band, for attacks on the Chippewas in 1829. Rolette in turn charged that Taliaferro had permitted a naturalized American named Laidlaw, a partner in the Columbia Fur Company, to distribute agency liquor to the Indians at Traverse des Sioux in order to promote the interests of that company. When in 1825 Taliaferro designated seventeen sites for trading posts within his jurisdiction, to be divided between the two competing companies, Rolette and his cohorts objected on the grounds that some of the forts were unnecessary and that their number gave the Indians too good a chance to lounge around them instead of hunting. [33] Thus the war of charges and countercharges went on.

Taliaferro may have exceeded his authority in designating so specifically the locations of the proposed trading posts, as he later did in suspending the traders' privilege of bringing liquor into the Indian country for their boatmen. They were permitted under the law to bring in one gallon per month for each boatman in their employ. Taliaferro charged that the men never saw more than a third of this, and even that "escaped" at a price of eight to sixteen dollars a gallon. So in August, 1830, he issued a circular forbidding the introduction of whiskey or high wines under this pretext. His action was not supported by higher authority, although General Clark conceded that Taliaferro's reasons were good. [34]

[32] Taliaferro Journal, January 12, 1822, and March 27, 1826.

[33] *Ibid.*, September 26, 1829, and October 22, 1830; Joseph Rolette to Lewis Cass, November 15, 1826, and to Clark, June 27, 1826; undated document in Indian Office files, accompanied by affidavit from Alexander Faribault, June 26, 1826, and Joseph Laframboise (undated), NARS, RG 75, LR. Faribault and Laframboise were in the employ of Rolette, whose hand is evident in the main document.

[34] Taliaferro to Clark, August 17, 1830; Clark to Secretary of War, September 22, 1830, NARS, RG 75, LR.

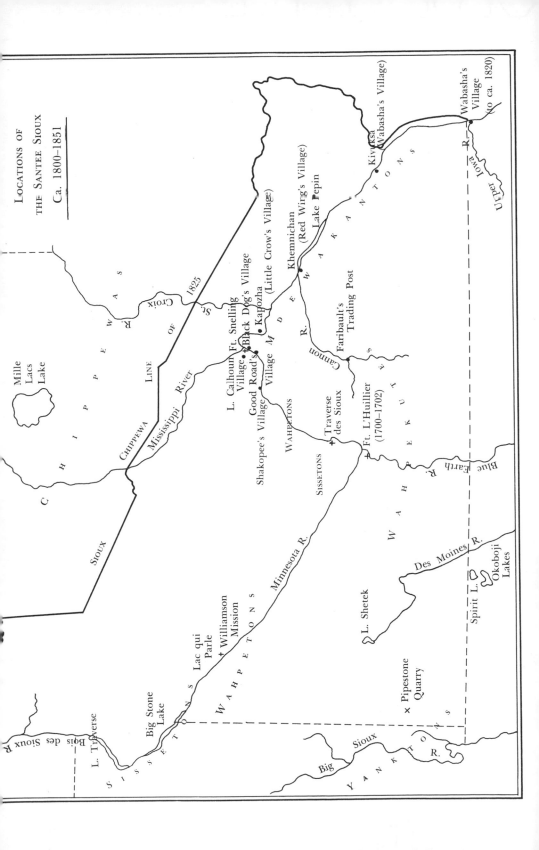

LOCATIONS OF
THE SANTEE SIOUX
Ca. 1800–1851

Although Taliaferro complained of the remoteness of his post in the 1820's, its isolation was rapidly being broken down, together with what remained of the insulation from the white man's world that the Sioux had enjoyed up to then. Three visitors to the upper Mississippi region in the early 1820's left detailed accounts of their experiences. The first was Henry Rowe Schoolcraft, who appeared in the summer of 1820 in the capacity of geologist and mineralogist for an expedition led by Governor Lewis Cass of Michigan Territory. Although the trip through the Sioux country was only incidental to Cass' primary purpose, the party did stop at the St. Peter's Agency long enough to help negotiate a treaty of peace between the Sioux and the Chippewas. The council was so poorly attended by the Indians and they manifested such indifference toward its objective that even Schoolcraft doubted that the peace would last.[35]

The treaty concluded, the party proceeded down the Mississippi to the villages of Little Crow, Red Wing, and Wabasha. Either Schoolcraft had not yet developed the ethnological bent that later led him to attempt an exhaustive study of American Indian cultures, or else he thought the Sioux less interesting than the Chippewas among whom he had been living, for his observations on these villages contain little that is not found in greater detail elsewhere. He seems to have been somewhat confused as to the divisions of the Sioux. His list includes both "Minokantongs" and "Mendewacantongs," of which the former are the Mdewakantons whom he visited; the "Mendewacantongs" he lumps with the Wahpekutes and locates vaguely south of the Minnesota River.[36]

Three years after Schoolcraft's visit, the silence of the upper Mississippi was broken by the shrill whistle of the first steamboat to penetrate that far into the wilderness, the *Virginia*, which on May 10, 1823, arrived at Fort Snelling. Welcome as it no doubt was to the garrison, it spread astonishment and consternation among the Indians, whose previous experience with the white man's boats had been limited to skiffs and keelboats, both powered by human muscle and not radically different from their own canoes.[37] Aboard the *Virginia* was an Italian

[35] Henry R. Schoolcraft, *Narrative Journal of Travels Through the Northwestern Regions of the United States*, ed. by Mentor L. Williams (East Lansing: Michigan State University Press, 1953), pp. 199–200.

[36] *Ibid.*, pp. 202, 209–210, 212, 218.

[37] William J. Petersen, *Steamboating on the Upper Mississippi* (Iowa City: State Historical Society of Iowa, 1937), p. 105.

nobleman, Count Giacomo Constantino Beltrami, who dreamed of following in the footsteps of Marco Polo, Columbus, Cabot, and Vespucci and making some discoveries of his own. Though a romantic in his response to nature, Beltrami treated everything American with derision, including the aborigines, who appear in his account merely as amusing curiosities. Red Wing, for example, is described as "an old man of hideous aspect, bent under the weight of years and atrocities," and a beggar withal.[38] On the whole, Beltrami does not add materially to our knowledge of the Sioux, but he provides an unusual vantage point from which to view them. Later on, when the trip up the Mississippi became a fashionable tour, his point of view became commonplace as genteel eastern ladies caught their first glimpses of the savage in his poverty and degradation.

Much more important than Beltrami's was the well-planned, well-executed expedition of Major Stephen H. Long in 1823, which passed up the Mississippi, followed the Minnesota to its source, then descended the Red River to the forty-ninth parallel, and returned by way of the international boundary to Lake Superior. In keeping with the aim of obtaining and recording scientific information on the native peoples along the route, the expedition's chronicler, William H. Keating, left a detailed description of the Sioux. The party first passed a small village of five lodges, evidently a remnant of Wabasha's village, a few miles above the Upper Iowa River, and two days later reached the main village. Even at the smaller outpost they saw about two acres of corn.[39]

At the Red Wing village an American flag was hoisted over the chief's cabin, and the visitors were invited to hold a council. Upon entering the lodge, they seated themselves on two bed frames for the smoking of the calumet and the inevitable speech-making. Presents of tobacco, powder, and shot were given, but the chief wondered if he and his warriors might have a little of their "Great Father's milk" to assuage their grief over the recent loss of friends and relatives in war with the Chippewas. When Major Long told them he had no whiskey along and pointed out that it was bad for people, the chief agreed but seemed regretful (pp. 259–261, 270).

In general, Keating's names for the various bands he encountered tally well with later accounts by reliable witnesses. He refers to the two villages of Wabasha as constituting the Keoxa band (usually spelled

[38] J. C. Beltrami, *A Pilgrimage in America* (Chicago: Quadrangle Books, Inc., 1962), 186–187.
[39] Keating, *Narrative of an Expedition*, p. 255.

"Kiyuksa"), to Red Wing's band as Eanbosandata, and to Little Crow's as Kapoja. Near the last village the party stopped for a time at an Indian cemetery consisting of several scaffolds holding coffins; "sometimes a trunk (purchased from a trader), at other times a blanket, or a roll of bark, conceals the body of the deceased." There were also several graves in which bones had been deposited after the flesh had decayed or been eaten by birds of prey. The village itself consisted of houses "formed by upright flattened posts, implanted in the ground, without any interval, except here and there some small loopholes for defence; these same posts support the roof, which presents a surface of bark." Before and behind each house was a scaffold used for drying corn, pumpkins, and other vegetables (p. 299).

Four Mdewakanton villages were passed on the Minnesota River. The first, which Keating called Oanoska, was presided over by Wamdetanka (Big Eagle), formerly dependent on Little Crow. This was what is usually known as Black Dog's village, located some three to five miles from the mouth of the St. Peter's, on the right bank. About seven miles farther upstream, also on the right bank, Long's party reached Tetankatane, or the Old Village, supposedly the center from which the Mdewakantons dispersed after their expulsion from the Mille Lacs region. It had been ruled by Wabasha's father before his removal to the Upper Iowa, and is the one referred to as Pinichon's village and later as Good Road's village. The next village was Taoapa, Shakopee's village, thirty miles up the river and on the left bank, consisting of fifteen large bark lodges and having a population of about three hundred, or about the same as Kapozha or Kiyuksa. The lodges and cornfields were in good order, arranged along the river, and there were the customary drying scaffolds, on which the explorers were told the Indians slept on very hot nights. One more Mdewakanton village, called Weakaote, was seen some six miles above the Little Rapids (near modern Le Sueur), a hamlet of two lodges and the ruins of a third. Later the party encountered the chief of the village, and were told that the Indians living there planned to move farther up the river (pp. 339–348, 401–402).

Except for Weakaote, the Mdewakanton villages reported by Keating are those which later white settlers found, in approximately the same locations. Some split-offs took place later, but in general the semi-sedentary Santees appear to have been settled in more or less permanent villages by this time. This was not, of course, true of the Wahpekutes, whose usual hunting grounds are given by Keating, although it does not appear that he actually saw many of them. According to Joseph Renville, who had joined the party as guide and interpreter at Fort Snelling, the Wahpekutes had the reputation among the other Indians of being a lawless band. They were said to live principally near the headwaters of the Cannon and Blue Earth rivers. Some of the Sissetons rendezvoused near the mouth of the Blue Earth, but a division of their people called the Kahra hunted mostly in the Lake Traverse–Red River area. The Wahpetons were found mainly near the headwaters of the Minnesota. Keating, relying on Renville's estimates, gave the population of the Mdewakantons as 1,500, of the Wahpekutes as 800, of the Sissetons as 2,500, and of the Wahpetons as 900. Adding to this 2,000 Yanktons, 5,200 Yanktonais, 14,400 Tetons, and 800 stragglers of one kind or another, he arrived at a total of 28,100 for the entire Dakota nation (pp. 396, 402–403). Despite some over- and underestimates for particular bands, this is probably as reliable a figure as was offered before the Sioux began receiving annuities and census rolls were prepared.

Like other visitors, Keating had views of his own on the Sioux and their prospects. He saw them as a "noble ruin," no longer meeting at a common council fire, no longer going on the warpath in armies (as he supposed they had once done) but only in small bands of marauders. He postulated a golden age which had passed: "When they lighted the common calumet at the General Council Fire, it was always among the Mende Wahkanton, who then resided near Spirit Lake [Mille Lacs], and who were considered as the oldest band of the nation, their chiefs being of longer standing than those of the other tribes. . ." (pp. 442–443). Despite some hopeful signs among the agricultural bands, he felt that the Sioux had been corrupted by the white man. He thought that "the occasional supplies of these articles which they receive from the Indian agents and officers of our government, whenever they are in want of food, no doubt tend to encourage their lazy habits." Colonel Snelling, it was said, had once offered a chief the use of a plow and someone to teach him how to use it, so that his people might raise potatoes. The chief thought the proposition over, then replied that he would be a fool to accept it, as "his father always supplied him with provisions, as often as he was in need of them" (pp. 439–440).

The Sioux may have seemed a "noble ruin" to Keating in 1823, but their deterioration still had a long way to go. If the occasional distribution of goods by Taliaferro was so injurious as Keating supposed, how much more so were the annuities provided by later treaties, which Sibley saw as the real beginning of the Indians' decline. Taliaferro was not blind to the dangerous potentialities of the annuity system, but he wished to see that his charges received the best possible bargain, and he apparently thought that his efforts to promote agriculture among them would offset the debilitating effects of gratuities from the government. In this supposition he was wrong, as the second decade of his tenure at the St. Peter's Agency demonstrated.

CHAPTER 3

Civilizing the Sioux

As THE third decade of the nineteenth century ended, the Santee Sioux were entering a period of crisis that was to last thirty years and end in catastrophe. In all probability none of them recognized the symptoms for what they were, although the signs of change were already evident. There were more white men in their country than ever before—the soldiers even had a fort in the heart of the Santees' territory—and steamboats were coming up the river with increasing frequency. But much of the old culture was still intact. The changes that had taken place within the memory of a man were largely accessions from the white man's world, many of which made life more comfortable and more interesting.

One change, however, that was alarming to Indian and white alike was the depletion of game. Schoolcraft had noted as early as 1820 that the nearest bison in abundance were a two days' journey west of the Mississippi River villages; in Hennepin's day they had roamed the prairies immediately back from the river. The smaller game was also disappearing from the vicinity of the Indian settlements. Keating mentions the almost total absence of game of any kind on the Minnesota River in 1823.[1] Under these conditions, and with agriculture a

[1] Henry R. Schoolcraft, *Narrative Journal of Travels Through the Northwestern Regions of the United States*, ed. by Mentor L. Williams (East Lansing: Michigan State University

negligible source of food, the Sioux were often hungry a good part of the year. The occasional handouts of provisions were not nearly enough to meet the needs of the recipients.

In Taliaferro's view, the solution was for the Indians to expand their meager farming and eventually become self-supporting. Whenever he held a council, he tried to impress on them the advantages of agriculture. He was much encouraged when, in his second summer at St. Peter's, the chief Black Dog remarked that every day he saw the whites plowing and wished that he had someone to show his people how to cultivate the soil in this fashion.[2] Apparently this wish led to no concrete results, but in the winter of 1828–1829 nature came to the agent's aid. During that severe winter the occupants of at least thirty lodges starved to death because of the shortage of game. Taliaferro had no supplies with which to help them, and he had been "compelled to be the witness of scenes the most unpleasant." The victims of this starving period were the nomadic Sioux from the upper Minnesota, but the Mdewakantons were also affected. The next spring they all left their villages in search of food of any kind.[3]

This was the psychological moment for Taliaferro to press his agricultural schemes. An Indian named Mahpiya Wichasta, or Cloud Man, had been one of those who nearly starved on the prairie the previous winter, and he had at that time made a resolution to give farming a try if he lived through the ordeal. Together with one Kee-e-he-ie (He That Flies), father-in-law of the interpreter-farmer Philander Prescott, Cloud Man took the great step in the summer of 1829. Taliaferro sent out a soldier from the fort and two yoke of oxen, under Prescott's supervision, and they plowed for about a month in the vicinity of Lake Calhoun. Few Indians ventured out the first year, but the second year more came than there was work for, and some had to dig with hoes. The agent hired men to collect materials for a log village and for a building to protect the property of such Indians as "might submit to become cultivators of the soil."[4]

Press, 1953), p. 212; William H. Keating, *Narrative of an Expedition to the Sources of St. Peter's River* (Minneapolis: Ross and Haines, 1959), pp. 302–303.

[2] Taliaferro Journal, September 26, 1821.

[3] Lawrence Taliaferro to William Clark, February 28, 1829, NARS, RG 75, LR; Taliaferro Journal, June 21, 1829.

[4] Samuel W. Pond, "The Dakotas or Sioux in Minnesota as They Were in 1834," *Minnesota Historical Collections*, XII (1905–1908), 326; Philander Prescott, "Autobiography and Reminiscences of Philander Prescott," in *Minnesota Historical Collections*, VI (1894), 482; Taliaferro to Secretary of War John H. Eaton, February 23, 1830,

Taliaferro took considerable pride in his experiment, which he named "Eatonville" after Jackson's Secretary of War. While in Washington early in 1830 he wrote to Eaton that the President had expressed a willingness to further the experiment; the agent thought that six or eight hundred dollars taken from the Indian civilization fund would "mature what has happily been begun. . . ."[5] His journal records frequent rides out to Eatonville, which was only six miles from Fort Snelling. Prescott was superintending work at the colony the next summer and, so far as he could, financing it out of his own pocket. When Taliaferro visited the village early in September, he found the Indians busy shucking and tying up their corn; as soon as they had finished collecting wild rice, they would dig their potatoes. Taliaferro instructed the women to save seed from the melons, squash, pumpkins, beans, peas, onions, cabbages, and other vegetables.[6] The Eatonville colony did not effect a revolution in the economy of the Sioux, and it eventually had to be abandoned because of its vulnerability to Chippewa attacks; but it demonstrated to Taliaferro's satisfaction that the Sioux could be taught to farm in a manner approximating that of white frontiersmen.

The project of civilizing the Sioux received a financial boost from a treaty negotiated in 1830 with the Sioux and several other tribes, who gathered at Prairie du Chien that July. Although the primary purpose of this treaty was to stop raids by the Sioux and the Sacs and Foxes into each other's territory, certain land cessions agreed to by the tribes involved payment. The Sioux ceded a twenty-mile-wide strip of land on their side of the dividing line set up in 1825, the Sacs and Foxes ceding a similar strip on their side. This forty-mile-wide "neutral strip" only aggravated relations between the tribes by tempting hunters from each to intrude upon it, but the land cession was compensated for by the government in the form of a $2,000 annuity to be paid for ten years in money, merchandise, or animals, at the chiefs' option. In addition, for the same period "and as long thereafter as the President of the United States may think necessary and proper," they were to be provided with

NARS, RG 75, LR. Prescott was confused as to the year this experiment started, for he mentions that during the first year he and his crew cut a large number of tamarack logs for use in rebuilding the agency council house. It did not burn until August, 1830, and entries in Taliaferro's Journal for 1829 make it clear that the Eatonville project was under way by the end of that summer. See also *The Recollections of Philander Prescott: Frontiersman of the Old Northwest*, ed. by Donald Dean Parker (Lincoln: University of Nebraska Press, 1966), pp. 126–129.

[5] Taliaferro to Eaton, February 23, 1830, NARS, RG 75, LR.

[6] Taliaferro Journal, August 24 and September 4, 1830. In the last entry he says the colony was established August 15, 1829.

one blacksmith and the necessary tools, agricultural implements, and iron and steel to the amount of $700. An education fund was also set up, of which the Sioux were to receive benefits to the amount of $500 annually. The signers of this treaty included twenty-six Mdewakantons, nine Wahpekutes, and two Sissetons; no Wahpetons signed. Besides names recognizable as those of Wabasha, Little Crow, and Big Eagle, the chiefs who signed included Wacouta, or the Shooter, who had succeeded Tatankamani as chief of the Red Wing band in 1829; Wakinyan Tanka, or Big Thunder, soon to become chief at Kapozha; and Tachunk Washtay, or Good Road, the next chief of the old Pinichon village.[7]

The annuities provided by the 1830 treaty were too small to have much effect, good or bad, on the Santee Sioux, but the blacksmith shop was a convenience for some. For years the bands near the agency had been having their work done by the agency smith; but because that location was inconvenient for Wabasha's band, now more than twice as large as any of the others, Taliaferro decided to place the new blacksmith shop at the Kettle Hills, just below the Kiyuksa village.[8]

Although most of the dividing line between the Sioux and the Sac and Fox tribes was surveyed in 1832 and 1833, neither it nor the neutral strip through which it ran had any effect on the perennial warfare between the two tribes. In any case, during the Black Hawk War in 1832, some of the Sioux had a chance to vent their hatred of their enemies without incurring the displeasure of the government. Wabasha's band was invited to join the military and played a brief and inglorious role in the later stages of the campaign. After Black Hawk and his warriors had been pretty well beaten, Wabasha's braves fell upon a band of a hundred or so fugitives, half-starved and nearly defenseless, and slaughtered at least sixty-eight of them, including many women and children.[9] Retaliation was inevitable as soon as the Sacs and Foxes were somewhat recovered, and raiding back and forth continued for at least another decade.

If Taliaferro met with no success in his attempts to halt intertribal

[7] Charles J. Kappler, comp. and ed., *Indian Affairs, Laws and Treaties*, II (Washington: Government Printing Office, 1904), 305–309. For the report of Tatankamani's death, see the Taliaferro Journal, June 1829.

[8] Taliaferro to Clark, September 1, 1834, NARS, RG 75, LR; Taliaferro Journal, July 16, August 24 and 28, 1831.

[9] Clark to Commissioner Elbert Herring, January 24, 1834, and July 5, 1833; Clark to Herring, July 21, 1833; A. S. Hughes to Clark, December 31, 1833, NARS, RG 75, LR; William T. Hagan, *The Sac and Fox Indians* (Norman: University of Oklahoma Press, 1958), pp. 191–192.

warfare, he could take some comfort from the slow but substantial success of his Eatonville experiment, which in six years grew from two families to forty-five. So encouraging were the prospects that the agent wrote Superintendent Clark in 1833 that he could use two instructors in farming for the Sioux, who were "in a most destitute condition from the great and increasing scarcity of game." The next year he presented a more formal request to Indian Commissioner Elbert Herring. Since the education fund provided by the 1830 treaty had never been spent, he asked that it now be used to employ two men of "respectable character to instruct [the Indians] in the art of cultivating the soil." [10]

Taliaferro had two men in mind when he made this request. That spring Gideon H. and Samuel W. Pond, young "volunteer missionaries" unconnected with any organized society, had come up the river to Fort Snelling with the intention of working among the Sioux. They were welcomed by Taliaferro and almost at once given an opportunity to show what they could do. The agent had always held that Indians must be civilized before being Christianized, but he had no objection to combining the two operations, as the Ponds proposed to do. They were given a place to live at the Lake Calhoun settlement, where about a year later they were joined by Thomas S. Williamson, Alexander G. Huggins, and their families, together with a sister of Mrs. Williamson. Bearing somewhat stronger credentials than the Ponds, they had been sent out by the American Board of Commissioners for Foreign Missions. Soon after their arrival Jedediah D. Stevens, who had made a preliminary visit to the agency in 1829, followed with his family. [11] Thus within a comparatively short time, the Santee Sioux, hitherto without missionaries, were virtually inundated with them.

Some rivalries developed at once, but a real impasse was avoided when Williamson accepted Joseph Renville's invitation to settle at his trading post on Lac qui Parle, near the headwaters of the Minnesota River. Gideon Pond joined him there the next spring. Stevens located at Lake Harriet, near the Eatonville colony, where Samuel Pond joined him in the spring of 1837, after being ordained the previous winter. That spring another missionary, Stephen Return Riggs, and his

[10] Taliaferro Journal, August 8, 1835; Taliaferro to Clark, August 2, 1833, and Taliaferro to Herring, July 23, 1834, NARS, RG 75, LR.

[11] Stephen R. Riggs, "Protestant Missions in the Northwest," *Minnesota Historical Collections*, VI (1894), 126–127; Riggs, "The Dakota Mission," *Minnesota Historical Collections*, III (1870–1880), 115–117.

wife came to the Sioux country and settled at Lac qui Parle, which became the most successful of the numerous missionary efforts in the next two decades.[12]

"Successful" is here a relative term. None of these mission stations accomplished much toward Christianizing the Indians before the reservation period of the fifties, and it was not until the morale of the Sioux was shattered by the aftermath of the Uprising in 1862 that wholesale conversions were made. For the missionaries those first years must have been extremely frustrating. The Lake Calhoun people were docile enough, and they were farming industriously, but they felt no desire to adopt the religion so assiduously preached by the white men who lived among them. At Lac qui Parle the support of Renville, who commanded great influence among the Indians, enabled the missionaries to gather a small congregation, made up almost entirely of women and mixed-bloods at first but eventually including a few men. But here too the work was slow and unrewarding.[13]

One of the most significant contributions of the missionaries was the reduction of the Dakota language to writing and the publication of books in that tongue. White men as far back as Hennepin had been compiling Dakota vocabularies, but nothing really systematic was done until the missionaries began their work. Their motive was not mere curiosity, of course, but a need to present their message in a form the Indians could understand. As Protestants, they regarded the use of the Bible in the vernacular as central to their task. Possessed of considerable linguistic ability, they availed themselves of such knowledge as had been accumulated by officers at Fort Snelling and others who had interested themselves in the Dakota language, and gradually acquired a knowledge of the grammar and vocabulary sufficient to enable them to translate portions of the Bible. Once books began to appear in Dakota, the missionaries' task of teaching the Indians to read and write was made easier. After they had been at work a little more than fifteen years, Riggs edited and the Smithsonian Institution published a monumental *Grammar and Dictionary of the Dakota Language*, which to a considerable degree fixed the written form of the language. From the very beginning the missionaries regarded the use of Dakota as a temporary expedient. They were convinced that its days as a living language were numbered, and in his introduction to the *Grammar* Riggs justified the project partly

12 Riggs, "Protestant Missions in the Northwest," pp. 128–129.
13 *Ibid.*, p. 130; Riggs, "The Dakota Mission," p. 118.

on the grounds that the work might prove useful to future philologists after the language itself had died out.[14]

During the years that Taliaferro was agent for the Sioux of the Mississippi, the conduct of Indian affairs was gradually being systematized, and a definite Indian department was taking shape within the War Department. When Taliaferro was first appointed in 1819, neither his duties nor the limits of his jurisdiction had been clearly defined. As time passed, however, many of the ambiguities of his position were resolved, along with those of other Indian agents. The Bureau of Indian Affairs was created in 1824, but it was not until 1832 that a commissioner was appointed. Two years later a massive revamping and codification of practices and policies was incorporated in the legislation collectively known as the Indian Intercourse Act of 1834, which superseded a series of congressional acts dating back to 1793. The new legislation grew partly out of recommendations submitted several years earlier by Lewis Cass and William Clark, recommendations which in turn may have reflected Taliaferro's experiences with traders, the introduction of liquor, intertribal warfare, and other matters relating to Indian affairs. Among other things, these laws increased the agents' discretionary authority in dealing with the whiskey traffic and the licensing of traders.[15]

Among the provisions of the new law was one amplifying earlier legislation dealing with Indian depredations on property owned by whites. This should not have been a serious problem at the St. Peter's Agency, since theoretically the only white people in the vicinity were government employees (including the Fort Snelling garrison), traders, and their families. As a matter of fact, however, there were squatters on the military reserve, chiefly refugees from the Earl of Selkirk's ill-fated Red River colony, and a number of mixed-bloods whose ties with the Indians kept them close to the Sioux villages. Members of all these groups had livestock, and it was inevitable that the Indians, whose legitimate hunting opportunities were diminishing, should occasionally kill a pig or an ox belonging to one of the whites, especially in the seasons of greatest hunger. Almost as soon as the new laws became known, depredations claims began coming in to the agent for his approval. It

[14] Riggs, "The Dakota Mission," pp. 120–124; Pond, "The Dakotas or Sioux . . . in 1834," p. 340; William W. Folwell, *A History of Minnesota*, I (St. Paul: Minnesota Historical Society, 1956), pp. 199–200, 203.

[15] Francis Paul Prucha, *American Indian Policy in the Formative Years* (Cambridge: Harvard University Press, 1962), pp. 50, 59–60, 252, 266–267; U.S. *Statutes at Large*, IV, 729–732.

was difficult for the claimants to obtain evidence that would stand legal scrutiny, since the Indians would rarely admit having destroyed any livestock. Consequently most such claims, at least in the early years, came to a dead end before ever reaching the Indian Office, which was extremely cautious about honoring those that did pass local inspection.[16]

Another problem aggravated by the presence of the settlers was the introduction of whiskey among the Indians and among the soldiers at Fort Snelling. Neither Taliaferro nor Major John Bliss, commander at the fort from 1833 to 1836, really wanted to expel the settlers, though they wished to discourage further immigration and to have those who tried to sell liquor removed. Taliaferro recognized that there would be occasional conflicts when whites and Indians were in close proximity but took the view that those who behaved themselves might as well be allowed to stay.[17]

Taliaferro's long tenure in office gave him a knowledge of his Indians and continuity enjoyed by few agents then or afterward. By the middle thirties he could look back over the years of his service and see what changes had taken place in the Indians over whom he exercised jurisdiction. What he saw did not please him. Despite his high hopes, the treaty of 1830 had not accomplished what it had been expected to, and the material and moral condition of the Santee Sioux was getting worse with each passing year. The answer, it seemed to the agent, lay in another treaty, by which the Indians could cede lands they no longer needed—specifically, those east of the Mississippi—and receive in return benefits that would set them on the road to civilization and security. Apart from the advantages such a cession would bring to the

[16] Statement of Jacob Falstrom, dated August 27, 1834; Remarks by Chiefs at Payment, July 2, 1835; Affidavit dated June 5, 1835, signed by Taliaferro, John Bliss, *et al.*, NARS, RG 75, LR. Falstrom claimed to have lost an ox to the Indians. J. B. Faribault swore that the Indians of Little Crow's band had killed fifteen hogs, a horse, and a bull, that those of Shakopee's band had killed thirty-five hogs and pigs, two horses, and a bull, and that Black Dog's band had killed nineteen hogs and a horse. Some of these losses, having been incurred in 1831, were rendered uncollectable under the law of 1834, which set a three-year limitation on claims. The Indians admitted killing thirteen of Faribault's pigs but denied all the other charges. They also claimed that white men had killed two of their horses. The commission that examined the evidence concluded that, except for the thirteen pigs, none of the claims could be allowed in as much as it was impossible to prove any particular band of Indians guilty.

[17] Bliss to Clark, April 30, 1835; Bliss to Lewis Cass, April 30, 1836; Taliaferro to Bliss, April 22, 1836, NARS, RG 75, LR.

Indians, it would satisfy the growing pressure for the opening up to exploitation of the timber resources in what is now western Wisconsin and east-central Minnesota. Taliaferro hoped that it would also reduce the chance of collisions between the Chippewas and the Mississippi bands of Sioux.[18]

A detailed proposal for a treaty was submitted to Superintendent Clark in 1836, but it received a cool reception from both Clark and Commissioner Herring. Later in the year, however, the St. Peter's Agency was transferred to the jurisdiction of Governor Henry Dodge of Wisconsin Territory, who looked upon it with more enthusiasm, as did the new Indian Commissioner, Carey A. Harris.[19] The only opposition to such a treaty seemed to come from the fur traders, whose prosperity depended on keeping the status quo in Indian affairs. Taliaferro knew that they could be reconciled to a treaty if they stood to gain by it through a stipulation that part of the price paid by the government would go directly to them as payment for uncollected debts owed them by the Indians. But he also knew that such an arrangement with the traders would either increase the cost to the government or diminish the benefits received by the Indians, or both; and in any case he was opposed to any strategy that would be advantageous to the traders.

The treaty that was finally hammered out and imposed on the Indians was partly a victory for Taliaferro, partly a victory for the traders. In the summer of 1837 the agent was instructed to arrange for a delegation of Sioux to go to Washington and there negotiate a peace settlement with a delegation of Sacs and Foxes. The twenty-six Sioux that he managed to round up seem to have been under the impression that this was the sole purpose of the trip, but when the Sacs and Foxes failed to appear, a treaty drawn up before they ever left the agency was signed, providing for the cession of the lands east of the Mississippi and the islands in that river.[20]

Taliaferro and his party left the agency August 18, went down the Mississippi and up the Ohio by steamboat as far as Pittsburgh, thence to Philadelphia and on to Washington by a combination of canal, railroad, and stagecoach. They arrived in the capital September 15 and were taken to the Globe Hotel, where they stayed for the next twenty-four days. The twenty-six Indians were housed and fed for a total cost

[18] Taliaferro to Clark, May 15, 1836, *ibid.*

[19] Clark to Herring, June 9, 1836; Taliaferro to Governor Henry Dodge, November 30, 1836; Dodge to Commissioner Carey A. Harris, April 18, 1837, *ibid.*

[20] Taliaferro to Dodge, August 2 and 21, 1837, *ibid.*; "Auto-Biography of Maj. Lawrence Taliaferro," *Minnesota Historical Collections*, VI (1894), 217–219.

of $640; Taliaferro and the interpreters were charged slightly higher rates. Presumably an effort was made to impress the Indians with the splendor and might of the white man's civilization, but no details of their entertainment appear in Taliaferro's correspondence. Six had their portraits painted (any smaller number would lead to ill feeling, the agent said), and all were given medals, some of which were stolen on the way home. The return trip began October 9 and took about a month. As on the way east, many of the Indians were ill, owing to the change of water and diet, but all made it back safely, despite a boiler explosion on board the *Rolla* below Rock Island.[21]

All manner of impediments had been placed in Taliaferro's way before, during, and after the trip. In the first place, many of the Sioux were reluctant to go because there had been an attack by the Sacs and Foxes just before their departure. Then the traders made a strenuous effort to prevent the delegation from going (after failing to write into the preliminary draft of the treaty all the provisions they wished to see in it) and interfered again at Prairie du Chien. Taliaferro was obliged to give the Indians presents to the amount of $1,200 before they would consent to move. Several traders accompanied the delegation, and others followed it. While in Washington the Indians were subjected to various pressures, of which perhaps the most pernicious was that of one Samuel C. Stambaugh, sutler at Fort Snelling and a sort of professional meddler, who succeeded in alienating some of the Indians from their agent, apparently in hopes of supplanting him. Taliaferro had previously objected to Stambaugh's being in on the negotiations, but he was unable to prevent his coming along. The interference of Stambaugh and the traders of course infuriated Taliaferro. In a note to James Maher, proprietor of the Globe Hotel, thanking him for the hospitality extended to the delegation, he apologized for his hasty departure, saying that he had "had many *rascals* to deal with." Stambaugh later had the effrontery to submit to the Indian Office a bill for his hotel expenses while in Washington.[22]

[21] Taliaferro to Captain Martin Scott, August 16, 1837; Taliaferro to Dodge, August 20 and 21, November 4, 1837; Taliaferro to Harris, September 5 and 8, n.d. [written in Washington], November 10, 1837; Bill for housing and feeding Indians, signed by James Maher (undated), NARS, RG 75, LR; "Auto-Biography of Maj. Lawrence Taliaferro," pp. 217–219. For a lively description of the typical treatment accorded Indian delegations visiting Washington, see Katharine C. Turner, *Red Men Calling on the Great White Father* (Norman: University of Oklahoma Press, 1951).

[22] Taliaferro to Dodge, August 21, 1837; Taliaferro to Harris, September 8 and n.d., 1837; Taliaferro to James Maher, October 11, 1837; Samuel C. Stambaugh to Secretary of War Joel R. Poinsett, February 23, 1838, NARS, RG 75, LR. Stambaugh

Considering its immense importance in the history of the Sioux, the treaty itself was brief. In return for the lands ceded, the United States promised to invest the sum of $300,000 and to pay to the chiefs and braves annually forever an income of not less than five per cent, "a portion of said interest, not exceeding one third, to be applied in such manner as the President may direct" (an "education fund" that was to cause trouble later), the rest to be paid in specie or in goods, as the Indians might specify. The relatives and friends of the tribe having not less than one quarter Indian blood were to receive a sum of $110,000, and the traders were to receive $90,000 in payment of the just debts of the tribe. Further, an annuity of $10,000 in goods was to be paid for twenty years and $8,250 spent annually during the same period for the purchase of medicines, agricultural implements and stock, and for the support of a physician, farmers, and blacksmiths, and for "other beneficial objects." In order to get the civilization program under way, upon ratification of the treaty $10,000 was to be spent for the immediate purchase of agricultural implements, cattle, and mechanics' tools. For twenty years the Indians were to receive provisions to the amount of $5,500 annually. Finally, they were to be paid $6,000 in goods upon their arrival at St. Louis on their way home. The twenty-one signers of the treaty, all Mdewakantons, included most of the chiefs and headmen whose names appeared on the treaty of 1830, with the exception of Little Crow and Wabasha, who had died, the latter in a smallpox epidemic that had carried off much of his band in 1836.[23]

Once back on their home ground, the Indians, traders, and others settled down to await ratification of the treaty. One of the weaknesses of the constitutional requirement that treaties be ratified by the Senate was the long delay that always intervened between the signing of a

---

asked $275 for hotel expenses and $140 for other expenses on the way. The St. Peter's Agency file for 1837 includes two undated letters to the Secretary of War, purporting to be from the chiefs but in Stambaugh's handwriting. One of them bears the notation by Taliaferro: "This paper is in Col. Stambaugh's own hand writing. Will go to show to the Dept. my objections to him generally."

[23] Kappler, *Indian Affairs, Laws and Treaties*, II, 493–494. Two treaties had been made in 1836 by which the eastern Sioux relinquished their shadowy claim to lands in southwestern Iowa and northwestern Missouri. On September 10 the "Lower Mdewakantons" (Wabasha's band) entered into such a treaty, for which they received $400, and on November 30 an identical treaty was made with the Wahpekutes, Sissetons, and "Upper Mdewakantons" (the other bands), who received $550 in goods. These treaties were of negligible importance to the bands concerned. See *ibid.*, II, 466–467, 481–482.

treaty and the beginning of the benefits it granted. In this case nearly nine months elapsed between the signing and the formal proclamation, and of course there was an additional delay before the promised annuities could begin arriving at the agency. It was a period of much anxiety. At the agency (from which Taliaferro was, as usual, absent most of the winter) hunger and unrest created a tense situation. Upon his return, he found that the nervousness and suspicion of the Indians had increased and that they were venting their feelings in violence. The son of the trader Provençalle had been killed and Joseph R. Brown wounded by angry Indians, and as a result the American Fur Company had withdrawn its trade from the Sioux. Together with the failure of the winter hunt, this deprivation contributed to a mood of reckless desperation among the Indians. As the weeks passed without news of ratification, Taliaferro's letters to his superiors became increasingly shrill, almost hysterical in tone. "Give me something satisfactory by which the feelings of the Indians may be calmed—otherwise I shall not deem my residence here safe among them—and of consequence must... leave the Agency," he begged, adding by way of defense, "What mortal man could do—has been done, and will continue to be done to keep my *miserable*, and *starving people* quiet until we hear from you." News of the ratification must have come shortly after this, for Taliaferro's letters were calmer a month later.[24]

The Indians still had a while to wait before receiving any tangible benefits from the treaty, and when these came they were far from satisfactory. The first annuities, distributed in October, created much ill feeling among the Indians, who claimed that the goods were both insufficient in quantity and inferior in quality. Only by promising that there would be an improvement the next year and that the annuities would arrive by June 1—a promise he was later to regret—was Taliaferro able to persuade the Indians to accept the goods.[25]

Implementing the treaty of 1837 presented several challenges for the agent. He decided to avoid ill feeling among the bands by hiring a farmer for each village if he could find that many who would work for the low salaries specified in the Indian Intercourse Act of 1834. He met

[24] Scott Campbell to Taliaferro, February 13, 1838; Taliaferro to Harris, February 21, June 5, and June 28, 1838; Taliaferro to Dodge, July 31, 1838, NARS, RG 75, LR. Campbell, Taliaferro's mixed-blood interpreter, was left in charge of the agency during the winter. In the letter cited he asked if Taliaferro had any news of the treaty: "Here I learn nothing but the blabbering of indian traders & other Idiots," he wrote.

[25] Taliaferro to Poinsett, August 27, 1839, *ibid.*

this problem by placing the missionaries, who received most of their support from their respective religious societies, on the payroll as farmers. Besides the stations previously mentioned, two Swiss missionaries, Samuel Denton and Daniel Gavin, were located at the Red Wing village; and a Methodist mission under Thomas W. Pope was working with little success at Kapozha. Denton, Samuel Pond, and Pope were hired in the fall of 1838, and the next year Stevens, formerly at Lake Harriet, was appointed farmer at Wabasha's village. The other three bands were supplied with men not connected with the mission stations.[26] Although blacksmiths were also hard to get at the salaries the Indian Office was willing to pay, Taliaferro filled this need late in 1838.[27] The accomplishments of the blacksmiths and farmers were not notable during the remainder of Taliaferro's term as agent, but they became fixtures on the local scene in the next decade and did something to prepare the Indians for the reservation period.

So far as the Indians were concerned, the treaty of 1837 solved few of the problems it was intended to solve, and it created some new ones. Besides postponing the day when they would become self-supporting, the Indians' growing dependence on annuities made for a decidedly uncomfortable situation when they arrived late, as they usually did. Payment in money proved disadvantageous to the Indians because the traders simply marked up their prices and extracted that much more for their goods. The "education fund," as it was called, proved an especially sore spot. When the Indians did not receive the $5,000 that the treaty had specified was to be supplied as the President might direct, they complained at the first payment.[28] Later, either on their own initiative or at the suggestion of the traders, they concluded that this fund was being secretly paid to the missionaries and that if they could somehow sabotage the schools, the money would be paid to them.

Yet another unfortunate effect of the treaty, which surely Taliaferro must have foreseen, was that the east bank of the Mississippi was soon lined with whiskey sellers. Though unable to enter the Indian country, they were in no way prevented from selling to any Indians who chose

[26] Taliaferro to Dodge, September 10, 1838; Dodge to Harris, October 16, 1838; Taliaferro to Governor Robert Lucas, May 24 and June 5, 1839, *ibid.*; 25th Cong., 3rd Sess., *H. Doc. 103*, pp. 14, 16, 18. Samuel Pond gave it as his opinion that the position of farmer was regarded as a sinecure and that most of the men so employed hired out their plowing and did little work themselves. See Folwell, *History of Minnesota*, I, 197 n.

[27] Taliaferro to Dodge, September 10, 1838, NARS, RG 75, LR.

[28] Remarks of chiefs at annuity payment, October 17, 1838, *ibid.*

to cross the river into their old hunting grounds. This problem became increasingly serious as the hamlet of St. Paul came into being in the forties, for it consisted chiefly of groggeries in its early years. All these unanticipated results of the treaty made Taliaferro's position a veritable hornet's nest during his last year at the St. Peter's Agency.

As if these troubles were not enough, the continuing warfare between the Sioux and the Chippewas reached a crescendo in 1839. There had been minor clashes in 1835 and 1836 and a bigger one in April, 1838, when a party of Chippewas appeared in the Sioux country, were hospitably entertained by a small hunting party, and then murdered nearly all of their hosts. An unsuccessful attempt at retaliation was made a few months later, but the real explosion came in the summer of 1839, when a close relative of Cloud Man was killed and the Sioux took terrible revenge on several bands of Chippewas who had come to Fort Snelling in the mistaken belief that their annuities would be paid there. Following their enemies toward their homes, the Kapozha and Minnesota River Mdewakantons fell upon them and killed nearly a hundred, while losing twenty-three of their own men. Folwell is probably right in saying that this outbreak "much weakened Major Taliaferro's confidence in his ability to control his red children by fine words and fair treatment." [29]

He was having even more serious troubles that summer. Although five steamboats had come up the river by June 3, the annuities, which he had promised the Indians would be there by June 1, had not arrived. By July 12 they had still not arrived, nor had the funds to pay the farmers and other employees. Shortly afterward part of the goods and provisions came, but there was still no money to pay the employees, and the blacksmith shops were idle for want of materials. Once more Taliaferro began to bombard the Indian Office with anxious appeals, climaxing the barrage with a letter of resignation. His officially stated reason was poor health, dating back to his service on the Niagara frontier in 1814, but in a letter to Secretary of War Joel R. Poinsett a few weeks later he made it clear that he had other reasons. Deprived of the means of holding the Indians' faith in him and threatened with assassination, he saw no course but to resign. [30]

[29] Thomas S. Williamson to Taliaferro, April 28, 1838, *ibid.*; Samuel W. Pond, "Indian Warfare in Minnesota," *Minnesota Historical Collections*, III (1870–1880), 131–133. This incident is given extended treatment in Folwell, *History of Minnesota*, I, 154–158. Folwell's account is based on the Taliaferro Journal, among other sources, and differs in some details from Pond's.

[30] Taliaferro to Lucas, June 3 and July 12, 1839; Taliaferro to Commissioner T.

Although Taliaferro's letter of resignation was so phrased as to leave the door open for its rejection (he had been given another four-year appointment in April), his remarks in a letter written after he had left the agency suggest that he was only too happy to be back at his home in Bedford, Pennsylvania. He wrote Commissioner T. Hartley Crawford that he was "most happy to be relieved from a *Post*, and *Country*, which must from the *nature*, and *designs* of a certain class of *Mongrels* . . . produce ere long a North Western Indian War." [31] Thus, on a note of savage bitterness, ended Lawrence Taliaferro's twenty years of service to the Santee Sioux.

Taliaferro had reason to be bitter. For nearly twenty years he had exerted himself to make the Sioux an agricultural people, but not until the last year of his service as agent did he have the funds to begin the project on a large scale, and then he was too harried to make adequate use of the opportunity. Ironically, it was his successors who received credit for whatever small success was finally achieved in the endeavors for which he had prepared the ground. His immediate successor, Amos J. Bruce, was a less aggressive man, and perhaps as a consequence his eight years as agent were more tranquil than Taliaferro's last two. He got on well with Taliaferro's old enemies, the traders—perhaps too well. There was less trouble with the Chippewas in the forties, and Bruce had more weapons at his disposal in dealing with such conflicts as there were. He was also aided by somewhat greater punctuality in the delivery of annuity provisions, although the money annuities and sometimes the funds for running the agency continued to arrive late.

Bruce's chief task was to persuade the Sioux to become farmers in the fashion of frontier whites so that they would no longer have to depend so heavily on the chase. The Indians' cultural crisis was primarily economic, as Taliaferro had recognized. Although the missionaries' preoccupation with saving souls led them unwittingly to introduce new sources of conflict, their efforts to induce the Indians to farm made them useful instruments in the agent's civilization scheme. Less can be said of the other tools he had to work with. Then as later, the Indian Bureau had to carry out its assigned task with imperfect materials.

Hartley Crawford, July 15, 1839; Taliaferro to Poinsett, July 16 and August 27, 1839, NARS, RG 75, LR. A postscript to his letter of resignation says: "I have the *sad consolation* of leaving after *twenty seven years* the public service as *poor* as when I first entered —*the only evidence of my integrity*. Will *Schoolcraft*, and some one or two others believe this? from the *oldest* agent in the Dept."

[31] Taliaferro to Crawford, December 12, 1839, *ibid.*

Bruce himself was a political appointee, and the people who worked for him were by and large animated by no burning zeal to help the Indians. Many of the government farmers, especially, were time-servers, some utterly incompetent.[32]

Even had these men been better qualified for their jobs, they would have been up against formidable obstacles. The semisedentary Mdewakantons practiced what was essentially a hoe culture, and their opposition to the use of the plow was not merely laziness but an actual religious objection, based on the notion that plowing would injure their fields. Besides, working in the fields was women's work, scorned by men who had been trained to be hunters and warriors. Despite occasional breakthroughs, such as when Cloud Man or the Sisseton chief Mazasha put their hands to the plow, practically all the farming was left to the women or the white employees. And when work oxen were issued to the Indians, they were as likely as not to be killed for food.[33]

Even if the Indians did show some industry, there was always a chance that a flood or drought would wipe out their crops. Flood damage was restricted to the villages on the lower Minnesota and occurred only infrequently. For the Indians living near the headwaters of that river, however, drought came often enough to cause them real hardship. The people living at Lac qui Parle, Lake Traverse, and Big Stone Lake, who were not parties to the treaty of 1837 and whose annuities under the earlier treaty expired in 1840, were repeatedly described as destitute and starving.[34]

[32] Amos J. Bruce to Representative John Miller, February 19, 1840; Bruce to Crawford, September 15, 1842, *ibid.* Stevens, the erstwhile missionary who had been appointed farmer at Wabasha's village, failed even to maintain a residence there but instead built himself a house some eight or ten miles away, on the Wisconsin side of the river. Bruce discharged him. There was a high rate of turnover among the government farmers, even under Bruce's mild regime, and his successor fired the entire lot.

[33] Bruce to Lucas, November 11, 1840; Robert Hopkins and Alexander Huggins to Superintendent Thomas H. Harvey, September 29, 1848, *ibid.*

[34] Governor John Chambers to Crawford, November 22, 1842; Bruce to Crawford, December 13, 1842; Crawford to Secretary of War John C. Spencer, October 7, 1842; Joseph R. Brown to Bruce, September 1, 1846; Bruce to Governor James Clarke, September 12, 1846; Clarke to Commissioner William Medill, October 5, 1846, *ibid.* Bruce reported in the spring of 1843 that the traders, missionaries, and the Fort Snelling garrison had rendered assistance to the destitute Indians. The squaws and children were admitted to the fort briefly every day to collect table scraps. Sibley had sent sixty bushels of corn to the band at the Little Rapids, along with some pork furnished by the officers at the fort. Bruce hoped "to keep life in most of them" until the ducks and geese arrived. See Bruce to Chambers, April 3, 1843, *ibid.* It is noteworthy that by this time the Sissetons and Wahpetons had to some extent adopted agriculture.

Because of all these hindrances, progress in making farmers out of the Sioux was extremely slow. In his last annual report Taliaferro spoke of the government's efforts in their behalf and provided statistics to show that some progress was being made. Yet he was not optimistic about the prospects. The Indians' habits of indolence and their "total disregard and want of knowledge of the value and uses of time and property" seemed to militate against any rapid progress toward self-sufficiency.[35] Seven years later Bruce, perhaps with Taliaferro's report before him, mentioned the same characteristics, which in his eyes almost forbade "any hope of their improvement, either in morals or intellect." Three years later Philander Prescott, now head farmer for the several bands, reported little progress, except among the Red Wing band, which appeared more willing than the others to adopt the customs of white men. The total acreage under cultivation was still small, and the plowing was still being done almost entirely by the government farmers.[36]

In comparison with the massive revolution that the Indian Office and its agents had hoped to effect, the farming done by the Sioux prior to the reservation period of 1853–1862 was negligible. This short-range view led the agent in 1848 to complain despairingly that the $4,200 a year that the farming enterprise had been costing was more than it would have cost the government to buy as much corn as the Indians raised.[37] If there had been anyone around who realized how slow and halting any culture change necessarily is, he might have felt that quite a bit had been accomplished in the decade of the 1840's.

At the same time that the agent and his employees were trying to transform the Sioux into farmers, the missionaries were teaching them to read and write. The missionary activities begun in the middle thirties expanded greatly in the next decade. Besides the remote Lac qui Parle station, which went on steadily with its work in the face of mounting difficulties, new missions were started and old ones moved to new sites. After the savage outbreak of war between the Sioux and the Chippewas in 1839, the Lake Calhoun village was abandoned out of fear of retaliation, and the band moved to a more protected site on the Minnesota River. In 1843 the Ponds rejoined Cloud Man's people there, and a few years later Samuel Pond accepted an invitation to open

[35] 26th Cong., 1st Sess., *S. Doc. 126*, p. 494.
[36] 29th Cong., 2nd Sess., *H. Ex. Doc. 4*, p. 245; 31st Cong., 1st Sess., *S. Ex. Doc. 1*, pp. 1054–1055.
[37] 30th Cong., 1st Sess., *H. Doc. 1*, pp. 474–475.

a school at Shakopee's village, now on the right bank of the Minnesota.[38]

A new station was opened in 1843 by Riggs and others at Traverse des Sioux, where Mazasha's small Sisseton band lived. Some of these people were hostile to the missionaries and persecuted them, while others were friendly enough, if incurably mendicant, and made occasional gestures in the direction of farming. The Methodist mission struggled along for a time but was finally abandoned in 1842. The Swiss mission at Red Wing was given up in 1846 and replaced two years later by an American Board mission, which sent John F. Aiton there. Aiton and Joseph W. Hancock, who arrived the following year, attempted to revive the school conducted earlier by Gavin and Denton. Although the chief, Wacouta, is uniformly described as a man of high character, friendly and co-operative toward the whites, the Indians' indifference to education and their habit of being away hunting a large part of the year made this school no more of a success than the others.[39]

Ironically, the biggest obstacle to the success of these mission schools was the education fund provided by the treaty of 1837. Although the Indian Office sent the money along each year with the rest of the annuities, no instructions for its disbursement ever accompanied it. Each year Bruce would ask for instructions, and then, receiving none, he would deposit the money in the Bank of Missouri at St. Louis. The only part of the fund he ever used was the sum of $500 given to the Methodist mission in 1841.[40] The Indians, who were acquiring a certain degree of sophistication where money matters were concerned, were understandably puzzled by the nonappearance of this portion of the annuity they were supposed to receive under the terms of the treaty. They apparently got wind of the $500 turned over to the Methodist mission and concluded that the rest of it was going to the other missionaries. Obviously, the way to get what was coming to them was to sabotage the schools and force them to close.

[38] Riggs, "Protestant Missions in the Northwest," p. 131; "The Dakota Mission," pp. 120, 123.

[39] Riggs, "The Dakota Mission," p. 121; Riggs, *Mary and I: Forty Years with the Sioux* (Boston: Congregational Sunday-School and Publishing Society, 1880), p. 100; 28th Cong., 1st Sess., *S. Doc. 1*, pp. 354–355; Thomas S. Williamson to Harvey, August 15, 1848, NARS, RG 75, LR; 31st Cong., 1st Sess., *S. Ex. Doc. 1*, p. 1064; [Joseph W. Hancock], *Goodhue County, Minnesota, Past and Present* (Red Wing: Red Wing Printing Co., 1893), p. 50. Hancock stayed at Red Wing after the Indians left and became a prominent citizen and the holder of several county offices.

[40] Bruce to Chambers, May 24, 1841; Bruce to Crawford, August 15, September 1, and October 31, 1841, and July 5, 1843, NARS, RG 75, LR.

When the Ponds reopened their school at Oak Grove, Cloud Man's new village, and the Traverse des Sioux station was started, they and the older schools suffered from the opposition of many of the Indians, including the influential chiefs. The trouble seems to have started in 1843, appearing first in the villages nearest Prairie du Chien and gradually moving up the Mississippi and the Minnesota, so that by the end of the summer it had reached even the remote Lac qui Parle post, whose Indians had no direct interest in the education fund. Here children were ordered to stay out of school, and those who defied the order had their clothes cut to shreds by members of the soldiers' lodge. The missionaries' cattle were killed and their lives threatened. So serious did the harassment become that when Bruce invited him, in 1846, to start a school at Kapozha, Williamson eagerly embraced the opportunity to leave Lac qui Parle.[41]

Williamson tended, like his fellows, to interpret their difficulties in spiritual terms. "God seems to have withdrawn his spirit and it is hard to interest the people in learning anything good," he complained, recalling that a few years earlier "numbers here [at Lac qui Parle] were inquiring what they must do to be saved."[42] Yet he understood very clearly the practical reasons for the difficulties he and his fellow missionaries were experiencing and had concrete proposals for remedying the situation. Like most of those who interested themselves in Indian education during the nineteenth century, he believed that the children should be separated from their parents as early as possible. By way of apology for the poor attendance at the Kapozha school, he insisted that an Indian village was no place to teach children to work or to speak English, "in sight of their relatives who think it disgraceful to do either and are spending most of their time in gaming ball playing swimming and other amusements." To overcome such evil influences, he proposed a manual labor boarding school, to be supported jointly by the government and the American Board.[43] But before he could impress his ideas on the policymakers in Washington, the Sioux had been removed from Kapozha and their other traditional villages.

The decade of the forties, like the previous one, was largely a period

[41] 28th Cong., 1st Sess., *S. Doc. 1*, pp. 354–355, 377–378; 29th Cong., 2nd Sess., *H. Ex. Doc. 4*, p. 313; Williamson to Bruce, June 30 and August 12, 1846, NARS, RG 75, LR.

[42] Williamson to Bruce, June 30, 1846, NARS, RG 75, LR.

[43] Williamson to Medill, October 19, 1847; Williamson to Harvey, August 15, 1848; Williamson to Commissioner Orlando Brown, February 26, 1850, *ibid.*

of failure and frustration for the missions. They recorded a few con-versions, taught a few people to read and write, and possibly created in the minds of the Indians a more favorable image of the white man than that produced by association with the traders, soldiers, and government officials. But in terms of their primary purpose they accomplished little. Samuel Pond was reporting objective fact when he wrote, many years later, "Before the outbreak of 1862 I saw very few Dakotas who seemed to give evidence of piety. A few at Oak Grove, a few at Lac Qui Parle, and that was all." [44] With the advantage of hindsight, the missionaries were later to speak of this as a period of sowing, the fruits of which were to appear later. Perhaps they were right, but at the end of the forties no fruition was in evidence.

Besides the mismanagement of the education fund and the cultural inertia that led the Indians to reject the efforts to make farmers of them, there were other obstacles to the work of the agents and missionaries, one of which was the failure of the government to fulfill its promises. When Governor James D. Doty of Wisconsin territory was negotiating with the Sioux for the cession of their lands in 1841, he listened sym-pathetically to their complaints of deficiencies in the annuity payments made up to that time. The Indians told Doty that they had no doubt that the Great Father had started their things on the way to them, "but after they leave Washington the road is very long and some of the boxes get holes in them . . . and their dollars and goods drop out." [45] When the annuity goods and provisions did arrive, they often were not what the Indians wanted or what the agent had requested. Bruce always sent in specific requisitions for articles the Indians could use, but the con-tractors had their own notions of what they would furnish, and the an-uity goods sometimes contained screw augers, knives and forks, pewter teaspoons, and other items for which the Indians had little use and less desire. [46]

[44] Samuel W. Pond, Jr., *Two Volunteer Missionaries Among the Dakotas* (Boston and Chicago: Congregational Sunday-School and Publishing Society, 1893), p. 219; S. W. Pond Narrative, I, 82 (cited by Folwell, *History of Minnesota*, I, 212).

[45] James D. Doty to President John Tyler, August 13, 1841, NARS, RG 75, LR.

[46] Bruce to Lucas, October 6, 1840; Bruce to Chambers, September 15, 1842, *ibid.* Bruce's first requisition included three hundred guns, with appropriate quantities of lead, powder, powder horns, flints, and the like; four thousand pounds of tobacco; fifty pounds of thread; 330 blankets of various colors and sizes; cloth handkerchiefs; yarn; a hundred dozen scalping knives (while he tried to keep the Indians at peace); fifty looking glasses; combs; tin pans; kettles; squaw axes; ribbon; vermilion; scissors; and other items to the amount of $10,000, as well as $700 worth of agricultural im-plements and work oxen, harnesses, etc.

Another source of difficulty in the 1840's was the increasing power that the traders came to wield over the Indians. The conditions under which they operated were radically altered during this period. The supply of furs dwindled rapidly, and the Indians, blessed with annuities, no longer hunted as assiduously as they had earlier. Instead of trading manufactured goods for peltries, the traders now exchanged them for the money the Indians were receiving. Credit was still extended liberally, since the traders had learned that debts owed by Indians could be collected from the government by means of a properly constructed treaty. As the ceded lands east of the Mississippi filled with settlers, a fierce tug-of-war began between the so-called independent traders, many of whom were chiefly dispensers of whiskey, and the licensed traders of the old American Fur Company. On the whole, the independent traders did the most harm to the Indians, whose addiction to whiskey brought them to new depths of degradation. Gideon Pond has left a striking description of the orgy that followed the payment in 1839, when the Indians

> bade fair to die, all together, in one drunken jumble. They must be drunk—they could hardly live if they were not drunk.—Many of them seemed as uneasy when sober, as a fish does when on land. At some of the villages they were drunk months together. There was no end to it. They *would* have whisky. They would give guns, blankets, pork, lard, flour, corn, coffee, sugar, horses, furs, traps, any thing for whisky. It was made to drink—it was good —it was wakan. They drank it,—they bit off each other's noses,—broke each other's ribs and heads, they knifed each other. They killed one another with guns, knives, hatchets, clubs, fire-brands; they fell into the fire and water and were burned to death, and drowned; they froze to death, and committed suicide so frequently, that for a time, the death of an Indian in some of the ways mentioned was but little thought of by themselves or others.[47]

Like the white man's liquor, his diseases wrought havoc among the Indians. Smallpox struck in the middle 1830's, and in 1846 and 1847 cholera and "bilious fever" raged through the river villages, "carrying [the Indians] off at a fearful rate," according to Bruce. Whooping cough was also a widely prevalent ailment and accounted for many deaths, especially among children.[48] Yet the Mdewakantons, the only

[47] Folwell, *History of Minnesota*, I, 209, citing "The Treaty with the Mdewakantonwan and Warpekute Bands of Dakotas," *Dakota Tawaxitku Kin, or the Dakota Friend*, I, No. 11 (St. Paul, September 1851).

[48] 26th Cong., 1st Sess., *S. Doc. 126*, p. 495; 30th Cong., 1st Sess., *H. Ex. Doc. 8*, p. 844; Bruce to Harvey, August 21, 1847, NARS, RG 75, LR.

band receiving annuities and thus the only one for which reasonably accurate figures are available, continued to increase throughout the 1840's. From 1,668 in 1839 they increased to 1,776 in 1841, and 1,938 in 1843. Despite the cholera epidemic, they were up to 2,141 in 1846 and to 2,200 in 1849. It is impossible to determine how much of this population growth is due to natural increase and how much to accessions from the non annuity bands, but it is unlikely that the Mdewakantons would welcome sizable additions to their numbers, since these would reduce their per capita benefits. Figures for the other subtribes are unreliable, but in 1846 Bruce reported 555 Wahpekutes, 862 Wahpetons, and 1,188 Sissetons, plus some mixed Sisseton and Yankton bands numbering altogether 2,612.[49]

Another obstacle to the agents' and missionaries' efforts to civilize the Sioux was the fondness of the Indians for war with their neighbors. The conflict with the Chippewas abated only briefly after the spectacular bloodshed in 1839, but the possible withholding of annuities provided the government officials with a new weapon. Still, non-annuity bands kept up the fight during the forties. Peace was made with the Sacs and Foxes in 1844, but trouble with the Winnebagos, now living in northeastern Iowa, began about that time and erupted in open attack by some Wahpekutes in 1847. The Sioux played an obstructionist role in the removal of the Winnebagos to central Minnesota in 1848, when Wabasha entertained the migrating tribe and offered them some land near his village. Another source of difficulty came from the invasion of the Sioux hunting grounds by half-breeds from the Red River settlements in Canada, who killed off the bison on which the prairie Sioux depended. Retaliation led in at least one case to the deaths of two innocent white men bringing a drove of cattle from Missouri to Fort Snelling.[50]

Despite all these obstacles, Bruce managed the St. Peter's Agency

[49] 28th Cong., 1st Sess., *S. Doc. 1*, p. 377; 31st Cong., 1st Sess., *S. Ex. Doc. 1*, p. 1017; Statistical table of Sioux bands, September 1, 1846, NARS, RG 75, LR.
[50] Bruce to Chambers, August 4, 1843; Chambers to Crawford, August 12, 1843; Bruce to Chambers, April 2, 1844; Chambers to Crawford, April 18, 1844; Bruce to Chambers, June 12, 1844; and July 1, 1845; Bruce to Medill, August 15, 1847; Henry M. Rice to Medill, April 3 and June 25, 1848; Bruce to Chambers, February 18, 1844; Bruce to Harvey, July 26, 1847; Bruce to Medill, August 12, 1847; Medill to Harvey, September 4 and 6, 1847; Chambers to Crawford, September 3, 1844; Bruce to Chambers, October 2 and November 2, 1844; *ibid.*; Russell Blakeley, "History of the Discovery of the Mississippi River and the Advent of Commerce in Minnesota," *Minnesota Historical Collections*, VIII (1895–1898), 382–385.

with reasonable success during his term of office. He weathered several attempts to have him removed, first by a Methodist missionary who accused him of being a "profane, dram-drinking agent" and of favoring the Catholics, and later by the independent traders and citizens allied with them, who charged him with favoring the licensed traders.[51] But in 1848 the agency was reduced to a subagency, as an economy move, and Robert G. Murphy became subagent. During Murphy's brief term of office—he was removed in favor of Nathaniel McLean, publisher of a Whig newspaper in St. Paul, in 1849—his chief accomplishment was reducing the amount of drunkenness among the Indians by the unlikely but apparently partially effective device of a temperance pledge.[52]

Momentous events were occurring in the land of the Sioux during the later 1840's. Minnesota Territory was created in the spring of 1849 and Alexander Ramsey of Pennsylvania appointed governor. In executing his function as ex officio superintendent of Indian affairs, a responsibility which he took with much seriousness, Ramsey made his first report to the commissioner a veritable compendium of historical and ethnological information on the Indians of the territory.[53]

As if to demonstrate beyond all question that civilization was moving in on the Santee Sioux, in April, 1849, a young lawyer named James

[51] Bruce to Crawford, June 14, 1842; Sibley to Crawford, October 31, 1842; Abstract of charges against Bruce, December 6, 1842; B. T. Kavanaugh to Charles A. Wickliffe, April 14, 1842; Petition of Sioux, prepared by H. Jackson, to President John Tyler [no date, but postmarked October 10, 1844]; Crawford to Secretary of War William Wilkins, October 31, 1844; Bruce to Crawford, February 7, 1845; Settlers' petition, n.d., accompanied by affidavits from Scott Campbell, April 9, 1846, and William Evans, April 9, 1846, NARS, RG 75, LR. Kavanaugh lived to regret his accusations against Bruce, for they elicited a countercharge from the trader Henry Hastings Sibley and other men, who offered sworn testimony that Kavanaugh had been guilty of voyeurism in drilling holes through the partition separating his stateroom from that occupied by the newly married Mr. and Mrs. Franklin Steele on the steamboat *Amaranth*. Kavanaugh left the mission that fall and later underwent an investigation by the officials of his church. Scott Campbell's testimony was evidently related to a grudge he bore Bruce, who had dismissed him for intemperance in the spring of 1843. The settler's petition, which his affidavit supported, charged Bruce with refusing to honor claims of private citizens against the government for damages done by the Indians, while paying those of the American Fur Company without question. Henry Jackson, one of the independent traders, was the first signer of this petition.

[52] Medill to Robert G. Murphy, May 6, 1848, and Medill to Bruce, May 6, 1848, NARS, RG 75, LS; Secretary of the Interior to Commissioner of Indian Affairs, November 6, 1849, NARS, RG 75, LR; 31st Cong., 1st Sess., *S. Doc. 1*, pp. 1049–1050; *Minnesota Pioneer* (St. Paul), August 23, 1849. The agent's salary was $1,500, a subagent's, $750.

[53] His report is contained in 31st Cong., 1st Sess., *S. Ex. Doc. 1*, pp. 1005–1117.

Madison Goodhue arrived in St. Paul with a printing press and proceeded to start the first newspaper in the territory, the *Minnesota Pioneer*. Goodhue was a highly articulate man, and, unlike some frontier editors, he entered upon his task with no strong prejudices against Indians. Goodhue's detailed account of the annuity payment in September, 1849, is the first by an observer sufficiently detached to be conscious of the color and pageantry of the ceremony. On the Saturday preceding the payment the Indians from Wacouta's and Wabasha's bands "came up the river with their hundred canoes, the paddles sparkling in the sunshine, and moored their multitudinous fleet to the island [below St. Paul], and fastened their bows to the beach." In ten minutes they had their canoes unloaded and were cutting and trimming willow poles for their tipis. In two or three hours they had more than forty erected, "and in the warm sunshine of an Indian summer day, the picture resting upon a rich back-ground of forest-trees now turning yellow, was really delightful." Sunday evening they left their encampment and embarked for the fort. Goodhue described the scene there with all the eye for detail of Parkman or Catlin:

> The Indians are seen straggling along the road—the males, with bows and arrows, pipes and guns—the females, laboring under huge packs of luggage slung by a strap across the forehead. Upon the ground about the Agency at Fort Snelling, while awaiting their turns for the hard handful of silver dollars, they are seen in every posture—some reclining in their tents (or lodges)—some a sitting on a rail—some stretched on their bellies and lazily picking at the ground with their toes—some smoking, and inducing a fuddle by fuming the smoke through the nose—some sauntering in squads of two or more, about the grounds, with the arms in school-boy fashion, about each other's necks—some outside the enclosure, running between two long rows of Indian spectators for a prize—and others of the dignitaries, seated by themselves, talking over the affairs of the invincible Sioux nation.

Inside the agency, four or five government officials with payrolls sat at a table and called the payees up one by one. As his name was called, each person or his sponsor stepped up, touched the secretary's pen, and reached for the money, which was usually deposited "by the hand of a white friend, in the box of his band." [54]

These, then, were the Sioux in 1849, still clinging to what remained of their traditional way of life in the face of vast changes taking place about them and threatening soon to disrupt that way of life and shatter it beyond all hope of recovery.

[54] *Minnesota Pioneer*, September 27, 1849.

CHAPTER **4**

The Monstrous Conspiracy

FROM COLONIAL TIMES the pattern of Indian-white relationships in this country was characterized by a steady and increasing white pressure on the lands claimed by the Indians. The pressure became especially intense after the Revolution, when settlers poured across the Appalachians. Between 1795, when the Treaty of Greenville was forced on a dozen tribes after the Battle of Fallen Timbers, and 1817 and 1818, when cessions having at least the coloration of Indian consent were made, the Indians ceded most of their lands in Ohio, Indiana, and Illinois. After Jackson's Indian removal bill in 1830, the small tracts reserved at the time of those treaties were also surrendered and the Indians obliged to emigrate across the Mississippi.[1] The Sioux were not subjected to this kind of pressure until comparatively late, the small cession made in 1830 having been of slight importance and that made in 1837 involving lands no longer extensively used by them.[2] Sooner or later, however, the advancing frontier was certain to reach the upper Mississippi valley.

Oddly enough, the first major land cession negotiated with the Santee Sioux was not an attempt to open territory to white settlement but

[1] Grant Foreman, *The Last Trek of the Indians* (Chicago: University of Chicago Press, 1946), pp. 18, 32–34, and *passim*.

[2] One village, Kapozha, was located on the east bank of the Mississippi and had to move across the river after the treaty of 1837.

72

rather part of an idealistic scheme to create a northern Indian territory to be occupied by the tribes expelled from the Old Northwest. The chief advocate of this scheme was Secretary of War John Bell, who, as chairman of the House Indian Affairs Committee, had studied the Indian problem and had become convinced that such a territory would offer the best solution to the problem created by the emigration of the eastern tribes. By a liberal construction of a provision in the Indian appropriations act passed March 3, 1841, Bell undertook to negotiate with the Sioux for the cession of a portion of their lands sufficient to accommodate the emigrating tribes. To conduct the negotiations he selected Governor Doty of Wisconsin Territory, who had accompanied Schoolcraft in 1820 and was somewhat familiar with the region desired and with its native inhabitants.[3]

In company with several traders whose services he regarded as essential, Doty arrived at Traverse des Sioux about mid-summer and met with the chiefs and braves of the Sissetons, Wahpetons, and Wahpekutes. He seems to have encountered remarkably little opposition to his proposal. Either the Indians did not understand what they were agreeing to, or else the traders had done a good job of softening them up for the kill. As a result, Doty not only made the desired treaty but exceeded his instructions as to the area of the cession. Bell had expected to buy not more than five million acres, but Doty found it expedient to purchase six times this area, for which the government was to pay $1,300,000.[4]

Doty's treaty is an interesting document, a strange mixture of the utopian and the practical. The tract ceded was a rough parallelogram, west of the territory claimed by the Mdewakantons and east of the crest of the Coteau des Prairies. Everything south of roughly the forty-sixth parallel and north of the present Minnesota-Iowa line was to be incorporated into an Indian territory, within which the Indians were to be encouraged to become farmers and, eventually, citizens. Specific tracts on the left bank of the Minnesota River were set apart for the various bands of Sioux who were parties to the treaty. Each of them was to be provided with an agent, a school, a blacksmith, a gristmill and

[3] Alice Elizabeth Smith, *James Duane Doty: Frontier Promoter* (Madison: State Historical Society of Wisconsin, 1954), pp. 257–258; U. S. *Statutes at Large*, V, 419.

[4] James D. Doty to Secretary of War John Bell, August 4, 1841, NARS, RG 75, LR. The treaty of July 31, 1841, may be found in Thomas Hughes, *Old Traverse des Sioux* (St. Peter: Herald Publishing Co., 1929), pp. 166–170. Three copies, in different hands, are to be found accompanying Doty's letter of transmittal (August 4, 1841). The treaty in Hughes is based on these.

sawmill (where water power was available), and other appurtenances of civilization. The whole was to be under the supervision of a governor or superintendent whose headquarters were to be at the mouth of the Blue Earth River. One of the innovations of Doty's plan was that it provided for more direct control of the Indian trade by the government. The traders became, in effect, government appointees, and the governor had the power to fix prices and otherwise regulate trade.[5]

The traders' services in making this treaty possible were recognized by a provision allowing up to $150,000 for the payment of claims against the Indians by them and by white settlers. Furthermore, Doty seems to have promised jobs to virtually every trader operating in the Sioux country. Nine of them were to be appointed traders at the various settlements, three more were to be appointed agents, another was to be superintendent of agriculture at Traverse des Sioux, and Henry H. Sibley was to be placed in charge of the whole enterprise.[6] Upon what authority Doty presumed to dispense promises of jobs so liberally is not clear, but he seems to have operated on the principle that the best way to solve the problem of the traders' influence over the Indians was to acknowledge it and accept it.

The date of the principal treaty was July 31, 1841. On August 11, at Mendota, Doty negotiated a supplementary treaty with five of the seven Mdewakanton bands, by the terms of which they ceded all their lands and agreed to move to the left bank of the Minnesota. They agreed to the relevant clauses of the earlier treaty and to provisions substituted for the others. The cession was estimated at about two million acres.[7] The two lower bands (Red Wing and Wabasha) refused to sell. Agent Bruce recommended that, if they did not change their minds about selling, they should be removed to a point on the river "Embaratz" (the Zumbro) about thirty miles south of the Red Wing village; this would have been south and southwest of the present town of Pine Island, a favorite hunting ground of the Red Wing band.[8]

[5] Doty to Bell, August 9, 1841, NARS, RG 75, LR.

[6] *Ibid.*

[7] Doty to Bell, August 14, 1841; and "Articles of a Treaty made and concluded at Mindota [sic] . . . between James Duane Doty . . . and the Minda Waukanto Bands of the Dakota Nation," *ibid.*

[8] 27th Cong., 2nd Sess., *S. Doc. 1*, p. 355. Doty fails to mention the refusal of these two bands to sell in his correspondence with the Secretary of War, and the treaty as found in RG 75 includes no signatures. Still a third treaty was made with the half-breeds for the relinquishment for $200,000 of a reserve on Lake Pepin provided by the

Although the Indians neglected their hunting and farming in the expectation of receiving large annuities and were in "deplorable" condition by the fall of 1842, the Doty treaties were destined never to be ratified by the Senate and the grandiose plan for an Indian territory never to reach fruition. Besides opposition from former agent Taliaferro, who denounced it as a plot by the traders to gain complete control over the Indians, it ran into more formidable resistance from the Senate on quite other grounds, notably from the expansionist Senator Thomas Hart Benton of Missouri. Cutting through the maze of stated legalistic objections, it is evident that Benton's real reason for opposing the treaty was that it would have locked up a valuable tract of country for the Indians instead of opening it to white settlement. The political motives that may have contributed to the defeat of the Doty treaties need not detain us here. Presented to the Senate at the very end of the session, the first treaty was tabled on September 13, 1841, resubmitted the next spring, and finally rejected on August 29, 1842.[9]

The idea of a cession of the lands claimed by the Sioux in Minnesota was allowed to rest through most of the decade of the forties, and Indian Bureau officials behaved as though they expected the Sioux to stay where they were for all time. The proposal was revived, however, shortly after Minnesota became a territory in 1849. Almost as soon as he had taken office as governor, Alexander Ramsey began urging his superiors to capitalize on what he represented as the Indians' eagerness to sell their lands. His suggestion met a favorable reception from Indian Commissioner Orlando Brown and from Secretary of the Interior Thomas Ewing, to whose charge Indian affairs had been transferred with the creation that year of the new Department of the Interior. In a twenty-one-page letter Brown set forth detailed instructions for

---

treaty of 1830 but never occupied. See Doty to Bell, September 19, 1841, and Doty to Secretary of War John C. Spencer, November 9, 1841, NARS, RG 75, LR.

[9] Lawrence Taliaferro to Bell, September 10, 1841, and Thomas Hart Benton to the President [John Tyler], September 14, 1841, *ibid.*; Smith, *James Duane Doty*, pp. 260–262. Calling the treaty the "most unjustifiable and *reprehensible* thing of the kind that ever came before the Senate," Benton argued that, in proposing to set up a government for the Indian territory, it constituted an attempt by the executive branch to arrogate to itself functions properly the prerogative of the legislative branch. Some of the missionaries looked favorably on the Doty treaties. Stephen R. Riggs, who was with Doty at Traverse des Sioux, wrote Samuel W. Pond: "I am pleased at the Gov. views about civilizing them [the Indians]. They are comprehensive and enlightened. The experiment must show whether they are *practicable* under present circumstances." See Riggs to Pond, July 29, 1841, in Pond papers, Minnesota Historical Society.

negotiations to be held at the fall annuity payment. All lands claimed by the Sioux north of the Iowa line were to be acquired—more if possible; the region south of the Minnesota River should be the absolute minimum accepted. The price paid should be determined by the value of the land to the Indians (not much, thought Brown), not by its value to potential white immigrants. Two or two and a half cents per acre would surely be ample, although the commissioners were authorized to go above this if they thought the President and the Senate would agree.[10]

The attempt to negotiate with the Sioux in the fall of 1849 was a dismal failure. Many of the western Indians had left on their annual buffalo hunt, and the Mdewakantons were unwilling to treat so late in the season "and for other reasons," as Ramsey cryptically expressed it. Their chief reason probably was that they did not wish to share their annuities under the 1837 treaty with the other bands, as Brown's instructions had specified. They evaded the proposal for a cession and spent their time complaining of various grievances, notably the disposition of the education fund. They demanded that their grievances be redressed before they would discuss any cessions, and they urged the other bands not to come to the negotiations.[11]

This abortive attempt to make a treaty had one benefit: it taught Ramsey something about Indians. He undoubtedly learned a good deal also by talking to his friend Henry H. Sibley, who had traded with them for nearly fifteen years. In December, 1849, the two men addressed a letter to Commissioner Brown, in which they urged a more realistic approach to the matter of obtaining the desired cession. In the first place, the Indians would not sell unless they had the assurance that they would be permanently located on some portion of the proposed cession. Ramsey suggested that they be allowed to remain on the lands north of the Minnesota, above the Little Rapids, and that they be further permitted to hunt anywhere on the cession not occupied by whites until the President might direct otherwise. Furthermore, the Indians objected to a limited annuity on the grounds that its expiration would work a hardship on them. A better method, thought Ramsey and Sibley, was to give them a fixed sum for twenty years, then reduce it if their numbers had diminished, and continue the practice "until the

[10] Alexander Ramsey to William Medill, June 19, 1849; James Ewing to Orlando Brown, July 16, 1849, NARS, RG 75, LR, Minnesota Superintendency; Brown to Ramsey, July 14, 1849, NARS, RG 75, LS; Brown to Ramsey and Governor John Chambers, August 25, 1849, NARS, RG 75, LR.

[11] Ramsey to Brown, September 18, October 4, and December 10, 1849; Chambers and Ramsey to Ewing, October 18, 1849, *ibid.*

bands should become extinct." Another difficulty was that the Doty treaties had made the Indians aware of the value placed on their lands by the whites. Hence there was no hope of buying the land for less than ten cents an acre. Buying twenty or twenty-five million acres at this price and deducting the traders' debts would leave a sum sufficient to give each Indian fifteen or sixteen dollars annually at an interest rate of five per cent. Liberality, the two men urged, was the true policy to follow.[12]

After the failure of negotiations in 1849, it was assumed that another attempt would be made the following year. Although Ramsey was advised early in September, 1850, to hold his Indians in readiness for forty days after the passage of the Indian appropriations act, no further instructions came, and the only result was that the Indians missed out on their fall hunt. In 1851, however, the government at last meant business. To assist Ramsey in making the desired treaty, no less a personage than the new commissioner of Indian affairs, Luke Lea, was detached from his duties in Washington and sent to the remote upper Mississippi valley. The instructions the two men received from Secretary of Interior A. H. H. Stuart were similar to those sent to Ramsey two years earlier, with two important exceptions. They were permitted to pay up to ten cents an acre for the lands; and if they thought it proper for the Indians to be allowed to remain on some part of the cession " during the pleasure of the President," they were authorized to include such a provision in the treaty, provided the locations were as remote as possible from the nearest white settlements.[13] The earlier instructions had expressly forbidden such reservations.

Many observers have noted the moral obliquity that seemingly afflicted white men in their dealings with Indians. Men justly respected for integrity and fairness in their relations with other white men saw nothing reprehensible about resorting to all manner of chicanery and equivocation when dealing with Indians. Starting from the axiom that the Indians were mere children and had a less enlightened view of what would serve their own best interests than the Great Father and his representatives did, government officials, especially treaty commissioners, felt themselves under no restraints in deceiving or bullying the Indians into acceptance of terms decided upon by higher authority.

[12] Ramsey and Henry H. Sibley to Brown, December 10, 1849, *ibid.*

[13] Acting Commissioner A. L. Loughery to Ramsey, September 5, 1850, NARS, RG 75, LS; Ramsey to Commissioner Luke Lea, December 21, 1850; Secretary of Interior A. H. H. Stuart to Lea and Ramsey, May 16, 1851, NARS, RG 75, LR; U.S. *Statutes at Large*, IX, 556.

They knew—or thought they knew—what was best for the Indians, and the end justified the means. By a remarkable coincidence, what was deemed best for the Indians was invariably also to the advantage of the government, the traders, and, above all, the land-hungry settlers.

If one were seeking a treaty tailor-made to illustrate this phenomenon, he could not do better than to examine the treaties of Traverse des Sioux and Mendota, negotiated with the Sioux in the summer of 1851. All the standard techniques were employed by the commissioners. The carrot and the stick—and at least once the mailed fist—were alternately displayed, as the occasion seemed to demand. If the Indians asked for time to consider the terms offered them, they were chided for behaving like women and children rather than men. If they asked shrewd, businesslike questions, the commissioners uttered cries of injured innocence: surely the Indians did not think the Great Father would deceive them! If they wanted certain provisions changed, they were told that it was too late; the treaty had already been written down. The Indians were flattered and brow-beaten by turns, wheedled and shamed, promised and threatened, praised for their wisdom and ridiculed for their folly. In such fashion was their "free consent" obtained.

Like Doty in 1841, Ramsey and Lea determined to treat first with the less sophisticated upper Sioux—the non-annuity bands—so that if they signed a treaty, the commissioners could present the lower bands with a *fait accompli* that would virtually force the Mdewakantons to follow their example. The Wahpekutes were permitted, at their own request, to meet the commissioners in company with the Mdewakantons. When Ramsey and Lea arrived at Traverse des Sioux late in June, they found few Indians on hand but plenty of traders and other hangers-on. Few treaties before or afterward were so thoroughly covered for the benefit of the general public. Two artists were present to memorialize the event on canvas, and the press was ably represented by editor Goodhue of the *Pioneer*, whose running journal furnishes the most detailed account of the proceedings.

After three weeks of waiting around for the remote bands to appear, during which time the Indians present lived well on beef, pork, and bread, the negotiations finally got under way July 18 in an outdoor arbor on a terrace well back from the river. In all the speeches by the commissioners, stress was laid on the Indians' desire to sell their lands, a wish which the government was represented as being willing to humor. Having heard that the game had nearly all disappeared "and that hunger and starvation, like wolves, were often in their lodges," the

President had decided to send the commissioner himself in order to guarantee that the Indians' wishes would be met. Naturally, he denied that the government had any desire to take advantage of them in any way. Since the Indians had much land, which they were unable to use, and the Great Father had money and goods, an exchange seemed perfectly logical. Lea pointed out that other tribes had sold their lands and were now "happier and more comfortable, and every year growing better and richer." His hearers had no way of verifying this assertion, but the modern reader, who can consult Grant Foreman's *The Last Trek of the Indians* for the details of the misery and starvation among the eastern Indians forced to emigrate, is in a better position to judge its accuracy.[14]

After Lea had outlined the benefits to be received under the terms of the proposed treaty, he invited comments from the Indians. This proved a tactical error in that it led to an incipient mutiny which had to be quelled by a threat of stopping the issue of rations. The commissioners did, however, honor the reasonable request that the treaty provisions as outlined by Lea be put in writing so that the Indians could consider them at length, and several amendments proposed by the Indians after a day's deliberation were incorporated into the final document.[15]

On July 23 the commissioners ordered blankets, knives, tobacco, ribbons, paint, and other articles piled up in tempting array, just in case there should be any inclination on the part of the Indians to back out at this late hour. At 1:40 that afternoon the commissioners took their places and were followed shortly by the Indians. The pipe passed among the parties to the negotiation, and then the treaty was read in English and translated into Dakota by Stephen R. Riggs. Soon the signing by the Indians began. Sleepy Eyes threatened to disrupt the harmony of the ceremony by some largely irrelevant objections, and another Sisseton requested that the treaty not be changed in Washington. Upon Lea's assurance that "everything we promise will be faithfully performed," the signing went forward. The Indian who had earlier asked that the treaty be written down now took occasion to point out to the

[14] William G. Le Duc, *Minnesota Year Book for 1852* (St. Paul: W. G. Le Duc, 1852), pp. 31, 37–38, 52–54. This is a reprint of a day-by-day account of the treaty negotiations, published in the *Minnesota Pioneer* from July 3 through August 14, 1851. Folwell attributes the authorship to James M. Goodhue, editor of the *Pioneer*. See also Lucile M. Kane, "The Sioux Treaties and the Traders," *Minnesota History*, XXXII (June 1951), 65–80.

[15] Le Duc, *Minnesota Year Book for 1852*, pp. 55–60.

white men that "you think it a great deal of money to give for this land, but you must well understand that the money will all go back to the whites again, and the country will also remain theirs." When the treaty had been signed by everyone concerned, Lea asked the Indians "to be as honest and faithful in its observance as the government will be upon their part." As matters turned out, meeting this obligation would not have demanded any great degree of honesty or faithfulness. The ceremony completed, Goodhue commented: "Thus ended the sale of twenty one millions of acres of the finest land in the world."[16]

The treaty of Traverse des Sioux provided for the cession by the upper Sioux of all their claims in what is today Minnesota and a small portion of South Dakota. For this cession they were to receive $1,665,000, divided as follows: $275,000 was to go to the chiefs to enable them to "settle their affairs" (i.e., pay their debts to the traders), pay the costs of removal, and subsist themselves and their people for one year; $30,000 was to be spent to establish schools, blacksmith shops, and mills, and to open farms on the new reservation. The remainder of the principal ($1,360,000) was to bear interest at a rate of five per cent for a period of fifty years. This interest was to be used for the benefit of the Indians, who would receive a $40,000 cash annuity and $10,000 worth of goods and provisions annually; $12,000 was to be spent for general agricultural and civilization purposes, and $6,000 was to be used for education. An important article, later stricken out by the Senate, provided for a reservation on the upper Minnesota, extending for ten miles on either side of the river and from the western end of the cession down to the Yellow Medicine River.[17]

Although treaty stipulations providing for direct payments for traders' debts had been outlawed by Congress, a way was found to evade the letter of the law at Traverse des Sioux. Each Indian, as he stepped away from the treaty table, was pulled to a barrel nearby and made to sign a document prepared by the traders. By its terms the signatories to the treaty acknowledged their debts to the traders and half-breeds and pledged themselves, as the representatives of their respective bands, to pay those obligations. No schedule of the sums owed was attached to the document, but after the ceremony was over the traders got together and scaled down their claims (originally estimated at $431,735.78) to the round sum of $210,000; the half-breeds were to get $40,000. The

16 *Ibid.*, pp. 64–68.

17 Charles J. Kappler, comp. and ed., *Indian Affairs, Laws and Treaties*, II (Washington: Government Printing Office, 1904), 588–589.

Indians later claimed that they had thought they were signing a third copy of the treaty, as did Thomas S. Williamson. The traders and some others insisted, however, that the whole matter had been discussed privately beforehand and that the Indians knew perfectly well what they were signing. The testimony later taken is voluminous and contradictory, but one thing is certain: the "traders' paper" and the manner in which the Indians were induced to sign it did more than any other single action on the part of the white men present at the treaty to engender bitterness among the Indians afterward.[18]

A few days after the signing of the treaty of Traverse des Sioux with the upper bands, a similar agreement was made at Mendota with the Mdewakantons and Wahpekutes. Because the first treaty was the more spectacular and because it made the second almost inevitable and a trifle anticlimactic, historians have tended to give it their almost exclusive attention and to dismiss the treaty of Mendota with a few words. This approach calls for correction, for the second treaty is more important than its surface appearance may suggest. It was at Mendota, among Indians who had made treaties before, that the commissioners were really put on their mettle and where the treaty-making techniques were most baldly displayed in all their ruthlessness. It was here that the hard questions were asked—and answered with equivocation and bullying.

"Once more unto the *beef*, dear friends, once more," wrote Goodhue as the council got under way in the upper room of a large warehouse. Ramsey opened the negotiations on the afternoon of July 29 with much the same speech he had delivered eleven days earlier, but with the additional remark that, since the upper Sioux had already sold their lands, there was really nothing for the lower bands to do but follow suit. Because these people, unlike most of the Sissetons and Wahpetons, would have to leave their homes, Lea made perfunctory obeisance to the natural love of one's homeland and added that he himself had moved several times. When the treaty terms had been outlined and a tract on the upper Minnesota below that reserved for the upper bands had been suggested as a reservation, he commented that there probably would be no remarks but that if there were he would entertain them. Wabasha injected a sour note into the council at once by asking that the Mdewakantons be paid the education fund that had so long been a source of ill feeling with them. And a Wahpekute warrior asked about

[18] William W. Folwell, *A History of Minnesota*, I (St. Paul: Minnesota Historical Society, 1956), 282–283.

the government's announced plans to pay his band for the killing of seventeen of their men by the Sacs and Foxes two years earlier. The commissioners parried both of these inquiries and then adjourned the council.[19]

When they met again the next day, it was, at Wabasha's request, outdoors, on a high plain near Pilot Knob, overlooking the landing at Mendota and within sight of Fort Snelling. The chiefs, harder bargainers than their Sisseton and Wahpeton counterparts, refused to commit themselves on the proposed treaty, and the council had to be adjourned again without action. When it reconvened on July 31, Little Crow brought the discussion back to the question of the unpaid annuities. Lea tried to evade the issue, but Ramsey gave as straightforward an answer as any the Indians were likely to get: "If this treaty can be arranged, so that we can be justified in paying you this money," he said, "as much of it will be paid down to you as will be equal to your usual cash annuities for three years." The chiefs seemed to assent, and Ramsey thought that work on the treaty might as well go ahead. Little Crow was not ready yet, however; "We will talk of nothing else but that money, if it is until next spring," he said. Ramsey's reply that the money would be paid when the treaty was finished seemed not to satisfy the Indians, for they remained silent when Lea tried to return to the discussion of the treaty. Trying a different tack, the commissioners abruptly terminated the session and left.[20]

The next day the Indians assembled and asked the commissioners to join them, but the discussions that followed were fruitless. Evidently a break was in order, to give everyone time to think matters over and come back with something concrete. So, despite the long wait at Traverse des Sioux, the commissioners allowed three days to pass without any formal negotiations. Then, on August 5, the council reassembled for what proved to be the decisive session. After the treaty had been read in English and translated by Gideon Pond, Little Crow was invited to sign. He made no move to do so. Then Wabasha arose and questioned the whole argument that the treaty would be for the Indians' benefit; the provisions in the earlier treaty for schools, farmers, etc., had been of no benefit to them, and he thought a straight cash payment would be preferable. Furthermore, he objected to the prairie country which had been selected as their future home; he had always lived near the woods and preferred that type of country. At this point Lea bared the mailed fist that always lay thinly concealed behind his

19 Le Duc, *Minnesota Year Book for 1852*, pp. 70–75.
20 *Ibid.*, pp. 75–78.

words. Addressing Wabasha and the other chiefs, he said: "Suppose your Great Father wanted your lands and did not want a treaty for your good, he could come with 100,000 men and drive you off to the Rocky Mountains." The matter had been thoroughly thought over, a treaty had been prepared and signed by the commissioners, and it was too late to talk of changing it. But even this bald threat did not produce the desired result, for when Ramsey again called for signers, no one offered to be the first.[21]

Objections continued to be voiced. After the commissioners had evaded some and made slight concessions in response to others, Wacouta spoke up to express a well-founded fear: Would the treaty be changed when it got to Washington? "If all prove true as you say, it will be very good indeed. But," he continued, "when we were at Washington [in 1837], the chiefs were told many things; which when we came back here, and attempted to carry out, we found could not be done. At the end of three or four years, the Indians found out very different from what they had been told, and all were ashamed." He also asked for a reservation south of his village, "a tract of land called Pine Island, which is a good place for Indians." The high regard in which Wacouta was held inhibited Ramsey from ridiculing him as he had the earlier chiefs, but he pointed out that it would be impossible to satisfy everyone with a single treaty. As a partial concession, he promised that the Indians could go on hunting in their old homes for many years, until the country filled up with settlers.[22]

Still the objections went on, Wabasha and Little Crow leading the attack. Ramsey seemed hurt by the implications of some of the Indians' remarks. The chiefs made the commissioners ashamed, he said: "They seem to think we have come here as the representatives of the Great Father to cheat them." The carrot having been ineffectual, the stick was now brought into play once more, as Lea obliquely threatened to cut off rations, saying, "No man puts any food in his mouth by long talk; but may often get hungry at it. Let the Little Crow and the chiefs step forward and sign." This peremptory demand had the desired effect, for Little Crow stepped up and wrote his name, Taoyateduta, and the other chiefs made their *X*'s, until all sixty-four had signed.[23] On that hill overlooking the meeting point of the two rivers, the lower Sioux had signed away their patrimony.

The treaty of Mendota contained essentially the same terms as the

[21] *Ibid.*, pp. 79–82.
[22] *Ibid.*, pp. 82–85.
[23] *Ibid.*, pp. 85–86.

earlier one, with the exception of a smaller payment ($1,410,000), a provision that in the future the entire annuity under the 1837 treaty would be paid in cash, and different specifications for the reservation. The article concerning the reservation, like that in the other treaty, was stricken out by the Senate. In order to gain the assent of the Wah-pekutes, a clause was included providing for their participation in benefits derived from the 1837 treaty. Like the treaty of Traverse des Sioux, this agreement provided that the principal sum, on which interest was to be paid for fifty years, should not revert to the Indians upon the expiration of that time.[24]

As soon as the treaties had been signed, whites began pouring onto the ceded lands. Within two weeks of the end of negotiations at Mendota, they were reported to be crossing the Mississippi "in troops," making claims, and building shanties on lands which they as yet had no legal right to intrude upon. Most were said to be speculators rather than prospective settlers. Agent McLean protested to his superiors, but he recognized that it would be useless to appeal to the local civil authorities for redress, since they were in sympathy with the intruders. He applied to the commandant at Fort Snelling but was told that the garrison could do nothing about the situation.[25] Expecting the treaties to be ratified shortly, Ramsey was disposed to allow this invasion to take place, having heard, he said, that the government had elsewhere adopted the practice of tacitly indulging "her citizens in entering upon Indian lands, in the period between a treaty, and its ratification by the Senate." His only fear was that there might be a clash between the intruders and the Indians, but thus far the latter had shown remarkable forbearance. Their patience was sorely tried, however, when settlers began laying out farms on the Indians' fields and hay ground and ordering the Indians off.[26]

In one sense the presence of these hordes of white settlers was fortunate for the Indians during the winter of 1851–1852. Having missed out on their summer hunt and having lost most of their corn to floods, living in momentary expectation of receiving payments under the new treaties, the Indians were destitute and in a starving condition much of the winter and spring. The settlers, motivated no doubt by considera-

[24] Kappler, *Indian Affairs, Laws and Treaties*, II, 591–593.

[25] Nathaniel McLean to Lea, August 19, 1851, NARS, RG 75, LR.

[26] Ramsey to Lea, January 28, 1852, *ibid.*; 32nd Cong., 2nd Sess., *Ex. Doc. 1*, p. 354. This last imposition was inflicted between the time of the ratification of the treaties and their proclamation by the President.

tions of safety, since many of the Indians were armed, contributed heavily to their support and, in the opinion of contemporary observers, saved them from mass starvation.[27]

The only solution, as the whites saw it, was the swift ratification of the treaties. Goodhue warned that unless the treaties were ratified, the Indians would lose their lands without compensation, and there would be an Indian war. As a matter of fact, the treaties did not even reach the Senate until February 13—more than six months after they had been concluded—and then no sense of urgency animated the men whose task it was to ratify them. Despite opposition from southern senators who had no wish to see another northern state enter the Union in a few years, the treaties were finally ratified, with bare two-thirds majorities, on June 23, 1852, with amendments striking out the provisions for reservations and thus leaving the Indians without a home.[28] In the general rejoicing over the passage of the treaties, the white people of Minnesota seemed to regard the amendments as of little moment. The *Pioneer* commented that the Indians were losing nothing "of any positive value to them." Many probably assumed that the assent of the Indians to the changes would not be necessary, but Congress included in the Indian appropriations bill, passed August 30, a proviso that none of the $690,050 appropriated to carry out the treaty terms could be expended until the Indians had agreed to the amendments.[29] This proviso looks suspiciously like a last-ditch effort to defeat the treaties, but it could also be interpreted as an honest attempt to deal justly with the Indians.

Obtaining their consent proved by no means easy. When Ramsey met with the chiefs late in August and explained the amendments to them, they refused peremptorily to give their assent unless they could be assured of the location of their future reservation. He was extricated from the awkward position in which he found himself by virtue of a vaguely

[27] McLean to Lea, August 19, 1851, NARS, RG 75, LR; *Minnesota Pioneer*, August 14, 1851, March 4 and April 1, 1852. Only the Mdewakantons had received any annuities the previous summer, and the $30,000 turned over to them after the treaty at Mendota was spent almost at once. By the spring of 1852 the Indians were said to have eaten their ponies, "and when that was all gone, [had] literally gnawed the bark off of the trees."

[28] *Minnesota Pioneer*, April 1, May 6, and July 1, 1852; Folwell, *History of Minnesota*, I, 290–291; Kappler, *Indian Affairs, Laws and Treaties*, II, 593. In theory they had a home outside the limits of the cession, but no such location had been chosen, and they had been led to expect a reservation within the cession.

[29] *Minnesota Pioneer*, July 15, 1852; U. S. *Statutes at Large*, X, 52.

worded letter to Lea from the chairman of the Senate Committee on
Indian Affairs, who said that the amendments authorized the President
to allow the Indians to remain on a portion of their lands until the whites
wanted it. With this slender assurance, Ramsey gave the chiefs a half-
promise which was probably converted into a guarantee in the process of translation, and they finally consented to the amendments.[30]

One further hurdle remained to be surmounted: the traders and
half-breeds had to be paid off. Theoretically, Ramsey could simply have
paid them the sums specified in the traders' paper out of the $690,050
he was authorized to disburse. He believed, however, that legal evidence in the form of witnessed receipts signed by the chiefs and headmen was called for. Early in November he undertook this delicate task.
Since the Wahpekutes had signed a traders' paper at Mendota and had
not repudiated it, they presented no problem. The Mdewakantons were
not so docile. Once more the carrot and the stick had to be used. The
stick in this case was a delay in the payment of the annuities due under
the 1837 treaty, as well as of the current annuity—a highly effective
weapon with Indians who had been hovering on the brink of starvation
much of the previous year. The carrot consisted of dividing a sum of
$20,000 equally among the seven chiefs, ostensibly to be paid to certain
half-breeds who had not benefited from the treaty. There was a fine
cloak-and-dagger scene late on the night of November 8, when Wabasha and Wacouta were presented with bags of gold and promptly
signed a receipt for the entire $90,000 supposedly due the traders and
a statement authorizing Ramsey to pay the remaining $70,000. The
other chiefs followed their example the next day, and on the eleventh
each signed a voucher for $2,857.14 2/7.[31]

The upper Sioux, who had protested as soon as they learned the
nature of the traders' paper they had signed, also proved refractory and
had to be reduced to submission by the withholding of their annuities
and by the arrest and deposition from his chieftainship of Red Iron,
leader of the opposition. It was almost the end of November before
Ramsey finally secured the signatures of eleven chiefs and braves of
sufficient stature to give the operation the appearance of legality.[32]

[30] Ramsey to Lea, August 28, September 4 and 10, 1852; Senator D. R. Atchison to
Lea, August 3, 1852, NARS, RG 75, LR; Folwell, *History of Minnesota*, I, 294. The
Wahpekutes also objected to the striking out of the clause that would have provided
for their participation in the annuities received by the Mdewakantons under the treaty
of 1837.

[31] Folwell, *History of Minnesota*, I, 284, 297–299.

[32] *Ibid.*, I, 299–303. In reply to the complaint about the traders' paper, Ramsey had
assured the upper Sioux in December, 1851, that, as the paper was not part of the

Newton H. Winchell, though no admirer of the Sioux, referred to the treaties of 1851 as a "monstrous conspiracy."[33] They were that and more. From beginning to end—the tactics used to get the Indians to agree to the treaties in the first place, the bad faith of the Senate in amending them, the devices employed to force the Indians to accept the amendments, the whole nefarious business of the traders' paper— it was a thoroughly sordid affair, equal in infamy to anything else in the long history of injustice perpetrated upon the Indians by the authorized representatives of the United States government in the name of that government. Despite all the fine talk during the negotiations about the welfare of the Indians, they seem to have been speedily lost sight of once their X's were down on paper. When the treaties reached the Senate, the Indians became mere pawns in a power struggle between sectional and political factions. Even the subsequent investigation of Ramsey's role in the affair—in which he was whitewashed by the Senate—seems to have been politically motivated and not the product of any real concern for the Indians.[34] When the whirlwind was reaped a decade later, the immediate victims were the comparatively innocent white settlers near the reservation, not the men ultimately responsible. In the end, of course, the ones who suffered most were, as always, the Indians.

---

treaty, the commisioners had no power, "and assumed none, in relation to the payment of debts to their traders." See McLean to Lea, December 13, 1851, NARS, RG 75, LR. His statement, which the Indians apparently accepted at face value, showed either ignorance of the terms of the paper (as he later testified) or disingenuousness. For a discussion of the role played by one Madison Sweetser in this affair, see Folwell, *History of Minnesota*, I, 299–303.

[33] Newton H. Winchell, *The Aborigines of Minnesota* (St. Paul: The Pioneer Co., 1911), p. 554.

[34] Folwell (in *History of Minnesota*, I, 462–470) traces the course of the investigation in some detail. His information is derived principally from the voluminous "Report of the Commissioners Appointed by the President of the United States to Investigate the Official Conduct of Alexander H. Ramsey, Late Governor of Minnesota, with the Testimony Taken in the Case by Them, Transmitted to the Senate with the Message of the President of the United States, January 10, 1854," 33rd Cong., 1st Sess., *S. Ex. Doc. 61*.

CHAPTER 5

Reservation Days

THE TREATIES of Traverse des Sioux and Mendota brought the Santee Sioux within the toils of the reservation system for the first time. They had previously been able to live and hunt pretty much as they pleased in the region they had occupied since their expulsion from the Mille Lacs country. But now, by submitting to the terms of these treaties, they became reservation Indians, subject to the humiliation and demoralization that condition implied in the nineteenth century. The practical impossibility of immediately confining them to the reservation prolonged their freedom for a few years; but as their old lands filled with white settlers and as strenuous efforts were made to keep them on the reservation, they gradually submitted to the dictates of authority.

Properly speaking, the Santees had no reservation under the terms of the 1851 treaties as amended by the Senate. But since the directive to locate them on some tract of land outside the ceded area was never acted upon, they were temporarily assigned to the reservation originally set apart by those treaties. The failure of the government to make any specific provision for them before their removal from their old homes is attributable in part to the confusion attending the changeover from a Whig to a Democratic administration in the spring of 1853 and the preoccupation of the new officials with other concerns. After a few months, however, the question began to be raised as to the exact status of the land assigned to the Indians. People charged with managing their affairs wondered about the anomaly of locating them on lands they had sold and from the sale of which they were already receiving payment. Early in 1854 the Secretary of the Interior submitted to President Pierce his recommendation that the Indians be permitted to occupy the reservation as their permanent home "until the President shall consider it proper to remove them."[1] Pierce gave his approval to this oddly phrased recommendation, and there the matter rested.

Some members of Congress must have recognized the paradox of a permanent home from which the residents might at any time be evicted, for the Indian appropriations act of July 31, 1854, contained a provision that "the President be authorized to confirm to the Sioux of Minnesota, forever, the reserve on the Minnesota River" then occupied by them, "upon such conditions as he may deem just."[2] No executive action was ever taken in line with this authorization, however, and the status of the lands occupied by the Indians remained uncertain until 1860, when, as will be seen, the Senate belatedly confirmed the Indian title to them.[3]

Although the treaties had been negotiated by the Whig governor of Minnesota, Alexander Ramsey, neither he nor the Whig appointee to the post of agent, Nathaniel McLean, had any part in the actual removal of the Indians to their new reservation. The treaties were not formally proclaimed until February 24, 1853; and before anything could be accomplished toward removing the Indians and establishing the agency, both men were out of office, together with the Indian commissioner, Luke Lea. Although the new Democratic governor, Willis A. Gorman, had no special qualifications for the job of superintendent of Indian affairs, the agent who replaced McLean, Robert G. Murphy, was better qualified, having held the post briefly in 1848–1849. And the new commissioner, George Manypenny, though sometimes wrongheaded, was an able man who took his responsibilities more seriously than did most holders of the office in the nineteenth century.

Overruling McLean's earlier plan, Murphy decided to locate the new agency at a fairly well timbered site on the south side of the Minnesota River, about fifteen miles above Fort Ridgely, a military post

[1] Governor Willis A. Gorman to Commissioner George Manypenny, September 13, 1853; Secretary of the Interior Robert McClelland to Manypenny, April 13, 1854, NARS, RG 75, LR.

[2] U. S. *Statutes at Large*, X, 326, 331.

[3] Charles J. Kappler, comp. and ed., *Indian Affairs, Laws and Treaties*, II (Washington: Government Printing Office, 1904), 780–789.

then being built. His ambitious plans for breaking land, erecting buildings to house the blacksmiths, farmers, and laborers, and cutting logs
for the next season's construction made little progress in 1853, chiefly
because he and Gorman had their hands full getting the Indians moved.
The superintendent held several councils in the spring, at which the
Indians pointed out that, since preparations for their reception on the
reservation were incomplete, they would be much better off continuing
to plant at their old homes until enough ground had been broken on the
reservation for their needs. Gorman, who seems to have regarded their
removal as a test of his competence as an administrator, argued with
them until they finally agreed to visit the reservation and decide then
whether preparations had progressed far enough to warrant their removal that summer.[4]

This concession served as an entering wedge to induce a majority of
the lower Indians to move that season. The emigration began in August
and progressed slowly. By September 10, Gorman had got the two
lower bands, who were the most strongly opposed to moving, as far as
Little Crow's village, where they rested for a few days. While there the
chiefs demanded in council that they be paid the funds accumulated
under the 1837 treaty. Gorman offered to disburse $4,000 of the money
in a per capita payment when they reached Shakopee's village. He
actually paid out only $1,500, and that was taken from the subsistence
and removal fund, but it was enough to pry them loose at Shakopee
late in October and get them the rest of the way to the new agency.[5]

Whatever his methods, Gorman was quite proud of his achievement
in removing the Indians. Except for sixty members of Wabasha's band,
who had fled to the Red Cedar River, all the Mdewakantons and Wahpekutes had been safely brought to the reservation, he boasted, together
with those Sissetons and Wahpetons who had resided on the lower Minnesota.[6] Most of them stayed only long enough to receive their annuities, however, and then took flight back to their old hunting grounds,
where they spent the winter and, in some cases, the next summer as well.
Conflicting accounts make it difficult to determine just what was accomplished in the first year on the reservation. Gorman's official reports

[4] Alexander Ramsey to Luke Lea, February 14, 1853; Gorman to Manypenny,
July 27, 1853; Robert G. Murphy to Gorman, September 3, 1853; Gorman to Manypenny, May 27, 1853, NARS, RG 75, LR; *Minnesota Pioneer* (St. Paul), June 9, 1853.

[5] 33rd Cong., 1st Sess., *S. Doc. 1*, p. 314; Gorman to Manypenny, August 23 and 31,
September 9, November 15 and 28, 1853, NARS, RG 75, LR.

[6] Gorman to Manypenny, November 15, 1853, *ibid*.

speak glowingly of extensive farming operations on the reservation. "It only requires a little energy to make the most wonderful progress in civilization among the Sioux," he complacently wrote in July, 1854. On the other hand, Moses N. Adams, a missionary at Traverse des Sioux, gave the impression that very little was done to establish the Indians as farmers. His version received partial confirmation from Superintendent of Farming Philander Prescott, who admitted that the Wahpekutes and three of the Mdewakanton bands were roving about the country most of that year, complaining of their treatment. It appears that only a small amount of land had been broken in 1853, and that so badly that it had to be plowed again before it could be planted.[7]

The unwillingness of the Indians to settle down on the reservation had been predicted by one who knew them well, Lawrence Taliaferro, who in 1853 had written to Commissioner Manypenny that they had been so deceived by the outgoing administration as to be skeptical of all the government's professed efforts in their behalf. "Never—*never* deceive an Indian *once even*," he warned; "if you do, you may expect never to hear the last of your promise."[8] There were also other, more immediate reasons why the Indians refused to stay put on their reservation. The fact is that there was practically nothing to keep them there. Even Agent Murphy himself did not see fit to reside at the agency, but bought a house at Shakopee, where he remained for the rest of his term. He defended his residence there on the ground that, since the Indians spent most of their time off the reserve, he was actually in a better location to attend their wants than he would have been at the agency. Furthermore, since their old traders were still located at such places as Wabasha, Red Wing, and Faribault, the Indians found it cheaper to buy there and transport the goods and provisions to the reservation themselves than to have the traders sell at a higher rate at the agency.

[7] Gorman to Manypenny, July 18, 1854; Moses N. Adams to Manypenny, August 3, 1854; Murphy to Manypenny, November 4, 1855, *ibid.*; Com. of Indian Affairs, *Annual Report*, 1854, p. 74. Adams charged that no special effort was made to have the Indians return to the reservation early in the spring of 1854 and that neither Gorman nor Murphy was around at the time they should have begun planting.

[8] Lawrence Taliaferro to Manypenny, July 12, 1853, NARS, RG 75, LR. Taliaferro continued to make gratuitous offers of advice and services for years after he had resigned his post as agent. In this letter he describes his achievements with the Indians —"deals a little in self-glorification," as the Indian Office clerk noted by way of summarizing the contents of the letter on the back—and announces that if the Indians should prove too refractory for the department, "*temporarily* I am at the service of my Country."

In any case, the roads from the settled parts of Minnesota to the reservation were so primitive that supplies could not be brought there in the winter.[9]

The Indians did not leave the reservation in the expectation of enjoying an easy life among the white settlers; they were driven by starvation. The annuities were paid so late and in such small amounts in both 1853 and 1854 that the Indians could not live through the winter on what they received; and since there was little game on the reservation, they had no choice but to hunt in the ceded territory. So long as they merely hunted and fished in the woods, they encountered no hostility from the settlers, but those who sought to return to villages that were now becoming towns met with opposition. In the spring of 1854, before the Wacouta band returned from their winter hunt, their bark houses were burned by the white residents of the growing town of Red Wing. The Indians made no hostile overtures when they arrived, but simply located elsewhere and planted their corn as usual.[10] They continued, however, to visit the Red Wing area during the entire reservation period, to the increasing annoyance of the white settlers.

The plowing done in 1854 was not impressive, in either quantity or quality, but some progress was made toward establishing an agency by the construction of eleven buildings, including two storehouses, a blacksmith shop, houses for the farmers and laborers, and boarding and work houses. There were still no houses for the agent, the interpreter, the head farmer, or the chiefs, however, and the single blacksmith was greatly overworked. In the next year twelve log houses were built for the employees and chiefs, a saw mill was raised and placed in readiness, and the frame was erected for a flour mill. More acreage was plowed for each band and for a few families who wished to farm individually. As a matter of fact, by September, 1855, the amount of land broken exceeded the immediate demands of the Indians, and some of it remained unplanted.[11]

[9] Gorman to Manypenny, January 9, 1854 (incorrectly dated 1853); Murphy to Gorman, January 6, 1854; Murphy to Manypenny, October 31, 1855; James Shields to Manypenny, n.d., 1855 (postmarked September 14), *ibid.*; *Minnesota Pioneer*, January 5, 1854. Shields, then a member of Congress, owned land near Faribault and took an interest in the welfare of the Indians who drifted into his locality.

[10] Shields to Manypenny, n.d., 1855, NARS, RG 75, LR. *History of Goodhue County* (Red Wing: Wood, Alley & Co., 1878), p. 338. This information is contained in an address delivered June 15, 1869, by Dr. W. W. Sweeney, who settled at Red Wing in 1852.

[11] Com. of Indian Affairs, *Annual Report*, 1854, pp. 74–75; 34th Cong., 1st and 2nd Sess., *S. Doc. 1*, pp. 378–380, 384–385.

Many of the Indians, especially the upper bands, for whom no plowing had been done, were still off the reservation in 1855, either farming at unauthorized locations or simply roaming around the settlements. Nearly all were dependent on hunting during the winter. They felt, with reason, that the representatives of the government were being grossly unfair in demanding that they stay on the reservation and yet not providing enough food for them to live on there. Possibly if they had made maximum use of the land broken for them, they might have produced enough food to sustain them through the winter, but it is doubtful.[12]

The Indians had other complaints as well. From the very beginning, there had been hitches of one sort or another in getting their supplies to them. Ramsey had used so much of the subsistence and removal fund in persuading the Indians to accept the Senate's amendments to the treaties that he had little to turn over to his successor in the spring of 1853. In addition, goods sent up in the fall of 1852 had been detained at La Crosse by the closing of navigation on the Mississippi and did not reach the agent until the next spring.[13] In the summer of 1853 the upper bands neglected their customary summer hunt on the prairies in the expectation of receiving their annuities about July 1, but these were not sent from Washington until October and not distributed until late in November. The next year such annuities as did arrive, late in the fall, were so niggardly that the Indians at first refused to accept the money, saying it was not the amount the government promised them and accusing Murphy of holding back part of what was coming to them.[14]

They may have been in error as to the amount of money they were entitled to, but if so they were to be pardoned. The officials responsible for keeping the accounts in order confessed themselves unclear about the amounts owed under the various treaties. The frequent changes of personnel of course contributed to the confusion. Murphy tried to untangle the complications involved in the education fund that had so long been accumulating; but he had only the figures of his predecessors to go by, and his pathetic appeal to the commissioner for specific instructions brought no immediate response. The Indians understood

[12] Murphy to Manypenny, May 25, 1855; Major H. Day to Manypenny, October 13, 1855, NARS, RG 75, LR. Day, then commanding officer at Fort Ridgely, was acting agent in Murphy's absence.

[13] Ramsey to Manypenny, April 16, 1853; Gorman to Manypenny, September 8, 1853, *ibid.*

[14] *Minnesota Pioneer*, October 20 and 27, 1853; Murphy to Manypenny, July 20, 1855; Murphy to Gorman, July 27, 1854; Murphy to Manypenny, December 30, 1854, NARS, RG 75, LR.

that Lea had told them in 1851 that the $30,000 paid upon the signing of the treaty of Mendota was about half the accumulated sum, and they kept asking for the other half. Gorman and Little Crow went to Washington in the spring of 1855 and were promised (so the chief thought, at least) that this sum would be paid. As the time approached when some of the provisions of the 1837 treaty would expire, Commissioner Manypenny got to work on the problem and finally submitted to the Secretary of the Interior a seventeen-page letter detailing the various appropriations made and the uses to which they had been put since 1838. The mouse which this mountain of labor brought forth was the conclusion that the government owed the Indians $30,041.58, which sum he recommended Congress be asked to appropriate, provided the Treasury Department concurred.[15] There the matter rested for a time.

The withholding of the education fund was not the only respect in which the government failed to meet its obligations to the Sioux. For reasons not clear, appropriations during the early 1850's were insufficient to fulfill the provisions of the 1851 treaties. Not only did the Indians receive less money, goods, and provisions than they had a right to expect, but funds for the management of the agency were not forthcoming. The employees' wages were months, even years, in arrears, and improvements promised to the Indians languished in the planning stage or half completed for lack of funds. Furthermore, the physical problem of transporting supplies to the comparatively remote Sioux agency sometimes exceeded the powers of human ingenuity to solve. The Minnesota River could never be relied upon to be navigable at the season when goods and provisions reached St. Paul, and sometimes contractors had to default on their agreements. Add to this the inflationary effect of a rise in prices, which in 1855 resulted in the Indians' receiving only two thirds as much goods as they were accustomed to getting, and you have a situation extremely unpleasant for the Sioux and decidedly uncomfortable for Agent Murphy, whom they held immediately responsible for any shortages in their annuities.[16]

The truth is that, even allowing for all the handicaps he labored under, Murphy does not seem to have exerted himself in behalf of the

[15] Murphy to Manypenny, September 28, 1855; Manypenny to McClelland, April 8, 1856, *ibid*. Congress did appropriate the sum of $42,841.47, which included the accumulated education fund, and $31,000 of it was paid in December of 1857. See William J. Cullen to Charles E. Mix, November 26 and December 24, 1857, *ibid*.

[16] Gorman to Manypenny, July 18, 1854, and August 30, 1855; Murphy to Manypenny, November 4, 1855, *ibid*.

Indians to the degree that a truly dedicated agent like Taliaferro would have. Even the missionaries, Riggs and Williamson, though not wishing to see him replaced by someone worse, had to qualify their testimonial in his favor with the remarks that "he may have given more attention to his own pecuniary interests than we suppose is compatible with the full discharge of the duties of a public officer"; and the best they could say for him was that he was as good as anyone else the Indians had had as agent for the previous sixteen years.[17] Like all his predecessors, Murphy came under attack from the traders, both licensed and unlicensed, who repeatedly tried to have him removed. Their grudge against him seems to have stemmed mainly from his refusal to license those living off the reservation and his later exclusion of all traders from the annuity payments. Although their complaints did not directly produce the desired effect, they may have undermined his position and thus prepared the way for his eventual dismissal.[18]

The axe fell on Murphy's neck when the Minnesota Superintendency was abolished in 1856 and Indian affairs in the territory were placed under the jurisdiction of the Northern Superintendency, then in the charge of Francis Huebschmann. When the superintendent visited the agency in June, his Teutonic sense of order was offended by the easygoing way in which affairs there had been managed by Murphy and Gorman. He found conditions on the reservation "deplorable" and a "spirit of lassitude" prevailing.[19] Within a few weeks Murphy had been replaced by Charles E. Flandrau, a man of considerable experience as an Indian trader and apparently also a man of integrity. Under Flandrau things began to hum around the agency, though the results of his more vigorous administration did not become evident until after he had left office. He inherited an unfortunate state of affairs and was confronted with some new and extremely serious problems before he could feel his way into the job. Then, in the summer of 1857, he was named to the territorial supreme court and also served as a member of the convention to draw up a constitution for the proposed state of Minnesota.

[17] Memorandum from Stephen R. Riggs and Thomas S. Williamson to Manypenny, March 17, 1855, *ibid*. The reference to "sixteen years" is interesting, as that was the length of time since Taliaferro had resigned.

[18] Murphy to Shields, January 28 and March 4, 1855; Murphy to Manypenny, March 21, 1855; Murphy to J. Ross Brown, March 24, 1855; Shields to Manypenny, n.d., 1855; Affidavit of James Wells, March 6, 1855, *ibid*.

[19] McClelland to Manypenny, January 23, 1856, NARS, RG 75, LR, Minnesota Superintendency; Francis Huebschmann to Manypenny, July 19 and June 28, 1856, NARS, RG 75, LR. If conditions on the reservation were as bad as Huebschmann describes them, he had reason for dismissing Murphy.

These responsibilities kept him away from the agency much of the time, and finally he resigned his position after only thirteen months as agent for the Sioux.

While the government was gradually establishing a presence on the reservation, the missionaries were also turning their eyes in that direction. Except for Lac qui Parle, all the missions among the Santee Sioux were located on the ceded lands and hence were left, officially at least, without any Indians to minister to after the removal in 1853. Most of the missionaries remained where they were and continued their work among the white settlers, but Williamson elected to stay with the Indians. After nearly four years at Little Crow's village, he moved in the fall of 1852 to a point a few miles above the mouth of the Yellow Medicine River and there, among the upper Sioux, established a new mission called Pajutazee. In the late winter of 1854 the Lac qui Parle mission burned to the ground, and Riggs moved his mission down the Minnesota to a site not far from Williamson's and started a new station called Hazelwood.[20] These were the only missions on the reservation until 1860, when the Episcopal church began its work with the Sioux. Since no government schools were opened until the later fifties, despite treaty provisions for education, the missionary establishments provided the only educational opportunities available to the Indians for several years. Both Williamson and Riggs remained with the Sioux throughout the reservation period and were instrumental in organizing the first substantial effort on the part of the Indians to become farmers.

Besides their other contributions, which included a short-lived periodical, the *Dakota Friend*, or *Dakota Tawxitku Kin*, the missionaries exerted some influence over the course of government policy toward the Sioux. Although their influence at this time was not as great as it became after the Civil War, when for a time the religious bodies virtually took over Indian policy, it was far from negligible. On June 6, 1850, more than a year before the treaties, the members of the Dakota Mission met at Kapozha and drew up a formal "Outline of a Plan for Civilizing the Dakotas," which Governor Ramsey later submitted to Commissioner Lea. Among other objections, they found the Sioux then living too close together in their villages and the villages too far apart, and recommended that they all be removed to the upper Minnesota and encouraged to settle there in separate family units, on tracts of land which would eventually become their individual property. A

[20] 33rd Cong., 1st Sess., *S. Doc. 1*, p. 315; *Minnesota Pioneer*, March 30, 1854.

system of laws and government should gradually be imposed upon them. The missionaries asked for an educational fund of $12,000, over which the Indians would exercise no control. They proposed village schools in which the Sioux would be taught to read and write in their own language and a system of small manual labor boarding schools in which English would be the medium of instruction. Annuities, they said, should be paid semiannually, in cash, to individual heads of families rather than to the chiefs. The object of this plan was to break up the community system among the Sioux and eliminate the favoritism that prevailed when the chiefs controlled the distribution of annuities. No money should be paid to creditors of the Indians. Finally, mixed-bloods should share in annuities and other benefits received by the Indians from the government.[21] Whether as a direct result of this outline or for other reasons, many of these provisions were written into the treaties of 1851, and others became official policy during the reservation period.

The most dramatic event during Flandrau's brief term as agent was the massacre early in 1857 of a number of white settlers in the Okoboji–Spirit Lake region of northwestern Iowa and the adjacent portion of Minnesota Territory by a renegade band of Wahpekutes under the leadership of an outlawed chief named Inkpaduta. The Wahpekutes had been split about 1840 by dissension leading to the murder of their old chief, Tasagi, by a rival, Wamdesapa. The followers of the latter, including Inkpaduta, had been expelled from the tribe and had since then led a nomadic life on the prairies of modern-day eastern South Dakota and adjoining parts of Iowa and Minnesota Territory. They had not taken part in the treaties of 1851, but had shown up now and then at annuity payments. According to one story, the brother of Inkpaduta had been wantonly slain, with all his family, in 1854 by a white whiskey-seller and horse thief named Henry Lott. Whatever the truth of this tale, Inkpaduta was fiercely hostile to the whites, although he concealed his hatred sufficiently when on his periodic begging expeditions among the whites, who by 1856 were beginning to settle on that remote frontier.[22]

[21] *Minnesota Pioneer*, November 28, 1850; Ramsey to Lea, February 6, 1851, NARS, RG 75, LR.

[22] Thomas Hughes, "Causes and Results of the Inkpaduta Massacre," *Minnesota Historical Collections*, XII (1905–1908), 264–269; Mankato *Independent*, August 1, 1857; Cullen to Commisioner James W. Denver, August 20, 1857, NARS, RG 75, LR. The literature of the Inkpaduta massacre is voluminous, and only the most useful primary and secondary sources are cited here. A good primary source is the official report of

The winter of 1856–1857 was unusually severe, with intense cold and much snow. Even the annuity Indians suffered, and Inkpaduta's band managed to survive only by begging and committing depredations in the white settlements. After killing a settler's dog which had bitten one of their number, they were forcibly disarmed by a posse of whites. Unable to hunt without weapons, they were incensed by this action, somehow recovered their guns or replaced them, and took out their wrath by a general slaughter of whites in the vicinity. On March 8 and 9 they descended upon a settlement on the Okoboji lakes, killed some thirty-four people, and took three women prisoner. Then they repeated the performance a few miles farther north on Spirit Lake, where they killed a settler and took his wife prisoner. A couple of weeks later they struck at another small settlement, called Springfield, near the present site of Jackson, Minnesota, where the people had been warned of their approach and had taken refuge inside one of the houses. The Indians killed the whites who had remained outside the improvised fort, plundered the store of the Woods brothers, and then disappeared.[23]

When word of the first murders reached Flandrau at the agency on March 18, he immediately enlisted the aid of the commandant at Fort Ridgely in organizing an expedition to protect the settlers at Springfield. Because of the heavy snow, which Flandrau thought rendered any military action futile, the party sent from the fort under the command of Captain Bernard E. Bee did not reach the Springfield vicinity until after the Indians had left. Attempts to catch up with them were unsuccessful, although it was later learned that the soldiers had come near enough to be seen by the Indians. It is perhaps just as well that the soldiers did not encounter their quarry, for the Indians would almost certainly have killed their captives if attacked. Upon mature consideration and after the passage of some weeks, it was decided that the safety of these women took precedence over the punishment of their captors; and early in May, Indian Bureau officials and the military commanders concluded to send out a party of friendly Indians to effect the rescue of the women before any more troops were employed.[24]

Meanwhile, there was intense excitement all along the frontier and

Captain Bernard E. Bee, addressed to First Lieutenant H. E. Maynadier, Adjutant, 10th Infantry, Fort Ridgely, April 9, 1857, NARS, RG 75, LR, Northern Superintendency. A sound secondary source is William W. Folwell, *A History of Minnesota*, II (St. Paul: Minnesota Historical Society, 1961), 400–415.

23 Folwell, *History of Minnesota*, II, 401–404.

24 *Ibid.*, II, 404–406.

well behind it. The size of Inkpaduta's force, actually composed of only twelve or fourteen men and some women and children, was greatly exaggerated, and rumors of a general Indian uprising spread throughout the territory. Petitions were received at Fort Ridgely calling for assistance to settlers on the Blue Earth and Watonwan rivers; people were "flocking in from the country by hundreds terribly frightened" to the infant towns of Mankato and St. Peter; hastily formed volunteer forces satisfied their hatred for Indians by attacking harmless bands who were hunting and fishing as they did every winter. Reports reached St. Paul and Faribault that Mankato and St. Peter had been sacked and that thousands of bloodthirsty warriors were sweeping down the Minnesota valley toward St. Paul. By the time the territorial legislature met on April 27, the excitement had largely abated, but there was a loud demand for the rescue of the prisoners and the punishment of the murderers. On May 15 the legislature appropriated $10,000 (which it did not have) for the rescue of the women held by Inkpaduta's band.[25]

Five days after this gesture by the legislature, two Wahpetons turned up at the Riggs mission with one of the captives, Mrs. Margaret Ann Marble, and asked $500 apiece for their efforts in ransoming her from the renegades. Their success prompted Flandrau to send out a party of three Wahpetons on the twenty-third to bring back any of the remaining captives who might still be alive. After a month they returned with Abbie Gardner, whom they had found living with a band of Yanktons; the other two women had been killed. Now that all the surviving captives had been delivered up, the way was open to the punishment of the Indians. Late in June word reached Flandrau that a member of the band, Inkpaduta's son, was at the Yellow Medicine agency. Accompanied by a small force from Fort Ridgely, he went in pursuit of the man, who was killed and his wife taken prisoner on July 1. On his return to the lower agency, Flandrau was surrounded by hostile upper Sioux, who forced him to release the woman. He was then allowed to proceed but remained a virtual prisoner at the agency until the arrival July 5 of an artillery battery from Fort Ridgely.[26]

[25] Charles E. Flandrau to Huebschmann, April 16, 1857, NARS, RG 75, LR; Franklyn Curtiss-Wedge, ed., *History of Rice and Steele Counties* (Chicago: H. C. Cooper, Jr., and Co., 1910), I, 338; Folwell, *History of Minnesota*, II, 406. The account in Curtiss-Wedge was written by Frederick W. Frink, who had started a newspaper in Faribault a few months before the massacre.

[26] Folwell, *History of Minnesota*, II, 407–409. For greater ease of administration, a second agency was established about 1856 near the mouth of the Yellow Medicine River. From this time on, the original agency was referred to as the "lower agency"

The next two weeks were extremely tense at the agency. After Flandrau left to participate in the constitutional convention at St. Paul, the newly appointed superintendent of Indian affairs, William J. Cullen, was in charge of the agency. Cullen had some anxious moments, especially after a Sisseton had stabbed a soldier and the superintendent was faced with the job of arresting the Indian. After some hostile displays by the Indians, the offender was finally delivered up on July 17, but he escaped shortly thereafter and was never recaptured. During that time Cullen was also trying to persuade the Indians to undertake the punishment of Inkpaduta themselves. He was under instructions from the new Indian Commissioner, James W. Denver, to accomplish the task in this way, without the aid of troops, and was authorized to withhold all annuities until Inkpaduta and his followers had been delivered up or killed. The Indians refused to go after Inkpaduta without a military escort, and for a time there was an impasse that had ominous overtones. Finally, on July 18, Little Crow offered his services, and in the next four days an expedition of more than a hundred men was fitted out and sent on its way. When they returned, on August 4, they reported the killing of three and possibly four of the band and brought with them two women and a child; Inkpaduta and four other men, they said, had separated from the rest of the band some weeks earlier and were now far to the west. Their mission only partly accomplished, the Indians refused positively to continue the campaign without troops. Cullen and a special agent, Kintzing Prichette, who had been sent from Washington, decided that the Indians had done all they could, that it was unjust to hold all the Sioux responsible for the misdeeds of a few, and that their annuities should be paid. The commissioner finally concurred late in August, and the payment was made about the middle of the next month.[27]

The Inkpaduta affair and its sequel in the crisis at the agency had profound effects on Indians and whites alike. One obvious result of the failure to punish Inkpaduta himself (he was never captured), noted at the time and later, was that the Indians learned that attacks on whites could go unpunished and that Indian Bureau officials could be induced

and the other one as the "upper agency." The Indian Office continued to use the name "St. Peter's" for both agencies.

[27] Cullen to Denver, July 26 and August 20, 1857; Kintzing Prichette to Denver, August 16, 1857, NARS, RG 75, LR; Mankato *Independent*, September 12 and October 3, 1857. The extensive correspondence carried on during and after the Inkpaduta affair by Indian Bureau officials and military officers is contained in 35th Cong., 1st Sess., *H. Ex. Doc. 2*, pp. 349–403.

to back down from previously stated positions. Another result was that white settlers on the frontier became jittery; in the following years, whenever difficulties occurred at the agency, rumors of an uprising swept the countryside. Perhaps the most significant result, in the long run, was that hostility toward the Indians increased enormously. Relations between the Sioux and their white neighbors had been passably friendly up to this time; they became progressively less so after the so-called Spirit Lake massacre. Thus the danger of a real uprising was intensified because of a shift in the attitudes of both whites and Indians.

The most perceptive observations made at the time were those contained in a long report submitted by Special Agent Prichette the following October. After summarizing the events of the previous six months, he warned Commissioner Denver that the "causes of alienation" which produced the hostility of the Indians at the agency went beyond the mere temporary excitement. The complaints that he heard from the Indians at their councils all pointed to "the imperfect performance or non-fulfillment of treaty stipulations." As to the possibility of a war against the United States, he said that the chiefs who had acquired some knowledge of the strength of the nation realized that they could not permanently resist but thought that a war might lead to better treaties and thus benefit them in the long run.[28]

So far as the civilization of the Sioux was concerned, Prichette believed that the hope of making them a permanent agricultural people, under existing circumstances, was "a vain dream of impracticable philanthropy." Why? Because experience had shown that "their advance towards such a condition, is but a new incitement to the desire of grasping their lands, increased in proportion, as they may have made them valuable by improvement and culture." He added the chilling comment that there was no chance of their being Christianized "so long as they are in direct contact with our own people." The only hope for the Sioux, as Prichette saw it, was their total isolation within limits "preserved and maintained inviolate by the plighted faith of the Nation." To accomplish this desired end, however, the "moral force of public opinion" would have to be enlisted. And the "moral force" of a people whose presence was a deterrent to the Christianization of the Indians was indeed a slender reed to lean on. The attitude of those people toward the Indians was suggested by an item in a Red Wing

[28] Prichette to Denver, October 15, 1857, NARS, RG 75, LR. Prichette said that the Indians cited Black Hawk as an example of one whose war, while outwardly futile, had actually brought more favorable treatment of the tribe afterward.

newspaper noted by Prichette: "We have plenty of young men who would like no better fun than a good Indian hunt." In Minnesota he found that "but one sentiment appeared to inspire almost the entire population, and this was, the total annihilation of the Indian race within their borders."[29] Thus the objectives of the Indian Bureau and the missionaries were impossible of attainment in the face of a populace who found no room in their world for live Indians.

Hopeless though their mission may have been, the men in charge of Indian affairs went ahead with their work seemingly convinced that what they were doing would be crowned with success if they went at it intelligently, diligently, and honestly. Joseph Renshaw Brown, Flandrau's successor as agent, was a good choice for the job. He had long acquaintance with the Sioux as a trader and was married to a woman of Sioux descent. Building on the foundations laid by Flandrau, Brown inaugurated an era of real progress toward the realization of the civilization clauses in the 1851 treaties. More acreage was brought under cultivation, schools were opened, and several buildings, including at long last an agency, were erected.[30]

Brown's achievement was not, of course, due entirely to his own initiative and driving energy. He had arrived on the scene when many of the Indians themselves were undergoing a fundamental change in their attitude toward farming and the white man's way of life. As game became increasingly scarce in their old hunting grounds—and as they themselves became increasingly unwelcome there—some of them began to consider more seriously the advice so persistently urged on them to cultivate the soil and live like white men. With the encouragement of missionary Riggs, a number of upper Sioux had in 1856 formed the "Hazelwood Republic," a voluntary association whose members agreed to abandon their native manners and dress and begin farming on individual allotments of land. Two years later a similar decision was made by a few of the lower Sioux, who elected a judge and council and threw off their tribal relations and customs. Superintendent Cullen

[29] Prichette to Denver, October 15, 1857, *ibid.*; St. Paul *Daily Times*, July 28, 1857.

[30] 35th Cong., 1st Sess., *H. Ex. Doc. 2*, pp. 345–349. During a brief stint as editor of the *Minnesota Pioneer*, Brown had written as though he accepted the prevailing notion that the Indian race was doomed to extinction and that it was only a matter of time before the new reservation would be ceded, but his conduct as agent belied this position. Likewise, although he had publicly sneered that Cullen would have been hard pressed to distinguish between a Sioux Indian and a snapping turtle, he seems to have got on well enough with his superior once installed as agent. See the *Minnesota Pioneer*, October 27, 1853, and the *Pioneer and Democrat*, July 18, 1857.

himself performed the symbolic act of cutting the hair of sixteen men, to each of whom he gave two suits of clothing, a cow, a yoke of oxen, and a house equipped with a cooking stove. To encourage others to follow the example, Brown that year had forty-five houses built and a small tract of two to five acres of land broken in connection with each. The following year Cullen cut the hair of a hundred more of the lower Sioux, including the chiefs Wabasha and Wacouta, and a hundred houses were framed. By this time the Indians were cutting their own rails and making fences, and in 1860 the use of white men for agricultural labor was abandoned and the work turned over to the Indians.[31]

Accepting the widespread conviction that individual ownership of land was essential to the civilization of the Sioux, Brown proposed to allot an eighty-acre tract to each head of family or other adult, with the expectation that eventually the Indians would qualify for fee patents to those allotments and become citizens. Since only that part of the reservation south of the Minnesota would be required for this purpose, the proposal was advanced by Cullen in his report to the commissioner in 1857 to dispose of the remainder of the reservation and use the receipts for the benefit of the Indians. Such a proposal would naturally meet with the favor of the white population of Minnesota, many of whom were already squatting on parts of the reservation. When the chiefs made their usual request for permission to visit Washington, Cullen took advantage of the opportunity to suggest to Acting Commissioner Charles E. Mix that this might be a good time to "effect a readjustment of their treaty" as he had advised in his annual report.[32]

The result of this combination of circumstances was the treaty of June 19, 1858, the principal outcome of a four-month visit to Washington and the East by a selected group of chiefs representing both upper and lower Sioux. Actually two treaties, one with each division of the Santees but signed the same day, this document provided for the allotment in severalty of the southern half of the reservation, with the excess land to be held in common for the future use of the tribe, the allotments to be exempt from taxation, sale, or alienation in other ways even after patents had been issued. (The tax-exempt status could be altered by

[31] Com. of Indian Affairs, *Annual Report*, 1858, p. 50; Cullen to Denver, December 7, 1858; Cullen to Commissioner A. B. Greenwood, August 13, 1859; Joseph R. Brown to Cullen, April 15, 1860, NARS, RG 75, LR; 36th Cong., 2nd Sess., *S. Ex. Doc. 1*, p. 280. Cullen claimed to have cut the hair of two hundred men at the 1859 payment, but Brown's official report says one hundred.

[32] Com. of Indian Affairs, *Annual Report*, 1857, p. 51; Cullen to Mix, December 24, 1857, NARS, RG 75, LR.

the state legislature with the consent of Congress.) It also authorized the Senate to determine whether the Indians had a sound title to the reservation, and if so, what compensation should be paid them for the northern half. Provision was also made for the payment of "just debts" and for the building of roads across the reservation, and there was a significant clause which amended all previous treaty stipulations regarding the payment of specific sums for particular purposes and left the management of those sums to the discretion of the President.[33]

This treaty was really an astonishing document, when one considers how much the Indians left to the discretion of the Senate or the President. In view of their experience in 1851, they might have been expected to drive a hard bargain and get all they could. Instead, they granted the government virtually carte blanche to do as it pleased with them and their property, including what they were entitled to under the terms of earlier treaties. As a matter of fact, there is some evidence that Little Crow, at least, put up a show of resistance. During the all-night council that climaxed the long stay in Washington, he told Commissioner Mix that "we have been so often cheated that I wished to be cautious, and not sign any more papers without having them explained, so that we may know what we are doing." There followed a dispute between the two, in the course of which Mix accused the chief of acting like a child. But the result was a foregone conclusion. After a "warm and protracted discussion," as one newspaper called it, the treaty was signed at 7 A.M., and the next day the delegation started for home, "strengthened in their purpose by what they [had] seen during their sojourn."[34]

The aftermath was in some respects even more interesting than the treaty itself. Although the Senate ratified the treaties on March 9, 1859, and they were proclaimed at the end of that month, nothing was done toward determining the validity of the Indians' title to their reservation until 1860, more than two years after the signing of the treaty. Then the Senate confirmed the Indians' title and allowed them the sum of thirty cents an acre for the area relinquished. This was a better price than the Senate amendments to the 1851 treaties had allowed them— ten cents an acre—but the 1860 resolution also gave settlers on those lands the right of pre-emption at a price of $1.25 an acre![35] Brown

---

[33] Kappler, *Indian Affairs, Laws and Treaties*, II, 781–789.

[34] *Pioneer and Democrat*, June 29 and July 8, 1858.

[35] Kappler, *Indian Affairs, Laws and Treaties*, II, 789. The Senate Committee on Indian Affairs had recommended that the Indians be paid at the rate of $1.25 an acre. See Folwell, *History of Minnesota*, II, 397.

thought the lands worth five dollars an acre. There was still worse to follow. When Congress finally appropriated $266,880 for the lands, nearly all of the payment to the lower Sioux and a large part of that to the upper bands went to pay the "just debts" of the traders, and the Indians saw but little of the money. Thus the disillusionment and bitterness they had come to feel toward the government was compounded by this treaty, supposedly designed for their benefit.[36]

At the same time, other difficulties were doing much to negate the effectiveness of Brown's work in civilizing the Sioux. There was, for example, the never ending feud with the Chippewas. Alexander Ramsey had tried in 1850 to resolve the quarrel by the usual method of calling a council, which ended with the contending parties in total disagreement.[37] The raids and counterraids continued through the years, despite the removal of the Sioux to their reservation and the gradual filling up of the ceded territory with white settlers. When the government intervened, as it did in 1856, its hesitant and inconsistent policy did nothing either to diminish the warfare or to raise its own prestige with the Indians.[38]

As a matter of fact, the government was rapidly losing the respect of the Sioux during these years. The agency warehouse was plundered in 1855, in 1856, and again in 1858, and no decisive retaliatory action was taken. The arrogance which this failure engendered among the dissatisfied Indians was heightened by the growing hostility of the Yanktons and Yanktonais, who resented the cession in 1851 of lands to which they thought they had a claim, and who sometimes showed up at annuity payments and extorted a "cut" from the Sissetons. In 1857 they burned several buildings and drove off white settlers who had established townsites in the area west of the present Minnesota line.[39]

[36] Folwell, *History of Minnesota*, II, 393–400.

[37] *Minnesota Pioneer*, June 13, 1850; Ramsey to Orlando Brown, June 15, 1850, NARS, RG 75, LR, Minnesota Superintendency.

[38] Newspapers of the time and correspondence of the Indian Bureau contain numerous references to continued raids, including one in which a party of Chippewas invaded the heart of St. Paul and fired into a store that some Sioux had entered. See the *Minnesota Pioneer*, April 28, 1853. As late as 1860 a Red Wing newspaper noted that about two hundred of Wacouta's band had gone over into the Wisconsin timber to hunt. In January a few members of the band appeared in Red Wing with furs and venison which they traded for provisions to take back to the rest of their party. Hunting had been good, they said; they had bagged over a hundred deer, twenty bears, and four Chippewas. See the Red Wing *Sentinel*, November 12, 1859, and January 7, 1860.

[39] Huebschmann to Manypenny, June 28, 1856; Huebschmann to Colonel E. B. Abercrombie, June 13, 1856; Flandrau to Cullen, August 7, 1857; Joseph R. Brown to Mix, May 23, 1858; Cullen to Mix, July 1, 1858, NARS, RG 75, LR.

The Yanktons were partially mollified by a treaty in 1858 confirming to them the Pipestone quarry, which was within the cession made in 1851, but the Yanktonais remained hostile and wanted no dealings with the United States government. The Indian Bureau finally decided to pacify them by the distribution of some goods, and in 1859 Cullen was delegated to handle the business at the time of the regular annuity payments. After paying off the lower Sioux, he stopped at the upper agency, located near the Yellow Medicine River, learned that the census rolls were not complete, and decided to make his visit to the Yanktonais before paying the upper bands. The Indians demanded their annuities, however, and would not permit him to pass their lines, a few miles above the agency. After some inconclusive wrangling, they seized the bridles of Cullen's horses and turned them around so that they were headed back toward the lower agency. Cullen had no choice but to return to the agency, where he sent in a request for troops from Fort Ridgely. With military aid, he was able to get past the angry Sissetons on a second attempt, and later the Indians who had treated him so roughly were jailed.[40]

Another source of trouble in the later fifties was the constant danger of clashes between Indians and white settlers. Despite a congressional appropriation in 1854 and repeated appeals by the agents and superintendents for a survey of the reservation boundaries, nothing was done until 1859 (and then done badly), by which time the General Land Office had already surveyed the adjacent territory and opened to settlement several townships wholly or partly within the reservation. The Indians, who had been accustomed to depredations in the white settlements farther east all through the decade, were even less inclined to respect the supposed rights of the settlers who innocently took up lands in these townships. The Indian Office was perpetually deluged with settlers' claims for damages, sometimes accompanied by petitions signed by large numbers of citizens and threatening drastic action in retaliation for the depredations.[41]

Some of these claims were undoubtedly legitimate, but many prob-

[40] Cullen to Greenwood, June 24, 1859, and August 15, 1859, *ibid.*; Mankato *Weekly Record*, July 5 and 12, 1859.

[41] U. S. *Statutes at Large*, X, 331; Henry M. Rice to Manypenny, January 18, 1855; Joseph R. Brown to Cullen, September 12 and December 5, 1858, and November 2, 1859; C. L. Emerson, Surveyor General, to Thomas A. Hendricks, Commissioner of the General Land Office, February 8, 1859; S. A. Smith, Commissioner of the General Land Office, to Greenwood, December 15, 1859, NARS, RG 75, LR; Mankato *Weekly Record*, November 1, 1859.

ably represented nothing more than a desire to get some money out of the government. And Special Agent Prichette was doubtless right when he analyzed the motives behind the repeated demands for volunteer forces to drive the Indians out: "The object of this in certain quarters is to occupy important points, in advance, as the nucleus of settlements, with a view to speculation in town sites. . . ." [42]

During Brown's last years in office, perhaps the most serious trouble at the agency stemmed from the growing hostility between those Indians who wished to adopt the manners of the whites and those who violently opposed any such move toward civilization. When the customary techniques of ridicule failed to deter the "farmer Indians" from their purpose, the "blanket" faction inaugurated a more or less systematic campaign of harassment intended to make life so uncomfortable for the farmers that they would abandon their efforts. Beginning with such forms of petty persecution as burning haystacks or stables, the campaign soon advanced to the stage of cattle-killing and from that point proceeded to the stage of open threats against the lives of those who persisted in the face of such persecution. In the winter of 1860 the farmer Indians were warned that no man who wore pantaloons the next summer would see the leaves fall.[43]

It took a great deal of courage for a man to continue farming in the face of such threats, especially among the upper Sioux, where the anti-civilization group was in the vast majority. In the spring of 1860 a succession of murders and retaliations led to the breakup of the Hazelwood Republic and the abandonment by its members of their claims. In August, 1860, an Indian of Mankato's band who had been shooting oxen used to haul materials for the building of houses announced that he would kill men as well as animals if necessary to stop the erection of more houses. Since Mankato was a chief of the lower Sioux, it was evident that by this time the infection was spreading down the Minnesota. Superintendent Cullen, like Brown, recognized the menace to their whole program and wrote the commissioner that summer: "There is no doubt that at the present time a great struggle for ascendancy is

[42] Prichette to Denver, July 28, 1857, NARS, RG 75, LR.

[43] Joseph R. Brown to Cullen, August 21, 1859; Brown to "Dear Col.," February 3, 1860; Brown to Cullen, February 6, 1860, *ibid.* Some of these threats were carried out in 1859 and 1860. The usual method was to induce the victim to drink whiskey and then draw him into a quarrel when he was drunk, thus making his death appear the result of one of the drunken altercations that were becoming increasingly common on the reservation as the proximity of white settlements made the introduction of liquor much easier than it had been before.

taking place among the Sioux between the civilized or improvement Indians who have adopted our habits and customs and those who still retain the savage mode of life." [44] But aside from imprisoning the insurgent who wanted to stop the building of houses, there was not a great deal the agent or superintendent could do without military assistance; and there were never enough troops at Fort Ridgely for any of them to be spared for continuous duty at the agency.

By 1860, therefore, it was clear that Agent Brown, his white and Indian employees, the missionaries, and the farmer Indians were sitting on a powder keg. The more successful Brown was in his efforts to make farmers out of the Indians, the more opposition was stirred up and the more violent it became. His hope was that, with the aid of troops to protect the farmers, he could induce enough Indians to follow their example so that they would constitute a majority. This goal seemed almost within sight among the lower Sioux, but at the same time the opposition there was growing at an alarming rate. Some of the most hostile of the upper Sioux were no longer showing up for their annuities, but had taken up residence with their wild Yanktonai cousins; at the same time the presence of those cousins just west of the reservation constituted a perpetual menace. What might have happened if Brown had been permitted to stay on the job for a few more years must forever remain in the realm of conjecture. The vagaries of political expediency dictated that he and nearly all of his employees, as well as Superintendent Cullen, should be turned out of office when a new administration took over in 1861 and replaced by inexperienced men who had been faithful servants of their party in the campaign of 1860.

[44] Joseph R. Brown to Cullen, March 3, May 17, and August 11, 1860; Brown to Captain G. A. De Russy, August 10, 1860; Cullen to Greenwood, July 16, 1860, *ibid.*

Dahcotah Encampment, by Seth Eastman

View of the Prairie du Chien treaty field, 1825. From an oil by J. O. Lewis.

Samuel W. Pond   Stephen Return Riggs

Lawrence Taliaferro. Portrait by an unknown artist

Signing of the Treaty of Traverse des Sioux, July, 1851. Oil by Francis
D. Millet in the Minnesota State Capitol

Sioux delegation to Washington, 1858. Standing, left to right: Akepa, Scarlet Plume (Wam-de-apeduta, or Red Feather), Red Iron (Mazasha), John Other Day (Ang-petu-to-ke-cha), Little Paul (Mazakutemani), and Charles R. Crawford. Seated, left to right: Iron Walker (Mazomani, or Walking Iron), Stumpy Horn, Sweet Corn, and Extended Tail Feathers

Physician's house, Upper Sioux Agency, built in 1859. Much altered, the building is now in a state park. Photograph taken in 1967

ief Little Crow (Taoyateduta). Photograph taken in 1858 by Z. Shindler.

Courtesy of the Nebraska State Historical Society

The execution of thirty-eight Sioux Indians at Mankato, Minnesota, December 26, 1862.

CHAPTER **6**

Catastrophe

THE TIME-HONORED practice of "cleaning out" officeholders of the defeated party and replacing them with stalwarts who had contributed to an election victory was never more sweepingly followed than by the Republicans after the election of 1860. In the Indian Service the process went so far, in some instances, as to include physicians, blacksmiths, and laborers. Among the Minnesotans who expected—and received—rewards for their service to the party were three men who were to be associated with the Santee Sioux in the next few years. Clark W. Thompson replaced Cullen as Northern Superintendent, Thomas J. Galbraith was nominated to the position of Sioux agent, and St. André Durand Balcombe was given the Winnebago Agency. None had had any previous experience with Indians.

Of these three the one who had the most to do with the Sioux before the outbreak of 1862 was, of course, Galbraith. Though a man of ability and probably of integrity, he was handicapped not only by his inexperience but by traits of character and personality that would have made him a dubious choice for the job of Indian agent at any time, and an extremely unwise selection for the post he received in the spring of 1861. His official letters show him to have been a man supremely confident of his own rectitude, scornful of advice, inclined to oversimplify situations, and doggedly determined to cling to his interpretation of a situation and to justify his course of action afterward, regardless of the consequences that might have followed. By the testimony of men who had no reason, decades later, to hold a grudge against him, he was arrogant, stubborn, emotionally unstable, and a hard drinker. John P. Williamson, son of the old missionary to the Sioux, wrote, as the Indians were being shipped into exile in 1863, that he hoped Galbraith would not appear at their new home. Galbraith's political enemies charged him with cowardice—an accusation that receives some support from the military men who observed him under stress just before the uprising.[1]

All this attention to the character and personality of Galbraith will not seem irrelevant if it is remembered that when Little Crow began to negotiate with Colonel Sibley in the dying days of the uprising, he started his letter with these words: "Dear Sir: For what reason we have commenced this war I will tell you, it is on account of Maj. Galbrait. . . ."[2] The causes of the Sioux Uprising are manifold and complex, but it is no exaggeration to say that Thomas J. Galbraith had more to do with bringing on the war than any other single individual. If the picture of him that emerges from contemporaneous and later testimony and from his own correspondence is substantially correct, his appointment as Sioux agent was a political blunder of major proportions.

When Galbraith arrived at the agency in May, 1861, he found the Indians disturbed by a rumor, allegedly spread by southern sympathizers, that the annuities would not be paid that summer. He denied this report and was able to make the payment almost on schedule, but not without military help and not without difficulty. The upper bands, described by the agent as "restive, turbulent, saucy, insolent, impudent and insulting," were furious over the deduction of some $9,000 from their annuities to pay depredations claims. Deductions for that purpose

[1] William W. Folwell, *A History of Minnesota*, II (St. Paul: Minnesota Historical Society, 1961), 222 n.; Mankato *Semi-Weekly Record*, September 10 and October 1, 1861; Lucius F. Hubbard and Return I. Holcombe, *Minnesota in Three Centuries* (Mankato: Publishing Society of Minnesota, 1908), III, 292–295. Folwell quotes Judge Martin J. Severance as saying, in an interview with the local historian Thomas Hughes, more than forty years after the uprising, that Galbraith "had no diplomacy and treated the Indians arrogantly," and adding that he was wholly unfit for his job. Holcombe's account of troubles at the upper agency in 1862, apparently based on interviews with Lieutenant Timothy J. Sheehan, includes the story that Galbraith tried to bolster his spirits with "Dutch courage," i.e., whiskey.

[2] Minnesota *Executive Documents*, 1862, p. 444.

had long been customary, but never had the amount been so great, nor the evidence to support the claims so skimpy.[3]

Although Galbraith forwarded to his superiors a memorial from the Indians protesting to Congress against this extortion, he showed no comprehension of certain other manifestations of their hostility. The most acutely dissatisfied and turbulent elements had formed a "soldiers' lodge," an institution observed as early as Hennepin's time and designed to enforce a temporary discipline on the normally anarchic Sioux. Galbraith supposed this organization to be identical with the anti-civilization faction that had caused so much unrest during Brown's last years as agent. No doubt the two groups included many of the same individuals, but Galbraith's insistence that they were the same organization was an oversimplification of the situation, as was his attempt to trace the origins of the group to Inkpaduta's band of renegades. He also succumbed to the conspiracy theory, so often used by Americans to explain the inexplicable, and exaggerated the influence of "rebel emissaries."[4]

The Civil War did, however, unquestionably complicate the government's problem of meeting its obligations to the Indians. Whatever the influence of "Copperheads," the Indians could see with their own eyes that the government was neglecting some of its responsibilities to them and that the country was being drained of young white men to fill the Union armies. Coupled with newspaper reports of defeats suffered by these armies, such observations inevitably led some of the Indians, already smoldering with resentment toward the government for its treatment of them, to wonder if the time might be approaching for them to strike back. The virtual loss of the corn crop to cutworms in 1861, followed by a winter of near-starvation, increased their discontent and spread it to people who heretofore had been largely passive.

The two months immediately preceding the outbreak of August,

[3] Thomas J. Galbraith to Clark W. Thompson, June 4 and July 31, 1861; Cyrus Aldrich to Commissioner William P. Dole, July 16, 1861, NARS, RG 75, LR. $5,500 of the sum charged against the Indians was for losses allegedly suffered by the trading firm of Carothers and Blake, whose post on Big Stone Lake had been robbed by some Indians. The Sioux considered the amount extortionate, in view of the fact that the robbery had been committed by two men, who could not possibly have run off with goods to that amount. They especially resented the fact that they had known nothing of the deduction until Galbraith informed them of it just before the payment.

[4] Galbraith to Thompson, July 30, 1861, *ibid.*

1862, were a period of alternating tension and relaxation. As the customary time for the annuity payments drew near, the Indians became increasingly anxious. The same rumors that had unsettled them the previous year sprang up anew, spread in some cases by the traders, who refused to extend further credit to the Indians on the ground that there would be no annuities from which the debts could be paid. Late in June representatives of the upper bands obtained assurance from Galbraith that the payment would be made, although not before July 20. On July 14, by which time the goods and provisions had arrived but not the money, Galbraith was confronted with some five thousand hungry Indians, including a thousand Yanktonais, demanding that the provisions be issued. In keeping with his inflexible character, he refused to make a separate issue of provisions and insisted that the whole payment await the arrival of the money, as was the established procedure.[5]

Although Galbraith did, under pressure, dole out enough food to keep the Indians alive, they did not go home as he wished them to do, and on August 4 violence broke out. Despite the presence of a detachment of troops from Fort Ridgely, the Indians decided that the time had come to go after the provisions, so tantalizingly near in the warehouse, trusting that they would be able to get away with it. After first surrounding the troops, whom they had previously advised that there would be a peaceful demonstration, they sent a party of braves to assault the warehouse door and carry off the provisions. Before they could get more than a few sacks of flour out, the military commander, Lieutenant Timothy J. Sheehan, trained one of his two howitzers on the door and then marched into the warehouse via the lane speedily formed by the Indians. Here he confronted Galbraith, who, according to some accounts, was too frightened to do anything on his own initiative, and urged him to make an issue of provisions to the Indians.[6] A small issue was made, but it did not satisfy the Indians, who still refused to leave until all their provisions were distributed. After two more days of tension the agent, on the advice of missionary Riggs and the military commander, held a council and offered to issue the annuity goods and provisions on condition that the Indians would then go home and not

[5] Folwell, *History of Minnesota*, II, 228–229. By common consensus, the best history of the Sioux Uprising, its causes, and its consequences is that by Folwell, pp. 109–301, and appendix, pp. 361–450. Because that volume has been readily accessible since its republication in 1961, in the following account citations are provided only for quotations and other information not found in Folwell.

[6] Hubbard and Holcombe, *Minnesota in Three Centuries*, III, 295.

return until summoned to receive the money annuities. The issue was then made, and on August 10 the Indians left the agency.[7]

The delay in the arrival of the money annuity was due in part to the exigencies of the war, in part to an experiment undertaken the previous year by the new administration. According to the best available evidence, it had been decided to shift from a cash annuity to one paid in goods. A start in that direction had been made in 1861, when a $20,000 advance on the 1862 cash annuity was paid in goods. The Indians objected so strenuously to the loss this would entail in their cash annuities for the next year that the Indian Bureau was persuaded to make up the deficiency out of the projected 1863 annuities. This course meant that the payment would have to await passage of the Indian appropriations act for 1863, which was not finally approved until July 5, 1862. Then the question arose as to whether the payment might not be made in greenbacks rather than in the customary gold coin. This issue was not settled until early in August, just about the time that matters were becoming critical at the Yellow Medicine agency. After some correspondence between Superintendent Thompson and Commissioner Dole, in which Thompson warned of the danger of an outbreak, $70,000 in coin was finally sent. The money arrived in St. Paul on August 16, just in time to reach Fort Ridgely at noon on the eighteenth, "by which hour some hundred white people lay in or about their homes dead or bleeding from wounds," as Folwell says.[8]

In all the troubles that the successive agents had had with the Sioux in the previous three or four years, it was the upper bands, sometimes in conjunction with the Yanktonais, who received the blame. True, the lower bands had the heaviest grievances. They had had to leave their old homes, as most of the Sissetons and Wahpetons had not; they had seen their payment under the 1858 treaty diverted to the traders, while the upper bands received at least something; and they were the principal sufferers from white intrusion on the reservation. Yet through all the years of turmoil at the Yellow Medicine the Mdewakantons and Wahpekutes had remained apparently docile. If the Sioux Uprising had been the carefully matured conspiracy that some contemporary observers believed it to be, all logic would have pointed to the upper bands as the ones most likely to erupt in violence. Why, then, was it the lower Sioux who did most of the fighting when the uprising came—and suffered most of the punishment? The answer is that the outbreak came

[7] Folwell, *History of Minnesota*, II, 230.

[8] *Ibid.*, II, 238; Thompson to Dole, August 5, 1862, NARS, RG 75, LR.

about by accident, not by plan, and that the accident which produced
it involved the lower Sioux more immediately than the upper.

Yet it was not entirely blind chance. In the last days before the war
began, several events happened that brought tempers to the boiling
point among the lower Sioux. First of all, Little Crow seems to have
been present at the payment reluctantly made by Galbraith to the upper bands on August 8 and 9, at which time he obtained a promise that
a similar issue of provisions would be made at the lower agency. This
promise was not kept. About a week later a council was held between
the Indians, represented by Little Crow, and the traders and Galbraith. When no information was received as to the time of the payment
and no concessions were made in the matter of credit by the traders,
Little Crow is supposed to have announced grimly: "We have waited a
long time. The money is ours, but we cannot get it. We have no food,
but here are these stores, filled with food. We ask that you, the agent,
make some arrangement by which we can get food from the stores, or
else we may take our own way to keep ourselves from starving. When
men are hungry they help themselves." Galbraith, apparently unequal
to making a decision himself, turned to the traders and asked them what
they would do. After some consultation among themselves, their spokesman, Andrew J. Myrick, first tried to evade the issue by leaving, but
when called back by the agent, snarled: "So far as I am concerned, if
they are hungry, let them eat grass." When this incredibly heartless
remark was interpreted for the Indians by the younger Williamson,
"there was a moment of silence, followed by savage whoops and wild
gestures, with which the Indians disappeared."[9]

Yet even the calculated insult of Andrew Myrick did not of itself
bring on the Sioux Uprising, though it rankled in the minds of Little
Crow and his people and turned up later in the chief's letter to Sibley.
The highly inflammable situation on the Sioux reservation in mid-
August, 1862, required something to ignite it—some incident that
would lead the Indians to feel that they had nothing to lose by going to
war, that their hand had been forced, and that there was no retreat for
them. Such an incident was provided on August 17, about forty miles

[9] Folwell, *History of Minnesota*, II, 233. In Little Crow's letter to Sibley he accuses
Myrick of telling the Indians that they could eat grass "or their own dung." See
Minnesota *Executive Documents*, 1862, p. 444. Victorian reticence may account for the
omission of the last phrase from Winifred W. Barton's mention of the incident, on
which Folwell relies. See her biography, *John P. Williamson, a Brother to the Sioux*
(Chicago: Fleming H. Revell Co., 1919), pp. 18, 46, 48–52.

from the agency, in Acton township, Meeker County. That Sunday morning four young men, members of a band that had seceded from Shakopee's village, were returning from a hunting expedition. The discovery of some hen's eggs along a fence on the land of a white settler led to an argument as to whether one of the party was brave enough to kill a white man. A dare was made and taken, and they went on to the home of the settler, Robinson Jones. Before the morning was over, Jones, his wife, an adopted daughter, and two other white men lay dead, and the four Indians were hurrying back to the reservation. The "Acton Massacre," trivial in its causes, is credited with setting off the bloody conflict known to history as the Sioux Uprising.

But for the combination of circumstances existing among the Sioux at that time, the Acton killings might have had no more serious consequences than the Inkpaduta affair of 1857. The culprits would have been delivered up to the authorities for punishment; or if they fled, pressure would have been put on the chiefs to have them captured, or perhaps troops would have been sent after them. But in August, 1862, the Indians were not disposed to wait to see what the white men would do. Little Crow may have believed that "the whites would take a dreadful vengeance because women had been killed," as he said in justification of his decision for war, but the Sioux had sufficient reasons for opening hostilities without this fear. Most of their grievances have already been mentioned: bitterness over the treaties of 1851; the non-fulfillment or tardy fulfillment by the government of obligations incurred under the terms of those treaties; the treaty of 1858 and the deception (as the Indians saw it) practiced upon them in turning over most of the proceeds from the ceded lands to the traders; the high-handed manner in which the white authorities had sought to punish the whole Sioux nation for the misbehavior of the outlaw Inkpaduta; the advantage which the Indians believed, with reason, was being taken of them by their traders; the increasing pressure of white settlement near and even on the reservation, which, coupled with the uncertainty of the Indians' tenure, seemed to foreshadow a time when they would again be bullied into signing a treaty and be forced to move once more.

To these grievances should be added a few others, mentioned by the Indians themselves and therefore evidently of substantial moment in their thinking. Some thirty years after the uprising, Big Eagle, one of the chiefs who had opposed war at the start but had later fought in most of the battles, told of the reasons his people had when they began a conflict which even some of their leaders recognized as suicidal from the start. Besides objecting to the sharp practices of the traders, whose word was always accepted in preference to that of an Indian, who kept no books, and to the abuse of Indian women by white men, Big Eagle complained of the agents' efforts to induce the Indians to become farmers. His words provide an insight into the Indians' point of view:

> Then the whites were always trying to make the Indians give up their life and live like white men—go to farming, work hard and do as they did—and the Indians did not know how to do that, and did not want to anyway. It seemed too sudden to make such a change. If the Indians had tried to make the whites live like them, the whites would have resisted, and it was the same way with many Indians.[10]

Underlying all of these actions that Big Eagle found objectionable was the ingrained and apparently ineradicable racial arrogance of the white man. Big Eagle said: "Many of the whites always seemed to say by their manner when they saw an Indian, 'I am much better than you,' and the Indians did not like this." [11] The same attitude of superiority is expressed in somewhat more sophisticated fashion in Galbraith's official report for 1863, in which he says: "To be clear, '*the habits and customs of white men are at war with the habits and customs of the Indians.*' The former are civilization, industry, thrift, economy; the latter, idleness, superstition, and barbarism. . . ." [12] The insufferable smugness and complacency of the white man finds its ultimate expression in the words of Charles A. Bryant, historian of the uprising. The conflict of Indian and white he saw as "a conflict of knowledge with ignorance, of right with wrong"; since the Indian did not obey the divine injunction to subdue the earth, he was "in the wrongful possession of a continent required by the superior right of the white man." [13] Big Eagle never read Bryant's book. If he had done so, perhaps he would have been impelled to precipitate another uprising.

[10] Return I. Holcombe, ed., "A Sioux Story of the War," *Minnesota Historical Collections*, VI (1894), 384.

[11] *Ibid.*, 385.

[12] Quoted in Charles S. Bryant and Abel B. Murch, *A History of the Great Massacre by the Sioux Indians in Minnesota* (Cincinnati: Rickey and Carroll, 1864), p. 51. Galbraith offered as a "settled fact" in his mind the theory that "the encroachments of Christianity, and its handmaid civilization, upon the habits and customs of the Sioux Indians, is the cause of the late terrible Sioux outbreak." Although to Galbraith the fault, of course, lay with the Sioux, he conceded (or perhaps boasted) that Christianity had in most instances "waded to success through seas of blood. . . ." See *ibid.*, p. 50.

[13] *Ibid.*, pp. 48–49. The title page of Bryant's book bears the legend: "For that which is unclean by nature thou canst entertain no hope; no washing will turn the Gipsy white. Ferdousi."

The military history of the Sioux Uprising has been told and retold so many times and in such detail that only the general outlines need to be sketched in here. When the Acton murderers returned to their village on Rice Creek on the evening of August 17, they made known the events of the day to the chief of their band, Hochokaduta, who sought the counsel of Shakopee. There seems to have been a general consensus that war was inevitable and might as well be initiated by the Indians, but before taking the fatal step these Indians naturally wanted to enlist the widest possible support from the other bands. A council was held that night at Little Crow's house, and his leadership in the forthcoming action was finally obtained. According to the received tradition, Little Crow recognized the futility of a war against the whites and argued against it until he was taunted with cowardice, whereupon he agreed to lead his warriors and ordered the massacre to begin the next morning at the lower agency. Little Crow had recently been defeated in a contest for speaker of the lower Sioux, and it is supposed that he saw the opportunity now offered him as a chance to regain face.[14]

The war broke in full fury on the morning of August 18. Soon after daylight a party of warriors attacked the lower agency, killing all the whites they could find, including both such long-time friends as Philander Prescott and men they had good reason to hate, such as trader Myrick, whose mouth they stuffed with grass. Soon they fell to looting the agency stores, however, and thus permitted many of the whites to escape by way of the ferry to the north side of the Minnesota and from there to Fort Ridgely. Since the uprising soon became general and spread over the countryside, some of them were killed before they could reach the safety of the fort. Likewise, settlers on both sides of the river were killed in great numbers during the first forty-eight hours of the war. News of the outbreak did not reach the upper agency at once, and when it did there was sharp division among the Sissetons and Wahpetons as to whether they should join. In later years members of those tribes were to insist that the uprising was all the work of the lower bands. This claim was exaggerated, but it does appear that the element opposed to the war was strong enough among the upper Sioux to prevent their wholehearted participation. Most of the whites at the upper

[14] Holcombe, "A Sioux Story of the War," 387. Big Eagle says that the Sioux looked upon the war as a means of healing dissension that had broken out in the tribe. For an imaginative reconstruction of what Little Crow may have said on this occasion, see "Taoyateduta Is Not a Coward," *Minnesota History*, XXXVIII (September 1962), 115. This oration is supposed to have been obtained from Little Crow's son, Wowinapa, after his capture.

agency were able to escape on August 19, with the help of the faithful John Other Day. The agency buildings, however, were burned and looted there, too.

It should be pointed out that most of the principal chiefs of both the lower and upper Sioux, such as Wabasha, Wacouta, Traveling Hail (who had won the election for speaker), Red Iron, and Standing Buffalo, were opposed to the uprising and either took no part or joined very reluctantly in a few battles, meanwhile giving all the aid they safely could to white victims. The Sioux were at no time united, at no time committed as a nation to the purposes of the hostile minority. Furthermore, even those chiefs who did take an active part in hostilities were able to exercise no really effective discipline over their men. These facts go far to explain why the Sioux Uprising was so brief in comparison with other Indian wars, despite certain initial advantages to the Indians, such as that of almost total surprise.

The Sioux Uprising divides itself into two phases: a short period of about a week when the Indians were on the offensive, and a longer period when they were gradually driven back by growing military forces. Even during the former period they won only one engagement, the battle of Redwood Ferry. As soon as news of the killings at the lower agency reached Fort Ridgely, the commander of the post, Captain John S. Marsh, set out for the agency, about thirteen miles upstream and across the river, with forty-six men and an interpreter. He and his men were ambushed at the ferry, and more than half the party killed. Marsh himself was drowned. Indian losses are supposed to have been one killed. The one-sided outcome of this skirmish was due mainly to Marsh's ignorance of the danger into which he was plunging himself and his men, but it had the effect of convincing the Indians that they could kill white men like sheep. Their overconfidence led them to exert less than their fullest energies in later, more important battles and thus indirectly contributed to their ultimate defeat.

The Sioux leaders were not without some conception of strategy. Although the uprising had not been planned in detail, there had doubtless been discussion at various times of the best way to conduct a war against the whites. Two points had to be taken to open the way for a sweep down the Minnesota valley: Fort Ridgely and the German town of New Ulm, on the south bank of the river a few miles below the reservation. Little Crow and other astute chiefs recognized that Fort Ridgely was the more vital and wished to attack that point first, but they were overruled by the young braves, who were attracted by the prospects of plunder in the poorly defended town. This lack of control over their warriors cost the Sioux leaders the opportunity to attack either position in full force, though either might have been taken with comparatively slight loss in the first two days of the war.

New Ulm was attacked twice, once on August 19 and again on the twenty-third. The first attack was a badly planned and badly co-ordinated affair and failed to accomplish its purpose or to inflict many casualties. The second, however, was a major assault, directed with some skill by competent Sioux leaders. With the advantage of superior numbers, the Indians nearly took the town. By that time the defenders had been reinforced, however, and they were finally able to turn back the assault, at a cost of thirty-four dead and sixty wounded and the loss by fire of most of the town, which was evacuated two days later. As Big Eagle was to say later, the defenders of New Ulm had "kept the door shut" to the projected push down the valley.

Between the two attacks on New Ulm an even more important battle was taking place at Fort Ridgely. Had the Indians attacked on the eighteenth or the nineteenth, as Little Crow wished to do, they could almost certainly have taken the fort, which was woefully undermanned after the debacle at Redwood Ferry. By the twentieth, however, when they finally did attack, reinforcements had come, and the Indians were unable to penetrate the fort's defenses without incurring heavier losses than their concept of warfare permitted. Attacking from concealed positions in ravines nearby, Little Crow and his warriors (probably fewer than four hundred) were driven back by artillery fire and finally abandoned the assault. After a day of heavy rain, they attacked again on the twenty-second, at least eight hundred strong, but failed to set fire to the rain-soaked roofs and were driven out of outlying buildings they had briefly occupied. The Indians then launched a final great as-sault which, well conceived and well directed, might very well have succeeded but for the devastating fire of the twenty-four-pound cannon. The second battle of Fort Ridgely was no mere raid or ambush; it was real war. Some hint of its ferocity can be gained from the official report, which concluded: "Thus, after six hours of continuous blazing con-flict, alternately lit up by the flames of burning buildings and darkened by whirling clouds of smoke, terminated the second and last attack." [15]

[15] Board of Commissioners, *Minnesota in the Civil and Indian Wars, 1861–1865*, II (St. Paul: Pioneer Press Co. [1893]), 186.

The military importance of the battles of Fort Ridgely, like those at New Ulm, is that they halted the momentum of the Sioux campaign, disrupted the strategy of the Indian leaders, and prevented the realization of the dream of a grand sweep down the Minnesota valley all the way to Fort Snelling.

While the main body of the Sioux warriors was alternately attacking Fort Ridgely and New Ulm, smaller parties were carrying out raids all over southwestern Minnesota. Among the places where white casualties were heavy were Milford Township in Brown County, Lake Shetek in Murray County, and portions of Kandiyohi County. In most cases the men were killed, the women and children taken prisoner and held until the final defeat of the Indians at Wood Lake. Much of our information about the uprising comes from the stories told by those captives. In addition to a good deal of brutality, these accounts frequently tell of kindness and even heroism on the part of individual Indians toward their white prisoners. Early accounts of the uprising seized upon the occasional instances of torture and mutilation, exaggerated them, and conjured up a picture of wholesale atrocities unparalleled in the history of Indian warfare. Some of the stories revel in details of babies nailed living to walls, of unborn infants torn from the maternal womb and flung in the faces of the dying mothers, of bodies hacked up beyond all recognition. Like Falstaff's story of the men he battled, however, the closer these stories are scrutinized, the less foundation there seems to be for them. Although the earth between Fort Ridgely and the lower agency was supposed to be virtually carpeted with multilated bodies, Dr. Jared W. Daniels, who accompanied a burial party and who should have recognized cases of mutilation if anyone would, categorically denied that the corpses he saw had been mutilated. Atrocities there no doubt were, as there have been in every war since the beginning of time, and they were not all committed by the Indians. But these isolated instances were multiplied in the imagination of refugees and their details exaggerated to such a degree that the early accounts can no longer be accepted by sober scholarship.[16]

Before the momentum of the Sioux attack had spent itself, countermeasures were put into motion by state officials, and soon the initiative passed from the Indians to their enemies. As soon as Governor Alexander Ramsey learned of the first attacks, he commissioned former

---

[16] Governor Ramsey gave official sanction to the atrocity stories by repeating some of the most lurid in his special message to the legislature, September 9, 1862, printed in Minnesota *Executive Documents*, 1862, pp. 3–15 (extra session).

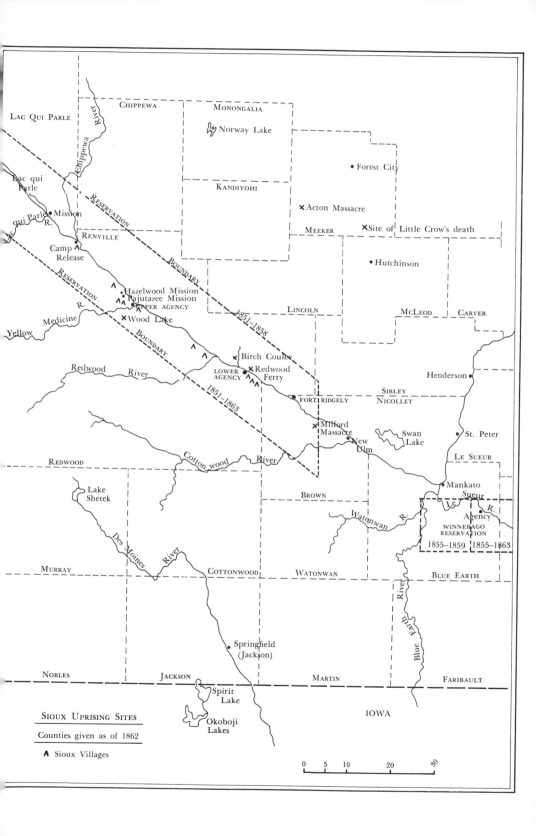

LAC QUI PARLE

CHIPPEWA

MONONGALIA

Norway Lake

KANDIYOHI

Forest City

Acton Massacre

MEEKER

Site of Little Crow's death

Lac qui Parle

Mission

RESERVATION

RENVILLE

Camp Release

Hutchinson

Hazelwood Mission
Pajutazee Mission
UPPER AGENCY

LINCOLN

McLEOD

CARVER

Wood Lake

Medicine

Yellow

R.

BOUNDARY

1851–1858

Birch Coulee

Redwood River

LOWER AGENCY

Redwood Ferry

Cotton wood River

BOUNDARY

1851–1863

FORT RIDGELY

SIBLEY

NICOLLET

Henderson

Milford Massacre

New Ulm

Swan Lake

St. Peter

LE SUEUR

REDWOOD

Lake Shetek

BROWN

Watonwan R.

Mankato

Le Sueur R.

Agency

WINNEBAGO RESERVATION

1855–1859   1855–1863

Des Moines River

MURRAY

COTTONWOOD

WATONWAN

BLUE EARTH

Blue Earth River

Springfield (Jackson)

NOBLES

JACKSON

MARTIN

FARIBAULT

Spirit Lake

Okoboji Lakes

IOWA

SIOUX UPRISING SITES

Counties given as of 1862

Δ Sioux Villages

0   5   10   20   30

Governor Henry H. Sibley to lead an expedition against the Sioux, with whom Sibley had traded and hunted in years past. Quickly assembling a force, Sibley moved toward the theater of war, and by August 27 his advance guard had reached Fort Ridgely, whose garrison was greatly strengthened by the arrival of the additional troops. After his arrival on the twenty-eighth, Sibley awaited reinforcements and sent out a party to reconnoiter and to bury any bodies they found. This party, under the over-all command of Joseph R. Brown, unwittingly provided the Indians with another chance to defeat the whites, an opportunity of which they again did not take full advantage. A portion of Brown's force camped on the night of September 1 near a small stream called Birch Coulee, across the river from the lower agency. Like Fort Ridgely, the site could easily be approached from cover, a fact which did not escape the Indians' notice. They began an attack before sunrise and continued it all day, with gradually decreasing intensity. Not until late on the morning of the third were the besieged troops relieved by forces sent out by Sibley. Thirteen killed and forty-seven wounded—the heaviest military losses of the war—were the result of an unwise selection of a campsite; as at the other battles, the Indian losses were slight—two killed, according to Big Eagle.

Although Little Crow was able to launch attacks on outlying settlements like Forest City and Hutchinson and although raids were to continue for many months, the fury of the uprising was spent by early September, and the main task facing the military commanders was to convince the Indians that they could not win and that the sooner they surrendered the better it would be for them. To take advantage of any wavering of purpose that might exist among the hostiles, Sibley had left a message for Little Crow on the Birch Coulee battlefield in hopes of opening negotiations for the release of the captives. A reply, dated September 7, rehearsed the Indians' grievances, including the delay in the issue of provisions "till our children was dieing with hunger," and mentioned the captives only enough to remind Sibley of their presence in the Indian camp.[17] No doubt Little Crow realized their utility as hostages and wished to make the best terms he could. Unfortunately for his purposes, dissension among his people was increasing day by day, and some important chiefs were only awaiting an opportunity to dissociate themselves from the war and its principal architect. On September 12, Sibley received a secret message from Wabasha and Taopi (chief of the farmer Indians) inquiring about terms of surrender. The lower bands

[17] *Ibid.*, p. 444.

had by this time evacuated the area of their reservation and were con-
gregating near the village of the upper Sioux chief Red Iron, in what
is now the eastern tip of Lac qui Parle County.

About the same time, the lower Sioux gave a feast which was attended by most of the men of both divisions. The advantages and disadvantages of surrender were thoroughly discussed at this council. Paul
Mazakutemane, formerly head of the Hazelwood Republic and a leading Christian Indian, made a speech in which he charged the lower
Indians with having started the war without consulting the upper
bands, pointed out the hopeless odds facing them now, and pleaded for
the surrender of the captives. In reply, Rda-in-yan-ka, Wabasha's son-
in-law, delivered an oration which, if correctly reported, probably summed up the position of the more intelligent among those who favored
continuing the war. The speech, as printed in the earliest history of the
uprising, deserves quotation at full length:

> I am for continuing the war, and am opposed to the delivery of the pris-
> oners. I have no confidence that the whites will stand by any agreement they
> make if we give them up. Ever since we treated with them their agents and
> traders have robbed and cheated us. Some of our people have been shot,
> some hung; others placed upon floating ice and drowned; and many have
> been starved in their prisons. It was not the intention of the nation to kill any
> of the whites until after the four returned from Acton and told what they had
> done. When they did this, all the young men became excited, and com-
> menced the massacre. The older ones would have prevented it if they could,
> but since the treaties they have lost all their influence. We may regret what
> has happened but the matter has gone too far to be remedied. We have got
> to die. Let us, then, kill as many of the whites as possible, and let the prison-
> ers die with us.[18]

Whether because of the eloquence of his appeal or for other reasons, the
decision was made to continue the war. As the council broke up, the
braves rode off, singing:

[18] Isaac V. D. Heard, *History of the Sioux War and Massacres of 1862 and 1863* (New
York: Harper and Brothers, 1863), pp. 151–152. The authenticity of this speech may
be questioned; Heard gives no source for it. Paul Mazakutemane provides a remotely
similar version, much less eloquent, in "Narrative of Paul Mazakootemane," trans. by
Rev. S. R. Riggs, *Minnesota Historical Collections*, III (1870–1880), 82–90. Still, it is
probably as accurate as most of the renditions of speeches by Indians, such as the
memorable words of Logan as recorded by Jefferson in *Notes on the State of Virginia*. It
has the flavor of the letter dictated by Rda-in-yan-ka four days before his death and
translated by Riggs.

> Over the earth I come;
> Over the earth I come;
> A soldier I come;
> Over the earth I am a ghost.[19]

The "friendlies" were thus not in a position to seize the captives from Little Crow and make a separate peace with the whites. Sibley realized that in order to bring about such an eventuality, he would first have to inflict a decisive defeat on Little Crow's forces. In the battle of Wood Lake he did so. That battle, which involved relatively large forces on both sides, started by accident when some soldiers in search of potatoes stumbled upon Indians hidden in the grass, awaiting the moment set for attack. After about two hours of fighting, the Sioux were defeated with a loss of sixteen killed, as compared to only seven on the other side—the only major clash in which the admitted Indian losses outnumbered those of the whites. The battle of Wood Lake, fought on September 23, ended Little Crow's last hope of winning the war. Soon thereafter he and his loyal followers fled to the Dakota prairies, where they assumed, correctly, that no military force would be able to pursue them so late in the season.

Their flight left the way open for those who had opposed the war or who had tired of it to deliver up the captives and make peace on such terms as they could obtain. Sibley entered the friendly camp three days after the battle and took possession of the 269 men, women, and children, both whites and half-breeds, who had been held by the Sioux since their capture early in the war. Although bitterly denounced by many Minnesotans for the extreme caution of his movements, Sibley almost certainly prevented a general slaughter of the captives by not rushing pell-mell into battle with the Sioux while Little Crow still had them in his possession. By recovering the prisoners and driving the hostile Sioux from the state, he had accomplished the two purposes of his expedition. Although Little Crow was still at large and raids conducted by small, irregular bands continued for more than two years afterward, the purely military phase of the Sioux Uprising may be said to have ended on September 27 at Camp Release.

There remained the question of what to do with the twelve hundred Indians taken into custody at Camp Release and the others who drifted in or were rounded up by detachments from Sibley's force later. The way this problem was met in the weeks that followed constitutes one of

[19] "Narrative of Paul Mazakootemane," p. 85.

the blackest pages in the history of white injustice to the Indian. In order to understand how it could have been countenanced by men of integrity and humanity like Sibley, one must attempt to comprehend the frame of mind in which the white population of Minnesota found itself during and after the uprising. Contemporary newspapers provide some indication of the popular mood. Far from the scenes of massacre, in a part of the state that could hardly have felt itself in immediate danger, a Red Wing editor wrote of the Sioux four days after the attack on the lower agency: "They must be exterminated, and now is a good time to commence doing it." [20] Closer to the scenes the same sentiment was expressed. A Mankato newspaper announced on August 30: "The cruelties perpetrated by the Sioux nation in the past two weeks demand that our Government shall treat them for all time to come as outlaws, who have forfeited all right to property and life." [21] The editor of the other Mankato newspaper told his readers that if its columns were not overflowing with news, it was because he had joined one of the volunteer companies formed "for the *extermination of Indians*. . . ." [22] A group of men involved in the defense of Fort Ridgely entered into a solemn compact that if they survived the attack they would not rest until they had exterminated every man, woman, and child in the Sioux nation.[23] As late as February, 1863, a Faribault newspaper published a letter that declared: "Extermination, swift, sure, and terrible is the only thing that can give the people of Minnesota satisfaction, or a sense of security." [24]

No doubt the sentiment reflected in the newspapers grew largely from the atrocities reported from the war zone. But in view of the remarks made in 1857 by Special Agent Prichette about the desire of the whites to use an Indian war as a pretext for seizing lands, one is justified in wondering how much that motive figured in the hysterical utterances of the newspapers and of public men in the weeks following the out-

[20] *Goodhue County Republican* (Red Wing), August 22, 1862.

[21] Mankato *Semi-Weekly Record*, August 30, 1862.

[22] Mankato *Independent*, September 11, 1862. The editor, Clinton B. Hensley, contracted pneumonia on this "Indian hunt" and died six days before the execution of the convicted Indians.

[23] *Pioneer and Democrat* (St. Paul), September 4, 1862 (citing the Stillwater *Messenger*, September 2, 1862).

[24] *Central Republican* (Faribault), February 18, 1863. The writer of the letter did not favor removal of the Indians: "The settlers are too generous to send as a blightly curse, to any portion of this fair earth, those fiends [who] would pollute the foulest regions of h-ll by being colonized there!"

break. Although the evidence would not support the contention that the Sioux Uprising was deliberately provoked by the whites as an excuse for exterminating the Sioux or driving them out of the state and opening their lands to settlement, there were undoubtedly plenty of Minnesotans who felt, and perhaps expressed the view privately, that the cloud had a silver lining, that though the murder of hundreds of settlers was a high price to pay to be rid of the Indians, yet one could not be blind to the advantages it now offered in terms of the opportunity to satisfy the greed of those safely behind the lines. And what better way was there to mask this greed than to wave the bloody shirt and call righteously for the extermination of the "inhuman fiends" who had heretofore stood in the way of Manifest Destiny, Minnesota brand?

Whatever the motives, vengeance was called for, and vengeance there had to be. Since the most clearly guilty among the Sioux were scattered over the prairies to the west, the popular demand for retribution had to be satisfied by punishing such Indians as were available. Although those who had voluntarily surrendered might reasonably be assumed to be innocent—and one of the captives who later wrote of her experiences was unable to recognize any of the murderers in that group—they were available and thus had to serve in the absence of more suitable material. According to missionary Riggs, who accompanied Sibley's expedition, as soon as the captives had been released, they began to tell of "Indian men who had maltreated these white women, or in some way had been engaged in the massacres. . . ." So the next day Sibley asked Riggs to serve as a medium of communication between the women and himself. The result was the apprehension of a few of the Indians and the organization of a military commission to examine others against whom charges might be made. This plan was innocuous enough at first, but pressure from public opinion forced a change in procedure; and in a few weeks, "instead of taking individuals for trial, against whom some specific charge could be brought, the plan was adopted to subject all grown men, with a few exceptions, to an investigation of the commission, trusting that the innocent could make their innocency appear."[25] Thus the revered Anglo-Saxon principle of law that a person is considered innocent until proved guilty was reversed in the case of Indians.

Riggs, writing years afterwards, admitted that it was impossible for

[25] Stephen R. Riggs, *Mary and I: Forty Years with the Sioux* (Boston: Congregational Sunday-School and Publishing Society, 1880), pp. 206–207; Stephen R. Riggs to Martha Riggs, September 27, 1862, copy in Riggs Papers, Minnesota Historical Society.

the Indians to "make their innocency appear," particularly since participation in battles was grounds for a conviction on a charge of murder. Isaac V. D. Heard, a lawyer who served on the commission and later wrote a history of the Sioux war, justified the departure from the usual rules of war on the grounds that "the battles were not ordinary battles." Since New Ulm was defended by civilians, an attack on it was not war but murder. Besides, wrote Heard, most of these Indians must also have been engaged in individual massacres and outrages. The marauding bands "undoubtedly" consisted of the same men who made the sustained attacks on Fort Ridgely and other fortified positions, so they were not engaged in war either. Heard's clincher, however, is this example of logic as employed by white men in 1862: "The fact that they were *Indians* . . . would raise the moral certainty that, as soon as the first murders were committed, all the young men were impelled by the sight of blood and plunder . . . to become participants in the same class of acts." 26

If the manner in which the trials were conducted represented a departure from normal legal procedure, the method used to disarm the bulk of the Indians was a violation of common decency. The first ones arrested were handled in a straightforward fashion, but a ruse was employed to place 236 others at the mercy of their captors. Informed that their annuities were to be paid and that they must first be counted, as had been the practice in previous years, the men were sent through a doorway and there asked to give up their arms, with the promise that they would receive them back shortly. As soon as they did so, they were chained by the ankles two and two, as those arrested earlier had been. No doubt Sibley and his officers thought they were being comparatively lenient, for some of the soldiers advocated making any agreement with the Indians to obtain the captives and then murdering all the Indians—men, women, and children.27

Sibley's intention when he began the trials was apparently to execute promptly all the men found guilty by his commission. Actually, he had no authority to take such action, nor did his superior, General John

26 Riggs, *Mary and I*, p. 207; Heard, *History of the Sioux War*, pp. 255-257.
27 Heard, *History of the Sioux War*, p. 187. According to Big Eagle, the half-breeds who served as intermediaries between the Sioux and the military had assured him and the other men that they would be kept prisoner only a short time; he served three years in prison and narrowly escaped hanging. See Holcombe, "A Sioux Story of the War," pp. 397, 399.

Pope, who had been placed in command of the Military Department of the Northwest in September. As the convictions multiplied, this intention faded, and Sibley merely kept on with the trials, meanwhile awaiting orders from superior authority. The procedure was to present certain charges against each prisoner, based on information provided by the half-breeds and others who had been held captive by the Indians. According to Heard, Riggs served as a virtual "Grand Jury" in assembling this evidence; Riggs later denied this ascription of authority to him. Although the missionary shared the general feeling that most of the Indians tried were guilty, and wrote President Lincoln that the "great majority" should be executed to meet the "demands of public justice," he had serious reservations about the manner in which they were convicted. The greater part, he said, "were condemned on general principles, without any specific charges proved. . . ."[28] For his suggestion that even Indians perhaps deserved a fair trial, he was roundly condemned, as were other missionaries, including the elder Williamson.

When the trials were finally concluded, on November 5, nearly four hundred Indians and half-breeds had gone through the process, which sometimes accommodated forty in a single day. Of them, 303 were judged guilty of murder and sentenced to death. One, Joseph Godfrey, a mulatto married to an Indian woman, though convicted on evidence as reliable as any offered in these trials, proved himself so useful at supplying evidence to convict his recent comrades-in-arms that his sentence was later commuted. The commissioners managed to persuade themselves that there was some doubt of his guilt, though they allowed no such doubts to intrude upon their judgment of men less pliable or less articulate.[29] The condemned Indians and a few women and children who accompanied them were removed from the camp on November 9 and marched to a hastily improvised prison just west of Mankato. As they passed through New Ulm, they were attacked by local citizens, then engaged in disinterring some of those who had been killed in the fighting late in August; fifteen prisoners and several guards were

[28] Riggs, *Mary and I*, p. 208; Stephen R. Riggs to President Abraham Lincoln, November 17, 1862, Riggs Papers.

[29] Godfrey served three years in prison, together with the Indians, and then accompanied them upon their release to the Niobrara reservation in Nebraska, where he became known as a quiet, industrious man who seldom left his farm. He died in 1909. Niobrara (Nebr.) *Tribune*, July 8, 1909.

seriously injured by the barrage of bricks and stones with which the "Dutch she devils," as Sibley called them, bombarded the now defenseless Indians.

Two days before the departure of the prisoners, the rest of the captured Sioux were sent down the river to Fort Snelling. They, too, were attacked along the way. As they passed through Henderson, they were set upon by the enraged populace with guns, knives, clubs, and stones. Several were injured, and one infant was so badly hurt that it soon died. Those who survived this assault and the following winter remained in a dismal encampment on the flats below Fort Snelling for about six months, tormented by wild rumors concerning the fate of their menfolk and perpetually in danger of being killed by parties of whites who repeatedly threatened to break through the wooden fence erected for their protection.

When the trials were completed, the general assumption was that all 303 of the men condemned to death would be speedily hanged. President Lincoln, however, intervened and ordered General Pope to send him the complete trial record, which he then turned over to two men with instructions to examine each case carefully, with special reference to those who had been convicted of rape or of murdering innocent settlers. Although under conflicting pressures from humanitarians who urged leniency and from citizens of Minnesota desirous of revenge, Lincoln apparently consulted his own conscience in the matter before him and reduced the number to be executed to forty, including Godfrey, whose sentence was commuted upon recommendation of the military commission that had tried him. Lincoln's action was, of course, displeasing to the people of Minnesota, whose spokesmen, Governor Ramsey and the congressional delegation, had been insisting that the Indians must all be executed or lynch law would prevail. After an abortive attack on the condemned by a Mankato mob on December 4, Ramsey issued a proclamation calling on the people of the state to refrain from mob violence. He assured them that even if the President should see fit to interfere with the rightful course of justice by saving any of the prisoners from the halter, they would still be subject to state law, and the will of the people would prevail through legal means.[30] There was no further violence, even after Lincoln's order was made public, though the newspapers continued their attacks on the "sickly sentimentalists" who had exerted a baneful influence on the President. Nevertheless,

[30] His proclamation is in Minnesota *Executive Documents*, 1862, pp. 64–66 (extra session).

the prisoners were removed from Camp Lincoln on the day after the attempted assault and placed in more secure confinement in what is now downtown Mankato.

After one postponement, the execution was set for December 26, across the street from where the prisoners were being held. Elaborate precautions were taken to prevent an outbreak of violence. Martial law was declared for an area ten miles around, the sale of liquor was suspended, and troops were concentrated in the town to guarantee that the Indians would meet their deaths in proper legal fashion. These precautions were unnecessary; the spectacle of thirty-nine Indians to be hanged at once was a good enough show to divert the citizens from any more active sports. The condemned men were separated from their comrades four days before the execution and were offered the services of both Protestant and Catholic missionaries. All but two accepted Christian baptism. Contemporary accounts make much of their last farewells to their friends and families. As on an earlier occasion, the most eloquent words were those of Rda-in-yan-ka, who dictated the following letter to his father-in-law:

> WABASHAW: You have deceived me. You told me that if we followed the advice of General Sibley, and give ourselves up to the whites, all would be well—no innocent man would be injured. I have not killed, wounded, or injured a white man, or any white persons. I have not participated in the plunder of their property; and yet to-day, I am set apart for execution, and must die in a few days, while men who are guilty will remain in prison. . . .
>
> My wife and children are dear to me. Let them not grieve for me. Let them remember that the brave should be prepared to meet death; and I will do so as becomes a Dacotah.[31]

A last-minute change of schedule was the removal of one name from the list of those to die. The remaining thirty-eight condemned mounted the scaffold chanting their death song, reluctantly allowed the white caps to be adjusted over their heads, and then attempted to grasp each other's hands in a final gesture of solidarity. The trap was sprung by William Duley, some of whose family had been killed at Lake Shetek. His personal desire for revenge and that of the spectators was satisfied

---

[31] Quoted in Heard, *History of the Sioux War*, p. 284. The execution of the Sioux is recounted in many places, notably in Thomas Hughes, *History of Blue Earth County* (Chicago: Middle West Publishing Co., [1901]), pp. 127–136. Comparison with contemporaneous newspaper accounts reveals several discrepancies in Hughes' account, which was evidently based largely on the recollections of John C. Wise, editor of the Mankato *Semi-Weekly Record* in 1862.

as thirty-eight Sioux corpses dangled from the scaffold. When all had been pronounced dead, the bodies were buried in a shallow grave near-by, from which they were shortly exhumed for use as cadavers by local physicians.[32]

As injustice had characterized every previous stage in the treatment of the Sioux, so it also figured in the selection of the men who were to die. Among the 303 originally condemned to death there were three or four by the name of Chaskay, and two or three Washechoons. All were numbered, but since no one could remember which number was attached to which individual, Joseph R. Brown was entrusted with the job of examining the charges so as to determine which men were intended in Lincoln's order. Riggs later wrote that, although "extraordinary care" was meant to be used, when he and Brown afterward compared the men's stories and confessions, made a day or two before their death, they were forced to conclude that two mistakes had occurred. And the marshal of the prison told Bishop Henry B. Whipple that on the day after the execution, when he went to release a man who had been acquitted for saving a woman's life, he was told: "You hung him yesterday."[33]

Although the Sioux still in custody, both at Mankato and at Fort Snelling, had to be disposed of, and although Little Crow was still at large, the execution that December day at Mankato brought the Sioux war to an end. It was a totally unnecessary conflict precipitated by an accident, disastrous for its white and its Indian victims alike. Did it have any redeeming features? The missionaries professed at the time to see in the mass conversion of the Indians an unlooked-for and welcome benefit, an example of good coming out of evil. Others saw in the selfless devotion of the loyal Indians and in the courage displayed by some of the white victims of the uprising evidence of heroism which compensated in part for the bestiality shown on both sides.[34]

Though the Sioux Uprising produced individual heroes and hero-

[32] *Minnesota Pioneer*, December 28, 1862; Nathaniel West, *The Ancestry, Life, and Times of Hon. Henry Hastings Sibley, LL.D.* (St. Paul: Pioneer Press Publishing Co., 1889), p. 291.

[33] Riggs, *Mary and I*, p. 211; Henry B. Whipple, *Lights and Shadows of a Long Episcopate* (New York: Macmillan Co., 1899), p. 132. The Washechoon who was executed was later discovered to have been a sixteen-year-old white boy who had been brought up among the Indians. See Hughes, *History of Blue Earth County*, p. 129.

[34] Besides the attacks on the prisoners at New Ulm and on their families at Henderson, white atrocities included throwing a wounded Indian into a burning building at Fort Ridgely. This "daring but somewhat cruel feat" was witnessed by Sergeant J. C. Whipple and reported to Charles S. Bryant. See Bryant and Murch, *History of the*

ines, it revealed no leader of heroic stature, as some earlier Indian wars had done. Noble deeds were performed by many of the participants in the conflict. Among the whites there was the ferryman who, according to legend, kept the ferry going until all who wished to use it had crossed or until he was killed by the Indians. Among the Indians there were John Other Day, Lorenzo Lawrence, Paul Mazakutemane, Simon Anawangmani, and others, who took very real risks to help their white friends. They were praised in the newspapers and from the pulpits, and some of them received a more tangible reward through a congressional appropriation for their benefit a few years later. But no amount of praise for their courage can disguise the fact that they were the betrayers of their people. Some, like Taopi, who testified in the trials, were so hated that they dared not go to live among their people after the uprising.[35]

The fashion once was to designate as heroes only the "good Indians" —those who cooperated with the whites in the despoliation of their people. The pendulum has swung the other way in recent times, and we have in such a book as Alvin M. Josephy's *The Patriot Chiefs* a long-delayed tribute to those who refused to collaborate—not the mere troublemakers but the leaders who fought for their way of life and sometimes chose to die rather than submit. An attempt could probably be made to "rehabilitate" Little Crow and invest him with the dignity of a tragic hero. Yet, though Sibley's biographer calls him the successor to Osceola, Black Hawk, Tecumseh, and King Philip, he lacks the stature of those men. If his final gesture in leading his people in what he knew to be a hopeless cause places him in a class with the great chieftains, his earlier collaboration with the whites—sometimes, it would seem, for personal gain— deprives him of the true heroic stature.

Other than Little Crow, only one of the hostiles who fought and died

---

Great Massacre, p. 201. Many of the depredations which the Indians' annuities were used to pay were actually committed by white looters who roved through the abandoned country picking up what the Indians had left.

[35] The conflicting stories about the ferryman are discussed in Joseph Connors, "The Elusive Hero of Redwood Ferry," *Minnesota History*, XXXIV (June 1955), 233–238. The *Pioneer and Democrat* for August 27, 1862, mentions that Other Day was currently quite a "lion" in St. Paul, where he addressed an audience at Ingersoll's Hall and where the familiar portrait of him was made by the photographer Joel E. Whitney. Taopi's testimony and that of his mother may have resulted in some convictions, but it brought no tangible rewards from the government. He died in extreme poverty in 1869. See the *Central Republican*, March 3, 1869, and the Faribault *Republican*, October 18, 1871, and also William Welsh, comp., *Taopi and His Friends, or the Indians' Wrongs and Rights* (Philadelphia: Claxton, Remsen and Heffelfinger, 1869), pp. 53–54.

in 1862, Rda-in-yan-ka, emerges as a candidate for the position of tragic hero. Fully knowing of the duplicity of white men and aware, at least by mid-September, of the futility of the war he was fighting, he deliberately chose death in preference to surrender. If there is in his final message to his father-in-law a note of petulance, there is also a stronger note of defiance, the defiance of one who is not afraid to die but who wants the reasons for his death and the manner of his death known and remembered by his own people and perhaps by his enemies. One would like to learn more about Rda-in-yan-ka. As it is, about all we know, besides the text of his two known utterances, is the sketchy information provided by the court record. He was accused, on the testimony of David Faribault, of being active in nearly all the battles and of functioning as a kind of exhorter to his fellows. In his defense he said only that he had gone to Little Crow and tried to stop the killings when he learned of them on August 18. He did not deny the charge, brought by Paul Mazakutemane and Lorenzo Lawrence, that he opposed surrendering the captives, and he "supposed that he was to be hung for that." [36] He was probably right in this supposition, for he was not accused of any of the classes of crimes specified in Lincoln's order.

Whatever the end of the Sioux Uprising may have meant to the white man—a chance to speculate in land or acquire a farm in lands previously unavailable, a demonstration of the Lord's saving power over men about to be executed, or something else—for the Sioux it meant just one thing: catastrophe. It meant their expulsion from the land where they and their ancestors had lived since the immemorial past, and, more than that, it meant the shattering of whatever unity the Santee bands had possessed. Never again were the Mdewakantons, Wahpekutes, Sissetons, and Wahpetons one people, occupying a single fairly well defined land area. Henceforth they were scattered over states and provinces, with hundreds of miles separating their dispersed settlements and the lands between rapidly filling up with white men, who learned eventually to tolerate the Indian, if only to exploit him, but never to accept him as an equal.

[36] Heard, *History of the Sioux War*, pp. 281–282. Heard reports (p. 292) one other grim tradition concerning this man. At the execution he suffered the final indignity of having the rope break, so that, although probably dead, he had to be strung up a second time. Hughes assigns this ignominy to Cut Nose, the most hated of the thirty-eight. See Hughes, *History of Blue Earth County*, p. 134. Contemporary newspaper accounts do not name the man who fell.

CHAPTER 7

Exile

ALTHOUGH THE execution of the men thought to be most deeply implicated in the massacres of 1862 partially satisfied the demand of the Minnesota citizens for vengeance, two more objectives remained to be realized: the Sioux had to be expelled from the state, and an effort had to be made to punish the fugitives still roaming the prairies to the west. The accomplishment of the second of these aims—to the degree that anything was accomplished—had little bearing on the Santees and can be summarized briefly.

Besides Little Crow's group of diehards, most of the upper Sioux had fled before Sibley's army in September, 1862, and spent the winter in the Devils Lake area. Although most of them had not been involved in the massacres, they judged it expedient to stay out of the way of white men not disposed to make fine distinctions between guilty and innocent Indians. In the spring of 1863 a campaign was planned to kill or capture these remaining "hostiles" and incidentally to demonstrate to all the Sioux that United States troops could invade their country with impunity. The projected campaign took the form of a gigantic pincers movement involving two bodies of troops, one moving northwest from Fort Ridgely, the other advancing up the Missouri from Fort Randall to cut off the retreat of those Indians driven west by the first. Sibley, now a brigadier general, commanded the first force, General Alfred Sully the second.[1]

Whether the 1863 campaign was a success or a failure, from the standpoint of the whites, depends on what standards of measurement are used. On the one hand, Sibley's enemies saw it as an ineffectual waste of the taxpayers' money which not only failed to kill or capture any large number of Indians but left the Minnesota frontier comparatively unprotected and subject to isolated raids by small bands of Indians. On the other hand, the expedition did drive the main body of the Sioux west of the Missouri, at least temporarily, and destroyed enormous quantities of their supplies and equipment. Three battles were fought in July: Big Mound, Dead Buffalo Lake, and Stony Lake, all in what is today east-central North Dakota. All resulted in one-sided victories for the military force, which had modern rifles and some artillery, while the Indians had to fight mostly with shotguns and bows and arrows and were chiefly concerned with protecting the retreat of their women and children. Sully's failure to move up the Missouri rapidly enough to effect a meeting with Sibley permitted the bulk of the Indians to escape west of the river. Sully did, however, achieve the biggest victory of the expedition in the battle of Whitestone Hill, fought in present-day Dickey County, North Dakota, on September 3. The Indians' casualties were heavy, and a large number of captives, mostly women and children, were taken.[2]

The dissatisfaction of many Minnesotans with the campaign of 1863 grew partly out of the continued hostility of Indians closer at hand. Beginning in April and continuing through July, the settlers were plagued by a series of petty horse-stealing raids, in the course of which

[1] The campaigns of 1863 and 1864 are treated in some detail in William W. Folwell, *A History of Minnesota*, II (St. Paul: Minnesota Historical Society, 1961), 265–301. The present account follows this treatment, supplemented by Robert Huhn Jones, *The Civil War in the Northwest* (Norman: University of Oklahoma Press, 1960). Among the primary sources consulted are *The War of the Rebellion: A Compilation of the Official Records of the Union and Confederate Armies* (Washington: Government Printing Office, 1886–1901); Board of Commissioners, *Minnesota in the Civil and Indian Wars, 1861–1865* (St. Paul: Pioneer Press Co., 1890, 1893); A. P. Connolly, *A Thrilling Narrative of the Minnesota Massacre and the Sioux War of 1862–63* (Chicago: A. P. Connolly, 1896); David L. Kingsbury, "Sully's Expedition Against the Sioux in 1864," *Minnesota Historical Collections*, VIII (1895–1898), 449–456; and "Diary Kept by Lewis C. Paxson, Stockton, N.J.," *North Dakota Historical Collections*, II (1908), Part 2, 102–163.

[2] The site of the battle of Whitestone Hill is in a state park today. There is an impressive shaft on the hill commemorating the soldiers who were killed there, and an inconspicuous marker below honoring the Indian dead.

several whites were killed. Not only did the raiders reach exposed frontier settlements like those on the Watonwan River and the edge of the Big Woods in McLeod and Wright counties, but they even penetrated as far as Le Sueur, Rice, and Dakota counties, east of Mankato and St. Peter. The profound sense of insecurity engendered by these raids led the state government to resort to extreme measures to end the menace. On July 4 a volunteer force of scouts was authorized and a $25 bounty on Sioux scalps declared. Sixteen days later a reward of $75 was ordered, payable to anyone not serving with this force who could provide satisfactory proof that he had killed a Sioux warrior. In September the reward was increased to $200.[3]

One of these raids resulted in the killing of Little Crow. The chief and his immediate followers had spent the winter without adequate provisions on the northern plains and had sought aid from the British authorities at Fort Garry. Although the governor of Rupert's Land refused to give them ammunition when they called on him late in May, he did relieve their starvation with an issue of provisions.[4] In June, Little Crow, his son Wowinapa, and a few followers invaded the area of McLeod and Meeker counties, where some settlers were murdered, probably by members of their band. On the evening of July 3, Nathan Lampson and his son Chauncey fired on two Indians picking raspberries in a thicket north of Hutchinson. They killed one, who was later identified as Little Crow, and the other, Wowinapa, was later captured by the military. The chief's body was thrown on a heap of entrails at a slaughter house; his scalp eventually ended up in the state historical society. Thus ignominiously perished the leader of the Uprising of 1862.[5]

The less than complete success of the 1863 campaign led to the outfitting of another the following year. Again two columns, one moving up the Missouri, the other west from Minnesota, were employed. They contrived to meet on the Missouri and then headed into the comparatively unknown country to the west, where they fought a major

[3] Minnesota *Executive Documents*, 1863, pp. 339–349, 192, 196, 198. This source lists only four beneficiaries under the terms of these orders, three of whom received $25 each, the other $75. See *ibid.*, pp. 223, 224, 226, 403. As Walter Trenerry pointed out in an article a century later, these orders, issued by the state adjutant general, were illegal. See Walter N. Trenerry, "The Shooting of Little Crow: Heroism or Murder?", *Minnesota History*, XXXVIII (September 1962), 153.

[4] Secretary of State William Seward to Secretary of Interior John B. Usher, July 2, 1863, NARS, RG 75, LR.

[5] Mankato *Weekly Union*, July 17, 1863; Folwell, *History of Minnesota*, II, 281–285.

engagement with the Indians in the Killdeer Mountains and did some desultory skirmishing in the Badlands. This expedition added to the geographical knowledge of what is now western North Dakota, and it probably also contributed to the starvation of the Indians whose supplies were destroyed, but it bore little relationship to the Sioux Uprising or its perpetrators. Most of the Indians encountered were Yanktonais and Tetons, who had taken no part in the uprising and were doubtless somewhat puzzled at the gratuitous invasion of their country. From this point on, the military campaigns on the prairies lose whatever connection they had with the 1862 outbreak and merge into the long series of wars with the Sioux that ended only with the Wounded Knee massacre in 1890.[6]

Although the newspapers of Minnesota were calling for the expulsion of all Indians from the state, attention naturally centered early in 1863 about the Sioux who had been taken into custody at Camp Release. These people—the prisoners held at Mankato and the larger group at Fort Snelling—spent a miserable and anxious winter. The condemned men probably fared better than their families. Out of the 350 or more, only thirteen died during the winter, as against about 130 in the camp at Fort Snelling. Under the stimulus of Thomas S. Williamson, who preached to them every Sunday, and Robert Hopkins, one of their number and a Christian, the men in prison underwent a mass religious conversion. Early in February, Williamson and Gideon Pond, satisfied that the professions of faith were in most cases sincere, baptized 274 of the prisoners. Eventually nearly all were baptized. Along with this burst of religious enthusiasm came a desire to adopt other features of the white man's culture, notably the written word. According to Riggs, the prison became one great school that winter. The prisoners practiced writing on slates and with pen and paper until they were able to express themselves with sufficient fluency to write letters to their families. One contemporary account had it that by March they were turning out one or two hundred letters weekly, which Williamson faithfully carried to the camp below the fort.[7] The knowledge acquired during the winter of 1862–1863 later proved valuable to the men who were released, some of whom became leaders among their people.

[6] Folwell, *History of Minnesota*, II, 296–300. Further expeditions in 1865 and 1866 encountered no Indians.

[7] *Ibid.*, II, 249–251; Stephen R. Riggs, *Tah-koo Wah-kan; or, the Gospel Among the Dakotas* (Boston: Congregational Publishing Society, 1869), pp. 342–354; Mankato *Weekly Record*, March 7, 1863.

The families of the condemned men, together with the rest of the captive Sioux, experienced a similar wave of religious enthusiasm and interest in learning. They too were under the influence of missionaries, to whom goes the credit for the transformation that swept over them. John P. Williamson, who had barely begun missionary work on the old reservation at the time of the uprising, joined them at their place of confinement and remained with them all winter, as did Samuel D. Hinman, the Episcopal missionary whose work on the reservation had likewise been cut short by the outbreak. Williamson held nightly prayer meetings in the garret of an old government warehouse large enough to seat five hundred. Although he proceeded more cautiously than his father, he did baptize at least 140. Hinman baptized 144, including all the chiefs of the lower Sioux, and soon had 300 under his care. These two men thus laid the foundations for the later strength of the Episcopal Church and the American Board of Commissioners for Foreign Missions among the Santees. Father Augustin Ravoux, who had ministered to the convicted prisoners before they were executed, baptized 184, but he did not remain in the camp and hence did not gain so lasting an influence for the Catholic Church as the other men did for their denominations.[8]

The number in these two concentration camps varied somewhat throughout the winter. At the end of February there were 322 prisoners at Mankato, plus about 20 cooks, laundresses, and other service personnel—all Indians—employed by the prison authorities.[9] The other group contained 1,601 on December 2 and 1,591 on March 10, the 130 deaths having been nearly offset by additions captured by the military during the winter. At the time of the earlier census, the total included 295 upper Sioux, 133 Wahpekutes, and 112 half-breeds without tribal affiliation; the rest were Mdewakantons.[10] The extreme congestion,

[8] Folwell, *History of Minnesota*, II, 252–254; Riggs, *Tah-koo Wah-kan*, pp. 355–361.

[9] Mankato *Weekly Record*, March 7, 1863.

[10] Com. of Indian Affairs, *Annual Report*, 1863, pp. 313–316; Henry H. Sibley to Usher, March 14, 1863, NARS, RG 75, LR. Among the Mdewakantons, the largest band was Wacouta's, with 221 members, followed by Taopi's with 214, Traveling Hail's with 193, Wabasha's with 165, Eagle Head's with 109, Good Road's with 98, and Black Dog's with 61. Taopi was chief of the "farmer Indians," a band made up of men from several of the traditional villages. Since he was originally from Kapozha, however, he may be considered the legitimate successor to the chief of that village, Little Crow. Traveling Hail was chief of the old Lake Calhoun band, and Eagle Head led an offshoot of the Shakopee band, most of whose members had taken flight with their chief as the uprising came to a close. Mankato, chief of the Good Road band, had

which encouraged the spread of measles and other diseases, together with exposure to cold, accounted for most of the deaths, which were heaviest among the children. Except for the cramped quarters, the Indians' physical circumstances were probably little worse than they would have been in a normal winter on the reservation. Anxiety over their fate added to the hardship of this dismal winter and created a psychological state only partly alleviated by the religious consolation afforded by their acceptance of Christianity.

The missionaries who devoted themselves to the welfare of the Indians were handicapped in their work by the continued vindictiveness of the surrounding white populace. The calumny directed indiscriminately at all Indians naturally fell to some extent on those whites who did not share the majority view. Hinman was attacked physically by a party of roughs who broke into the stockade and beat him unconscious. Riggs, the elder Williamson, and others who defended the Indians publicly were denounced as "avaricious priests" who, like other dogs, had had their day.[11] When it was rumored that these men had interceded with the President and urged him to stay the execution of some of the condemned prisoners, they were denounced as mawkish sentimentalists or, by the more extreme, as "contemptible fools" and "cold hearted scoundrels."[12]

Even Bishop Henry B. Whipple, perhaps the most respected churchman in the state, came in for his share of obloquy for his role—an important one—in preventing this legalized murder. In 1859, at the age of thirty-seven, he had been consecrated Episcopal Bishop of Minnesota. Almost at once he began interesting himself in the welfare of the Indians. Besides opening a mission at the lower agency in 1860, he had begun work among the Chippewas. Several months before the uprising he had written to President Lincoln attacking the government's Indian policy, and that fall he had gone to Washington and appealed in person for clemency in the matter of the condemned prisoners. For the latter action and for his frequent and public calls for moderation he was roundly condemned by a large segment of the population.[13]

---

been killed at Wood Lake, and Big Eagle, chief of the Black Dog band, was one of the condemned men held at Mankato.

[11] Henry B. Whipple, *Lights and Shadows of a Long Episcopate* (New York: Macmillan Co., 1899), p. 133; *Central Republican* (Faribault), February 18, 1863.

[12] *Central Republican*, May 13, 1863.

[13] Bishop Whipple's service in the cause of the Indian reform movement had only begun at this time. In the next twenty-five years he was to interest himself in virtually every phase of the movement and to become a powerful influence on government

After several letters from him had appeared in the newspapers, some-one purporting to speak for "many citizens" asked publicly, "Has'nt [*sic*] Bishop Whipple, relative to the condemned Indians in this State, nearly written himself into the ground?" In his autobiography he tells that at one time he was warned that some frontiersmen had been over-heard saying that they "must go down to Faribault and clean out that bishop." And he said that after he had issued the sacrament of confirma-tion to some of the captives at Fort Snelling, a newspaper account was headlined "Awful Sacrilege—Holiest Rites of the Church Given to Red-handed Murderers." [14] The most stridently and ferociously anti-Indian newspaper in the state was the *Central Republican* of Faribault, the Episcopal seat and Bishop Whipple's residence. Referring to another visit of the bishop to the camp, it commented: "God was mocked and his religion burlesqued by the solemn farce of administering the sacred ordinances of baptism and confirmation to a horde of the treacherous fiends at Fort Snelling not long since." [15]

The ferocity of the sentiments expressed by contemporary newspapers was aggravated by political considerations, each party trying to outdo the other in catering to what it believed to be the popular mood. At a time when the motto was "Extermination or Removal!"—the former preferred—it was impossible for any political figure or party organ to remain neutral or even to approach neutrality. Hence the savagery of public statements by Governor Ramsey and the congressional delega-tion from Minnesota is attributable in part at least to their feeling that it would have been political suicide to urge restraint and sweet reason-ableness where the Indian question was concerned.

Under such pressure from their constituents and their political op-ponents, both the Minnesota legislature and the congressional delega-tion moved rapidly to bring about the expulsion of the Sioux from the state. As early as Governor Ramsey's special message to the legislature

---

policy as the spokesman for the humanitarian groups that were seeking to recast that policy along new lines.

[14] St. Paul *Pioneer*, December 6, 1862; Whipple, *Lights and Shadows of a Long Episco-pate*, pp. 136, 160. The editor of the *Pioneer*, comparatively moderate on the Indian question, said that Whipple deserved a respectful hearing, even if his views were unpopular.

[15] *Central Republican*, June 10, 1863. The editor of this newspaper was Orville Brown, known among his many enemies as "Awful Brown," who later bought the Mankato *Record*, transformed it into a Republican organ, and served several years as postmaster of Mankato. Born in 1810 in New York, he died in 1901, doubtless still regretting that all the Sioux had not been exterminated.

on September 9, 1862, the idea was broached of abrogating all treaties with the Sioux and reimbursing victims of the uprising from the annuities still due under the treaties. His proposal at that time was to ask that two million dollars be applied to this purpose, but the bill introduced in Congress by Representative Cyrus Aldrich on December 2 reduced the sum to $1,500,000. Although this amount was further reduced in the Senate, the notion expressed in Ramsey's message was accepted in principle by both houses. More important to most white Minnesotans was the expulsion of the Sioux. On December 16, Senator Morton S. Wilkinson introduced a bill calling for their removal, together with one providing for the removal of the Winnebagos.[16]

After some weeks in the congressional hopper, the desired legislation was finally obtained, in the form of two acts, the first approved February 16, the second March 3, 1863. The first of these was titled "An Act for the Relief of Persons for Damages sustained by Reason of Depredations and Injuries by certain Bands of Sioux Indians" and concerned chiefly the mechanics of paying the victims of depredations. The first section, however, specifically abrogated all treaties entered into by the government with the four bands of Santee Sioux and denied them any further benefits under the terms of these treaties, including all rights to occupancy of lands in the state of Minnesota.[17] The second piece of legislation, titled "An Act for the Removal of the Sisseton, Wahpaton, Medwakanton, and Wahpakoota Bands of Sioux or Dakota Indians, and for the disposition of their Lands in Minnesota and Dakota," was the necessary sequel to the first, which had left the dispossessed bands without a place to live. The act of March 3 did not specifically designate a future home for them, but it did call upon the President to assign to them a tract of land, outside the limits of any state, large enough to provide each member of the tribe willing to farm with "eighty acres of good agricultural lands, the same to be well adapted to agricultural purposes." It further provided that the proceeds from the sale of their former reservation should be invested for their benefit. None of the money was to be paid directly to the Indians, as under the old system, but it was to be used to advance them in farming so that they would become self-sustaining. On the same date Congress approved an appro-

16 Minnesota *Executive Documents*, 1862, p. 11 (extra session); Folwell, *History of Minnesota*, II, 246; *Minnesota Pioneer*, January 6 and 15, 1863; *Congressional Globe*, 37th Cong., 3rd Sess., pp. 100, 104.

17 U. S. *Statutes at Large*, XII, 652–654, 819–820.

priation of $50,016.66 for the removal of the Sioux and their establishment in their new homes.[18]

These two pieces of legislation constituted something of an innovation in United States Indian policy. Heretofore it had been the practice always to employ the treaty-making power in altering the relationship between the government and an Indian tribe; even though the tribe had been defeated in war and the pretext of a treaty between sovereign entities was patently absurd, the hoary farce was enacted. Now a precedent had been set for unilateral abrogation of treaties and the management of Indian affairs by Congress, without even the illusion of the Indians' consent. If there seemed to be some justification for this action in the case of the Sioux, there was none for the bill, approved February 21, calling for the "peaceful" removal of the Winnebagos, who had not, as a tribe, taken any part in the uprising.[19] In a sense, these acts anticipated the abandonment, seven years later, of the whole practice of negotiating treaties with Indian tribes.

Since the act of March 3, 1863, did not specify where the Indians' new home would be, this became the topic of considerable discussion. Various theories had been advanced in the months since the uprising as to what should be done with the Indians. The advocates of outright extermination, though noisy, were not numerous among people whose opinion carried much weight in the determination of policy. Even Galbraith, who confessed to "feelings of exasperation against these savages" and who was emotionally involved by the need for self-justification, conceded in his official report that "few will contend that the Sioux and all other Indians can be '*exterminated*' just now."[20]

Galbraith's suggestion for a reservation was a reasonable one. He proposed placing the Santees on a tract of land at the northern end of the Coteau des Prairies, an area partly included in the later Sisseton Reservation in northeastern South Dakota and southeastern North Dakota. The rest of his proposal was not so reasonable. He wanted to surround the Indians with a military guard to keep them from all but

[18] *Ibid.*, XII, 819–820, 784. This sum was one third that heretofore stipulated to be paid under the terms of the various treaties. A supplementary appropriation of $137,293.40 was made June 25, 1864, for deficiencies in the subsistence and removal expenses of both Sioux and Winnebagos. See *ibid.*, XIII, 172.

[19] *Ibid.*, XII, 658–660.

[20] Com. of Indian Affairs, *Annual Report*, 1863, pp. 294, 296. Galbraith's report, pp. 266–298, is one of the major primary sources of information on the Sioux Uprising.

authorized contacts with white men and put them to work in a fashion not easily distinguished from slavery. His personal vindictiveness emerges clearly from his recommendation:

> The power of the government must be brought to bear upon them; *they must be whipped, coerced into obedience.* After this is accomplished, few will be left to put upon a reservation; many will be killed; more must perish from famine and exposure, and the more desperate will flee and seek refuge on the plains or in the mountains. . . . A very small reservation should suffice for them.[21]

Sibley offered a somewhat similar proposal, with the exception that the reservation he proposed would have been around Devils Lake. He, too, wanted the Indians surrounded by a military cordon and reduced to beneficent servitude. One suggestion, which apparently received serious consideration for a time, was to send the convicted men to the Dry Tortugas, off the Florida coast, there to live out their lives. Surely the wildest proposal was that of James W. Taylor, who wanted to send all the Minnesota Indians—Sioux, Winnebagos, and Chippewas, numbering some 47,000—to Isle Royale in Lake Superior, to survive or starve as they could.[22]

Whatever the merits of these various suggestions, none of them was adopted. Instead, Secretary of Interior Caleb B. Smith recommended to Congress in December that the Santee Sioux be placed on the Missouri River and drafted a bill to this effect. The site for their new home was later narrowed down to a point within a hundred miles of Fort Randall. Because the country below that post was beginning to fill up with white settlers, this instruction effectually limited the choice to some point above the fort—not too far above, however, for there was a supply problem to consider. The decision as to the exact site of the reservation was left to Superintendent Thompson, who received both oral and written instructions while in Washington in the spring of 1863. Thompson went exploring late in May, after the Indians had already been started on their way, and rather hastily, it would seem, decided upon a site about eight miles above the mouth of Crow Creek, some eighty miles above Fort Randall. He had been disappointed to find most of the country above the fort utterly unsuitable, devoid of timber or other resources; and knowing that the boat carrying the Indians was only a couple of days behind him, he apparently selected the first spot

[21] *Ibid.*, 1863, p. 296
[22] Folwell, *History of Minnesota*, II, 256–257.

that seemed remotely acceptable. In his report to Commissioner Dole, made the day he arrived, he said: "I believe this is about the location the Secretary expected me to make; it is the best there is here anyway, so that I hope for your and his approval." Four days later he had almost convinced himself that it was a good place. "This is decidedly the best country above Fort Randall on the ceeded [*sic*] lands," he wrote the commissioner. "It has good soil, good timber and plenty of water." It was not perfect, however: "The only drawback that I fear is the dry weather. On the hills the grass is already dried up; but this is said to be an unusual season."[23] The three seasons the Santees spent at Crow Creck all proved to be "unusual," but Thompson kept right on justifying his desperate choice of a reservation in the face of irrefutable evidence that he had made a disastrous error.

The first Sioux to leave Minnesota upon the opening of navigation in the spring of 1863 were the prisoners at Mankato. In order to forestall any possible violence by local mobs, plans for their removal were kept more or less secret until almost the last minute. There had been rumors that they were to be removed, but nothing definite was known until the *Favorite* docked at Mankato on the evening of April 21. The next morning four companies of infantry were on guard duty, in lines across the street in front of the prison. About 15 or 20 women went first, followed by 48 men who had been acquitted of formal charges but had been kept in confinement for no better reason than that they had been caught in bad company. These men were dropped off at Fort Snelling and joined their tribesmen who had spent the winter there. The 278 remaining prisoners came next, chained in pairs (3 who were ill were carried on blankets by their companions), and finally a company of troops who were to accompany them. Although there were many spectators, there was no disorder. The Mankato *Weekly Record* commented: "All believe they richly deserve hanging," but since this was not the President's will, "the next best thing was to take them away."[24] Many whites still refused to credit the story that these men had undergone a religious conversion and treated this report with ridicule. Commenting on a prayer-meeting said to have been held on board the *Favorite*, the *Central Republican* thought it would have been fine if the boiler had exploded:

[23] Commissioner William P. Dole to Clark W. Thompson, April 8 and 9, 1863, NARS, RG 75, LS; Thompson to Dole, May 28 and June 1, 1863 (in Com. of Indian Affairs, *Annual Report*, 1863, pp. 310–311, 316).

[24] Mankato *Weekly Record*, April 25, 1863; *Minnesota Pioneer*, April 24, 1863.

What a glorious termination of Father Riggs' life-long Christian labors
among the heathen it would have been if in the midst of that prayer season
[*sic*] on the Favorite an explosion had occurred, which would have landed
our land-lubber soldiers in some muddy marsh . . . while Father Riggs, with
his pet lambs cleansed from all their sins in the blood of the innocents they
slaughtered last Fall, purified through the gospel of [John] Beeson, and
sanctified by faith in Riggs—went home to glory![25]

On the day before their departure Bishop Whipple wrote the Secretary of the Interior inquiring about the fate of the prisoners. Mentioning
trials conducted in the heat of anger and errors made then and later,
he suggested that perhaps they deserved a better fate than being sent to
prison, far from their families. He thought some sort of reform school
would be preferable, where they could learn to read and to practice
trades that would be useful to them on their release.[26] These recommendations may have been given some attention, but they do not seem
to have altered the immediate plans of the government, which were to
confine the men at Camp McClellan, an army barracks near Davenport, Iowa, erected at the beginning of the Civil War for the reception
of recruits. Except for some nineteen, who had been sentenced to specific prison terms, they were to be held here indefinitely, or until other
plans for their disposition were decided upon.[27]

The part of Camp McClellan in which the Indians were confined
consisted of four barracks, one of which was used as a hospital and as
quarters for the women and children who had accompanied the men.
The camp, located on a high elevation, covered an area two or three
hundred feet square and was enclosed by a board fence fifteen feet high.
The barracks were of a temporary sort and afforded little shelter in the
winter. Since the fuel the prisoners were allowed usually lasted only
half a day in the coldest part of the winter, they spent their afternoons
shivering in their worn blankets. Many developed tuberculosis and
other diseases, and about 120 died during the three years they spent
there. In the summer this "prison" was not a bad place. The inmates
were permitted a good deal of freedom. They could work on nearby
farms or go into town and trade mussel-shell rings, bows and arrows,
and other products of their labor, all without a guard. No attempt at
escape was ever made, although one is said to have been contemplated

[25] *Central Republican*, May 6, 1863.

[26] Henry B. Whipple to Usher, April 21, 1863, NARS, RG 75, LR.

[27] Stephen R. Riggs, *Mary and I: Forty Years with the Sioux* (Boston: Congregational
Sunday-School and Publishing Society, 1880), p. 220; Mankato *Weekly Record*, May
9, 1863.

at one time. The interest in religion and education which had begun at Mankato continued here. Some of the money earned by trade went for books, which were thus in good supply among the prisoners. The elder Williamson had charge of the prisoners for the first two years and ministered to their needs diligently. Early in his stay with them, he ran into difficulty and was for a time excluded from the prison on the grounds that they were "such abominable villains, incarnate devils, guilty of murder, rape and countless other atrocities, that it was wrong to show them any kind of sympathy even so far as to preach the gospel to them." But later the ban was lifted, after Williamson protested that it constituted a violation of religious freedom. The Indians divided themselves into bands, according to their old village allegiances, each under a *hoonkayape*, or elder, and carried on their religious activities in this fashion.[28]

Meanwhile, the main body of the Sioux at Fort Snelling were shipped out early in May, also by steamboat. Although an overland route would have been much shorter, Sibley had written Secretary of Interior Usher in March recommending shipment by water as cheaper and safer and pointing out that to send them by land would expose them to attack by hostile whites and also provide too many opportunities for escape.[29] While Superintendent Thompson was in St. Louis arranging for the transportation and subsistence of the Indians and buying farm implements and other necessary items, the actual removal was entrusted to his brother, Benjamin Thompson. On May 4 the first installment, made up mostly of women and children, boarded the *Davenport* and started on their way down the Mississippi. The boat, 35 feet wide and 205 feet long, carried 771 Indians and a military escort of 40 men. In such fashion did the contractor, Pierre Chouteau, Jr., and Company, fulfill the terms of the contract that called for "ample space for comfort, health, and safety" of the Indians. The next day the *Northerner*, pulling three barges and hence less crowded, departed with 547 Indians aboard.[30]

Thompson's contract contained a provision that the passengers might

[28] *Minnesota Pioneer*, April 29, 1863; Mankato *Weekly Record*, May 9, 1863; Riggs, *Mary and I*, pp. 221–223; Riggs, *Tah-koo Wah-kan*, pp. 369–374; Thomas S. Williamson to Dole, July 25, 1863, NARS, RG 75, LR; Thomas S. Williamson to Stephen R. Riggs, May 9, 1863, August 18, 1863, and September 11, 1863, Riggs Papers. Williamson's first letter to Riggs cited here contains a detailed description of the prison camp.

[29] Sibley to Usher, March 14, 1863, NARS, RG 75, LR.

[30] William E. Lass, "The Removal from Minnesota of the Sioux and Winnebago Indians," *Minnesota History*, XXXVIII (December 1963), 355–359; *Minnesota Pioneer*, May 5 and 6, 1863.

be transported by rail from Hannibal to St. Joseph. This was done with the second shipment. The Indians, accompanied by the younger Williamson, were jammed into freight cars, 60 to a car, for the trip across Missouri two days after their arrival at Hannibal on May 9. The first party, which included Hinman, went by boat all the way, transferring at St. Louis to the *Florence* for the slow ascent of the Missouri. At St. Joseph the two groups were reunited and completed the trip in incredible congestion. Williamson wrote his mother from St. Joseph that if all 1,300 were crowded onto one boat, it would be "nearly as bad as the Middle Passage for slaves." [31] He later described conditions on board the *Florence*, saying that

> when 1300 Indians were crowded like slaves on the boiler and hurricane decks of a single boat, and fed on musty hardtack and briny pork, which they had not half a chance to cook, diseases were bred which made fearful havoc during the hot months, and the 1300 souls that were landed at Crow Creek June 1, 1863, decreased to one thousand. . . . So were the hills soon covered with graves. The very memory of Crow Creek became horrible to the Santees, who still hush their voices at the mention of the name.[32]

They had good reason to recall Crow Creek in after years with feelings of horror. The site chosen for their new home was as unsuitable as anything their nightmares might have conjured up in the months they remained at Fort Snelling anxiously awaiting the government's decision. Historian Heard, writing with evident relish, described it as "a horrible region, filled with the petrified remains of the huge lizards and creeping things of the first days of time. The soil is miserable; rain rarely ever visits it. The game is scarce, and the alkaline waters of the streams and springs are almost certain death." [33] If it was not quite that bad, it was certainly not a country "well adapted to agricultural purposes," as called for by the removal act. After a year's residence there, the agent described it in his annual report for 1864 as a drought-stricken desolation, a land with no lakes, almost no timber—"the whole country being one wilderness of dry prairie for hundreds of miles around." [34] The hope that the Indians might support themselves was

[31] John P. Williamson to Mrs. Thomas S. Williamson, May 13, 1863 (in Frances H. Relf, ed., "Removal of the Sioux Indians from Minnesota," *Minnesota History Bulletin*, II [May 1918], 422–423).

[32] Quoted in Riggs, *Mary and I*, p. 224.

[33] Isaac V. D. Heard, *History of the Sioux War and Massacres of 1862 and 1863* (New York: Harper and Brothers, 1863), p. 295.

[34] Com. of Indian Affairs, *Annual Report*, 1864, p. 411.

obviously incapable of fulfillment the first year because they had arrived too late and inadequate preparations had been made for them. Besides that, the region, never subject to heavy rainfall, was passing through a cycle of extreme drought in the 1860's, and "literally nothing" was harvested in 1863 and 1864. Furthermore, there was not much game in the area, and the Indians were forbidden to leave the reservation and hunt on the prairies, though a party accompanied by Williamson did go out during the first winter and brought back enough meat to save the colony from starvation.[35]

Since the Indians could not support themselves at Crow Creek, the only way to save them from starvation was for the government to supply them with their necessities. This proved difficult because of the distance from all sources of supply, the brief period of navigability on the Missouri (and it was unusually low during the drought), the loss of cattle on the hoof in transit, and the exorbitant prices charged by suppliers. To prevent the scandal that would have resulted if the Indians had all starved, Thompson contracted for a quantity of pork and flour, together with three hundred head of beef cattle, to be shipped overland from Mankato in the late fall of 1863. This "Moscow expedition," as the newspapers called it, may have saved the Santees from extinction, but the pork and flour shipped to them had been condemned as unfit for consumption by soldiers, and the beef cattle became emaciated during their 292-mile trip to the reservation. The meat and flour, with appropriate quantities of water, were dumped together into wooden tanks made of fresh cottonwood logs, and the "rotten stuff" was ladeled out to the squaws.[36]

The condition of the Indians at Crow Creek was relieved only temporarily and in indifferent fashion by the "Moscow expedition" of 1863 and its successor in 1864. It remained desperate during the entire period they were exiled there. The meager sum of $100,000 appropriated annually by Congress was insufficient to provide adequately for the Indians' needs. The three hundred deaths that occurred during the first

[35] *Ibid.*, 1864, p. 410; Folwell, *History of Minnesota*, II, 260–261; J. P. Williamson to Riggs, March 2, 1864, Riggs Papers. The younger Williamson wrote to Riggs that there was not even enough grass for prairie fires. He also remarked that on Isle Royale the Indians could at least have caught fish. See J. P. Williamson to Riggs, June 9 and July 22, 1863, Riggs Papers.

[36] T. S. Williamson, *et al.*, to Dole and Usher, September 8, 1864 (in Com. of Indian Affairs, *Annual Report*, 1864, p. 421); Folwell, *History of Minnesota*, II, 439–441; J. P. Williamson to Riggs, December 26, 1863, and January 16, 1864 (dated 1863), Riggs Papers.

few months were due largely, said the missionaries, to the lack of suitable food and clothing. As late as 1865 the absence of a physician or any medicines made it impossible to treat the great amount of illness aggravated by exposure and malnutrition.[37] As an illustration of the extremities to which the Indians were reduced, one of the soldiers who accompanied the first relief expedition reported on his return to Mankato that the squaws were picking half-digested kernels of grain out of horse manure and boiling them up for soup. Bishop Whipple repeated this story in numerous letters to government officials and also asserted that many previously respectable women had turned to prostitution as the only means of keeping themselves and their children alive. So desperate did the exiles become that some fled across the prairies in midwinter and arrived, half-starved and nearly frozen, at Faribault, having eaten nothing but roots dug from the frozen ground along the way.[38] The Winnebagos, whose number included a higher proportion of men, started leaving the reservation almost as soon as they arrived, most of them going to the Omaha reservation. Eventually, in 1865, the *fait accompli* of their flight was recognized by the government, and a treaty was made with the Omahas granting the Winnebagos part of their reservation.[39]

[37] T. S. Williamson, *et al.*, to Dole and Usher, September 8, 1864 (in Com. of Indian Affairs, *Annual Report*, 1864, p. 421); U.S. *Statutes at Large*, XIII, 180, 550, 559; Com. of Indian Affairs, *Annual Report*, 1865, pp. 189, 221. The amount appropriated in 1864 and 1865 was $100,000 each year, supplemented in the latter year by $54,711.83 for the Santees, the Winnebagos, and the Yanktons, to replace goods lost by the burning of the *Welcome* at St. Louis on July 15, 1864. The second "Moscow expedition" is discussed in the Mankato *Weekly Record*, November 26, 1864. For a complete account of these expeditions, see William E. Lass, "The 'Moscow Expedition,'" *Minnesota History*, XXXIX (Summer 1965), 227–240.

[38] Mankato *Weekly Record*, January 16, 1864; Whipple to Secretary of Interior James Harlan, June 1, 1866, NARS, RG 75, LR; Faribault *Democrat*, March 31, 1876 (quoting a letter from Whipple to New York *Times*, March 3, 1876). The letter to the *Weekly Record* from "One Who Has Been There" said of conditions at Crow Creek: "The condemned and rotten pork which was sold at the old Agency in this county [Winnebago Agency] last fall for $1.25 per hundred, was carted across the country with us, and is now being retailed to the Indians by the traders at 25 cents per pound." The soldiers were said to have tried to burn the pork in their stoves, "but the stench was so awful that they could not remain in their tents."

[39] Com. of Indian Affairs, *Annual Report*, 1863, pp. 321–323; George B. Graff to Dole, March 27, 1864; O. H. Irish to Dole, March 28, 1864; John A. Burbank to H. B. Branch, December 23, 1863; Burbank to Dole, January 11 and October 19, 1864; Robert W. Furnas to William M. Albin, September 28, 1864, NARS, RG 75, LR,

The blame for keeping the Santees at Crow Creek rests partly with Superintendent Thompson, who refused to admit that he had made a mistake, partly on the preoccupation of the country with the Civil War, and partly on a failure of communication between the agent at Crow Creek and his superiors in Washington. Although Galbraith put in a brief appearance at the reservation, he was speedily assigned to work with the commission evaluating depredations claims, and the Winnebago agent, St. A. D. Balcombe, was placed in charge of the Santees.[40] Whatever Balcombe may have thought of Crow Creek, he does not seem to have exerted himself at first to have the Indians moved. Even when Indian Bureau officials requested his opinion on the suitability of the reservation, he apparently neglected to reply until prodded again and again. When he did write, no attention was paid to what he said. Once the commissioner refused to approve an additional expenditure for provisions on the ground that the Indians should sustain themselves partly by hunting. Yet Balcombe had earlier informed him that they had been disarmed and that the military commanders refused to let them hunt off the reservation.[41]

Miserable as conditions at Crow Creek were, some effort was made to re-establish the institutions of the old reservation. As soon as Thompson had arrived, late in May, he had set about erecting temporary buildings, surveying the reservation, and plowing the ground on which it was hoped a crop might be raised. Since the Sioux and the Winnebagos were to be given adjoining reservations, he thought it advisable to locate the agency on the line between them so that it could serve both. A stockade four hundred feet square was constructed for the protection of

---

Winnebago Agency; Mankato *Weekly Record*, March 19, June 4, and September 3, 1864; Charles J. Kappler, comp. and ed., *Indian Affairs, Laws and Treaties*, II (Washington: Government Printing Office, 1904), 872–874.

[40] Dole to Thomspon, May 30, 1863, NARS, RG 75, LS; Thompson to Galbraith, June 23, 1863; Thompson to Dole, June 24, 1863; Thompson to St. A. D. Balcombe, December 18, 1863, NARS, RG 75, LR, Northern Superintendency; Dole to Balcombe, February 8, 1864, NARS, RG 75, LS. John Williamson wrote Riggs: "I think that Supt Thompson will bring every influence to build up this Agency and as long as this Administration lasts will succeed." Thompson, he thought, was involved in a scheme to divert trade to the upper Missouri via Mankato by building a line of forts of which that at Crow Creek was one. See J. P. Williamson to Riggs, December 26, 1963, Riggs Papers.

[41] Acting Commissioner Charles E. Mix to Balcombe, August 12, 1863, NARS, RG 75, LS; Thompson to Balcombe, December 18, 1863, NARS, RG 75, LR, Northern Superintendency.

the agency buildings and personnel. A sawmill was set up to prepare the cottonwood and other timber for use in the buildings, and roads were cut so that the cattle could be brought to the river for watering. Except for the plowing, which was wasted effort, these undertakings produced quite a satisfactory agency plant by the end of the summer.[42]

The stockade and the small contingent of troops stationed there were insufficient protection, according to Balcombe, who reported in 1864 that it had been a year "full of fears anxieties and misfortunes." The agent and the Indians alike were acutely aware that they were surrounded by hostile Sioux, who looked with contempt on both their tribesmen who had surrendered and the alien Winnebagos. Consequently both tribes "lived in fear and trembling close to the stockade, in one consolidated community" instead of scattering on farms as they were supposed to do. When a report reached the agency that even the few troops stationed there would be withdrawn, Balcombe, in a paroxysm of terror, appealed to the commissioner for two companies of soldiers, to be subject exclusively to his orders, independent of the commanding officer of the district. He insisted that if the troops left, no whites or Winnebagos would stay at the agency. Commissioner Dole called this request "strange" and refused to consider it. Shortly afterward General Sully took away the cannon and all the troops except an infantry lieutenant, twelve infantrymen, and ten cavalrymen. One of the bastions to the stockade had never been completed, and another had recently burned. The agency was obviously in no condition to defend itself against a determined attack by the western Sioux whom Sully's campaign had stirred up.[43]

Balcombe's personal anxiety may account in large measure for the semihysterical quality of his reports, but he had become convinced, by the end of the second summer of drought that the Indians were right in believing that nothing could be grown at Crow Creek. Unless it was the government's plan to let them become extinct, they would have to be placed in a more satisfactory location. Thompson did not, however, share Balcombe's feelings. In his report to the commissioner accompanying that of the agent, he largely negated the effect of the latter by saying that the Sioux were well pleased with the location, and if it were not for the faultfinding of the Winnebagos and the disposition of the whites to tell them the reservation was no good, all would be well.[44]

[42] Com. of Indian Affairs, *Annual Report*, 1863, pp. 310–311, 317–318; 1864, p. 408; J. P. Williamson to Mrs. Stephen R. Riggs, September 26, [1863], Riggs Papers.

[43] Com. of Indian Affairs, *Annual Report*, 1864, pp. 408–411, 422–423.

[44] *Ibid.*, 1864, pp. 411–412, 402.

The missions provided the only hopeful note in Balcombe's report for 1864. The two missionaries who had accompanied the Indians to their new home had soon made an effort to re-establish the schools they had operated in Minnesota. Williamson opened a day school early in December which ran during the following winter with an average attendance of about a hundred. Most of the scholars were large, said Williamson, adding, "Nearly all the small children died in 1863. . . ." He reported that, whereas in 1862 only 20 of these people professed Christianity, now his congregation numbered 222. Balcombe reported that 412 Sioux had withdrawn from the tribe and wanted the "religion of civilization." Intemperance was no longer a problem, even though transients passing through provided an occasional source of whiskey.[45]

The condition of the Santee Sioux improved somewhat in 1865. For one thing, they escaped from the obstinacy of Thompson and the timorousness of Balcombe. As part of a general administrative reorganization in the Indian Bureau, the Northern Superintendency was transferred that spring from St. Paul to Omaha, and the Crow Creek agency was placed under the Dakota Superintendency. Newton Edmunds, governor of Dakota Territory and ex officio superintendent of Indian affairs, was a native of Michigan who had previously served as a clerk in the Surveyor General's office. His older brother, James M. Edmunds, was commissioner of the General Land Office. After his nomination to the governorship, Edmunds had taken an especially active interest in Indian affairs. Now he followed the time-honored practice of replacing the agent and other personnel at the agency with men of his own choosing. Balcombe, who had never been formally appointed agent for the Sioux, was instructed to follow the majority of the Winnebagos and locate his agency on the land purchased for them from the Omahas. Simultaneously James M. Stone was appointed agent for the "Sioux of the Mississippi," as the Santees were still officially called.[46]

Stone seems to have made a favorable impression on missionary Williamson, who wrote his father that the new agent was a "quiet unassuming man" and told Riggs: "I think the Agent will treat the Ind's kindly, and make a fair distribution of what is sent them, but that the funds will all be managed by the Governor (Edmunds) and other men

[45] *Ibid.*, 1864, pp. 413–415.

[46] *Ibid.*, 1865, pp. 47–48; Dole to Thompson, March 24, 1865; Dole to Balcombe, March 25, 1865; Dole to James M. Stone, March 27, 1865; Dole to Newton Edmunds, March 27, 1865, NARS, RG 75, LS; Herbert S. Schell, *History of South Dakota* (Lincoln: University of Nebraska Press, 1961), pp. 105–106.

not here."[47] Like most Indian agents in their first report, Stone professed to have found everything in wretched shape on his arrival. One bastion of the stockade had no roof; plastering was needed; the fences were in poor condition; the prairie sod was badly broken; only 2 cows and 17 wagons, mostly in poor condition, had been turned over to him; of 170 ox-yokes, only 30 could be made serviceable; the boiler in the sawmill was leaky; the logs turned over to him were largely rotten; the powder magazine was a damp hole seven by nine feet; and beef that had been packed in snow had spoiled when warm weather came.[48]

But Stone had great faith in the future of Crow Creek. The corn crop looked good, and although the potatoes had been ravaged by grasshoppers and bugs, he felt sure that the Indians were on their way to self-sufficiency. The supply problem was improving, too. Disdaining another Moscow expedition, Governor Edmunds industriously set about supplying Crow Creek from local sources, cutting some bureaucratic corners to do so. In justification of his failure to follow official directives, he reported that the Indians said "they have never before had as good beef or as much of it." According to Edmunds, they were also well pleased with their new agent and were generally doing better. About 3,000 bushels of corn were raised that year, enough to save many from starvation.[49]

All was not rosy, however, despite Edmunds' optimistic view of the situation. Many of the Indians were still living in the cloth tipis they had brought with them from Minnesota or in bark shanties, which the governor described as "totally unfitted for winter." Stone persuaded fifteen of the most industrious to build log houses, and Edmunds urged the expenditure of a thousand dollars toward the construction of more. The hundred or so able-bodied men in the group were now permitted to hunt off the reservation, but when a party tried to enter the area east of the James River, where bison were plentiful, they were turned back by scouts acting under instructions from Joseph R. Brown and had to return with but little meat. Any Sioux from west of the James were regarded as hostile, regardless of their pedigree. Major Robert H. Rose, commanding at Fort Wadsworth, wrote Stone to that effect in the sum-

    [47] J. P. Williamson to T. S. Williamson, June 20, 1865, Williamson Papers, Minnesota Historical Society; J. P. Williamson to Riggs, June 21, 1865, Riggs Papers.

    [48] Com. of Indian Affairs, *Annual Report*, 1865, pp. 219–220.

    [49] *Ibid.*, 1865, pp. 228–229; Edmunds to Commissioner Dennis N. Cooley, January 31, 1866, NARS, RG 75, LR.

mer of 1865, adding ominously *"And I take no prisoners."* Edmunds thought this threat should be sufficient grounds for removing Rose from his command, if not for dismissing him from the service, but the military were not accustomed to paying much attention to the opinions of men in the Indian Service. The Santees were unhappy about their exclusion from the area east of the James, especially since their relatives, the Sissetons, now gathered around Fort Wadsworth, were permitted to hunt there.[50]

The Santee Sioux diminished steadily in number throughout the years they spent at Crow Creek, despite occasional accessions as the military rounded up fugitives during the expeditions of 1863 and 1864. Late in August, 1863, 116 prisoners were turned over to Colonel Stephen Miller at Fort Snelling, and the next winter 60 or 70 more surrendered. Most if not all of them were eventually delivered to Crow Creek, as were those who fled the reservation that winter and returned to Minnesota. Then, in 1864, some of the convicted men at Davenport were released and sent, together with a number of women and children—54 in all—to the agency. Yet when Stone took charge in June, 1865, he found only 1,043 Indians, more than 900 of them women, at Crow Creek.[51] Thus the death rate must have remained high even after the first six months, when casualties were heaviest.

Unknown to the hapless Indians, events were taking place in Washington and elsewhere that were to result in their removal from Crow Creek in the spring of 1866. Brief as it was, the Crow Creek episode was an important period in the history of the Santee Sioux. Following upon the total disorganization of their society at the end of the uprising, it marked the beginning of new patterns of organization. The seven Mdewakanton bands had retained their identity, despite split-offs, during the reservation period of 1853–1862. They were still used for census purposes in the camp at Fort Snelling and seem to have formed the basis for the organization of the convicts at Camp McClellan. But the removal to Crow Creek and the three years there proved too much for the survival of these long-established tribal divisions. Early in 1866,

[50] Com. of Indian Affairs, *Annual Report*, 1865, pp. 189, 221; Stone to Cooley, October 4 and November 2, 1865, NARS, RG 75, LR.
[51] C. G. Wykoff to Dole, September 24, 1863; Sibley to Thompson, May 14, 1864; Thompson to Dole, June 16, 1864, NARS, RG 75, LR; Sibley to Thompson, October 12, 1864; Thompson to Balcombe, October 14, 1864, NARS, RG 75, LR, Northern Superintendency; Com. of Indian Affairs, *Annual Report*, 1865, p. 228.

Agent Stone reported that he had appointed a chief of a band of Santees made up of remnants of six old bands.[52] Although he probably
overestimated his ability to make chiefs that the tribe would accept, his
statement suggests that the old loyalties were breaking down and also
that the initiative had passed from the Indians themselves to the representatives of the white man's government in Washington. As with so
many other Indian tribes in the period after the Civil War, the dependence on the white man for much of their material culture was being
extended to a dependence on him for their social and political organization as well. Coupled with the mass acceptance of Christianity, this
meant that the Santee Sioux were losing their specifically Indian cultural identity. The rest of their story is essentially a chronicle of the
process by which this loss came about and the sporadic and largely ineffectual efforts to arrest it.

[52] Stone to Edmunds, February 6, 1865, NARS, RG 75, LR.

CHAPTER **8**

Recovery at Niobrara

CROW CREEK was visited in the fall of 1865 by a peace commission consisting of Governor Edmunds, who acted as chairman; Edward B. Taylor, newly appointed Northern Superintendent; Generals Henry H. Sibley and Samuel R. Curtis; Orrin Guernsey; and the Reverend Henry W. Reed, who had been previously appointed to investigate conditions there. Their visit was brief, but in their official report they spoke "in the strongest possible terms" on the "state of semi-starvation for two years" and recommended that the Santees be moved.[1] Although several possible sites for a new home were considered, Superintendent Taylor, who seems to have been the most influential member of the commission, favored an area at the mouth of the Niobrara River in northeastern Nebraska Territory. He plugged for this location while in Washington in February, 1866, and Indian Commissioner Dennis N. Cooley, after consultation with Reed and the two generals, approved the recommendation. On February 27 an executive order was issued withdrawing from pre-emption and sale four townships in what is now Knox County.[2]

[1] Com. of Indian Affairs, *Annual Report*, 1866, p. 230.

[2] *Ibid.*, 1866, p. 223; Charles J. Kappler, comp. and ed., *Indian Affairs, Laws and Treaties*, I (Washington: Government Printing Office, 1904), 861. The establishment of the Santee Reservation is discussed in greater detail in my article "The Establishment of the Santee Reservation, 1866–1869" in *Nebraska History*, XLV (March 1964), 59–97, of which the first part of this chapter is a summary.

The chief advantage of this site, as Taylor saw it, was that it had plenty of timber and at least two thousand acres of tillable land. In addition, being lower on the Missouri, it would be much easier to supply than Crow Creek. Taylor estimated that the cost of transportation could be cut in half at once, and he professed to believe that the Indians could be made self-supporting by October of 1867, after which the only cost to the government would be that of running the agency. Although a few settlers—not over half a dozen, Taylor thought—had taken claims on the land, their claims could be repurchased at a cost only slightly above the government price of public lands.[3]

As soon as Taylor's plan became known, opposition developed in Dakota Territory, where commercial interests wanted to retain the patronage of the Crow Creek agency. The Yankton newspaper charged that the removal plan was a scheme concocted by Nebraska politicians for the benefit of their state, and Governor Edmunds, who seems not to have been consulted in the choice of a new location, argued that, given another year, Agent Stone could raise an abundance of food at Crow Creek, where the soil was just as good as at Niobrara and where the government had erected several thousand dollars' worth of buildings.[4]

Nothing came of Edmunds' pleas, made early in April, for by that time plans for the removal of the Indians were well under way. The first to go to the new reservation were the prisoners at Davenport. The number of fugitives captured by the military since 1863 almost equaled the 120 deaths in the prison, so that by 1866 there were still 177 prisoners and 70 women and children. After the pardoning of 30 or 40 in 1864, Thomas S. Williamson and others had worked actively for the release of the rest. Commissioner Cooley was kindly disposed toward them, saying in his report for 1865: "The only offence of which many of them appear to have been guilty is that of being Sioux Indians, and of having, when a part of their people committed the terrible outrages in Minnesota, taken part with them so far as to fly when pursued by the troops," and indicating that plans were under consideration for their release.[5]

The stage was thus set for their removal to Nebraska. Upon the rec-

[3] Com. of Indian Affairs, *Annual Report*, 1866, pp. 223–224; Edward B. Taylor to Commissioner Dennis N. Cooley, April 6, 1866, NARS, RG 75, LR.

[4] *Union and Dakotaian* (Yankton), May 26, 1866; Governor Newton Edmunds to Cooley, March 17 and April 6, 1866, NARS, RG 75, LR.

[5] Stephen R. Riggs, *Mary and I: Forty Years with the Sioux* (Boston: Congregational Sunday-School and Publishing Society, 1880), pp. 220–223; Com. of Indian Affairs, *Annual Report*, 1865, p. 27; George E. H. Day to Stephen R. Riggs, October 27, 1865, Riggs Papers.

ommendation of General Alfred Sully, commanding the Department of Iowa, and General John Pope, the War Department agreed to turn the prisoners and their families over to the Indian Bureau. After some confusion caused by conflicting orders as to whether the War Department or the Interior Department was to furnish transportation and the failure of the agent assigned to receive and accompany them to appear before their departure from Davenport, the 247 Indians were finally placed on board the steamboat *Pembina* on April 10 for the trip to St. Louis, where they were transferred to the *Dora* and sent up the Missouri.[6] The trip was tedious and uneventful. The Indians took in the sights of St. Louis during their stop there, and one is said to have boasted of killing and scalping a dozen white women during the uprising. For the most part, however, they spent their time making pipes and other articles for sale along the way. They held twice-weekly religious services and devoted much time to reading books in Dakota.[7]

After their arrival at the Niobrara about the middle of May, the *Dora* went on up the river with supplies for Fort Rice. It had been expected to bring down the Crow Creek people on its return trip, but hitches developed, and the Indians and their property had to be transported by land. The failure of the *Dora* to bring a hundred sacks of flour, as it had been expected to do, left the people at Crow Creek in a difficult plight. With supplies on hand for only ten days, Reed, serving as special agent, decided to send the old and infirm in wagons with some provisions, in hopes of reaching Fort Randall before their supplies were exhausted. They were sent on their way May 28, and the rest of the population went on foot or horseback, reaching Niobrara on June 11.[8] The whole operation had been rather badly managed, through the fault of no one in particular, but the reunion of the former prisoners with their families compensated for much of the inconvenience.

[6] General Alfred Sully to John P. Sherburne, Assistant Adjutant General, Department of the Missouri, December 29, 1865; Secretary of Interior James Harlan to Secretary of War E. M. Stanton, January 13, 1866; E. Schriver, Inspector General, to Harlan, January 30, 1866; Cooley to Harlan, March 26, 1866; Harlan to Cooley, March 27, 1866; General John Pope to Harlan, March 29, 1866; Jedediah Brown to Harlan, April 14, 1866; E. Kilpatrick to Cooley, May 3, 1866; Kilpatrick to Harlan, April 10 and 14, 1866, NARS, RG 75, LR; Com. of Indian Affairs, *Annual Report*, 1866, pp. 233–234.

[7] Com. of Indian Affairs, Annual Report, 1866, p. 234; St. Louis *Democrat*, April 14, 1866 (cited in Mankato *Weekly Record*, April 28, 1866).

[8] Kilpatrick to Harlan, April 14, 1866; E. B. Taylor to Cooley, May 3, 1866; Henry W. Reed to Cooley, May 25, 1866; J. Brown to Harlan, June 18, 1866, NARS, RG 75, LR; Com. of Indian Affairs, *Annual Report*, 1866, p. 232.

Preparations for their arrival had been under way for some time. Before the prisoners had arrived, Taylor had requisitioned a large hotel building at the Niobrara townsite and had bought two small buildings for storehouses. When the first Indians arrived, they were set to work planting corn and potatoes on some land already broken by one of the white settlers in the vicinity. The first site of the agency was at the townsite, about a mile east of the present town of Niobrara. There the Indians lived in tents, and the missionaries, their families, and other white people occupied the hotel. Very few improvements were made here, and those of a temporary nature. Because of lack of wood and also because of complaints from settlers that the Indians were committing minor depredations, they were removed that fall to winter quarters near the mouth of Bazile Creek, three or four miles down the Missouri from the townsite. The agency was re-established there, and various buildings, including warehouses, sleeping quarters for the employees, an agency office, a blacksmith shop, and an interpreter's house, were erected before cold weather set in. All the buildings were one-story, sod-roofed affairs of logs, intended for only temporary occupancy. The missionaries built their own houses, of the same materials and much the same construction.[9]

The tentativeness of these successive locations cannot have failed to impress the Indians with the uncertainty of their tenure in this new home. Although the amount of land withheld from entry and sale had been nearly doubled by a second executive order on July 20, the lands cannot be spoken of as a reservation in the customary sense of a permanent home guaranteed to the Indians by treaty with the United States government. Secretary Harlan's letter requesting the original withdrawal of four townships from the market stipulated that the withdrawal should be only temporary, "until the action of Congress be had, with a view to the setting apart of these townships as a reservation for the Santee Sioux Indians. . . ."[10] And until such action should be taken, there was nothing to prevent the government from moving the Indians anywhere it pleased.

[9] E. B. Taylor to Cooley, May 3, 1866; Hampton B. Denman to Commissioner Lewis V. Bogy, January 8, 1867; E. B. Taylor to Cooley, October 20, 1866, NARS, RG 75, LR; Com. of Indian Affairs, *Annual Report*, 1866, p. 243; Riggs, *Mary and I*, p. 232; Winifred W. Barton, *John P. Williamson, a Brother to the Sioux* (Chicago: Fleming H. Revell Co., 1919), p. 109; John P. Williamson to Thomas S. Williamson, September 17, 1866, and to Mrs. Thomas S. Williamson, November 3, 1866, Williamson Papers; John P. Williamson to Stephen R. Riggs, November 12, 1866, Riggs Papers.

[10] Kappler, *Indian Affairs, Laws and Treaties*, I, 861–862.

The uncertainty of the Indians' position, coupled with their own dissatisfaction, provided an opportunity for the Dakota politicians to work for their removal. Even before they arrived at Niobrara, a storm of protest went up from the white settlers on the opposite side of the Missouri. Although the complaints stressed the danger to the white population from "these hell hounds of Minnesota notoriety," as territorial delegate Walter A. Burleigh called them, the real motives seem to have been a desire to regain the patronage of the agency. When the Dakota politicians proposed a new home for the Santee Sioux, they suggested not some remote spot farther west, but a tract of land between the James and Big Sioux rivers, in eastern Dakota. This scheme was opposed, for different reasons, by the congressional delegations from Nebraska, Iowa, and Minnesota, by Episcopal missionary Samuel D. Hinman, and by the Indian Bureau itself. The plan went as far as the issuance of an executive order, dated March 20, 1867, closing the proposed reservation to white settlement, but Hinman persuaded the chiefs to reject it, and nothing further came of it.[11]

Although the scheme was defeated, the Santees were not quite through moving. In the spring of 1867 they were instructed to move to a point a few miles below the agency and plant there one season, "with the assurance that if they were pleased with the location it would be secured to them as a permanent home."[12] This proposed new location, called Breckenridge after a city projected for the site in the early days, was said to be favored by the Indians and had the advantage, as the new superintendent, Hampton B. Denman, saw it, of being well supplied with hardwood timber. The Bazile Creek site had been virtually denuded of timber during the Indians' brief stay there, and the nearest timber was at Breckenridge, where much of the lumber used in the construction of houses and other buildings the previous fall had been obtained.[13]

On the strength of the promise made to the Indians, Agent Stone

[11] Com. of Indian Affairs, *Annual Report*, 1866, p. 229; Memorial to the President of the United States Relative to the Removal of the Santee Band of Sioux Indians, January 10, 1867; Ignatius Donnelly and William Windom to Secretary of Interior Orville Browning, March 20, 1867, NARS, RG 75, LR; *Congressional Globe*, 39th Cong., 1st Sess., p. 3062; Kappler, *Indian Affairs, Laws and Treaties*, I, 897–898; J. P. Williamson to Riggs, May 3, 1867, Riggs Papers.

[12] Com. of Indian Affairs, *Annual Report*, 1868, p. 246.

[13] James M. Stone to Denman, May 27, 1867; Denman to Bogy, January 8, 1867, NARS, RG 75, LR; J. P. Williamson to Mrs. T. S. Williamson, November 3, 1866, Williamson Papers.

went ahead during the summer of 1867 and moved the agency buildings to the new site. As soon as the breaking plows that had been ordered arrived, early in June, he set part of the teams to breaking new
land there while the rest were used to haul the buildings. About two
thirds of the plowing that year was done in the Breckenridge vicinity,
the rest at the old Bazile Creek site. A good deal was accomplished that
summer, and if grasshoppers had not made one of their periodic incursions and destroyed the crops, it might have marked a real step
toward self-sufficiency for the Santees.[14]

Grasshoppers were not the only source of trouble that summer, however. Although the new agency site was on previously reserved lands,
some of the most valuable timber lay just east of the reservation boundary, and in order to acquire it (and for other reasons), Denman recommended the addition of one full and one fractional township to the
east of the reservation as it then existed. He also recommended that two
of the originally reserved townships, including that on which the townsite of Niobrara was located, be restored to the market. His suggestions
were not acted upon immediately, and in the interval certain Dakota
citizens got wind of the plan and set about taking claims on the sections
containing the timber Denman especially wished to reserve. Technically
within their rights, since no order had been issued withdrawing this
land from entry, they refused to move away when Stone informed them
that the land where they were cutting timber and building a house had
been reserved for the Indians.[15] Under the impression that the lands
had already been withdrawn, Hinman had begun building a mission,
when he was interrupted by a pair of "meddlesome squatters from
Dacota," as Denman called them. The wheels of bureaucracy grind
slowly, and it was not until November 16 that an executive order was
finally issued adding to the reservation the lands desired by Denman
and restoring to the market the township containing the townsite.[16]

A delegation of Indians who had gone to Washington early in 1867
to consider the proposal to remove them to Dakota had been told then
that another peace commission would visit them the next summer.
When it arrived, about harvest time, its message was not calculated to
please the Indians. According to Agent Stone, they were told "that

[14] Stone to Denman, May 31, June 5, and September 21, 1867, NARS, RG 75, LR.

[15] Denman to Bogy, January 8, 1867; Stone to Denman, August 30, 1867, *ibid.*

[16] Samuel D. Hinman to Denman, August 30, 1867; Denman to Acting Commissioner Charles E. Mix, September 5 and 6, 1867, *ibid.*; Kappler, *Indian Affairs, Laws
and Treaties*, I, 862.

they must leave here next Summer, that none would be allowed to remain unless they abandoned their tribal relations and relied upon their own exertions for support."[17] Although this threat was doubtless intended to stimulate the Santees to greater efforts in their own behalf, its effects were in fact demoralizing. The tribesmen were unwilling to give up their tribal relations, and they were unprepared to take upon themselves the full task of their support. The result was that instead of working harder, they almost gave up working at all. Stone and Denman believed that, after the "debased and indolent life led by these Indians" since leaving Minnesota, it would take several years of intensive training before they could be placed on their own, and instead of being hauled off to a new reservation, they should be allowed to sink their roots deeply into the one where they were.[18]

This recommendation, sensible as it was, did not coincide with the plans of the peace commissioners, who wished to set up a vast reservation—a northern Indian territory—bounded by the forty-sixth parallel, the Missouri River, the Nebraska border, and the 104th meridian. In their report to the President the next January they included the Santees among the tribes to be placed on the reservation, although they added that it might be advisable to let them and the other Nebraska tribes remain where they were and become incorporated with the citizens of the state. They persuaded the Santees to allow their chiefs and headmen to inspect the country that had been designated for them on the proposed reservation, but it was found to be much like Crow Creek. To their objections, voiced by the agent and superintendent, the only comfort Commissioner Nathaniel G. Taylor could give was the instruction to tell the Indians that it would be "perfectly safe" for them to plant and that they would "not be removed from their present location against their own consent."[19]

His promise apparently did not satisfy the Indians, for at the end of April, 1868, Stone wrote that even those who had formerly been the most industrious were refusing to plant this year. They expected the peace commission back that summer, to tell them to move. With an unconscious irony that one more familiar with their history would have noticed, Stone observed that their uncertainty tended to weaken their

[17] Stone to Denman, November 30, 1867, NARS, RG 75, LR.

[18] Stone to Denman, January 31, 1868; Denman to Commissioner Nathaniel G. Taylor, February 3 and 17, 1868, *ibid.*

[19] Com. of Indian Affairs, *Annual Report*, 1868, pp. 46, 246–247; N. G. Taylor to Denman, March 3, 1868, NARS, RG 75, LR.

respect for the government and for their agent, and might eventually destroy their faith in the integrity of the men in charge of that government.[20] Denman repeatedly went to bat for the Santees. Submitting Stone's remarks to the commissioner, he added his own comment that they had suffered enough in the previous six years to atone for any crimes they might have committed during the uprising and that it was now time to show "magnanimity and kindness." In his official report for 1867 he had stressed their atonement:

> All treaties with these Indians have been abrogated, their annuities forfeited, their splendid reservation of valuable land in Minnesota confiscated by the government, their numbers sadly reduced by starvation and disease; they have been humiliated to the dust, and in all these terrible penalties the innocent have suffered with the guilty.

He asked for a treaty commission to guarantee them their present reservation and recommended that part of their annuities be restored.[21]

When another peace commission went up the Missouri in June, 1868, it stopped at the Santee Agency just long enough to gather the chiefs and virtually force them to accompany the party to Fort Rice. The outlook was ominous. Williamson wrote to his father that "Stone says the Commissioners talked more independent than last year. They said they had made up their minds the Santees could not stay in Nebraska so they were going [to] tell them at once that they had to go up in the new T[erritory] when they came to council. It was all a humbug to ask what they wanted when the dose was all ready cut & dried."[22] The outcome was not so bad as he and the Indians expected, however. When the chiefs returned from Fort Rice, they had signed, on behalf of the Santees, the 1868 treaty of Fort Laramie with the Sioux. The provisions of that treaty which affected the Santees were those providing for the allotment of lands to anyone desiring to farm. The act of March 3, 1863, had contained a similar provision, but now the Indians' consent was obtained and the size of the proposed allotments increased from 80 to 160 acres. According to Stone's annual report, the commissioners assured the Indians that if they would adopt white customs, take land in severalty, and begin farming, the government would allow them to remain where they were and assist them generously in their efforts.[23]

[20] Stone to Denman, April 30, 1868, *ibid.*

[21] Denman to N. G. Taylor, June 12, 1868, *ibid.*; Com. of Indian Affairs, *Annual Report*, 1867, p. 265.

[22] J. P. Williamson to T. S. Williamson, June 19, 1868, Williamson Papers.

[23] Com. of Indian Affairs, *Annual Report*, 1868, p. 247; Kappler, *Indian Affairs, Laws and Treaties*, II, 999–1000.

The 1868 Fort Laramie treaty, the last participated in by the Santee Sioux, provided the basis for most legislation concerning them in subsequent years. If its terms left their situation still somewhat indefinite, the allotment provision gave them some measure of security.

The stage which may properly be called the establishment of the Santee Reservation came to an end in the summer of 1869, when the boundaries were finally determined. To forestall threatened immigration into a township adjacent to the reservation, an executive order was issued on August 31 withdrawing it from entry and sale; at the same time three townships south and southwest of Niobrara which had never been occupied by the Santees were restored to the market. These changes left the Santee Reservation a compact rectangular tract of land, twelve miles from east to west and averaging about fifteen miles from north to south, encompassing 115,075.92 acres. It included some good agricultural land, particularly in the southern and eastern parts and along the streams, but a great deal of it was suited only for grazing. One superintendent, after examining the reservation, described it as "the roughest and least valuable tract of country I have seen in Nebraska, a large part of it being bluffs and steep hills only fit for pasturage." His successor doubted that the bluff land, covered with wild sage and cactus, was good even for pasture, except in the ravines. In the 1890's, when the potentialities of the area had been more fully revealed, a member of Congress commented that "for the past three or four years, on account of the extreme drought, it would be difficult to graze one steer on five acres of these high lands on the Missouri bluffs." [24] Though parts of the Santee Reservation, especially the wild, rugged area called the Devil's Nest, possess a certain austere beauty, agriculturally it was no substitute for the rich lands of the Minnesota valley taken from the Indians by Congress in 1863.

The year 1869 brought other changes to the Santee Sioux. As part of President Grant's revamping of Indian policy, the Northern Superintendency was turned over to the Society of Friends. Samuel M. Janney replaced Denman as superintendent, and his brother, Asa M. Janney, was appointed Santee agent. The Janneys, natives of Loudoun County, Virginia, were both in their late sixties when they came to Nebraska and were lifelong members of the Society. Samuel, the elder by two years, was the author of at least ten books and pamphlets, including

[24] Hinman to Commissioner Ely S. Parker, June 29, 1869, NARS, RG 75, LR; Samuel M. Janney to Parker, August 19, 1871; Barclay White to Parker, January 11, 1872, NARS, RG 75, LR, Santee Sioux Agency; Kappler, *Indian Affairs, Laws and Treaties*, I, 862–864; 54th Cong., 2nd Sess., *S. Rpt. 1362*, p. 7.

some poetry on Indian themes. He had at one time operated a girls' boarding school in Virginia and had interested himself in Negro education before the Civil War. The two men were full of ideas about the management of the agency, ideas which, for better or worse, continued to affect the Santee Sioux long after the Janneys had left office.[25]

One of the pet schemes nursed by Agent Janney, who had been a miller in his home state, was to build a gristmill on Bazile Creek, move the agency there, and establish the Indians on farms surrounding this administrative center. There was no flour mill within forty miles, and it was thought that a considerable saving could be made by grinding the wheat raised by the Indians rather than shipping in flour, as had been done in the past. Shortly after he took office, Janney began drawing up specifications for a mill, and construction got under way in 1870. After several delays, the mill was finally ready to start grinding in June, 1871. No sooner had it begun operating, however, than portions of the dam gave way because of the porous nature of the soil. Such accidents continued to interrupt milling activities throughout the years the mill was in operation. A fine three-story chalkstone structure, it speedily became a liability rather than an asset to the agency and eventually had to be abandoned.[26]

Janney's hopes for moving the agency to Bazile Creek were never realized, but another project of his, an Indian police force, did become a reality. The idea originated when the chiefs refused to take action against one Mazazidan, who was charged with abusing his wife and stealing horses. Janney and his employees were finally obliged to arrest Mazazidan themselves, but the agent thought it would be better to have a corps of men, carefully selected for reliability, who would be responsible to the agent for the maintenance of law and order. In October, 1869, he asked for, and shortly received, authority to organize a police force to consist of one man from each of the six bands, chosen by the chiefs. At first he tried paying them on a fee basis, so much for each arrest, but he found them overzealous and had to abandon that policy

---

[25] Com. of Indian Affairs, *Annual Report*, 1868, p. 5; Henry E. Fritz, *The Movement for Indian Assimilation, 1860–1890* (Philadelphia: University of Pennsylvania Press, 1963), pp. 73–74; William Bacon Evans, "Dictionary of (American) Quaker Biography," ms in Quaker Collection, Haverford College.

[26] S. M. Janney to Parker, August 20, 1869, and June 17, 1870; Asa M. Janney to S. M. Janney, September 17, 1869, January 10, June 27, and November 12, 1870, NARS, RG 75, LR; A. M. Janney to S. M. Janney, June 4 and 21, 1871, NARS, RG 75, LR, Santee Sioux Agency; Com. of Indian Affairs, *Annual Report*, 1883, p. 108.

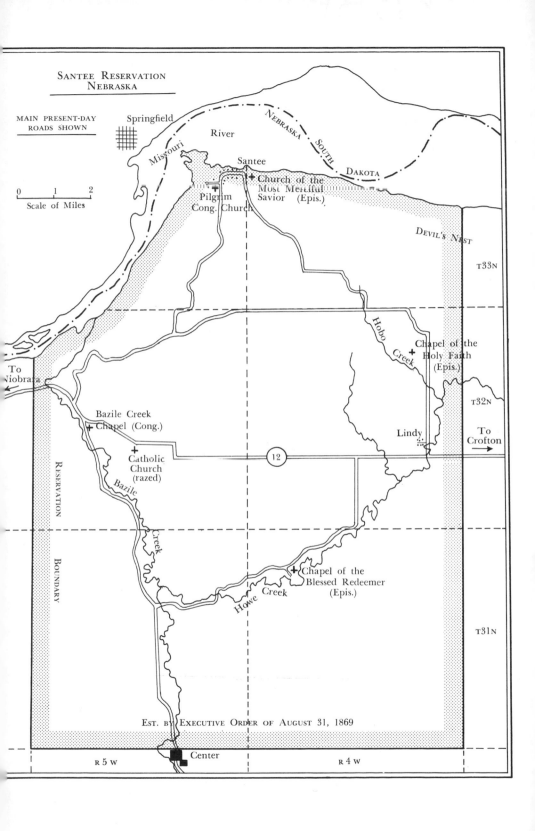

SANTEE RESERVATION
NEBRASKA

MAIN PRESENT-DAY
ROADS SHOWN

0   1   2
Scale of Miles

Springfield

Missouri   River

NEBRASKA   SOUTH

DAKOTA

Santee

Church of the
Most Merciful
Savior   (Epis.)

Pilgrim
Cong. Church

DEVIL'S NEST

T33N

To
Niobrara

Hobo Creek

Chapel of the
Holy Faith
(Epis.)

T32N

Bazile Creek
Chapel (Cong.)

Lindy

To
Crofton

Catholic
Church
(razed)

Bazile

12

RESERVATION   BOUNDARY

Creek

Chapel of the
Blessed Redeemer
(Epis.)

Howe   Creek

T31N

EST. BY EXECUTIVE ORDER OF AUGUST 31, 1869

Center

R 5 W

R 4 W

in favor of a flat wage of five dollars a month.[27] Except for a few intervals, the police force, one of the first such experiments on any reservation, remained a permanent institution at Santee for the rest of the nineteenth century.

Janney's most important achievement during his two years as agent was the allotment of land to the Indians and their settlement on farms scattered over the reservation. The uncertainty of their tenure led some of the more thoughtful to the conviction that their only security lay in the allotment of land in severalty. Fearing that nothing would be done toward this end at Santee, and resenting the authority of the old chiefs, a number of the men who had emancipated themselves from tribalism while at Davenport left the reservation in the spring of 1869, together with their families, and took up homesteads in the valley of the Big Sioux River, in the vicinity of the later town of Flandreau, South Dakota. To forestall similar action by others, Janney began to press strongly for allotment almost as soon as he became agent. He called the Indians together in the summer to tell them of his plans and to get their reaction. He was able to report a favorable response, and sent to Commissioner Ely S. Parker a petition from the chiefs and headmen asking for allotment as a means of preventing a further exodus by men who believed "that the Government does not intend to give them here a permanent home."[28]

Although Janney's first intention was to allot 160 acres to each of two hundred heads of families, under the terms of the 1868 treaty, he later adopted the plan of allotting smaller farms of 40 and 80 acres, as specified in the act of March 3, 1863. He proposed to spend $329 per family, this sum to cover a house (for fifty dollars), a yoke of oxen, a stove, a cow, six sheep, two goats, and two hogs. It would be best, he thought, to settle the valleys first, since they contained the land best suited for the Indians and also because there was a threat of a land grant to a railroad that would follow the course of Bazile Creek.[29] As with his other projects, the allotment did not proceed quite as Janney wished. There were delays in the survey, and the agent was faced with knotty problems such as how much land to give a man with more than one wife. By the end of May, 1870, however, two hundred farms of 80 acres and two

[27] A. M. Janney to S. M. Janney, October 19, 1869, and January 22, 1870, NARS, RG 75, LR.
[28] A. M. Janney to S. M. Janney, June 19, 1869; Chiefs and Head Men to Commissioner Parker, July 19, 1869, *ibid.*
[29] A. M. Janney to S. M. Janney, October 1, 1869, and January 10, 1870; S. M. Janney to Parker, January 3, May 31, and June 17, 1870, *ibid.*

hundred of 40 acres had been laid out. Some Indians had already settled on their farms then, and by the next spring about sixty families
were thus located, despite a drought the previous year which had resulted in an almost complete crop failure.[30]

In his last annual report, made in July, 1871, Janney wrote that about
80 houses had been built on individual allotments and furnished with
windows and doors from a sawmill which he had set up two years
earlier. Most of the houses had tables, often covered with oil cloth; bed-
steads, cupboards, and benches or seats were common now. Over 150
bed quilts had been made in the previous eighteen months. Some
women were raising chickens, and nearly half the families had cows.[31]
It should perhaps be mentioned that the Indians did not receive patents
for these allotments. Instead, they were given certificates which stated
that the United States would hold the title in trust for the holder and
his heirs so long as they continued to occupy the land. It was specified
that these certificates conferred no right except that of possession; further legislation by Congress would be required to convey a fee simple
title.[32]

The decade of the 1870's witnessed a gradual decline in the numbers
of the Santees. From 974 in 1870, the population dwindled to 791 four
years later and to 736 by 1879.[33] The most important single event
among many that conspired to bring about this decline was a devastating smallpox epidemic in 1873. About the middle of August a Santee
prostitute returned from Fort Randall with a case of what the agency
physician diagnosed as syphilis. A scattering of other cases appeared in
following weeks, but not until September 25 was the disease recognized
as smallpox. By that time it was out of control and the physician himself was down with it. In response to an appeal from the agent, Joseph
Webster, the Indian Office sent a special agent to take over and employed a Yankton physician, who hurriedly erected a crude hospital
and vaccinated everyone he could. By mid-December the epidemic had
run its course, after causing at least 70 deaths out of 150 cases. The
effects of the outbreak were similar to those accompanying the great

---

[30] S. M. Janney to Parker, February 8, March 11, and May 31, 1870, *ibid.*; S. M.
Janney to Parker, February 21, 1871; A. M. Janney to S. M. Janney, May 1 and
July 5, 1871, NARS, RG 75, LR, Santee Agency; Com. of Indian Affairs, *Annual
Report*, 1870, p. 227.

[31] Com. of Indian Affairs, *Annual Report*, 1871, pp. 441–443.

[32] Sample certificate (no date), NARS, RG 75, LR, Santee Agency.

[33] A. M. Janney to S. M. Janney, August 20, 1870, NARS, RG 75, LR; Com. of
Indian Affairs, *Annual Report*, 1874, p. 36; 1879, p. 236.

plagues of the past. People fled their homes and camped in isolated places, or else turned the sick out of doors and left them to die in the bushes. Many fled the reservation entirely and never returned.[34] Thus the Santee population was considerably reduced both through the deaths themselves and through the panic-stricken flight of many who did not catch the disease.

Despite this outbreak and repeated crop failures, which also caused many departures from the reservation, the population did not diminish fast enough to suit the white population, now filling up the surrounding country. In 1871 a Niobrara merchant wrote Senator P. W. Hitchcock demanding the restoration to the market of the Santee Reservation. "The Counties below are pretty well settled up," he wrote, "most of the good Land that is not occupied by settlers is in the hands of speculators, the emmigration to our County has been good this year and I think next year all the Land will be taken by actual settlers and if you will be kind enough to get those Santee Indians out of Nebraska, the emmigration will be much larger yet." He claimed, with some exaggeration, that the reservation constituted the best part of the county.[35] When the town of Niobrara acquired a newspaper, it served as a medium of expression for those who wished to have the Indians removed. Edwin A. Fry, the spitfire editor of the Niobrara *Pioneer*, argued that the Indians were kept there in order to furnish jobs for the agency employees, who "generally see that their red charge get paid for loafing."[36]

In the next years hostility to the Sioux, following the Battle of the Little Big Horn and other conflicts, was extended to the Santees, although no one could by that time have taken very seriously any talk of an uprising by them. When removal of the Poncas to Indian Territory was broached in 1877, local sentiment demanded that the Santees accompany them, and an effort was made in Congress to include them in the Ponca removal bill. It was true, said the *Pioneer*, that they dressed as white men, but this was at government expense, as was their farming. When the Poncas were removed, there was some agitation to have the

[34] Dr. George Roberts to Commissioner Edward P. Smith, November 6, 1873; White to E. P. Smith, December 22, 1873, NARS, RG 75, LR, Santee Agency.

[35] H. Westermann to Senator P. W. Hitchcock, November 3, 1871, *ibid.* Westermann was later said to be a contender for the post of Santee agent, to the dismay of the Indians, who got up a petition protesting against his appointment, on grounds that he was a drunkard, "a man who defies God," and an Indian-hater. "For ten years he has been working to drive off the Santee people from this land," said the petition. See Petition to Commissioner Hiram Price, March 14, 1882, *ibid.*

[36] Niobrara (Nebr.) *Pioneer*, October 20, 1874.

Santees placed on the old Ponca Reservation as a buffer between the Teton Sioux and the white settlements. When all these efforts failed, the tactics were changed to a demand that the Indians be allotted lands in severalty, without restrictions. "If the Santee Indians would consent to abandon their tribal relations and receiving government aid, we apprehend that no one would object to their locating in our country," wrote editor Fry—meaning, of course, that their lands would soon find their way into white possession.[37]

Despite the sense of insecurity this constant agitation for removal engendered in the minds of the Santees, there was fairly steady progress toward adoption of the white man's way in the 1870's. Perhaps the most significant evidence of change was the increasing pressure during the decade for abandonment of the old political system with its chiefs, and the substitution of an elective system patterned after that of the white community. Growing out of the experience with the Hazelwood Republic on the old reservation in Minnesota, and encouraged strongly by the American Board missionaries, this movement began to manifest itself in 1873, although there had been tentative moves in that direction before the Flandreau exodus four years earlier. A petition from the Indians requesting the change was prepared in August, 1873, misplaced during the smallpox epidemic, and recovered the next spring, at which time it was forwarded to the Secretary of the Interior. Noting that there was opposition from elements of the tribe, Secretary Delano recommended taking no action until the Indians had discussed the matter in council and determined the will of the majority.[38]

The proposal was presented to the Indians for a vote in June, 1874, and defeated by a slender margin. Agent Webster thought that the republican element was growing in strength and that the Indians should be allowed to work the matter out among themselves.[39] When the subject came up again the next February, the hereditary chiefs, most of whom were old men, presented a petition in which they charged that they could not legally be removed without an act of Congress "at the behest of a mean sentiment, attractive to all young and half-enlightened people, 'that the right of suffrage brings always prosperity.'" Behind the chiefs in promoting this Tory point of view was the Episcopal missionary, Hinman, then as usual at odds with the American Board

[37] *Ibid.*, February 15, 1877; May 31, 1878; and February 28, 1879.
[38] Petition to Commissioner E. P. Smith, August 27, 1873; Webster to E. P. Smith, March 12, 1874; Secretary of Interior Columbus Delano to E. P. Smith, March 28, 1874, NARS, RG 75, LR, Santee Agency; Niobrara *Pioneer*, April 26, 1878.
[39] Webster to E. P. Smith, June 16, 1874, NARS, RG 75, LR, Santee Agency.

people. In reply, the advocates of an elective system, supported by the latter faction, presented a petition pointing out that if the Indians were to adopt white ways, the institution of the chieftainship would have to go.[40]

The movement for elective officers received a stimulus from the death of the head chief, Wabasha, on April 23, 1876. By that time even Hinman had come around to the point of view that perhaps the Santees had outgrown the chieftainship, especially since the chiefs and headmen exerted little influence over the tribe. He suggested that another election be held to determine the future political pattern of the Santees. If they should decide upon an elective system, let the reservation be divided into four districts, with two councilors from each, to hold office for two years.[41] With the missionaries in substantial agreement on the policy to be adopted, the principal obstacles to another election had been removed. When the election was finally held, on January 22, 1878, all seventy-four votes cast favored the abolition of the old system. There were another forty-one eligible voters, ten of whom were also in favor of a change, thought the agent. The pattern proposed by Hinman was followed in the subsequent election for councilmen. Most of those elected were of the "progressive" faction, but Napoleon Wabasha, son of the late chief, was returned from his district.[42] Although the actual power wielded by the council was negligible, the peaceful adoption of the elective system was evidence of the transformation that was taking place among the Santees.

The Indians' relatively rapid acceptance of the white man's political methods was not accompanied by comparable progress toward economic self-sufficiency, despite the best efforts of the successive agents. Perhaps the most serious hindrance to their attempts was the region's susceptibility to drought, grasshopper infestation, and other obstacles to successful agriculture. During the early and middle seventies, years of passably good crops alternated with years of partial or total crop failure.[43] Although conditions toward the end of the decade were better, drought was to return in the 1880's.

[40] Webster to E. P. Smith, February 27 and June 5, 1875; Petition from Chiefs to E. P. Smith, February 19, 1875, *ibid.*

[41] Hinman to Commissioner John Q. Smith, January 16, 1877; Charles Searing to J. Q. Smith, January 8, 1877, NARS, RG 75, LR, Nebraska Agencies.

[42] Isaiah Lightner to Commissioner Ezra A. Hayt, January 23 and April 20, 1878, *ibid.*; Niobrara *Pioneer*, April 26, 1878.

[43] A. M. Janney to Parker, February 21, 1871; Webster to E. P. Smith, June 19, 1874; Webster to White, July 17, 1874, NARS, RG 75, LR, Santee Agency; Com. of Indian Affairs, *Annual Report*, 1871, pp. 442–443; 1872, p. 217; 1873, p. 188; 1874, p. 208; 1875, p. 323; 1876, p. 100.

Convinced that self-sufficiency could be attained if only the Indians would work harder, the Indian Office did its best to encourage them to greater exertions; but it was too far from the scene to time its inducements to the vagaries of the weather. The 1868 treaty had provided for prizes to be awarded to the farmers raising the best crops. Offered at Santee in 1870, they went to two men, both past sixty; no mention was made of the premiums in later years.[44] Another type of stimulus, used repeatedly, was the threat to withdraw rations. But the Indians could hardly be blamed if grasshoppers took their crops, and the government was always prepared, if sometimes tardily, to provide the necessities in such cases. All through the seventies there was talk of reducing or eliminating rations altogether. In 1873—a good year—the Indians received with equanimity the news that their subsistence would be discontinued after the next fiscal year. But after the almost total failure of crops the following summer, missionary Alfred L. Riggs wrote the commissioner that if this policy were carried out, there would be great distress and some Indians would wander off, perhaps permanently.[45] In view of the predicament the Indians were in, the issue of rations was reinstated. Nevertheless, the agent proposed to continue a policy, begun in 1874, by which all able-bodied men between the ages of eighteen and forty-five were required to work for any rations they received. The terms were modified at the beginning of 1876 to include work on their own allotments.[46]

The principal crop on the Santee Reservation was wheat. Wheat-raising began on a significant scale in 1876, when 166 acres were sown, and the agent requested a smaller quantity of wheat in his quarterly estimates for subsistence. The acreage increased rapidly, until in 1879 more than 1,200 acres were sown. Threshing machines, reapers, and cradles became important articles in the agent's requests beginning in

[44] A. M. Janney to Parker, February 21, 1871, NARS, RG 75, LR, Santee Agency; Kappler, *Indian Affairs, Laws and Treaties*, II, 1002.

[45] Com. of Indian Affairs, *Annual Report*, 1873, p. 188; Alfred L. Riggs to E. P. Smith, August 7, 1874, NARS, RG 75, LR, Santee Agency. The food given the Indians was no more than enough to sustain life. In the fall of 1874, for example, each individual received a weekly ration amounting to $4\frac{1}{2}$ pounds of beef, $3\frac{1}{4}$ pounds of flour, $5\frac{1}{2}$ ounces of pork, 3 ounces of sugar, and $1\frac{1}{2}$ ounces of coffee, plus 8/13 ounce of soap and $\frac{1}{4}$ ounce of tobacco. The last four items were issued only once per quarter. The usual practice was to give each head of family a ration ticket, with the number of rations he was entitled to, at the start of each quarter. These were presented at the agency warehouse each Saturday. See Webster to White, December 17, 1873, and Webster to E. P. Smith, November 6, 1874, *ibid.*

[46] Searing to J. Q. Smith, December 15, 1875, *ibid.*

1876. He did not always get what he asked for, but in 1877 three reapers were at work in the fields, and two years later there were thirteen. The increase in other machinery was equally impressive. By the end of the decade sixteen horse rakes and thirteen mowing machines were in operation.[47] All this activity on the reservation, however, did not by any stretch of the imagination mean that the Santees were self-sufficient. There was probably a measure of justice in the *Pioneer*'s charges that government employees were doing their work for them.

Intermittent drought and grasshopper invasions were not the only reasons for the failure of the Santees to become self-supporting. As has always been the case in the management of Indian affairs, the effort in their behalf was subject to frequent interruptions and changes of direction. For one thing, the agency changed hands more often than was desirable. Webster, who had taken over from Janney in 1871, remained only until 1875 and was under attack during much of his term for displaying a lack of energy. Upon his resignation, Charles H. Searing, who had previously been steward at the agency school, took over and held the office for less than two years. Then Isaiah Lightner was nominated for the post, but because his nomination was not acted upon by the Senate, he had to be content with the position of "farmer-in-charge" for about a year, under the jurisdiction of the Yankton agent, John G. Gassman. Conditions at the agency suffered a regression during this interregnum, for Gassman, according to a later special agent, on the first day of his administration, "placed his hand improperly into the U.S. Treasury" and undermined the morale of his employees by his practices. Gassman was removed after a few months and another agent appointed at Yankton. Shortly afterward Lightner's appointment as agent was confirmed, and affairs at the Santee agency began to run more smoothly.[48] All the Santee agents during the seventies were Quakers, apparently hard-working, conscientious men, at least in so far as their correspondence and the absence of evidence to the contrary can furnish a key to their character.

[47] Searing to J. Q. Smith, April 26 and May 1, 1876, *ibid.*; Com. of Indian Affairs, *Annual Report*, 1877, p. 147; 1879, pp. 104–105.

[48] A. M. Janney to S. M. Janney, July 5, 1871; S. M. Janney to Parker, July 11, 1871; William Dorsey to Parker, June 20, 1871; White to Webster, May 29, 1874; B. R. Cowen, Acting Secretary of Interior, to E. P. Smith, August 12, 1875; Searing to E. P. Smith, October 6, 1875, NARS, RG 75, LR, Santee Agency; Lightner to J. Q. Smith, May 1, 1877; White to Hayt, December 8, 1878; John W. Douglas to Hayt, July 2, 1878; White to B. Rush Roberts, October 11, 1877, NARS, RG 75, LR, Nebraska Agencies.

Another reason for the lack of continuity on the reservation was the vulnerability of the Indian Office itself, which was politically controlled and had to respond to the same pressures as other government agencies. The panic of 1873 brought a general retrenchment that was bound to affect the Santee agency in time. Agent Searing complained in 1876 that the "sweeping reduction in the employé force" had produced unfortunate effects at Santee. There was no money to pay the police force, for example, and their services, which had become quite valuable, had had to be dispensed with. During that summer the gristmill was idle and the various shops closed most of the time owing to a lack of men to operate them.[49] Janney's white elephant, the gristmill, was a source of much annoyance and may have played a role in delaying the agricultural progress of the Santees. At times when it was idle due to low water or a washout at the dam, the agent had to contract for flour at a price much higher than that charged for wheat. About the most that could be said for the mill was that the constant need for repairs provided employment for a number of Indians and thus enabled them to collect rations.[50]

Yet despite all these handicaps there was progress in the direction desired by the men who formulated and executed Indian policy. Not only were the Santees cultivating more land each year, but they were adopting a good many of the customs and conveniences of white men. Houses were built; wagons, plows, harrows, and other implements were issued; and some Indians were encouraged to build up cattle herds. As early as 1873, Webster submitted a list of forty-eight men who could be trusted to take care of cows. That year the carpenter and his apprentices were kept busy making door and window frames, cupboards, benches, tables, and chests; about half the houses then boasted some or all of these conveniences.[51] For a time a matron was provided by the Society of Friends to visit the Indian women in their homes and instruct them in such household arts as soapmaking. The epidemic of 1873 may have had something to do with the emphasis on soap in the next year or so, as it undoubtedly did with the effort to substitute shingles for dirt roofs, and board floors for the bare earth. By 1877, 50 of the 153 houses had shingle roofs, and most of them had board floors. By

[49] Com. of Indian Affairs, *Annual Report*, 1878, p. 100.

[50] Edw. C. Kemble, U.S. Indian Inspector, to J. Q. Smith, January 22, 1877, NARS, RG 75, LR, Nebraska Agencies.

[51] Webster to White, June 2, 1873, NARS, RG 75, LR, Santee Agency; Com. of Indian Affairs, *Annual Report*, 1873, p. 189.

that time the men were reported to have adopted white man's dress in full, the women partially.[52]

Another evidence of progress was that Indians were taking over an increasing proportion of the skilled and semiskilled labor at the agency. In 1875 the miller had an Indian apprentice, and another was being taught to run the steam engine at the sawmill. Three years later the blacksmith shop and gristmill were operated entirely by Indians, and another served as office clerk. As a consequence, the expenses for white labor had fallen from $9,760 in 1874 to $4,020 in 1878.[53]

In his official report for 1879, Agent Lightner summed up the progress achieved by the Santees in the thirteen years they had been in Nebraska:

> A few years ago it was necessary for a white man to be with them to give directions in plowing, sowing, and caring for the crops; now they do their own plowing, planting, sowing, reaping, gathering, and threshing without the aid of a white man, and they are as capable of taking care of their machinery as many white people.

He cited the nearly 2,000 acres planted that year, the 1,300 tons of hay put up, the 71,000 feet of cottonwood lumber cut, and the 8,000 bushels of wheat ground at the mill as evidences of their advancement. (The wheat had been purchased from white men, but for the season then just ending the Indians would have a surplus from their own crop.) The Indians, said Lightner, "look well as to where their pay is to come from for work," but they would work at the mill without pay. There was no loafing around the store, the agency was quiet at night, and doors could be left unlocked. About the only complaints he had were that some of the Indian couples lived together without benefit of marriage and that the inevitable designing whites were still trying to drive the Santees from their land. Later that fall, when he talked with the Indians on the subject of ending the weekly issue of rations, he told them that they would have to become self-supporting before they could become citizens. To this ultimatum they suggested that the issue be reduced to once every two weeks, which "would make them half citizens."[54]

[52] Webster to E. P. Smith, April 23 and May 8, 1874, and January 7, 1875; A. L. Riggs to E. P. Smith, September 25, 1875, NARS, RG 75, LR, Santee Agency; Com. of Indian Affairs, *Annual Report*, 1874, p. 208; 1877, p. 147.

[53] Com. of Indian Affairs, *Annual Report*, 1875, p. 232; 1878, p. 100.

[54] *Ibid.*, 1879, pp. 104–105; Lightner to Hayt, October 7, 1879, NARS, RG 75, LR, Nebraska Agencies.

That is what the Santee Sioux were at the end of the decade of the seventies: half-citizens. In their adoption of the externals of white customs, they were well in advance of their relatives in Dakota Territory (except for the Flandreau colony) and probably living much like white pioneers on the Great Plains at the same period. In their economic thinking, particularly as concerned the relative merits of self-reliance and dependence on the government, they had quite some distance to go before their attitudes corresponded to those of the pioneers. In their religious and educational progress, they were a mixture of aboriginal and European elements, the proportions varying from individual to individual in a manner bewildering to white observers. All things considered, the Santees had come a long way since the misery of Crow Creek. In terms of assimilation to white culture, they had advanced far since their days in Minnesota; in terms of the integrity of their own culture, they had declined even more conspicuously.

CHAPTER 9

The Quiet Decades

BY COMPARISON with the agencies for the wild Sioux to the northwest, the Santee Agency had a remarkably placid history during the last three decades of the nineteenth century. There were no periodic outbreaks of violence, no frightened appeals by the agent for military protection, no mass flights from the reservation by the Indians. Instead, there were the singing of hymns, the daily routine of the classrooms, the seasonal round of planting and harvest. The contrast was so great that George Hyde, historian of the Oglalas and Brulés, was led to say of the Santees, with considerable exaggeration, that in 1870, when Spotted Tail visited them, "They had placed themselves absolutely under the control of their missionaries, and they had little thought for anything in the world beyond piety."[1] To the extent that this generalization has any truth to it, the piety and docility of the Santees were due largely to the activities of the missionaries who had worked among them on the reservation in Minnesota, during the traumatic period of exile, and since their settlement in Nebraska.

John P. Williamson and Samuel D. Hinman followed the Indians down from Crow Creek in the spring of 1866. The American Board missionaries attempted, without much success, to conduct school in tents that summer at the Niobrara townsite, and then moved in the fall

[1] George E. Hyde, *Spotted Tail's Folk* (Norman: University of Oklahoma Press, 1961), p. 167.

to Bazile Creek, where they remained until 1868. When they moved to Breckenridge, that spring, they began their work quite modestly, in a long log house used as a combined church and school.[2] The Episcopal mission started more ambitiously, with substantial buildings at Breckenridge in 1867, including a church that Agent Stone said would be the finest in Nebraska west of Omaha. The next year Hinman began work on a school, to cost $9,000, and followed it in 1869 with an addition to be used as a hospital. A tornado struck in June, 1870, however, and destroyed nearly everything. Although the mission was rebuilt in the next few years, its progress was considerably interrupted by this disaster.[3]

Meanwhile the American Board people entertained larger ambitions than their initial efforts suggested. Williamson moved to the Yankton reservation in 1869 but was replaced the next year by Alfred L. Riggs, son of the Hazelwood missionary. Riggs' plan was to establish at Santee "a normal academy for the training of native teachers." Within a few months of his arrival a building program had been inaugurated, and by the winter of 1870–1871 the "Santee Normal Training-School" had an enrollment of 111 and an average attendance of 69. Although the great bulk of the enrollment in the early years was composed of day students from the immediate vicinity, even in that first year 13 came from other Sioux communities, mainly from Flandreau. By 1873 both the American Board and the Episcopalians had extended their operations and were reaching at least some of the children in outlying parts of the reservation with day schools.[4]

Despite the promise held out by the denominational schools, the successive agents continued to recommend the establishment of a government manual labor school at the Santee agency. Their reasons are readily explainable in terms of traditional American notions about the separation of church and state and of the then current beliefs about the best way to lead the Indians to civilization. Although Indian education

[2] Winifred W. Barton, *John P. Williamson, a Brother to the Sioux* (Chicago: Fleming H. Revell Co., 1919), p. 109; Com. of Indian Affairs, *Annual Report*, 1867, p. 284; 1868, p. 248; Stephen R. Riggs, *Mary and I: Forty Years with the Sioux* (Boston: Congregational Sunday-School and Publishing Society, 1880), p. 234; Mary Buel Riggs, *Early Days at Santee* (Santee: Santee Normal Training School Press, 1928), p. 9.

[3] Com. of Indian Affairs, *Annual Report*, 1869, pp. 341–342; 1870, pp. 234, 240; 1871, pp. 443–445; James M. Stone to Hampton B. Denman, January 31, 1868; Denman to Nathaniel G. Taylor, June 12, 1868; Asa M. Janney to Ely S. Parker, June 2, 1870, NARS, RG 75, LR.

[4] Com. of Indian Affairs, *Annual Report*, 1870, pp. 234, 240; 1871, pp. 443–445; 1874, pp. 36–37; Mary B. Riggs, *Early Days at Santee*, p. 9.

had been carried on exclusively by churches and missionary societies up to about 1860, government-operated schools gained in popularity after the Civil War, and eventually government support was withdrawn from the mission schools.[5] Besides the widespread feeling that education, for Indians as for white children, was primarily the business of the state, there was a strong prejudice among Indian Bureau officials against conducting any schooling in the Indians' native language. Agent Janney, who first began agitating for an industrial school in 1871, said that although the mission schools, which taught in Dakota, might be doing a satisfactory job of preparing their graduates to become missionaries to their people, they were not giving the Indians the kind of education needed to fit them for eventual citizenship. So long as they were educated in their native tongue, said Janney, they were still Indians. And, as everyone knew, the primary aim of our Indian policy was to transform Indians into white men. In vain did Riggs point out that "*education* is *more than language*, and must use a *medium* that is *understood*. We cannot afford to wait for our scholars to know the English language before we begin their education."[6] Not until 1934 did the Indian Bureau finally recognize that the eradication of the Indian's native language was not necessary to his education and initiate a policy that aimed at giving the student a functional command of English without depriving him of the tongue of his ancestors.

Janney resigned his position as agent before any concrete moves toward setting up an industrial school were taken, but his successor, Webster, pushed the project to completion. Opened in 1874, with thirty-six pupils and three teachers, the school seems to have been operated with reasonable success until 1877, when the Yankton agent briefly placed in charge at Santee nearly sabotaged it by first recommending that it be turned over to the Episcopal Church and then closing it at the end of the fiscal year.[7] It survived this blow, however, and, although its enrollment was down to twenty-five when Gassman closed it, by late in the next year it had increased to the point that

[5] Hildegard Thompson, "Education Among American Indians: Institutional Aspects," American Academy of Political and Social Science *Annals*, CCCXI (May 1957), 96–97.

[6] Com. of Indian Affairs, *Annual Report*, 1871, p. 442; Joseph Webster to Barclay White, December 6, 1872; Alfred L. Riggs to Ezra A. Hayt, December 22, 1877, NARS, RG 75, LR, Santee Sioux Agency.

[7] Webster to White, December 6, 1872; White to Acting Commissioner H. R. Clum, February 3, 1873; White to B. Rush Roberts, October 11, 1877, NARS, RG 75, LR, Santee Sioux Agency; Com. of Indian Affairs, *Annual Report*, 1874, pp. 36, 208–209.

another teacher was needed. As the term "manual labor" suggests, much of the work carried on at the school was vocational, chiefly agricultural, in nature. In 1878 twenty-three acres were cultivated, a figure which increased year by year.[8]

Meanwhile, the mission schools were also expanding. The Episcopal mission was operating two day schools by 1875, one in connection with the Church of the Blessed Redeemer on East Bazile Creek (now called Howe Creek), the other at Wabasha's village, near where the Church of the Holy Faith was later erected. The American Board people were also operating a district school at their Bazile Creek outstation near the gristmill. All these schools were conducted by native teachers. The Normal Training School then had an enrollment of eighty-two, still drawn mostly from the immediate locality. A small press had been put into operation in 1871, and four years later the *Iapi Oaye*, or *Word Carrier*, a bilingual monthly periodical, was being issued in an edition of twelve hundred. A number of books of the Bible had been published, along with textbooks for use locally and in other schools among the Sioux.[9]

Agent Lightner reported in 1877 that the agency was becoming a center of education for all the Sioux. During the previous winter the enrollment at the Normal School included two men from Flandreau, seven from the Cheyenne River Agency, and six men and seven women from the Yankton Agency. Altogether, forty-nine students, including those from remote portions of the Santee Reservation, were boarded at the residence halls. By this time the achievement of the school was impressive enough to draw praise from even so hardened a skeptic as editor Fry of the Niobrara *Pioneer*, who visited it in February, 1878. After describing the buildings and the service he attended, he concluded his article with what was, for him, high praise: "We spent a very pleasant day and came away convinced that many of the Indians we saw at the Mission were well along in civilized life."[10]

Although the educational work was the missionaries' most conspicuous achievement, they were at least equally concerned with the spiritual growth of their Indian charges. As during the reservation days in

[8] White to Hayt, December 8, 1878; Roberts to Hayt, November 19, 1878, NARS, RG 75, LR, Nebraska Agencies; Com. of Indian Affairs, *Annual Report*, 1878, p. 99.

[9] Samuel D. Hinman to Webster, April 3, 1875, NARS, RG 75, LR, Santee Sioux Agency; Com. of Indian Affairs, *Annual Report*, 1875, pp. 323–324.

[10] Com. of Indian Affairs, *Annual Report*, 1877, pp. 147–148; Stephen R. Riggs to Edward P. Smith, August 5, 1873, NARS, RG 75, LR, Santee Sioux Agency; Niobrara *Pioneer*, February 8, 1878.

Minnesota, they felt that the two aspects of their work should go hand in hand. Hence besides their academic training, which had strong religious overtones, they conducted church services of various kinds. The Santees, if not quite so fanatically pious as they looked to Spotted Tail and his pagans, were assuredly "praying Indians" by this time. The missionaries tried to inculcate in them the same sense of stewardship and self-reliance that their clerical counterparts serving white congregations tried to stimulate. To keep the people from becoming beggars, a weekly collection was taken almost from the beginning of the American Board's mission work at Santee. Despite the protest that they were all poor, the Indians managed to scrape together $44.47 in pennies in the first eight months of 1871. By 1875, when their circumstances were somewhat improved, they had contributed during the previous year $65.20 for pastoral support, $23.04 for relief of the poor and sick, and $7.48 for missions elsewhere.[11]

Among the less savory aspects of mission work among the Santees was the sharp sectarian rivalry between the American Board and the Episcopal Church. The complex and enigmatic personality of Samuel D. Hinman seems to have been one of the catalysts that precipitated this unseemly quarrel. A native of Connecticut, he had come as an orphan to Bishop Whipple's divinity school in 1859. His devotion to the Indians, both on the old reservation and during the months following the uprising, had confirmed the bishop's faith in him. He seems to have possessed certain traits of temperament, however, that made it impossible for him to work in harmony with ministers of other denominations.[12]

Although government officials tried to stay clear of the controversy, they were inevitably drawn in. In defending Agent Webster against charges of favoritism by one of the religious bodies, Superintendent White described the situation at the agency with gentle sarcasm:

> Such is the zeal of said missionaries for the advancement of the Christian religion among the heathen . . . that a difficulty seems to have arisen between them, and it is notorious in the tribe that the missionaries themselves, have of late years, not been upon terms of ordinary civility and courtesy with each other.[13]

As if this were not enough, Hinman was investigated by his own church

[11] Com. of Indian Affairs, *Annual Report*, 1871, p. 444; 1875, pp. 323–324.
[12] Henry B. Whipple, *Lights and Shadows of a Long Episcopate* (New York: Macmillan Co., 1899), pp. 61–62.
[13] White to William Dorsey, May 4, 1874, NARS, RG 75, LR, Santee Agency.

authorities on charges of "gross immorality, misconduct and the dishonest and unfaithful use of money entrusted to him for the work of the mission," found guilty, and expelled from the reservation. When he tried to return and claim his property (which term he apparently construed to cover the mission property), there was actual violence, with armed white men, half drunk, coming from Niobrara to espouse either Hinman's cause or that of his adversaries. The situation finally quieted down in September of 1880, but Agent Lightner described the Indians as having been appreciably "unsettled" by the whole business.[14]

As on other reservations occupied by relatively acculturated Indians, the biggest event at Santee in the last two decades of the century was the allotment of lands and the opening of the reservation to white settlement. But whereas this momentous event took place on most reservations after the passage of the General Allotment (Dawes) Act of 1887, allotments at Santee preceded the Dawes Act by two years. Many of the original allotments made by Janney in 1870 and 1871 were later canceled because of the death or departure from the reservation of the allotees, and those of people who remained were later increased to 160 acres, wherever possible, to conform to the terms of the 1868 treaty. Although a number of the Santees met the requirements of that treaty in regard to improvements made and amount of land brought under cultivation, the years were allowed to pass without any action toward issuing patents to them. The delay was due partly to some uncertainty concerning whether the lands allotted should be inalienable and, if so, for how long. By 1877, Lightner believed that the Indians were ready to become citizens and take their lands in severalty, but he did not think that government guardianship should be withdrawn or that the reservation should be thrown open to white settlement.[15]

In 1881, Congress passed a bill that provided a precedent for a policy on the Santee allotments. The important provision of this legislation, which concerned the Wisconsin Winnebagos, was a twenty-year inalienability clause. Lightner thought that it should open the way to the

[14] Niobrara *Pioneer*, March 1, July 28, 1877, and June 7 and July 14, 1878; Arnoux, Ritch & Woodford (counsel for Hinman) to Commissioner Roland E. Trowbridge, June 8, 1880; Isaiah Lightner to Trowbridge, June 24 and 28, 1880; William W. Fowler to Trowbridge, October 1, 1880; William H. Hare to Trowbridge, August 2, 1880, NARS, RG 75, LR, Nebraska Agencies. Hinman made several later attempts to regain "his" property, without success.

[15] Acting Secretary of Interior M. H. Smith to E. P. Smith, August 21, 1874; Webster to E. P. Smith, August 5, 1874, NARS, RG 75, LR, Santee Agency; Charles Searing to John Q. Smith, August 9, 1876, NARS, RG 75, LR, Nebraska Agencies; Com. of Indian Affairs, *Annual Report*, 1877, pp. 147–148.

issuance of patents to the Santees.[16] Nothing was done until late the next year, however, when a Sioux commission visited the agency. Lightner had prepared the way by calling a council late in October, at which the Indians expressed a desire that patents be issued but also indicated a reluctance to allow any part of the reservation to be opened to white settlement. The old fear of being moved somewhere else still troubled them. When the commission arrived, in November, the Santees' assent was obtained to an agreement substantially embodied in the Indian appropriations act approved the next March 1. The relevant provisions of the act stated that patents issued under the terms of the 1868 treaty "shall be of legal effect," the United States to hold the land in trust for twenty-five years.[17]

The Indians immediately began applying for patents, and by August, 1884, Lightner reported that application papers had been given to 127 landowners. No patents had yet been received, however, to the annoyance of the agent, who wanted them issued promptly so that the Indians could "come under the laws of the land and could vote—(for Blaine and Logan)."[18] Blaine and Logan did not win the election, and the lame duck administration of Chester A. Arthur received credit for opening the Santee Reservation to white settlement, by means of an executive order dated February 9, 1885, which specified that all lands remaining unalloted and unselected by April 15 should on that date be restored to the public domain and be made subject to settlement and entry on May 15. Immediately there came a protest from the white people of Knox County, who feared that not enough of the reservation would be left after Lightner had finished alloting lands. They objected especially to the allotment of 80-acre tracts to women and children under the terms of the act of March 3, 1863, in addition to the 160-acre tracts on which patents were then to be issued. Fortunately for the Indians, they had a friend in Alfred L. Riggs, who sent off a series of letters to influential men in and out of the government, pointing out that to limit allotments to the 160-acre homesteads would leave many Santees with no land at all. The smaller allotments were made, though certificates rather than patents were issued to the recipients.[19]

[16] Com. of Indian Affairs, *Annual Report*, 1882, p. 117; U.S. *Statutes at Large*, XXI, 317.

[17] Robert S. Gardner to Commissioner Hiram Price, July 3, 1882; Lightner to Price, November 8 and 22, NARS, RG 75, LR, Santee Agency; U.S. *Statutes at Large*, XXII, 444.

[18] Com. of Indian Affairs, *Annual Report*, 1884, p. 122.

[19] Charles J. Kappler, comp. and ed., *Indian Affairs, Laws and Treaties*, I (Washington: Government Printing Office, 1904), 864; A. L. Riggs to M. E. Strieby

After some delay, owing to a general relocation of families since the allotment made in the later 1870's, the process of assigning homesteads was completed before the deadline set by Arthur's executive order. The Santees now held 71,784.56 acres, plus 1,310.7 acres reserved for agency, school, and missionary use; 42,160.56 acres were opened to settlement. By the time of Lightner's annual report for 1885, white farmers were scattered about the reservation, taking up land and putting up buildings. The agent thought that, on the whole, they were a good class of people, from association with whom the Indians stood to benefit. Of the 210 allotments made under the 1868 treaty, 132 of the allotees had complied with the terms of that treaty so as to be entitled to patents. Further legislation needed before patents could be authorized on the 485 smaller allotments was not forthcoming until 1898.[20]

All was not well, however. White men began meddling in the Santees' affairs even before allotment had been completed. Some tried to determine the Indians' selections so as to be able to rent or run cattle on Indian lands adjacent to their own. Others began exerting pressure on the Indians to request that the twenty-five-year clause be waived. A petition bearing fifty-four signatures of Indians and asking for repeal of this clause was submitted to the commissioner in April, 1886. Denounced by the agent as an attempt by white men to get the Indians' lands, it presumably received no consideration at the Indian Office.[21]

The Santees were better prepared for allotment than many other Indian groups, on whom it was virtually forced after the passage of the Dawes Act. They had been farming, after a fashion, for many years, and were less dependent on the rations issued to them than their Sioux relatives west of the Missouri in Dakota Territory. Lightner's plan to issue rations every two weeks had worked a hardship on the old and in-

(Corresponding Secretary of the American Missionary Association), March 9, 1885; Senator Charles F. Manderson to Commissioner John D. C. Atkins, March 22, 1885; petition from citizens of Knox County to Commissioner of Indian Affairs (undated, received April 10, 1885), NARS, RG 75, LR, Santee Agency; Com. of Indian Affairs, *Annual Report*, 1885, p. 136.

[20] Lightner to Atkins, April 14, 1885, NARS, RG 75, LR, Santee Agency; Com. of Indian Affairs, *Annual Report*, 1885, pp. lxiv, 136; U.S. *Statutes at Large*, XXX, 583.

[21] Lightner to Atkins, May 27, 1885; Charles Hill to Atkins, April 17, 1886, NARS, RG 75, LR, Santee Agency; Com. of Indian Affairs, *Annual Report*, 1886, p. 189. In 1886 a rumor was being circulated among the Indians that if they could get the restrictive clause repealed, they could buy lands at their old homes in Minnesota— a story to which some credence was lent by the purchase that year of lands for Sioux who had been living in Minnesota. See Chapter 13.

firm and had been abandoned, but he continued to press steadily for a reduction. There were problems, however. After he had divided the tribe into those who were self-supporting and those who still required rations, he began to wonder about the wisdom of such discrimination. His somewhat ungrammatical summary of his thinking on the subject expressed the dilemma faced by any conscientious Indian agent during that period:

> Now then here is A and B living side by side each have had the same care extended over them and because A has went to work and done as we wished him to do and been a good Indian and raised some wheat for sale you say stop his rations but B, because he has been careless and lazy you say feed him as I said I wish to advocate justice and nothing more and to stop the rations on the good ones and feed the bad ones would not in my judgement be justice. . . .[22]

Despite his qualms, this was roughly the policy adopted in the early 1880's. But in 1883, Lightner was able to report that the issue of rations had "quite recently" been discontinued except to school children and about a hundred old and infirm persons. This policy had its drawbacks, however, in that those still receiving rations were sharing them with their relatives. Lightner thought an almshouse the proper solution to the problem, but none was ever provided.[23]

The discontinuance of rations was symptomatic of a continuing improvement in the condition of the Santees during the early eighties. The amount of land under cultivation increased steadily until 1887, when it began to level off as a result of a succession of droughts. As early as 1880, 7,000 bushels of wheat were raised, 2,000 bushels of oats, and 3,000 bushels of corn. The heavy emphasis on wheat led, as elsewhere, to soil exhaustion and crop failures. By 1887 the acreage sown to wheat had dropped to little more than a quarter of the land under cultivation.[24] The amount of machinery also increased from year to year. By 1884 farming operations were conducted with the aid of 184 wagons, 134 cross-plows, 75 breaking plows, 28 mowing machines, 22 horse-rakes, 10 reaping machines, and 3 threshing machines. The machinery

[22] Lightner to Hayt, February 4, 1880; Lightner to Trowbridge, March 20, 1880, NARS, RG 75, LR, Nebraska Agencies; Com. of Indian Affairs, *Annual Report*, 1883, p. 107.

[23] Com. of Indian Affairs, *Annual Report*, 1881, p. 127; 1883, p. 107; 1885, p. 137.

[24] *Ibid.*, 1880, pp. 121–122; 1883, p. 107; 1885, p. 137; 1887, p. 154; Lightner to Price, August 9, 1881, NARS, RG 75, LR, Santee Agency.

was used by too many people, not all of whom were careful of it, however, and some of the mowing machines had been in use since 1868.[25]

Another evidence of progress was the gradual assumption by the Indians of the management of most work at the agency. In 1883, Santees were serving as blacksmiths, issue clerk, cattle herder, miller, harnessmaker, and brickmaker. Except for the physician and one clerk, all employees were Indians by 1888. "We do not inquire if the Indians will work," said Lightner, "for we know that by far the majority of them will work, and when we have it to be done, we ask, and the necessary labor is performed." The Indians built their own houses, drilled wells, and planted shade and fruit trees on their homesteads. The police force was revived during this period, and in 1884 a court of Indian offenses was instituted. Both the police force and the court were eliminated about 1891, to the regret of the agent, who claimed that drunkenness and gambling increased afterward.[26]

Despite the unmistakable evidence of advance toward civilization on the part of the Santees, there was a continuing need for an agency to supervise their affairs. In fact, the agency plant grew more impressive during the eighties. In 1881 it consisted of a council house or office, two warehouses, a machine house, a sawmill, a smokehouse, an icehouse, a jail, a physician's office, a harness shop, two school buildings, three workshops, a trader's house and store, and six houses for employees; there were in addition two granaries, a gristmill, and a dwelling ten miles from the agency. The mill at Bazile Creek was finally abandoned in 1883 and the machinery moved to a new building erected at the agency, where it was powered by steam until 1891, when water from an artesian well was put to work turning its machinery. During the last twenty years of the century, other agency buildings were improved, log structures replaced by frame, or new roofs put on.[27]

Lightner's long tenure as agent came to an end in 1885, perhaps as a consequence of his bold advocacy of the Republican ticket the previous year, and he was replaced by Charles Hill, formerly superintendent at the government school. Both men were investigated as a result of complaints by Indians and employees, but no evidence of dishonesty on the part of either was discovered. Like many other Indian agents of the

25 Com. of Indian Affairs, *Annual Report*, 1884, p. 122; 1888, p. 172.

26 *Ibid.*, 1880, p. 122; 1883, p. 108; 1881, p. 127; 1884, p. 124; 1887, p. 155; 1888, p. 172; 1890, p. 145; 1891, p. 295.

27 *Ibid.*, 1881, p. 127; 1883, p. 108; 1891, p. 294; Lightner to Price, September 5, 1882, and September 28, 1883, NARS, RG 75, LR, Santee Agency.

time, they were unwilling to brook any opposition to their will from the Indians, and both seem to have employed physical violence against Indians who refused to submit to their authority. In later years Lightner served on the Philanthropic Committee of the Illinois Yearly Meeting of Friends, making Indian affairs his special concern. He settled at Monroe, Nebraska, only eight miles from the government Indian school at Genoa, in which he took a continuing interest.[28]

Hill's successor in 1890 was James E. Helms, a young man who speedily got himself into difficulty with the Episcopal missionary and others. Although he was investigated, he was let off with "a very pointed message of reproof and counsel" by his superiors. Helms was succeeded in 1894 by Joseph Clements, who served without particular distinction through a trying period at Santee and was followed in 1898 by Henry C. Baird, a rather typical Indian agent of the old school who alienated Indians and white employees alike by his domineering manner.[29]

It is probably fair to say that none of these men, except Lightner, the last Quaker to serve as agent, left any significant impress on the Santees. The power of an agent to do either good or harm had been much circumscribed since the days of Lawrence Taliaferro, when only the presence of the military provided any effective restraint on his actions. Exercising a limited jurisdiction over a fairly articulate Indian population living in close proximity to missionaries with powerful outside backing, and hemmed in by a white community that kept them under constant surveillance, the agents at Santee in the last two decades of the nineteenth century were mere functionaries of the Indian Bureau, already on their way to becoming anachronisms.

Increasingly as the nineteenth century drew to a close, the primary instrument of government policy toward the Indians came to be the school. The government school at Santee had a checkered career during the 1880's and 1890's, plagued by fires and by frequent changes of administration. In its early years it was under the immediate direction

[28] Lightner to Atkins, December 1, 1885; Hill to Atkins, December 1, 1885; Gardner to Price, July 3, 1882; Petition of Indians to Price, January 30, 1884, NARS, RG 75, LR, Santee Agency; Petition of Chiefs to Commissioner, January 6, 1880; Lightner to Hayt, January 22, 1880, NARS, RG 75, LR, Nebraska Agencies; *Friends' Intelligencer*, LXXX (March 31, 1923), 231.

[29] Marie L. H. Steer to Commissioner Thomas J. Morgan, November 17, 1891; J. A. Leonard to Morgan, December 26, 1891; President Grover Cleveland to James E. Helms, January 8, 1894; Joseph Clements to Commissioner Daniel M. Browning, March 15, 1894; Clements to Commissioner William A. Jones, October 2, 1897; Henry C. Baird to Jones, March 5, 1898, NARS, RG 75, LR, Santee Agency.

of the agent and was staffed, like the agency itself, by members of the Society of Friends; but after the creation in 1882 of the post of Superintendent of Indian Schools, a local superintendent was appointed, and regular government appointees occupied the teaching positions. Congress annually appropriated $3,000 for its operation, a sum described by the agents as inadequate.[30]

Despite a declining general population, enrollment at the school continued to hold its own or sometimes even increase. Listed as having a capacity of 45, it had a total enrollment in 1884 of 84. Although the average daily attendance was much less, congestion was severe, especially after each of the successive fires. A special agent who visited in June, 1888, found 36 girls occupying a single sleeping room, three or four to a bed; much the same conditions existed among the boys. A new school was built, steam heated in order to minimize the danger of fire, and on June 22, 1889, it was formally opened. Its capacity of 100 was almost immediately exceeded, and 120 children were crowded in. By 1891 the number of students had increased to 142, as pressure was brought upon parents who neglected sending their children to school.[31]

In the 1890's clashes between the superintendent and the agent were chronic, and between March, 1895, and February, 1896, a series of four fires, two of which were deliberately set by students, practically destroyed the school. In 1897 a $17,700 brick building, complete with hot and cold water in the lavatories and showers, was erected to replace those recently burned. At the end of the century the Santee Industrial School consisted of the two-story brick building, containing boys' and girls' dormitories, a kitchen, a dining room, a playroom, lavatories, and teachers' quarters, and a two-room frame structure valued at $600.[32]

The Santee Industrial School was probably operated in much the same way as other Indian boarding schools of the period. To counteract the tendency of the children to come and go as they pleased, a stern regimen was imposed, which no doubt aggravated their dissatisfaction with school life. The published reports of the various superintendents reveal a strong concern for efficient operation but little or no sympathy for Indian children. On the other hand, there is no doubt that most

[30] Com. of Indian Affairs, *Annual Report*, 1880, p. 103; 1883, p. 109; 1885, p. lxx; 1874, p. 209.

[31] *Ibid.*, 1884, p. 123; 1888, pp. 174–175; 1889, p. 244.

[32] Charles D. Rakestraw, Supervisor of Indian Schools, to W. N. Hailmann, February 27, 1896; Clements to D. M. Browning, August 7 and December 26, 1896; Baird to Jones, June 3, 1899, August 24, 1899, and May 24, 1898, NARS, RG 75, LR, Santee Agency; Com. of Indian Affairs, *Annual Report*, 1896, p. 204; 1897, p. 184.

of the students found the physical conditions of school life more comfortable, particularly after the brick building was finished, than life in the ill-heated log houses in which most of their families lived. Whether this comparative luxury compensated for the rigid discipline imposed by the school authorities and the absence of parental affection is another question.

While the Santee Industrial School was running its hectic course, the mission schools were proceeding steadily with their work. The Episcopal Church ran three day schools and a girls' boarding school for a number of years, and about 1882 opened Hope School, a small institution for boys across the river at Springfield, Dakota Territory. After the burning of the mission buildings at Santee in 1884, the girls' school, called St. Mary's, was closed and re-established the following year at Springfield. These church schools were later consolidated and at the beginning of 1896 rented to the government, which conducted the combined institution as a school for about fifty boys.[33]

The Santee Normal Training School reached its high point in the 1890's, when it became in reality what its founder had envisioned it as being: a center of education for all the Sioux. Although Asa Janney wrote in 1871 that neither of the mission schools expected or desired government aid, requests for aid in the form of rations to nonresident scholars soon began reaching the commissioner; and in 1879, Riggs asked for a subsidy in the form of tuition payments of $20 per quarter per student. Knowing the commissioner's prejudice against teaching in Dakota, he requested support only in proportion to the amount of English taught. An agreement was entered into on September 21, 1880, for the support through tuition payments of an average of thirty pupils, and it was renewed the following year.[34] For more than a decade government aid in this form was extended to the school. In the early years the total amount was a modest sum—$2,271 in 1883—but it rose year by year, averaging over $12,000 annually from 1886 to 1893 and contributing importantly to the institutional budget. Although the support received from religious societies usually amounted to more than that amount, there were years in which the government contributed

[33] Com. of Indian Affairs, *Annual Report*, 1878, p. 99; 1879, p. 105; 1882, p. 115; 1884, p. 123; 1885, p. 138; 1887, p. 156; 1895, p. 206; 1896, pp. 203–204.

[34] A. M. Janney to S. M. Janney, February 1, 1871; A. L. Riggs to E. P. Smith, August 5, 1873; John O. Means, Secretary of the American Board of Commissioners for Foreign Missions, to Price, August 25, 1881, NARS, RG 75, LR, Santee Agency; S. R. Riggs to Hayt, January 24, 1879, NARS, RG 75, LR, Nebraska Agencies.

more than half of the total budget of the school, including rations
issued.[35]

Government subsidies were far from an unmixed blessing, however,
for with aid came the threat of control. Santee Normal's most vulner-
able point was its use of the Dakota language in its teaching, and Riggs
was constantly obliged to defend the practice to each new commissioner.
He managed to keep the anti-vernacular forces at bay for a time, but
an uneasy peace reigned, interrupted frequently by grumblings from
the Indian Office. In 1880 the Bureau adopted a regulation requiring
the exclusive use of English but providing a loophole that permitted
Santee Normal to continue its operations as before, but followed it in
1884 with a more stringent ruling and a threat to withdraw government
support from any school using the vernacular.[36] The real blow came in
1886, when Commissioner John D. C. Atkins issued this peremptory
order: "In all schools conducted by missionary organizations it is required that all instructions shall be given in the English language." In
another order, dated February 2, 1887, Atkins went on to say: "The
instruction of the Indians in the vernacular is not only of no use to
them, but is detrimental to the cause of their education and civilization,
and no school will be permitted on the reservation in which the English
language is not exclusively taught."[37]

When these instructions reached Riggs, he complied, but with great
reluctance. In his official report he pointed out that in the normal department of the school the use of Dakota was "indispensable to the best
instruction." "Things, not names," he said, "are what the true teacher
must grasp; then names come afterwards." The theological classes had
had to be suspended, he said, as the instruction had been almost entirely in Dakota, and the training of interpreters had likewise been terminated by the commissioner's order. Pointing out that the Santee
Normal Training School represented "the high water mark of Indian
advance more than any other school in the country," he reviewed its
history and described its impressive physical plant, concluding: "And
now this is to be dismembered and eviscerated by the order of the
Government."[38]

Complaints from Riggs and other missionaries drew from Commis-

[35] Com. of Indian Affairs, *Annual Report*, 1883, p. 245; 1884, p. 123; 1885, p. 138;
1886, p. 193; 1887, p. 318; 1888, p. 377; 1889, p. 391; 1890, p. 329; 1891, pt. 2, p. 16;
1892, p. 771; 1893, p. 626.

[36] *Ibid.*, 1887, pp. xx–xxi.

[37] *Ibid.*, 1887, p. xxii.

[38] *Ibid.*, 1887, p. 162.

sioner Atkins a lengthy defense in his next annual report. Seeking precedents for his position, he noted that the peace commission of 1868 had advocated the establishment of schools for the Indians in which "their barbarous dialect should be blotted out and the English language substituted," and mentioned the regulations and orders of 1880 and 1884. In his own report of the previous year he had said: "The English language as taught in America is good enough for her people of all races." Now he appealed to patriotic impulses for support. "Every nation is jealous of its own language," he wrote, "and no nation ought to be more so than ours, which approaches nearer than any other nationality to the perfect protection of its people."[39] The possibility that the Indian nations might also be jealous of their own languages seems not to have crossed his mind.

The literal application of Atkins' order might conceivably have included a ban on religious services in an Indian language. Although the Indian Bureau denied any such intent, some officials took it upon themselves privately to attack the practice of vernacular services. A special agent who visited Santee in 1888 questioned the propriety of prayers at the school delivered in the native language. He wrote: "It may be none of my business to invade the Sanctum Sanctorum, where infallibility is supposed to exist, or to make any remarks on this subject. I think the English vernacular is good enough for the Indians and more acceptable to the Deity than the Choctaw harangue delivered this morning." He thought that it would be best for the Indians to "forget their native habits with their native tongue as well, as soon as possible."[40] The flippancy of his comments, made in an official report, only underscores the basic lack of understanding of the Indian and the hopeless ethnocentrism of white Americans of the time.

The financial support given the Santee Normal Training School by the government was too valuable to surrender at once, and Riggs submitted to the commissioner's order, though continuing to plead for its repeal. Finally, however, the strain of trying to accommodate the school's work to the demands of the government proved disproportionate to the benefits received, and in 1893 the government contract was terminated.[41] Santee Normal Training School had expanded greatly

[39] *Ibid.*, 1887, pp. xx–xxii.

[40] Hill to Atkins, December 27, 1887; W. H. Tallmadge to Acting Commissioner A. B. Upshaw, June 20, 1888, NARS, RG 75, LR, Santee Agency; Com. of Indian Affairs, *Annual Report*, 1888, p. xvii.

[41] Com. of Indian Affairs, *Annual Report*, 1894, pp. 194, 198. Perhaps Riggs saw the handwriting on the wall when he read Commissioner Morgan's report in 1891. Morgan expressed the hope that the day was not far off when the government would take sole

during the years it received government assistance, but the loss of that support did not mean the end of the school. In 1883 it had been turned over by the A.B.C.F.M. to the American Missionary Association, a Congregational body, which operated it until the fourth decade of the twentieth century.[42] As conditions changed among the plains tribes, its function was altered, and it ceased to be exactly what it was in the 1880's and 1890's: a torch shedding its light throughout the Sioux country, working to build up a cadre of educated Sioux capable of extending its influence to other reservations. If Sioux outnumber Indians of any other tribe in a recent biographical dictionary of prominent Indians, part of the credit must go to the Santee Normal Training School, where some of them received their education.[43]

Important though the educational history of the Santee Reservation is, it does not tell the whole story of the Santee people in the last years of the nineteenth century. To approach completeness, it is necessary to consider some of the problems that confronted the Indians and their agents in those years. Generally speaking, there were three categories of problems at Santee, as the agents saw the situation: those blamable to the vagaries of nature, those resulting from the persistence of old habits among the Indians, and those created by allotment and citizenship.

Except for a great flood in 1881, which forced the town of Niobrara to move to a new site, most of the difficulties caused by weather and climate had to do with drought. After a series of fairly good seasons in the early eighties, a cycle of drought began in 1886 and continued for the next decade, with only occasional years of normal rainfall. By 1893 the agent referred to it as the "never failing drought."[44] White farmers in the surrounding area were hit as hard as the Indians, of course, but,

charge of Indian education. Public support for sectarian schools he found "contrary to the letter and the spirit of the Constitution" and "utterly repugnant to our American institutions and our American history. . . ." Beginning in 1896, Congress started gradually reducing the annual appropriations for denominational schools, until 1900, when it appropriated only 15 per cent of the amount provided in 1895, "this being the final appropriation for contract schools." See *ibid.*, 1891, p. 68; 1895, p. 10; 1896, p. 14; 1897, p. 13; 1898, p. 15; 1899, p. 16; 1900, p. 24.

[42] Com. of Indian Affairs, *Annual Report*, 1883, p. 108.

[43] Marion E. Gridley, ed., *Indians of Today* (3d ed.; Chicago: The Council Fire, 1960), lists twenty Sioux, as compared to seventeen Cherokees, who form the second largest tribal representation. An earlier edition (1947) lists fourteen Sioux, ten Cherokees.

[44] Lightner to Trowbridge, April 1, 1881, NARS, RG 75, LR, Santee Agency; Com. of Indian Affairs, *Annual Report*, 1881, p. 127; 1886, p. 190; 1893, p. 199.

as someone has said, they could usually return to the "wife's folks back east," while the Indians had nowhere to go. The situation became so serious that in 1893 the councilmen requested a return to the issuance of rations, after a decade of at least nominal self-support. The next year Agent Clements called attention to the "miserable, starving condition of many of the Indians under my charge."[45] Conditions were better in 1895 and 1896, but the next year drought struck again, as it did to some extent in 1898. The fact was, though the Indian Bureau refused to admit it, that the Santee Reservation (what was left of it) was incapable of supporting the number of people then living on it, given the climatic conditions of the region. The land was better suited to the range cattle industry, but allotment in severalty had so broken up the Indians' holdings that cattle could not be run over large expanses of territory.

The problems arising from the survival of the old culture were not so serious as the agents thought they were, but some of them did constitute hindrances to the drive to make the Santees self-sufficient. The successive agents expended a great deal of ink and energy inveighing against the Indian dances, partly because they were seen as remnants of the barbarous past but mainly because they involved gift-giving on a large scale. Although Lightner reported in the early eighties that they had been entirely abandoned, this was only wishful thinking on his part. He permitted dances on Christmas, New Year's, and the Fourth of July because he saw them merely as social affairs at which the participants no longer recited brave deeds of the warlike past, but collected money for charity.[46]

Unfortunately, the charitable intent of the dances tended to get out of control, especially when it took the form of generosity toward visiting tribes. When a party of Winnebagos paid a friendly call on their Santee friends in 1881, they put on a dance, in defiance of Lightner's orders, and took home eleven or twelve horses donated by their hosts. The agent, his authority flouted in the presence of his own Indians, was infuriated and wrote the commissioner: "I do not object to the giving so much as the manner in which the present was made, at a dance which they knew I had forbidden. . . ."[47] The same thing happened in 1890, much to the mortification of Agent Helms, who asked for authority to

[45] Santee Councilmen and James Garvie to Secretary of Interior Hoke Smith, September 5, 1893; Clements to D. M. Browning, June 22, 1894, NARS, RG 75, LR, Santee Agency.

[46] Com. of Indian Affairs, *Annual Report*, 1882, p. 115; 1885, p. 137.

[47] Lightner to Price, August 22, 1881, NARS, RG 75, LR, Santee Agency.

withhold annuities from the Indians who had given away their horses and other property. In 1893 it was said that eighty-five horses and ponies, in addition to other stock, had been given away to a party of some 250 Winnebagos.[48]

Although the official attitude was one of opposition to these survivals of old custom, at times the Indian Office was more lenient than the local agent. When Helms tried to stop the dancing in 1893, someone he characterized as a "half-breed agitator" telegraphed the Washington officials that the men who had served as scouts wanted to celebrate Cleveland's election. A department letter in reply said that as long as they violated no laws, there should be no interference. Helms sputtered about the harm done by the dances in delaying acculturation, but apparently did not interfere with them. By then they had become sufficiently exotic that white people in the surrounding towns were willing to pay to watch them. Riggs objected strongly, saying that the revival of "heathen war dances, as shows to gratify the white people, is a practice that works great damage."[49] Despite official proscription, this aspect of the traditional culture managed to persist down to the end of the century and beyond.

It should perhaps be mentioned that the Santee Sioux appear never to have adopted the sun dance, which occupied a central position in the ceremonial life of the true plains tribes. Nor do they seem to have been affected by the ghost dance mania that caused so much unrest among the Tetons about 1890. At least there is no mention of it in the agents' correspondence from that period, except in reference to other groups. The dances indulged in by the Santees may have had their origin in the aboriginal religion and in the practice of war, but by the last decades of the century they had been shorn of most of their earlier significance and had become primarily social in function. They were not, of course, any more acceptable to the missionaries and government officials on that account.

The agents also objected to the tendency of some of the Santees to go on periodic visits to other agencies. Usually these visits had no purpose other than pure sociability, but at times they took on a religious coloration, as when an Episcopal convocation was held at Rosebud in 1880. Lightner, who had no quarrel with the Episcopalians, objected to the Indians' absence for three weeks just at the time when they should have

[48] Helms to Morgan, November 24, 1890.; *ibid.*; Com. of Indian Affairs, *Annual Report*, 1893, p. 202.

[49] Com. of Indian Affairs, *Annual Report*, 1893, p. 202; 1895, p. 204; 1889, p. 248.

been breaking new land and taking care of their wheat. Experience had shown, he said, that their cattle often got into the grain when the people were away from home.[50] Besides such brief visits and convocations, there was a certain amount of moving back and forth between Santee and the Minnesota colonies, and between Santee and Flandreau, depending on where benefits were currently being received. It is no accident that the biggest gains in the Santee population occurred when lands were being allotted and when cash payments were being made there, while the biggest losses in the eighties and nineties coincided with the distribution of land and other benefits to the Minnesota Sioux.[51]

Some of the agents found sinister overtones in perfectly innocent Indian customs—customs which in some cases existed among white frontiersmen as well as among Indians. For example, Helms reported in 1891 that the Santee farmers had a tendency to form "bees" to do jobs most expeditiously managed by several people. He was encouraged, however, to think that the practice was on the wane.[52] In other respects, too, when the Santees behaved much like the typical wasteful frontier farmer, their actions were denounced as characteristically Indian. One agent complained that they bought farm machinery on credit, then left it outdoors to be ruined by rain and snow. Sometimes stock that had been issued to them was sold or neglected, and during the worst of the drought years they ate their hogs as fast as they were issued. When stallions were bought, the Indians sold the colts to white men or traded them for ponies. The limited amount of timber on the reservation had been used so prodigally that by 1892 there was little fuel left.[53]

The allotment of lands, the issuance of patents, and the entry into full-fledged citizenship created difficulties for the Santees and their agents not foreseen by those who imagined that the Indian problem would be solved once the Indian became a landowner and a citizen. On one level there was the question of who was responsible for the roads and

[50] Lightner to Trowbridge, May 17, 1880, NARS, RG 75, LR, Nebraska Agencies.

[51] The largest gains registered in any one year came in 1886 (gain of 44), when allotment was being completed; in 1893 (gain of 45), when a substantial payment had just been made; and in 1898 (gain of 30), when another payment was made. The greatest loss came in 1887 (loss of 18), just after lands had been purchased for the Sioux in Minnesota. See Com. of Indian Affairs, *Annual Report*, 1885, p. 135; 1886, p. 189; 1887, p. 156; 1888, p. 170; 1892, p. 311; 1893, p. 198; 1897, p. 183; 1898, p. 332.

[52] *Ibid.*, 1891, p. 293.

[53] *Ibid.*, 1895, p. 204; 1884, p. 121; 1890, p. 141; 1892, p. 311.

bridges in what had formerly been the Santee Reservation. In 1894, Helms wrote that since no tax could be levied on Indian lands and the poll tax could not be collected, it was impossible to keep the roads fit for travel.[54] The problem was eventually solved, after a fashion, by the gradual passing of Indian lands into white possession and the consequent increase in the tax base, but it remained to perplex agents and county officials until well into the twentieth century.

Citizenship brought other, more serious problems. Helms wrote in 1892 that the Santees "vote, pay some taxes, . . . electioneer, and many of them drink whisky." Their voting was an advantage to them, in that it made them more desirable neighbors when an important election rolled around, and some took to politics in a small way. By the early 1890's two Santees were on the county board and worked to see that the agency got its share of the county road and bridge fund. A. J. ("Joseph") Campbell served as county coroner for a time.[55] If this participation in the political life of the community was seen as largely beneficial, the freedom to drink whiskey was not. With the coming of allotment, old laws regarding the introduction of whiskey into the "Indian country" became obsolete and were not immediately replaced by laws adapted to the new conditions. In the meantime (and afterward) the liquor problem gave much concern to the agents and missionaries. A temperance society was organized early in 1887, but its membership was so small that it probably had little influence on the Santees. In 1889, when the court of Indian offenses was functioning, twenty-one out of thirty-eight cases heard during the year were for drunkenness.[56]

White men received much of the blame for the situation. Besides providing the Indians with liquor (for which there were many prosecutions in the later 1890's), they set anything but a good example, according to the Episcopal missionary. Agent Helms was charged with, among other offenses, bringing liquor to the agency and allowing what he did not himself consume to fall into the hands of the Indians. The agent who followed him attributed the drinking problem to the fact that the Indians considered themselves citizens, with the same rights as white people. The county was unwilling to take costly action, since the Indians paid few taxes and there was a general feeling that they were the respon-

[54] Helms to D. M. Browning (no date, received February 19, 1894), NARS, RG 75, LR, Santee Agency.

[55] Com. of Indian Affairs, *Annual Report*, 1892, p. 312; 1887, p. 154; Hill to Atkins, June 5, 1888, NARS, RG 75, LR, Santee Agency.

[56] Com. of Indian Affairs, *Annual Report*, 1888, p. 173; 1889, p. 243.

sibility of the federal government. When liquor sellers were indicted, they sometimes pleaded guilty, were fined a dollar each, and were "sent home to repeat the work of debauchery." Some even charged that the liquor law was unconstitutional and threatened to carry their cases to the Supreme Court if necessary.[57] As long as there was no effective way of preventing white men from selling liquor to the Indians, the problem of drinking could not be solved.

A different type of problem growing out of allotment was that of the children born since the reservation had been opened. As early as 1888 nearly a hundred children had been born since the land was allotted and were without hope of receiving farms when they reached maturity. On March 2 of the following year Congress passed a bill containing a provision that Santees who had not received allotments in 1885 should be entitled to farms of from 40 to 160 acres, on their reservation. Since there was no land available there, the provision remained a dead letter and was modified in 1891 by an appropriation of $32,000 for the purchase of lands elsewhere for those, mostly children, who had missed out on the earlier allotment. No such purchases were made, and the following year a clause was inserted in the Indian appropriations act permitting the payment in cash of this sum, together with the proceeds from the sale of the old Minnesota reservation. Payment of the latter sum was made in December of the same year, and the rest was paid in 1893. Besides the $32,000, the Santees received $34.93 per capita from the sale of the old reservation, and some of them were paid additional sums from an appropriation made for the benefit of scouts and their heirs.[58]

The money came at a good time, in the midst of the drought years, but unfortunately it was not all spent as wisely as it might have been. Furthermore, the expectation of more such windfalls did irreparable damage to such habits of prudence, thrift, and industry as the Santees had acquired since 1866. The Episcopal missionary wrote in 1896: "Most if not all of what they expect is disposed of by credit at the stores long before it is received, and much is spent in rioting and drunkenness when obtained." The agents agreed that farming had fallen off, and habits of indolence had become prevalent. In 1896, Congress amended

[57] *Ibid.*, 1888, p. 177; 1896, p. 202; 1897, p. 185. James J. Janney to Morgan, February 10, 1891; Steer to Morgan, November 17, 1891; Clements to D. M. Browning, March 16, 1894, NARS, RG 75, LR, Santee Agency.

[58] Hill to Atkins, April 6, 1888; Helms to Morgan, December 2, 1892, NARS, RG 75, LR, Santee Agency; Com. of Indian Affairs, *Annual Report*, 1893, p. 200; U.S. *Statutes at Large*, XXV, 890, XXVI, 720–721, XXVII, 145.

the act of March 2, 1889, so as to provide further benefits to the Santees. This legislation brought another payment, which, together with
additional payments of interest on funds in the Treasury, made the
Santees temporarily richer by $89,015.75 in cash, plus $18,499.13 in
stock and farm implements.[59]

Besides all the cash payments, the Santees were enjoying another kind
of unearned income in the 1890's. Soon after allotment they discovered
that they could make more money with less work by leasing part of
their lands to white farmers than by trying to farm them by themselves.
Abuses soon crept in. A farmer might lease an eighty-acre tract and
then let his cattle roam far beyond the confines of that unfenced unit.
As the years passed, the practice of leasing became more widespread
and the abuses more flagrant. The early leases were entirely unofficial,
based on mere oral agreements, but in time the Indian Office began
making legal contracts with farmers and stock raisers, in the hope of
thereby exercising some control over the manner in which the land was
used. Most of the agents opposed leasing, on the ground that it contributed to the laziness of the Indian and postponed indefinitely the day
when he would be truly self-supporting.[60] From a purely economic point
of view, however, it was probably the best arrangement that could have
been made for the use of lands like those on the Santee Reservation.
Only a farmer or rancher with access to large amounts of land could
hope to make a success of his operations in an area with so unpredict-
able a climate.

To one who had watched the course of events since 1866, the condition of the Santees at the turn of the century was anything but encouraging. True, their numbers had been increasing steadily since 1879,
until the population had risen from 736 in that year to 1,019 in 1898—
about the same number who had come down from Crow Creek and up
from Davenport thirty-two years earlier. Educationally they had progressed far in those years. Not only did they enjoy the facilities of the
Santee Normal Training School and the Santee Industrial School, but
by the middle nineties contracts were being made with school districts
in Knox County, and Santee children were sharing classrooms with
white children. But they were as far as ever from self-sufficiency and in
many respects were retrograding. Worst of all, the Indian Bureau and

[59] Com. of Indian Affairs, *Annual Report*, 1896, p. 205; 1897, p. 184.
[60] Helms to Morgan, July 19, 1892, NARS, RG 75, LR, Santee Agency; Com. of
Indian Affairs, *Annual Report*, 1894, p. 193; 1896, pp. 41, 202; 1898, p. 332; 1900,
p. 280.

other government agencies seemed unaware that earlier hopes had not been realized. In 1894 the House subcommittee on Indian affairs was considering abandoning the Santee agency, presumably because the Indians were thought to be almost assimilated and able to look out for themselves.[61] Fortunately, the agency was not discontinued then, or for more than twenty years afterward, but the fact that abandonment was being considered was an augury of things to come.

At the end of the nineteenth century the belief was widespread that the Indian problem was nearly solved. Indian wars were a thing of the past, many reservations had been allotted, and the Indians were decreasing in numbers. Government responsibility in the future toward those who remained was thought to be primarily a matter of education. The mass of the American people were busy with other concerns, including their newly acquired overseas empire, and they did not wish to be reminded that Indians still lagged behind the rest of the population in education, in health, and in their economic and social condition. If the Indians were ready to be "turned loose," as a later generation expressed the abdication of public responsibility for their welfare, the Santees should have been as ready as any. This notion probably underlay the talk of closing down the agency. As elsewhere, however, such talk reflected more a wish to be rid of the Indian problem than any actual readiness of the Indians to get along without government help and guidance. Although the most serviceable features of the Santees' culture had been successfully beaten out of them, what had been acquired from the white man's culture was insufficient to compensate for the loss. The residue of the old culture, much of it an economic liability, together with the legacy of more than a half-century of exploitation and robbery by the white man, left the Santees unprepared to confront the twentieth century on a basis of equality with white Americans.

[61] Com. of Indian Affairs, *Annual Report*, 1895, p. 204; 1898, p. 332; Joseph Hollman to D. M. Browning, April 10, 1894, NARS, RG 75, LR, Santee Agency.

CHAPTER 10

The Fate of the Upper Sioux

WHILE THE main body of the lower Sioux were adjusting to reservation life on the Great Plains, a parallel course was being followed by the upper bands, in a somewhat more northerly setting. In the closing days of the Sioux Uprising, most of the Sissetons and Wahpetons, though largely innocent of participation in the massacres, fled before the advancing military force under General Sibley and scattered over the plains of Dakota Territory. For the next few years they led a nomadic life, wishing to re-establish themselves in the good graces of the white man's government but fearing to give themselves up. Gradually, however, the bulk of them gathered on the Coteau des Prairies, just west of the Lake Traverse–Big Stone Lake area, where in the fall of 1864 the army established Fort Wadsworth, partly for their benefit but chiefly to protect the frontier. Some Dakota politicians, notably Walter A. Burleigh and Governor Newton Edmunds, tried to have them removed to Crow Creek. Failing in this effort, Edmunds, at least, came around finally to advocating that they be given a reservation on the Coteau and restored to treaty relationships with the government.[1]

After two inconclusive attempts to negotiate with those bands had been made in 1864 and 1866, Benjamin Thompson, who had been serving with the commission to appraise the former reservation lands in

[1] Clark W. Thompson to William P. Dole, January 14, 1865; Walter A. Burleigh to Dennis N. Cooley, July 23, 1865; Newton Edmunds to Cooley, August 7, 1865, NARS, RG 75, LR; Com. of Indian Affairs, *Annual Report*, 1866, p. 180.

Minnesota, took the initiative late in the latter year and proposed bringing a hand-picked delegation to Washington to make a treaty. Thompson argued that these people had been friendly in 1862, had saved many white captives, and would prove a useful buffer between the white settlements and the wilder Indians to the west. His recommendation was endorsed by General Sibley, who also urged that Joseph R. Brown be given a role in the negotiations. Commissioner Bogy was sufficiently impressed by his arguments to instruct Thompson to bring a delegation, not to exceed twenty-one men, to Washington in January and to associate himself with Brown in the enterprise.[2]

The delegation was brought to Washington as requested and on February 19, 1867, signed a treaty including pretty much the same terms as the one that had been rejected the previous summer. As finally concluded and amended by the Senate, it provided for two reservations, one a wedge-shaped piece of land between Lake Traverse and Fort Wadsworth, its apex at Lake Kampeska (near present Watertown, South Dakota) and its base along, but not parallel to, the later South Dakota–North Dakota boundary. The other reservation, which will be discussed in the next chapter, was a tract extending south from Devils Lake. The most interesting provisions of the treaty were those designed to encourage the civilization of the Sisseton and Wahpeton Sioux. In line with Brown's thinking during his term as Sioux agent, they called for the allotment of the reservations into 160-acre tracts, the owners to receive inalienable patents after five years if they had brought under cultivation at least 50 acres. Furthermore, no goods, provisions, etc., were to be issued except in return for labor performed or produce delivered (the aged and infirm were exempted from this provision), and no trade in furs was to be permitted. Despite Brown's most strenuous efforts, he was unable to incorporate into the treaty a restoration of the tribe's annuities.[3]

Certain other provisions, specifying the amount of money to be expended each year for the benefit of the Indians and allowing the payment of traders' debts to a certain sum, were stricken out by the Senate, which chose instead to leave the expenditures to the discretion of the

[2] Joseph R. Brown to Dole, January 31, 1864; Benjamin Thompson to Lewis V. Bogy, November 19, 1866; Henry H. Sibley to Alexander Ramsey, December 14, 1866, NARS, RG 75, LR; Cooley to Sibley, March 19 and April 25, 1866, NARS, RG 75, LS; Bogy to Benjamin Thompson, December 20 and 22, 1866, NARS, RG 75, LS; Com. of Indian Affairs, *Annual Report*, 1866, pp. 180, 227, 240.

[3] J. R. Brown to Bogy, February 4, 1867, NARS, RG 75, LR; Charles J. Kappler, comp. and ed., *Indian Affairs, Laws and Treaties*, II (Washington: Government Printing Office, 1904), 957–959.

Secretary of the Interior and omitted all reference to traders' debts. The treaty thus amended was approved by the Indians on April 22 and proclaimed May 2.[4] Signing as head chief of the Sissetons and Wahpetons was Gabriel Renville, nephew of the illustrious Joseph Renville and a relative by marriage of Joseph R. Brown. Scarlet Plume signed as chief of the Sissetons, but most of the other hereditary chiefs, such as Standing Buffalo, were still roaming the prairies and had no share in the treaty. Their nonparticipation, as well as that of several of the leading "farmer Indians" from the old reservation days, was unfortunate in that it caused a split which contributed to the extreme factionalism that later plagued the Sisseton-Wahpeton group.[5]

Benjamin Thompson was appointed agent shortly after the treaty was ratified and assumed his duties that summer. Even before his arrival, there had been efforts by the government to aid these Sioux in their farming endeavors. Beginning in 1865 the government had attempted to provide them with hoes and other articles, but some of the purchases never reached them, and grasshoppers and drought rendered their efforts at farming ineffectual. By the fall of 1866 they were in such a state of destitution that they were kept alive only by the timely issuance of some soldiers' rations from Fort Wadsworth that had been condemned as unfit for human consumption.[6] The next spring they received garden and field seeds, which they dutifully planted with the aid of hoes and pointed sticks. Much of the crop was again destroyed by grasshoppers, but they managed to raise 120 bushels of potatoes and 230 bushels of corn. This was not enough to tide them over the winter, however, and once more they hovered on the brink of starvation while efforts to provide them with emergency supplies were hampered by the usual bureaucratic red tape and slowness of communication between Washington and the remote frontier post. Eventually assistance in the form of more condemned rations and some agricultural implements was sent.[7]

[4] Kappler, *Indian Affairs, Laws and Treaties*, II, 958–959; U.S. *Statutes at Large*, XV, 505–511.

[5] U.S. *Statutes at Large*, XV, 511; Henry B. Whipple to Ely S. Parker, August 24, 1869, NARS, RG 75, LR, Sisseton Agency.

[6] C. G. Wykoff, Chief Clerk, Northern Superintendency, to Dole, May 22, 1865; Sibley to Ramsey, December 14, 1866, NARS, RG 75, LR; Colonel S. B. Hayman, commanding at Fort Wadsworth, to Lieutenant Colonel Smith, Acting Assistant Adjutant General, Department of Dakotah, November 21, 1866, NARS, RG 75, LR, Northern Superintendency; Charles H. Mix to Nathaniel G. Taylor, July 10 and August 10, 1867, NARS, RG 75, LR, Sisseton Agency.

[7] Mix to N. G. Taylor, July 10, 1867; Benjamin Thompson to N. G. Taylor, March

The plight of the upper Sioux was extremely serious at this time. Since one of the objects of making a treaty was to keep them from indiscriminate roving, they were expected to remain on their reservation at all times and ran the risk of being treated as hostile if they strayed outside its boundaries. Because the game in the locality was not nearly enough to supply their needs, they were largely dependent on such provisions as were issued by the commanding officer at Fort Wadsworth or by the designated agents of the Indian Bureau. As other members of their tribe had discovered, however, they had a powerful friend in Bishop Henry B. Whipple, who now argued so eloquently in their behalf that he not only persuaded Congress in 1868 to appropriate $30,000 for their benefit but inadvertently saddled himself with the responsibility of expending the sum.[8]

The language of the appropriations act created an awkward situation in which the money to be used for the Indians was not subject to the control of the Indian Bureau, which could do no more than provide Bishop Whipple with suggestions in response to his inquiries. Agent Thompson, who was nominally in charge of the Indians although he spent very little time on the reservation, had no funds at his disposal and repeatedly asked that some be provided out of the proceeds of the sale of the old reservation. Bishop Whipple, who was unable to carry out the terms of the congressional directive in person and who seems not to have wished to entrust the execution of his charge to Thompson, turned over the task of actually purchasing and delivering provisions, clothing, farm implements, and seed for the Indians to his old friend and family physician, Dr. Jared W. Daniels, one-time physician on the old Sioux reservation. When Daniels arrived at Fort Wadsworth in October, 1868, he found the Indians in great need and immediately began issuing a pound of food per day, once a month, plus sugar, coffee, and tobacco to those who paid for it with work. He also provided axes and plows and, to those who had hay, cattle as well. The next spring he started the Indians breaking land, with hoes if necessary, and beginning April 1 he had a farmer visit each dwelling to keep a record of work done.[9]

Bishop Whipple himself visited the reservation in the late fall of 1868

30, 1868, NARS, RG 75, LR, Sisseton Agency; Com. of Indian Affairs, *Annual Report*, 1867, p. 245; 1868, pp. 194–195; U.S. *Statutes at Large*, XV, 217.

[8] U.S. *Statutes at Large*, XV, 217; Whipple to Parker, August 24, 1869, NARS, RG 75, LR, Sisseton Agency; Com. of Indian Affairs, *Annual Report*, 1869, pp. 326–330.

[9] Benjamin Thompson to N. G. Taylor, August 19, 1868; Whipple to Bogy, August 19, 1868, NARS, RG 75, LR, Sisseton Agency; Com. of Indian Affairs, *Annual Report*, 1869, pp. 320–321.

and was so appalled by the destitution he found that he decided to ignore the provision of the 1867 treaty and issue food and clothing to those in greatest need, without regard to whether they had worked or not. Brown and Thompson both opposed this practice. Thompson complained that

> These indiscriminate issues, although relieving their necessities at the time, lead to evils by encouraging the idle to hang around the post, and if encouraged will certainly retard if not entirely prevent the success of the auspicious commencement under the treaty on this reservation. It is not to be expected that Indians, any more than white men, will work from choice if they can obtain a living without doing so. . . .[10]

An element of professional jealousy may have entered into this criticism, for Thompson was acutely sensitive to the ambiguity of his position and became more so when, in March, 1869, Congress appropriated $60,000 for the Sisseton and Wahpeton Sioux and again placed its disbursement entirely in the hands of Bishop Whipple. The awkwardness was resolved, after a fashion, by the appointment the next month of Daniels as agent, but it was several months before Thompson could be persuaded to turn over the government property to him.[11]

Thompson had accomplished some good during his term as agent. He had induced many families to select farms and begin improvements, and he had built houses for 150 families. Handicapped by a lack of funds, he had nevertheless broken about 550 acres of land, including 50 acres plowed by the Indians themselves and a hundred acres broken with hoes. Under Daniels' direction, the work of establishing the upper Sioux on their reservation continued at an accelerated pace. Dissatisfied with Thompson's practice of residing alternately at Fort Wadsworth and in Brown's house at Lake Traverse, he invited the chiefs and headmen to choose an agency site. At the location they selected, about nine miles south of the present town of Sisseton, he had a warehouse, an agency office, a boarding house, and an interpreter's house built, all of logs and costing only $2,100. By the fall of 1869 about 160 families had taken farms, widely scattered about the reservation.[12]

[10] Whipple to N. G. Taylor, December 10, 1868, NARS, RG 75, LR, Sisseton Agency; Com. of Indian Affairs, *Annual Report*, 1868, p. 195.

[11] U.S. *Statutes at Large*, XV, 315; N. G. Taylor to Jared W. Daniels, April 22, 1869; Parker to Benjamin Thompson, July 13, 1869; Acting Commissioner W. F. Cady to Whipple, September 25, 1869, NARS, RG 75, LS; Whipple to Parker, August 24, 1869, NARS, RG 75, LR, Sisseton Agency.

[12] Benjamin Thompson to N. G. Taylor, December 23, 1868, and April 12, 1869;

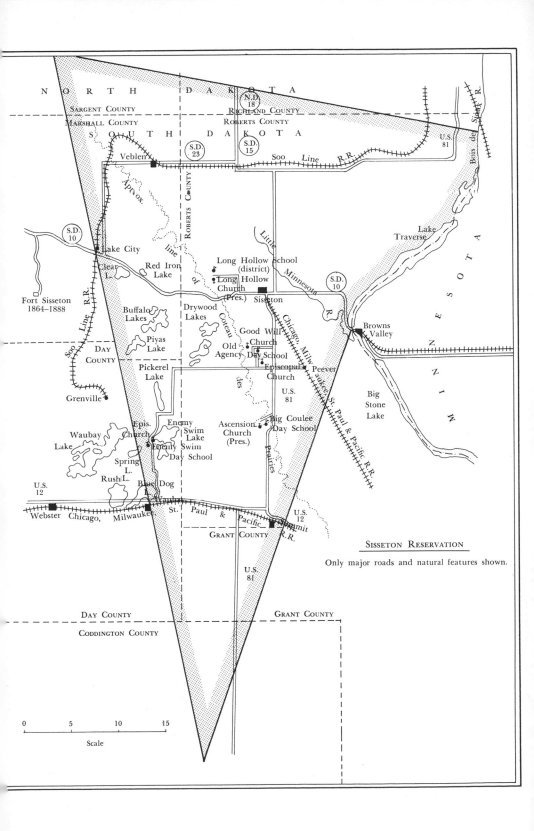

NORTH DAKOTA

SARGENT COUNTY

N.D.
18

RICHLAND COUNTY

MARSHALL COUNTY

ROBERTS COUNTY

SOUTH DAKOTA

S.D.
23

S.D.
15

Veblen

Soo   Line   R.R.

U.S.
81

ROBERTS COUNTY

S.D.
10

Lake
Traverse

Approx.

line

of

Little

Minnesota

Lake City

Clear
L.

Red Iron
Lake

Long Hollow School
(district)

Long Hollow
Church
(Pres.)

R.

Fort Sisseton
1864–1888

Soo

Line

R.R.

Buffalo
Lakes

Drywood
Lakes

Coteau

Sisseton

S.D.
10

Browns
Valley

Piyas
Lake

Good Will
Church

DAY
COUNTY

Pickerel
Lake

des

Old
Agency

Day School

Episcopal
Church

Peever

Chicago, Milwaukee,

Big
Stone
Lake

Grenville

U.S.
81

St. Paul & Pacific R.R.

Waubay
Lake

Epis.
Church

Enemy
Swim
Lake

Enemy Swim
Day School

Ascension
Church
(Pres.)

Big Coulee
Day School

Prairies

Spring
L.

Rush L.

Blue Dog
L.

Waubay

U.S.
12

Webster   Chicago,   Milwaukee,

St.   Paul   &   Pacific

U.S.
12

Summit

R.R.

GRANT COUNTY

SISSETON RESERVATION

Only major roads and natural features shown.

U.S.
81

DAY COUNTY

GRANT COUNTY

CODDINGTON COUNTY

0   5   10   15

Scale

The number of Indians on the reservation, variously estimated at the time of the treaty, fluctuated considerably in the early years. Thompson reported a population of 1,637 in 1868, but the next year he counted only 1,164. Daniels found 1,498 in 1870, and there were just two fewer in 1872. By the next year the number had increased to 1,540 and in 1874 to 1,677.[13] The probability is that people kept drifting in from the plains as the news reached them that they need not remain pariahs any longer. As fast as they arrived, they were encouraged to take up farms, send their children to school, and generally accommodate themselves to the government's beneficent intentions.

In their slow progress toward civilization the Sissetons and Wahpetons were subjected to the influence of missionaries almost from the beginning of their life on the new reservation. Stephen R. Riggs and Thomas S. Williamson, who had been their spiritual mentors on the old reservation, promptly took up the work again in the new location. The Indians themselves, some of them ordained ministers, played an active part in re-establishing the missionary activity. After holding services in homes for some time, Daniel Renville and a number of others early in 1869 petitioned Agent Thompson for assistance in building a church. In the summer of 1870, Riggs began building a church and school to be named "Good Will." When Gabriel Renville questioned his authority to build, he wrote to the Interior Department for instructions. Although ordered to suspend operations until it was decided which denomination was to have charge of the agency, he went ahead with the building and later received authorization to do so. Daniel Renville became pastor of the church, and late in the fall of 1870 a school was opened under the direction of Wyllys K. Morris, Riggs' son-in-law. As on the old reservation, teaching was conducted in both English and Dakota. Another church was built at Ascension and John B. Renville, a native clergyman, placed in charge.[14] Thereafter mission work grew year by year, even though Williamson remained only a short time and Riggs spent only the summer months at Sisseton.

All significant missionary activity among the upper Sioux, both

Benjamin Thompson to Parker, June 30, 1869, NARS, RG 75, LR, Sisseton Agency; Com. of Indian Affairs, *Annual Report*, 1869, pp. 321–323.

[13] Com. of Indian Affairs, *Annual Report*, 1868, p. 194; 1869, p. 324; 1870, p. 225; 1873, p. 226; 1872, p. 255; 1874, p. 254. Daniels counted 1,613 in 1869, but 321 of those belonged at Devils Lake. Still, his figure is substantially higher than Thompson's.

[14] Stephen R. Riggs, *Mary and I: Forty Years with the Sioux* (Boston: Congregational Sunday-School and Publishing Society, 1880), pp. 254, 258–259, 261–263; Com. of Indian Affairs, *Annual Report*, 1869, pp. 322, 325.

before the uprising and afterward, had been conducted by the American Board, which was at that time under Presbyterian control. Hence it was natural that when President Grant distributed the various agencies among the different denominations, the Sisseton agency should come under the control of the American Board. Daniels was an Episcopalian, and although he was well liked by the Indians and apparently effective as an agent, control of the agency by the American Board necessitated his replacement by a Presbyterian. The man selected for the post was Moses N. Adams, who had been a missionary at Traverse des Sioux before the treaties of 1851. The choice was an unfortunate one from the standpoint of harmony on the reservation, for it exacerbated the factionalism already existing and led to a period of nearly continuous strife between the opposing forces. From Adams' arrival at the agency in December, 1871, until his departure in 1875, charges and counter-charges were exchanged, and there was acute dissatisfaction leading on occasion to violence, which in turn resulted in retaliation by the agent. Because this period of contention almost certainly contributed to the ultimate failure of the civilizing experiment at Sisseton, it warrants more attention than such squabbles usually do.

The conflict was between the "church party," made up of those Indians who had been most strongly under missionary influence on the old reservation and who often surpassed their teachers in moralistic rigidity, and the "scout party," headed by Gabriel Renville, who preserved many of the "heathen" customs, such as polygamy and dancing, and paid little attention to Christian observances. The dichotomy was not simply between civilization and anti-civilization factions, for Renville and some of his followers were the most progressive farmers on the reservation, and they accused some of the ministers belonging to the other group of devoting so much time to their spiritual duties that they neglected their farms. Generally, however, the least progressive members of the tribe tended to side with Renville in his disputes with the agent, with the result that he was tarred with the same brush so far as Adams was concerned.[15]

Shortly after Adams took over as agent, the chiefs and headmen charged in a petition that he had made indiscriminate issues of supplies instead of adhering to the terms of the treaty and had thereby weakened the incentive to labor which the treaty had been intended to provide.

---

[15] Everett W. Sterling, "Moses N. Adams: A Missionary as Indian Agent," *Minnesota History*, XXXV (December 1956), 167–168; Gabriel Renville, *et al.*, to Sibley, May 2, 1871, NARS, RG 75, LR, Sisseton Agency.

They accused him of conspiring with Riggs to "feed their flock of idlers," i.e., the native ministers, who were of course expected to farm like their parishioners. Adams dismissed the charges as reflecting personal animosity toward him. Matters took a more serious turn late in 1873, when a self-constituted police force tried to drive two native ministers off the reservation by seizing their oxen, wagons, plows, and other equipment issued by the government and turning these items over to the agency for reissue to more deserving members of the tribe. With assistance reluctantly provided by the garrison at Fort Wadsworth, Adams took two of the leaders into custody and then removed Gabriel Renville, the two culprits, and another man from the "executive board" that he had set up, and replaced them with members of the church faction.[16]

Apparently thinking the battle won, Adams then proposed a new system of government for the reservation. The rules and regulations included in his plan reveal much about the man's mentality and the attitude with which he approached his duties as Indian agent. One stipulation was that "ample provision should be made for them . . . guaranteeing to each one protection in the liberty to worship and serve God, according to the dictates of his own conscience." But this expression of religious freedom was followed immediately by the sentence "All idolatrous and pagan worship and service should be forbidden with suitable penalty attached." When he had been on the job less than a year, Adams wrote the commissioner that changing the Indians' ways would be difficult, "for in all the work of educating and elevating this people, socially and morally, we encounter their native and peculiar habits; their ignorance and prejudice, and their amazing slowness to believe and do what is right."[17]

Adams' stern measures did not silence the discontent of the scout party, who got up another petition and finally brought about an investigation of affairs at the agency in 1874. The upshot was the formal censure of the agent, who had by this time alienated even Riggs by his autocratic and sometimes violent methods. Before his replacement in the spring of 1875, Adams got in a few Parthian shots, accusing the

16 Chiefs and Head Men to Great Father, February 7, 1872; Moses N. Adams to Commissioner Francis A. Walker, April 3, 1872; Adams to Edward P. Smith, December 15, 17, 18, 23, and 26, 1873, NARS, RG 75, LR, Sisseton Agency; Sterling, "Moses N. Adams: A Missionary as Indian Agent," pp. 171–173.

17 Adams to E. P. Smith, January 28, 1874; Adams to Walker, April 3, 1872, NARS, RG 75, LR, Sisseton Agency; Sterling, "Moses N. Adams: A Missionary as Indian Agent," pp. 169–170.

government inspector, E. C. Kemble, of having "covered the Cross of Christ with shame among the pagan portion of this people" by saying that the agent was not there as a minister and should not interfere with the feasting and dancing. Kemble had called the scout party "the most industrious, enterprising and prosperous members of the tribe" (which they probably were); Adams replied, irrelevantly, that they were "largely pagans, polygamists, bigamists and drummers who, almost to a man, retain many of their old heathen habits and customs."[18]

Despite the contention between rival factions during Adams' tenure as agent, some progress was made on the reservation, notably in education. As early as 1869 four buildings erected by the Indians were in use as schools. Although Adams doubted the value of such scattered institutions and wanted a manual labor school, he had to be content with day schools for his first two years as agent. By the fall of 1872 two brick schools were completed to house classes previously conducted in homes and churches, and soon afterward the church building at Ascension was taken over by the government as a school. Two more district schools were built in 1874. These schools seem not to have been very successful in their early years. Adams' successor, John G. Hamilton, remarked of the educational system on the reservation that "results are hardly commensurate with the amount of money expended." Dissenting from Adams' view that all five of the schools should be taught the year around, he operated them for only four and a half months. Later they were largely abandoned because of irregular and unsatisfactory attendance and general indifference on the part of the Indians. Daniels had observed much earlier that the novelty of school wore off after about two months.[19]

Adams wanted a central institution to train native teachers for the outlying schools, much as Santee Normal Training School was doing. His first request was turned down by the Indian Bureau, but in 1873 he was authorized to begin construction on a manual labor school. Although not entirely finished, it was opened that fall with an enrollment of eighteen girls. It was a small operation for a number of years, kept

[18] Adams to E. P. Smith, February 14, 1874, and March 20, 1875; Dr. George H. Hawes to E. P. Smith, November 2, 1874, NARS, RG 75, LR, Sisseton Agency; Sterling, "Moses N. Adams: A Missionary as Indian Agent," p. 175.

[19] Adams to Walker, February 26 and May 18, 1872, and January 24, 1873; Adams to E. P. Smith, March 29, 1873; John G. Hamilton to E. P. Smith, June 23, 1875, NARS, RG 75, LR, Sisseton Agency; Com. of Indian Affairs, *Annual Report*, 1869, p. 321; 1871, p. 531; 1872, p. 256; 1873, p. 226; 1874, p. 256; 1875, p. 252; 1876, p. 37; 1878, pp. 41–42.

open for only nine months a year during Hamilton's term of office.[20] Besides the government schools, the Sissetons also had the facilities of one or more mission schools, which, though they never acquired the importance of those at Santee, supplemented the government schools for a time. In 1876, for example, the mission school was in session longer than the district schools, and two years later both the Good Will and the Ascension mission schools were in operation for ten months. In that year the American Board spent $2,510 for its work on the Sisseton Reservation.[21]

When the Sisseton Reservation was established, the land surrounding it was as yet unceded by the Indians. Although their claim to some eight million acres in the eastern part of Dakota Territory was considered somewhat shadowy, the language of the 1867 treaty implied that such a claim existed. As the tide of settlement began to sweep into the area, pressure for its cession grew, until in 1872 Congress instructed the Secretary of the Interior to examine and report on any claim the Sissetons and Wahpetons might have to that region and, if their claim was found to be valid, what compensation, if any, should be made to them for the extinguishment of their title. Agents Adams and William Forbes, of the Devils Lake Reservation, and James Smith were appointed commissioners to investigate the matter. Their instructions specified that, although the act of Congress contemplated payment, because these lands were "not only of no advantage to the Indians, but positively mischievous, as tending to keep alive their savage habits and traditions, the consideration if any thus to be paid ought to be very moderate." The consent of the Indians was not required, but it was deemed expedient that they should voluntarily and freely accept relinquishment of their claim.[22]

The council held with the chiefs and headmen of the Sissetons and Wahpetons was not altogether a love feast, but the Indians had learned by then that whatever terms the white man chose to offer them might as well be accepted. Hence they put up only token opposition to the offer of ten cents an acre, to be paid in ten annual installments of $80,000 each. Smith pretended that this sum was really more than the lands were worth to the Indians, but Adams and Forbes more frankly advised

[20] Adams to Walker, February 26, 1872, and January 24 and March 29, 1873, NARS, RG 75, LR, Sisseton Agency; Com. of Indian Affairs, *Annual Report*, 1872, p. 256; 1873, p. 226; 1874, p. 256; 1876, p. 37.

[21] Com. of Indian Affairs, *Annual Report*, 1876, p. 37; 1878, pp. 41, 43.

[22] U.S. *Statutes at Large*, XVII, 281; Walker to William Forbes and Adams, July 19, 1872, NARS, RG 75, LR, Sisseton Agency.

the Indians to accept it as the best they could get. The agreement signed in September, 1872, contained nine paragraphs, of which Congress later struck out all but the first two, which provided for the cession and the amount of compensation. These sweeping amendments were agreed to as a matter of course in May, 1873, and the last claims of the Sisseton-Wahpeton Sioux, except for the two reservations, were done away with for a ridiculously low price.[23]

About the most that could be said for the agreement was that it provided, for the next ten years, a badly needed source of revenue for the Indians. The treaty of 1867 had been, in its amended form, deliberately vague as to the amount of money to be expended for these people, and appropriations were always subject to the exigencies of the budget. Following the panic of 1873, for example, appropriations for the Indian Service generally were cut drastically. Theoretically the Sissetons and Wahpetons were entitled to benefits from the sale of the old reservation in Minnesota, but the sums realized from that source were usually tied up in one way or another so that practically none of the money reached the Indians until the 1890's. Hence the pittance they received for the cession of their lands in eastern Dakota gave their agent something to work with for a decade, at the end of which time they were expected to have become entirely self-supporting.

Although the Sissetons had begun locating on farms during Thompson's term as agent, no thoroughgoing survey of the reservation was made at that time. Consequently people had settled pretty much where they pleased, without regard to whether their farms were susceptible to description in the customary surveyor's terms. By 1874, "all sorts of difficulties had grown out of local contentions about timber, land, &c," as Adams commented. The next year C. C. Royce was sent out by the Interior Department to survey the Indians' claims preparatory to issuing certificates of allotment. Royce also found "numerous and very vexatious disputes" among the Indians as to the boundaries of their claims. In many cases they had settled too close together to permit the assignment of 160-acre tracts to each family without requiring some to move.[24]

[23] Proceedings of Council, September 18, 1872; Adams to Walker, September 19, 1872, NARS, RG 75, LR, Sisseton Agency; Com. of Indian Affairs, *Annual Report*, 1872, pp. 118–123; U.S. *Statutes at Large*, XVIII, 167.

[24] Com. of Indian Affairs, *Annual Report*, 1874, p. 257; 1875, p. 253; Secretary of Interior Columbus Delano to E. P. Smith, April 23 and May 10, 1875; C. C. Royce to E. P. Smith, June 14 and September 25, 1875; Acting Secretary of Interior B. R. Cowen to E. P. Smith, October 1, 1875, NARS, RG 75, LR, Sisseton Agency.

In making the allotments Royce was guided by a principle necessitated by the nature of the country embraced in the reservation. Most of the timber, highly prized by the Indians, was located in the coulees along the eastern slope of the Coteau, whereas the best farm land lay well to the east, beyond a rather sterile strip at the base of the Coteau. Thompson had recognized this problem and in 1868 had recommended that each family be given forty acres of timber in one piece and the remainder of his quarter section in another tract. Royce followed that principle in making the allotments in 1875, with the result that most of the Indians had two pieces of land, rather widely separated. If the homesteads had been situated on the tracts of good agricultural land, no difficulty would have ensued; but the Indians, regarding the availability of timber more highly than the quality of the soil, had settled mostly in the coulees. Years later, when they had received patents, they found it convenient to lease their farmland and practice a kind of subsistence agriculture on the remote timber claims where they lived.[25]

Despite a rapid turnover in agents and slow progress in farming, life on the Sisseton Reservation during the 1870's had an appearance of stability. In accordance with the terms of the 1867 treaty, rations, clothing, stock, and farm implements were issued only in return for labor performed. The labor might include hauling supplies from the nearest railroad terminus (Morris, Minnesota, until 1876, when a road was surveyed to Herman, a few miles nearer) or construction work around the agency, but there was not enough work of this kind for the number of men who needed to draw rations. Consequently, the practice was adopted early and long continued of including work on one's own claim. The men were paid, not in cash but in credit, at a rate comparable to the going rate for labor outside the reservation. Breaking new sod was worth five dollars an acre, ordinary plowing, three dollars an acre. The transportation of supplies by ox team from Herman paid twenty dollars.[26]

Keeping track of the amount of work done by each man involved a tremendous amount of bookkeeping on the part of the agent and his clerk. An account of every man's work was kept in a set of "Indian

[25] Benjamin Thompson to N. G. Taylor, July 11, 1868; Royce to E. P. Smith, September 25, 1875, NARS, RG 75, LR, Sisseton Agency; Com. of Indian Affairs, *Annual Report*, 1900, p. 385.

[26] Hamilton to John Q. Smith, February 14, May 15, and July 28, 1876; Edward H. C. Hooper to Ezra A. Hayt, May 13, 1878, NARS, RG 75, LR, Sisseton Agency; Com. of Indian Affairs, *Annual Report*, 1871, p. 532; 1870, p. 226.

books"; the transactions covered an average of over 250 pages of ordinary ten-quire journal pages. Goods were issued by the storekeeper on requisitions signed by the agent or the clerk. The storekeeper kept a ledger showing the amount of goods received and issued and posted it weekly. Supplies were issued monthly in this fashion to more than four hundred individuals. In addition, Indians whose credit was notably good or who brought in produce for sale were allowed to draw on the warehouse at any time, even though this procedure placed an additional burden on the storekeeper. Ironically, the further the Indians advanced—that is, the more labor they performed—the more work devolved upon the agency employees. Issuing weekly rations to "wild" Indians at the agencies west of the Missouri was relatively simple compared to the task at Sisseton.[27]

There were a good many Indians, of course, who contributed little or nothing to their own support. These people, who constituted the "poor list" as distinguished from the "working list," made up a remarkably large proportion of the tribe. In 1872, for example, they numbered 660 out of a total of 1,496. Some of them were doing a little farming, but many were the elderly, the infirm, and the incompetent. During the decade their numbers diminished, as more and more families located on farms and thus qualified for inclusion on the "working list."[28]

In many respects, the history of the Sisseton Reservation during the last three decades of the nineteenth century parallels that of the Santee Reservation. At both places efforts were made to render the Indians economically self-sufficient, and on both reservations those efforts were hampered by drought and grasshopper plagues, by the Indians' uneven co-operation with their agents, and by the uncertainty and instability of the government's policy toward them. Some circumstances at Sisseton were peculiar to that reservation, however. Because the reservation was nearly nine times the size of the Santee Reservation as finally constituted, the Indians were scattered more widely and the agents had more difficulty keeping track of them. Located as it was in country not yet settled, it did not for several years include all the Indians nominally attached to the agency. Some continued to plant on Big Stone Lake, with the tacit permission of the agent, until at least 1870; another band, who practiced little or no agriculture, remained west of the reservation until the death of their chief, Big Eagle Feather, in 1873; still another

[27] Hamilton to J. Q. Smith, February 14, 1876, NARS, RG 75, LR, Sisseton Agency.

[28] Com. of Indian Affairs, *Annual Report*, 1872, pp. 255–256; 1875, p. 251.

group lingered around Fort Ransom, on the Sheyenne River, for two or three years before they were persuaded to join their tribesmen on the reservation.[29]

As at Santee, there was a steady increase in the number of agency buildings and Indian houses during the 1870's and 1880's. Daniels and Adams had operated with primitive facilities—log buildings of various sizes—but their successors replaced the more vital of these with better structures. A brick warehouse, in which the agent's office was located, was built in the later seventies. A steam-operated saw- and gristmill served the area surrounding the agency, though later, as towns grew up around the reservation, many of the Indians found it more convenient to haul their grain to mills in those towns and were given passes for that purpose. As late as 1875 a substantial number of the Indians were still living in tipis, but then a campaign was initiated to provide a log house for each family. Frame houses were not common until much later, and most families kept a tipi for occasional use in the summer even after they had made the transition to log houses as permanent residences.[30]

The attempt to train Indian apprentices to do the agency work was not as successful as at Santee, partly because a large proportion of the industrious men were farming and partly, it would seem, because some of the agents used their position to employ their relatives. Adams, in defending himself against Inspector Kemble's unfavorable report, said that most of the Indians who were not farming were unstable and unreliable and hence unsatisfactory as apprentices. Nevertheless, he employed an Indian as apprentice to the agency carpenter, and two were then working with the miller and learning his trade. In time, the apprentice system became an anachronism, and the Indians asked to be paid as hired help on the same basis as irregular employees hired from outside the reservation.[31] The employment of Indians as teamsters was not wholly successful, for some fell into temptation when at Morris to pick up supplies and became drunk; one agent recommended that supplies be brought in by a contractor. In 1879 the agent tried the

[29] *Ibid.*, 1867, p. 245; 1868, p. 193; 1869, p. 321; 1871, p. 532; 1873, p. 226; 1874, p. 255; Captain L. M. Kellogg, commanding at Fort Ransom, to Horace Capron, Commissioner of Agriculture, July 5, 1869; Daniels to Sibley, November 30, 1869, NARS, RG 75, LR, Sisseton Agency.

[30] Com. of Indian Affairs, *Annual Report*, 1869, p. 321; 1872, pp. 255, 257; 1878, p. 40; 1890, p. 67; Hamilton to E. P. Smith, December 1, 1875, NARS, RG 75, LR, Sisseton Agency.

[31] Adams to E. P. Smith, January 8, 1875; Charles Crissey to Hayt, August 26, 1879, NARS, RG 75, LR, Sisseton Agency.

experiment of replacing the white farmer with ten Indians, whom he placed in different parts of the reservation to instruct their fellows in agriculture and aid the agent in keeping tabs on affairs in the outlying areas. This innovation worked for a time but fell into disuse under a later agent.[32]

In the later seventies the Indians became increasingly independent in their behavior, if not in their economic condition. Those who left the reservation to have their wheat and corn ground at mills in nearby towns often sold a part of their grain or other produce for cash, with which they began making small purchases. About 1878 they began buying harvesters and other farm machinery, signing notes for them and paying for them out of the next crop. By 1880 ten reapers and ten fanning mills had been bought in this manner.[33] Their doing business in neighboring towns was a natural development in the assimilation process, but it caused stresses and strains in the somewhat rigid system evolved from the provisions of the 1867 treaty. By the end of the seventies the Indians could no longer earn enough by labor to buy the household articles and clothing they needed, and the prices paid for produce at the agency were well below those paid in off-reservation areas. By 1880 the pass system was clearly anachronistic at Sisseton, as the agent pointed out to the commissioner in requesting a relaxation of the policy. He admitted that some who left the reservation got drunk but pointed out: "The fact still presents itself, if this people are to become all the Dept is trying to make them, they must meet temptation and learn sooner or later, what our civilization is, by contact with it in neighboring towns." The Indian Office responded by issuing an order to the effect that men holding patents to their land need no longer carry passes. Since only two had thus far met the fifty-acre requirement, this ruling had practically no effect.[34]

As might have been expected, many of the Indians were leaving the reservation without passes, not always on legitimate business. In 1879 there was a flurry of excitement over the discovery that some had been cutting timber on the reservation and selling it, at prices well above those paid at the agency, to the contractor supplying wood to Fort Sis-

[32] Hamilton to J. Q. Smith, May 15, 1876; Crissey to Hayt, July 8, 1879, *ibid.*

[33] Hamilton to J. Q. Smith, March 14, 1876; Crissey to Hayt, August 26, 1879, and February 27, 1880, *ibid.*; Com. of Indian Affairs, *Annual Report*, 1878, p. 41.

[34] Crissey to Hayt, August 26, 1879, and February 27, 1880, NARS, RG 75, LR, Sisseton Agency.

seton, as Fort Wadsworth had been renamed in 1876. The practice seems to have been stopped with the co-operation of the commanding officer, but with the settling up of the surrounding country, the Indians found a ready market for wood smuggled from the reservation and for the oxen that had been issued to them. Their usual practice was to trade the oxen for horses or else sell them and buy horses or ponies. The absence of any single authority such as existed at the fort made it impossible to put a stop to this illegal trade. The introduction of whiskey among the Indians became a more serious problem in 1880, with the sudden development of the town of Browns Valley that year. The agent complained that it was impossible to obtain witnesses or to get the Indians to tell where they were buying the liquor.[35]

As at Santee, there was at Sisseton a gradual discontinuance of rations as the Indians approached self-sufficiency. The series of grasshopper plagues ended in 1877, and the next year a good crop was raised. Charles Crissey, who became agent in 1879, decided that the time was ripe for some major moves toward self-support. In the spring of 1880 only those who began farming that year were issued seed wheat; the rest used seed saved from the previous year. By the end of that growing season, only one-fourth of the Indians' subsistence was being provided by the government. Great quantities of farm machinery were being purchased by the Indians then, and more than four hundred cows were issued the following year, most of which were cared for by the farmers who received them.[36] The process of achieving self-support in food was hastened in April, 1882, by the burning of the warehouse. No subsistence supplies were issued after that date except for school children, apprentices, and the police force. In September, Agent Crissey reported: "After five months trial of a lesson, which, probably, is as hard a one as this people has ever been called upon to learn, and harder than any they will ever be obliged to learn in the future, I can safely say that the question of self-support of this people is forever settled."[37] His prediction was a trifle too sanguine, as was the statement of Benjamin Thompson, who returned as agent in 1884, that the Sissetons were "entirely self-supporting," but for several years they did provide their own

[35] Acting Commissioner E. J. Brooks to Secretary of Interior Carl Schurz, September 12, 1879; Crissey to Hayt, February 27, 1880; Crissey to Roland E. Trowbridge, August 4 and October 13, 1880, *ibid.*

[36] Com. of Indian Affairs, *Annual Report*, 1879, p. 44; 1880, p. 49; 1881, p. 56; 1882, pp. 41–42.

[37] *Ibid.*, 1882, p. 43.

subsistence and appeared to be progressing rapidly toward the goal the Indian Office had set for them.[38]

In some respects the parallels between Santee and Sisseton during the later nineteenth century are so close that the story of one reservation is the story of the other. On both reservations all the agents made sporadic efforts to stamp out "heathen" practices such as the old dances, but somehow they never achieved complete success. Soon after one agent had reported that the dances were virtually extinct, his successor would discover that they were reviving. In this campaign the agents were always assured of the co-operation of the missions, whose career at Sisseton much resembled that of the missions at Santee. During the period when Indian agencies were parceled out among religious denominations, the American Board had a monopoly on religious activities at Sisseton, but in 1881 an Episcopal mission was established by Bishop Hare. By 1883 the Episcopalians had two outstations in addition to their church at the agency. In subsequent years they expanded their activities until their membership at least equaled that of the Presbyterians.[39]

The manual labor boarding school followed a course much like that of the comparable institution at Santee, though without the spectacular misfortunes that marked the history of the latter. After a slow start in the seventies, it grew rapidly in the next decade, until it became too small for the needs of the reservation. Late in 1883 an addition costing more than $10,000 was put into use, and the school was soon enjoying an average attendance of nearly one hundred. Its enrollment fluctuated toward the end of the century, as the reservation was opened to white settlement and country schools began dotting the landscape. Some $7,000 was spent for another addition to the school in 1891, but mismanagement in the following years, coupled with substantial cash payments to the Indians, which had the same demoralizing effect as at Santee, tended to keep the enrollment from expanding in proportion to the population growth and educational needs of the reservation.[40]

One of the more striking parallels between Sisseton and Santee was that each spawned an offshoot colony. In 1875 some twenty-five families belonging to the church party, who feared that Adams' removal would leave them at the mercy of the other faction, fled the res-

[38] *Ibid.*, 1884, p. 49.

[39] *Ibid.*, 1881, p. 56; 1883, p. 46.

[40] *Ibid.*, 1883, p. 45; 1884, p. 50; 1885, p. 48; 1889, p. 164; 1891, pp. 419–420; 1895, p. 301.

ervation and took up homesteads about forty miles to the southeast. Although Agent Hamilton at first seized the issue oxen and farm implements they had taken with them, the missionaries later induced the Interior Department to replace those items and to give the Brown Earth colony, as it was called, other assistance in the way of seed, farm animals, and machinery. A school was built in 1880, with government support, and operated, unsuccessfully, until 1884. Led by the native minister, Daniel Renville, the Brown Earth people built themselves a log church in the second year of their self-exile from the reservation.[41]

The Brown Earth colony did not acquire the permanence of Flandreau, however, perhaps because the enterprise was ill-conceived by its initiators and insufficiently aided by the government. Although many of the colonists filed for homesteads, they do not seem to have been able to make the improvements necessary to meet the existing requirements. When Thompson investigated the colony in 1884, he found that few had more than five acres broken, and most were living by fishing, hunting, trapping, and selling wood to the neighboring whites. When the Sisseton Reservation was allotted under the provisions of the Dawes Act, most of these people returned to the reservation and took farms there. A few wanted nothing further to do with reservations, however, and migrated to Minnesota, where they formed the nucleus of the present Upper Sioux community near Granite Falls.[42] If the Brown Earth experiment had ended in failure, it had none the less taught the participants something about the pitfalls of independence and may possibly have prepared them for the trials that the whole tribe underwent following allotment.

Allotment was the biggest event on the Sisseton Reservation during the last two decades of the century. Sisseton was one of the earliest reservations to be allotted, and today it serves as the classic example of the evils of allotment. Because of the fifty-acre requirement in the 1867 treaty, the issuance of patents proceeded very slowly after the survey of farms carried out by Royce in 1875. Gabriel Renville received a patent almost at once, and Charles Crawford, like Renville a mixed-blood,

[41] Hamilton to E. P. Smith, June 21, 1875; Daniels to J. Q. Smith, April 9, 1877; Stephen R. Riggs to Hayt, November 19, 1877; Hooper to Hayt, June 4, 1878, NARS, RG 75, LR, Sisseton Agency; Com. of Indian Affairs, *Annual Report*, 1878, p. 43.

[42] Com. of Indian Affairs, *Annual Report*, 1878, p. 43; 1880, p. 50; 1884, pp. 50–52; 1885, p. 50; Sterling, "Moses N. Adams: A Missionary as Indian Agent," p. 177; James W. Balmer to Commissioner John Collier, November 7, 1938, NARS, RG 75, Pipestone School Agency (enclosing "Historical Data of Early Settlement of Upper Sioux Indian Community").

followed within a few months. After that, however, only one more was issued until 1883, when nine were issued. As late as 1886 the agent reported that a total of only thirty-three patents had been issued, mostly to older men.[43] At that rate it would have taken many decades for all the Sissetons to become landowners, and white settlers were clamoring to have the reservation opened.

Although the Sissetons had petitioned Congress in 1884 to be recognized as a civilized tribe and given the privileges granted the Five Civilized Tribes in Indian Territory, no action was taken until February 8, 1887, when the Dawes Act became law. It authorized the President to order allotment of any reservation when, in his opinion, the Indians were ready to take on the responsibilities of citizenship. Since the Sissetons were by this time largely self-supporting and were living under a fairly complex system of reservation government, it was natural for their reservation to be chosen as one of the first to undergo the experiment. The former Santee agent, Isaiah Lightner, went to Sisseton in the summer of 1887 and began making the allotments called for. Completion of the job required two years, at the end of which time 1,971 allotments had been made and 1,341 patents issued.[44]

Once allotment had been carried out, the next step was to arrange for the opening of the reservation. Here as elsewhere, the supposition was that no additional lands would ever be needed by the Indians. When the proposition to sell part of the reservation had been broached in 1884, the Indians had stoutly opposed it; but in November, 1889, when a commission met with the governing body of the tribe, they agreed without much discussion. The agreement signed December 12, 1889, provided that the unallotted lands should be sold at $2.50 per acre, the money to be held at 3 per cent interest and used by Congress for the "education and civilization" of the Indians, as provided by the Dawes Act. Together with other matters relating to the Sissetons, this agreement was ratified by Congress and became law on March 3, 1891. A proclamation was issued the next month opening the reservation to settlement. Of the original 918,770.58 acres, 310,711.06 had been allotted, 34,187.26 were reserved for agency, school, and church purposes, and the remaining 573,872.26 acres were made available for purchase by white settlers. As at Santee several years earlier, the houses of white

[43] Com. of Indian Affairs, *Annual Report*, 1883, p. 46; 1885, p. 49; 1886, p. 86.

[44] U.S. *Statutes at Large*, XXIV, 388–391; D'Arcy McNickle, "Rescuing Sisseton," *The American Indian*, III (Spring 1946), 23; Com. of Indian Affairs, *Annual Report*, 1887, p. 47; 1888, p. 56; 1889, p. 16.

pioneers soon dotted the prairies in every direction. Railroads had begun building through the reservation in 1880, and now towns sprang up at various points.[45]

The effects of allotment were much the same as at Santee. There was an immediate decline in farming activities among the Indians and a corresponding rise in the practice of leasing to white operators. Coming on the heels of drought in the later 1880's, these developments produced an abrupt halt in the civilizing process and a partial retrogression to an earlier stage. As early as 1889 the agent reported that his Indians would need assistance during the coming winter; and in 1891, $5,000 was spent up to April 1 for pork, flour, beef, and beans for the "destitute and starving." School attendance fell off markedly during this period, too, though the hope of obtaining rations induced some children to return to school with the coming of winter.[46]

All these evidences of decline were not due solely to allotment, however, for the Sissetons, like the Santees in the same period, received large cash payments during the early nineties. The agreement signed in December, 1889, also provided for the payment of $342,778.37 in back annuities to members of the tribe who had served as scouts with the United States Army during the Indian wars. This was calculated to be the amount that they would have received between July 1, 1862, and July 1, 1888, if their annuities had not been cut off by the act of February 16, 1863. The scouts (or their heirs) were also to be paid $18,400 annually from July 1, 1888, to July 1, 1901, the date on which the treaty of Traverse des Sioux would have expired. These provisions were incorporated into the Indian appropriations act of March 3, 1891, and payment was made in July. Although up to then two traders were scarcely making a living on the reservation, after that date three did a lively business as long as the money lasted.[47]

Together with the payment for the ceded lands, this money had much the same effect on the Indians as at Santee. Whiskey was relatively easy

[45] Com. of Indian Affairs, *Annual Report*, 1884, p. 51; 1890, p. 65; 1891, pp. 664–665; 1892, pp. 469, 728–729, 81; 1888, p. li. The figures on acreage are from the general report for 1892. The Sisseton agent in 1895 offered a somewhat different breakdown. According to him, 316,907 acres were retained by the Indians, including only 1,187 acres for agency, schools, and churches; 601,873 acres were thrown open for settlement. The early stages in the attempt to negotiate for a right of way for the Chicago, Milwaukee and St. Paul railway are treated in 48th Cong., 1st Sess., *H. Ex. Doc. 71*.

[46] Com. of Indian Affairs, *Annual Report*, 1889, p. 163; 1890, pp. 66, 69; 1891, p. 420.

[47] *Ibid.*, 1891, pp. 421, 664–665; Kappler, *Indian Affairs, Laws and Treaties*, I, 430–431, 485.

to obtain now that white settlers were everywhere and towns had sprung up; the agent reported in the fall of 1891 that the agency jail had been well filled for a time after the payment of annuities. The death of Gabriel Renville in August, 1892, removed an influence which, despite the attacks of Agent Adams and others, had been prevailingly good. Conditions were so bad that year that the agent, D. T. Hindman, resigned his job after only three or four months of duty. Captain George W. H. Smith, who served as acting agent the next year, was disillusioned by what he saw at Sisseton. Although the Indians there had received more advantages than most Indians, he thought, they were not as far advanced as they should have been. Contrary to what he had supposed before coming to the agency, only a few were self-supporting; most depended entirely on the per capita payments. Fewer than half the eligible children were in school. Although there had been a "fair" crop that year, drought returned again in 1894 and brought an almost total loss of crops and vegetables.[48]

The Sisseton population grew rapidly during the years of cash payments. From 1,520 in 1887 the number rose to 1,730 in 1891 and 1,863 in 1895. Since most of this increase came after the allotments had been made, the additional members of the tribe had no land of their own. Neither they nor the more fortunate members of the tribe were living under conditions much better than they had enjoyed years before. In 1890 there were on the reservation 77 frame houses, 22 log houses with shingle roofs, and 103 log houses with dirt roofs. Not all of them were occupied at one time; some of the frame houses were vacant during cold weather, and some of the log houses were unoccupied during warm weather. Tipis were still popular in summer, when the houses were used for storage.[49]

Citizenship brought with it new problems at Sisseton as elsewhere. The tax-exempt status of Indian land created ill feeling among the white population and made for difficulties in punishing Indian offenders in local courts. So far as civil actions were concerned, the Indians had no money for litigation and tended to go to the agent with their problems, as they had done before allotment. Many of them proceeded on the assumption that citizenship conveyed the right to buy and consume alcohol. In 1895 all but eleven of sixty-two arrests made by the agency police were for assault and disorderly conduct while under the

[48] Com. of Indian Affairs, *Annual Report*, 1891, p. 420; 1892, pp. 469, 471; 1893, pp. 303–305; 1894, p. 302.

[49] *Ibid.*, 1887, p. 45; 1891, p. 419; 1890, p. 67; 1895, p. 302.

influence of liquor. The next year all but nine of forty-three arrests were for similar causes. That year an Indian woman was shot and killed in Browns Valley by another Indian, who was tried in the Minnesota courts and sentenced to the state penitentiary at Stillwater. In 1899 the agent reported that six deaths that year were traceable to drinking. Prosecution of whiskey dealers in the last years of the century resulted in some decrease in the liquor trade, but the problem lingered on into the twentieth century.[50]

The outlook at the end of the century was even less promising at Sisseton than at Santee. When in 1898 and 1899 a total of $304,000 was paid out over a twelve-month period, the agent reported that only half the Indians had used it wisely. The other half wanted the agency abolished and their lands deeded to them without restrictions, presumably so that they could sell them and use the proceeds as they had their recent payments. In 1900 most of the older Sissetons were living on their forty-acre tracts in the coulees and leasing the rest of their allotments. The distance of their good lands from their homes, the lack of large horses, and the shortage of machinery and grain were cited as reasons for leasing. Most of them were so heavily in debt for what they did own that they dared not appear in town with good horses. At least half the Sissetons were then living entirely on the income from the leases and on the interest on their annuities. The agent thought that the money remaining to their credit should be paid to them so that they could liquidate their debts. As if this were not enough, drought that year had reduced the crop to a third of what it had been in better years.[51]

Thus the history of the Sisseton Reservation in the late nineteenth century followed much the same pattern as Santee: a brave beginning, with considerable enthusiasm among both Indians and agents, followed by gradual progress toward self-sufficiency, culminating in allotment, which proved to be not the crowning achievement of the process as intended, but actually a disaster for the Indians, succeeded by deterioration and a return to poverty. This time, however, the sense of urgency and the idealism that had characterized thinking on the Indian question in the 1860's and 1870's were gone, replaced by a widespread wish to ignore the whole problem, now that the government had done all it could to help the Indian. So the Sissetons, like their Santee cousins, faced the twentieth century unequipped to meet the challenges it presented.

[50] *Ibid.*, 1890, p. 66; 1895, pp. 301–302; 1896, p. 301; 1899, p. 346.
[51] *Ibid.*, 1899, p. 346; 1900, pp. 385–386.

CHAPTER 11

The Devils Lake Reservation

THE TREATY of 1867 with the upper Sioux provided for a reservation between Devils Lake and the Sheyenne River, chiefly for those Santees who were still fugitives on the plains but also for the Cuthead bands of Yanktonais who claimed that area. When five hundred Indians had gathered there, an agent was to be appointed for them. Four years passed before this provision was complied with, and in the meantime the Indians who resided in the vicinity were largely under the supervision of the commanding officer of Fort Totten, established in 1867 on the south shore of Devils Lake.[1] In the fall of that year 57 lodges—some 250 souls—were said to be living permanently there, and more were expected during the winter. Later reports mentioned 80 and even 130 lodges; the Indians were all in "great destitution" by December, when efforts were made to subsist them out of military stores. Those efforts failing, Sisseton Agent Benjamin Thompson arranged with Joseph R. Brown to supply a limited amount of provisions, to be paid for when an appropriation was made by Congress. Justus C. Ramsey, brother of the former Minnesota governor, was designated to receive the supplies from Brown, accompany them to Devils Lake, and there distribute them to the Indians. The mission, carried out in mid-winter under conditions of extreme hardship, kept life in the Indians till spring.[2]

[1] Charles J. Kappler, comp. and ed., *Indian Affairs, Laws and Treaties*, I (Washington: Government Printing Office, 1904), 957–958.

[2] Benjamin Thompson to Nathaniel G. Taylor, October 17, November 29, and

Although it may be supposed that humanitarian considerations were uppermost in the minds of those who arranged for this emergency relief shipment, there were other reasons for making a gesture in behalf of the Indians at Devils Lake. Charles A. Ruffee, who was then engaged in establishing an overland mail route across present-day North Dakota, received reports from his agent at Devils Lake that the Indians there and on the Mouse (Souris) River were "positively in a starving condition" and had eaten their horses and those of the mail carriers. There were also a number of Santee Sioux on the Missouri River 150 miles west of Fort Buford who were waiting to be joined by the Hunkpapas the next spring in hostile displays against the whites, and Ruffee thought that if those at Devils Lake were fed, the more remote bands might get the word and be influenced to settle down on the reservation.[3]

Partly in response to Ruffee's recommendation, the appointment of an agent was considered early in 1868, but the absence of an appropriation for these Indians rendered such an appointment superfluous, in the eyes of Secretary of Interior Browning. The congressional act that year which appropriated $30,000 for the Indians at Fort Wadsworth also provided $15,000 for the Devils Lake group and placed Bishop Whipple in charge of the expenditure. When Dr. Jared W. Daniels was appointed agent for the Sissetons and Wahpetons in 1869, he investigated the situation at Devils Lake and found a population of just over four hundred, of whom only ninety were men. The commandant at Fort Totten had provided them with some seed corn, which they planted with the aid of pointed sticks and elk and deer horns, but none of it ripened before frost. Daniels had fifty acres broken—as much as they would need the next season. Only a few really wanted to cultivate the soil in the white man's fashion, he thought; the rest wanted to plant "the same as they always have as Blanket Indians."[4]

The Indians complained, through the military, of Daniels' management of their affairs. The "acting head chief" of the Sissetons at Devils

---

December 14 and 30, 1867, and January 17 and July 14, 1868; Benjamin Thompson to Justus C. Ramsey, January 15, 1868; Joseph R. Brown to N. G. Taylor, August 11, 1868, NARS, RG 75, LR, Sisseton Agency.

[3] Charles A. Ruffee to Charles E. Mix, December 2, 1867; Ruffee to N. G. Taylor, March 2, 1868, *ibid.*

[4] N. G. Taylor to Benjamin Thompson, March 25, 1868, NARS, RG 75, LS; Orville Browning to N. G. Taylor, April 6 and August 17, 1868; Captain L. M. Kellogg to General O. D. Greene, Assistant Adjutant General, Headquarters, Department of Dakota, October 24, 1869, NARS, RG 75, LR, Sisseton Agency; Com. of Indian Affairs, *Annual Report*, 1869, p. 332.

Lake, Tiwashte, or Good Lodge (usually called Little Fish), protested to the garrison at Fort Ransom that all that his people had received out of the appropriation in 1869 were a tin cup of corn, a bucket of seed potatoes, and one paper each of carrot, beet, turnip, and rutabaga seed per family. They had arrived too late in the season to mature, so the Indians would again face starvation unless aided by the military.[5] Although Little Fish may have exaggerated, Daniels did favor holding assistance to the Devils Lake group to a minimum, so that the serious farmers there would be induced to move to the Sisseton Reservation, and he seems to have spent very little time at the more northerly reservation. He employed Peter Sutherland as a sort of subagent at Devils Lake, but Sutherland's residence there was not continuous and may not have been of much benefit to the Indians.[6]

By 1870 it was generally accepted that there were enough Indians permanently located at Devils Lake to warrant the appointment of a regular agent. Daniels admitted his inability to look after them and thought that an agent stationed there would keep them from drifting back to the Missouri River, where they would be in contact with hostile elements. Early in the next year William H. Forbes, an old friend and employee of Sibley, was appointed agent. Forbes had been a resident of Minnesota since 1837, had operated a trading post on the old reservation, had served as provost marshal during the trials in the fall of 1862, and was thoroughly acquainted with the Sioux.[7] After a flying trip to Fort Wadsworth to confer with Daniels and receive $3,147.20 intended for the Devils Lake Indians, he returned to St. Paul to buy clothing and other supplies before entering upon his work at the agency early in May. Finding the Indians in a "deplorable condition," he immediately ordered quantities of flour and pork, as well as seed potatoes. More than twenty adults had died the previous winter, chiefly, Forbes thought, because of a lack of animal food. Game was almost nonexistent in the country around Devils Lake; a party that arrived

[5] Kellogg to Greene, October 24, 1869, NARS, RG 75, LR, Sisseton Agency.

[6] Com. of Indian Affairs, *Annual Report*, 1869, p. 332; Major George A. Williams, commanding Fort Totten, to Greene, December 10, 1869, NARS, RG 75, LR, Sisseton Agency.

[7] Ely S. Parker to Henry H. Sibley, April 5, 1870, NARS, RG 75, LS; Jared W. Daniels to Parker, September 26, 1870, NARS, RG 75, LR, Sisseton Agency; William H. Forbes to Parker, February 8 and 21, 1871, NARS, RG 75, LR, Devils Lake Agency; J. Fletcher Williams, "A History of the City of St. Paul, and of the County of Ramsey, Minnesota," *Minnesota Historical Collections*, IV (1876), 54–56. Forbes had also served in the territorial council.

from the Missouri shortly after Forbes reached the agency reported that they had seen no buffalo in thirty days' travel across the prairies.[8]

If Forbes worked no miracles in his first months at the agency, it should be pointed out that he was forced to operate under considerable handicaps. Like Thompson at the beginning of his work at the Lake Traverse reservation, Forbes was dependent on the military for a place to live, to conduct agency business, and to store supplies. Fortunately, the commanding officer turned over to him some log buildings that had served as temporary quarters while Fort Totten was being erected. Forbes described them as unfit for occupancy, but he nevertheless put one to use as an agency office and another as a storeroom; he found living quarters for himself and his family in the fort itself. This made for an extremely awkward situation, especially considering the jealousy then prevailing between the military and the Indian agents. There was always the possibility that as the garrison was increased, the quarters assigned to Forbes would be needed, and the site where the log buildings stood might also be needed for other purposes. Although he promptly requested authority to build a storeroom, an agent's house and office, and other necessary adjuncts to an agency, the Indian Office granted his request only grudgingly and in piecemeal fashion. Forbes remained a guest of the fort all during his term as agent, and as late as the 1890's some of the log buildings were still being used, though then only as a guardhouse.[9]

One of Forbes' handicaps was that the Indians who settled at Devils Lake were less advanced than those at Fort Wadsworth. The Christianized members of the tribe had largely located on the Sisseton Reservation, and it was the pagan element who predominated at Devils Lake. The Cutheads had scarcely come under the influence of missionaries and agents at all. Although their head chief, Wanatan, seems to have been one of the most sensible and stable of the Indian leaders, his influence was partially negated by constant additions to their numbers from other segments of the tribe, either homeless wanderers from as far away as the Milk River region of Montana, or families nominally attached to the Standing Rock agency. Thus Forbes had to contend with inexperience and some reluctance when he attempted to induce his Indians to farm, and in addition had to face the repeated disruptions

[8] Forbes to Parker, March 20 and 25, and May 4, 1871, NARS, RG 75, LR, Devils Lake Agency.

[9] Forbes to Parker, May 10, 1871; Forbes to Edward P. Smith, August 4, 1873, *ibid.*; Com. of Indian Affairs, *Annual Report*, 1893, p. 229.

caused by new and even less civilized groups joining the Indians already on the reservation.[10] Although the official correspondence makes no mention of them, there were probably also some lower Sioux who drifted down to Devils Lake from the Turtle Mountain area, after fleeing to Canada in 1862 and 1863. In 1869, General Henry A. Morrow, sent out to report on the number and tribal affiliation of these Indians along the international boundary, wrote to his superior that some Santees were moving back and forth across the border, living by hunting and by robbing supply trains. Reputed to be the most intelligent Indians on the plains, they were said to have retained enough of their religious training so that they chanted psalms around their campfires and on occasion substituted some of Isaac Watts' hymns for their own songs at scalp dances.[11]

Although the cultural diversity of the Indians who settled at Devils Lake constituted something of a hindrance to the government's attempt to make them self-supporting, the reservation had the advantage of much greater continuity of personnel than did the Sisseton Reservation. Except for an interregnum of ten months, only three agents served here for the first nineteen years that the agency existed. More important, all three men had been there, in one capacity or another, from the beginning of the agency and pursued essentially the same policy as agents. The available evidence indicates that all three executed their trust with diligence and honesty. Few complaints from the Indians reached the commissioner's office, though of course this dearth of criticism may have been the result of an inability to communicate their troubles to higher authority rather than evidence of satisfaction with the way the agency was being run. Usually, however, when a military post existed on an Indian reservation, discontented Indians found a ready ear for their complaints, which were then forwarded indirectly to the commissioner without the agent's knowledge. Thus it seems likely that Forbes and his successors managed to stay on good terms with the Indians while at the same time pressing forward the objectives of their superiors in regard to the civilization of their charges.

Of the men Forbes hired before taking over the agency, easily the most valuable was James McLaughlin, later to become agent himself.

[10] Forbes to Parker, May 10, 1871; Forbes to E. P. Smith, August 1, 1873; James McLaughlin to Acting Commissioner S. A. Galpin, October 6, 1876; McLaughlin to John Q. Smith, February 27, 1877, NARS, RG 75, LR, Devils Lake Agency; Com. of Indian Affairs, *Annual Report*, 1872, p. 259.

[11] General Henry A. Morrow to Greene, November 19, 1869, NARS, RG 75, LR, Fort Berthold Agency.

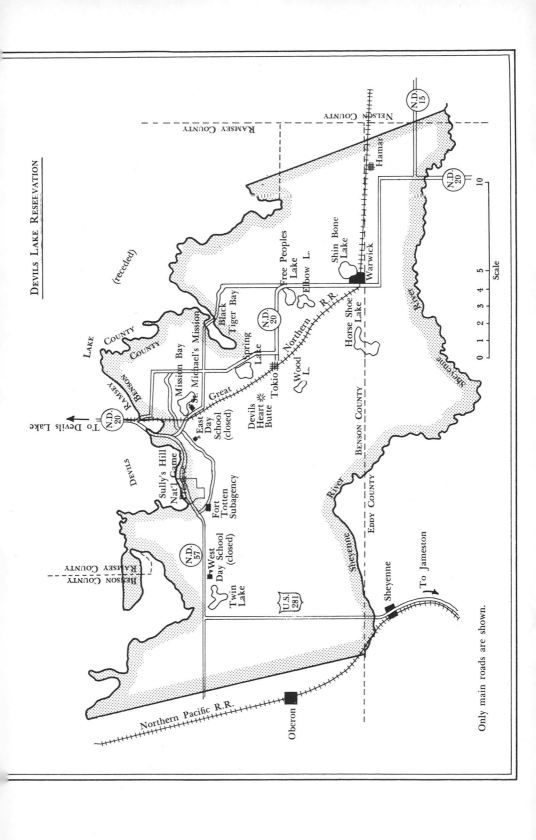

DEVILS LAKE RESERVATION

Only main roads are shown.

Not quite thirty when he came to Devils Lake, he had lived in Minnesota since 1863, had married a woman of Sioux descent, and had acquired at least a rudimentary knowledge of the Dakota language. A couple of months after Forbes entered upon his duties, McLaughlin left St. Paul with a bull train consisting of ten wagons and twenty yoke of oxen, bound for the remote Devils Lake agency. Although officially employed as a blacksmith, he was given to understand by Forbes, who was in poor health, that most of the agent's work would fall on him. His salary was later raised, and eventually he was designated as Forbes' overseer.[12] He was a good choice, as became more evident when he assumed the post of agent in 1876.

Forbes also brought with him a practical farmer of mixed blood, George W. Faribault, who began at once instructing the Indians in more efficient farming methods. Some of them had hidden a supply of seed corn, which they now brought out and planted. Together with forty bushels of seed potatoes brought from Fort Abercrombie and some turnip seed turned over by the local quartermaster, it provided them with quite a good crop in the summer of 1871—fifteen hundred bushels of corn, five hundred bushels of potatoes, and a thousand bushels of turnips, according to the agent's official report. The Indians that season also put up two hundred tons of hay and cut more than ten thousand fence rails. With the aid of a sawmill lent by the post quartermaster, Forbes had enough logs cut for twenty houses.[13] During the course of that year he obtained eight work oxen, and by selecting four more from the beef cattle purchased that fall, he provided the agency with enough oxen to begin the spring work in 1872. The acreage under cultivation was substantially increased that year, although seed wheat ordered by the agent arrived too late for planting, and grasshoppers consumed most of the other small grains. That season the agency received a mower-reaper, a horse rake, and a two-horsepower thresher, the first farm machinery of consequence in use at Devils Lake.[14]

Despite these and other evidences of progress, the bulk of the Indians' subsistence continued for some years to be provided by the government. Before Forbes' arrival, Sutherland had been issuing one pound of

[12] James McLaughlin, *My Friend the Indian* (Boston: Houghton Mifflin Co., 1910), pp. 8–9; Forbes to Francis A. Walker, January 6, 1873, NARS, RG 75, LR, Devils Lake Agency; H. R. Clum to Forbes, March 26, 1873, NARS, RG 75, LS.

[13] Forbes to Parker, May 10, 1871; Forbes to Clum, September 30, 1871, NARS, RG 75, LR, Devils Lake Agency; Com. of Indian Affairs, *Annual Report*, 1871, p. 535.

[14] Forbes to Walker, January 6, 1872, NARS, RG 75, LR, Devils Lake Agency; Com. of Indian Affairs, *Annual Report*, 1872, p. 259.

flour per day to each working Indian and two barrels of pork per month, to be divided among all five hundred. Since this ration was grossly insufficient, Forbes borrowed powder and lead from the post trader and gave them to trustworthy Indians so that they could kill ducks and other waterfowl while awaiting the arrival of supplies. The supplies, which never seemed to come in sufficient quantity for the constantly increasing number of Indians on the reservation, were issued in accordance with the terms of the 1867 treaty—exclusively in return for labor performed except for the elderly and infirm.[15] One reason for the inadequacy of the supplies was that the apportionment of funds to the two reservations set up by the treaty never accurately reflected the actual number of Indians present. In 1872, Forbes complained that Devils Lake had received only $25,440.22, as against $49,440.22 for the other reservation, despite the fact that there were then between nine hundred and a thousand Indians at the former. Furthermore, the Sisseton agency had been in existence since 1867, and the agent already had much equipment to work with which had to be purchased for Devils Lake out of current appropriations. In response to the agent's complaints, the appropriation that year was reapportioned on a basis of a thousand at Devils Lake to fifteen hundred at Sisseton, but the division of funds between the two remained a sore spot with Forbes, who repeatedly urged that appropriations be made separately for the two agencies.[16]

Other problems plagued the agent in the early years of his administration. Prior to his arrival, several white men had settled on or near the reservation, ostensibly to establish farms but really to ply the liquor trade with the military garrison. Since the nearest "seat of justice" was at Pembina, some 140 miles away across trackless prairies, Forbes found it impossible to take legal action against the men, who were also charged with selling whiskey to the Indians.[17]

The military post presented a more direct menace early in 1872, when Forbes was notified that the military reservation encompassed more than half the Indian reservation, including all the best land, all the fresh water, and nearly all of the timber. Except for eighty acres, all the Indians' improvements and houses were included, and they were for-

[15] Forbes to Parker, June 8, 1871, NARS, RG 75, LR, Devils Lake Agency; Com. of Indian Affairs, *Annual Report*, 1871, pp. 536–537.
[16] Forbes to Walker, July 8, 1872, NARS, RG 75, LR, Devils Lake Agency; Com. of Indian Affairs, *Annual Report*, 1872, p. 260.
[17] Forbes to Clum, December 5, 1871; Forbes to E. P. Smith, August 22, 1874, NARS, RG 75, LR, Devils Lake Agency.

bidden to cut wood on this portion of what they supposed to be their reservation. There followed a period of uncertainty, during which the dispute was carried all the way to the Secretaries of Interior and War. General Philip H. Sheridan, then commanding the Military Division of the Missouri, recommended that, pending a top-level decision, the Indians be allowed to enjoy all the privileges they had been used to. His recommendation was passed along to Forbes, who asked that the status quo be maintained until the land had been allotted according to the treaty, and promised that in the meantime no improvements would be made or farms opened nearer than four miles from the fort. Secretary of War Belknap wrote Secretary of Interior Delano in October, approving Forbes' recommendation, with the proviso that his concurrence not be construed as a renunciation of the military's claims to the land. The military reservation was eventually reduced, by stages, but it remained a source of irritation until Fort Totten was finally abandoned in 1890.[18]

Another development in 1872, which proved both an annoyance and a convenience, was the construction of the Northern Pacific Railroad west from Fargo. It was a convenience in that it permitted supplies to be shipped by rail to Jamestown, eighty-two miles from the agency. Eight hundred barrels of flour had cost $7,960 delivered at the agency before the coming of the railroad; in 1873, the first year the new line was used, the cost was $4,704.10.[19] But the railroad was not welcomed by the Indians. Although they had agreed in the 1867 treaty to permit the building of railroads through the unceded country, they resented the appearance of white settlers who followed in the wake of the construction crews. It was this dilemma that led to the negotiations for the cession of the unceded lands in 1872 and 1873. The Devils Lake Indians offered more opposition to signing the agreement than those at Sisseton did, and were finally persuaded to sign only by the inclusion of an article later stricken out by the Senate. Although Forbes doubted that they would ratify the amendments, they did so in May, 1873, after opposition from some who wanted payment made in cash rather than deposited in the civilization fund.[20]

[18] Forbes to Walker, February 3 and April 19, 1872; Secretary of War W. W. Belknap to Secretary of Interior Columbus Delano, March 23 and October 16, 1872, NARS, RG 75, LR, Devils Lake Agency. The successive orders defining the boundaries of the Fort Totten military reservation are printed in 53rd Cong., 3rd Sess., *S. Ex. Doc. 79.*

[19] Forbes to Walker, July 10 and October 9, 1872; Forbes to E. P. Smith, August 24, 1873, NARS, RG 75, LR, Devils Lake Agency.

[20] Forbes to Walker, July 10, 1872; Forbes to Clum, March 28, 1873, *ibid.*; Com. of Indian Affairs, *Annual Report,* 1872, p. 259; 1873, p. 229.

When the Indian agencies were parceled out among the various religious denominations, Devils Lake was assigned to the Catholic Church. Hence it was logical that when a school was started there, it should be placed under the management of a religious order of that church. Forbes began agitating early for a manual labor school and was authorized to start building one in 1873. Arrangements were then made to put it under the supervision of the Sisters of Charity, more commonly known as the Grey Nuns of Montreal, but delays of one sort or another prevented the school from opening until the fall of 1874. The two-story brick structure, sixty by forty feet, was made available to girls of all ages and to boys under twelve. The four sisters who operated it were paid only $150 per year, in addition to their rations drawn from the agency supplies. In order to induce parents to send their children, Forbes permitted double rations to be issued, one set to the children at school, the other to their parents at home. His argument (besides the need for some special inducement) was that single rations would not be enough to subsist the children at school, since at home they enjoyed the benefit of any crops their parents raised. The scheme seems to have worked, for the school was soon filled to capacity and Forbes was calling for an addition.[21]

Although the agency site was turned over by the War Department in 1873—permanently, as Forbes understood the arrangement—the manual labor school was erected some seven miles away, presumably to have it as far as practicable from the fort. This decision meant that the administrative and educational functions of the agency were separated and carried on at a considerable distance from each other. When an agency building was begun in 1874, to replace the sod-roofed log buildings of the "old post," it was located on the old site, and the bifurcation of administrative function was made permanent. As for the Indians, they were even more dispersed. At first they had settled in five or six encampments, mostly in wooded areas, but after a few years they began to scatter over the reservation on individual farms, as desired by their agent. Nothing approximating a survey was undertaken until 1875. Many of the Indians wished to retain their lands in common ownership and opposed the suggestion of surveying the reservation until 1874, when good crops the previous year had enabled them to pass the

[21] Forbes to Parker, May 10, 1871; Forbes to E. P. Smith, July 9, 1874, and February 26, 1875; McLaughlin to J. Q. Smith, January 31, 1877, NARS, RG 75, LR, Devils Lake Agency; Com. of Indian Affairs, *Annual Report*, 1873, pp. 227–229; 1874, pp. 238–239.

Courtesy of the Minnesota Historical Society

Bishop Henry B. Whipple

Pilgrim Congregational Church, Santee Agency. The main part was built in the early 1870's. Photograph by Grant for the National Park Service, 1952.

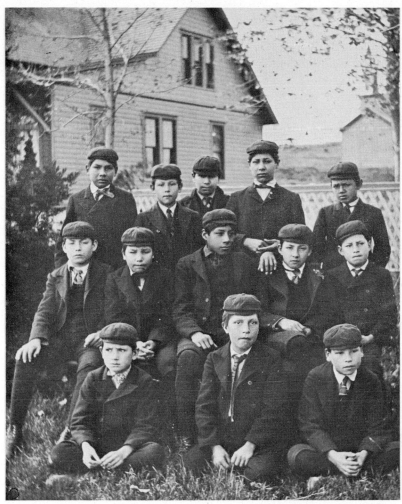

Boys' Junior Endeavor, Santee Normal Training School

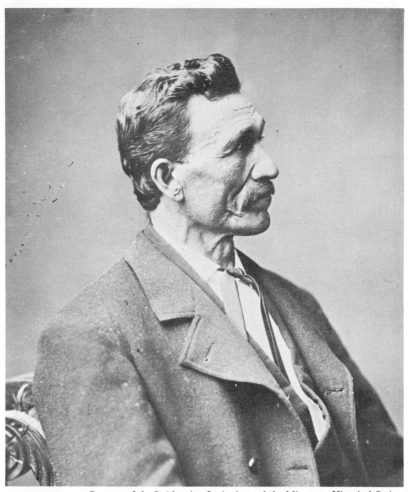

Courtesy of the Smithsonian Institution and the Minnesota Historical Society

Gabriel Renville (Ti-wakan). Photograph by C. M. Bell, 1880–1881

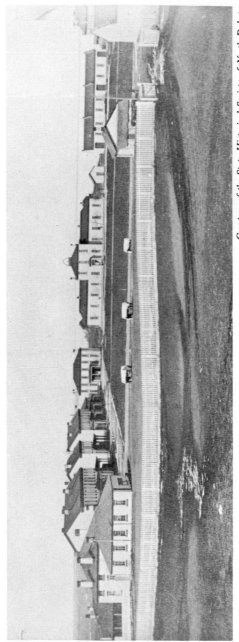

Fort Totten, 1878

Payment to Minnesota Mdewakantons, 1885

Joseph La Framboise and a group of Sioux at the door of the Sisseton
Agency, 1896. Photograph by E. A. Bromley

Fort Totten Indian school band

winter in fairly comfortable circumstances and they became convinced that farming in the white man's fashion was worth a try. The survey made in 1875 was not complete enough to permit allotment of homesteads, as had been done at Santee and Sisseton. In only two townships were even the section corners established, and part of the reservation was not surveyed at all.[22]

From what has already been noted, it is evident that progress in the direction desired by the Indian Bureau was slower at Devils Lake than at Sisseton. Perhaps it would be more accurate to say that, because the Devils Lake people were less advanced to begin with, their condition at any given time was somewhat behind that of the Sissetons. Still, there was progress. As early as 1872 Forbes reported that more than fifty men dressed like the whites, and the next year he said that seventy-five were living in houses and most had adopted white dress. His successor claimed in 1875 that 275 were then dressed in " citizen's garb." A later agent encouraged this transformation by reducing the quantity of blankets issued and substituting clothing; he even went so far as to issue only white blankets, which the Indians almost had to use exclusively as bed covering. At that time, in 1878, the agent wrote of the Indians: "They are all anxious now for white mans full dress since many of them have cut their hair."[23] They may not have been "anxious," but they had little choice but to accept what was given them.

Although Devils Lake and Sisseton were subject to the same general regulations regarding rations and annuity goods, there were differences in the manner of distribution. For one thing, until 1877 the issues were made weekly at Devils Lake, despite the waste of time involved in having the heads of families come to the agency each Monday to receive supplies. Biweekly issues were adopted in 1877 and replaced two years later by a monthly issue, which had been the practice at Sisseton for several years. Fortunately, the Indians were not restricted solely to these periodic issues for needed supplies. Those who performed labor around the agency or on their farms or who helped haul supplies from

[22] Forbes to E. P. Smith, August 4, 1873, February 5, 1874, and February 26, 1875; Moses K. Armstrong to E. P. Smith, June 28, 1875; Paul Beckwith to J. Q. Smith, January 22, 1876, NARS, RG 75, LR, Devils Lake Agency; Com. of Indian Affairs, *Annual Report*, 1873, p. 230; 1875, p. 239. Beckwith wanted the agency moved to where the school, mill, and Indian farms were located in order to reduce conflict between military and Indian service personnel.

[23] Com. of Indian Affairs, *Annual Report*, 1872, p. 259; 1873, p. 228; 1875, p. 239; McLaughlin to Ezra A. Hayt, March 7, 1878, NARS, RG 75, LR, Devils Lake Agency.

Jamestown were paid in "checks" printed in various denominations and usable as a medium of exchange at the agency storeroom. Even though a force of white employees was maintained, there was enough work around the agency to furnish employment to quite a number of Indians. They hauled wood, brick, and stone when the school building was going up, and they brought in and stacked wheat and made the agency hay. In addition, they did their own farm work, including the building of stables.[24]

As at Sisseton, the agents discriminated in the issuance of rations between the industrious and the "disobedient or indolent," as one called them. The latter group received the basic issue of pork, flour, and tobacco, but only the workers were entitled to soap, sugar, coffee, tea, candles, and kerosene. In 1877 the agent was issuing a pound of soap per month to each family who owned and occupied a log house.[25] There was, of course, some opposition to this regimen. As at Sisseton, some of the Indians objected to working for the annuities to which they were entitled under the terms of the agreement providing for the cession of their lands. Their resentment sometimes had deeper origins. Forbes remarked, with unusual insight, that it was hard to teach an Indian to farm, "especially as he views his teachers as belonging to the race who brought him to this necessity of manual labor for support." Frequent visits from Indians of other reservations not only interfered with work going on at Devils Lake but apprised the local Indians that at some of the agencies west of the Missouri rations were issued to people who did nothing to earn them.[26]

Except for this rather low-key resentment, relations between the successive agents at Devils Lake and their Indians appear to have been largely harmonious during the seventies and eighties. The self-contained little community was spared the extreme factionalism that so disrupted the Sisseton Reservation. Possibly one reason for the comparative harmony prevailing at Devils Lake was the fact that Forbes did not try to push the Indians too far or too fast or interfere seriously with their traditional customs. There is little mention in his official reports of dances, though unquestionably they continued throughout the period. A later agent complained that several work oxen had been sacrificed at one of

[24] McLaughlin to J. Q. Smith, September 18, 1876, and March 28 and July 7, 1877; McLaughlin to Hayt, October 4, 1879; Forbes to E. P. Smith, September 6, 1873, NARS, RG 75, LR, Devils Lake Agency.

[25] McLaughlin to Hayt, December 24, 1877, *ibid.*

[26] Com. of Indian Affairs, *Annual Report*, 1873, p. 229; 1874, p. 239; 1875, p. 240; Forbes to E. P. Smith, September 6, 1873, NARS, RG 75, LR, Devils Lake Agency.

the dances, and he clamped down on the "medicine dance," at which property was given away. Nor was there any wholesale assault on native marriage practices. Forbes noted in his second annual report that more than one hundred children and several adults had been baptized and "some few have been married legally," but neither he nor his immediate successors exhibited the fanatical zeal for the extirpation of polygamy and Indian marriages that Moses N. Adams displayed at Sisseton.[27]

Agent Forbes, whose health had been undermined by military service in the Civil War, died in the summer of 1875. McLaughlin applied for the position of agent, but the Catholic Board recommended an outsider, Paul Beckwith, who was appointed and took charge of the agency early in September. Beckwith may have been a capable man, but the continued presence of McLaughlin on the agency staff created an awkward situation, which Beckwith tried to remedy by discharging his rival, ostensibly for reasons of economy. Ironically, at the very time that Beckwith was announcing the discharge of McLaughlin, the head of the Catholic Board, General Charles Ewing, was recommending the removal of Beckwith as agent and McLaughlin's appointment to the post. When McLaughlin took charge, on July 3, 1876, he found that his predecessor had used up nearly all the provisions and returned the remaining cash to the Treasury, so as to embarrass the new agent, and had even taken with him all the agency records and blank forms needed to carry on the staggering amount of bookkeeping demanded by the Indian Office.[28]

With so inauspicious a beginning, McLaughlin might have been pardoned if he had spent the first few months of his administration merely undoing the damage of his predecessor. As a matter of fact, however, he set to work with commendable energy, following roughly the same approach initiated by Forbes, and executed the government's purposes so

---

[27] Com. of Indian Affairs, *Annual Report*, 1872, p. 260; 1876, p. 25; McLaughlin to J. Q. Smith, February 16, 1877, NARS, RG 75, LR, Devils Lake Agency. The first serious attempt to regularize the Indians' marriage practices came in the winter of 1881–1882, when the new agent, John W. Cramsie, called together the chiefs and headmen and set up rules that no man should have more than one wife and all should be married by a clergyman. As a result of this order, said the agent, some Indians who had lived together for years, and had married sons or daughters, had come to be married by the priest. See Com. of Indian Affairs, *Annual Report*, 1882, p. 21.

[28] Beckwith to J. Q. Smith, February 20 and March 21, 1876; Charles Ewing to Secretary of the Interior, March 31, 1876; McLaughlin to J. Q. Smith, July 3, 1876, NARS, RG 75, LR, Devils Lake Agency.

successfully that he stayed on as agent for more than five years. Some of the Indians who had fled the reservation when Beckwith became agent now returned, and soon McLaughlin had about 1,100 Sioux under his jurisdiction. As if this increase in the reservation population did not constitute enough of a challenge, he assumed control of the agency at a critical time, just after the Battle of the Little Bighorn, when every white settler on the northern plains lived in momentary expectation of an Indian attack. Rumors of an impending raid on Fort Totten were given some credence by the agent, who sent out a scouting party of twenty trusted men to verify the reports. They found nothing, but the rumors kept circulating. McLaughlin felt obliged to testify to the loyalty and docility of his Indians, for irresponsible or frightened whites repeatedly spread reports of depredations and possible massacres by the Devils Lake Sioux.[29]

The war scare eventually died down, and the agent was able to move ahead with his plans for the civilization of his Indians. Among his accomplishments was the distribution, in 1877, of 50 cows, 14 calves, 2 bulls, and 187 pigs. He believed that diversified agriculture offered a better prospect for ultimate self-support than the heavy reliance on corn, potatoes, and root vegetables which had been the Indians' chief products thus far. Although some efforts had been made to raise wheat, the Indians preferred corn because it yielded more per acre. They grew the northern variety called "Ree" corn, cultivated by the Arikaras and other sedentary tribes of the upper Missouri. They ordinarily used it in soup, flavored with a small amount of meat, or pounded it into a coarse hominy. McLaughlin's experiment with cows and pigs was not conspicuously successful, and in 1878 he turned to wheat raising, which was shortly to become the mainstay of white settlers in that region. Only five hundred bushels were produced that year, in comparison with ten thousand bushels of corn, an equal quantity of potatoes, more than five thousand bushels of turnips, and fifteen hundred bushels of oats; but the acreage increased rapidly after that, from seventy-five acres in 1879 to over a thousand four years later.[30]

Because the amount of grain raised soon exceeded the capacity of the Indians to harvest and thresh it with the means at their disposal, McLaughlin kept nagging at the Indian Office to provide him with

[29] McLaughlin to J. Q. Smith, June 21 and August 14, 1876, *ibid.*; Com. of Indian Affairs, *Annual Report*, 1876, p. 25; McLaughlin, *My Friend the Indian*, p. 22.

[30] Forbes to E. P. Smith, May 2, 1874; McLaughlin to Hayt, February 19, 1878, NARS, RG 75, LR, Devils Lake Agency; Com. of Indian Affairs, *Annual Report*, 1877, p. 57; 1878, p. 27; 1879, p. 28; 1883, p. 24.

machinery. In 1879 he promised the Indians that anyone raising more than one acre of wheat could have it cut by machine. The Indian Office enabled him to keep his promise and also fulfilled his request for a threshing machine, though not the kind he had requested. Among Mc-Laughlin's other accomplishments were the organization of a police force, the increased employment of Indians as apprentices to the blacksmith, carpenter, and other agency employees, and the construction of a gristmill. When the nucleus of his police force had been organized, he asked that they be allowed to carry carbines or revolvers or both. To the query as to whether they might not use these weapons too freely, he replied: "My experience has shown me that Indians are less excitable, more collected, and much more prudent in such matters than white men are, and will never resort to the use of arms unless oblidged to protect themselves."[31] He may have revised his thinking on this point after Indian police under his direction at Standing Rock killed Sitting Bull in 1890.

The boarding school continued to operate during McLaughlin's time, although the Indian Office almost killed it at one time by trying to transform it into a day school and requiring the nuns to subsist themselves. Running it as a day school would have meant the end of the duplicate ration system that Forbes had devised, and McLaughlin feared that without this inducement not one child would come to school. The Sister Superior was ready to close the school, but McLaughlin ordered it continued while he haggled with the authorities in Washington. For a total cost of $1,255 a year, exclusive of rations, the government received the services of the four nuns, three helping girls, and a chaplain; one of the nuns doubled as physician and performed most of the medical services required on the reservation. It was a good bargain, as the agent hastened to point out. The matter was finally resolved by a compromise: after July 1, 1878, the school personnel subsisted themselves but received an increase in pay; the school continued as a boarding school, but the children received only single rations.[32]

[31] McLaughlin to Hayt, July 10 and August 30, 1879, and September 28 and December 19, 1878; McLaughlin to Roland E. Trowbridge, November 15 and 30, 1880, NARS, RG 75, LR, Devils Lake Agency; Com. of Indian Affairs, *Annual Report*, 1878, pp. 27–28; 1879, p. 28; 1880, p. 30.

[32] McLaughlin to J. Q. Smith, January 31 and June 20, 1877; McLaughlin to Hayt, July 20, 1878; J. B. A. Brouillet to J. Q. Smith, February 9, 1877; Brouillet to Acting Commissioner of Indian Affairs, February 2, 1880; McLaughlin to Brouillet, January 22, 1880, NARS, RG 75, LR, Devils Lake Agency. According to Agent Beckwith, each sister received $150, or a total of $600 per year. Adding fourteen cents exchange per dollar, this amounted to $684. Three helping girls received a total

Since the sisters had stipulated that only boys under twelve would be taken into their school, the older boys were left without educational facilities. Beckwith had experimented with two day schools for them, but nothing seems to have come of his attempt. In 1877, McLaughlin began agitating for an addition to the old school, and the next year he submitted a proposal for a new building, in which a school for older boys could be maintained. The addition was erected in 1878 and part of it put to use as a hospital, something the various agents had long thought desirable. In the spring of 1879 a lay brother of the Benedictine Order joined the mission and took charge of the manual labor part of the school. Early in 1880 the Reverend Claude Ebner opened a school for older boys in some of the old log buildings. Included with the school was a forty-acre tract to be used in the teaching of practical agriculture. Two years later a building was erected especially for this school.[33]

In 1881, McLaughlin was transferred to the more lucrative post of agent at Standing Rock, and his place at Devils Lake was taken by John W. Cramsie, who had run a store near the agency since 1877. Cramsie's acquaintance with the reservation extended much farther back than his four-year term as trader, however. He had first come there in 1867 as an employee of the Quartermaster Department at Fort Totten and, because of his knowledge of Dakota, was speedily given work in connection with the Indians. He had taken the first census of them and issued their first rations. For a time during Forbes' term, he served as interpreter. Thus he was thoroughly familiar with the situation at Devils Lake and apparently in sympathy with the policies followed by Forbes and McLaughlin. Appointed while James A. Garfield was President, he served through the administrations of Arthur and Cleveland and well into the Harrison administration—more than nine years in all, important years for the Indians of the Devils Lake Reservation.[34]

Under Cramsie's direction, the Indians made some long strides toward the goal of complete self-support through agriculture. Assuming that their chief reliance, like that of the white settlers who were swarm-

---

(including exchange) of $171. The chaplain received $400. See Beckwith to J. Q. Smith, December 30, 1875, *ibid.*

[33] Beckwith to J. Q. Smith, January 18, 1876; McLaughlin to Hayt, January 3, 1880; McLaughlin to Brouillet, January 22, 1880, *ibid.*; Com. of Indian Affairs, *Annual Report*, 1877, p. 56; 1878, p. 28; 1880, p. 30; 1882, p. 20.

[34] Com. of Indian Affairs, *Annual Report*, 1881, p. 35; 1882, p. 20; 1887, pp. 27–28; Walker to Forbes, July 26, 1872, NARS, RG 75, LS.

ing in around the reservation, should be on wheat-raising, he increased the acreage devoted to it year by year and continued McLaughlin's policy of acquiring ever more farm machinery. His annual reports show a rapidly increasing acreage: 1,500 in 1882, 2,480 in 1884, 3,850 in 1886, over 4,000 in 1887, 5,500 in 1889. Even before McLaughlin's departure, all of the actual farming was done by the Indians themselves, though with supervision by the agent and his employees. Not all of the machinery required to harvest and thresh the crops then being raised was provided by the government. In 1883, Cramsie reported that ten Indians had raised $88.50 toward the purchase of a McCormick self-binder, and he offered to contribute $192 from his own funds. The next season the harvest was carried on with the aid of seven self-raking reapers provided by the government, twelve Indian-owned reapers, and three self-binders.[35]

It should perhaps be mentioned that by the 1880's the Indians were moving into the area of a cash economy. The machinery they owned had been purchased with money earned by delivering wood to the schools and by selling wheat to the Turtle Mountain reservation. They had made $1,813 in that way and had used $1,370 for machinery. Cramsie commented that the Sioux took satisfaction in selling their surplus wheat to the Chippewas at Turtle Mountain. Some cash was also earned from the sale of down timber and buffalo bones collected on the prairie. During at least part of this time the Indians also filled the wood contract for the military post.[36]

Among Cramsie's other contributions to the progress of the agency were the issue of mares, which he thought better suited to the climate than oxen, and the erection of a number of new buildings long needed. He made an addition to the gristmill and paid the miller out of a 1/10 toll taken from all grain brought to be ground there. Despite all these improvements, the Indians' production of grain outran the capacity of the machinery and horses available. In 1887, Cramsie complained that the lack of the essential machinery constituted a bottleneck which limited further increases in production. Apparently the bottleneck was relieved, for acreage continued to increase in the following years, as did total production when the weather permitted. Symptomatic also of progress was the discontinuance of rations in 1884 to all but the old and infirm. The Indians had been prepared for this change by the expiration

[35] *Ibid.*, 1882, p. 20; 1883, p. 24; 1884, pp. 30–31, 34; 1886, p. 54; 1887, p. 29; 1889, p. 140.
[36] *Ibid.*, 1884, p. 31; 1878, p. 27.

of their annuities under the 1872 agreement the previous year, and there seems to have been no such period of crisis as occurred at Sisseton. An agent's official reports can conceal as much as they reveal, of course, but Cramsie's long acquaintance with the reservation and his manifestly realistic attitude toward his job lend credence to the picture of steady progress presented by his annual summaries of activities at the agency.[37]

Cramsie's realism and his willingness to change his mind are illustrated by his attitude toward the innovation of a court of Indian offenses. The Secretary of the Interior had proposed such an institution in 1882, and early the next year appropriate rules and regulations were drawn up by the Indian Office. Although Cramsie had doubts about the willingness of Indian judges to incur the displeasure of their friends and relatives for no compensation, he dutifully appointed such a court at Devils Lake the same year. By 1884 he saw the institution in a more favorable light. His court had tried forty-two cases in the previous year and administered thirty-four sentences.[38] The court became a permanent institution and was apparently accepted by the Indians. In 1891 it was meeting every second Saturday, with the agent in charge and the head farmer serving as clerk. An Indian policeman would call up a case and make a statement; then the prisoner would defend himself, after which the judges would confer and decide upon the penalty. That year the court tried six cases for damage done by stock, six for drunkenness, ten for gambling, three for desertion, three for adultery, six for assault and battery, and one each for theft, rape, and bastardy. The Indian police force, which had started with only five men, later increased to fifteen but by 1891 was down to eleven.[39]

During the eighties the Devils Lake Reservation gradually became part of the world around it, as railroads moved closer and white settlers and towns followed. In 1880, James J. Hill began pushing his St. Paul, Minneapolis and Manitoba Railroad (later the Great Northern) west from Grand Forks, and the supply point for the agency changed from Jamestown to the end of the track, about twelve miles west of Grand Forks. By 1883 the nearest station was just northeast of the reservation boundary. From this time on, the freighting of supplies to the agency lost its importance as a source of income for the Indians. In 1883 an

[37] *Ibid.*, 1884, pp. 30, 32; 1886, p. 55; 1887, p. 29.

[38] *Ibid.*, 1883, pp. xv, 27; 1884, pp. 32–33. In 1885 the court tried forty-eight cases and imposed fines amounting to $186. See *ibid.*, 1885, p. 27.

[39] *Ibid.*, 1891, p. 317; McLaughlin to Hayt, September 28, 1878, NARS, RG 75, LR, Devils Lake Agency.

agreement was signed by the Indians granting a right-of-way to a line called the Jamestown and Northern. Although the railroad was built and in operation by the spring of 1885, no action on the agreement was taken by Congress until 1901, when it was finally approved and compensation to the Indians authorized.[40]

Congress acted somewhat more rapidly to compensate the Indians for another cession of land. When the reservation was established, the western boundary was described as a line extending from the westernmost tip of Devils Lake to the nearest point on the Sheyenne River. Such a line was drawn in 1875, and white settlers a few years later began taking up lands to the west of it. When a resurvey was made in 1883, it was discovered that the nearest point to Devils Lake on the Sheyenne was some distance to the westward. About 64,000 acres of land then being homesteaded really belonged to the Indians. The Secretary of the Interior declined at that time to take any action toward removing the white settlers or passing on the justness of the Indians' claim. He seemed skeptical of the whole business, suggesting that perhaps the river had changed its course in the intervening years. In 1887, however, Commissioner John D. C. Atkins asked that Congress take action to compensate the Indians for the loss of this land. Cramsie recommended that they be paid a dollar an acre for it and that the money be used to buy stock, machinery, and other items needed for the Indians' further advance in agriculture. The wheels of bureaucracy ground slowly, and this recommendation did not reach Congress until 1890. Finally, in 1891, when allotment was being pressed on the Indians and meeting unexpected resistance, Congress got around to paying the Indians—at a rate of $1.25 per acre, which gave the Indian Bureau $80,000 to expend in behalf of the Devils Lake people. Immediately contracts were let for 200 brood mares, 100 cows, 100 steers, 4 bulls, 75 plows, 100 sets of harness, and 50 sets of ox harness, and estimates were submitted for material and labor to repair 217 houses.[41] This windfall—for such it really was—thus was not dissipated in per capita payments, but was spent for articles and services of long-term benefit to the tribe.

The passage of the Dawes Act in 1887 led eventually, though not immediately, to the allotment of the Devils Lake Reservation. As soon

[40] McLaughlin to Trowbridge, April 8 and September 6, 1880, NARS, RG 75, LR, Devils Lake Agency; Com. of Indian Affairs, *Annual Report*, 1883, p. 27; 1885, p. xxxiii; U.S. *Statutes at Large*, XXXI, 1447.

[41] Com. of Indian Affairs, *Annual Report*, 1887, pp. liii, 26–27; 1891, pp. 107, 318; U.S. *Statutes at Large*, XXVI, 1010.

as the act had been passed, Cramsie began allotting farms but suspended operations upon learning that the act required the services of a special agent to perform this task. Not until two years later did actual work get under way, and then it ran into opposition from the Indians, who objected to paying taxes and being subject to the white man's laws, which they suspected would be enforced to their disadvantage. They announced that if they were paid for the portion of the reservation that had been inadvertently opened to settlement and for the right-of-way granted the Jamestown and Northern, and had their annuities under the 1851 treaties restored, they might be willing to accept citizenship. Nonetheless, allotment continued, interrupted once by the death of the special agent originally sent out to do the job, and was finally completed in 1892. Patents were issued the following year.[42]

Allotment in severalty proved to be the same tragic failure at Devils Lake as elsewhere. Although it cannot be assigned sole blame for all the misfortune that subsequently befell the Indians of that reservation, it certainly contributed importantly. Despite Cramsie's optimistic reports of yearly progress toward self-sufficiency, even he recognized that his efforts were not meeting with complete success. In his last report he remarked of his Indians that he was "not very sanguine that they will ultimately become absolutely self-supporting and civilized," but he did not elaborate on this observation. Earlier reports give some hint of his reasons, however. Starting in 1886, drought began to reduce the crops raised by the Indians. Like the grasshopper plague of the seventies, it was not as destructive at Devils Lake as it was farther south, but there were years when the crop was almost a total failure. The Indians were not, of course, the only ones to suffer from the uncertainty of the climate, but they were perhaps more easily discouraged than many of the white settlers. The agent at Devils Lake in 1895 wrote that the Indians had "on account of rigidity of soil, unfavorable seasons, inexperience, and a multiplicity of causes, done what even experienced white farmers with better advantages have—signally failed in agriculture for the last number of years. . . ."[43]

Comprehending the nature of the problem and solving it were, unfortunately, two different things. Before he left office, Cramsie pointed out that Congress failed to appreciate the size of the job it was attempt-

---

[42] Com. of Indian Affairs, *Annual Report*, 1887, pp. 32–33; 1889, pp. 143–144; 1890, p. xlvi; 1891, p. 317; 1892, p. 350; 1894, p. 217.

[43] *Ibid.*, 1886, p. 54; 1889, p. 146; 1895, p. 229.

ing to do with an annual appropriation of $6,000, $5,000 of which went
to pay employees. Some blame also attaches to the Indians. There were
years of good crops, such as 1891, the year in which stock in large
quantities was issued to the Indians. The evidence provided by the
agents' official reports suggests that they did not take full advantage of
the opportunity thus presented. Hostility to allotment may have accounted for much of their failure to capitalize on the opportunity; a
return of drought during the next three seasons may have canceled the
benefits received from the issue. Whatever the reasons, the acreage
cultivated remained stationary or dropped during the nineties, and the
total output declined even more sharply. By 1892 the crop was described as just enough to provide the Indians with a little credit at
stores.[44]

From a condition at least approaching self-sufficiency, the Devils
Lake Indians slipped back in a few years to almost total dependence on
government assistance. In 1893 they were said to be living largely on
parched corn and wild turnips. Hunger obliged them to slaughter many
of the cattle issued in 1891, and they were too poor to buy replacements.
After many years in which the birth rate exceeded the death rate, in
1894 the agent reported forty deaths and only twenty-seven births; the
next year about seventy deaths occurred—the cause: want and destitution. Although the death rate was down by 1897, the Indians were
described as being farther from self-support that winter than the previous one. The number of cattle, 150 that year, was down to 68 the
next, and the agent remarked that the Indians were "surrounded by
disadvantages, and their nearest neighbors are poverty, hunger, and
failure. . . ."[45]

Evidence of decay and deterioration was visible on every hand in the
nineties. As at Sisseton, attendance at the reservation schools fell off,
although the school system had progressed admirably during the previous decade. The original manual labor school, destroyed by fire in
1883, was replaced three years later, and the two educational institutions showed a steadily increasing enrollment for several years. In

[44] *Ibid.*, 1889, p. 146; 1891, p. 318; 1892, p. 351; 1893, p. 229; 1894, p. 217; 1895,
p. 228.

[45] *Ibid.*, 1893, p. 229; 1894, pp. 217–218; 1895, pp. 228–229; 1897, pp. 211–212;
1898, pp. 221, 223. The agent reported in 1893 that only twenty or thirty families were
really self-sustaining; the rest lived from hand to mouth. In 1895 he reported that
about 118 elderly people were wholly dependent on the government.

1890 the military post was abandoned and the buildings—thirty-nine in all—turned over to the Indian Bureau. They provided the agency with a capacious school plant, though some of the buildings were not suited to such purposes. Both schools were taken over by the government, but the Grey Nuns were retained as teachers. Although the enrollment was very large in the nineties—as high as 380 in 1895—the children were mostly Chippewas from Turtle Mountain. In 1898 only 65 children at the old school and 4 at the new one were from Devils Lake. The Indians objected to sending their children to the school because there were "too many Chippewas" there, but other reasons may have been more important. As soon as allotment had been carried out and the Indians had become citizens, they became negligent about sending their children to the school. Some complained that the children were ill-treated—and one agent conceded that there might be justice to their complaint; another story was that the Indians had expected to find a market for their produce at the school when the military post was abandoned. When this hope did not materialize, as the school raised its own provisions, they became bitter and refused to send their children, saying they would prefer to do without rations than let the children go. As a result, by 1900 only 109 out of 235 children on the reservation were in the local school.[46]

Congress at length showed some signs of recognizing the seriousness of the situation at Devils Lake. In 1895 the customary $6,000 appropriation was doubled, and in each of the four following years $10,000 was appropriated. Though nominally intended to aid the Indians in becoming self-supporting, this money was actually in the nature of direct relief and did little more than keep them alive from year to year.[47] Thus the picture at Devils Lake by the end of the century was essentially the same as that at Sisseton. Despite superficial differences— greater continuity of policy and less dissension at Devils Lake—the results at the two reservations were much the same at the time white

[46] *Ibid.*, 1883, p. 25; 1886, p. 56; 1891, pp. 578–579; 1893, p. 437; 1895, p. 389; 1896, p. 385; 1898, p. 222; 1899, p. 270; 1900, p. 310.

[47] When the ten annual installments of the $800,000 paid for lands ceded ended in 1883, Congress began appropriating $8,000 annually for the Devils Lake Reservation. In 1886 the amount was reduced to $6,000, at which level it remained until 1895, when it was increased to $12,000, of which $7,000 was to be made immediately available. Even the highest of these figures represents an amount much smaller than the proportion assigned to Devils Lake from the $80,000 annuity provided under the terms of the agreement. See U.S. *Statutes at Large*, XXII, 447; XXIII, 91, 378; XXVII, 135, 628; XXVIII, 303, 892; XXIX, 338; XXX, 78, 586, 938.

Americans decided that they had done all that duty required of them toward the civilization of the Indian. On both reservations undue haste on the part of the government to force the Indians into full citizenship conspired with an adverse climate to bring about a reversal of the steady progress perceptible during the seventies and eighties and left the Indians, like those at Santee, poorly prepared for the new century.

CHAPTER 12

The Flandreau Colony

MOST OF THE Santee and Sisseton Sioux were willing to settle down on the reservations provided for them in 1866 and 1867. A few, however, found reservation life too confining and struck out on their own. Significantly, they were not the least civilized members of their tribes, but, in most cases, the very people who had progressed the farthest in adopting the white man's way of life. Mention has already been made of the Sissetons who established the Brown Earth settlement in 1875. This colony proved unsuccessful and did not last, but the one of which it was an imitation, that at Flandreau, South Dakota, was more firmly grounded and has endured for nearly a century.

In the spring of 1869, while Agent James M. Stone was accompanying a delegation to Washington, twenty-five families left the Santee Reservation without authorization of any kind and settled on unoccupied land in the valley of the Big Sioux River, near where Charles Flandrau and others had made their abortive attempt to establish a town before the Sioux Uprising. According to John P. Williamson, the missionary who took the most active interest in them, they did so because they wished to break away from tribalism and domination by chiefs and agents and live like white men. Some of them had spent three years in prison at Davenport and while there had undergone not only a religious conversion, but a psychological transformation that substituted the white man's individualism for the Indian attitude of common ownership. Upon settling at Niobrara, they found their old chiefs firmly re-established in power and backed by the authority of a paternalistic government. Rebelling against this state of affairs and at least vaguely aware that the Sioux treaty of 1868 had included a provision permitting Indians to take up homesteads outside the "Great Sioux Reservation" as well as within its boundaries, they decided to test the government's sincerity and good faith. As Williamson pointed out, they had done of their own accord "just what the Government has been for generations trying to get the Indians to do."[1]

Without denying the essential correctness of Williamson's analysis of their motives, it is possible to see other reasons for their unprecedented move. The Indians themselves argued that the land was better at Flandreau than on the Santee Reservation, more like the country they had occupied before the uprising. No doubt some members of the group were chronic malcontents such as were found on every reservation, people who resented being subject to any authority, whether exercised by chiefs or by agents. In justification for their actions, the Flandreau settlers wrote the commissioner that they did not wish "to suffer the extortion of our chiefs and agents appointed over us and who collude together and between them both we get well stripped. . . ." This was stating the case rather strongly, for, bad as some agents were, there is nothing in the available evidence to show that Agent Stone was guilty of extortion or of "colluding" with the chiefs to cheat the mass of the Indians. In all probability, these Indians had imbibed, along with the rest of the white man's culture, a sizable measure of selfishness, and they thought they could accomplish their personal objectives better without the agent's supervision. Ownership of land was one means of gratifying their desire, and they were growing impatient with the delay in allotting individual farms at Santee. Coupled with their wish to own their own farms was the fear of another removal which constantly agitated the Santees for nearly two decades. All of these reasons, together with others less apparent, conspired to induce two dozen families to take what can only be described as an extremely daring, even foolhardy, step.[2]

[1] Stephen R. Riggs, *Mary and I: Forty Years with the Sioux* (Boston: Congregational Sunday-School and Publishing Society, 1880), pp. 265–267; John P. Williamson to John A. Burbank, October 22, 1869, NARS, RG 75, LR; Com. of Indian Affairs, *Annual Report*, 1871, p. 270.

[2] Petition of Flandreau Indians to Commissioner of Indian Affairs, December 23, 1869, NARS, RG 75, LR.

Besides the natural uncertainty over whether they would be able to make a success of farming unaided, these Indians had to consider the possibility that they would not even be allowed to attempt it. The men who exercised authority over them in the name of the United States government were by no means in sympathy with the experiment at the outset. Asa M. Janney, who succeeded Stone as Santee agent soon after the exodus took place, wrote in August that the Indians were not capable of competing with white men in the accumulation of property and would be subjected to great pressures when settlement of the Big Sioux country began and the value of the lands chosen by the Indians became known. Concerned about their morals as well, Janney thought they would be better off in close proximity to schools and missionaries than surrounded by unscrupulous whites who would corrupt their women.[3] Commissioner Parker was of the same mind. In November of that year he wrote Governor John A. Burbank of Dakota Territory, advising him that the Santees should be kept together and instructing him to take steps to induce them to return to their reservation, where Janney was about to begin allotting lands. When Burbank inquired whether they could be aided out of funds being used to encourage the Santees to become self-sustaining, he was told that regulations did not permit diversion of tribal funds to Indians who had voluntarily separated themselves from their tribe and that those people would progress more rapidly if they returned to the reservation and submitted to the government's plans for them.[4]

Fortunately for the survival of the Flandreau colony, they had a stalwart friend in missionary Williamson, who seems to have impressed Burbank with the wisdom of letting the Indians try their experiment. He wrote the governor in October that they had raised some corn the previous summer and had put up a number of log houses, evidently planning to hang on if they were allowed to do so. Although their corn amounted to only an acre or so per family and that had been injured by frost so as to be useless as seed, they were hard at work trapping muskrat in the hope of earning enough from the sale of furs to tide them over the winter and give them a start the next season. With no working stock other than their light Indian ponies, they had hired oxen from the three or four whites in the neighborhood and had broken patches of prairie sod, which they had cultivated with hoes and spades. William-

[3] Asa M. Janney to Ely S. Parker, August 6, 1869, *ibid*.
[4] Parker to Burbank, November 2 and December 14, 1869, NARS, RG 75, LS; Burbank to Parker, November 20, 1869, NARS, RG 75, LR.

son thought the government ought to aid them by providing oxen, wagons, plows, and other farm implements. "Our Government is spending millions of dollars to support whole tribes of overaged Indian papooses, hoping that some day they will have moral strength enough to undertake the care of themselves," he pointed out. "Here is a small colony that have started out for themselves."[5]

Burbank was inclined to agree with Williamson. He had written Commissioner Parker first on July 15 and had received, four months later, only the instructions to have them return to the reservation. He wrote again in November, stressing the benefit of their example to other Indians if they succeeded. Then, in December, the Indians themselves addressed a letter to the commissioner, giving their reasons for their action and asking permission to stay where they were. Parker finally acceded to their request but continued to refuse them any assistance from the government. Although there was no intention of forcing them to return to Santee, he said, if they chose to remain off the reservation, of course they would "forfeit their claim to any part of the payments made to their tribe."[6]

Parker had earlier informed Burbank, in reply to a request for information as to whether Indians could avail themselves of the Homestead Act of 1862, that they could do so only if they "permanently and wholly dissolved" all tribal connections. Only then could they exercise the rights and assume the obligations of citizens. Acting on this advice, Burbank had twenty-four members of the colony come to Yankton, the territorial capital, and execute a document renouncing their tribal ties and all benefits due them as members of their tribe. Homestead certificates were then issued to all but two of the group who were unable to pay the fourteen-dollar fee. Many had the exact amount, carefully wrapped, in small coins, showing that they had saved it up over a period of time. Burbank accompanied them to Vermillion, the location of the land office, and helped them in perfecting their titles.[7] Thus the Flandreau colony was formally launched.

Abandoning all claim to benefits as members of their tribe seemed a high price to pay for independence. Although the Indians were willing

[5] Williamson to Burbank, October 22, 1869, NARS, RG 75, LR.

[6] Burbank to Parker, August 20, 1870, and November 20, 1869; Petition of Flandreau Indians to Commissioner, December 23, 1869, *ibid.*; Parker to Burbank, March 22, 1870, NARS, RG 75, LS.

[7] Parker to Burbank, March 10, 1870, NARS, RG 75, LS; Burbank to Parker, June 10, 1870, NARS, RG 75, LR.

to pay it, some of their white friends did not think they should have to. Williamson though it was penalizing them for doing precisely what the government wanted all Indians to do—strike out on their own and become like white men. Of all the members of their tribe, these people most deserved the attention and encouragement of the government. He did not favor restoring their annuities or issuing rations to them, but he thought it only just that the government restore to them a part of what had been taken from them through the cession of their lands in Minnesota.[8] In time Agent Janney also came around to his view. In 1870 appropriations under the 1868 treaty were held up because of a dispute between the two houses of Congress arising from the House of Representatives' wish to assert its importance and abolish the treaty-making power enjoyed by the Senate. When the squabble was settled and an appropriation was voted early in 1871, Janney inquired of the commissioner whether the Flandreau people could share in the fund. A penciled endorsement, evidently by an official in the Department of the Interior, on Janney's letter reads: "This has been up several times and we have invariably directed that we can do nothing for them."[9] They had to wait another year before any official notice was taken of them.

Meanwhile, the Flandreau people were gaining a favorable reputation among their white neighbors. C. K. Howard, a Sioux Falls merchant, wrote Burbank in 1870 that he and his brothers had lent them money which they had repaid more punctually than white men usually did. He remarked that their settlement gave more indications of civilization and industry and "a show of living like white people than the same number of Norwegian families located a few miles below which the government protects and leaves the Indian in doubt." Although some whites were disposed to drive them out, it was probably, as Burbank said, because of a deep-seated prejudice against Indians as a race. Whereas a white man among others of his race was presumed to be honest in the absence of evidence to the contrary, an Indian was ordinarily thought to be a rogue until he proved himself otherwise. Hence the Indian had to be above suspicion if he was to be accorded the respect of white men. This the Flandreau Indians were able to do with surprising success.[10]

[8] Williamson to Burbank, July 30, 1870, NARS, RG 75, LR.

[9] A. M. Janney to Samuel M. Janney, April 18, 1871, NARS, RG 75, LR, Santee Sioux Agency.

[10] C. K. Howard to Burbank, May 15, 1870; Burbank to Parker, August 20, 1870, NARS, RG 75, LR.

For the first three years of their experiment, the Flandreau people would perhaps not have been able to survive without help of various kinds from such white neighbors as they had, for their farming did not afford them even a bare subsistence, and the amount of money they could make by trapping and hiring out to white farmers was not enough to make up the difference between what they produced and what they needed to live. Williamson kept up his campaign to have them aided by the government, however, and in 1871 he succeeded to the extent of having a report on their condition published in the commissioner's annual report to the Secretary of the Interior. After describing their struggle and pointing out that among them were four signers of the 1868 treaty, he asked specifically that each family be provided with one yoke of oxen, a wagon and log chain, a plow, a cow, a scythe, a fork, and a hoe. Though the expenditure might judiciously be extended over a period of years, $5,000 should be made available at once. Since the American Board missionaries had been working with the Santee people for decades, he deemed it proper that the money should be expended under the Board's direction.[11]

Presumably acting on the recommendation of the Indian Office, Congress included the "Families of Santee Dakota Sioux who have taken Homesteads at or near Flandreau, in Dakota Territory," in the Indian appropriations act of May 29, 1872, though without allocating any specific sum to that group. Some weeks later Sisseton Agent Moses N. Adams was instructed to take steps to build a school for the Flandreau Sioux and to determine what stock, tools, and other items were most needed there. When Adams visited the colony in October, he found 227 people living in 51 log houses. The original 25 families had doubled by the fall of 1869, and more had been arriving since. Their equipment was pitifully meager. Although they had 42 ponies, they were fit only to ride, and the Indians had broken the prairie by exchanging work with the whites. They had a total of 33 hay forks, 35 scythes, 77 hoes, and 1 plow. With these they were attempting to raise corn and potatoes on 152 acres, to which had just been added 61 acres of newly broken ground. They had that season raised nearly 3,000 bushels of corn and nearly 2,000 bushels of potatoes and had cut and stacked over 200 tons of hay. A small log church had been built the previous year and was now offered for sale as a schoolhouse for $1,000. Adams submitted an estimate for $20,000 worth of food, clothing, goods, seeds, and farm implements, and asked an additional $1,800 to

11 Com. of Indian Affairs, *Annual Report*, 1871, pp. 269–270.

248 of the Santee Sioux

cover purchase of the school, purchase of desks and a bell, and payment of a teacher's salary for one year.[12]

Once the precedent had been established, it was easier to persuade Congress to appropriate funds for the Flandreau people. They were included in a deficiency appropriation of $350,000 for the "Sioux of Different tribes," made March 3, 1873, and thereafter what they received was determined by the Indian Bureau, acting upon the advice of those on the scene. Agent Adams lived too far from Flandreau to exercise any very effective supervision over affairs there; and late in 1873, John P. Williamson was appointed special agent (at an annual salary of $480) to determine the needs of these people and distribute supplies to them. Williamson was then living at the Yankton agency at Greenwood, D.T., and was able to pay only periodic visits to Flandreau. Neither he nor the Indians wanted an agent located there, since it was just that kind of government supervision that they had rejected, but there was no objection to his looking after their temporal needs in the course of his attention to their spiritual condition.[13]

During the brief time that Adams had charge of government assistance to the Flandreau colony, he made two issues, one of clothing worth about $1,800 in the late winter of 1873, and another of oxen, wagons, plows, hoes, scythes, and other tools to the amount of nearly $10,000 the following June. When Williamson visited them in August, he found them using the articles to good advantage and expecting a good crop. Although he opposed issuing food or clothing, he thought the half of the group who had not received oxen, wagons, etc., should be issued those items before the start of the next season. Each family, he thought, should also receive a cow. In addition, Adams had opened a school. Although described as "flourishing" in Adams' official report for 1873, it actually stumbled along with light enrollment for many years. The Indians had taken homesteads scattered along the Big Sioux River for twenty miles or more, and it was impossible to get any large number of children in the school, even though it was centrally located. Williamson kept calling for a boarding hall to accommodate the children who lived too far from the school to travel back and forth every day, but the Indian Office never saw fit to honor his request.[14]

[12] U.S. *Statutes at Large*, XVII, 182; Moses N. Adams to Parker, October 9 and 23, 1872, NARS, RG 75, LR, Sisseton Agency.

[13] U.S. *Statutes at Large*, XVII, 539; Acting Secretary of Interior B. R. Cowen to Commissioner Edward P. Smith, September 10, 1873; Williamson to E. P. Smith, October 16, 1873, NARS, RG 75, LR, Flandreau Special Agency.

[14] Com. of Indian Affairs, *Annual Report*, 1873, p. 227; Williamson to E. P. Smith, September 1, 1873, NARS, RG 75, LR, Santee Agency; Moses K. Armstrong to E. P.

Despite his reluctance to issue provisions and thus place the Flandreau people in the same position of dependence on the government as the reservation Santees, Williamson was obliged by repeated crop failures to ask authority to do just that. Except for the first year, however, when he issued $314 worth of pork and flour, he insisted that provisions should be issued only during the season when the Indians were planting and cultivating their crops and when, without such assistance, they would have to leave their farms and hunt to keep their families alive. No matter how poor the crop, he afterward refused to issue provisions during the winter to any but old women, widows, and school children. The precedent for this practice was established in 1873, when the Indians, in compliance with Adams' request that they stay home to receive another issue of supplies, neglected their customary fall hunt, only to learn that no issue could be made that year. Their plight led to some dissatisfaction, expressed in a letter from their most articulate member, David Faribault, and others to Commissioner Edward P. Smith just before the end of the year. Faribault had kept track of every penny expended in behalf of his people and thought, incorrectly, that they were entitled to more.[15]

With Williamson's assistance, the Flandreau people made it through the hard winter of 1873–1874 (Williamson said that most white farmers in western Minnesota and Iowa were supplied with seed wheat at public expense the next season) and set to work the following spring with a determination to show what they could do with the equipment provided by the government. Unfortunately, they were hard hit the next summer by that scourge of the 1870's, the grasshopper. Somewhere between three-fourths and four-fifths of the expected crop was destroyed, leaving them with nothing to fall back upon for the winter. The following winter was one of real hardship. Williamson stuck to his determination not to make any general issue of rations until the planting season. He gave out rations for about a month during the winter to some fifty indigent persons but withheld the rest until March. Meanwhile, the men (and in many cases their families) went out in October and November for an unusually successful trapping season. They went out again in March but found that the bitter cold had frozen the lakes and creeks to the bottom and killed the muskrats. The Flandreau

Smith, December 28, 1873, and June 12, 1874, NARS, RG 75, LR, Flandreau Special Agency.

[15] Williamson to E. P. Smith, November 25, 1873, and January 7 and April 18, 1874; Armstrong to E. P. Smith, December 28, 1873, NARS, RG 75, LR, Flandreau Special Agency.

people were the best trappers in the Sioux nation, thought their agent; whereas the Yanktons would hardly bother to trap on their own reservation, these people would "go 50 miles away from timber and settlement, camp at some lake in the cold snow, and work day and night to catch and preserve a few rat and mink skins."[16]

Not everyone in the colony approved of the agent's methods of handling rations. David Faribault, who seems to have been ambitious for recognition as the leader of the group, composed a petition and submitted it to Moses K. Armstrong, territorial delegate to Congress, with the signatures of a number of his fellows. He complained that Williamson failed to understand that fur trapping was played out and hence no credit was extended to the Indians on the strength of their expected harvest of furs. Nor was there any longer a market for the Indians' ponies or for cordwood, which they had been selling to the whites before the economic depression had settled over the country. He accused Williamson of distributing the food and clothing to only a few people and of having selfish motives in seeking the position of special agent. Williamson reported later that he had heard that "some political schemers and soft-hearted sympathizers" had been trying to damage his reputation with the Indians, but that he had called them into council and explained the matter, with the result that the criticism died down.[17]

Political motives there unquestionably were. Late in 1875, when R. L. Pettigrew, a political figure in the territory, submitted to the territorial delegate, J. P. Kidder, a pair of petitions asking that Faribault be paid for his services, he remarked: "I hope you will take some interest in the matter as with a little care these Indians are inclined to vote the republican ticket and would have done so last year if the matter had been managed right."[18] Citizenship had come to the Flandreau people who had received patents to their land, and they were reaping the benefits.

The Flandreau Special Indian Agency remained in existence until 1879, and Williamson served as agent for all but the last few months of this time. On the whole, these were difficult years for the Flandreau people, as they were for other Indian groups living in the same region

[16] Williamson to E. P. Smith, April 18 and August 31, 1874, and January 14 and 28 and April 10 and May 15, 1875, *ibid.*; Com. of Indian Affairs, *Annual Report,* 1874, p. 42.

[17] David Faribault, *et al.*, to Armstrong, February 1, 1875; Williamson to E. P. Smith, March 12, 1875, NARS, RG 75, LR, Flandreau Special Agency.

[18] R. F. Pettigrew to J. P. Kidder, December 3, 1875, *ibid.*

as well as for the white pioneers who were gradually settling up the country. The annual incursions of grasshoppers were the principal reason that farmers on the plains were unable to gain a firm foothold. In 1875, for example, crops at Flandreau looked excellent until July 23, when millions of the insects, properly called Rocky Mountain locusts, descended on the fields and took half the wheat, nearly all the ruta-bagas, and much of the corn, potatoes, and other vegetables. An early frost nipped the corn and reduced the crop to half what had been ex-pected. Yet Williamson was able to report, somewhat prematurely, that the Indians would harvest 3,485 bushels of corn, 2,470 bushels of potatoes, 1,605 bushels of wheat, and substantial quantities of vegeta-bles—enough to tide them over the winter.[19] The following year only half a crop was realized, and by April, 1877, Williamson had to report that the Flandreau people were starving. They did better the next season, however, for the grasshoppers, though seen, did not settle but flew on. Williamson attributed the deliverance of his people and their white neighbors to the day of prayer declared by the governor. What-ever the cause, the invasions were never so serious in later years, and the Flandreau people began to get on their feet—or would have if other difficulties had not interfered.[20]

All through the early 1870's Williamson kept up a running battle for funds with which to encourage the Indians in their efforts. Their right to participate in benefits accorded the various Sioux groups under the treaty of 1868 had been recognized officially in 1874. In May, 1875, they received $5,000 from the proceeds of the sale of the old reservation in Minnesota, and three years later Williamson was authorized to buy them three reapers out of this fund, which thus came to be an important source of money in the lean years of the depression.[21]

In another respect their situation changed in 1875. Congress that year extended the benefits of the Homestead Act to Indians without exacting from them a renunciation of benefits to which they might be entitled as members of a recognized tribe. Since this law contained a provision making their homesteads inalienable for five years, the

[19] Williamson to E. P. Smith, August 6, 1875, *ibid.*; Williamson to John Q. Smith, April 10, 1877, NARS, RG 75, LR, Nebraska Agencies; Com. of Indian Affairs, *Annual Report*, 1875, p. 240.

[20] Com. of Indian Affairs, *Annual Report*, 1876, p. 28; 1877, p. 59.

[21] Cowen to E. P. Smith, February 13, 1874; Columbus Delano to E. P. Smith, February 14, 1874, NARS, RG 75, LR, Flandreau Special Agency; Williamson to J. Q. Smith, April 10, 1877; Williamson to Ezra A. Hayt, April 22 and May 21, 1878, NARS, RG 75, LR, Nebraska Agencies.

Flandreau Indians who acquired title to their farms after that date were protected—for a short time—against loss of their land. Unfortunately, most of their homesteads had been taken up earlier and were not so protected. Some (those under the 1868 treaty) had no restrictive clause and were speedily encumbered with mortgages. By 1876, out of eighty-five homesteads taken, only thirty were patented; on those the owners were paying taxes—excessive taxes, in Williamson's opinion—as they were on their personal property.[22]

The living conditions of the Flandreau Indians at this time were similar to those of white pioneers in the same locality. Although most had taken 160-acre claims, they cultivated only from one to ten or perhaps twenty acres of their farms, which were so situated as to have the Big Sioux River running through most of them. Five years after the arrival of the first contingent, they were all living in log cabins with earth roofs and earth floors; most had put up stables of a crude kind and stored enough hay to carry their stock through the winter. As the years passed, their circumstances gradually improved. Beginning in 1878, a concerted effort was made to replace their log cabins with frame houses. That year the government built eight houses at $350 each, and in 1882 it provided twenty more at a total cost of $5,000. With the addition of another twenty in 1884 and a few built by the Indians themselves, by 1887 all were housed in frame dwellings.[23] Gradually during the same years their household furnishings improved and increased. At first few had stoves or much of anything else, but as time went on they provided themselves with what they needed, following their white neighbors' examples. From the very beginning they wore clothing like that of the whites; and in 1875, Williamson hired a seamstress to make clothing for the school children and to teach the women sewing. He and others repeatedly noted that there was little about the dress of these people or their way of life to show that they were Indians. Though nearly all were literate in their own language, few knew much English for a number of years, and they were therefore handicapped in their dealings with white businessmen and farmers.[24]

[22] U.S. *Statutes at Large*, XVIII, 420; Com. of Indian Affairs, *Annual Report*, 1876, p. 27; 1878, p. 31.

[23] Williamson to E. P. Smith, January 7, 1874, NARS, RG 75, LR, Flandreau Special Agency; Com. of Indian Affairs, *Annual Report*, 1878, p. 31; 1882, p. 116; 1884, p. 124; 1887, p. 159.

[24] Williamson to Burbank, October 22, 1869, NARS, RG 75, LR; Williamson to E. P. Smith, January 14, 1875, NARS, RG 75, LR, Flandreau Special Agency; Williamson to J. Q. Smith, April 16, 1877; Petition of Flandreau Indians, June 24, 1878, NARS, RG 75, LR, Nebraska Agencies.

Williamson tried to function as an intermediary between the Indians and whites, along with performing his other duties. As he remarked shortly before he left his position, he had been "agent, carpenter, farmer, clerk and interpreter by turns," all of these tasks requiring much labor on his part. When authorized to build eight houses that year, he accompanied sixty Indians to Luverne, Minnesota, the nearest railhead, and bought lumber, then superintended the construction and did much of the work himself. He was insistent, however, that government services to the Flandreau people be held to a minimum. He opposed the appointment of David Faribault as a government employee both because he considered him unqualified and because he believed the Indians would do better with no employees other than an agent and a teacher, and he hoped that the agent could soon be dispensed with. At various times they had asked for a farmer, a blacksmith, and a physician, but he had always opposed such requests.[25]

His successor, William H. Wasson, who assumed charge of the agency in August, 1878, apparently had other ideas, for he immediately complained of the lack of facilities and submitted estimates for an agency building and other items that he deemed necessary. The Indian Office was not moved by his request, however, and disallowed all but fifty dollars (for a windmill and pump) out of his estimate of $3,575. Early in 1879 it went even further and consolidated the Flandreau Special Agency with the Santee Agency. Wasson and his wife were retained for a short time as superintendent and teacher, but by November of that year the Reverend John Eastman, a member of the colony, had been placed in charge of the school and was the only government employee.[26]

Santee Agent Isaiah Lightner visited Flandreau at the end of April, 1879, and found the Indians "quite indifferent as to having any one to come among them as an Agent. . . ." Three of the men spoke at a council held by Lightner and questioned the need for a government school, inasmuch as they were paying local school taxes. Lightner explained that he had no intention of forcing himself on them but would help them if they wanted help. He had been directed to buy oxen, cows, stoves, and other items for them, but if they did not want these, he would not do so. "They laughed some and did not know exactly

[25] Williamson to Hayt, July 3, 1878; Williamson to J. Q. Smith, October 3, 1876, NARS, RG 75, LR, Nebraska Agencies.

[26] William H. Wasson to Hayt, August 17 and 26, 1878; Secretary of Interior Carl Schurz to Hayt, March 17, 1879; Isaiah Lightner to Hayt, May 7 and November 26, 1878, *ibid.*

what to say but soon I found they were willing to accept of the goods,"
wrote Lightner. Clearly the Flandreau people wanted to preserve their
self-respect but at the same time did not wish to miss out on anything
the government might see fit to give them. Lightner endorsed Williamson's policy and proposed to use as few employees as possible "and to
act myself in as unassuming [a] manner as I can to be in charge of
them." Since about forty families had less than ten acres broken, he
saw the need to supply provisions during the breaking season to keep the
Indians from going off on trapping expeditions.[27]

Circumstances around the Indian colony were changing by the late
1870's. The town of Flandreau was growing rapidly, and white settlers
were filling up the vacant lands between the Indian homesteads. In a
petition to Lightner signed by twenty-six members of the colony, the
Indians expressed the view that they needed help and guidance more
than ever now that "our lands are being cut by R. R. Corporations and
are in great danger of Minipulations [*sic*] and frauds," In his last
official report, Williamson pointed to whiskey, debt, and taxes as the
chief problems facing the Flandreau people then and in the future. As
early as 1875 he had seen the penchant for strong drink as the one
exception to their otherwise good conduct, and later he said that there
would be no trouble between them and the whites if whiskey were kept
out of the country. Their tendency to fall into debt did not distinguish
them from their white neighbors, but it constituted a problem for them
as it did for the latter. By 1878 they were paying eight hundred dollars
a year in taxes—a heavy load for them to bear. Inattention to the
principles of sanitation, as practiced by white people, was another
source of difficulty among the Indians and accounted for the high
mortality, which in some years exceeded the number of births. As
frame houses with board floors gradually replaced the log cabins, that
problem became less serious.[28]

Perhaps the greatest threat to the colony was that a combination of
pressures and temptations would induce many of the Indians to sell out.
This began happening on an alarming scale about 1879, when Lightner
called the commissioner's attention to it. "They are getting nicely
started and their lands are becoming valuable," he wrote, "and the
Indians have not received more than half price for what they have

[27] Lightner to Hayt, May 7, 1879, *ibid.*

[28] Com. of Indian Affairs, *Annual Report*, 1874, p. 241; 1875, p. 240; 1878, pp. 30–31;
Williamson to Hayt, July 3, 1878; Petition of Flandreau Indians to Lightner, July 28,
1879, NARS, RG 75, LR, Nebraska Agencies.

disposed of to white men." Those whose lands carried no restrictions could sell out whenever they wished, and those who took claims under the act of 1875 could sell upon the expiration of their five-year restrictive clause. Lightner felt that it would take some effort to make them hold fast. They had by that time 86 homesteads, ranging from 40 to 320 acres and totaling 13,527 acres. About a third, Lightner thought, were progressing, another third were at a standstill, and the rest were retrograding. Few cultivated enough land to live on or to accumulate stock, and consequently they were readily susceptible to the pressures brought upon them to sell out. As Lightner noted, they were not unlike the generality of white pioneers in their willingness to move on when offered what they considered a good price. As a matter of fact, he thought that a higher proportion of the Flandreau Indians had become permanent settlers than of the whites who first settled the area.[29]

Still, they were not holding fast in the early 1880's. The population decreased from 365 in 1878 to 221 in 1888, and their acreage went down to 5,042 by 1886, when 234 people remained in the colony. It is not difficult to surmise where the people went who left Flandreau in those years. In 1885 allotment was carried out at Santee, and some returned to take advantage of the opportunity thus afforded. In 1884, Congress began appropriating sums for the support and civilization of small Sioux groups in Minnesota, and many from Flandreau joined these even smaller colonies. Big Eagle, for example, who had been among the leaders of the 1869 exodus from Santee, now migrated again and shortly established himself in the old reservation area. The movement away from Flandreau took place in spite of diligent efforts to provide the Indians with houses, implements, and stock. In 1883, for example, they were issued 128 oxen, 10 bulls, 325 heifers, 320 hogs, and 50 sheep; some of the animals were sold to white farmers. By this time the government was employing not only an Indian overseer and a teacher but also a contract physician and thus was more deeply involved in the affairs of the settlement than ever before.[30]

By the later eighties the loss of land became so alarming that the Indian Bureau authorized a per capita payment, made in May, 1887, to help the Indians pay off their mortgages. This was the first of several financial windfalls in which the Flandreau people shared. They received

[29] Lightner to Hayt, November 26, 1879, NARS, RG 75, LR, Nebraska Agencies; Com. of Indian Affairs, *Annual Report*, 1880, p. 122; 1881, p. 128; 1884, p. 124.
[30] Com. of Indian Affairs, *Annual Report*, 1878, p. 30; 1883, pp. 109–110; 1886, p. 193; 1888, p. 170.

substantial benefits from the series of congressional acts relating to
the division and sale of the "Great Sioux Reservation," mentioned
earlier. In 1891 they received $42,000 in lieu of the land they were
entitled to under Section 7 of the Sioux act of 1889. The Santee agent
reported that they used the money wisely. In 1893 they received a per
capita payment amounting to about $7.03 each from proceeds of the
sale of the old reservation. The act of June 10, 1896, also brought them
financial largess to the extent of $43,516.80 in cash. Perhaps as a result
of all these and smaller payments, their numbers began once more to
increase, and the Flandreau population hovered around three hundred
through the 1890's.[31]

The decade of the nineties brought a benefit of another kind to the
Flandreau people, although it was not limited to them. Williamson's
repeated appeals for a boarding school had met with a cold reception
from the Indian Office, and Lightner declined to renew the request,
though urged by the Indians to do so. In 1885 he had the day school
repaired and painted and the grounds enclosed with a fence and planted
with shade trees. Five years later, however, the town of Flandreau was
selected as the site for a non-reservation boarding school to serve
Indian children in the Dakotas and adjacent states. A quarter section
just north of the town was chosen by Santee Agent James E. Helms and
the teacher at the day school, Hosea Locke, and purchased by the
government for $2,000. The first four buildings of the boarding school
were constructed in 1892, at a cost of $52,425.30, and it was put in
operation in March, 1893, with the former day school pupils as a
nucleus. By the end of the fiscal year the school had an enrollment of
ninety-eight, including many students who were not from the local
Indian community.[32] Since the Flandreau Indian School has not been
identified closely with the Flandreau Santee Sioux colony, its subsequent history does not properly come within the scope of this study;
but in its early years it filled an educational need not adequately met by
the day school or the district schools which had followed in the wake
of white settlement.

By the end of the nineteenth century the Flandreau Sioux were
better off economically than the other Santees, the Sissetons, or the
Devils Lake people. Although they had lost much of their land and
were to lose more in the next decades, they had shown a tenacity and

[31] *Ibid.*, 1887, p. 159; 1891, p. 295; 1893, p. 200; 1897, p. 184.
[32] *Ibid.*, 1885, pp. 139–140; 1892, p. 895; 1893, p. 457; U.S. *Statutes at Large*, XXVI,
358–359, 1012.

ingenuity that helped them overcome apparently insuperable obstacles and become moderately successful. Besides their farming, they had found other ways of earning a living. In 1874 one man held the contract for carrying the mail through Flandreau and received $1,000 a year for his services. Before the turn of the century they were also exploiting the resources of the nearby Pipestone quarry and making pipes, rings, and other articles for sale. They realized an income of $2,250 from the sale of such items in 1888 and doubtless similar amounts in other years for which no figures are available.[33] More important, they had established a reputation for honesty and reliability among their white neighbors. Lightner was probably expressing a view shared by those neighbors when he wrote in 1881 that the Flandreau Indians "pay their taxes promptly, their word can be relied upon, and they make good neighbors." There was factionalism among them, of course, as there is in any group of people. When John Eastman had been appointed teacher at the school, a petition was got up for his removal and his replacement by Walter L. Pettijohn. Upon investigation, the move was found to be the work of Pettijohn's mother, and the charges against Eastman were false, some of the signatures forgeries.[34]

Such factionalism did not detract from the essential achievement of the Flandreau people in breaking out of the nest and testing their own wings. If they received government support, those who stayed in the colony used that support on the whole wisely. The amount and kind of help they received from their white neighbors cannot be measured, but it is not likely that it outweighed the advantage taken of them by other whites, nor was the government support given them disproportionate to the handicaps under which they labored as Indians in a frontier community. All things considered, the Flandreau colony in 1900 was the most successful and most securely based of the various fragments into which the Santee Sioux had been dispersed since 1862.

[33] Com. of Indian Affairs, *Annual Report*, 1874, p. 242; 1881, p. 306; 1888, p. 173; Lightner to Roland E. Trowbridge, April 2, 1880, NARS, RG 75, LR, Nebraska Agencies.

[34] Com. of Indian Affairs, *Annual Report*, 1881, p. 306; Lightner to Hayt, April 2, 1880, NARS, RG 75, LR, Nebraska Agencies.

CHAPTER **13**

Those Who Stayed

OF ALL THE splinter groups into which the Santee Sioux were fragmented after the uprising, none have so quietly dramatic a history as those few who never left Minnesota or who returned to the state after a discreet interval. Defying both hostile public opinion, which persisted long after the outbreak, and the poverty that was their lot for having renounced the benefits extended to the tribe, they hung on at or near their old homes until the government finally, in 1884, extended belated and limited recognition to them. After that their numbers were gradually augmented by migration from outside the state, until by 1960 there were more Santee Sioux living on the small reservations in Minnesota than there were on the Santee Reservation in Nebraska.

The story of the Santees who stayed behind goes back to 1853, when the bulk of the Mdewakantons and Wahpekutes were removed, albeit temporarily, to the reservation on the upper Minnesota. For several years, many of them spent most of their time in their old territory, showing up at the agency only for the annuity payment, and some never did establish residence on the reservation. A few families lingered around Faribault, aided by Alexander Faribault, who helped them send their children to the local schools and gradually merge with the white community. There is evidence that some also hung on in the Wabasha vicinity, perhaps members of that portion of the old Wabasha band who refused to move to the reservation in 1853. The naturalist and author Henry David Thoreau reported seeing "Dacotah shaped wigwams" just below Wabasha when he passed up the Mississippi in the spring of 1861, and several months after the uprising a group of nineteen Sioux who had lived peaceably there all through the hostilities were captured by the military and taken to Fort Snelling. A record kept by the Prairie Island people says that one of their number went up to the Redwood to make maple sugar in the spring of 1862, lingered through the summer, and was caught up in the war that fall.[1] Passing references in newspapers of the 1850's and early 1860's also suggest that many of the lower Sioux remained in the vicinity of their old villages throughout the reservation period.

In addition to those who had partly or completely severed their ties with their tribe before the uprising, there was a larger number who were not removed with the main body in 1863. When 1,318 Sioux were shipped out of Fort Snelling that May, 137 were left behind to serve as scouts against the hostile Indians on the frontier. To this figure, which included women and children, must be added an indeterminate number who had testified against their fellows the previous autumn and believed that their lives would be jeopardized if they were forced to rejoin the tribe.[2] The fate of these "friendly Sioux" was a matter of concern, not only to themselves, but to friends of the Indians like Bishop Whipple and General Sibley; even Galbraith expressed concern about what might happen to them if they were made to accompany their tribesmen. On December 18, 1862, a petition was signed by five chiefs of the lower Sioux, five of the upper, and by other braves and headmen, disavowing participation in the uprising and asking that they be permitted to return to the reservation and the farms they had cultivated before the outbreak. The fact that the petitioners were among the very few not tried by the military court the previous fall indicates that their protestations of innocence were sincere. Although Antoine Freniere, a mixed-blood as vindictive as any of the whites, charged that these men merely wanted to return to the reservation in order to dig up plunder they had buried during the fighting, several

[1] *Central Republican* (Faribault), June 10, 1863; *Goodhue County Republican* (Red Wing), January 16, 1863; "History of Prairie Island Sioux, Begun by Thomas Rouillard— Related by Eliza Wells and Translated by Grandson, Norman Richard Campbell," ms, Minnesota Historical Society; Walter Harding, ed., *Thoreau's Minnesota Journey: Two Documents* (Geneseo, N.Y.: Thoreau Society, 1962), p. 4.

[2] Charles E. Mix to William P. Dole, May 18, 1863, NARS, RG 75, LR, Northern Superintendency.

prominent citizens were inclined to give them at least the benefit of the doubt.[3]

An early version of the bill to abrogate all treaties with the Santee Sioux contained a provision which would have awarded 160 acres of land to each Indian who had helped the whites during the uprising, provided him with agricultural implements, stock, etc., and given him a lifetime annuity of fifty dollars.[4] This clause of the bill was widely denounced in the newspapers, on the ground that Little Crow's case demonstrated that the "good Indian" of today might be the hostile of tomorrow. The Mankato *Weekly Record* predicted that the signers of the petition—the "pets," as it called them—might in five years be re-enacting the scenes of the previous August. "Christianizing Indians has proved an expensive undertaking to Minnesota," wrote editor John C. Wise, "and our people want no more experiments in that line."[5]

Despite the opposition, the removal bill that became law on March 3, 1863, contained a provision authorizing the Secretary of the Interior to grant eighty acres of land on the old reservation to "any meritorious individual . . . who exerted himself to save the lives of the whites in the late massacre." No mention was made of any other assistance or annuity. Perhaps because the land itself would be of no use to the Indian without implements, stock, and seed, which he was quite unable to purchase for himself, nothing was done to carry out this provision until 1865, when Congress passed a bill that enabled the Secretary of the Interior to assist the Indians financially in establishing themselves.[6]

Meanwhile, the friendly Sioux had been living in extreme poverty, preserved from starvation only by the charity of their white friends. When Sibley's spring campaign of 1863 was about to begin, Bishop Whipple asked him what was to be done with the families of his scouts and the other Indians who had rescued whites. Upon Sibley's reply that they would have to go to the new reservation on the Missouri with the rest of their tribe, the bishop suggested that they be turned over to him and sent to Faribault. An appeal to Alexander Faribault brought an offer of part of his farm as a camping place for these unfortunates. Only Faribault's reputation in the city named for him enabled him to so defy public opinion as to harbor members of the hated Indian race on his

---

[3] 54th Cong., 2nd Sess., *S. Rpt. 1362*, pp. 16–17; St. Paul *Pioneer*, December 14 and 18, 1862. According to Freniere, only one Indian, John Other Day, and two half-breeds, Joseph Coursoll and Jack Frazer, were free of complicity in the uprising. Someone, probably Sibley, wrote to the *Pioneer*, denying Freniere's charge.

[4] St. Paul *Pioneer*, January 15, 1863.

[5] Mankato *Weekly Record*, February 7, 1863.

[6] U.S. *Statutes at Large*, XII, 819–820; XIII, 427.

property. As it was, he was threatened and had to publish in the local newspaper a detailed statement identifying the Indians who were living on his land. None of those camping there in June, 1863, had taken any part in the uprising, he asserted, other than to help the whites escape; some had never lived on the reservation at all; one, a widow, had a son in the Union Army at the time.[7]

Although this public notice of the innocence of Faribault's guests prevented any violence that might have been planned, the four years that the Indians lived on his land were not altogether pleasant ones, for either him or them. They had no money, and their attempts to raise crops were largely unsuccessful. Faribault, who owned a mill, employed them when he could and sustained them by outright charity the rest of the time. They dug and sold ginseng, which had a certain popularity at the time, until the land had been so dug over that several years would be required for the ginseng to recover. They were not allowed to dig on other people's land. At the beginning of April, 1866, Faribault presented a claim for $3,871.44 to the government, partially covering his expenditures since March 1, 1863. His account included such items as "One coffin for child—$6.00" and "One coffin for son—$12."[8] His claim was eventually honored by the government, but it is unlikely that Faribault, who died in comparative poverty himself, was ever fully compensated for his generosity to his Sioux relatives.

The bill passed by Congress and approved February 9, 1865, was due largely to the exertions of Bishop Whipple, who made six trips to Washington at his own expense on behalf of the Sioux in Minnesota and elsewhere. Called "An Act for the Relief of certain Friendly Indians of the Sioux Nation, in Minnesota," it noted that these Indians were destitute because of their services to the whites in 1862, authorized the President to investigate their condition and "make such provision for their welfare as their necessities and future protection may require," and appropriated $7,500, one third of which was to be paid to John Other Day, the rest to "such other Indians as shall appear specially entitled thereto, for their friendly, extraordinary, and gallant services in rescuing white settlers from massacre in Minnesota."[9]

[7] Henry B. Whipple, *Lights and Shadows of a Long Episcopate* (New York: Macmillan Co., 1899), pp. 133–134; *Central Republican*, June 10, 1863.

[8] Com. of Indian Affairs, *Annual Report*, 1866, p. 235; Alexander Ramsey to Secretary of the Interior, enclosing Faribault's account dated April 1, 1866, NARS, RG 75, LR.

[9] Henry B. Whipple to Lewis V. Bogy, December 25, 1866, NARS, RG 75, LR; U.S. *Statutes at Large*, XIII, 427.

The determination of who was to share in the appropriation took some time and the actual distribution even longer, but action toward carrying out the provision for the Indians' welfare began almost at once. In the absence of Bishop Whipple, who was in Europe, his protégé, Samuel D. Hinman, immediately began agitating to have the government fulfill the clause in the removal act that provided for eighty-acre farms on the old reservation to be granted to the friendly Sioux. Hinman, in Washington at the time, wrote Commissioner Dole on March 15, 1865, asking that twelve sections of land be withdrawn from pre-emption and sale until each deserving head of family had received the allotment promised in 1863. Two days later the Secretary of the Interior authorized him to select the lands to be reserved. The tract Hinman proposed to locate his Indians on was on the south bank of the Minnesota River, in the vicinity of the old agency, including what is today the Lower Sioux Indian Community. Hinman was authorized to gather and establish the Indians on these lands, and Superintendent Clark W. Thompson was instructed to spend $800 to buy farm implements and seeds and to have lands plowed for the Indians.[10]

Although Hinman must surely have realized that there would be widespread public sentiment in Minnesota hostile to such a scheme as he envisioned, he went blithely ahead with the plan and collected at Faribault as many Indians as he could preparatory to establishing them on their lands. At this point his efforts were abruptly halted. General Sibley wrote him late in April that he had received orders from General John Pope forbidding any settlement of Indians on the old reservation without further orders from Pope or from higher authority. Even at this point the opposition of the whites might have been overcome but for the sudden revival of anti-Indian feeling that followed the murder by a small party of half-breeds of a family living south of Mankato. On the second day of May this group of renegades, led by John Campbell, a son of old Scott Campbell and a deserter from the Union Army, fell upon the Andrew Jewett family and killed or fatally wounded all four members of the family. A few days later Campbell was taken into custody on suspicion, subjected to a brief and somewhat irregular trial, and summarily hanged on the present site of the Blue Earth County courthouse. Although Campbell and his companions

[10] Samuel D. Hinman to Dole, March 15, 1865; Secretary of Interior John P. Usher to Dole, March 17, 1865, NARS, RG 75, LR; Dole to Hinman, March 23, 1865, NARS, RG 75, LS.

were outlaws primarily and Indians only secondarily, the savagery of their behavior led to such an upsurge of hatred for all Indians as to render impracticable any further efforts to locate the friendly Sioux on their old reservation. There followed an exchange of letters between Pope, backed by Sibley, and General Ulysses S. Grant, with the result that Grant finally sustained Pope's action in forbidding Hinman to proceed further with his plan. Grant remarked, with a degree of detachment not possible to those closer to the scene, that perhaps the Indians needed protection from the whites as much as the whites needed protection from the Indians.[11] Thus ended the first and only really serious attempt in the sixties to let the Sioux return to their old reservation.

On the chance that another attempt might be made, however, the citizens of Minnesota made known their opposition through appropriate channels. On February 28 of the following year a joint resolution of the state legislature and a memorial to the Secretary of the Interior were submitted in protest against the rumored proposal to settle "certain meritorious Indians upon our frontier." It complained that such Indians would have intercourse with the hostiles on the plains who had been harassing the Minnesota frontier since 1862. Furthermore, said the memorial, "The experience has shown, that even under ordinary circumstances a settlement of Indians in a body among whites is very detrimental and injurious both to the Indians and whites." Although the whites were said to entertain the kindest feelings toward these Indians individually, they insisted that the lands in question be opened to settlement.[12] The inconsistency of their argument and the absurdity of the prediction that Indians who had remained in Minnesota out of fear of the hostiles would now make common cause with the latter may have been noticed by the Secretary of the Interior, but he took no further action to settle the friendly Indians on the lands chosen for them by Hinman.

The failure of Hinman's plan left Alexander Faribault reluctantly footing the bill for the support of the Sioux on his land, with no

[11] Henry H. Sibley to Hinman, April 27, 1865, NARS, RG 75, LR; Mankato *Weekly Union*, May 5, 1865; Thomas Hughes, *History of Blue Earth County* (Chicago: Middle West Publishing Co., [1901]), pp. 149–154; *The War of the Rebellion: A Compilation of the Official Records of the Union and Confederate Armies*, First Series, Vol. 48, Pt. 2, pp. 347, 359, 367, 480. The story of the attempt to settle the Indians on their old reservation is summarized in Hinman to Whipple, May 30, 1866, NARS, RG 75, LR.

[12] Joint Resolution of the Minnesota State Legislature and Memorial to the Secretary of the Interior, March 16, 1866, NARS, RG 75, LR.

certainty of ever being reimbursed by the government. Besides presenting his claim, he requested in the spring of 1866 that the Indians be removed from his land and otherwise provided for. They were doing irreparable damage to his standing timber, and this he knew he would never be compensated for.[13] So long as the main body of the Santees were at Crow Creek, there was an understandable reluctance to send those in Minnesota to rejoin their tribesmen, but when the Crow Creek people had been removed to the Niobrara, supposedly a satisfactory home, pressure for the removal of the remnants at Faribault and elsewhere became stronger. Sibley wrote the Commissioner of Indian Affairs, Dennis N. Cooley, in April, 1866, that, with the exception of eight men and their families, these people would be willing to go to the new reservation and should be removed in time to plant crops there that season. The next month their removal was authorized by the Secretary of the Interior, but for reasons not clear no action was taken at that time, and by the first of June the plan had been temporarily abandoned.[14]

Since the Indians were not going to be removed as Sibley had recommended, the Indian Office decided to make temporary provision for them and to investigate their situation more thoroughly before taking further action. As soon as the altered intention of the government was known, Bishop Whipple set the Indians to work plowing some thirty or forty acres of Faribault's land, on which they put in a crop of corn, potatoes, and vegetables. The expenses, over a hundred dollars, were borne by the bishop himself, though Faribault continued to give what financial aid he could. The Department of the Interior also appointed a special agent, Shubael P. Adams, to investigate the condition of the Indians, submit suggestions for action, and attend to the distribution of the $7,500 appropriated by Congress the previous year. Adams arrived at Faribault late in June and spent several weeks collecting information on the "Scattered Sioux," as they came to be called.[15]

Adams found that there were 374 Sioux in Minnesota, including

[13] Ramsey to James Harlan, March 10, 1866; Alexander Faribault to Secretary of the Interior, June 2, 1866; Hinman to Whipple, April 6, 1866; Hinman to Secretary of the Interior, March 29, 1866, *ibid.*

[14] Sibley to Dennis N. Cooley, April 13, 1866; Harlan to Cooley, May 5, 1866; Whipple to Harlan, June 1, 1866, *ibid.* In his official report Cooley gave the "various delays" as the reason for not removing the Indians that spring. See Com. of Indian Affairs, *Annual Report*, 1866, p. 46.

[15] Cooley to Whipple, June 12, 1866, NARS, RG 75, LR; Com. of Indian Affairs, *Annual Report*, 1866, p. 235.

those at Big Stone Lake, who spent part of their time in Dakota Territory. He found 65 at Faribault, 12 at Wabasha (most of whom had fled from Crow Creek that spring), 158 on the Yellow Medicine and at the scouts' camp about seventy miles south of there, and 139 at the head of Big Stone Lake. More than half of them were mixed-bloods. Those at the scouts' camp received rations (but no pay) and spent a good share of their time hunting; except for about 40, he did not recommend their removal to Niobrara. Likewise, those at the Yellow Medicine, some of whom were farming, and those at Big Stone Lake constituted no annoyance to white settlers where they were and might well be left there. The Faribault and Wabasha groups, however, lived mostly on charity, having no hunting grounds and being able to raise only a small part of their necessities. Adams said, probably incorrectly, that they had no attachment to their present locations and were willing, even anxious in many cases, to go to the Niobrara.[16]

On the strength of Adams' recommendations, it was decided to remove the Indians that year, and Alexander Faribault was designated, at Bishop Whipple's and Sibley's suggestion, to do the job. His appointment did not reach him, however, until early in September, which he regarded as too late in the season for such an operation. The Indians were scattered around the woods, some of them gathering wild rice, and assembling them would take a considerable time. For these reasons, as well as on the grounds of poor health, Faribault declined the appointment but expressed a readiness to remove the Indians the next spring, provided the compensation were raised from five to ten dollars a day.[17] So another winter passed without any action toward the removal of the friendly Sioux.

These people were somewhat better provided for during the winter of 1866–1867 than in previous years, for some of them had received their shares of the $7,500 Adams had been ordered to disburse. The selection of those who were to receive the money was a difficult task. Bishop Whipple had the primary responsibility, but he enlisted the aid of the other missionaries, such as Riggs and the Williamsons, General Sibley, and everyone else who had personal knowledge of the circumstances. A list containing thirty-six names was finally submitted to Commissioner Cooley in June, 1866, and approved by him soon afterward. Besides such well-known individuals as Other Day (whose share

---

[16] Shubael P. Adams to Cooley, August 10, 1866, NARS, RG 75, LR.

[17] Sibley to Cooley, August 9, 1866; Harlan to Cooley, August 29, 1866; Faribault to Cooley, September 9, 1866; Orville Browning to Cooley, September 26, 1866, *ibid.*

of $2,500 Bishop Whipple thought outrageously large), Taopi, Lorenzo Lawrence, and Paul Mazakutemane, the list included eleven names suggested by Sibley; they were men who had performed no acts of marked heroism but who had by their moderating influence helped prevent the slaughter of the white captives. Adams did not disburse the money himself, but delegated Dr. Jared W. Daniels of Faribault to perform that part of the job. Daniels paid the Faribault Indians at once, in the fall of 1866, a few more the next winter, and nearly all the rest the following spring. Those who received the money early enough bought seed and tools and set about farming in the summer of 1867.[18]

Since those at Faribault had been assured that they would be removed the next summer, they apparently spent their money for food and other necessities. Alexander Faribault reported in the fall of 1866 that they were well supplied with provisions for the winter. Their condition was by no means enviable, however. They were still living in the worn-out tipis they had owned before the uprising, they had had no new blankets nor much clothing for four years, and their crops the previous summer had been washed out by a freshet. Ralph Waldo Emerson, on a lecture tour that winter, visited their encampment "in a wild piece of timber" late in January. In a letter to his daughter Ellen, he told of entering one of their tipis, in the company of Faribault's son, and finding them sitting on the ground, about to eat their supper, which was placed on a board. In one tent two young girls were singing psalms in Dakota. Emerson, nurtured on the romantic ideal of the early nineteenth century, regretted that "the light was not birch-bark nor pine-knot, but a kerosene lamp."[19]

The next spring Secretary of Interior Orville Browning authorized Superintendent Edward B. Taylor to have the Minnesota Sioux removed to the Santee Reservation under Hinman's supervision. No sooner had the news that they were to be removed become generally known than a chorus of protests arose, emanating primarily from those Indians who had all along objected to joining their tribesmen, but echoed also by some people who might have been expected to rejoice at the prospect. Not only were objections received from such friends of the Indians as Stephen R. Riggs, Thomas S. Williamson, and ex-Senator

[18] Whipple to Cooley, June 2, 1866; S. P. Adams to Cooley, June 26, 1866; Jared W. Daniels to Cooley, August 24, 1866, and June 10 and August 31, 1868, *ibid.*

[19] Faribault to Cooley, September 9, 1866; Whipple to Bogy, December 25, 1866, *ibid.*; Ralph L. Rusk, ed., *The Letters of Ralph Waldo Emerson* (New York: Columbia University Press, 1939), V, 493.

Henry M. Rice, but similar sentiments were expressed by Governor William R. Marshall, former Governor Ramsey, and sixty-one citizens of Faribault, who signed a petition asking that certain members of the group there be permitted to stay. The principal objection was the compulsory nature of the proposed removal. Riggs asked that the order be modified so as to permit those who wished to stay to do so. Governor Marshall thought it an injustice that Indians who were farming and were "to all intents and purposes ... citizens" should be removed against their will. Rice pointed out that "to send them amoung [*sic*] their own people whom they opposed and openly fought during the Indian war would be, I fear, sending them to their graves." His rather visionary recommendation was that they be sent to some place suitable to them and unobjectionable to the whites.[20] As might be expected, the most moving of the pleas came from the Indians themselves. Accompanying one of Governor Marshall's letters was an undated petition from Taopi and six others, partly in the handwriting of Bishop Whipple and bearing evidences of his literary style throughout. Pathetically the petitioners begged,

> Reward not we beseech thee our father our loyalty by delivering us up to the vengeance of our enemies We are but a little band all that remains of a once powerful nation upon the soil which was the hunting grounds of our fathers We shall need but a little space but for a little while Our white brothers now lords of soil once ours should not deny us this little boon.[21]

When the removal was finally carried out, in July, 1867, it was voluntary, although the Indians who chose not to leave were informed that no further provisions for their removal at government expense would be made. Hinman left the Santee Agency June 10 and arrived twelve days later at Faribault, from which base he visited all the Indian groups in southern Minnesota and took a census of them. This proved more difficult than he expected, for some of the Indians kept moving back and forth between the Missouri River and the Redwood area. Since the Sissetons and Wahpetons now had a reservation of their own, he omitted them from his figures, though they had accounted for the great majority of those Adams had found the previous year. Except for three lodges

[20] Browning to Edward B. Taylor, April 19, 1867; Stephen R. Riggs to Browning, March 11, 1867; Henry M. Rice to Browning, April 10, 1867; William R. Marshall to E. B. Taylor, April 18, 1867; Ramsey to Whipple, July 6, 1867; petition from Faribault citizens, July 30, 1867, NARS, RG 75, LR.

[21] Petition from Taope [*sic*], *et al.*, (undated), accompanying letter of Marshall to Commissioner of Indian Affairs, May 29, 1867, *ibid.*

whom Colonel Sam McPhail, proprietor of the town of Redwood Falls, had permitted to live in that vicinity, all the upper Sioux had been ordered away to their reservation. Hinman found seventy-five Sioux at Faribault, two at Mendota, four at Wabasha, and one lodge above Fort Snelling. All those at Faribault seemed willing to go except Taopi and his relatives and another man who had bought land in the vicinity. Those at Mendota and near Fort Snelling were cultivating large fields under the protection of their friends and relatives who were citizens, and they had no wish to leave. Two of the four at Wabasha seemed willing to leave but were deterred by the others, including one who lived across the river in Wisconsin. Hinman also learned that John Bluestone had bought a farm near Shakopee and was doing well at farming. All of these people he left behind. Those he took with him to Santee numbered five lodges, or thirty-nine individuals—slightly more than half the number at Faribault. Because of flooding due to recent rains, Hinman and his party had a miserable trip to Nebraska, but they arrived safely on August 15, exactly a month after their departure.[22]

Although the Hinman expedition of 1867 marked the end of the long struggle to remove the Sioux from Minnesota, it did not end efforts to locate the remnant on their old reservation. The next spring Bishop Whipple wrote to Sibley and to the Commissioner of Indian Affairs asking that Taopi and his friends be granted eighty-acre tracts there. Taopi he described as "poor, homeless, destitute, and yet worthy of our gratitude for rescuing our captives."[23] The wheels again ground slowly; and in May, 1869, Whipple was authorized to make new selections, not to exceed twelve sections of land, in a locality where there would be no conflict between the white settlers and the Indians. By this time, of course, it was difficult to find any land on the old reservation that had not been occupied by whites. Even in 1865, when Hinman had first tried to locate the Indians there, he was told that several pre-emption claims had been made on the tract chosen by him. In 1869 the land then withdrawn from sale was restored to the market, and now there was nothing available below the Yellow Medicine. McPhail, asked by Bishop Whipple to examine the country above there, was able to find only two suitable locations, one at the extreme western end of the old reservation, on the Dakota border, the other at the foot of Big Stone Lake. Since

[22] Hinman to Hampton B. Denman, August 20, 1867, *ibid.* See also *Central Republican,* July 17, 1867.

[23] Whipple to Sibley, April 7, 1868; Whipple to Commissioner of Indian Affairs, April 30, 1868; Sibley to Browning, April 20, 1868, NARS, RG 75, LR.

both of them were close to the new Sisseton Reservation, the bishop suggested that Sisseton Agent Daniels be given charge of such Indians as might be placed there.[24]

Nothing came of this scheme. It would not have helped Taopi in any case, for he had died on February 19, 1869, after falling ill on a hunting trip far north of St. Paul and returning to Faribault to die. He had earlier told Bishop Whipple that he expected never to have another home except his grave.[25] The rest of the little colony at Faribault stayed on, generally accepted by their white neighbors and gradually rising out of the abject poverty that had characterized their early years. In 1884 the Faribault *Democrat* presented a rather favorable picture of them:

> Here in Faribault there are a number of Indian families, who have comfortable homes, and clothed in the garments of civilization, provide for themselves as do their white neighbors. They are all faithful Christians and every Sunday, no matter what the weather, finds them in their places in the Cathedral and at least once a month reverentially kneeling at the altar to receive the Holy Communion.[26]

Less than five years later they left Faribault to join the newly established colony near the old agency site, where Hinman helped them to build a church and where the largest of the Sioux enclaves in Minnesota today is situated.

During the sixteen years after Hinman's removal of those at Faribault, the history of the Sioux in Minnesota is almost a total blank. The government having no further obligations toward them, they are scarcely mentioned in the correspondence of the Indian Bureau. It appears, however, that the fifty or so remaining in the state when Hinman removed the rest in 1867 were joined in succeeding years by a good many who preferred the risks of independence in their old homeland to the security of reservation life. Once the initiative had been taken by the people who went to Flandreau in 1869, others followed their example,

---

[24] Secretary of Interior Jacob D. Cox to Ely S. Parker, May 25, 1869; Joseph W. Wilson, Commissioner of the General Land Office, to Cox, May 27, 1869; Parker to Whipple, June 11, 1869; Samuel McPhail to Whipple, August 24, 1869; Whipple to Parker, September 1, 1869, *ibid.*

[25] *Central Republican*, March 3, 1869; William Welsh, comp., *Taopi and His Friends, or the Indians' Wrongs and Rights* (Philadelphia: Claxton, Remsen and Heffelfinger, 1869), pp. 53–54; George C. Tanner, *Fifty Years of Church Work in the Diocese of Minnesota 1857–1907* (St. Paul: Published by The Committee, 1909), p. 401.

[26] Faribault *Democrat*, June 27, 1884.

choosing to migrate all the way to Minnesota, where they were later joined by some of the Flandreau colonists. The 1870 census showed 175 Indians, nearly all of whom were presumably Sioux, scattered through the southern counties. Aside from 34 in Chippewa County, probably the remnants of the scouts' camp, the largest concentrations were at Faribault and Traverse des Sioux, with smaller groups at Bloomington (the residence of Gideon Pond), in the Shakopee–Prior Lake area, and on Grey Cloud Island in Washington County. The number continued to increase in subsequent years, until in 1883 a special census revealed 237 Sioux in Minnesota.[27]

Only once between 1867 and 1883 was a serious attempt made to bring the Minnesota Sioux back within the pale of government benefits. Late in 1875 the Reverend David Buel Knickerbacker, rector of Gethsemane church in Minneapolis, wrote Commissioner Edward P. Smith in behalf of the Sioux Indians then living at Mendota, Shakopee, and elsewhere in the state. He estimated their numbers at perhaps 125 or 150, of whom 75 were living at Mendota. He described them as industrious, temperate, and honest, all professing Christians. Besides cultivating about ten acres of land and collecting wild rice, they supported themselves by making moccasins and working on farms during harvest. The church helped supply them with clothing and provisions. The land they occupied at Mendota was owned by Sibley, who offered to donate a few acres if the government would buy some more and put up a few small houses. Knickerbacker believed that $500 a year judiciously expended would protect them from want in the winter, and they would soon be independent. "It seems impossible to persuade them to leave here to go to their people in Nebraska," he remarked, indicating that their removal was still regarded as a desirable solution to the problem.[28]

Commissioner Smith replied that, although these people had treaty rights at the Flandreau, Sisseton, or Santee agencies, it would probably be best to leave them where they were rather than try to remove them. There were unfortunately no funds available to help them in their present locations, except possibly the civilization fund, which was running low. All he was willing to suggest was that perhaps the Bureau

[27] A. T. Andreas, ed., *An Illustrated Historical Atlas of the State of Minnesota* (Chicago: Lakeside Building, 1874), pp. 14–15; "Memorial Notices of Rev. Gideon H. Pond," *Minnesota Historical Collections*, III (1870–1880), 371.

[28] David B. Knickerbacker to Edward P. Smith, October 13, 1875, NARS, RG 75, LR, Santee Agency.

could help them if Sibley would provide them with the land he had offered.[29] Knickerbacker wrote back that Sibley would sell about one hundred acres for $2,000, less $200 which he would deduct as his donation in place of the ten or twenty acres promised. The commissioner's line had hardened by this time, however, and the project went no further. He replied early in 1876 that he considered the proposed purchases an expense not justified by the financial condition of the Indian Office at the time. He added, rather sharply, "I do not recognize that these Indians, failing to comply with previous requirements as to their removal, have any claim upon this office. If they choose the privileges of independence, they must also assume its burdens."[30]

Information on the Sioux in Minnesota during the seventies is scarce indeed. Yet it is evident, from scattered references in newspapers and Indian Bureau correspondence, that some were more or less permanent residents in the Red Wing and Wabasha areas and that others paid periodic visits to their old homes.[31] A Dakota County history published in 1881 provides the information that there were a few Indians living there at that time. The picture it gives of the Mendota colony is not as favorable as that offered by the Reverend Knickerbacker. The settlement then consisted of an encampment of seven tipis, containing, when visited, thirty-five women and children and only one or two men; the rest of the men were away hunting in Dakota Territory. They lived in a "primitive and savage manner" and were said to "speak no English,

[29] E. P. Smith to Knickerbacker, October 21, 1875, *ibid.*

[30] Knickerbacker to E. P. Smith, November 22, 1875; E. P. Smith to Knickerbacker, January 20, 1876, *ibid.*

[31] In 1877, Santee Agent Isaiah Lightner wrote Commissioner Smith that Charles Hedges, an industrious Indian, had bought some land near Red Wing and wished to take with him the property issued him by the government. Lightner thought there would be a number of his charges going to Minnesota. The same year the Red Wing *Argus* complained of the number of drunken Indians seen almost daily on the streets, but the editor was more concerned about where they were getting the stuff than with the convenience of future historians, and he provided no further information. There were Indians at Wabasha two years later, when Francis Talbot, an old trader who had worked under Alexis Bailly, inquired about getting an appointment as trader at Santee. He professed to be well known to "some of the chiefs there and their relatives here [at Wabasha]." In the spring of 1879 and again in the fall small parties of Indians passed through Lake City on their way to Wabasha; the second party was made up of three squaws, one brave, three broken-down horses, one papoose, and "one gamin of a brave," according to the Cannon Falls *Beacon.* See Lightner to John Q. Smith, May 16, 1877, and Francis Talbot to Superintendent of Indian Bureau, January 27, 1879, NARS, RG 75, LR, Nebraska Agencies; Red Wing *Argus,* June 28, 1877; Cannon Falls *Beacon,* March 7 and September 12, 1879.

profess no religion and own no land." It treated another group more generously. These were "the few quiet people who cultivate a little land on the bottoms below Hastings, and sell pipes and beadwork to the whites. They are regular attendants of the Episcopal church." Their principal man was Ma-pi-awa-con-sa, locally known as Indian John.[32]

The picture we get from these varied sources is that of a people striving for obscurity, a goal which the whites were perfectly willing to help them attain. Their poverty was due not so much to laziness, as the whites charged, as to economic and cultural handicaps which unfitted them for competition with the white population and obliged them to live on the fringes of society, the objects of charity, contempt, or, at best, good-natured condescension. Too few to be feared any longer, they were looked upon by their white neighbors much as the village idiot might be: harmless, useless, a burden to society. Although the whites doubtless wished the government or some other agency would take upon itself responsibility for the Indians' support, they were really not a big enough burden to cause much concern. If they had been picturesque, they might have been more popular; then they could have put on war dances at county fairs and Fourth of July celebrations, as some of them later did. But for the most part they were not picturesque but pitiably drab, people the community would just as soon not have strangers see. Fortunately, as the white settlers saw it, the Indian was said to be the vanishing race; no doubt these little encampments of aborigines would soon die off.

[32] Edward D. Neill, *History of Dakota County and the City of Hastings* (Minneapolis: North Star Publishing Co., 1881), pp. 195–196.

CHAPTER 14

Up from Oblivion

THE SIOUX in Minnesota did not vanish, nor were the white people of the state permitted to forget them. In fact, as people from Santee and from the Flandreau and Brown Earth colonies drifted back, perhaps only temporarily at first, then settled down to stay, their numbers gradually increased. The returnees were as mixed in their motives as they were in their origins. Some left Santee because they resented living under the authority of an Indian agent. Some fled the reservation because, like the Flandreau colonists, they wanted to dissociate themselves from the tribe. Some of them no doubt sincerely wished to take up farms and live like white men; unfortunately, not all were qualified by experience or temperament for the life of a farmer, competing with white farmers. Some had tried farming at Flandreau or Brown Earth, had lost their lands in mortgages or sold them for a pittance, and now wanted to try again, in a country where a crop was somewhat more certain. More than a few of those who came back were mere restless drifters who would never have succeeded anywhere. Whatever their motives, all these people had one characteristic in common with the Europeans who emigrated to America in the same period: they were dissatisfied where they were and hoped to better their lot somewhere else.

The special census of 1883 showed that they numbered 237, scattered throughout the southern third of the state. None of the fourteen localities in which they had settled accounted for many families. The largest, Shakopee, had eleven families, or forty-seven individuals; the second largest, near Wabasha, had nine families, or forty individuals. Thirty-three were camped on Grey Cloud Island, twenty-four at Mendota, and twenty at Bloomington. The other groups were even smaller: six families at Faribault, three at Hastings and Redwood, two at Red Wing, one each at Prior Lake, Kapozha, West St. Paul, and St. Peter, and four families at Maiden Rock, Wisconsin.[1] Most of them lived in tipis, set up on the lands of white men who did not object to the Indians' presence. Some had made down payments on land which they were trying to farm with inadequate equipment. One of them was Good Thunder, one of the heroes of the uprising, who had appeared in July, 1883, near the site of the old Redwood agency. Later that year a few more tipis were seen on the bluff overlooking the Minnesota River, and in the spring of 1884 Good Thunder, who had sold his Flandreau homestead for $400 and a team of horses, bought eighty acres of land for $694.[2] His example was followed by Charles Lawrence, who bought an adjacent eighty, and within a few years quite a little colony had formed, consisting mostly of more or less uninvited guests who set up their tipis on the lands of their more affluent relatives. Located across the Minnesota from the old Birch Coulee battle site and from the town of Morton (called Birch Cooley post office until 1894), this Indian community was commonly called Birch Coulee.

The manner in which the Birch Coulee settlement began was probably to some extent typical of the way all of the colonies started. A few brave souls took the leap, and others followed. For the most part, these people were wretchedly poor. Few had land enough to farm successfully, and those who did lacked the necessary stock and equipment. So they depended largely on the bounty of their white neighbors for their survival and thus did not endear themselves to those neighbors, whose attitude toward Indians was conditioned by what they had seen, or perhaps only heard, of the 1862 Uprising. Old friends of the Sioux, such

[1] List of Dacotah Indians in Minnesota, October 1, 1883, NARS, RG 75, LR, Sioux in Minnesota file. Unless otherwise indicated, all Indian Office documents cited in this chapter are in the file labeled "Sioux in Minnesota" rather than included under any particular agency.

[2] J. G. Larsen, "Indian Mission Dates from 1860," Morton (Minn.) *Enterprise*, February 27, 1936; Benjamin W. Thompson to John D. C. Atkins, December 31, 1885, and January 2, 1886, NARS, RG 75, LR; Redwood County Register of Deeds, Deed Record 10, p. 301.

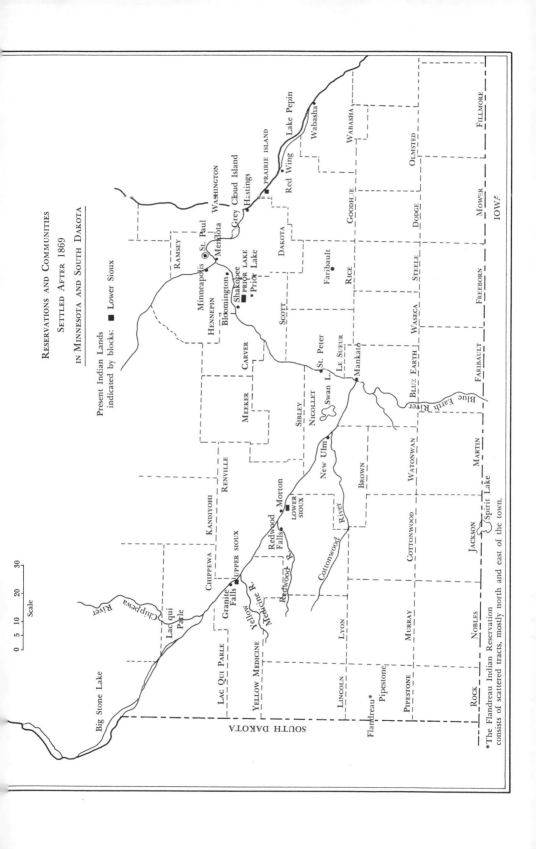

RESERVATIONS AND COMMUNITIES
SETTLED AFTER 1869
IN MINNESOTA AND SOUTH DAKOTA

Present Indian Lands
indicated by blocks: ■ Lower Sioux

Scale
0 5 10   20   30

*The Flandreau Indian Reservation
consists of scattered tracts, mostly north and east of the town.

as Bishop Whipple and General Sibley, noticed their plight, however, and continued their long campaign to right the wrongs the Indians had suffered. The Indians had new friends, too, such as Representative Horace B. Strait of Shakopee, who in 1884 engineered through Congress an appropriation for their benefit.[3]

The Indian appropriations act for 1885, passed July 4, 1884, contained a short paragraph under the section headed "Sioux of Different Tribes, Including Santee Sioux of Nebraska," providing the sum of $10,000 for "the purchase of stock for the Medewakanton band of Sioux Indians, in the State of Minnesota, and other articles necessary for their civilization and education, and to enable them to become self-supporting. . . ." An amendment approved March 3, 1885, provided that the Secretary of the Interior might disburse the money "for agricultural implements, lands, or cash," as in his judgment might seem best, and that $720 should be expended to pay a practical farmer to teach the Indians agriculture. The appropriation was intended to benefit only those Sioux who had been uniformly friendly to the whites during the uprising and had therefore found themselves unwelcome with the rest of the tribe. This restriction was eventually found unworkable, but for a time at least lip service was paid to it.[4]

When this innocuous piece of legislation was passed by Congress, there was no intention to provide reservations for the Minnesota Mdewakantons or to return them to a wardship status, for that was precisely what they had just left. Yet when money is appropriated, someone must be appointed to disburse it, and this implies a government agent. Once an agent is appointed, he is soon making many of the Indians' decisions. If land is to be purchased and the Indians are at a disadvantage in buying it from white owners, a government agent is needed to make the purchases. And if the Indians prove themselves unable to hold onto the land, it must be placed in a restricted status, under government trusteeship. Hence, although the present-day Minnesota Sioux are technically correct in saying that their people

[3] Surprisingly few facts have been discovered concerning the preliminaries that must have led to this appropriation. The Shakopee *Argus*, July 24, 1884, credits Strait with the insertion of the item in the Indian appropriations act.

[4] U.S. *Statutes at Large*, XXIII, 87, 375; Robert B. Henton to Commissioner John H. Oberly, December 31, 1888, NARS, RG 75, LR. The directive from the Indian Office specified that the appropriations were intended "for the benefit of those of the Mdewakanton Band, who remained faithful to the whites during the outbreak of 1862–3, and thereby incurred the enmity of other Indians, and for the descendants of those friendly Indians."

were pioneers in the same sense as the white squatters of an earlier period, it is none the less equally true that their settlements soon became Indian reservations, except for fee patented land, and have remained so.

Preparatory to distributing the appropriation, the Indian Bureau designated Walter S. McLeod, mixed-blood son of the trader Martin McLeod, to conduct a census of the Indians and determine their most pressing needs. In order to prevent a rush into Minnesota by Indians from Dakota and Nebraska wishing to share in the largess, the act was made applicable only to those who were residents of the state on October 1, 1883.[5] With the assistance of Good Thunder, Phillip Chaska of Mendota, and John C. Wakeman of Grey Cloud Island, McLeod prepared a census roll containing the information on the location and numbers of Sioux in Minnesota given earlier in this chapter. According to McLeod and the Reverend William C. Pope, Episcopal rector of the Church of the Good Shepherd in St. Paul, they were most in need of land and houses; some already in possession of farms wanted teams, cows, harness, stoves, or wagons. They also needed clothing for their children who were attending white schools. McLeod said they objected to being paid like annuity Indians and suggested that half the money be given them in cash to use as they saw fit. Bishop Whipple was not so confident of their ability to handle money wisely; he thought they should be paid a specified sum monthly if the money was to be used for rations.[6]

Before the payment was made, there was disagreement over whether mixed-bloods should share. Commissioner Hiram Price was prepared to include them in the payment, but McLeod argued that their inclusion would make each person's share so small that it would scarcely buy a spelling book. Besides, it was his understanding that the appropriation had not been intended to apply to mixed-bloods, but only to full-bloods who desired to "assimilate with the population generally in dress, habits, custom[s] and association in society. . . ."[7] McLeod's wishes were allowed to prevail this time, but the problem remained to

[5] Horace B. Strait to Hiram Price, July 19, 1884; Secretary of Interior William Teller to Price, February 26, 1885; Walter S. McLeod to Price, August 21, 1884; Strait to Price, March 21, 1885, NARS, RG 75, LR.

[6] McLeod to Price, August 21, 1884; Henry B. Whipple to Strait, August 28, 1884; William C. Pope to Price, December 9, 1884, accompanying list of "Wants of Minnesota Dacotahs," NARS, RG 75, LR.

[7] Strait to Price, September 5, 1884; McLeod to Price, September 15, 1884, NARS, RG 75, LR.

vex disbursing agents in the future, for the great majority of the Sioux in Minnesota were of mixed blood, and there was no reliable way to discriminate among people with varying degrees of Indian ancestry.

The payment, consisting of cash and articles deemed of use to the Indians, was made in April, 1885, at Shakopee, by W. H. Robb, a bonded employee of the Indian Bureau appointed for the purpose. As the first payment to the Mdewakanton Sioux since 1861, it was a memorable occasion. Some of the descendants of those who participated still retain photographs taken then, showing the Indians in full tribal regalia. The *Scott County Argus* reported on March 19 that Shakopee had been full of Indians the previous Thursday and Friday. "They kept coming from every direction until about four hundred aboriginees were among us," the paper said. This gathering was for the purpose of enrolling; the actual payment came a few weeks later, after the rolls had been carefully examined to see that no unauthorized persons shared in the distribution. Each applicant was subjected to a rigid examination in the presence of the rest of his band. The payment was completed by April 15, and all the Indians dispersed to their homes.[8]

Later in the year a detailed statement of how the cash portion of the payment had been spent was submitted to the Indian Office, signed by Wakeman, Chaska, and Charles Lawrence and endorsed by Sibley and Reverend Pope. Most of it was used to buy land or to make further payments on land already purchased. A group of Wabasha citizens wrote the commissioner that the Indians there had spent their share wisely and that another like appropriation would be useful in helping them to be self-sufficient.[9] There were, of course, some dissident voices. The Reverend Samuel D. Hinman, who had joined the Birch Coulee colony, wrote the next year that after the payment a dance had been held at Mendota at which the old heathen practice of sacrifice was revived— only now they sacrificed "one keg of beer or two." For weeks thereafter it was "one grand carouse," he wrote. The Indians drank to the new President, Grover Cleveland, "a democrat, the party which treated with us of old and gave us money to buy whiskey and beer."[10] Another

[8] *Scott County Argus* (Shakopee), March 19, 1885; Strait to Price, March 21, 1885; W. H. Robb to Atkins, April 15 and 16, 1885, NARS, RG 75, LR.

[9] John Wakeman, Phillip Chaska, and Charles Lawrence to Atkins, November 27, 1885; Citizens of Wabasha to Atkins, October 3, 1885, NARS, RG 75, LR.

[10] Samuel D. Hinman to Whipple, September 3, 1886, *ibid.* If Hinman's rendition of the toast to Cleveland is accurate, it is not clear what incident the Indians were referring to. The treaties of Traverse des Sioux and Mendota in 1851 and the Doty

kind of protest came from the Indians living at Maiden Rock, Wisconsin, who had been excluded from the payment on the ground that they were not residents of Minnesota. Five days after the business at Shakopee was over, a white resident of Maiden Rock wrote the commissioner on behalf of John and Jacob Walker, who had been refused payment, and a year later Felix Rock wrote in behalf of "those Indians in and about Red Wing and those who did not get their share of the appropriation in 1884." If there was to be another $10,000, he thought they should get an extra allowance.[11] Since the Walkers, who had left Santee in the seventies, later lived at Prairie Island, it seems likely that they moved there about this time in order to qualify for the next payment.

The rumor of a second appropriation was well founded, for on May 15, 1886, Congress authorized another $10,000 for the Minnesota Mdewakantons. The need for another distribution of money was increased by the presence of a growing number of Sioux in Minnesota. Good Thunder had been making satisfactory progress in paying for his farm and raised enough food for his own needs in 1885, but the influx of newcomers was "eating him up," as Special Agent Benjamin W. Thompson wrote at the end of the year. By this time there was an encampment of Flandreau people a mile or two east of Good Thunder's farm, and others were scattered around in the woods near the river. Some Sissetons from the Brown Earth settlement had been so excited by the promises of two or three agitators that they had left their farms, on which there was a five-year restriction, and made pretended sales for a yoke of cattle, in hopes of becoming Mdewakantons and sharing in the benefits now coming to the Minnesota Sioux.[12]

The language of the 1886 appropriation bill was identical with that of the earlier one, as amended, giving considerable latitude to the Secretary of the Interior in the expenditure of the money. Believing that the Indians' most immediate need was for farms, Bishop Whipple recommended that the greater part of the fund be spent to purchase

---

treaties in 1841 (at all of which liquor was consumed) were negotiated under Whig administrations. The 1837 and 1858 treaties were made with small delegations brought to Washington, and it is unlikely that much drinking went on then. The beneficiaries of the 1885 payment could have had but dim recollections of the Prairie du Chien treaties of 1825 and 1830.

[11] A. Cook to Atkins, April 21, 1885; Felix Rock to Atkins, April 26, 1886, *ibid.* Rock (or Rocque), a promising young mixed-blood, died at Prairie Island in 1888, at the age of 29.

[12] U.S. *Statutes at Large*, XXIV, 39; Benjamin Thompson to Atkins, December 31, 1885, and January 2, 1886, NARS, RG 75, LR.

land in the Birch Coulee area. Although he recommended Strait as a good man to negotiate for it, the Indian Office decided to employ McLeod, already serving as farmer and general handyman. He was formally commissioned as farmer and special disbursing agent on October 16, 1886, his earlier commission having expired the previous month.[13] McLeod recommended that all purchases be made at Birch Coulee, Shakopee, and Prairie Island, the last site to be used for all the Indians not residing at the other two or willing to move there. Beginning in April, 1887, he bought seven small tracts, aggregating nearly 330 acres, plus a ten-acre plot at Hastings. The largest block, 147 acres, was bought at Birch Coulee, part of it from Charles Lawrence, who was having difficulty paying for the land he had bought earlier. Two adjacent tracts totaling 98 acres were purchased in Scott County, not far from the village of Prior Lake. Nearly half of that area belonged to John Bluestone, on whose land many of the Shakopee group were living. Nearly 85 acres were purchased on Prairie Island in Goodhue County. Altogether, these purchases accounted for more than $4,100 of the appropriation. McLeod also spent $549.17 in paying off mortgages on the land belonging to Good Thunder and Charles Lawrence.[14]

Together with some 447 acres previously owned by the Indians, these purchases gave the Minnesota Mdewakantons a small but not insignificant land base, enough for them to practice a subsistence agriculture of sorts. The land was divided into small tracts ranging from three to fifteen acres and deeded to individual Indians in fee simple, without restrictions. At Prairie Island, for example, the principal eighty-acre unit was divided into eleven narrow strips a half-mile in length and ranging from six to nine rods wide. The next step was to provide houses for the Indians. Six had been built on Prairie Island by the next December, apparently strung out along one end of the land purchase, and it was understood then that six more would be built. Most of the fourteen families living there at that time occupied tipis. Similar conditions existed at the other colonies, although McLeod had reported in August, 1886, that there were then thirty-seven frame and four log houses among the Minnesota Sioux.[15]

[13] Whipple to Atkins, July 5, 1886; McLeod to Atkins, September 2, 1886; Commission dated October 16, 1886, NARS, RG 75, LR.

[14] McLeod to Atkins, September 2, 1886, and November 28, 1887, *ibid.*; Com. of Indian Affairs, *Annual Report*, 1891, Part 1, pp. 111, 178–179.

[15] McLeod to Atkins, August 11, 1886; Hastings H. Hart to Atkins, December 10, 1887, NARS, RG 75, LR; Com. of Indian Affairs, *Annual Report*, 1891, Part 1, pp. 178–179.

Bishop Whipple's intention was to establish a single Indian community at Birch Coulee, under the auspices of the Episcopal Church, and he regretted the purchases made at other points. Late in 1887 he wrote Representative John L. Macdonald, Strait's successor, reviewing the accomplishments of the two earlier appropriations and requesting another, of $20,000, of which $1,000 should be earmarked for a school, complete with furniture, books, and other equipment. The earlier appropriations had largely failed, he said, because much of the land had been bought in places that were unsuitable for farming. With the larger sum now proposed, used exclusively to build up the Birch Coulee settlement, he believed it would be possible to "remove all of these scattered Sioux and have a model Christian village."[16] As might be expected, Hinman strongly endorsed this view. He wrote his bishop that the Indians at Faribault, Mendota, and Birch Coulee were doing reasonably well but that the others were living like vagabonds, "drinking and eating what their women earn—by work, or begging or bylines of shame." The Prairie Island group was especially distasteful to him. He accused them of being the chief offenders in putting on the old heathen dances, "for purposes of gain, at the time of the Winter Carnival and Ice Palace at St. Paul." The affair lasted only ten days, but the participants spent at least three months preparing for it and much longer recovering afterward. He charged that they spent thirty dollars per person for "finery and dissipation" and then begged the rest of the year. He added that they were not wanted at Birch Coulee and should be deprived of any share in the benefits enjoyed by their more industrious brethren.[17] The Whipple-Hinman view carried considerable weight, but it was partially offset by other friends of the Sioux, such as Francis Talbot of Wabasha, who argued that the Indians were attached to their old homes and should not be forced to move to Birch Coulee.[18]

The next legislation in behalf of the Minnesota Mdewakantons, which became law on June 29, 1888, reflected Whipple's wishes in large part, although it did not require the beneficiaries to join the Birch Coulee colony. Out of the $20,000 appropriated, $1,000 was to go, as he had requested, to build a school "at the most suitable location." The expenditure of the rest was again to be at the discretion of the Secretary

[16] 50th Cong., 1st Sess., *H. Ex. Doc. 228*, pp. 2–3.

[17] Hinman to Whipple, September 3 and December 31, 1886, and October 23, 1888, NARS, RG 75, LR.

[18] Francis Talbot to Representative Thomas Wilson, April 5, 1888, *ibid.* Talbot's view was concurred in by the Reverend J. C. Birch, rector of Grace Episcopal church in Wabasha, and other citizens, whose supporting statements were submitted, along with Talbot's letter, to Commissioner Atkins on April 19, 1888.

of the Interior. Perhaps the most important new provision contained in this bill was that setting May 20, 1886, rather than October 1, 1883, as the date by which all who were entitled to benefit must have been living in Minnesota; it was also specified that they must have severed their tribal relations.[19]

McLeod's commission expired in the fall of 1888, and he was replaced by Robert B. Henton, a long-time acquaintance of the Minnesota Sioux, strongly recommended by Bishop Whipple, who had been lukewarm about McLeod. Henton had lived near the old agency before the uprising—one of his sons had been born on the third day of the outbreak—and he had later become a businessman in Morton and owner of most of the townsite. Soon after his appointment he made a thorough investigation of conditions among the Indians under his charge and submitted some recommendations to the Indian Office. He found that important changes in their population distribution had taken place since the census of 1883. The Birch Coulee settlement was now the largest, with eighty-six people; that near Prior Lake was second, with sixty-two. These groups and the three families at Hastings and the two at Bloomington he considered to be well situated and permanent, even though they all needed more land. The few at Faribault were about to move to Birch Coulee.[20]

The rest were badly situated, and Henton thought they would have to be removed. Mendota and Grey Cloud Island, each of which now had only eleven Indian residents, were mere squatters' camps and should not be allowed to continue, since land could not be bought there except at prices too high for the limited appropriation. The Wabasha location, where seven families now lived, was unsuitable for farming; most of the people lived in town, anyway. Prairie Island, now the third largest colony, with forty-six inhabitants, was reserved for Henton's severest condemnation. Though a good location on the ground of its seclusion, it was otherwise unfortunate, for it had no hay or timber, and the land was unsuitable for farming. Local whites encouraged the Indians to stay in the hope of selling land to them, and the county poor fund aided them "liberally" to the extent of one to three dollars doled out weekly per family. "It seems necessary that these should be removed

[19] U.S. *Statutes at Large*, XXV, 228–229.

[20] Secretary of Interior William F. Vilas to Oberly, November 19, 1888; Henton to Oberly, December 31, 1888, NARS, RG 75, LR; Morton *Enterprise*, November 4, 1898. After McLeod's appointment late in 1886, Hinman wrote Whipple: "He has entirely adopted our views, and we wish to withdraw all opposition to him." Hinman described him as a Democrat, not a Christian but not an opponent of Christianity. See Hinman to Whipple, December 31, 1886, NARS, RG 75, LR.

elsewhere," he wrote. "They must select a new location or stop asking aid from the County poor fund." Elsewhere the Indians were poor but self-reliant; those at Prairie Island seemed to be "complaisant beggars" who brought themselves into continual disrepute. Though it would be impossible to sell the land except at a loss, he suggested inducing as many as possible to leave and dividing their holdings among those who stayed. No more purchases should be made there.[21]

Despite Henton's convictions, supported by Bishop Whipple, when he came to making more land purchases, he was obliged to include not only the despised Prairie Island site but also Wabasha, where no land had previously been bought. His position and that of Bishop Whipple were further undercut by a proviso in the appropriations act of March 2, 1889, which specified that "as far as practicable lands for said Indians shall be purchased in such locality as each Indian desires, and none of said Indians shall be required to remove from where he now resides and to any locality or land against his will." About all the comfort the Birch Coulee advocates could take from this bill was that it earmarked $1,000 more for the completion of the school. Another $8,000 was appropriated on August 19, 1890, with the specification that $2,000 of it was to be expended for the Prairie Island settlement—the only time any of the Sioux colonies were mentioned by name in such a bill. This provision virtually ended Bishop Whipple's dream of concentrating all the scattered Sioux at Birch Coulee.[22]

The actual purchase of land under these appropriations began in April, 1889, when slightly over 650 acres were bought adjoining the earlier purchases in the Birch Coulee vicinity. The next month Henton bought 40 acres at Hastings for five families and 120 acres at Prairie Island. He would have preferred removing the eleven families at the latter site, but, as he wrote, "These Indians are of the Red Wing or Wacoute band and this is their old home, therefore though the soil is poor they are loth to leave it and we have no means of compelling their removal." There was a school adjacent to the settlement there, and the Indians went to church in Red Wing. Fortunately, the white neighbor from whom the land was bought was a "young, industrious Swede with a family, who is their friend and aids them in every way by advise and example."[23] Under the provisions of the appropriations made in 1889 and 1890, Henton also bought 110.24 acres of Mississippi River bottom-

[21] Henton to Oberly, December 31, 1888, NARS, RG 75, LR.
[22] U.S. *Statutes at Large*, XXV, 992–993; XXVI, 349.
[23] Com. of Indian Affairs, *Annual Report*, 1891, Part I, pp. 110–111; Henton to Oberly, April 8 and 9, 1889, NARS, RG 75, LR. This "young Swede." A. A. Johnson,

land near Wabasha, of no value as farm land but of use as camping grounds to the Indians, who obtained most of their living from the river. He added to the previous holdings in Scott County by purchasing nearly 170 acres near Prior Lake and rounded out the tract at Birch Coulee by another 99 acres, 9 of which were bought from Samuel Taopi for use as a site for the new school.[24]

Henton made one important innovation in these land purchases. Before he began buying up lands, he discovered that of the tracts previously bought and deeded directly to the Indians, one had been sold, two mortgaged, and several denuded of timber. He thought that future purchases should be retained by the government, at least until it could be determined which Indians were reliable.[25] His policy was followed in the later purchases, with the result that all of this land, except for the tracts at Wabasha and Hastings, is still in Indian possession, whereas most of the earlier purchases had slipped out of the Indians' hands by 1900. The few that they still clung to by the early 1930's were so encumbered with mortgages and unpaid taxes that the government at that time tried to buy up as many as possible for incorporation into the tracts still held in federal ownership.

Although Henton spent $16,581.42 for land, and $2,000 went to complete and furnish the school at Birch Coulee, a considerable part of the various appropriations was used for other purposes, ranging from the purchase of cattle and machinery for Indians seriously attempting to farm, to food and clothing for the aged and indigent. Henton periodically submitted detailed statements of his expenditures which provide a good picture of what the government was trying to do for the Minnesota Sioux. In 1890, for example, he spent $1,568 at Prairie Island, $900 of which went for three teams and sets of harness, $150 for three wagons, $30 for two plows, $15 for three cultivators, $50 for a mower, $23 for a rake, and $400 for twenty acres of timber, a purchase that was never consummated. At the same time he spent $987 at Birch Coulee, $3,712 at Prior Lake, $970 at Bloomington (including a land purchase which did not go through), $728 at Wabasha, and $378 at Hastings.[26]

---

later wrote of the Indians that "the most of them are industrious. And I think would make good farmers if they had a start." See A. A. Johnson to Commissioner Thomas J. Morgan, February 26, 1890, NARS, RG 75, LR.

[24] Com. of Indian Affairs, *Annual Report*, 1891, Part 1, pp. 110–111; Henton to Oberly, April 7 and 12, May 15, 1889, NARS, RG 75, LR.

[25] Henton to Oberly, March 5, 1889, NARS, RG 75, LR.

[26] Com. of Indian Affairs, *Annual Report*, 1891, Part 1, p. 111; Henton to Morgan, May 1 and October 29, 1890, NARS, RG 75, LR.

Later the same year he submitted another statement, which included $713 for aid—principally food and clothing—to a few of the older people at Prairie Island, Hastings, and Wabasha. Out of the $8,000 appropriated that year, he proposed to spend only $500 on aid to the old and infirm, mainly several women ranging in age from seventy to ninety who had no particular homes but lived irregularly with various families. The Birch Coulee settlement required no such assistance that year, but the other groups all had some members who were destitute.[27] The next summer Henton delivered two teams of horses, three wagons, four harrows, four plows, and ten cows to the Indians there and a similar quantity to the Prior Lake colony.[28]

White attitudes toward these little Indian settlements varied widely. Although it may have been true, as Henton charged, that some whites encouraged the Indians to stay in hopes of selling unproductive land to the government, the general feeling toward them seems to have been unfriendly. In May, 1889, a group of local farmers met in a rural school near the Birch Coulee community to protest against the presence of the Indians in the locality. Although the resentment was ostensibly directed mainly at the exemption of the Indians' lands from taxation (those recently purchased and held in government ownership), a newspaper report in the Redwood Falls paper said that the "farmers living in this locality do not regard them in any respect as desirable neighbors." One of the speakers at the May 7 meeting argued that the first Indians to return should have been ordered away; but since that had not been done, the only course was to "employ the best means at hand to get rid of an element of society we do not want." A petition was drawn up for presentation to Congressman John Lind. The Reverend Nathan N. Gilbert, an official of the Episcopal Church, wrote the commissioner that the best people in Redwood County did not sympathize with this movement, which, however, should be watched in order "to check it at the outset."[29]

Opposition to the Prairie Island people stemmed mostly from the drain their chronic poverty produced on the county poor fund. The county officials wished some other agency to accept responsibility for them; and, after learning from the State Board of Corrections and Charities that the Indians were legally a charge on the county, they

[27] Henton to Morgan, October 29 and November 11, 1890, NARS, RG 75, LR.
[28] Morton *Enterprise*, June 5, 1891.
[29] Redwood *Reveille*, May 8, 1889; St. Paul *Pioneer Press*, May 9, 1889; Nathan N. Gilbert to Morgan, May 11, 1889, NARS, RG 75, LR.

began corresponding with the Indian Office. A Red Wing newspaper reported late in 1887 that they had received from one to three hundred dollars a year from the poor fund and urged that they be sent to their proper reservation. Despite efforts by the government to come to their assistance, they remained a burden on the county. In 1891, Henton reported the complaint of the Goodhue County Board of Commissioners that the Indians there were constantly calling for aid.[30]

It is impossible to determine how much of the opposition to the Indian colonies was due to the stated reasons and how much to the latent hostility to Indians left over from the days of '62. The phrase "dirty redskins" continued to be used in weekly newspapers, without quotation marks and without humorous intent, for many years after the uprising. As late as 1893, when the Minnesota Board of World's Fair Managers issued a booklet titled *Minnesota: A Brief Sketch of Its History, Resources and Advantages*, the Red Wing *Daily Republican* commented that there was too much about the Indian in it. "We cannot believe it desirable to associate the thought of the Indian with the current idea of the Minnesota of today," observed the editor.[31] If the more articulate and presumably better educated members of the community looked upon Indians in general as outcasts, there is every reason to suppose that the mass of the white population at least shared this attitude and probably went much further in anti-Indian sentiment.

Objection to government recognition of the Sioux in Minnesota came from another source: the agents and missionaries on the Santee Reservation. In 1886, Alfred L. Riggs wrote Commissioner Atkins that aid given these renegades would only create ferment among the Santees. He charged that there was a movement afoot among certain white men and Indians to re-establish the Redwood agency and that some of the Indians expected to recover the annuities forfeited in 1863 and the old tribal organization that had been broken up at Santee by majority vote. If assistance were given them, it would be a "premium upon laziness, a step backward towards barbarism, and encouragement to idle dreams," he wrote; and if the dream of re-establishing the agency should be realized, it would "establish a perpetual Indian community in the heart of civilization."[32] Agent Hill added his voice to the chorus

[30] Hart to Atkins, December 10, 1887; Henton to Morgan, March 16, 1891, *ibid.*; Red Wing *Argus*, December 22, 1887; Goodhue County Board of Commissioners, "Proceedings," 1888, pp. 128, 131.

[31] Red Wing *Daily Republican*, September 11, 1893.

[32] Alfred L. Riggs to Atkins, April 29, 1886, NARS, RG 75, LR.

in 1888, complaining that the conduct of the Minnesota Sioux in holding the old pagan dances was having a disquieting effect on the Santees,
some of whom had gone to West St. Paul the previous winter to take
part in the festivities there. Though credited with breaking away from
the reservation and becoming self-supporting, the Minnesota Sioux
were actually more uncivilized than many of the Santees, as evidenced
by this reversion to barbarism. He called their conduct "quite disgraceful" and reported that "a few of the least progressive" at his
agency had been induced to leave their homes on visits to their relatives
in Minnesota.[33]

If the whites had objections to the presence of the Indians, the latter
had complaints of their own. There were essentially three groups who
felt themselves discriminated against in the distribution of benefits under
the various appropriations: those who lived at Mendota, Grey Cloud
Island, Bloomington, and other points at which no land was purchased
and who therefore derived no benefit from land purchases; those who
were excluded on the ground that they were mixed-bloods; and those
who arrived in Minnesota after the May 20, 1886, deadline. The first
two groups were made up to a considerable extent of the same individuals, people who had lived in and around the Twin Cities, regarding
themselves and being regarded, not as Indians, but as members of the
general population. Even those who qualified as Indians could not
benefit substantially from the appropriations unless they moved to one
of the settlements where land had been purchased. Henton believed that
pressure should be brought on them by withholding food and clothing
in order to persuade them to move.[34]

Since the line between mixed-bloods and full-bloods was never precisely determinable, the former were gradually admitted to participation in the benefits enjoyed by their Indian relatives. Henry Belland,
Jr., writing under the name of Tewasdakeduta, asked early in 1891 that
they be paid in provisions in such amounts as would assure equality
among them and their Indian relatives who had received land and
stock. By July, 1892, clothing and food had been distributed to 132
mixed-bloods, most of whom supported themselves by day labor; more
names were later added to the list, and there were many others who
expressed no wish to participate.[35] Henton was always opposed to per-

[33] Com. of Indian Affairs, *Annual Report*, 1888, p. 173.

[34] Henton to Morgan, July 24, 1889, NARS, RG 75, LR.

[35] Tewasdakeduta [Henry Belland, Jr.] to Secretary of Interior John W. Noble,
March 26, 1891; Henton to Morgan, July 24, 1892, and February 14 and March 3,
1893, *ibid.*

mitting mixed-bloods to share, arguing that the 198 full-bloods objected to sharing the small appropriations with the 722 mixed-bloods who were on his census roll by 1898. He believed that at least the payments should be restricted to full-bloods, half-bloods, and minor children of the latter.[36]

Complaints also came from members of the outlying communities who charged that Hinman dominated Henton and was trying to exclude from the appropriations all those who refused to move to Birch Coulee. The Reverend John Eastman, one of the spokesmen for the dissatisfied element, wrote that only Hinman's friends received any benefits. Henton denied these charges and said that delays in consummating the land purchases had created suspicion among the Indians.[37] There is no doubt, however, that Hinman wished to concentrate the Indians at Birch Coulee, and he may have let fall some remarks that sounded like threats. Hinman's zeal for his church also left him open to accusations of another kind of discrimination. Complaints came from Big Eagle, John and Moses Wakeman, and several others who had come to Minnesota from Flandreau after the 1886 deadline. They were Presbyterians, Eastman an ordained minister of that faith. Henton's refusal to admit them to benefits or to assign them land was seen as an effort by Hinman to discriminate against anyone who did not join the Episcopal Church. Henton denied the charge, claimed that Big Eagle and the Wakemans had been hostile in 1862, and expressed the opinion that they were trying to break up the settlement, which they were unable to control.[38] Whatever the truth of these charges and countercharges, the little Sioux colonies were already rent with factionalism, an evil that has persisted ever since.

The Birch Coulee settlement, if it did not realize all of Bishop Whipple's hopes for it, did achieve a measure of prosperity and stability beyond any of the other Sioux communities in Minnesota. Hence its early history deserves separate consideration. As we have seen, its population grew rapidly after Good Thunder had established himself there in 1883. By the end of 1885 there were sixteen tipis, fifty-four souls, in the vicinity. That year Hinman, fresh from his unhappy

[36] Henton to Commissioner William A. Jones, January 13, 1898, *ibid.*

[37] John L. Macdonald to Oberly, January 27 and February 9, 1889; David Wells to Morgan, February 21, 1890; John Eastman to Morgan, March 12, 1890; Henton to Oberly, February 26, 1889; Henton to Morgan, March 4, 1890, *ibid.*

[38] Henton to Morgan, February 26 and March 15, 1889, *ibid.* In view of Hinman's record at Santee, there may have been some substance to the charges made against him now.

experience at Santee, visited the growing community. At the request of Bishop Whipple, he returned in the spring of 1886 to resume the mission work that had been broken off by the uprising nearly twenty-four years earlier. Good Thunder offered the church twenty acres of his land, on condition that a house of worship be erected there. The offer was promptly accepted, and by the end of 1887 the bishop was able to report that he had built "a mission house with a room attached large enough for worship."[39] This structure proved inadequate to the needs of the flock, and in 1889, after the Faribault group had moved to Birch Coulee, a stone church was begun. Although the site was not the same as that of the church almost completed in 1862, the stone that remained from the old building was used in the construction of the new one. At the laying of the cornerstone, on August 27, 1889, Good Thunder brought a written request from the Indians that the church be named St. Cornelia's, in honor of the wife of their beloved bishop.[40]

The consecration of St. Cornelia's, on July 15, 1891, was a major event in the history of the little Indian community. Bishop Whipple opened the service by leading the procession and reading a part of the liturgy in Dakota. The lesson was then read by Napoleon Wabasha, who had settled at Birch Coulee too late to benefit from the various appropriations and who had recently been made lay reader to give him some employment. At the regular morning service Bishop Whipple told how, thirty-three years earlier, Taopi, Good Thunder, and Wabasha had requested him to send a missionary to the lower Sioux, and he had sent Hinman. He then reviewed the more recent history of the congregation, with special emphasis on Good Thunder's contribution.[41] Hinman was not present at this dedication, for he had died on March 24,

[39] Whipple to Atkins, December 11, 1885, *ibid.*; George W. Tanner, *Fifty Years of Church Work in the Diocese of Minnesota 1857–1907* (St. Paul: Published by the Committee, 1909), p. 404; Henry B. Whipple, *Lights and Shadows of a Long Episcopate* (New York: Macmillan Co., 1899), pp. 181–182; Morton *Enterprise*, February 27, 1936; Redwood County Register of Deeds, Deed Record 19, p. 66. The indenture for the transfer of Good Thunder's twenty acres is dated August 7, 1889, but the transfer had presumably been made two years earlier and not recorded until then. It conveys the tract from Good Thunder and Sarah Good Thunder to "Rt. Rev. Henry B. Whipple, Episcopal Bishop of Minnesota, and his successors in office in Trust for to be used as a site for church, Parsonage, School and Burial Grounds for the Mdewa[ka]nton Sioux Dakota Indians of Minnesota." A consideration of one dollar was given, as in the case of the nine acres bought from Taopi for a school site.

[40] Tanner, *Fifty Years of Church Work in the Diocese of Minnesota*, p. 404; Whipple, *Lights and Shadows*, p. 182; Faribault *Democrat*, June 6, 1890.

[41] Morton *Enterprise*, July 24, 1891.

1890. For a number of years after his death the little stone church was served by the rector at Redwood Falls. Then, in 1899, Henry Whipple St. Clair was made deacon and placed in charge of the church. In 1904 he was ordained to the priesthood. Of Sioux blood himself, he was the son of the Reverend George Whipple St. Clair, the first of his people to be ordained by Bishop Whipple.[42]

Bishop Whipple was responsible also for the other institution started in the little village about this time. It was at his behest that the 1888 appropriations act had contained a provision for a school. Though he seems to have hoped that the school would be placed under the management of the Episcopal Church, it came to be conducted as a day school by the Bureau of Indian Affairs. When bids were let for its construction, they all exceeded the $2,000 limit set by Congress, and the size of the building had to be reduced. It was finally built, however, and was ready for use by the spring of 1891. The first teacher was Robert H. C. Hinman, son of the missionary, who had charge of it for nearly thirty years.[43]

With the advantage of better soil than the other Sioux communities had, Birch Coulee prospered more than they did. In 1894, when dry weather had virtually destroyed the crops on the sandy soil of Prairie Island, Henton was able to report that the people at Birch Coulee were doing well. He added that they were more industrious than the people of the other localities; "Many of their homes are indications of refinement and thrift," he remarked. Although their principal reliance was on agriculture, lace-making was introduced in the nineties as a means by which the women could find useful employment and supplement the meager income from farming. The idea originated with Miss Sibyl Carter while on a trip to Japan. She first introduced it on the White Earth Reservation in 1886 and then persuaded Bishop Whipple's niece, Miss Susan Salisbury, to teach the Sioux women at Birch Coulee the art. It caught on well, and soon they were turning out some pieces of fine workmanship.[44]

The gradual improvement in the material condition of the Minnesota

[42] Tanner, *Fifty Years of Church Work in the Diocese of Minnesota*, pp. 404–405; Whipple, *Lights and Shadows*, p. 176.

[43] Whipple to Atkins, July 6, 1886; Henton to Morgan, December 6 and 20, 1890, NARS, RG 75, LR; 50th Cong., 1st Sess., *H. Ex. Doc. 228*, p. 3; 50th Cong., 2nd Sess., *H. Ex. Doc. 61*, p. 3; Morton *Enterprise*, June 26, 1891; *Pioneer Press*, June 24, 1891.

[44] Henton to Daniel M. Browning, February 21, 1894, NARS, RG 75, LR; Morton *Enterprise*, September 23, 1892; Tanner, *Fifty Years of Church Work in the Diocese of Minnesota*, pp. 406–407.

Sioux was more apparent at Birch Coulee than it was at the other colonies, but everywhere they gradually came to be accepted by the white community. References to them in newspapers, though often condescending and patronizing, lack the asperity and undisguised contempt of earlier years. Their activities are mentioned, not in quite the same tone as those of the whites, but with the implied assumption that these activities would interest the general public. The Morton *Enterprise* might report the result of a baseball game between the local Indians and a team from Wabasha (won by the latter, despite partial umpiring by a local merchant) or might mention an exchange of visits between the Birch Coulee Sioux and those of the Sisseton Reservation. On their return from one such trip, the local group brought back thirty-three head of ponies and several cattle. As if to demonstrate their assimilation, in 1897 the Birch Coulee men organized a brass band and toured the countryside, giving concerts in various towns.[45]

The Prairie Island people were more noteworthy for such distinctively Indian activities as pow-wows held in the traditional manner. Early in 1887, when they had been there only a year or two, they played host to a traveling company of Winnebago and Omaha dancers. In 1892 (and probably on many other occasions) they presented war dances in a tent as part of the Fourth of July celebration in Red Wing.[46] Here and elsewhere the Indians made and sold moccasins, catlinite pipes, drums, and similar articles to supplement their income. Not all of the activities they indulged in were approved by the church, which continued to exercise a close surveillance over them. The old prejudice against Indian dances, even though they might be quite devoid of religious significance now, remained strong, however much appeal the dances might have to the general public. And certainly the church did not approve of the considerable amount of drinking that went on, even at Birch Coulee, despite federal and state regulations forbidding the sale of liquor to Indians. Newspaper reports of drunkenness are too numerous to be dismissed merely as isolated cases blown up out of proportion for journalistic purposes.[47]

Economically, the condition of the Minnesota Sioux worsened during the early 1890's. This deterioration was due in large part to the poor quality of the land purchased at most of the colonies, aggravated by several years of drought. The Indian Office received an increasing

[45] Morton *Enterprise*, June 19 and July 31, 1891, and May 7, 1897.
[46] Red Wing *Daily Republican*, February 17, 1887, June 29 and July 5, 1892.
[47] Morton *Enterprise*, September 11 and 18, 1891.

number of letters telling of "destitution" among these people as the $60,000 appropriated between 1884 and 1890 gradually dried up, and local newspapers contained a discouraging number of items like one in the Hastings *Democrat* early in 1895, telling of the death of a woman from starvation at Prairie Island. The newspaper commented that almost all of the Indians in the locality were in want of the necessities of life; one family had lost two pigs and thirty chickens because they had nothing to feed the animals. Calling for charity, the paper pointed out that the Indians "cannot make their wants known, and they don't know how to work, and could not obtain employment if they did."[48]

In response to the situation confronting the Minnesota Sioux, Congress in 1895 resumed the practice of appropriating funds for their benefit. Then and for the four following years the sum of $5,000 was appropriated annually for the "temporary support and civilization of Sioux, Medawakanton Band, in Minnesota."[49] There is no indication that these small gratuities did more than relieve the counties of part of the burden of keeping the Indians alive. When Special Agent James McLaughlin toured the Sioux communities in 1899, he found poverty everywhere except at Birch Coulee and recommended that the lands elsewhere be disposed of, since the Indians were unable to make use of them. After talking with Episcopal Rector C. C. Rollit, of Red Wing, he concluded that the Prairie Island people were "neither thrifty nor industrious, and were it not for the aid given them by Mr. Rollit at intervals, there would be considerable want among them at times." The county was willing to bury them at public expense but had no funds to give them medical assistance.[50]

The immediate reason for McLaughlin's visit was the resignation in the summer of 1898 of Robert B. Henton as special disbursing agent. With Henton's resignation the question arose whether the services of an agent were any longer needed for the Minnesota Sioux. Except for

[48] Michael McHugh to Secretary of Interior Hoke Smith, August 8, 1893; Henton to Hoke Smith, January 11, 1894; Henton to Representative O. M. Hall, February 22, 1894, NARS, RG 75, LR; Hastings *Democrat*, quoted in Red Wing *Daily Republican*, February 13, 1895. McHugh claimed to have originated the idea of asking government help for the Minnesota Sioux and said that he was spending two or three dollars a week helping those in and around Hastings. He also asked to be appointed agent. Hall, a native of Red Wing, endorsed Henton's request for an appropriation, saying that he knew of the destitution of those Indians living between Red Wing and Hastings.

[49] U.S. *Statutes at Large*, XXVIII, 873, 892; XXIX, 338; XXX, 78, 144, 586, 938.

[50] James McLaughlin to Secretary of Interior E. A. Hitchcock, March 17, 1899; McLaughlin to Jones, March 17, 1899, NARS, RG 75, LR.

those at Birch Coulee, they all opposed the appointment of another agent and wanted a straight cash payment. On the recommendation of the Reverend W. H. Knowlton of Redwood Falls and Representative J. T. McCleary, a local man, George L. Evans, was appointed in 1899. His term of service was brief. The last appropriation was made on March 1 of that year, and in June, 1900, Evans was notified that his services would no longer be needed after the end of the fiscal year.[51] Thus ended the first stage of the history of the Minnesota Sioux following their return from exile.

Although only sixteen years had passed since their recognition by the Indian Office and by Congress, certain important changes had come over them in that brief period. In 1884 they were unwelcome vagabonds, with no legal title to the lands they occupied, except for that which had been purchased with their own money; by 1900 most of them were established on land bought for them by the government, most of it securely held in government ownership. The location of their settlements had changed considerably, too. Since the younger, more ambitious people tended to gravitate to the places where land was available, the settlements near the Twin Cities had dwindled away until they were occupied only by the elderly, who were cared for by local churches and relief agencies. Thus Mendota, Grey Cloud Island, and Bloomington had been virtually abandoned by the turn of the century. Furthermore, the people assigned plots of land at Wabasha had not chosen to occupy them but had mostly moved to Prairie Island or one of the other colonies, and the Hastings group dwindled to one woman, who finally consented to have the land there sold to the state of Minnesota. To all practical purposes, therefore, by 1900 the Minnesota Mdewakantons were concentrated at three points: Birch Coulee, Prairie Island, and Prior Lake.[52]

As the twentieth century dawned, the Minnesota Sioux were far from the self-sufficiency that Bishop Whipple had thought they would

[51] Morton *Enterprise*, August 19 and November 4, 1898; McLaughlin to Jones, March 17, 1899; W. H. Knowlton to Jones, January 27, 1899; George L. Evans to Jones, June 20, 1900, NARS, RG 75, LR. Henton, who died shortly after his resignation, had served under two Democratic and two Republican administrations and had always been reappointed even though local Republicans applied for the post during the Harrison and McKinley administrations.

[52] J. F. Jacobson to Representative C. R. Davis, January 14, 1906; Emma Judson to Commissioner Francis E. Leupp, May 8, 1906; Acting Secretary of Interior Thomas Ryan to Commissioner of the General Land Office, August 27, 1906, NARS, RG 75, LR; U.S. *Statutes at Large*, XXXIV, 78.

achieve if the government would give them a helping hand. Perhaps they were no better off than they would have been if they had remained on their reservations in Nebraska and South Dakota. But they had satisfied the homing instinct that made them restless on those reservations, and they had established permanent communities which, small though they were, stood as authentic survivals of the Sioux people in their ancient homeland.

CHAPTER 15

The Twentieth Century: Santee

THE HISTORY of the Santee Sioux in the twentieth century can be understood only against the background of the general trend of Indian affairs during the period. The policies pursued by the Indian Bureau during the first quarter of the century were essentially a continuation of those followed in the last decade of the previous century. The Dawes Act had come as the culmination of a long period of reform agitation, and it was hard for those in charge of Indian policy to admit that allotment had been a failure. The continuing attrition of the Indians' land base was not seen as a misfortune so long as Bureau officials and the American public persisted in the assumption, contradicted by the census returns, that the Indian was a vanishing race. As one recent writer has commented, "Authorities responsible for policy continued to refer to a diminishing population long after the growth curve had turned upward."[1] And in the face of what should have been convincing evidence that the Indian was far from self-sufficiency, the Bureau gradually withdrew its services to tribes that seemed relatively far along in the acculturation process.

The first real indication of an approaching change in government policy came in 1926, when Secretary of the Interior Hubert Work asked

[1] D'Arcy McNickle, *The Indian Tribes of the United States: Ethnic and Cultural Survival* (London: Oxford University Press, 1962), p. 53.

the Institute for Government Research, a privately endowed foundation, to carry out an economic and social survey of conditions among the
American Indians. Two years later the survey staff submitted a statement of its findings, usually called the Meriam Report after Lewis
Meriam, who served as technical director. The Meriam Report was an
eye-opener to those who had supposed that the Indian problem was
solved or well on the way to solution. It described the economic plight
of the Indian in sober prose, backed by statistics, and emphasized the
failure of allotment. It offered specific recommendations for the reform
of Indian policy—recommendations that amounted to a repudiation
of the time-honored thesis that the Indians must ultimately be totally
assimilated to the larger society.

Charles J. Rhoads, who became commissioner in 1929, and his assistant commissioner, Henry Scattergood, made some policy changes in
line with the Meriam Report's recommendations, but there was no
major change of direction until the appointment in 1933 of John Collier
as commissioner under the Roosevelt administration. Collier's approach,
embodied in the Indian Reorganization Act of 1934, proposed not
merely to stop the loss of Indian lands but to recover some of what had
been already lost. Instead of being told to "hurry up and get assimilated" and to give up the remnants of their culture, Indians were encouraged to preserve what they had left. And they were given an
opportunity to organize as legal entities and draw up constitutions for
effective tribal government. In addition to substantive changes in policy,
the Collier program brought to the management of Indian affairs a
missionary fervor not heretofore seen in the twentieth century. In Indian
policy, as in other areas of American life, the Depression shook old
beliefs and made innovation easier than in normal times.

Although Collier remained commissioner until 1945 and his basic
philosophy was shared by his immediate successor, William A. Brophy,
the vigor and much of the effectiveness of his program were lost with
the coming of World War II and the diversion of the national energies
to other purposes.[2] After the war a mood of retrenchment in the country,
and especially in Congress, led to efforts to reduce expenditures in the
Indian Service and, indeed, to abolish the Bureau altogether. Reflecting a sense of frustration at the failure of government policy to accomplish its purpose of incorporating the Indian into the fabric of American
life, Congress in 1953 passed House Concurrent Resolution 108, which
called on the government, "at the earliest possible time," to get out of

---

[2] John Collier, *From Every Zenith* (Denver: Alan Swallow, 1963), p. 369.

the Indian business.[3] The bywords of the 1950's came to be "termination" and "relocation"—the unilateral severance of Bureau services to
individual tribes and the Bureau-sponsored movement of Indians from
reservations to cities where more jobs were available.

In the later 1950's the pendulum began to swing back in the other
direction, after the policies of the previous few years had been repeatedly attacked and their deficiencies pointed out by responsible critics;
and with the election of John F. Kennedy in 1960 the policy of termination was officially declared dead. Once again emphasis was placed on
helping the reservation Indian to make a living where he was and on
continuing Bureau services until a tribe considered itself ready to dis-
pense with them. As in the Collier administration, the Indian was to
play the major role in policy decisions on individual reservations.

No sooner did the new approach begin to show results, however, than
involvement in the Vietnam civil war brought a demand for cutbacks
in domestic programs, and the call for termination began to be heard
again. When Philleo Nash, the anthropologist appointed commissioner
by President Kennedy, resigned in the spring of 1966, his successor,
Robert L. Bennett, was subjected to close scrutiny by a Senate committee, which reportedly demanded, as a price for confirming his nomination, that he promise to speed up the withdrawal of the federal
government from Indian affairs.[4] To the distress of Indians all across
the country, termination, far from being dead, appeared by 1966 to be
once more an extremely live issue.

To a degree, the Santee Sioux have all been affected by the general
course of Indian policy in the twentieth century, and their history has
consisted in part of puzzled reactions to these increasingly frequent re-
versals of policy. Yet their responses have not been uniform. In fact, the
interested observer is less likely to be struck by the common elements in
their recent history than by the divergent courses followed by the
various fragments of the Santee Sioux in the present century.

On the Santee Reservation there was a gradual withdrawal of government services, marked by the closing of the agency in 1917. Although
this group took advantage of the Indian Reorganization Act, a mass
exodus followed in the 1940's and 1950's, amounting almost to abandonment of the reservation. At Sisseton and Devils Lake the dissipation

[3] McNickle, *Indian Tribes of the United States*, pp. 61–62.
[4] *New York Times*, April 10, 1966. The Senate Interior Committee complained that
there had been virtually no legislation in recent years to terminate federal control of
Indian tribes.

of the Indians' land base went on for the first three decades of the century, and the failure of both groups to accept the IRA prevented proposed land purchases from materializing. Meanwhile, a growing population created an increasingly desperate situation. The Flandreau and Minnesota Sioux were largely neglected until the 1930's, but then their condition improved. The IRA was accepted by the Flandreau colony and by both Lower Sioux (Birch Coulee) and Prairie Island; extensive, though insufficient, land purchases were made, and a revival of community spirit occurred.

Any discussion of the history of these groups in the twentieth century is bound to be sketchy, and any judgments rendered are inevitably inconclusive, since not all the returns are yet in. Even Santee, whose history a superficial observer might think finished, still retains much of its identity as an Indian community after more than seventy-five years of attempted assimilation, and probably will continue to do so for some time to come. Yet its history for the first thirty years of the century was largely one of decay and deterioration. One cause may have been that, judging from their official reports, the men placed in charge there lacked the evangelical zeal displayed by such men as Janney and Lightner in the 1870's.

H. C. Baird, whose term of office carried over into the new century, was the last to bear the traditional title of agent. In keeping with the belief that the Indian Bureau's responsibility toward its wards was in the future to be primarily educational, the old-time agents were replaced early in the century by superintendents. Early in 1902, Wilbert E. Meagley was appointed superintendent of the Santee government school and was charged with all the duties "heretofore devolving upon the Indian agent at the Santee Agency as to agency matters. . . ."[5] After some delay, Meagley took office in February, 1903, and retained the position for more than six years. Although the school was closed in 1909, Meagley's successor, Frank E. McIntyre, kept the title of superintendent, as did the man who followed him in 1914, Charles E. Burton, who remained in charge of the agency until it was discontinued.[6]

---

[5] Commissioner William A. Jones to Wilbert E. Meagley, January 27, 1902, NARS, RG 75, LR, Santee Agency.

[6] Jones to E. A. Hitchcock, December 24, 1902, *ibid.* Meagley's appointment was withdrawn when George W. Saunders was appointed. The Civil Service Commission did not approve Saunders' appointment, however, and Meagley became superintendent early in 1903. See Meagley to Jones, February 24, 1903, *ibid.*

These first seventeen years of the twentieth century were marked by the loss of much of the Santees' remaining land and by the continued erosion of what was left of their culture. Both losses came about as a result of a combination of circumstances for which the Indians and the government shared culpability. The premature attempt to make farmers out of the Indians by legislative fiat through allotment was a failure from the beginning. The practice of leasing, well established by 1900, withstood official disapproval, and the Bureau was finally forced to accept it in order to exercise any measure of supervision over it. Besides collecting the rentals, so as to protect the Indian from dishonest whites, the agency deposited the money and paid it out only on authority from the Indian Office. Furthermore, a regulation was long in effect requiring every able-bodied Indian to reserve at least forty acres of his allotment for his own use. This rule was manifestly inappropriate at Santee, where much of the reservation was unsuited for farming and where few of the Indians had enough stock or equipment. Hence in 1902 it was modified to permit Indians whose allotments were rough and broken to lease their entire farms for grazing purposes.[7] Although leasing provided the Indians with some income, it was never enough to give them an adequate livelihood.

A more serious problem was that of the loss of Indian land. This came about in two ways: through the sale of inherited and "non-competent" interests and through the issuance of patents. As the original allottees died, their allotments came into the possession of their legal heirs, who sometimes were quite numerous. Since ordinarily none of the heirs were financially equipped to buy out the others, the land thus inherited became "fractionated," i.e., the undivided property of several individuals. Subdividing the allotments was impracticable because it would have left the heirs with uneconomically small units. The solution usually resorted to was to sell the lands and divide the proceeds among the heirs. The same easy way out was taken with regard to allotments owned by people who, because of age or physical handicaps, were unable to farm them.

Land sales under these two categories began before 1900 and continued until well into the third decade of the century. By 1904 eighty-

[7] George W. Saunders to Jones, September 9, 1902; Assistant Secretary of Interior Thomas Ryan to Jones, September 26, 1902, *ibid*. Leasing was first legalized by Congress in 1891, to the extent that allottees unable to use their allotments because of age or disability were permitted to lease them for a three-year period, under conditions prescribed by the Secretary of the Interior. See U.S. *Statutes at Large*, XXVI, 795.

five tracts had been sold, for a total of $95,895. From then until 1923 local newspapers frequently contained notices of prospective sales, with descriptions of the tracts offered and the names of the allottees. Some allotments were offered for sale repeatedly, since they were virtually worthless, even for grazing purposes. The Indian Office did all it could to encourage buyers. In 1910 regulations were changed so that only 15 per cent of the price needed to be paid at once; another 10 per cent was to be paid when the legal papers were signed, and 25 per cent would be paid yearly thereafter.[8] Most of the sales were to land dealers rather than to individual farmers or ranchers. Examination of a marked reservation map shows that the tracts sold were widely scattered and followed no perceptible pattern. So the purchasers could not expect to block out large acreages. It made little difference, however, for cattle could be run on leased lands quite as conveniently as on purchased lands.

A great part of the land lost by the Santees in the half-century following allotment was patented to individual owners and then sold. The issuance of patents began as soon as the twenty-five-year restrictive clause expired in 1910. A competency board was appointed to determine which Indians were qualified to receive patents and which would require a longer period of government guardianship. It was understood by local whites, and presumably by Bureau officials, that most of the patentees would promptly sell their lands. At least there was no hypocrisy in the Niobrara newspaper, which saw the competency hearings as offering "a considerable opening of lands to settlement since it will give the [Indians] first class patents to their lands." Recalling the efforts to have the Santees removed back in the 1870's, Edwin A. Fry, erstwhile editor of the Niobrara *Pioneer*, remarked that this end would shortly be realized. "As we begin to see things now, it will not be more than another dozen years before the Santee lands will have passed from their control and the white man in possession," he wrote.[9]

The process did not move quite as swiftly as Fry expected. For one thing, the competency board displayed some sense of responsibility and did not classify all the Indians as competent. Enough were so classified, however, that many tracts of land promptly came into the market. Some of the allottees were living at Prairie Island or elsewhere in

[8] J. F. House, Supervisor of Indian Schools, to Jones, July 6, 1904, NARS, RG 75, LR, Santee Agency; Niobrara *Tribune*, December 22, 1910. At one sale in 1917, a total of $88,000 was realized. See the Niobrara *Tribune*, January 18, 1917.

[9] Niobrara *Tribune*, November 10, 1910.

Minnesota and had no interest in their lands other than a pecuniary one. A surprisingly small number of patents were issued annually—usually only three or four—but the lands were almost invariably sold. Interestingly, the superintendent was often less inclined to grant patents than the Indian Office. McIntyre asked authority to suspend recommendations on applications for patents, and when it was denied, he tried to delay the procedure as much as possible.[10]

Technically, the Indian Bureau no longer exercised any supervision over an Indian once a patent had been issued to him, but in practice the distinction between wards and nonwards was shadowy. Often a man would receive a patent and sell his farm, but his wife would remain under guardianship, and both would continue to benefit from whatever meager services the government still offered her. Despite the attempt to represent the Santees as self-sustaining, they were still very far from that condition early in the twentieth century. Meagley pointed out in 1903 that the government then still employed for the Santees and Poncas "seven mechanics, an engineer, and a miller, supplying all necessary material for their work; two doctors with the necessary drugs have been furnished; large gratuities in the way of wagons, plows, harrows, mowers, harnesses, twine, etc., have been furnished. . . ." Yet, thought Meagley, the average Santee believed himself to be self-supporting.[11]

The fact that the Indians were still to some extent beneficiaries of services not accorded the general population was often a source of resentment on the part of local whites. This feeling occasionally found expression in the newspapers, as when the Niobrara *Tribune* remarked that, although the Indians in the vicinity owned some good farms, "the shiftlessness and worthlessness prevalent among them [had] been a serious drawback to the town." The industrious ones were in a minority, said the paper, and those who had attended Carlisle, Haskell, or other Indian schools seemed not to have profited much from their training. The Indians had their complaints, too, though they less frequently found expression in print. Occasionally a letter might appear in the newspaper. One published in 1911 criticized "our white neigh-

[10] Meagley to Francis E. Leupp, July 25, 1906; Superintendent's Annual Reports, 1910, 1911, 1913, and 1916, NARS, RG 75, Santee Agency. After 1906 the superintendents' reports were no longer published in the *Annual Reports* of the Commissioner of Indian Affairs, but they continued to be submitted, in typewritten form, and are preserved in the National Archives. Normally, they consist of a narrative and a statistical part, both of which come to be increasingly routine with the passage of the years.

[11] Meagley to Jones, August 31, 1903, NARS, RG 75, LR, Santee Agency.

bors, who are always ready to give us advice and who claim that they are doing so for our personal benefit," and wondered why, if they were such good neighbors, they attacked the superintendent. Why didn't they help fight the whiskey problem instead of contributing to it? Why didn't they want the Indians to attend school? The letter ended: "All that they do tell us is that we are thoroughly competent to handle our own affairs, boost us and endorse us for our patents to our allotments, but when our land is sold and the money spent, Where-Do-We-Stand."[12]

Besides the services afforded by the agency, the Santees received benefits of other kinds during the early 1900's. Until 1907 they continued to receive income from the "Sioux Fund"—the proceeds from the sale of the Great Sioux Reservation, in which the Santees had been adjudged to have an interest. About 160 of them also shared in the settlement of the Sisseton-Wahpeton claims case and received $154.70 each. The Sisseton-Wahpeton claims case has a long and tangled history, to which only passing attention can be paid here. It stemmed from the argument that the upper Sioux had not taken part in the Uprising of 1862 and should not have been deprived of their share of the annuities due them under the terms of the treaty of Traverse des Sioux. After being in and out of Congress many times, it was finally accepted and turned over to the Court of Claims. The case was settled in 1907, and payment made in 1909.[13] A few of the upper Sioux had surrendered in the fall of 1862 and had accompanied the lower Sioux to Crow Creek and thence to the Niobrara. There had also been some intermarriage and a certain amount of drifting back and forth between the Santee and Sisseton reservations.

The Santees had their own claims case repeatedly before Congress. Though originating in a council held at Santee in 1884, the case received little attention until the 1890's, when two factions, one led by James Garvie, the other by John Eastman of Flandreau and former Santee Agent Charles Hill, later a banker in Springfield, South Dakota, joined forces and pressed their cause with vigor. In order to counter the government's claim that the 1868 treaty nullified all previous treaties, Garvie obtained testimony from the two surviving members of the

[12] Niobrara *Tribune*, January 29, 1914, and June 29, 1911.

[13] Meagley to Commissioner Robert G. Valentine, October 27, 1906, NARS, RG 75, LR, Santee Agency; Niobrara *Tribune*, March 4, 1909. The Sisseton-Wahpeton claims case is discussed at length in William W. Folwell, *A History of Minnesota*, II (St. Paul: Minnesota Historical Society, 1961), 418–437.

delegation that signed the treaty to demonstrate that pressure was used to induce them to sign.[14]

The Santee claims case finally passed Congress in 1917. The Indians claimed the sum of $2,468,878.40, after deducting the benefits received from the government. The government found other benefits, however, and revised the figures so that the Santees wound up owing a substantial sum! This led to further revision of the figures by their lawyers, with the result that the Santees were finally judged to be entitled to $386,597.89, less about 10 per cent to their lawyers. Payment was made in the winter of 1924. After thirty years of waiting, the Santees finally received $129.30 each. This was perhaps enough to justify the premature rejoicing of the Niobrara *Tribune*, which had commented, upon the passage of the bill in 1917, that "it looks good to the auto dealer and the merchant and the man who has anything to sell and who resides near Santee at the present time." It may also have staved off outright destitution for a time, though its effects must necessarily have been brief.[15]

Despite the earnest endeavors of missionaries and Indian Bureau officials, the Indian culture had not been completely stamped out by the beginning of the twentieth century, as evidenced by the survival of the old dances. In 1901, the fiftieth anniversary of the treaties of Traverse des Sioux and Mendota, some of the Santees held a celebration in honor of the chiefs who had signed those treaties. This became an annual event and included dancing by a handful of old men who had served as scouts in 1863 and 1864. In an effort to exercise some control over it, Superintendent McIntyre tried in 1910 to combine it with an Indian fair, but the only result was that for several years there were two such affairs.[16]

[14] Folwell, *History of Minnesota*, II, 437–439; Niobrara *Tribune*, July 22 and 29, August 5 and 26, and September 2 and 9, 1920, August 3, 1922, April 12, 1923, and February 7, 1924. The account by Garvie in the *Tribune*, July 22 to September 9, 1920, is extremely detailed but should be read with caution, as the writer was the leader of one of the factions in contention for the honor of winning the case.

[15] Folwell, *History of Minnesota*, II, 438–439; Niobrara *Tribune*, March 8, 1917, and February 7, 1924.

[16] Niobrara *Tribune*, August 5, 1909, August 18, 1910, July 20 and 27 and August 10, 1911, September 12, 1912, and July 10, 1913; Edward H. Eastman and David Graham to Valentine, July 17, 1911; Frank E. McIntyre to Valentine, August 5 and 25, 1911, NARS, RG 75, Santee Agency. A group calling itself "an Indian Committie organized for the purpose of management of celebration of the old Chief Made Wa Kan Ton" wrote the commissioner complaining of McIntyre's innovation. The phraseology led Indian Bureau officials to suppose that "Made Wa Kan Ton" was the

It is well to remember that the policy of discouraging or even forbidding these dances continued in force far into the twentieth century. Although professing to follow a "policy of persuasion," McIntyre actually forbade dancing by the old scouts at the fairs in 1913 and 1914 and thereby stirred up ill feeling. His successor, Burton, was more liberal. When he requested permission for the old men to dance for an hour, he was told by the assistant commissioner that there would be no objection provided the dances were held in the daytime only and no "immoral dances" were allowed. "No school children or young Indians of your reservation should be permitted to be spectators at these dances," the official wrote, "as the Office thinks it would be better to keep their ideas away from these old-time customs as much as possible."[17]

How much of the impetus for these dances came from the Indians themselves and how much from white people is debatable. Certainly they were encouraged by the merchants of nearby towns for commercial purposes, and most of the spectators were whites. When the official celebration was merged with the fair, every effort was made by the superintendent to subordinate the distinctively Indian features to those that might be found at any county fair. For a few years the Indian Bureau furnished $200 in premiums, and one of the largest landowners on the former reservation offered another $105 by way of encouraging the Indians to exert themselves in agriculture.[18] Although the fair may have served in some degree as a means of hastening the acculturation process by satisfying the Indians' wish for a celebration of their own, it had certain features that displeased the superintendent, and it never succeeded in getting a monopoly on the reservation festivities. Some drinking inevitably accompanied it (though sometimes this was carried on mostly by whites), and the appearance of Winnebagos, Yanktons, and other tribes naturally required return visits by the Santees when those tribes held their fairs. As for unauthorized celebrations on patented land, the superintendents were uniformly opposed to them and did

name of a chief, and subsequent correspondence contains numerous references to this nonexistent chieftain.

[17] Superintendent's Annual Report, 1911; Charles E. Burton to Commissioner Cato Sells, March 30, 1915; Assistant Commissioner E. B. Merritt to Burton, May 18, 1915, NARS, RG 75, Santee Agency.

[18] Niobrara *Tribune*, August 5, 1909, August 10 and 31 and September 28, 1911, September 12, 1912, and September 23, 1915; McIntyre to Valentine, August 25, 1911; Burton to Sells, March 26, 1915, and February 12, 1916, NARS, RG 75, Santee Agency.

what they could to discourage Indians from attending them, though of course they had no direct control over them.[19]

Although it might not seem evident from the close supervision still exercised by the superintendent over the personal affairs of the Indians, there was during this period a phased withdrawal of agency functions and Bureau services. Meagley closed down the gristmill in 1904, since it was costing far more to operate than the slight benefits warranted.[20] A month or so after McIntyre's arrival in the summer of 1909, he closed the boarding school. Since the plant was in poor shape and "not well thought of by the Indians," his action met with little opposition. The presence of the Santee Normal Training School and of a number of district schools on the reservation made the boarding school superfluous in the superintendent's eyes. As a matter of fact, however, the district schools did not provide an adequate substitute, chiefly because of hostility from whites. When a Bureau school official visited the reservation in 1916, he found the situation quite unsatisfactory. Since the teachers were not employed by the government, they felt no responsibility toward the Indian children. "The irregularity of attendance and the natural timidity of the Indian children rather annoy the teacher," he reported, "and, in most cases, no doubt, the teachers feel relieved when the Indians drop out."[21]

Discontinuance of the agency, considered even before 1900, became apparently feasible in 1917, after both Nebraska and South Dakota had adopted prohibition ordinances, and one of the principal obstacles to freeing the Santees from supervision seemed to have been removed. A special agent sent to determine the advisability of closing the agency reported that of the 1,173 Indians on the reservation, 734 were considered competent, and another 300 were probably so. Aside from 74 elderly, indigent, or diseased Indians, all could safely be released from

---

[19] McIntyre to Sells, October 9, 1914; B. J. Young to Valentine, August 3, 1911, NARS, RG 75, Santee Agency; Niobrara *Tribune*, September 23, 1915.

[20] Meagley to Jones, July 27, 1904; Meagley to Leupp, December 12, 1904, NARS, RG 75, LR, Santee Agency.

[21] Superintendent's Annual Report, 1910; Sam B. Davis, Supervising Superintendent, to Sells, June 12, 1916, NARS, RG 75, Santee Agency; *Word Carrier*, XXXVIII (September–October, 1909), 3. The attendance problem was complicated by Nebraska law, which did not require children to attend school if they lived more than two miles away or did not have an open road to school; many of the Santees lived in isolated crooks and corners of the rugged country and did not have ready access to good roads or schools nearby. See Key Wolf, Day School Inspector, to House, May 6, 1922, NARS, RG 75, Santee Agency.

guardianship; these exceptions could be placed under the Yankton Agency. Only 18,000 acres of land remained in Indian hands, and the quantity was diminishing steadily.[22] Commissioner Cato Sells, on the strength of this recommendation, advised the Secretary of the Interior that the agency be discontinued and all employees except the agency physician, the interpreter, the government farmer, and a single police private be discharged. The decision having been made, Superintendent Burton turned over the government property to Yankton Superintendent A. W. Leech, and one September morning residents of the agency noticed that for the first time in many years the 7:50 work bell failed to ring. Local newspapers treated this event as evidence of the completion of the government's task with the Santees and complimented the Indians on their signal achievement. But an inspector who visited Santee the next year reported that more rations were issued there than at the Yankton Agency.[23]

The agency plant, including the school, was not disposed of for nearly a decade, while the Bureau carried on unsuccessful negotiations with Knox County for the assumption by the county of responsibility for the aged and indigent. Meanwhile the buildings deteriorated and became a resort of bootleggers and a "loafing ground for worthless, shiftless Indians and whites of questionable character," as one Yankton superintendent reported. After several crimes had been committed in the vicinity, the superintendent called for the removal of the subagency that had been retained after 1917, in order to break up "this cesspool of inequity [*sic*]." The recommendation was carried out in 1926, when the government farmer was transferred to the old Ponca agency west of Niobrara, and the crumbling buildings were sold at auction. Except for the campus of the Santee Normal Training School and the Episcopal mission, the auction left the old Santee Agency a virtual ghost town.[24]

[22] Superintendent's Annual Report, 1917; H. S. Taylor to Sells, July 26, 1917, NARS, RG 75, Santee Agency.

[23] Sells to Secretary of Interior Frank K. Lane, August 6, 1917, *ibid.*; Superintendent's Annual Report, 1918; R. E. L. Newberne, Special Supervisor, to Sells, April 20, 1918, NARS, RG 75, Yankton Agency; Niobrara *Tribune*, September 13 and 20, 1917.

[24] Burton to Sells, August 27, 1917, NARS, RG 75, Santee Agency; Superintendent's Annual Report, 1919; H. W. Sipe to R. E. L. Daniel, March 27, 1925; Daniel to Commissioner Charles H. Burke, April 15, 1924, and March 1, 1926; Burke to Daniel, October 8, 1924; Hearing on matters relating to Santee reservation, Nebraska, before E. B. Merritt, Assistant Commissioner of Indian Affairs, March 30, 1926; Daniel to Burke, August 24, 1926, and August 11, 1927; H. M. Gillman, Jr., to Burke, June 18,

Withdrawal of government services to the Santees was premature, but the Indians' complaints were dismissed as the natural reluctance of the recipients of unearned benefits to part with them. Superintendent Leech reported in 1921 that the Santees were "living in hopes of the United States placing them back on the ration roll again and supporting them in idleness after they have dissipated their means, which most of them have already done." Because neither Leech nor his successor, R. E. L. Daniel, appears to have had much sympathy for the Indians, one may legitimately question the objectivity of their evaluation of the situation at Santee.[25]

The government got an inside look at conditions there from a source other than the superintendent in 1926, and the spectacle was not cheering. After receiving resolutions from the Knox County Board of Commissioners, the Niobrara Commercial Club and the village council, and the Santee Indian Mission, Representative Edgar Howard of Nebraska visited the reservation late that year, in connection with the disposition of the agency buildings, and reported that conditions were "deplorable beyond words." Because of drought, no corn had been harvested in the previous two years, and many of the people were destitute. Howard asked, not for a survey (which had been promised), but for an immediate issue of food. An issue of rations was promptly made, and an investigation was also ordered. District Superintendent

1927; Merritt to Secretary of Interior Hubert Work, August 27, 1927, NARS, RG 75, Yankton Agency; Niobrara *Tribune*, February 21 and July 3, 1924, November 19, 1925, and November 4, 1926. About the time the agency was discontinued, an attempt was made to promote a land boom in the vicinity. The town of Santee was platted, a bank was organized, and there was even talk of getting a railroad. Not much came of this effort, and when the bank folded in 1926, the high hopes for a sizable town on the site of the old Indian agency collapsed. See the Niobrara *Tribune*, April 12 and 19, 1917, January 31, 1918, May 8, 1919, July 3, 1924, and July 1, 1926; *Word Carrier*, LV (March–April 1926), 3.

[25] A. W. Leech to Sells, March 21, 1921, NARS, RG 75, Yankton Agency. Stephen S. Jones, a Santee, characterized Daniel as "hard-boiled" and charged that he had ordered patents issued to allottees who wished their land to remain in restricted status. He had attempted to discharge the agency physician, Dr. George J. Frazier, also a Santee, but appeals from Frederick B. Riggs, superintendent of Santee Normal Training School, and others frustrated this intention. See Jones to John M. Green, March 6, 1930; Daniel to Burke, April 15, 1924; William Abraham and Joseph Johnson to Burke, January 11, 1926; Gillman to Burke, June 18, 1927, NARS, RG 75, Yankton Agency; Niobrara *Tribune*, February 4, 1926. Daniel was not Leech's immediate successor, but the two men who served as Yankton superintendent between these two had very brief terms. J. F. House was placed in charge April 1, 1922, and relieved the following June 30. Harvey K. Meyer was superintendent for a time in 1922 and 1923.

O. C. Upchurch of Pierre, accompanied by the agency physician, Dr. George J. Frazier, visited seventeen homes, met with members of the tribal council, and recommended immediate relief for needy families. Upchurch also reported that Daniel had tended to ignore the Indians' pleas. "It is claimed," he said, "that he has a brash way of dealing with his charge and in some instances really [has] put a deaf ear to any pleas." Relief funds were made available for use at Santee, but this was a stopgap measure only and did not get at the roots of the problem.[26]

The general economic depression that followed the stockmarket crash in 1929 brought the Santee situation to a crisis and precipitated the government back into the Indian business to a degree unanticipated in earlier years. Transfer of the welfare burden to Knox County worked only indifferently in normal times; the Depression found that county, like other units of local government all over the country, utterly incapable of meeting the welfare needs of its white population, let alone the Indians. It not only cut off poor relief, but sent a bill to the Department of the Interior for $9,011.20 for expenditures made for Indians between 1919 and 1932. The government took the position that to honor this requisition would be to set a precedent, and "we would find ourselves deeper in the Indian problem than we have been for many years."[27] On the Great Plains the situation was aggravated by drought. The crop in 1931 was the smallest ever known, everyone was in debt, and the Farmers Union elevator in Niobrara was going out of business because there was no grain to be shipped out and the farmers had no money to pay for grain that might be shipped in.[28]

That summer a meeting was held at Santee to ask for government help to the destitute Indians before the arrival of cold weather. Some assistance was rendered by the Red Cross and by government agencies, largely in the form of direct relief. The distinction between wards and nonwards complicated the handling of benefits, since government appropriations were restricted to those in the former status. Like it or not, the government *was* deeper in the Indian problem than it had been for years. The Meriam Report had pointed out, before the Depression, that people unable to support themselves, whether Indian or non-Indian, were a social responsibility requiring help from some government

[26] Niobrara *Tribune*, November 18 and 25 and December 23, 1926.

[27] *Ibid.*, January 21 and February 11, 1932; Peyton Carter to Commissioner Charles J. Rhoads, February 24, 1933; Rhoads to Representative Edgar Howard, March 30, 1933, NARS, RG 75, Yankton Agency.

[28] Niobrara *Tribune*, August 6, 1931.

agency—federal, state or local—or from private charities. In the Depression only the federal government, which had a long history of responsibility to the Indians, was big enough to cope with the problem.[29]

The Santee Sioux accepted the Indian Reorganization Act by a vote of 260 to 27 at an election held November 17, 1934. In a way, it is rather surprising that they voted to accept the act, for they had been proceeding in the opposite direction so long that some major psychological reorientation must have been required of them. Furthermore, their recent experience with the Indian Bureau had not been pleasant. Their dissatisfaction with the successive Yankton superintendents was transferred to a new object when, in 1933, the Yankton Agency was abolished and the Santees were placed under the Winnebago Agency. Complaints against the Winnebago superintendent, Henry M. Tidwell, and members of his staff began reaching Representative Howard, including a telegram from the Knox County Board describing Tidwell as "absolutely incompetent" and demanding immediate relief for fifty destitute families. An investigation by the Indian Bureau substantiated the charges, and shortly thereafter Tidwell was replaced by Gabe E. Parker, a man of Choctaw descent and sympathetic to Collier's policies.[30]

Aid to the Santees under the new administration did not, of course, await the appointment of Parker. Federal Emergency Relief Administration funds were made available in 1933, and many of the Indians were set to work building and improving roads that summer. Some were employed in an Indian Emergency Conservation Work project to develop a public campground on the old agency site. The new government farmer, James W. Brewer, encouraged the Indians to grow subsistence gardens, but no attempt was made at that time to get them back into the wheat and cattle business. They were encouraged, however, to devote some of the proceeds from their road work to the purchase of seed. Direct relief in the form of surplus mutton bought from the

[29] *Ibid.*, August 6, 1931; Lewis Meriam *et al.*, *The Problem of Indian Administration* (Baltimore: Johns Hopkins Press, 1928), pp. 89–93.

[30] John D. Forsythe to Howard, March 19, 1934; Clyde W. Flinn to A. L. Hook, June 9, 1937, NARS, RG 75, Winnebago Agency; Gillman to Commissioner John Collier, June 27, 1933, NARS, RG 75, Yankton Agency; B. G. Courtright to Louis R. Glavis, Director of Investigations, March 22, 1934; Courtright to Collier, March 23, 1934; Ray Ovid Hall to Mary McGair, April 30, 1934, NARS, RG 75, Winnebago Agency. A petition from Howard Redwing and others to Representative Howard, dated June 26, 1933 (NARS, RG 75, Yankton Agency), said that one family was so near starvation that they used as food some dead and partly decomposed chickens thrown onto a barn roof by whites.

Navajos, blankets, shoes, and other clothing was also furnished in 1933 and 1934. When about 130 cattle were issued in October, 1934, the Indians were given complete freedom to keep their cows or butcher them.[31]

Important as these various forms of assistance were, they were in the final analysis palliative rather than remedial. The Santees could not achieve self-support by rebuilding roads or constructing a campground, and the land base remaining to them was insufficient for successful farming. The Meriam Report had stressed the Indians' dependence on agriculture in the future as in the past and had proposed methods to retain and make usable the land resources left to them. One of the objectives of the Indian Reorganization Act had been to permit tribes organized under its provisions to undertake land acquisition programs, the land thus acquired to remain in tribal ownership. In response to a circular from the Bureau in June, 1935, the Santee tribal council prepared recommendations for purchases which they felt would give their people an adequate land base. By this time they had only 3,132.29 acres left out of the amount allotted in 1885, plus about 1,800 acres of fee patent land, nearly all of which was encumbered with unpaid taxes and mortgages. The members of the council estimated that only 2,352 acres of this land was suitable for agriculture. The government farmer thought that out of 105 families only 3 had enough land to provide a cash income from farming, and only 15 had enough for subsistence needs; the remaining 87 families were, to all practical purposes, landless.[32]

Land purchases made with IRA funds ultimately came to 3,368.54 acres, mostly in 1936 and 1937. This was far less than the Bureau had planned to buy and fell short of the Santees' needs, just as purchases for other tribes failed to meet their needs. Funds dried up with the coming of World War II and the diversion of appropriations to defense purposes. As late as the summer of 1940 the landless Santees were said to be "anxiously awaiting the acquisition of additional areas in order that further benefits to individuals, families, and the tribe might be realized." They have continued to wait ever since. Pending completion of

[31] Niobrara *Tribune*, July 20 and September 7 and 14, 1933; February 8, April 19, May 3, June 14, July 5, and October 11, 1934.

[32] Meriam, *The Problem of Indian Administration*, p. 488; James W. Brewer to Gabe E. Parker, August 3, 1935; Resolution to Commissioner of Indian Affairs from David Frazier and Ulysses Redowl, September 24, 1936; Hook to J. M. Stewart, Director of Lands, March 24, 1937, NARS, RG 75, Winnebago Agency.

expected purchases, some twenty-five families were set up on leased, white-owned lands and furnished with livestock and farm equipment. Although they were said to be doing well in 1937, rentals on the land were taking a third of the profits.[33]

Besides the purchase of land, several other measures were taken to improve the condition of the Santee Sioux. The Indian Reorganization Act had provided for a sum of $10,000,000 to be used for reimbursable loans to tribal groups. The principle of reimbursable loans was not new, but previous experience with it had been discouraging. More intelligently managed, it proved much more successful in the 1930's, although at Santee as elsewhere the amount of money available was never enough for the needs of the tribe. Rehabilitation funds were also obtained for construction of houses and farm buildings, a project that did much to improve living conditions among those families that were able to benefit. In line with the Collier administration's emphasis on encouraging community spirit, a "community self-help building" was completed in 1937, containing a large room with a capacity of nearly two hundred, a kitchen at the rear, and smaller rooms for sewing projects, committee meetings, or a tribal office; in a wing were spaces for weaving and other arts and crafts activities and a carpentry shop.[34]

It is important to note that in all those projects the Indians themselves were consulted and did much of the planning. Though opposed to the withdrawal of government supervision, Commissioner Collier and his allies had no brief for paternalism. Everything was done to encourage the Indians to take the initiative, apparently with good results, for many of the ideas discussed by Indian Bureau officials came originally from the Indians themselves. Superintendent Parker reported after one meeting at Santee, concerned with a plan for subsistence garden plots for the old and needy: "It would do your heart good, as it certainly did mine, yesterday afternoon to sit through long hours of serious expectant

[33] 82nd Cong., 2nd Sess., *H. Rpt. 2503*, p. 62; Flinn to Hook, June 6, 1937; Fred H. Daiker to Thomas H. Kitto and David Frazier, June 5, 1940, NARS, RG 75, Winnebago Agency.

[34] Parker to Collier, February 24, 1936; Isaac Redowl to Parker, August 18, 1938; David Frazier *et al.*, to Collier, October 15, 1936; Xavier Vigeant to William Whipple, December 22, 1938; Vigeant to Ralph Bristol, January 14, 1939; Samuel H. Thompson, Supervisor of Indian Education, to Collier, December 2, 1938, *ibid.*; Niobrara *Tribune*, July 2, 1936, and October 7 and 14, 1937. The community building was burned in the spring of 1965, after serving the Santee tribe more than twenty-seven years.

and profoundly appreciative attitudes and discussions of the members of the Santee Sioux Tribal Council."[35]

The constitution and bylaws drawn up after acceptance of the IRA were designed to reflect the peculiar status of the Santees as Indians in an advanced stage of acculturation. For example, whereas many tribal constitutions gave the tribe jurisdiction over marriage and divorce practices, such a provision was omitted from the Santee constitution because these Indians "wanted to move in the direction of comprehensive State control over law and order and domestic relations rather than in the direction of tribal regulation of Indian custom marriages and Indian conduct."[36] After being approved by the Department of the Interior, the constitution and bylaws were accepted by the tribe, 284–60, on February 29, 1936. The council elected that year proved a more effective instrument of community policy than the old rubber-stamp body that had been instituted late in the nineteenth century and had existed nominally since then.[37]

Education was a central concern of the Collier administration, though at Santee it was distinctly subordinate, as a government activity, to other objectives, inasmuch as the reservation had long been incorporated into the county public school system. A specialist in Indian education visited six one-room schools and one two-room school in 1935 and found conditions markedly better than a similar tour of inspection nineteen years earlier had found them. Out of a total enrollment of 194 in those schools, 98 of the children were Indian. Their tuition was paid by the government. The rates varied from twenty-five to thirty cents a day at the smaller schools, and was forty cents at the two-room school, that at Santee village, where a lunch of soup, sandwiches, meat, fruit, doughnuts, and cocoa was served. Ten of the nineteen pupils there were Indians, all of whom attended regularly except for four from one family. The teachers all reported that the Indians did as well as the white children. In 1938 the same specialist found a great increase in enrollment, and a higher proportion of absenteeism among whites than among Indians.[38]

[35] Parker to Collier, June 24, 1937, NARS, RG 75, Winnebago Agency.

[36] Charlotte T. Westwood to Daiker, November 10, 1937, *ibid.*

[37] Niobrara *Tribune*, March 12, 1936. Some of the superintendents considered the old council more of a nuisance than an aid to them. See Superintendent's Annual Report, 1910, NARS, RG 75, Santee Agency.

[38] S. H. Thompson to Collier, January 29, 1935, and December 2, 1938, NARS, RG 75, Winnebago Agency.

In the middle 1930's the Santee Normal Training School was still functioning, under the direction of Rudolph Hertz, who had succeeded Frederick B. Riggs, son of Alfred L. Riggs, in 1933. Its enrollment was down to seventy-four boarding pupils and seven day pupils, but it employed twenty people, including six teachers, all with college degrees. In the spring of 1936 it ceased its long service to Indian young people and was transformed the following autumn into an institution for adult education, designed chiefly to provide refresher courses to families engaged in missionary work. Its career in this capacity was brief, however, and in 1938 the American Missionary Association disposed of several of the buildings, which were promptly wrecked for the lumber. The tribal council leased the land and some of the remaining buildings for use as living quarters for families who had not been benefited by the housing program.[39]

It would be pleasant to conclude this account of the Santee Reservation by reporting that the aims of the Collier administration were all achieved and the Indians placed in a position of economic security. Unfortunately, such was not the case. Just as the nation as a whole recovered very slowly from the effects of the Depression, so the Santees at the end of the 1930's were still far from self-sufficiency. Superintendent Parker was obliged to report in 1940 that the condition of all the Nebraska Indian groups was "one of almost total dependence upon Federal Government for work and direct relief; Agency allotments and WPA, Social Security, ADC, Old Age Assistance, NYA, and the like. . . ." He attributed the situation to more than ten years of drought and grasshopper infestations, livestock diseases, and lack of available employment for Indians off the reservation.[40]

During World War II the situation was somewhat alleviated because of the availability of work in war plants and the temporary employment of many men in the armed services. Judging from the census figures since 1940, many of the Santees who left the reservation during and after the war never returned. Between 1940 and 1960 there was a 65 per cent loss in the Indian population of the five townships that comprised the old Santee Reservation, as contrasted to a 13 per cent increase

---

[39] S. H. Thompson to Collier, January 29, 1935; lease dated May 1, 1939, between Board of Home Missions of the Congregational and Christian Churches and the Santee Tribe of Nebraska, *ibid.*; Niobrara *Tribune*, May 14, 1936, December 10, 1936, and June 30 and November 10, 1938.

[40] Parker to Collier, August 13, 1940, NARS, RG 75, Winnebago Agency.

between 1930 and 1940.[41] By 1960 there were only 317 Santees still living in the reservation area. In general and with many exceptions, it has been the most industrious and best-qualified who have left, with the result that the Indian Bureau and local agencies have continued to face many problems among those who have stayed behind.

One may wonder why the Nebraska reservation, alone among those occupied by the Santee Sioux, has suffered so extreme a decline in its resident population. Although no definitive answer can be given, certain factors, cultural and geographical, may go far toward accounting for the phenomenon. Cultural variations probably affect the differential rates of population increase or decline on the respective reservations. The people at Sisseton and Devils Lake are less acculturated than those at the other reservations and hence less likely to leave home and try their wings in the white-dominated society of the cities. The more highly acculturated people at Flandreau and the Minnesota colonies have more employment opportunities in the reservation area or within commuting distance than do those on the Santee Reservation. Santee is the only Santee Indian community that does not have a fair-sized town within reasonable commuting distance. Niobrara, the only nearby town, had a population of 736 in the 1960 census, as contrasted to 3,218 for Sisseton, South Dakota (in addition to Watertown [14,077] and others near the Sisseton Reservation); 2,129 for Flandreau, South Dakota, with its Indian school employing a sizable staff; 6,299 for Devils Lake, North Dakota; 2,728 for Granite Falls, Minnesota; 4,285 for Redwood Falls, Minnesota; and 10,528 for Red Wing, Minnesota.[42]

---

[41] *United States Census,* 1930, *Population,* Vol. III, Pt. 2, p. 117; 1940, Vol. II, Pt. 4, p. 681; 1960, Pt. 29B, pp. 60–61. The decennial census figures cannot be taken as entirely reliable. Only those who identify themselves as Indians are so classified, and it is possible that part of the increase in the 1930's reflects a greater willingness by some individuals to be regarded as Indians then. The figures given here are taken from the column headed "other," i.e., other than white or Negro.

[42] As will be noted in Chapter 17, the Flandreau people have in fact abandoned their "reservation" and are living in the town. The marked population growth noted among most of the Santee Sioux groups in the United States has been paralleled by an even more spectacular increase among the descendants of the Santees who fled into British territory after the Uprising of 1862. The total population of the seven reserves in Manitoba and Saskatchewan occupied by those people grew from 830 in 1904 to 1,922 in 1964. See Dominion of Canada, *Annual Report of the Department of Indian Affairs,* 1904, Pt. II, pp. 76–79; and *Traditional Linguistic and Cultural Affiliations of Canadian Indian Bands* (Ottawa: Indian Affairs Branch, Department of Citizenship and Immigration, 1964), pp. 25, 26, 27, 28.

Norfolk, Nebraska, with more than 13,000 people and a number of industries, is over seventy-five miles away—too far for convenient commuting but not too far to draw people permanently. Another factor is that conditions for successful agriculture are probably poorer at Santee than at any of the other locations. Though few Indians on any of the reservations do much farming, those at Santee may be indirectly affected in that they have a harder time making a living by leasing than the other groups do.

At the same time that the reservation population was declining, the alienation of allotted land, halted during the 1930's, was resumed. Although the tribal land purchased with IRA funds has remained intact, the amount of allotted land dropped from 3,252 acres in 1936 to 3,012 in 1952 and to 2,563 in 1960. In the next five years the acreage held almost steady.[43] The land remaining in Indian possession is widely scattered over the old reservation area, though there is some concentration at Santee village and along the streams. Because the topography is sharply dissected by ravines and lightly timbered with deciduous trees and brush, the acreage left to the Indians is not well suited to agriculture, except for occasional patches of bottomland. The scattered tracts of upland prairie are not occupied by the Indians, but are leased to white operators. Even here the land is rolling; and the roads, built on section lines, dip and rise with such frequency as to give the motorist a feeling of riding a roller coaster. Much of the old reservation, both Indian-owned and white-owned, is used only for grazing or is simply wasteland.

In the later 1940's and early 1950's, when there was much talk about "turning the Indians loose," it was inevitable that the Santee Sioux should be caught up in the controversy. Although they do not seem to have been among those most seriously considered for termination, the possibility was discussed. As on other reservations, there have been Indians at Santee who strongly favored such a move. They were usually either people who had themselves adapted successfully to white society and thought their tribesmen should do likewise, or people at the opposite extreme who resented the supervision of the Indian Bureau and wanted to be free to dispose of their land and spend the proceeds.

[43] Resolution to Commissioner, September 24, 1936, NARS, RG 75, Winnebago Agency; 82nd Cong., 2nd Sess., *H. Rpt. 2503*, p. 70; United States Department of Interior, *Reports*, September 1960, *United States Indian Population and Land: 1960*, p. 16; interviews, July 9, 1962, with Mr. Llewellyn Kingsley, and July 20, 1965, with Mr. Alfred Dubray, successive superintendents, Winnebago Agency, Winnebago, Nebraska.

An early and unsuccessful move in the direction of termination was made in 1941, when several members of the tribal council went to Washington to seek "full citizenship" for the Santees. Again in 1948 the Niobrara *Tribune* carried a bitter attack on the Indian Bureau for not having brought the Indians out of poverty. Despite the "enormous salaries dished out to its many millions of employees," there were still Indians living in poverty. Perhaps, suggested the writer, the Indian Service was able to help the Indians only once every fifteen years. In any case, he concluded, "It is about time that an investigation be made but very secretly in order that not one stone shall be left unturned."[44] The Santees were generally opposed to termination, however, and their opposition, coupled with their poor economic status, kept the proposal from going beyond the talking stage when it was revived in the 1950's.

The condition of the Santees in the mid-1960's remains depressed in comparison with that of the non-Indian population in the same region. Few are trying to farm the small tracts they have left, and it is doubtful that those farms could be made economically productive, even if the needed capital were available. In Knox County, as elsewhere on the Great Plains, there has been a general decline in the rural population in the past few decades. Between 1930 and 1940, when the Indian population of the reservation area was increasing, the *total* reservation population declined by 23 per cent. And between 1940 and 1960, when the Indian population declined 65 per cent, the *total* population dropped by more than 73 per cent.[45] It may be presumed that where white farmers are unable to make a satisfactory living, Indians, with fewer advantages and more handicaps, will also be unable to do so. Though there has been talk of starting a concrete plant on the reservation, no capital for the purpose has been made available. The area appears to have no other natural resources, except for the recreational potential of Lewis and Clark Lake, the reservoir created by the Gavins Point Dam. Most of the shoreline is owned by the Army Corps of Engineers or by the state, however, and the Santee tribe is not in a position to profit, except indirectly, from the tourist trade.[46]

[44] 83rd Cong., 2nd Sess., *H. Rpt. 2680*, pp. 95–96, 483; Niobrara *Tribune*, February 6, 1941, and January 22, 1948. *House Report 2680*, containing information submitted by field officers of the Bureau in 1953, stated that except for the tribal lands and government, the Santees had "practically ceased to exist as a tribe" and recommended termination in a period not to exceed fifteen years.

[45] See decennial census references in Note 41.

[46] Interview with Mr. Dubray, July 20, 1965. The Santee tribe requested $10,000 for the development of recreational facilities, but according to a Bureau official, "the entire sum was dissipated to minor stands and service facilities located near the lake

Younger people continue to leave the area for urban centers, ranging from small nearby cities like Norfolk to distant metropolises like Los Angeles. Some of them have found a satisfactory place in American life; others may only have exchanged rural poverty for urban poverty. The resident population at Santee has continued to decline in recent years, dropping from 317 in 1960 to 299 in 1962, and it includes a high proportion of the elderly and unemployable.[47] In this respect, as in others, Santee resembles many other Indian reservations in the country. If the Santees are no worse off economically than most other Indians, this fact is small comfort to them—and slight balm to the conscience of the white man.

---

with unrealistic salary payments." See R. E. Miller, Acting Area Director, to Acting Commissioner of Indian Affairs, July 18, 1961, Flandreau School Agency; correspondence in possession of Bureau of Indian Affairs Central Office, Washington, D.C.

[47] *United States Indian Population and Land: 1960*, p. 16; interview with Mr. Kingsley, July 9, 1962.

CHAPTER **16**

The Twentieth Century: Sisseton and Devils Lake

THE PRINCIPAL THEMES on the Sisseton and Devils Lake reservations during the first thirty years of this century were the rapid attrition of the Indians' land base, the disappearance of most of the externals of their aboriginal culture, and the gradual reduction of government services and supervision. Although these processes went on everywhere on allotted reservations, the pattern varied from one to another, depending on the degree of acculturation achieved before 1900, the nature and quality of the land on each reservation, the density of white settlement around and among the Indians, and the personalities of the various men who represented the Indian Bureau at each agency.

Like the Santees, the Sissetons were vitally affected by two pieces of legislation passed in the first decade of the century: a provision in the Indian appropriations act of 1902 permitting the sale of inherited lands, and the Burke Act of 1906 authorizing the Secretary of the Interior to issue patents to any Indian thought competent to handle his own affairs. The sale of inherited lands began at once, and by the summer of 1903 more than two hundred tracts had been advertised and most of them sold. So prodigal were the Indians with the money received that in 1905 the Indian Office issued an order requiring that all funds received from the sale of lands be deposited in banks and all checks on those deposits be approved by the agent. Although this order caused sales to fall off sharply for a few years, the total deposits by 1910 amounted to $271,441, which, at the average price of $14 per acre realized on the early sales, represented nearly 20,000 acres.[1] In the next decade annual sales rose once more. In 1911 alone, nearly 5,000 acres of inherited lands were sold, together with more than 3,500 acres of land belonging to Indians judged "non-competent" by the criteria mentioned earlier (see p. 298). For the next several years it was unusual when sales from these two sources totaled less than 3,000 acres.[2] Still, the Indians had started out with 300,000 acres; at that rate it would take nearly a century for all the lands to be lost.

The Burke Act provided another means by which their lands might be diverted into the hands of the eagerly waiting white men. Between the passage of the act in May, 1906, and September 1, 1907, thirty-one applications for patents had been favorably acted upon, and the only reason there were not more was that the Sisseton agent and his clerks were so weighted down with paper work connected with farming and grazing leases and the sales of inherited and non-competent lands that they were unable to process the applications as fast as they were presented. This bottleneck was to some degree relieved in the following years. In 1911, for example, forty patents were issued, for a total of more than 3,500 acres. The next year the number was down, however, and it continued to decrease in subsequent years, mainly because the superintendents saw the iniquitous effects of issuing patents and did what they could to discourage it. As early as 1910, Superintendent S. E. Allen reported that 90 per cent of the fee patent land had been sold.[3]

Despite such observations by men in a position to know the situation, the process of granting patents and selling inherited lands continued. In 1917, Commissioner Sells attempted to "liberalize" the issuance of patents by ordering them given to Indians regardless of the individual's wishes. He was frustrated in this policy, but not before more land had

[1] Com. of Indian Affairs, *Annual Report*, 1903, p. 321; U.S. *Statutes at Large*, XXXII, 275; XXXIV, 182.

[2] Com. of Indian Affairs, *Annual Report*, 1904, p. 338; 1905, pp. 279, 347; 1907, p. 73; Superintendent's Annual Reports, 1910, 1911, and 1912, NARS, RG 75, Sisseton Agency.

[3] *Ibid.*, 1907, p. 63; Superintendent's Annual Reports, 1910, 1911, 1912, 1913, NARS, RG 75, Sisseton Agency.

been disposed of.[4] High land prices during World War I led to a renewal of large sales of inherited lands. An exceptionally large sale in 1919 made it possible to equip many of the Sissetons with good houses and outbuildings, but this ready money, together with high wages during the war, caused them to neglect their farming, so that when land prices fell and the agricultural depression of the 1920's settled over the Middle West, they were in a poorer position than ever and more dependent on a government less willing to help them.[5]

As at Santee, of course, much of the land remaining in Indian hands was not actually used by them. Leasing began here early and soon developed into the principal source of regular income for a large proportion of the landowners. The Indians' logic was quite understandable. In a country where crop failure was a frequent occurrence, they preferred the security of a fixed, if small, payment to the risk of losing everything in a year of drought or grasshopper infestation. Leases negotiated through the agent brought them from twenty-five or forty cents an acre for grazing land to a dollar an acre for broken farm land. Together with what they raised in subsistence gardens or earned by day labor, it was enough to keep them alive, though not enough to enable them to live in anything approaching comfort.[6]

Although a later superintendent thought the Indians made more off their lands by leasing than they could by farming, the effort to make farmers out of them did not cease during this period. Some cheerful statistics were provided by the superintendent in 1910, but by 1929 it was said that only about twenty-six Indians were really farming like white men; most of the rest had nothing but gardens and a few chickens.[7] This decline—and one does not have to take the earlier figures literally to accept the fact of a decline—occurred in spite of strenuous efforts by the government and its local representatives to get the Sissetons on their feet. The number of supervisory personnel was increased, a reimbursable loan plan was instituted, a five-year plan was inaugurated in the early 1920's, and stock was issued to Indian farmers. None of these experiments seems to have accomplished much, partly because of drought and economic depression, partly because the Indians did not

[4] Harold E. Fey and D'Arcy McNickle, *Indians and Other Americans* (New York: Harper and Brothers, 1959), p. 81.

[5] Superintendent's Annual Reports, 1922 and 1923, NARS, RG 75, Sisseton Agency.

[6] Com. of Indian Affairs, *Annual Report*, 1903, p. 231; 1904, p. 338.

[7] Superintendent's Annual Reports, 1910, 1921, and 1929, NARS, RG 75, Sisseton Agency.

pay back the loans, partly because the government farmers were not retained. Other, more or less peripheral, measures to encourage farming among the Indians included the initiation of a reservation fair in 1911 and the organization of farmers' clubs in the 1920's.[8]

Besides the climatic and economic obstacles to successful farming, the superintendents at Sisseton complained that their efforts were impeded by certain characteristics of the Indians, presumably survivals of the aboriginal culture. They objected to the persistence of the old dances, for the same reasons that their counterparts at Santee did, and they attempted, with partial success, to suppress them. Some of the superintendents thought that the Sisseton's collective ethical system militated against their success as farmers in an individualistic economy. So long as the successful ones were obliged to share the proceeds of their efforts with the rest of the tribe, there was little hope of progress, thought one. Some of the Indians were prodigal with what they raised. In spite of the superintendent's urging to save seed each year, they would sell the whole crop and then appear at the agency office the next spring asking for seed wheat, to be paid for out of the money on deposit there from land sales. Such a request placed the superintendent in an awkward position. Although he thought they should be taught to exercise more foresight, he also knew that if he refused to allow them to buy seed, they would not farm at all.[9]

Not all of the habits and practices that prevented the Sissetons from becoming good farmers were distinctively Indian, however. Superintendent E. D. Mossman meant no compliment when he said that the Indians cared for their farm machinery the same as white men in that region, for he added that they let it stand out in all weather. "They have an idea that as soon as a mower has two or three guards broken, and sickle rusts," he remarked, "that instead of spending $5.00 for a new sickle or guards, they should purchase a new mower."[10] Nor was the drinking done by the Indians noticeably worse than that among white men. Since it was more difficult for them to obtain liquor, they resorted to some expedients that whites did not discover until prohibition. As early as 1914 they were buying Peruna and other patent medicines with a high alcohol content, as well as lemon and other extracts. Prohibition brought stills, mostly operated by white men who

[8] *Ibid.*, 1910, 1911, 1913, 1915, 1916, 1919, 1920, 1921, 1922, 1924, 1926, 1927, 1928, and 1929.
[9] *Ibid.*, 1915, 1917, 1918, and 1929.
[10] *Ibid.*, 1915.

sold to Indians quite as freely as to others. By that time the Indians (and whites) were drinking canned heat, body rub, hair tonic, and anything else that contained alcohol or a passable substitute. A favorite practice was to drive to a garage, have the car radiator filled with denatured alcohol, then drive home and drain the radiator. One superintendent wrote that in this way the Indians had "two and one-half gallons of intoxicant that will keep the family drunk for a week for less than $3.00."[11]

Except for their willingness to sell moonshine to the Indians, lease their lands (illegally if possible), and buy up the farms of those who had been issued patents, the white people on and around the Sisseton Reservation were not inclined to have much to do with their Indian neighbors. Although the Indians were permitted to vote and to sit on juries, many whites were prejudiced against them as a race because of the laziness and shiftlessness of a few. As one superintendent remarked, "Many persons fail to observe the industrious Indian working in his field, but always see and remember the Indian loafing on the street corner or drunk in the ditch."[12] Here as elsewhere the tax-exempt status of Indian land was a source of resentment on the part of the white community, evidenced by the reluctance of local officials to prosecute cases involving crimes by or against Indians and also by their opposition to admitting Indian children into district schools. The fact that the Indians paid property and poll taxes did not impress their white neighbors, who were opposed to much intermingling of the races on other grounds.[13] The closing of the boarding school in 1919 and the removal of the agency into the town of Sisseton in 1923 conspired to encourage more contacts between Indians and whites. Yet the separation continued, despite the efforts of at least one superintendent to make local whites aware that the Indian was not a vanishing race but was "to live with the white man for all time to come. . . ."[14]

To assign the blame for this de facto segregation exclusively to the white population would be to oversimplify the situation. No doubt there was discrimination on the part of the whites, as when the barbers in Browns Valley refused to shave Indians, but it does not wholly account for the continued separation of the races in a locality where they were geographically intermingled and where the Indians necessarily

[11] *Ibid.*, 1914, 1915, 1917, 1923, 1924, and 1926.
[12] *Ibid.*, 1910 and 1913.
[13] *Ibid.*, 1915, 1917, and 1918.
[14] *Ibid.*, 1919, 1920, 1923, 1925, and 1926.

came into frequent contact with white businessmen. The Indians had their own churches and their own social and other organizations, and they were to a considerable extent indifferent to association with the whites. Those who did associate freely were mostly mixed-bloods of predominantly white ancestry. The Dakota language continued to be used as the daily medium of conversation, and the extreme irregularity of attendance at any school meant that as late as 1915 many young people were unable to speak English. When the attempt to Christianize the Indians was in full swing, one of the arguments was that a common religion would forge a bond between red man and white. Yet as religion manifested itself at Sisseton, the Christian churches contributed to the separation of the races. In 1911 all but one of the twelve churches on the reservation were served by native clergymen, who used the Dakota tongue almost exclusively. Their associations with churches off the reservation were confined largely to other native congregations.[15]

Although the Indians remained in most cases a race apart, it cannot be said that they retained much of their aboriginal culture into the twentieth century, except for the Dakota language. Aside from a little beadwork, the superintendent in 1910 could report no native arts and crafts. The old dances, as we have seen, became less frequent as the years passed. They had long since lost their religious significance and had become merely a form of entertainment. Christian church organizations had usurped their former position, and most of the social activity on the reservation was connected with the churches and guild halls in the various neighborhoods. Something of the old collectivism may have persisted within these neighborhood groups, but any sense of tribal unity was dying out during this period. After a spell of factional dissension, the tribal council was voted out of existence in 1911. In the early 1920's a committee was appointed to look after the tribe's pending

---

[15] *Ibid.*, 1911, 1914, 1915, 1916, and 1922. The denominational composition changed gradually after the Presbyterian monopoly was broken. By 1911 four of the twelve churches were Episcopal, and one was Catholic. One superintendent's observation in 1915 that the Presbyterians were less effective as missionaries than the other groups would seem to be borne out by the fact that by the middle of the century about 46 per cent of the Sissetons were Episcopalians, as against nearly 28 per cent Catholics and less than 25 per cent Presbyterians. A handful belonged to millennialist or pentecostal groups. Until 1912, however, the Presbyterians maintained the Good Will mission school, which supplemented the work of the government boarding school. See Superintendent's Annual Reports, 1911 and 1912, in *ibid.*; 83rd Cong., 2nd Sess., *H. Rpt. 2680*, p. 147. The percentages are based on 1,813 Indians and do not include the entire reservation population.

Bishop Whipple School, Lower Sioux Indian Community (Birch Coulee), built in 1891. Photograph taken in 1961

Sioux family and tipi, Prairie Island, 1902

Traders' stores, with unused agency building between them, Santee
Agency, 1912

Santee Sioux dancers, Santee Agency, 1918

Courtesy of the Minnesota Historical Society

Dance at the dedication of the Lower Sioux community building, 1938

Old agency day school and community building, Sisseton Reservation. Photograph taken in 1965.

Encampment on the Big Sioux River at the Flandreau "Siouxtennial,"
1962.

Indian farm and typical Devils Lake Reservation landscape. Photograph taken in 1965.

claims, but its powers were severely limited. In short, the Sisseton Sioux were neither a tribe nor a people, but merely an aggregation of families and individuals scattered over an expanse of country, separated from one another by members of a culture still alien to many of them, a culture which did not fully accept them and which many of them did not wish to participate in.[16]

Events on the Devils Lake Reservation followed much the same course as at Sisseton during the first three decades of the twentieth century. Perhaps the most significant difference was that the "surplus" lands left after allotment were not disposed of until 1904, and the Indians enjoyed the benefits from the sale of the lands for the next ten years. James McLaughlin, serving as a special agent of the Indian Office, drew up an agreement in November, 1901, by the terms of which the Indians agreed to cede about 100,000 acres. The original agreement, providing that they should be paid a flat sum of $345,000, was amended by Congress so that the total amount paid would be determined by the price at which the lands were sold. In this form the agreement was ratified on April 27, 1904, and the greater part of the cession was opened to settlement the next September.[17] The price initially asked was $4.50 an acre, but the lands left unsold by 1907, mostly hilly and stony or else in small tracts, were made available at $2.50 an acre. Although the lands did not sell rapidly, their gradual sale provided a regular income for the Indians, since the proceeds were distributed in per capita payments. The last payments were made in 1914, after which the Devils Lake Indians were in much the same position financially as those at Sisseton.[18]

Although beginning later, the sale of inherited land and the issuance of patents went on at Devils Lake as at Sisseton. Because of an unusually high mortality rate among allottees, land sales were proportionately more extensive than at Sisseton or Santee. In 1906, for example,

[16] Superintendent's Annual Reports, 1910, 1911, and 1923, NARS, RG 75, Sisseton Agency.

[17] Com. of Indian Affairs, *Annual Report*, 1902, p. 263; 1904, p. 4; 1905, p. 279; U.S. *Statutes at Large*, XXXIII, 319–324. Available acreage figures are not consistent. The *Annual Report* for 1901 gives the "surplus" lands as 98,224 acres, whereas that for 1902 gives the figure as 110,576 acres. In 1904 it was listed as 104,000 acres.

[18] Charles J. Kappler, comp. and ed., *Indian Affairs, Laws and Treaties*, I (Washington: Government Printing Office, 1904), 597–598; U.S. *Statutes at Large*, XXXIII, 2368–2372; XXXV, 2143; Superintendent's Annual Report, 1914, NARS, RG 75, Fort Totten Agency.

$51,212.53 was received from the sale of inherited lands, and the next year 3,253.61 acres went for $33,944.10. In 1912, $64,743.23 was realized from the sale of such lands, and three years later the superintendent reported, jubilantly, that the sale just completed had been the best in several years.[19] Clearly the process could not go on for many more years without leading to almost total loss of the Indians' land. Fortunately, by 1917 the agency was in the charge of a superintendent, Samual A. M. Young, who realized what was happening. "Extensive land sales help to give the appearance of prosperity," he wrote, "while an analysis of the situation shows that capital is daily being used up and not replaced." He believed that the inevitable end would be financial ruin and a return to the ration system. He asserted his intention of holding the line on future land sales, saying, "It is much easier to retain lands than it is to retain funds after they are placed to the credit of the Indian."[20]

The issuance of patents seems at first not to have led to the sale of lands, but by 1912 the superintendent had to admit that some of the Indians who had been given patents were selling out. After the restrictions on the allotments at Devils Lake expired in 1918, the period of inalienability was extended another ten years. Superintendent Young strongly recommended this action and even went so far as to utter heresy: "I am convinced that the Dawes Act and the Burke Act, held as being so great a boon to the Indians, have been very baneful in their effects."[21] Unfortunately, his views were not shared by some of his successors. W. R. Beyer, who was superintendent in 1925, expressed the view that every young, able-bodied Indian who spoke English should be given a patent and cut off from government supervision.[22] The issuance of patents, together with the sale of inherited lands, went on throughout the 1920's and virtually up to the passage of the Indian Reorganization Act in 1934.

The Indians at Devils Lake were encouraged to farm for themselves by means of the same devices employed at Sisseton, and with no more success. Several years of drought, the temptation to lease lands, dwindling government assistance, and, after 1914, a lack of capital all con-

[19] Com. of Indian Affairs, *Annual Report*, 1901, p. 297; 1904, p. 267; 1906, p. 293; 1907, p. 73; Superintendent's Annual Reports, 1912 and 1915, NARS, RG 75, Fort Totten Agency.

[20] Superintendent's Annual Report, 1917, NARS, RG 75, Fort Totten Agency.

[21] *Ibid.*, 1910, 1912, 1918.

[22] *Ibid.*, 1925.

tributed to the failure of this effort. For a time the agents tried to induce the Indians to make flax their principal crop, in imitation of the surrounding white farmers, but this venture into a one-crop economy failed because of soil exhaustion and competition from better-equipped white men. The reimbursable loan plan was tried at Devils Lake, first in 1915, when $8,000 was used for the purchase of seed grains, and then revived in the later 1920's as a means of supplying the Indians with cows and sheep. By that time, however, drought had been a regular visitor too long for any half-measures to accomplish much toward the Indians' rehabilitation.[23]

Besides their chronic poverty—which was only increased during World War I as a result of the high cost of living—the Devils Lake Indians suffered more from disease than the Sisseton group. F. O. Getchell, their agent in 1901, attributed their susceptibility to pulmonary diseases to the shift from a healthy outdoor life to one spent largely indoors, in unventilated and overheated cabins. Most continued to live in log houses throughout the early 1900's, supplemented by tipis in the summer. The health situation was somewhat alleviated by the construction of a hospital in 1915, but many Indians were reluctant to use it. In World War I a dozen or more tried to volunteer but were rejected because of tuberculosis, trachoma, or other diseases. The Indians' poor health was given as one reason the whites were unwilling to send their children to the same schools as the Indian children.[24]

Educationally, the Devils Lake reservation was better supplied than Sisseton. Although as late as 1921 only six children were in public schools, the Fort Totten Boarding School, including the Grey Nuns' department, provided facilities for most of the children, though under appallingly crowded conditions. In 1916 they were said to be crowded twelve to eighteen in a room, with just enough room between the beds for a small child to walk. Supervisor Otis B. Goodall remarked that "the condition of the air when they arise in the morning is easier imagined than described." Infection traveled swiftly under such conditions, especially with only six bathtubs for 120 boys and one roller towel serving for a week.[25]

[23] *Ibid.*, 1910, 1913, 1914, 1915, 1916, and 1917; Com. of Indian Affairs, *Annual Report*, 1904, p. 268.

[24] Com. of Indian Affairs, *Annual Report*, 1901, p. 298; 1904, p. 268; Superintendent's Annual Reports, 1915 and 1918, NARS, RG 75, Fort Totten Agency.

[25] Superintendent's Annual Reports, 1916 and 1925, NARS, RG 75, Fort Totten Agency.

The boarding school proper, located at the old military post, enrolled mostly children from other reservations, while the Grey Nuns' school accommodated the girls and younger boys from Devils Lake. A day school was opened in 1902 for the older boys, but the bonded superintendent who succeeded Agent Getchell two years later thought it unnecessary and apparently did away with it. The anomaly of a government school in which all but two of the employees were nuns struck one or two of the superintendents, and in about 1920 government support was withdrawn from the Grey Nuns' school, which thereafter was supported entirely by the Catholic Church. It burned late in 1926, and was rebuilt and reopened in 1929 as the Mission School of the Little Flower. By that time nearly forty children, mostly mixed-bloods whose parents lived on fee patent land, were enrolled in the public schools.[26]

More of the old culture persisted at Devils Lake than at Sisseton. Besides the survival of the Dakota language, there were certain institutions such as a police force and a court of Indian offenses that tended to keep the Indians separate from the white community. In time the tribal court came to be used chiefly as a means of conciliation in family and neighborhood disputes, effective only if all parties accepted its nonmandatory decisions. Although as early as 1901 the Episcopal missionary was encouraging the Indians to take their cases to the local courts, the state and county authorities showed the same reluctance to act that we have noted at Sisseton. This refusal left a gap in the law-and-order system on the reservation, which was partly filled in 1920 when a federal judge in Fargo ruled that the state had jurisdiction in the case of the murder of one Indian by another. When the superintendent tried in 1929 to revive the institutions of the tribal judge and police force, outside groups threatened to bring suit against him on grounds that such a judge was illegal, and he abandoned the effort.[27]

The survival of authentic aboriginal culture was much less in evidence than this persistence of group identity. Nevertheless, the old dances continued. Each of the four districts into which the reservation was divided had its own dance hall, where the ceremonies were carried on, mainly by older members of the tribe. Superintendent Young saw no harm in the dances and thought that any suppression would produce

[26] *Ibid.*, 1918, 1927, and 1930; Com. of Indian Affairs, *Annual Report*, 1903, p. 231; 1904, p. 267; 1905, p. 280.

[27] Com. of Indian Affairs, *Annual Report*, 1901, pp. 297–298; 1903, p. 230; Superintendent's Annual Reports, 1920 and 1929, NARS, RG 75, Fort Totten Agency.

resentment and thereby frustrate his exercise of a beneficial influence in other respects. Whatever other survivals of the old culture there were did not come to the notice of the agents and superintendents. One official reported in 1911 that, although beadwork and basketry were taught at the school, there were no native industries left among the Indians.[28]

The Sioux of the Sisseton and Devils Lake reservations had reached approximately the same point by the end of the 1920's. As on the other reservations, the Depression revealed their true condition, which had been partially concealed behind a superficial appearance of progress. There was much tentative groping for a solution to the problem by all who were concerned in the matter. On the Sisseton Reservation it took the form of suggestions for meeting the heirship situation, which by the early 1930's had become so serious that at least 25,000 acres of land lay idle because potential lessees were unwilling to hunt up the scattered heirs whose signatures were needed on leases. With the land base down to less than 120,000 acres and the population up to 2,700, something had to be done, and soon. One superintendent suggested in 1932 that all inherited land be bought up by the government and divided into forty-acre tracts to be used as subsistence farms by young Indians who had no allotments of their own. If this was impossible, the only alternative he could offer was to sell all the inherited lands and close the agency.[29]

The heirship problem was to become worse before any real attempt was made to improve it; and, pending basic reforms, there were other needs that had to be met. As at Santee, the first step was to provide jobs, through the various public works agencies, for Indians who would otherwise have required direct relief. Men were employed in building roads, repairing houses, clearing out and thinning woodlands to reduce the fire danger, and performing other tasks of a useful though not essential nature. Fred A. Baker, who became superintendent in 1933, regretted that the $92,000 used for this purpose by June 30, 1934, had not been expended for subsistence homesteads. As it was, he felt that the Indians were not really any better off than they had been before, whereas if they had been placed on subsistence homesteads they would

[28] Superintendent's Annual Reports, 1911 and 1917, NARS, RG 75, Fort Totten Agency.

[29] Superintendent's Annual Reports, 1931 and 1932; Fred A. Baker to John Collier, February 12, 1934, NARS, RG 75, Sisseton Agency. Baker gives the figure of 68,000 acres lying idle.

have received the same amount of employment and would have been "better fitted to make their way in life."[30]

Baker was convinced that the Indians' future was bound up with the reservation and that efforts to aid them should be concentrated on helping them to become self-sustaining on the land they had left. He thought that if the idle land and that leased to whites could be made available for use by the landless members of the tribe, there would be enough to go around without substantial additional purchases. To accomplish this, the government would have to provide a revolving reimbursable fund from which the lands could be purchased from the heirs. When his proposal was first broached to the Indians in February, 1934, at a council called to discuss the Collier administration's plans for Indian self-government, it received a favorable vote of 81 to 45. But when they voted on acceptance of the Indian Reorganization Act, the result was a decisive rejection of the central feature of the Collier policy.[31] With the defeat of the IRA, Baker's plans for land purchases went out the window, and with them went the major hope for rehabilitating the Sisseton people.

Why did the Sissetons reject the IRA? Baker provided the answer, or a good part of it, in the text of a proposal for a rehabilitation program prepared some time before the vote. Remarking that little sense of tribal unity survived among the Sissetons, he pointed out that individualism had become predominant, and "collective effort in a cooperative way has found but little place in the life of the Indians of this reservation." According to Baker, they took pride in their progress toward civilization, and in the fact that they were like white people; hence they had "little inclination to resume tribal government or tribal customs" and wished to continue in the path they had been following since before allotment. When an early draft of the Wheeler-Howard Act (IRA) was presented to them, they had "expressed themselves as deeply resenting the formation of Indian communities" as provided there.[32] So well had Joseph R. Brown, Moses N. Adams, and other agents—not to mention Henry L. Dawes—accomplished their task that the Sisseton Sioux were psychologically unable to accept the proffered hand of the government when it was finally extended in the spirit of co-operation and friendship rather than as the mailed fist of authority.

[30] Baker to Collier, February 17, 1934, NARS, RG 75, Sisseton Agency.

[31] Baker to Collier, February 12, 1934; Superintendent's Annual Report, 1934–1935, in *ibid.*

[32] "Rehabilitation Program for the Sisseton-Wahpeton Sioux Tribe of Indians, Sisseton Indian Agency, South Dakota, Fred A. Baker, Supt.," June 4, 1935, in *ibid.*

The course of events at Devils Lake resembled that at Sisseton. Work relief and the dole were the first forms of government assistance, but soon the superintendent, Orrin C. Gray, began to think in terms of subsistence homesteads, to be set up on submarginal land purchased for the purpose. Here, too, individualism had progressed far enough to make the outlook dim at best. Some of the Indians had qualms about the subsistence homestead idea, for they objected to paying for communal property that they might not use. The land situation was nearly as bad as at Sisseton, except that the population had not been growing so alarmingly. About two-thirds of the land originally allotted had been disposed of, and two-thirds of what was left was tied up in a complex heirship tangle. Less than 50,000 acres remained, and 10,000 of that was either entirely useless or rough grazing land.[33] Although a subsistence homestead program might provide a solution for a few families, clearly a massive land exchange and consolidation project was in order if the situation were really to be remedied.

When the Devils Lake Indians voted on the IRA, on November 17, 1934, they rejected it, though not as decisively as the Sissetons. According to a member of the tribe who favored the act, anti-New Deal agitators had contributed to its defeat by spreading false rumors, "like no Indian will hold any property individually and the whole Act was a scheme to strip the Indians of whatever lands they have left and that they will be subject to forced labor and will be no better than convicts under government and such stuff."[34]

Even though rejection of the IRA on both reservations frustrated the hope of a thoroughgoing land reform, much was done to help the Sisseton and Devils Lake people during the 1930's. At Sisseton the Indian Division of the Civilian Conservation Corps built roads and truck trails, constructed a dam near the old Good Will mission, developed springs, carried out a rodent control program, and developed two picnic and camping areas. The dam was used to impound water for a small

[33] Superintendent's Annual Reports, 1931 and 1932; Orrin C. Gray to Collier, February 7, 1934; Elna N. Smith to A. C. Cooley, October 27, 1934, NARS, RG 75, Fort Tottten Agency.

[34] Louis DeWolf to Collier, n.d. (received January 22, 1936); Fred H. Daiker to DeWolf, February 18, 1936; Joseph Twobear to Collier, January 23, 1936, *ibid*. The vote showed 144 in favor, 233 opposed, and 144 eligible voters who did not participate. In its original form, the Wheeler-Howard Act specified that a majority of the eligible voters of a tribe had to vote against it for it to be rejected. Under this interpretation, the Devils Lake Indians were understood to have placed themselves under its provisions. But in 1935, Congress amended the act so as to require a majority of the votes cast for acceptance. This amendment barred Devils Lake from participation in the IRA.

irrigation project. A four-and-one-half-acre garden plot was irrigated, and ten houses were built, together with some outbuildings. At the site of the old boarding school a root cellar was constructed. When emphasis was placed on canning and preserving food for winter use, many Indian women used the cellar as a canning room. Later a community self-help building was erected for that purpose. All of these projects were designed both to give temporary employment to some of the men and to provide several families with part of their subsistence.[35]

Housing was a major problem on the Sisseton Reservation. As late as 1936 there were 517 families on the reservation, living in fewer than 300 houses. It was common for as many as five families to be occupying one house, with perhaps ten people to a room. To alleviate the situation, Baker proposed the construction of 100 houses and repairs to 150 others. As with all the other projects deemed necessary at Sisseton, this one fell far short of the superintendent's wishes. Although about 85 houses were built or repaired between 1936 and 1940, some people were still living in tents at the end of the decade.[36]

Health and education were two other major concerns on the Sisseton Reservation. In 1934 Baker listed construction of a thirty-five-bed hospital as the most immediate need of the people there; and in May, 1937, such a hospital was opened. So long as extreme congestion in living quarters remained the rule, however, the general health of the Sisseton people could not be radically improved. The effort to improve educational facilities for the Indians centered about the establishment of day schools. Baker and his successor, W. C. Smith, faced up to the fact that not enough children were attending the district schools, which had been located with reference to the convenience of the white farmers and not of the Indians. Although a great many went to Flandreau, Pipestone, or Wahpeton, or to mission schools, Baker and Smith did not see the off-reservation boarding school as the answer to local educational needs. After an experiment with day schools conducted in guild halls, in 1939 a day school was erected at Big Coulee, followed by another at Enemy Swim. Besides their primary function, they also served as community centers, since the dispersion of the Indians over a wide area made it impossible for all to use the community self-help building.[37]

[35] Baker to Collier, February 17, 1934; W. C. Smith to Collier, August 19, 1939; Charles L. Ellis to Collier, October 26, 1940, NARS, RG 75, Sisseton Agency.

[36] "Rehabilitation Program," June 4, 1934; W. C. Smith to Collier, July 9, 1938; Superintendent's Annual Reports, 1936–1937 and 1938–1939, *ibid.*

[37] "Rehabilitation Program," June 4, 1934; Superintendent's Annual Reports, 1936–1937 and 1938–1939, *ibid.* A day school was later built at Long Hollow, and the

Similar progress took place at Devils Lake. The central project there was the subsistence homestead plan, which got under way in April, 1936, with the construction of thirteen log houses on concrete foundations. The experiment began at an inauspicious time, for North Dakota was then in the throes of the worst drought in its history. The attempt to provide subsistence for thirteen families from the land proved unsuccessful, and the participants in the experiment became discouraged. Since there was not enough work available in the locality, they had to turn to "made" jobs with the agency. By the beginning of 1940 several of the original participants had left, most of them delinquent in their rent payments, and all but one of the remaining occupants of the houses were delinquent.[38]

A few other developments at Devils Lake merit mention. The Fort Totten boarding school was closed in 1935 and reopened the same year as a preventorium school for children with tubercular tendencies. Two day schools were opened in outlying parts of the reservation in 1937 but later abandoned. About 140 children were attending public schools by the later 1930's, and about 150 were at the Little Flower mission.[39] A central canning kitchen and community sewing room was started in 1936, the former benefiting at least fifty families, the latter, about a hundred. Some effort was made to revive native arts and crafts. The principal handicraft project was the manufacture of moccasins, Indian dolls, and other articles out of buckskin decorated with beadwork designs. Eighteen workers, mainly women with families, were employed on this project. Road work under the CCC provided jobs for a number of men, and others were employed in repairing and painting the agency buildings.[40]

In spite of all these measures taken by the Indian Bureau to improve the condition of the Sisseton and Devils Lake Indians, no fundamental

community self-help building was converted to use as a day school. Except for the one at Long Hollow, which was sold to the district, all the schools were still in operation by the Bureau in 1965.

[38] E. N. Smith to Cooley, October 27, 1934; List of Homestead Assignees, January 8, 1940; James H. Hyde to Collier, January 8, 1941; Superintendent's Annual Reports, 1934, 1936, and 1938, NARS, RG 75, Fort Totten Agency.

[39] Superintendent's Annual Reports, 1935, 1936, and 1937, *ibid.*

[40] Gray to Collier, June 8, 1936; Superintendent's Annual Report, 1938, *ibid.* In 1938, a fairly typical year, the income from work relief amounted to $43,341.79; an additional sum of $54,566.99 was received from federal, state, and county relief, and $12,477.62 was received from leases, hay permits, grazing and trespass—a total of $110,346.30 for the year, in addition to surplus commodities distributed through the county welfare board and an undetermined but small amount of earned income from off-reservation employment.

change could be effected without coming to grips with the land situation. Baker recognized from the start of his administration that the basic problem stemmed from the allotment of land in severalty. In his first annual report he denounced the allotment system, which he said had destroyed the economic unity of the land, made its use by livestock associations impossible, and deprived later generations of the land-holdings to which they were entitled. The issuance of patents had brought about the loss of lands; the sale of inherited lands had further depleted the reservation resources; and the inheritance of allotted lands had produced endless confusion, destroyed the Indians' initiative, and fastened on them the leasing system. About 92 per cent of the land at Sisseton was in heirship status, most of it so fractionated as to be virtually useless to its owners or to anyone else. It was even difficult to make contracts for repairs to houses on allotments because of the time needed to track down all the heirs whose signatures were required.[41]

The degree to which fractionation had progressed by the 1930's is almost incredible. An individual equity in a 160-acre farm might amount to as little as a 20-foot square. When Superintendent Smith was called upon to divide the wheat produced on an 80-acre tract, he found that the eleven Indians who owned the smallest equities would each receive 1,344 grains. The extreme case was that of the allotment of Akipa (Joseph Renville), who had died in 1891 and whose land was now owned by more than 150 heirs. Probating the estate cost $2,400 and required more than 250 typewritten pages. If the land were sold at its appraised value, Arie Redearth's share would have been 1.6 cents. Rentals would have had to accumulate to $250 before she would be entitled to one cent in income; and since checks were not normally issued for less than a dollar, it was estimated that 1,600 years would have to elapse before sufficient funds would accumulate so that a check might be issued, assuming that the current rate of rentals continued. Smith reported in 1937 that unless something was done shortly, the agency would have to buy larger adding machines to use in making the divisions of equities on rentals coming in; his clerk was then using 56,582,064,000 as a common denominator.[42]

[41] Superintendent's Annual Report, 1934–1935; W. C. Smith to Baker, February 17, 1937; W. C. Smith to Collier, July 9, 1938, NARS, RG 75, Sisseton Agency.

[42] Superintendent's Annual Reports, 1936–1937 and 1938–1939; W. C. Smith to Collier, April 30, 1937; Memorandum of Information relating to proposed legislation which would authorize the consolidation of the lands on the Sisseton Indian Reservation, North and South Dakota (accompanying letter from Secretary of Interior Harold L. Ickes to Representative Henry M. Jackson, Chairman, House Committee on Indian Affairs, n.d.), *ibid.*

Such figures as these are not evidence of wasted ingenuity on the part of the superintendent and his clerks. They dramatize the desperate situation that had evolved during a half-century of allotment, a situation made even worse by the fact that some fourteen or fifteen hundred Sissetons did not own even a fractional equity in an allotment and were absolutely landless. In 1937, Charles West, Acting Secretary of the Interior, wrote to Will Rogers, chairman of the House Committee on Indian Affairs, that, since the situation at Sisseton would be duplicated on other allotted reservations in ten or twenty years, action should be taken at once to make Sisseton a sort of pilot project, where a land consolidation and exchange program could be tried out. Bill after bill was introduced in Congress to effect this end, but each one either died in committee or was defeated in one house or the other.[43]

After nearly a decade of the Collier administration, the Sisseton Reservation remained an economically depressed area. In 1942 the number of families on the reservation had risen to 591, two-thirds of whom had an annual income of less than $300. The next year more than 400 families had to be given some form of relief. The situation became especially acute in the winter of 1947–1948. Mission workers who visited the reservation in January found "near-famine conditions" prevailing. In one family consisting of a middle-aged couple (the husband ill), a daughter, and her two children, the only income was $30 a month from the wife's pension. Another household was found to have no food but coffee and a little flour. Mercy flights of food were made in March to aid destitute families isolated by storms. Two years later the relief situation was described as even worse.[44]

The situation at Devils Lake was similar. Nearly 1,500 acres had been bought there and retained in government ownership, but the basic land problem was not solved. Apathy among the Indians made it difficult to get sufficient representation to elect a business council. The officers serving in 1938 were predominantly elderly—all but two were over sixty—and their discussions were carried on in Dakota, which Superintendent Gray did not understand. The very limited success of the subsistence homestead project left the Devils Lake people in not much

[43] Charles West to Will Rogers, November 24, 1937; William Zimmerman, Jr., to W. C. Smith, April 18, 1939; J. M. Stewart to Ross D. Davis, August 21, 1939; W. C. Smith to Collier, May 13, 1940, *ibid.* The first of the bills was H. R. 6047, introduced in Congress on March 31, 1937; H. R. 5451 followed two years later, and in April, 1945, H. R. 2947 was introduced. There were further attempts in the later 1940's and in the next decade.

[44] Ickes to Jackson, n.d., *ibid.*; Sisseton *Courier*, January 22 and March 18, 1948; January 19 and 26, 1950.

better economic shape than the Sissetons on the eve of World War II.[45]

The plight of these two reservations in the post-war period is suggested by the responses of the Indians and their superintendents to requests for information as to their readiness for termination. In a report prepared for Congress in 1953 many reservations were recommended for almost immediate termination, and usually the Indians were represented as favoring such action. Not so those at Sisseton and Devils Lake. The superintendent at Sisseton reported talking to scores of Indians and finding only one who wanted government supervision ended, and he was a man who had sold his land, had no income, and was generally regarded as incompetent. At Devils Lake the chief objection to termination was the extreme poverty of the group, growing in part out of the heirship problem. About 60 per cent of the trust land was in heirship status, and even the Bureau officials did not consider the Devils Lake people competent to manage their own affairs until that situation had been cleared up.[46]

Conditions at Sisseton and Devils Lake have not improved appreciably in recent years, although some figures show a rise in average family income. Since there has been no exodus comparable to that at Santee, while the birth rate has remained high, the reservation population is still far in excess of available resources. The resident population at Sisseton in 1960 was 2,315; at Devils Lake, 1,463, and it has probably increased since then. Although the land situation lies at the root of the present problem, a land exchange and consolidation program would no longer solve the Indians' predicament. Recent economic changes in agriculture have rendered subsistence farming and small-scale commercial farming impracticable, and the Indians have neither the capital nor the training nor the inclination to compete with large white operators.[47]

[45] Superintendent's Annual Report, 1938, NARS, RG 75, Fort Totten Agency.

[46] 83rd Cong., 2nd Sess., *H. Rpt. 2680*, pp. 78, 85, 406–407, 431–432. Despite the attitude of the Indians, as reported by their superintendent, the Bureau's view was that a large majority of the Sissetons were competent to manage their own affairs, however reluctant they might be to do so. According to the report, they had come to regard the Bureau as a "combination foster-father, Santa Claus, and scapegoat." The views expressed in that House Report must be accepted only with great caution, however, for a definite attempt was made to represent the Indians as prepared for termination. So single-minded was this effort that it sometimes led to strange paradoxes, as in the following statement about a Utah Indian group: "Indian Peak Paiute Indians are not competent to manage their own affairs. The Indian Peak Paiute Band of Paiute Indians are ready for complete Bureau withdrawal . . ." (p. 87).

[47] United States Department of Interior, *Reports*, September 1960, *United States*

A social and economic survey of the Sisseton Reservation completed at the end of 1955 showed that the Indian lands could support only one-fourth of the families then living on the reservation. Leasing had increased 30 per cent over the previous year, 50 per cent since 1952. In 1957 it was reported that 34 per cent of the Indians received no cash income from their land, another 30 per cent less than $100 a year. Only three farmers were regarded as successful. Many Indians had moved into the town of Sisseton, where relations between them and the non-Indian population were described as poor; the city auditor estimated that 85 to 90 per cent of arrests made there were of Indians.[48]

Off-reservation employment offers little hope for these people, unless they move away from the vicinity, for there is not much industry in nearby towns. Most of the Indians with regular jobs work for the Indian Bureau or the Public Health Service; others derive some income from seasonal farm work. The great majority of families on both reservations receive welfare assistance at least part of the year. Since Roberts County, South Dakota, where most of the Sissetons live, refuses direct relief to Indians, the burden falls on the Bureau to provide what help it can. Other sources of welfare are Aid to Dependent Children, old-age assistance, Aid to the Totally Disabled, and veterans' pensions.[49] Relocation, in progress since the late 1940's, had removed 163 families from the Sisseton Reservation, at least temporarily, by April, 1957. Fourteen months later it was reported that 250 people had been relocated in the previous two years, but 50 of them had returned. On-the-job training and adult vocational education programs were instituted during the 1950's, and efforts were made to attract industry.[50]

The Sisseton and Devils Lake reservations present a depressing spectacle to the visitor. Small log or frame shacks dot the countryside, most of them well back in the coulees at Sisseton, scattered over the wooded hills at Devils Lake. A housing project at Fort Totten in 1964 provided twenty new dwellings, and more are planned. Except for these, the only bright spots are the public buildings—the three day schools at Sisseton, the new central elementary school and the community hall at Fort Totten, a few of the churches on both reservations. Mere surface appearances may, of course, be deceptive, but at Sisseton and Devils Lake

Indian Population and Land: 1960, pp. 21, 25; interview with Mr. Wray P. Hughes, Superintendent, Sisseton Agency, July 26, 1965.

[48] Sisseton *Courier*, December 22, 1955, January 19, 1956, and June 6, 1957.

[49] Interview with Mr. Hughes, July 26, 1965.

[50] Sisseton *Courier*, April 25, 1957, June 19, July 31, and December 25, 1958.

they reflect all too accurately the bleakness of the lives of those who live there. Not only are their individual lives blighted by the apathy that is normally found among the poverty-stricken, but the collective life of the community suffers from the general atmosphere of futility. Despite their rejection of the IRA, both reservations later organized under constitutions granting limited advisory powers to tribal councils. Neither council seems very effective. Though capable individuals serve on both, the offices are not actively sought, chiefly because council members tend to become whipping boys for the tribe. The council at Devils Lake is described by agency personnel as "native-oriented" and still composed mainly of older men. Poor communication on the reservation also contributes to the ineffectiveness of tribal organization.[51]

Sisseton and Devils Lake illustrate even more forcibly than Santee the ongoing nature of the Indian problem—the failure of nearly a century of work by the Indian Bureau on the present reservations to accomplish the purposes that seemed so easy of realization in the 1870's and 1880's. The solution, if there is to be one, will require even more ingenuity than will be called for at Santee.

[51] Interview with Mr. Richard Drapeaux, Employment Service Officer, and Mr. James S. Yankton, Realty Officer, Fort Totten Subagency, July 28, 1965; T. N. Engdahl to Commissioner, April 3 and September 25, 1946, Sisseton Agency; Homer B. Jenkins, Acting Assistant Commissioner, to Alfred McKay, July 22, 1957, Turtle Mountain Agency. This correspondence is on file at the Bureau of Indian Affairs Central Office, Washington, D.C.

CHAPTER 17

The Twentieth Century:
Flandreau and the Minnesota Sioux

THE DEPLETION of the Indians' land base, with its attendant evils, which characterized the Sisseton and Devils Lake reservations from 1900 to 1930, occurred also at Flandreau and among the Minnesota Sioux colonies; but the consequences were less devastating, and in the 1930's the process was reversed by means of substantial land purchases. Together with greater opportunities for off-reservation employment, the improved land situation enabled these smaller groups at least to hold their own and present a more cheerful exterior to the world. Their land resources are still inadequate to their needs, and they have experienced a steady draining off of young men and women, but the population loss has been largely compensated for by a high birth rate among those who have remained.

Before the end of the nineteenth century the Flandreau people had lost the greater part of their homesteads and were living on small remnants insufficient to give them more than a bare living. Most of the farms were mortgaged, and in many cases the taxes were allowed to go unpaid until the lands were sold at tax sales. As early as 1895, the Santee agent complained that the Flandreau people were selling the barns and houses built by the government and permitting them to be moved away by the white purchasers.[1] This is the condition in which the settlement was found by Superintendent Charles F. Peirce when he took charge in 1901. Since his primary responsibility was the Flandreau Indian Industrial School, and since the local Indians seemed to require little attention, Peirce allowed them to do pretty much as they wished about disposing of their land and spending the proceeds. He thought that many could be given their pro rata share of the tribal funds and separated from government supervision.[2]

This is essentially what was done in 1905. Two years earlier the Flandreau Indians had petitioned for their share of the permanent Sioux fund, and now it was distributed, each person receiving $159.42. Except for some thirty or forty elderly people who had to be cared for, this payment in Peirce's opinion terminated all government aid to the Flandreau Sioux. As a matter of fact, however, it turned out not to be the final payment, for there still remained $8,063.01 to their credit in the Treasury, which was not paid until 1909. Many expected momentarily to become the beneficiaries of sizable payments from the Santee claims, and for a few years around 1905 they went deeply into debt and neglected their farming. As we have seen, the claims case was not finally settled until the 1920's, and then the amount received by each member of the tribe was small.[3]

The Flandreau Indians did little but survive during the first thirty years of the twentieth century. Numbering 288 in 1900, they lost numbers in the next decade, chiefly through departures for the Minnesota colonies, and were down to 275 in 1910. Then their population began to climb again, to 286 in 1920 and 328 in 1930. After most of their land was gone, they made a living as farm laborers until the farm depression of the twenties, when they took up skilled and semiskilled vocations such as carpentry, masonry, and auto mechanics. Still showing the resiliency that had carried them through the difficult early years of their experiment, they managed somehow to keep going without much official aid. Those who owned houses on their small tracts tried to pay their taxes; the rest rented when they could and moved on when unable to pay the rent. The old and helpless (numbering forty-six in 1910) continued to receive a semimonthly issue of beef, flour, coffee, and sugar; and the children were educated at government expense. Except for those ser-

[1] Joseph Clements to Daniel M. Browning, March 10, 1895, NARS, RG 75, LR, Santee Agency.

[2] Com. of Indian Affairs, *Annual Report*, 1902, pp. 266–267, 283.

[3] *Ibid.*, 1905, pp. 336–337; Charles F. Peirce to Francis E. Leupp, April 29, 1901, NARS, RG 75, LR, Flandreau School Agency.

vices, the Flandreau Sioux were as much on their own as the white people surrounding them.[4]

The depression of the 1930's revealed how slender the economic margin of safety the Flandreau people had enjoyed was. The effects were severe enough to induce them to appoint a council, which in May, 1933, reluctantly petitioned the new Indian Commissioner for assistance. "Due to unemployment, and with most of the Indians having homes and land here sixty years and beyond in age," they wrote, "it has been rather hard for the Indians to pay any taxes on their land for the last few years. Nearly all the homes consist of from three to five acres of land, with buildings."[5] In response to a circular sent out by the Bureau to various Indian groups early in 1934, the Flandreau council met and worked out recommendations for land purchases. Superintendent Byron J. Brophy also suggested legislation to permit the paying off of mortgages and delinquent taxes owed by those twelve families who still had land. He also thought the purchase of small homesteads of twenty acres or so for the landless would be desirable. He urged the development of self-supporting projects and recommended that everything should be on the reimbursable plan.[6]

During the course of the year two plans emerged: a subsistence homestead project for Indians who wished to earn most of their income by working in the town of Flandreau, and land purchases under the IRA

[4] Henry C. Baird to William A. Jones, May 2, 1901; Charles H. Dickson to Robert G. Valentine, April 7, 1910; Jess M. Wakeman to John Collier, February 14, 1934; Henry J. Flood, "Flandreau Homestead Subsistence Project" (enclosed in Byron J. Brophy to Harold L. Ickes, November 22, 1934, NARS, RG 75, Flandreau School Agency. The government did continue for a number of years to use a couple of buildings erected earlier. The tract of land on which the former day school was located came to be partially surrounded by the town of Flandreau, and in about 1890 a street was run through it. Fifteen years later the warehouse and granary were moved to the boarding school premises, and the day school building was converted into a warehouse. Part of this tract was transferred to the city in 1916, but the remaining building was moved to the part still in government possession. Peirce said that it provided a good place for rations to be issued and also for the Indians to leave their teams when they came to town, "feeling they are not encroaching upon other peoples property. . . ." Something of the old independence still persisted in spite of poverty and humiliation. See Peirce to Cato Sells, May 19, 1915, *ibid.*; U.S. *Statutes at Large*, XXXIX, 524.

[5] George Eastman *et al.*, to Collier, May 31, 1933, NARS, RG 75, Flandreau School Agency.

[6] Wakeman to Collier, February 14, 1934; Brophy to Collier, February 19, 1934, *ibid.*

for those who wanted to resume farming. The subsistence homestead project received the most attention at first. Several women were employed in a small garment factory, started in December, 1933, which made clothing, mainly for children, used in the Indian Service. For a number of years some of the local Indians had been employed in the boarding school. It was now believed that those people could be successfully established on subsistence tracts of from ten to forty acres. They could not be absorbed by agriculture even if they wished to farm; but if provided with houses, outbuildings, and a few cows and chickens, they could supplement the income they received from wage labor. When Mrs. Elna N. Smith, Assistant Supervisor of Indian Subsistence Homesteads, visited Flandreau in October, 1934, she noted that the Indians there were used to working and had not been pauperized; hence they were better material for such a project than some groups.[7]

Legal obstacles, centering about the fact that the subsistence homestead statute had been intended for already existing reservations, delayed action at Flandreau and created some unrest. Although the plan was not linked to acceptance of the IRA, anti-New Deal elements tried to persuade the Indians that it was all a trick to get them to accept the act, as they in fact did. During the delay, options taken on land for the project expired, and prices began rising.[8] When $25,000 was finally made available for land acquisition at Flandreau in May, 1935, the project had changed its complexion somewhat. Instead of small subsistence homesteads, the plan was now to assign forty-acre tracts to families, in the expectation that they would make farming their principal occupation. Work got under way after the formal proclamation of the Flandreau Indian Reservation on August 17, 1936. During the next three years some 2,100 acres were purchased and divided into forty-acre tracts. Eventually it was realized that forty acres was too small a unit for successful farming, and the amount of land assigned to each family was increased to eighty acres.[9]

[7] "Capital Needs for Indian Land Use, Flandreau Sioux Jurisdiction, S. D.," n.d. (received September 20, 1934); Elna N. Smith to A. C. Cooley, Director of Extension, October 23, 1934; William Zimmerman, Jr. to Ickes, December 11, 1934, *ibid.*

[8] Nathan R. Maragold, Assistant Solicitor, Interior Department, to Assistant Secretary of Interior Oscar Chapman, January 17, 1935; Brophy to Collier, March 12 and April 19, 1935; Collier to Brophy, April 25, 1935; E. N. Smith to Cooley, April 27, 1935, *ibid.*

[9] Zimmerman to Brophy, August 16, 1935; J. N. Stewart to Brophy, n.d.; Brophy to Stewart, November 11, 1936, *ibid.*; 82nd Cong., 2nd Sess., *H. Rpt. 2503*, p. 65. In some cases a person received two noncontiguous forties, but usually it was possible to assign the tracts so as to provide a workable unit.

The land-acquisition program, by far the most important Bureau activity at Flandreau in the 1930's, represented a sharp departure from the previous history of the community in that it created an Indian reservation composed of tribally owned land held in trust by the United States government. Apparently the experience of the previous sixty years had led the Indians to question the advisability of individually owned farms. By this time only two of the original homesteads remained intact, and one of them was in a complex heirship tangle and leased to white farmers; three or four small tracts scattered around and unused by the owners remained in Indian hands. Despite their history of factionalism, the Flandreau people seem to have co-operated to the extent of successfully managing the newly purchased lands and assigning them without stirring up charges of favoritism.[10]

The old individualism persisted, however. Though opposed to bills introduced in Congress to repeal the IRA, the Flandreau people were divided on termination. When interviewed on the question in 1953, some wanted to buy the farms they were occupying; others wanted the land given to them; still others wanted it sold and the proceeds divided among them. Although most were spending their money as fast as they made it, they were apparently doing all right financially. Most of their cash income was then being earned by the women working in the garment factory.[11]

The closing of the factory in 1956 was a blow to the Indians' economy. About the same time, the large farming enterprise of the Flandreau Indian school was discontinued, and the local Indians were deprived of the services of the agriculture teachers, who had functioned as extension agents. Most of the people formerly employed at the factory found jobs at the school, which experienced a large increase in enrollment at that time, and some moved away from the area. The resident population in 1965 was about 210. Few were actively farming by the mid-1960's. The assignments were leased to white farmers, and most of the Indians were living in town. With employment available at the school and some other jobs to be had locally (the tribal chairman in 1965 was a mail carrier for the Flandreau post office), it was the opinion of knowledgeable

[10] Brophy to Division of Extension and Industry, BIA, February 6, 1936; Kenneth W. Green, Assistant Land Field Agent, to Stewart, January 26, 1936, NARS, RG 75, Flandreau School Agency. Green proposed that the Flandreau community be made a pilot project because of unusually favorable conditions and a relatively small area and population. See Green to Fred A. Baker, Land Field Agent, April 30, 1936, *ibid.*

[11] Joe Jennings and Benjamin Reifel to Collier, September 25, 1939, NARS, RG 75, Flandreau School Agency; 83rd Cong., 2nd Sess., *H. Rpt. 2680*, pp. 320–321.

people that the average income of the Indians was about the same as that of the general population, and in some cases higher.[12]

Despite their determination in 1869 to become like white men, the Flandreau Sioux have come to take pride in their Indian heritage. In 1962 and again in 1965 they presented a "Siouxtennial" in co-operation with local civic and business groups. The flats across the Big Sioux River from the community building (a Bureau project of the 1930's) were covered with the tents and trailers of visiting Indians, many of whom participated in a parade through the streets of Flandreau.[13] As one watched cars and trucks pass by, filled with Wisconsin Winnebagos and Fort Thompson Sioux in full regalia, drums beating, old-time chants blaring from loudspeakers, one could not help wondering what had become of the determination of the original Flandreau homesteaders to give up everything that smacked of their Indian past. A further question inevitably suggested itself: Could it be that the more prosperous an Indian group becomes, through acceptance of the white man's way of life, the more vigorous their sense of Indian identity becomes?

The same question might occur to one following the history of the Minnesota Sioux groups in the twentieth century. Nearly as acculturated as the Flandreau people, they accepted the Indian Reorganization Act even more decisively, and one group has in recent years held an annual pow-wow drawing Indians and whites from a wide area. Their history since 1900 is much more complex and full of incident than Flandreau's, but it has followed generally the same lines.

After the last congressional appropriation in 1899, the Minnesota Mdewakantons were under no agent, received no rations, and were the beneficiaries of no government services in their communities except for a day school at the Birch Coulee settlement. Almost the only business relations they had with the government concerned the disposition of the Sioux fund and the Santee claims case, and those matters were handled through the Santee Agency. Many of them lived on fee patent lands; others occupied portions of the tracts bought about 1890 and retained

[12] Carl W. Beck, Assistant to the Commissioner, to Mrs. Mary W. Hemingway, May 7, 1956, Flandreau School Agency (correspondence in possession of Bureau of Indian Affairs Central Office, Washington, D.C.); interviews with Superintendent B. B. Warner and Tribal Chairman Richard K. Wakeman, July 22, 1965. The tribal executive committee continues to hold monthly meetings, but it is difficult to obtain a quorum (20 per cent of the resident population), for the semiannual general council meeting called for by the constitution.

[13] *Moody County Enterprise* (Flandreau), July 22, 1965.

in government ownership. The picture one gets of them very early in the century varies from one colony to another. The Indians near the old agency site were described in 1901 as "practically self-supporting, honest, moral, and good citizens." Those living at the other settlements, however, were said to be living a gypsy life in tents or shacks, fishing and catching driftwood, picking berries, and occasionally working for white men. They were largely untouched by church influences, and their children were not being sent to any school.[14]

As the years passed, the Scattered Sioux tended to gather mainly at Birch Coulee and Prairie Island. The forty-acre tract at Hastings was sold to the State of Minnesota in 1906 for inclusion in the state hospital property, and the Wabasha land, never permanently occupied, was finally transferred to the Fish and Wildlife Service in 1944. There was a gradual movement away from the Prior Lake lands, until by the 1930's only six families still lived there. Many of the people who owned or inherited assignments there actually lived in cities and towns throughout southern Minnesota and only occasionally tried to obtain a little income by leasing their lands. A few elderly people at Mendota continued to be cared for by the rector of Gethsemane church. Every month a ladies' committee would visit them and supply the really destitute ones with food and clothing to the amount of $1.25 or $1.50 per week. Elsewhere the old and indigent were cared for by relatives or by public and private charities in the communities where they lived. Some lived by begging.[15]

The Minnesota Mdewakantons were paid their share of the Sioux

[14] Com. of Indian Affairs, *Annual Report*, 1901, p. 541; A. O. Wright to W. A. Jones, October 15, 1902, NARS, RG 75, LR, Sioux in Minnesota file.

[15] U.S. *Statutes at Large*, XXXIV, 78; LVIII, 274; Henton to Morgan, July 24, 1889; Plat of Indian Lots, Scott County, dated October 8, 1904; Henry W. St. Clair to Andrew J. Volstead, October 24, 1904; John J. Faude to Acting Commissioner A. C. Tanner, June 1 and 8, 1900, NARS, RG 75, LR, Sioux in Minnesota file; Brief Memorandum Relating to Outlying Districts of the Pipestone Jurisdiction, May 1, 1937, NARS, RG 75, Pipestone School Agency. As early as 1898 only five out of the original sixteen assignments made at Prior Lake remained in Indian hands, and by 1904 only one Indian still held onto his land. Some died and some moved away; in either case the lands were usually sold. See *Plat Book of Scott County, Minnesota* ([Philadelphia]: North West Publishing Co., 1898), p. 8. When an elderly Prairie Island woman died in 1914, a Red Wing newspaper commented that she had been a familiar figure on the city's streets: "Scarcely a week passed for years that she did not call on her friends in the business district for aid, which was always forthcoming." See Red Wing *Daily Republican*, February 16, 1914. Such items continued to appear in the newspapers until well into the 1930's.

fund in 1907, and most of them shared in the proceeds of either the Sisseton-Wahpeton claims case in 1909 or the Santee claims case in 1924. Aside from those benefits, they were largely ignored by the government during the first three decades of the century. In 1915 the Episcopal Bishop of Minnesota, Samuel Cook Edsall, wrote Superintendent Frank T. Mann of the Pipestone Indian School, who had nominal supervision over the Minnesota Sioux, suggesting that those at Birch Coulee be issued some farm implements, which they might use collectively. Their land tracts were too small to be farmed profitably and were mostly leased to whites. Although Mann endorsed the proposal, it seems to have received no consideration at the Indian Office.[16] These people had been "turned loose," and, aside from operating a day school for their benefit, the government had no wish to involve itself with them again.

The day school lasted only until 1920. Taught until 1918 by Robert H. C. Hinman, son of the missionary buried at Birch Coulee, it followed the state course of study, slightly modified, and normally enrolled about twenty children. A school garden was raised on a nine-acre tract adjoining the building, and Hinman provided milk and butter for the children from his own dairy herd of four cows. Less than a year after Hinman retired to edit the Morton *Enterprise*, the school was ordered closed but was kept open until the summer of 1920 at the request of Superintendent Mann. It subsequently was taken over by Redwood County and has since been operated as part of the rural school system of the county. Elsewhere the Indian children attended either local district schools or boarding schools such as Pipestone or White Earth. The only other Mdewakanton colony large enough to have a predominantly Indian school was Prairie Island, where the Indian Bureau provided financial assistance to the district for Indian pupils.[17]

For many years the Pipestone superintendent's dealings with the Indians were limited to matters relating to education, but gradually he was drawn into a closer relationship that more nearly resembled that of the ordinary agency superintendent toward the Indians under his jurisdiction. By 1927, Superintendent James W. Balmer was visiting the

[16] Samuel Cook Edsall to Superintendent Frank T. Mann, June 21, 1915; Mann to Sells, June 17, 1915, NARS, RG 75, Pipestone School Agency.

[17] Report of L. F. Michael, Supervisor of Schools, December 18, 1913; Sells to Mann, November 24, 1919; Mann to Sells, November 28, 1919, and June 2, 1920; Peyton Carter, Supervisor of Schools, to Charles H. Burke, December 22, 1921; Ora Padgett to Burke, July 17, 1922; Tony Kuhn to Senator Henrik Shipstead, November 1, 1924, *ibid.*; Redwood Falls *Sun*, March 21, 1919.

various settlements two or three times a year. At that time two years of drought had rendered most of the Indians destitute and in need of assistance from some agency—local, state, or federal. Balmer found that county officials, especially those in Goodhue County, were willing to co-operate in providing relief supplies and medicine. On his visit to Prairie Island he was accompanied by the county agent and other local authorities, who went with him from house to house issuing free seed for the coming planting season.[18]

Despite the tendency to settle at the two main colonies, the Scattered Sioux were still widely scattered at this time. Besides mixed-bloods living like whites in Minneapolis, St. Paul, and Wabasha, there were colonies of Indians at Granite Falls, Shakopee, Savage, and Red Wing, as well as at Birch Coulee and Prairie Island. In 1929, Balmer counted 554 in all. This was the first accurate estimate of their numbers in many years.[19] Many of the Sioux residing in Minnesota continued to be carried on the rolls of the Santee, Flandreau, Sisseton, and Yankton jurisdictions. Not until the 1930's, when the larger communities organized under the IRA and drew up tribal rolls, were any really accurate population figures available, and they were not particularly helpful in determining the numbers of the Minnesota Sioux who had become virtually assimilated to the general population.

The Depression struck the Minnesota Sioux much as it did the Flandreau colony, and early efforts to meet it followed the same pattern. Continued drought greatly reduced the amount of crops the Indians could grow on their small tracts, especially on the light, sandy soil of Prairie Island. The widespread unemployment of the early thirties eliminated off-reservation jobs as a source of income. Thus the economic situation of these Indians, poor enough in normal times, became

[18] James W. Balmer to Burke, April 14 and May 17, 1927, NARS, RG 75, Pipestone School Agency.

[19] Balmer to Burke, April 14, 1927, and January 7, 1929, *ibid.* The figures of 150 at Birch Coulee and 779 elsewhere, first published in the Commissioner's *Annual Report* for 1899 and 1901, respectively, were repeated year after year. When new figures were adopted, they fluctuated so much from year to year as to be quite unreliable. In 1911 the figure of 350 is given for all Mdewakantons in Minnesota (p. 60). In 1913 the number is given as 300, including "Mdewakanton, Wapaquta, Sisseton, and Wahpeton at Birch Cooley" (p. 53). In 1914 there were supposed to be only 303, a figure which had fallen to 160 in 1916 and 164 in 1918 (pp. 80, 77, and 87, respectively). A more detailed breakdown in 1920 listed 303 Mdewakanton Sioux and 105 at Birch Coulee (p. 67). Another source gives 271 in 1920, 371 in 1930, and 548 in 1940 (Governor's Interracial Commission, *The Indian in Minnesota* [St. Paul?], 1947, p. 37). The federal census reports tell a still different story.

fully as serious as that of the Santees, Sissetons, and Devils Lake Indians, though involving fewer people. To meet the immediate crisis, Balmer distributed aid to the needy during the winter of 1929–1930 but found the available funds too small to take care of everyone. The next winter the home of one of the oldest Prairie Island women was repaired and painted, and fifty blankets were issued by the county nurse. Purchase orders were issued to twenty people there. Essentially the same kind of aid went to the other settlements.[20] Work relief was slower in being initiated here than on reservations, where the superintendent was in daily association with the Indians and had them as his primary responsibility. On the other hand, the relatively small number of Indians concerned and the comparative wealth of the counties where they lived made it possible for their most pressing welfare needs to be met, for a time at least, by local agencies.

The first significant assistance from the Indian Bureau came through the Indian Emergency Conservation Work program in 1934, when $5,347.63 was paid to men at Birch Coulee and Prairie Island for road construction and the development of springs and wells. The Indians received 90 per cent of that money in the form of pay checks issued at the end of each month; the remainder was withheld and paid in two installments the following winter, when there was no work to be had. Although the amount of IECW funds used in the next few years dropped sharply, the loss was more than compensated for by employment provided by the WPA. By 1937, WPA checks accounted for nearly 60 per cent of all income received by the Birch Coulee group. Because there was no WPA unit in Goodhue County, work of this kind did not begin at Prairie Island until that year.[21]

The rehabilitation projects were woefully underfinanced at first. In 1936, Superintendent Balmer requested an appropriation of $16,425 but received only $6,400 for all the Minnesota groups. The money was

[20] Balmer to Charles J. Rhoads, July 18, 1930, and January 14, 1931, NARS, RG 75, Pipestone School Agency.

[21] Peter J. Lightfoot to Collier, February 1, 1935; Lightfoot, "The Rehabilitation Program Pipestone Jurisdiction, Minnesota," [1937]; Shirley N. McKinsey, "An Economic Survey of the Lower Sioux Indian Community, Morton, Minnesota," 1937, *ibid.* The McKinsey survey and a similar one done on Prairie Island by Clyde G. Sherman ("An Economic Survey of the Prairie Island Indian Community in Minnesota," 1937) are extremely useful studies. They include inventories of the economic potential of each community and list all livestock, farm machinery, etc., available to the Indians. They were intended as the starting point for a thoroughgoing rehabilitation of the communities.

to be disbursed in the form of loans to those who might be expected to repay them, or as outright grants to the elderly and infirm. About two-thirds of it was used for loans at Birch Coulee, about one-third at Prairie Island and Prior Lake. With this money a start was made toward repairing existing houses and building small one-room dwellings to relieve overcrowding and provide living space for the homeless.[22] In 1937 another $6,500 was made available, and the program moved into high gear. Larger sums were allotted in 1938 and 1939, with the result that living conditions among the Minnesota Sioux were greatly improved. Many houses had basements for the first time, and the additional storage space thus provided served as an incentive to the Indians to increase their gardening. Many were also inspired to buy furniture or paint what they had and make other improvements on their own initiative.[23]

Besides the benefits to individual families, an important item in the program for each of the two principal communities was to provide the people with a community building. At Birch Coulee county officials were so impressed with the rehabilitation program that they offered to furnish the materials for such a building. Half the crew of WPA laborers who had been working on houses were transferred to the project, which got under way in the summer of 1937 and was virtually completed by the end of that year, although the formal dedication did not take place until the next spring. More than a thousand people attended the ceremony, at which talks were made by Episcopal Bishop Stephen E. Keeler of Minnesota, Superintendent Balmer, state WPA director Victor Christgau, and Xavier Vigeant, representing the Washington office of the Bureau. The building, constructed of red tile blocks, contained a main hall seating 125, a stage, a basement with kitchen, a dining room, a cloak room, and a furnace room. A somewhat similar but less pretentious community building was erected at Prairie Island in 1939.[24]

All the improvements had a stimulating effect on the Indians at the two communities. Early in 1938, Thomas Columbus, secretary of the

[22] Lightfoot, "Rehabilitation Program"; McKinsey, "Economic Survey"; Balmer to Collier, February 21 and March 9, 1936, *ibid.*; Morton *Enterprise*, April 2, 1936.

[23] D. E. Murphy to Balmer, March 3 and 15 and April 7, 1937; Balmer to Collier, August 28, 1937, and August 1, 1938, NARS, RG 75, Pipestone School Agency; Morton *Enterprise*, June 25, 1936, and December 16, 1937.

[24] Balmer to Collier, February 3, 1938; Thomas Columbus to Collier, January 25, 1938; Clara Madsen to Collier, August 2, 1939, NARS, RG 75, Pipestone School Agency; Morton *Enterprise*, June 3 and December 16, 1937, and June 2, 1938.

Birch Coulee council, wrote Commissioner Collier that as a result of the program nearly all the houses were in good repair, health conditions had improved, and the people were looking forward to their farming program. "Words could not convey to you," he concluded, "the thanks and gratitude from our people for the many wonderful things done for our community in the past year."[25] Balmer had earlier written that the Indians took great pride in their rehabilitated homes and were expressing their appreciation in many ways. Since the program had begun, "an entirely different atmosphere" had prevailed among the Indians, who were "more contented and happy" and doing what they could to better their economic condition.[26]

Unfortunately, IECW and WPA work provided only temporary employment, and the appearance of prosperity created by the rehabilitation program would be only a mockery unless a stable economic foundation could be provided for these people. As elsewhere, the Bureau saw the long-range solution in terms of increasing the Indians' land base, which was then obviously inadequate. Their holdings at the beginning of the Depression consisted of 470 acres at Birch Coulee, 120 acres at Prairie Island, and 258 acres at Prior Lake, all in government possession, and small tracts of fee patent land at each of those places. Some of the latter were in immediate danger of being lost because of long unpaid taxes. The small assignments of government land—thirteen to twenty-two acres to a family—were insufficient for anything but subsistence gardens. Balmer now outlined purchases that would not only provide enough land for those living in the existing Indian communities but increase the holdings sufficiently to permit those living in towns and cities to settle on farms if they wished.[27]

Before land purchases could be made under the IRA, the communities concerned had to accept that important piece of legislation. They did so by the decisive margin of 94–2, in an election held October 27, 1934; at Birch Coulee the vote was unanimous. The next step was to form councils and draft constitutions and bylaws. A problem arose in this connection, in that the Minnesota Mdewakantons, having ex-

[25] Columbus to Collier, January 25, 1938, NARS, RG 75, Pipestone School Agency.

[26] Balmer to Collier, August 28, 1937, *ibid.*

[27] Balmer to Cooley, December 26, 1935; "Brief Memorandum Relating to Outlying Districts," May 1, 1937; Balmer to Collier, July 18 and August 14, 1935, *ibid.* At Prairie Island 38.07 acres remained in Indian possession, 38.92 had been sold or otherwise disposed of to white owners, and the rest of the original 80 acres had been taken over for a railroad right-of-way, except for a tract of less than an acre which belonged to the Episcopal Diocese of Minnesota.

pressly abandoned their tribal relations as a condition of receiving the benefits provided in the 1880's, were ineligible to organize as a tribe. Inasmuch as each community had been more or less on its own for many years, the first intention was for each to organize independently, as an Indian community. By mid-summer of 1935, Birch Coulee had drafted a tentative constitution and bylaws, and Prairie Island had begun work on one. Although a speech by Henry Roe Cloud at a mass meeting later that year led the Minnesota Sioux temporarily to discard this plan in favor of organizing as a single group, they finally decided, after further discussion with Bureau representatives, to return to their original plan for separate organizations. Both groups voted on their constitutions in 1936 and on corporate charters the next year and approved them by decisive margins.[28]

The land purchases made for the Minnesota Mdewakantons were much more modest than Balmer had envisioned. Although something over 1,200 acres were added at Birch Coulee (now officially renamed Lower Sioux), Prairie Island was increased by only 414 acres, and no land was bought at Prior Lake. The people at Lower Sioux thus enjoyed a substantially improved land situation, but the amount available at Prairie Island was altogether inadequate, especially in view of the limited agricultural possibilities of the land there. The insufficiency of the purchase at Prairie Island was partially disguised by the fact that the Indians were permitted to use a larger tract of flowage land behind Lock and Dam No. 3 on the Mississippi. Although this land was periodically subject to inundation and thus unusable as farm land, it was thought that the Indians could trap, hunt, fish, obtain firewood, make maple sugar, harvest wild rice, and dig swamp potatoes and swamp bananas there.[29] It might have been of real benefit to an earlier generation, but by the 1930's the Minnesota Sioux were no longer making much use of the native resources of the soil that their ancestors had exploited with considerable success.

Although the Minnesota Sioux were all served by district schools by

[28] Lightfoot to Indian Office (telegram), October 28, 1934; McKinsey, "Economic Survey"; Balmer to Collier, July 18 and December 19, 1935; Charlotte T. Westwood and J. R. Venning to Collier, December 21, 1935, *ibid.* The Prior Lake community was deemed too small for separate organization and was placed under the jurisdiction of Lower Sioux.

[29] "Brief Memorandum Relating to Outlying Districts," May 1, 1937; Madsen to Collier, August 2, 1939, *ibid.*; 82nd Cong., 2nd Sess., *H. Rpt. 2503*, p. 62; United States Department of Interior, *Reports*, September 1960, *United States Indian Population and Land: 1960*, p. 14.

the 1930's, the Bureau played some part in improving educational facilities for them and inducing more of the children to attend. At Lower Sioux the former day school was still in use and enrolled about thirty pupils. With the aid of their WPA earnings, the local people cleaned up and beautified the school grounds.[30] At Prairie Island the situation was somewhat different. With the removal of the recently purchased lands from the tax rolls, District 132 no longer had a tax base sufficient to maintain the school, and in 1939 the district was dissolved and the school placed directly under county administration. When the community hall was built, the small school building was moved to a site near it so that the hall could be used for shop work and noon lunches. In return, the school authorities agreed to furnish heat for both buildings. A well-qualified male teacher was hired in the fall of 1939, after several years when inadequately trained young women had held the job. Among the innovations adopted here was inviting the sixth, seventh, and eighth graders to attend council meetings, so that they could become familiar with the work of the council, on which they might eventually serve.[31]

The discussion so far has concerned exclusively the old Mdewakanton colonies at which land purchases had been made between 1887 and 1891. There was another settlement of Sioux in Minnesota, however, which had never been recognized by the Indian Bureau, despite the fact that it came into being about the same time as the other communities. About 1887 some of the Sissetons who had established the Brown Earth colony drifted back to the old reservation area in Minnesota, just below the town of Granite Falls. Although county officials tried as early as 1891 to persuade the federal government to take responsibility for those people, who were then destitute, nothing was done toward obtaining land for them. Most of them owned small tracts purchased with their own funds. A few had bought land with trust funds derived from the sale of restricted allotments, and their tracts carried restrictive clauses. Except for these few, the lands came to be so encumbered with delinquent taxes that by the 1930's the Indians occupying them had only squatters' rights.[32]

[30] Morton *Enterprise*, September 24, 1936; Columbus to Collier, January 25, 1938, NARS, RG 75, Pipestone School Agency. In 1937 the Morton newspaper reported that the children were studying Indians; the first grade had learned such words as "travois," "moccasin," and "tipi." See the Morton *Enterprise*, April 29, 1937.

[31] Madsen to Collier, August 2, 1939; Balmer to Collier, December 21, 1939, NARS, RG 75, Pipestone School Agency.

[32] "Historical Data of Early Settlement of Upper Sioux Indian Community," accompanying Balmer to Collier, November 7, 1938; Balmer to Collier, June 14,

Although the original members of the Granite Falls group were Sissetons or Wahpetons, in about 1910 a number of Santees arrived, both from the Santee Reservation and from Flandreau. They were later joined by a scattering of Minnesota Mdewakantons and Yanktons, so that in time the settlement came to consist of a not-altogether-harmonious collection of people of different origins, enrolled under several jurisdictions. Because most of them were reluctant to send their children to school in Granite Falls, a district school was built for them in 1920. Called upon by the clerk of the Granite Falls school to explain their status, the Pipestone superintendent investigated the Indian settlement but did not actively take charge of it at that time. After the Collier administration took office and the IRA was passed, their status became a matter of greater moment, and they were placed under Balmer's supervision on March 1, 1936.[33]

The immediate reason for this action was that the Granite Falls group wished to organize under the IRA but found itself unable to do so because the Sisseton Reservation, where most of its members were enrolled, had rejected the act. The Granite Falls people had voted 42–35 in favor of the IRA at an election held April 6, 1935, but their votes were counted at the various jurisdictions under which they were enrolled. The principal demand for organization came, not from the Sisseton majority, but from a few families of mixed origins calling themselves Santees or Mdewakantons. Their spokesman was Mrs. Sophie Wilson, a woman of one-fourth Indian blood whose four marriages had given her a large number of relatives and in-laws. Throughout the 1930's she bombarded Superintendent Balmer, Commissioner Collier, Secretary of the Interior Ickes, President Roosevelt, and several congressmen with letters concerning the Granite Falls group.[34]

When Balmer took over supervision of the group, he found them on

---

1935, *ibid.*; Mair Pointon, Yellow Medicine County Auditor, to Thomas J. Morgan, January 7, 1891, NARS, RG 75, LR, Sisseton Agency. The Indians in their correspondence commonly refer to themselves as Wahpetons; they are referred to here as Sissetons because they were enrolled at the Sisseton Reservation.

[33] "Historical Data"; Clerk of Granite Falls schools to Padgett, December 20, 1920; Padgett to Sells, December 22, 1920; Balmer to Collier, April 13, 1936, NARS, RG 75, Pipestone School Agency.

[34] Lightfoot to Baker, January 16, 1935; Baker to Indian Office, April 12, 1935, Sophie Wilson to Collier, October 1, 1935; Archie Phinney to M. L. Burns, March 29; 1938; Phinney to Collier, March 19, 1939, NARS, RG 75, Pipestone School Agency. The correspondence concerning the Granite Falls group is voluminous and the information contained in it sometimes conflicting.

the horns of a legal dilemma. They could not organize under the IRA because they were not on a separate reservation, and land could not be purchased for a reservation until they had organized under the IRA. A legal way out was eventually found, but organization was temporarily stalled when it was discovered that each member of the group would have to renounce his rights at the jurisdiction where he was enrolled. When the Sissetons agreed to do that, plans went ahead once more.[35]

Land purchases amounting to 745.66 acres were made in 1938, but the New Upper Sioux Indian Community, as it called itself, did not organize under the IRA. The legal obstacles having been removed or bypassed, only internal dissension could prevent consummation of the plan, and that is precisely what happened. A semblance of harmony was maintained while the constitution was being drawn up in 1936 (somewhat prematurely), but by late 1937 friction between the Sissetons and the Santee faction was so great that the suggestion was made that the latter join the Lower Sioux for organizational purposes. At one point a plan was approved by which only the non-Sissetons would be permitted to organize; it of course drew a protest from the Sissetons.[36]

Curiously, although the majority had agreed to give up their rights on the Sisseton Reservation, their opponents were not willing to relinquish their reservation rights. Mrs. Wilson refused to give up her membership at Santee or forty acres of land she had acquired on the Sisseton Reservation through one of her husbands. She carried sufficient weight to guarantee that the first assignments made after the Upper Sioux reservation was proclaimed, on October 6, 1938, were given to members of her group. In 1939 she and some of her relatives visited Wash-

[35] Balmer to Collier, June 14, 1935, April 13, 1936, and September 22 and November 9, 1937; John Herrick to Balmer, August 11, 1936; Zimmerman to Balmer, April 19, 1937, *ibid.* The Yanktons were under the Rosebud jurisdiction after the Yankton Agency was closed in 1933. Balmer wrote Augustine L. Hook, Land Field Agent for the Bureau, on April 13, 1936, that there were seventeen Sisseton families, three Flandreau, one Mdewakanton, and six Santee and Yankton (no distinction made) at Granite Falls. At Birch Coulee there were twenty Mdewakanton families, eighteen Flandreau, and one Sisseton; and at Prairie Island there were twenty Mdewakanton families, three Flandreau, two Santee, and one Sisseton. The composition of those groups was actually more varied even than these figures show, for the McKinsey survey also showed seven whites, two Mexicans, and one Negro at Birch Coulee. Prairie Island has at various times included whites, Winnebagos, Chippewas, and even a Cherokee.

[36] Wilson, William R. Cavender, and Fred Pearsall to Balmer, May 14, 1936; Joe Jennings to Indian Organization, December 10, 1937; Phinney to Burns, March 29, 1938; Balmer to Collier, August 29, 1938, *ibid.*

ington and talked with Bureau officials and with Senator Henrik Shipstead. Members of the Sisseton faction promptly wrote to Shipstead that the group he had met with were only a small minority in the community. Although this was true, upon her return Mrs. Wilson carried a roll of paper bearing the words "Ind Off Wash D.C.," with which she impressed people. Later she endeavored to gain support at Prairie Island, tried to prevent the Sissetons from using the community building erected in 1941, and kept up her agitation for years, always arguing that the Sissetons were intruders and should be excluded from any organization that might be set up.[37]

In view of the factionalism prevailing and the reluctance of the majority to start a community organization under such circumstances, a Bureau field representative advised that the matter be dropped for the time. A board of trustees was set up, however, chiefly to advise the superintendent on the use of rehabilitation funds. The officers elected in 1942 were entirely from the Sisseton group. Torn by factionalism and lacking an effective community organization, the Upper Sioux colony has remained something of a thorn in the side of Bureau officials and the subject of controversy among the local white population. More than half the families live on fee patent lands along the highway between the IRA purchase and the city of Granite Falls. The center of their community is the Presbyterian church, which bears the name "Pejuhutazizi," a variation of the name of the Williamson mission. Upper Sioux thus lacks the unity of the other groups, though it is economically better off than Prairie Island, and in recent years the internal dissension may have diminished somewhat.[38]

The Minnesota Sioux groups were caught up in the termination controversy during the 1950's. An effort was made to show that they were as nearly ready as any other Indians in the country to get along without Bureau supervision. It was pointed out that their educational, health, and welfare needs were handled largely by local agencies and

[37] Jennings and Phinney to Collier, October 17, 1938; John Roberts, Walter A. LaBatte, and Herbert Ironheart to Shipstead, February 17, 1939; Wilson, *et al.*, to Collier, February 14, 1939; Balmer to Collier, March 22, 1939; affidavits from Wilson *et al.*, to Shipstead, February 13, 1941; Phinney to Collier, August 9 and September 9 and 10, 1941, *ibid.*

[38] Phinney to Collier, September 9, 1941; John McGue to Christian H. Beitzel, August 27, 1947; Zimmerman to D. E. Murphy, April 7, 1947; Balmer to Collier, September 25, 1943, *ibid.*; interview with Mr. Casimir L. LeBeau, Acting Superintendent, Minnesota Agency, Bemidji, Minnesota, July 30, 1965; Granite Falls *Tribune*, April 6, 1957.

that most of the Indians were employed in nearby towns or in the Minneapolis–St. Paul area. The land-assignment system had not worked because of the uncertainty of the individual's tenure and the restrictions imposed on the use of the land. The best solution, it was asserted, was to prepare an up-to-date census roll and divide up the lands and land proceeds as equitably as possible.[39] Discussions between Bureau representatives and the Indians went on in 1953 and 1954, and the councils at Prairie Island and Lower Sioux drew up resolutions calling for legislation to grant individuals fee simple title to the tribal lands. At Upper Sioux there was opposition to the plan, though the majority were represented as favoring it. On January 26, 1955, Senator Edward Thye introduced a bill (S. 704) in Congress to provide for termination of federal supervision over those lands. While the bill was in committee, opposition developed, not only from the Indians (who probably had not understood all the implications of termination when they went on record as favoring it), but also from some local white people, who realized that their welfare burden would be increased, and from the Governor's Commission on Human Rights, which said the bill "would not adequately protect the interests of the Indians in the interim period."[40] The bill never reached the Senate floor, and termination talk died down in the later 1950's.

The three little Sioux communities in Minnesota are scarcely visible in the midst of the general white society. Because they are Indian colonies in an overwhelmingly white area, however, they receive more attention than their size would warrant. Prairie Island especially has been given considerable publicity in recent years, perhaps because of

[39] 83rd Cong., 2nd Sess., *H. Rpt. 2680*, pp. 73, 402–403.

[40] Resolution adopted February 7, 1953, by Prairie Island Community Council; Area Director Don C. Foster to Commissioner Glenn Emmons, August 27, 1953; Mrs. William Lee to Senator Edward Thye, March 2, 1954; Acting Area Director K. W. Dixon to Emmons, March 25 and May 12, 1954; Emmons to Lee, April 7, 1954; Acting Area Director R. G. Fister to Emmons, October 28, 1954; Mrs. Joseph Campbell to Representative August H. Andresen, March 28, 1955; Emmons to Andresen, April 8, 1955; Area Director R. D. Holtz to Emmons, February 14, 1956; *Congressional Record*, 84th Cong., 1st Sess., pp. 11954–11955. The above correspondence is on file at the Bureau of Indian Affairs Central Office, Washington, D.C. Portions of it were consulted at the Minneapolis Area Office. When the Pipestone jurisdiction was discontinued in 1951, these groups were placed temporarily under the Minneapolis Area Office and then, in 1954, turned over to the new Minnesota Agency. See "Background data relating to the Sioux Indians in the Southern part of Minnesota," August 1958 (BIA release in possession of Prairie Island Community Council officers).

the apparent survival there of more of the old culture than at the other settlements.[41] The interest being shown in these communities suggests two things: that they have not been assimilated and that at least some white people familiar with them are concerned about the fact. To those who still see the solution to the Indian problem exclusively in terms of total assimilation, the survival of these colonies as identifiable social units reflects the failure of whites and Indians alike to achieve the desired goal. To others, who see nothing inherently bad in the retention of racial and community identity in the face of external pressures for conformity, the failure, to the extent that there is one, seems to be not the existence of these communities, but the persistence of poverty and its attendant evils in them.

There is no doubt that people living at Prairie Island and Upper Sioux are poor. Nor is there much doubt that their poverty is due largely to the limited economic opportunities available to them. But one should not therefore conclude that more extensive land purchases in the 1930's would have solved the economic problem. No doubt the Indians would be better off if they had more land; but, given the recent trends in agriculture, it is unrealistic to suppose that many would succeed in the present highly competitive world of farming. Besides, most of them, like most white Americans, prefer jobs that take them off the land, either temporarily or permanently. Since all the Minnesota Sioux groups are fairly close to towns large enough to afford some employment, many of their people commute to work; others have moved away to cities where jobs exist.

Although the Minnesota Sioux are more fortunately located than their tribesmen in Nebraska or the Dakotas—a fact reflected in their relatively superior economic state—they live in the midst of a rural

[41] Among the more important articles about Prairie Island are Cynthia Kelsey, "Changing Social Relationships in an Eastern Dakota Community," Minnesota Academy of Science *Proceedings*, XXIV (1956), 12–19; Bud Ehlers, "Brotherhood Starts at Home," Red Wing *Daily Republican Eagle*, February 20, 21, 23, 24, 25, 1961; Jay Edgerton, "Sioux Once Driven from Prairie Island," Minneapolis *Sunday Tribune*, October 30, 1949; and United States Public Health Service, "Basic Data: Prairie Island Sioux Community," December 7, 1959, ms. My own article, "The Prairie Island Community: A Remnant of Minnesota Sioux," *Minnesota History*, XXXVII (September 1961), 271–282, is based principally on these and other published sources, the Sherman "Economic Survey," and personal interviews and correspondence with local people. An interesting, though not wholly reliable, article is Gareth Hiebert, "Sioux Village Offers Color of the Past," St. Paul *Sunday Pioneer Press*, August 7, 1960.

population that is also more prosperous than that of the more westerly states, and the contrast is apparent to all concerned. Furthermore, they account for a disproportionate share of welfare cases and arrests for misdemeanors and petty crimes; the illegitimacy rate is much higher than among their white neighbors, and the number of behavior problems among school children is greater. And no one should be surprised to learn that discrimination against them as Indians exists, however muted and disguised it may be.

Yet it is possible to dwell too exclusively on the poverty and crime among the Indians and the prejudice against them among whites. Beyond question, these people are better off economically and socially than most of the other fragments of the Santee Sioux. To a visitor who has traveled widely on Indian reservations or even in poverty-stricken white rural areas, their communities, especially Lower Sioux, present a relatively prosperous appearance.[42] The shabbiness in evidence at Prairie Island and Upper Sioux may not be due entirely to poverty but may in part reflect a value system that places less emphasis on externals. Some Indians whose front yards are strewn with discarded beer cans and old tires may be earning as much money as the white owner of a house that is the epitome of neatness and order. Part of the effort that a white man might put into maintaining a house and yard that his neighbors are expected to envy may, among Indians, go to satisfy less tangible (but no less worth-while) desires.

The celebrating and visiting other reservations that so many of the agents inveighed against in the nineteenth century still play an important role in the lives of the modern Sioux. Although the old ceremonies had largely died out among the Minnesota people before the ban was lifted in the 1930's, they continued to visit other reservations and take a more or less passive part in the celebrations there. In 1958, many years after the last drummer had died, the Prairie Island group inaugurated an annual pow-wow at which Indians from other places put on most of the show. Though never much of a financial success, the affair has continued ever since, chiefly as a means of bringing together Indians of various tribes and reaffirming their common identity as

---

[42] The appearance of prosperity may, of course, be deceptive. The neatness of houses and yards at Lower Sioux is probably due more to community spirit than to a superior economic position. No one there attempts to farm any more, and off-reservation employment is not always readily available. As a result, many younger people moved away in the middle 1960's. By 1967, the community numbered only nineteen families, and there were nine empty houses. (Interview with Mrs. Pearl Blue, Secretary, Lower Sioux Community Council, April 8, 1967.)

Indians. White visitors are welcome—sometimes they even take part in the dances—and account for a sizable share of the gate receipts, but the pow-wow is not primarily for their benefit. One may quibble about the authenticity of the dances and the costumes, but there is no denying that here is a small group of Indians, surrounded for the better part of a century by a wall of white people, who are asserting their racial identity and their determination to retain it.

Nor is this pow-wow the only way the Minnesota Sioux demonstrate that they are Indians, sharers in the culture, history, and destiny of their race. In 1961 five delegates—two from Prairie Island, two from Lower Sioux, and one from Upper Sioux—attended the American Indian Chicago Conference, at which a "Declaration of Indian Purpose" was drawn up. It was a valuable experience for them, one which gave them perspective on the Indian problem as it concerns Indians of diverse backgrounds and degrees of acculturation.[43] If there is more hope for the Minnesota Sioux and the Flandreau group than for the Santees elsewhere, it is partly because they seem to be seeking a way to reconcile the need for improved material circumstances with the need to retain their Indianness. They may not have found the solution, but they are aware of the problem and are not lost in apathy and defeatism. Together with the geographical advantages they enjoy, this willingness to face their problems and to specify conditions for its solution makes the outlook for them brighter than for any of the other Santee groups.

[43] American Indian Chicago Conference, *Declaration of Indian Purpose* (Chicago: American Indian Chicago Conference, 1961), pp. 41, 45. Two delegates from Devils Lake and one from Flandreau also attended; Santee and Sisseton were apparently unrepresented.

CHAPTER 18

The Santee Sioux
and the Indian Problem

THE SANTEE SIOUX have come a long way since their first encounter
with the white man in the winter of 1660. The course they have followed
in the past three centuries has, unfortunately, been mostly downward.
This is not to deny that the European invader brought material advantages which the Indians might have been centuries in attaining unaided. The life of the Santee Sioux in his aboriginal state was no doubt
nasty, brutish, and short. His descendants today live longer, eat more
regularly, and enjoy greater control over the natural environment than
he ever imagined possible. Yet the world of the Indian before the European intrusion was one of immense potentialities, comparable to the
Mediterranean world a few centuries before Christ. In Middle America
a relatively advanced civilization had been developed, and its influence
had spread into the southern and southwestern portions of the present
United States. Although the Sioux, like the Germans and Scandina-
vians at an earlier time, were still stone-age savages when white men
first broke in on them, who can say that they would not, like the northern Europeans, have received the torch of civilization from the south
in time? Except for the absence of large animals susceptible of domesti-
cation, there is nothing about the American environment to indicate

that the Indian would not have paralleled the white and yellow races in his progress toward civilization.

Unfortunately his progress—if it was that—was interrupted, his world shattered, and his culture largely supplanted by that of his conqueror. Unlike the peoples of Asia and Africa, he was displaced by the white invader and left with pitiful parcels of land, where he was constantly under pressure to abandon even his identity and become a white man. It must be admitted, however, that nineteenth century Americans, like their colonial predecessors, had tenderer consciences than most conquerors. Early in the process of conquest, a few of them sensed at least dimly that the Indian was being deprived of his traditional way of life and that it was morally incumbent upon the white man to offer him a substitute. Because of the ethnocentrism of European man and especially Anglo-Saxon man, the only substitute even considered was European civilization in what was assumed to be its highest form—that embraced by the men whose uneasy consciences were prodding them to think about the fate of the Indian. This meant that the Indian had to become an independent farmer and a Christian—there was some disagreement as to the order in which these transformations were to take place—after which the rest would follow in due course. Tribal customs and language would disappear, the white man's way of life and the English language would be universally adopted, and eventually the Indian, if he did not literally die out, would be absorbed into the general population.

This neat theory contained several fallacies. For one thing, almost all of those who sincerely wanted to find a way for the Indian to survive on a continent being overrun by white people failed to discriminate between the essential and the nonessential—between aspects of the white man's culture that the Indian would have to adopt in order to accommodate himself to the dominant civilization and aspects which he could very well ignore if only the white man would let him do so. Granted the inevitability of the occupation by Europeans of most of the American continent, there were two respects in which the Indian had to modify his culture if the two races were to share the continent in peace and harmony: Agriculture had to take the place of an economy based on hunting, fishing, and food-gathering; and intertribal warfare had to lose its centrality in the Indian system. Inasmuch as most tribes who originally occupied the present United States had some agriculture and some were almost totally dependent on it, the first of these necessary modifications would not have required so radical a transformation as many white men once believed. Because of the intimate connection of war with virtually every other aspect of life among most Indians, the second change would have been more difficult to effect, though an increased emphasis on agriculture would presumably have removed much of the motivation for warfare.

These changes were necessary. But there was no necessity for the Indian to give up his language, his religion (except as it was connected with war), his dress, his family relationship system, or his preference for collectivism over individualism. Yet the agents and missionaries insisted that the whole cultural apparatus had to be jettisoned—quickly. They did not understand that culture change is selective; some features of the new culture are adopted and others rejected, and old traits are not abandoned until they have lost their usefulness and their hold on the imaginations of the people possessing them. There was no necessity for the native languages to be expunged; the advantages of knowing English would ultimately have become evident to those Indians most able to profit from a knowledge of the invader's language. Nor was there any good reason why a loincloth was less suitable attire for a farmer than pantaloons, why collective use of land was less satisfactory for people accustomed to such a system than ownership in fee simple, or why polygamy could not be tolerated until altered economic and social conditions made it no longer practicable. As for religion, there was no reason why an Indian farmer who danced to produce rain should be less successful than the white farmers who observed a day of prayer in hopes of bringing an end to the grasshopper plague of the 1870's.

The people who wanted to save the Indian might have accomplished more if they had tried to do less. But two conditions were required for the necessary culture change to take place: time for the Indian to see the necessity for the change and to make it himself, and a place for him to work out his destiny in comparative freedom from overt external pressure. Neither of these was granted him. The whites wanted the land, and if the Indian were to survive, he would have to change his way of life in a hurry. There was always—and still is—a certain irritation with the slowness of the Indian to come around to the position designated for him by his conquerors. As Roy Harvey Pearce has said:

> Americans had always felt that the process of acculturation, of throwing off one way of life for another, would be relatively simple. To be civilized the Indian would have merely to be made into a farmer; this was a matter of an education for a generation or two. . . . But acculturation was not a simple process, as we know now, at least. For a culture is a delicately balanced

system of attitudes, beliefs, valuations, conditions, and modes of behavior; the system does not change and reintegrate itself overnight, or in a generation or two.[1]

Even if the white man had been more modest in his demands for culture change by the Indian, he did not permit the Indian time enough to accomplish even the necessary changes.

Nor was the Indian allowed to stay in one place long enough for the experiment to be tried. Two possibilities for acculturation existed: Indian tribes might either be permitted to remain as enclaves within predominantly white communities, learning from their neighbors much as European immigrants did, or they might be placed beyond the white settlements and there guided toward civilization by agents and missionaries, protected meanwhile from undesirable influences. Both techniques were tried, sometimes successively with a single tribe; all too often when the second expedient was adopted, white settlement caught up with the Indians, and they had to be moved repeatedly. There was much to be said for keeping the Indians in substantial isolation from the whites and letting this highly adaptable race pick and choose what it wished from the cultural inventory of the European within the framework of the existing system. That approach was tried repeatedly, by the British government late in the colonial period and by the United States government with its successive "Indian frontiers," and was finally abandoned only in 1907, when Indian Territory and Oklahoma became a single state.

When Columbus landed in the Bahamas, the chance for the American Indian to develop a civilization independently of the Old World was doomed. But at any time between then and the end of the nineteenth century it would still have been possible to permit him to accept what he wanted of European civilization at his own speed and in his own way, if only the white man had exercised restraint and understanding. The various attempts to secure for the Indian an opportunity to adjust gradually to the encroaching civilization show that there were men of good will, often in positions of authority and influence, who possessed some measure of those qualities. But the mass of the American people did not. It is well to remember that the Indian's worst enemy was not the whiskey dealer, the rapacious fur trader, or the corrupt Indian agent, but the American frontiersman, whom every school child has been taught to revere as the embodiment of all that is

---

[1] Roy Harvey Pearce, *The Savages of America: A Study of the Indian and the Idea of Civilization* (Baltimore: Johns Hopkins Press, 1953), p. 66.

admirable in the national character. We should not forget that the pioneer pictured by Walt Whitman as proudly bearing the torch of civilization into the wilderness was also the man who saw the Indian mainly as an obstacle to be removed, preferably with a bullet.

That is why the idea of Indian enclaves in settled country never really worked so long as the land they occupied was good enough to attract white men. The Cherokees did the impossible and accepted the white man's civilization in the hope of being allowed to stay in their homeland of northwestern Georgia. But even this remarkable achievement did not save them from expulsion when popular sentiment became strong enough and when the President of the United States refused to back up the decision of the Supreme Court in their favor. In Ohio, Indiana, Illinois, Iowa, Kansas, and finally Indian Territory itself the process was repeated. Grant Foreman tells, in *The Last Trek of the Indians*, how the civilized Wyandottes and the partially civilized Shawnees and Delawares were persecuted and harried out of Kansas by white men who wanted the farms they were successfully cultivating. If Doty's treaty had been passed by the Senate, the same thing would undoubtedly have happened in Minnesota sooner or later, as indeed it did when the Winnebagos were hustled off their reservation in 1863 on the pretext that they had at least sympathized with the Sioux during the uprising.

Corrupt as the old Indian Bureau often was, its leaders were nearly always more sympathetic toward the Indian than the typical white frontiersman. So were many of the men in Congress, though they usually bowed to political expediency when their constituents brought pressure on them to get a particular band of Indians off some land that was wanted for settlement. Such responsiveness to public opinion, coupled with the fact that the men who formulated Indian policy, sympathetic though they might be, knew nothing about the processes of culture change and would have rejected with horror the notion of cultural relativity if it had been presented to them, largely explains the course taken by the United States government in its relations with the Indians in the nineteenth century. The amazing thing is that the Indians survived at all, with anything of their old culture clinging to them.

Not all of the harm done to the Indians was the work of their enemies. So far as the assault on their culture is concerned, perhaps the greatest damage was done by those who regarded themselves as their best friends—the missionaries. Neither the loftiness of their motives nor the selflessness of their devotion to the Indians they sought to convert is questioned here, nor does there seem to be any doubt that many of them knew the Indians better than any other white men did. But their single-minded determination to Christianize the Indians, born of their unshakable conviction that Christianity—their own particular brand of Christianity—was the true religion, blinded them to everything good in the Indian character that grew out of or could be identified with the native religions. In their reduction of the Dakota language to writing they performed a valuable service, just as some of the Ponds' writings provide much of the evidence on which modern ethnologists base their reconstructions of the aboriginal culture. A Mennonite missionary named H. R. Voth studied the Hopis intensively and made important contributions to the science of ethnology, but by his frontal assault on the value system of those people he also contributed to the factionalism and individual psychological instability that exist today among them.[2] Likewise the missionaries to the Sioux, with their stress on man's innate sinfulness and the need to accept Christianity, not only undermined the sanctions and controls of the old faith but probably damaged the emotional and psychological balance of those who came under their influence.

Under the combined assault of the missionaries and the government officials, the culture of the Santee Sioux was shattered—not only those portions of it that were irreconcilable with the altered conditions imposed upon the Indians by European conquest, but also those features which in no way prevented the Indian from becoming a farmer and which might have had great utility as something to hold to during the transitional period. One can go further: much was lost that might have enabled the Indian to live in the modern world more successfully than the white American, whose extreme individualism often creates psychological tensions and sometimes renders him a menace to his fellows. If this thesis is accepted, then it becomes possible to argue that the greatest crime committed by the white man against the Indian was not in stealing from him a continent, but in denying to him the right to be an Indian—trying to deprive him of his racial and cultural identity.

At the same time that the effort was being made to transform the Indian into a white man, he was losing the land base that afforded him

[2] Harry C. James, *The Hopi Indians* (Caldwell, Idaho: Caxton Printers, 1956), p. 30. James describes the church erected by Voth as "an offensive eyesore on the landscape and a monument to religious persecution and intolerance." See also Laura Thompson, *Culture in Crisis* (New York: Harper & Brothers, 1950), pp. 35–36, 136–141.

the only means of competing economically with other Americans. In these two deprivations—loss of culture and loss of land—may be found the roots of the "Indian problem" as it exists today. Even if the cultural transformation had been as rapid and as complete as its proponents expected, most Indians could not have made a satisfactory living on the land left to them after allotment. Excoriation of nineteenth-century Indian policy and those who made and administered it will not seem like beating a dead horse if we recognize that the problem this policy was supposed to solve still exists, in different form. Most Indians, including the Santee Sioux, continue to be poorer than other Americans and to constitute a financial burden on the more prosperous segments of our society. For the federal government to renege on its promises and abandon its services to the Indians would only transfer the problem to agencies less capable of handling it. Hence the termination talk of the 1950's was at best premature and at worst merely the latest disguise for a design to get at the Indians' remaining resources.

If the Indian problem is to be solved within any finite period of time, the solution will have to proceed along the lines suggested by Gordon Macgregor in *Warriors Without Weapons*. Speaking of the Pine Ridge Sioux, he says: "They need a way of working themselves out of the present poverty through a permanent economy based on available resources. They need also greater self-direction to permit the regeneration of society."[3] The implication here and elsewhere in Macgregor's book is that, although outside guidance and help will be needed, the solution will ultimately have to come from the Indians themselves. If external influences can work to relieve the anxiety and insecurity that beset them, he suggests, perhaps something will happen within the group that will enable them to improve their condition. Since the psychological problem of the Santee Sioux much resembles that of the Pine Ridge people, though in less acute form, the same principles ought to apply in any discussion of remedies for their plight.

What can non-Indians do to bring about an improvement in the condition of the Indian? Even though the role white people can play in the regeneration of Indian society must and should be only a minor one, there are some things they can do. In the first place, they need to rid themselves of some stereotyped notions and hackneyed opinions. In the nineteenth century the standard argument was that the Indians' culture needed to be destroyed because it constituted an obstacle to their

[3] Gordon Macgregor, *Warriors Without Weapons* (Chicago: University of Chicago Press, 1946), p. 212.

success in a white-dominated world. In the twentieth century the line more commonly heard runs something like this: It's a pity that our grandparents insisted on stamping out the Indian culture, but they did a good job, and now there isn't enough left to bother trying to preserve; so the Indians had better hurry up and go the rest of the way to total acculturation. The fact is, however, that the Indian culture is not dead. Among some tribes it retains remarkable vitality, and enough survives even among the Santee Sioux to be taken into account whenever policy decisions are made with regard to them. Though some of the survivals of the aboriginal culture constitute a handicap to the Indians possessing them, non-Indians should not arrogate to themselves the right to decide which traits are serviceable and which are not and to deliberately try to wipe out the latter. There are enough pressures for conformity, both within the law and outside it, to accomplish this end indirectly.

Throughout the long period that the United States government has been trying to solve the Indian problem, it has been faced with a series of dilemmas which really boil down to one. In the late nineteenth century the agent worried about how to get his Indians to support themselves by farming, when every step in that direction brought a loss in government assistance but Indians who made no effort to help themselves received rations and supplies gratis. The modern form of this dilemma amounts to this: How can the freedom necessary to develop responsibility be reconciled with the protection and guidance needed to prevent disaster? The Indian Bureau has again and again been accused of paternalism, and no doubt there was at one time ample justification for the charge. On some reservations the average Indian lacks initiative and tends to go to the superintendent about all sorts of trivial matters. This is the result of decades of paternalism and decision-making *by* white men *for* Indians. Beginning with the Meriam Report and more noticeably in the Collier administration, there was a concerted effort to turn more and more of the decision-making over to the Indians. If they make mistakes, those mistakes have a certain educational value, provided they are not too serious.

The Santee Sioux have not, in the present century, been faced with decisions of such magnitude as the one the Indians of the Fort Berthold Reservation had to contend with when they received a settlement for land lost through the construction of the Garrison Dam and had to decide whether to use it for a tribal program or expend it in per capita payments. Furthermore, many of them have been making most of their own decisions for a long time; the Flandreau people and the Minnesota

colonies have experienced little of the paternalism that was characteristic at Fort Berthold and Pine Ridge in the late nineteenth and early
twentieth centuries. Because of their comparative freedom, they tend to
resent evidences of paternalism. When a Red Wing newspaper published a series on "Brotherhood Begins at Home," the president of the
Prairie Island community council replied with a courteous but critical
letter, in which he objected to the assumption that non-Indians know
better than the Indian what is good for him and that they are therefore
justified in determining the course of Indian policy, regardless of the
wishes of the beneficiaries. Whether these implications were really
present in the series is less important than the Indian reaction. The
Prairie Island leader also stressed the right of a group of people to retain its own identity—a "peculiarity in the Indian character elsewhere
called patriotism by other Americans."[4]

His comment may have been an oblique reference to the view, ex-
plicitly stated in the series, that the ultimate destiny of the Indian is to
be biologically as well as culturally assimilated to the dominant white
race. This notion, expressed by William Byrd in the early eighteenth
century, seems to have more staying power than almost any other myth
about the Indian, despite the fact that, while full-blood Indians are a
dwindling minority, the proportion of Indian blood in people who
identify as Indians may well be increasing. Not only are Indians growing in numbers; they are remaining Indians. Despite a constant
draining off to urban centers, most reservations continue to be over-
populated; and those individuals and families who move away tend
to gather in Indian communities and to associate chiefly with Indians in their new homes. In 1954 participants in the Wenner-Gren
Conference at the University of Chicago discussed the question of assimilation and concluded that, although individual Indians are disappearing
into the general population, most Indian tribes are holding onto their
identity. Speaking of the possibility that the present Indian communities
might vanish within the foreseeable future, they expressed the view that
no one could expect "such group assimilation within any short, pre-
dictable time period, say, one to four generations. The urge to retain
tribal identity is strong, and operates powerfully for many Indian
groups."[5]

[4] Letter from Norman Campbell, in Red Wing *Daily Republican Eagle*, March 6,
1961. Campbell wondered, in view of our record in Indian affairs, "How can a nation
like ours venture forth to solve human relations problems on a world wide scale?"

[5] John Provinse *et al.*, "The American Indian in Transition," *American Anthropologist*, LVI (June 1954), 388. Another symposium on Indian affairs concluded that

Although the people at the Wenner-Gren Conference were probably thinking mainly of the large western reservations, their conclusion applies with almost equal validity to the small groups of Santee Sioux scattered through the Dakotas, Nebraska, and Minnesota. Everywhere except at Santee and Lower Sioux their numbers are increasing or at least holding their own. The number of colonies in Minnesota has dwindled since the first census was taken in 1883, but those that have disappeared Faribault, Hastings, Wabasha were gone by the first decade of the twentieth century. Except for Prior Lake, where the land holdings are scattered, the others at which land was purchased have survived and give no indications of disappearing. If anything, the Indians' group consciousness and sense of identity seem to be increasing.

Another phenomenon observed among Indians today is pan-Indianism—the tendency for people to think of themselves as Indians rather than as Sioux or Chippewas or Winnebagos and to exchange surviving elements of their once diverse cultures. Besides such surface manifestations as the almost universal adoption of the Plains Indian headdress, pan-Indianism is evident in the growing awareness by Indians of their common problems and a growing consciousness that the old tribal differences are insignificant in comparison to what they all have in common. At times, when old grudges against the white man are aired, it can take a somewhat belligerent form. A newspaper report of the 1963 meeting of the National Congress of American Indians was headlined "Indian Battles for Rights—in Reverse" and went on to say that Indians want, not integration, but recognition of their identity as a separate race. Robert Burnette, retiring president of the NCAI, was reported as saying, "We are first-class citizens and more."[6] Although this attitude has not manifested itself openly among the Santee Sioux, it promises to become a force to be reckoned with there as elsewhere.

Perhaps such an attitude, though to a white person it may sound chilling or ludicrous, depending on how seriously he takes it, carries

---

"Indian groups residing on reservations (homelands) will continue indefinitely as distinct social units" and that "even though many Indians continue to live in separate communities with some distinctive cultural patterns, integration into the life of the larger society can still take place." See Edward P. Dozier, George E. Simpson, and J. Milton Yinger, "The Integration of Americans of Indian Descent," American Academy of Political and Social Science *Annals*, CCCXI (1957), 165. These authors distinguish sharply between "integration" and "assimilation."

6 "Indian Battles for Rights—in Reverse," Minneapolis *Star*, September 13, 1963. A useful discussion of pan-Indianism is James H. Howard, "Pan-Indian Culture of Oklahoma," *Scientific Monthly*, LXXXI (November 1955), 215–220.

with it the real hope for the Indian. The nonwhite peoples of the world have been asserting themselves in recent years, and the long domination by Europeans of Asia and Africa has been broken. Why should not the American Indian demand more for himself, now that the emperor has been discovered to have no clothes on, the growling dog to have no teeth? The growing strength of such organizations as the NCAI, with their potential for influencing the course of legislation, suggests that Indians are becoming more articulate. In the nineteenth century too few Indians had acquired enough education to be really articulate, and those who had were inclined to identify with the whites and to share the prevailing views on civilizing the Indian. But now that educational opportunities are reaching the reservation Indian, there is hope that a considerable body of educated Indians will emerge who are not alienated from their people and who will insist on a better life for those who choose not to migrate to the cities where young people of all races have traditionally sought jobs.

Indians would, of course, be less reluctant to leave the reservation if they could be reasonably sure of a friendly reception elsewhere. This does not mean simply a job for which they are qualified; so long as an Indian is second choice for a job, he has little opportunity to demonstrate his qualifications. And so long as the stereotype of the lazy, unreliable Indian persists, he will be second choice at best. Since it is currently unfashionable to express such racial stereotypes publicly, one seldom encounters this view in books, magazines, or newspapers, but anyone who lives near an Indian reservation or even talks casually with non-Indians in such a community soon hears it expressed. And occasionally it finds its way into print. In 1960, *Desert* magazine received a letter from a reader protesting against the amount of "Indian rot" published in the magazine. "If you would like to see Indians as they really are," the writer advised, "go up to Parker, Arizona any weekend and hang around the beer joints. Parker is a real Indian town."[7] Discrimination against Indians is an established fact in both Dakotas and exists in less obvious form in Nebraska and Minnesota. Racial prejudice among school children is one of the reasons for the high drop-out rate among Prairie Island Indians attending the Red Wing school, according to a study prepared in 1964.[8] Although the burden of conquering prejudice

[7] Letter from Will T. Scott, in *Desert*, XXIII (October 1960), 4. Scott claimed to know Indians, having lived most of his life in Indian country and shared his blankets with the Apache scouts who were tracking Pancho Villa in 1916.

[8] Red Wing *Daily Republican Eagle*, September 11, 1964. This study was conducted

falls mainly on the non-Indian, there is much that the Indian can do to prove the inaccuracy of sweeping generalizations about his race.

Not all of the Indians' unwillingness to leave their reservations is due to fear of discrimination against them elsewhere. Many Indians, like people of other races, feel a deep attachment to their home territory, however limited its resources may be and however dreary it may look to the casual visitor. Whatever its limitations, the reservation is a place where an Indian can be an Indian, where he does not have to adapt himself to alien manners and alien values. This desire to remain an Indian is something else that white Americans find difficult to understand, perhaps because most of them are descended from people who gave up their traditional ways to become Americans. Yet until it is understood, non-Indians cannot fulfill their rightful role in helping the Indian to achieve his destiny. So long as this determination to remain an Indian is thought of in purely negative terms—as sheer stubbornness or as a defense mechanism to cover a sense of inadequacy—the general public will continue to propose solutions that demand a reorientation of the Indian personality along white American lines.

The Meriam Report stressed the need to consider the desires of the individual Indian in any policy planning. Specifically, it said, "He who wishes to merge into the social and economic life of the prevailing civilization of this country should be given all practicable aid and advice in making the necessary adjustments. He who wants to remain an Indian and live according to his old culture should be aided in doing so."[9] Under the Collier administration this philosophy was adopted and practiced, but during the 1950's attention was concentrated on helping the Indian to leave the reservation and "join the mainstream of American life," to quote the cliché so overused by the advocates of termination and relocation. As long as there are plenty of white Americans who have no desire to "join the mainstream of American life," what wonder is it that an even higher proportion of Indians do not?

In a pluralistic society that professes to prize diversity (even while it embraces a surface uniformity), surely there is room for groups as well as individuals who depart noticeably from the norm. Every society

---

by a "committee of welfare, juvenile and school officials." Children questioned said that about 25 per cent of the white children were unfriendly toward Indians; teachers were said to give fair treatment to all.

[9] Lewis Meriam *et al.*, *The Problem of Indian Administration* (Baltimore: Johns Hopkins Press, 1928), p. 88. The Meriam commission pointed out that unless the Indians who wished to stay Indians were aided, they might become a menace.

needs its marginal men—its Thoreaus and its Veblens—who are in it
but not of it and hence are in a position to criticize it more perceptively
than those who participate fully in it. Can American society not profit
from marginal groups as well as marginal men—provided, of course,
that they are not marginal simply in the sense of being economically
deprived? Indians have often proved shrewd critics of the white world.
A body of educated, articulate Indians who remained outside the mainstream of American life could be of incalculable benefit to the society
surrounding them. Perhaps Americans would get along better with the
rest of the world if they were more frequently reminded that they have
in their midst people who do not wholly share the prevailing value
system. They need to know that their value system is not the only one
that men have found worth embracing. The *Sentinel*, the organ of the
National Congress of American Indians, stated the case well for the
preservation of Indian value systems:

> We must have a variety of real values and differences so that any person has
> many real options for living in our society. We believe that allowing total
> development of Indian communities on their own basis will be a major step
> in providing that variety in American life which is so necessary to a healthy
> society.[10]

Understanding the Indian's point of view and his desire to remain an
Indian requires knowledge. Hence perhaps the most important way
the white man can help solve the Indian problem is to inform himself
on the history and present condition of these people about whom he
really knows very little. Indifference and apathy are more serious obstacles to true understanding than outright prejudice, if only because
they are vastly more widespread. For every white man who nourishes
active hostility toward Indians, there are hundreds who neither know
anything about them nor care to know anything. Those who think they
know something may only be the victims of myths and stereotypes. To
stir people out of their ignorance and complacency is one of the tasks
of the Bureau of Indian Affairs. In 1948, Gordon Macgregor wrote that
an agency superintendent "must always continue to enlighten the
general public on Indian affairs for better Indian-white relations, and
to overcome the unbelievable amount of mis[in]formation and prejudice about Indians."[11] But superintendents are usually too busy with

[10] *NCAI Sentinel*, XI (Winter 1966), 2.

[11] Gordon Macgregor, "The Resources, People and Administration of Fort
Berthold Reservation North Dakota," Missouri River Basin Investigations Reports,
No. 60, p. 15. Mimeographed ms loaned by the Aberdeen Area Office, Bureau of
Indian Affairs.

their main job to be able to devote much time to public relations work. The ball must be carried a good share of the time by people outside the Indian Service, people whose access to information may be more limited than that of the Bureau official.

In enlightening the general public, as in dispelling prejudice, considerable responsibility rests on the Indian himself. Some forward-looking tribes are undertaking their own public relations programs. Museums, usually run jointly by the tribe and the Bureau, can be found here and there; newsletters are published by several groups; and of course many Indians contribute letters to newspapers and thus reach a wider audience than they could perhaps reach in any other way.[12] Indians can also help improve their collective image by cooperating, as most do, with serious investigators belonging to other races. Like other people, especially those in lower economic groups, Indians resent anything that looks like snooping into their private affairs, and the line separating a mere frivolous curiosity from a scientific or scholarly interest is sometimes pretty thin. The more thoroughly and objectively their history and contemporary culture are studied, however, the better chance there is that the American public, which finally determines the general course of Indian policy, will awaken from its complacency and lend its support to a sound program.

The history of the Santee Sioux is the history of the American Indian. Mutually profitable early contacts with Europeans were followed by a massive onslaught on the native culture, partly deliberate, partly fortuitous. Then came forced land cessions, removal to a reservation, smoldering resentment that erupted in a bloody but abortive protest, vindictive punishment, and a long, dismal period of attempted acculturation, ending in poverty and demoralization. If the outlook has been brighter since 1933, the flicker of hope has by no means yet been fanned into a real flame. Like their past, the future of the Santee Sioux will probably parallel that of the rest of the Indians in this country. A gifted, resilient, durable people, they may yet realize something of their potential if the white man will give them a chance.

[12] The anti-Indian tirade that appeared in the letter in *Desert* magazine elicited a response (among many others) from an Indian who remarked: "The white man looks down on the Indian for some unexplained reason. Those who claim to 'know' Indians take it for granted that some mysterious law of life made them superior to the Indian people—or any other dark skinned race, for that matter." See letter from Jimmie James, in *Desert*, XXIII (December 1960), 6. An agency superintendent, who prefers not to be identified, told the author: "This town is full of 'Indian experts,' who know less about Indians than people a thousand miles away."

Appendix

TREATIES WITH THE SANTEE SIOUX

Pike's Treaty of 1805
Conference Between the United States of America and the Sioux Nation of Indians.

WHEREAS, a conference held between the United States of America and the Sioux Nation of Indians, Lieut. Z. M. Pike, of the Army of the United States, and the chiefs and warriors of the said tribe, have agreed to the following articles, which when ratified and approved by the proper authority, shall be binding on both parties:

ARTICLE 1. That the Sioux Nation grants unto the United States for the purpose of the establishment of military posts, nine miles square at the mouth of the river St. Croix, also from below the confluence of the Mississippi and St. Peters, up the Mississippi, to include the falls of St. Anthony, extending nine miles on each side of the river. That the Sioux Nation grants to the United States, the full sovereignty and power over said districts forever, without any let or hindrance whatsoever.

ARTICLE 2. That in consideration of the above grants the United States (*shall, prior to taking possession thereof, pay to the Sioux two thousand dollars, or deliver the value thereof in such goods and merchandise as they shall choose*).

ARTICLE 3. The United States promise on their part to permit the Sioux to pass, repass, hunt or make other uses of the said districts, as they have formerly done, without any other exception, but those specified in article first.

In testimony hereof, we, the undersigned, have hereunto set our

373

hands and seals, at the mouth of the river St. Peters, on the 23rd day of September, one thousand eight hundred and five.

Z. M. PIKE, [SEAL]
First Lieutenant and Agent at the above conference.

LE PETIT CARBEAU, his x mark. [SEAL]
WAY AGA ENOGEE, his x mark. [SEAL]

From Charles J. Kappler, comp. and ed., *Indian Affairs, Laws and Treaties*, II (Washington: Government Printing Office, 1904), 1031.

Treaty of 1837

Articles of a Treaty, made at the City of Washington, between Joel R. Poinsett, thereto specially authorized by the President of the United States, and certain chiefs and braves of the Sioux nation of Indians.

ARTICLE 1st. The chiefs and braves representing the parties having an interest therein, cede to the United States all their land, east of the Mississippi river, and all their islands in said river.

ARTICLE 2d. In consideration of the cession contained in the preceding article, the United States agree to the following stipulations on their part.

First. To invest the sum of $300,000 (three hundred thousand dollars) in such safe and profitable State stocks as the President may direct, and to pay to the chiefs and braves as aforesaid, annually, forever, an income of not less than five per cent. thereon; a portion of said interest, not exceeding one third, to be applied in such manner as the President may direct, and the residue to be paid in specie, or in such other manner, and for such objects, as the proper authorities of the tribe may designate.

Second. To pay to the relatives and friends of the chiefs and braves, as aforesaid, having not less than one quarter of Sioux blood, $110,000 (one hundred and ten thousand dollars,) to be distributed by the proper authorities of the tribe, upon principles to be determined by the chiefs and braves signing this treaty, and the War Department.

Third. To apply the sum of $90,000 (ninety thousand dollars) to the payment of just debts of the Sioux Indians interested in the lands herewith ceded.

Fourth. To pay to the chiefs and braves as aforesaid an annuity for twenty years of $10,000 (ten thousand dollars) in goods, to be purchased under the direction of the President, and delivered at the expense of the United States.

Fifth. To expend annually for twenty years, for the benefit of Sioux Indians, parties to this treaty, the sum of $8,250 (eight thousand two hundred and fifty dollars) in the purchase of medicines, agricultural implements and stock, and for the support of a physician, farmers, and blacksmiths, and for other beneficial objects.

Sixth. In order to enable the Indians aforesaid to break up and improve their lands, the United States will supply, as soon as practicable, after the ratification of this treaty, agricultural implements, mechanics' tools, cattle, and such other articles as may be useful to them, to an amount not exceeding $10,000 (ten thousand dollars.)

Seventh. To expend annually, for twenty years, the sum of $5,500 (five thousand five hundred dollars) in the purchase of provisions, to be delivered at the expense of the United States.

Eighth. To deliver to the chiefs and braves signing this treaty, upon their arrival at St. Louis, $6,000 (six thousand dollars) in goods.

ARTICLE 3rd. [Stricken out by Senate.]

ARTICLE 4th. This treaty shall be binding on the contracting parties as soon as it shall be ratified by the United States.

In testimony whereof, the said Joel R. Poinsett, and the under-signed chiefs and braves of the Sioux nation, have hereunto set their hands, at the City of Washington, this 29th day of September A. D. 1837.

[Signatures omitted.]

From Charles J. Kappler, comp. and ed., *Indian Affairs, Laws and Treaties*, II (Washington: Government Publishing Office, 1904), 493–494.

Doty Treaties of 1841

Articles of a Treaty made and concluded at Oeyoowarha, on the Minnesota River, in the Territory of Iowa, between James Duane Doty, Commissioner on the part of the United States, and the Seeseeahto, Wofpato and Wofpakoota Bands of the Dakota (or Sioux) nation of Indians.

ARTICLE I. The said Bands do hereby cede to the United States all their right, title and claim to the country occupied or claimed by the said Dakota nation, and particularly to the Tract of country now occupied and owned by the said Bands which is bounded and described as follows to wit: On the South, by the boundaries of the cession made to the United States by the said Bands by their Treaty concluded on the 15th of July 1830: On the East, by a line commencing on the said boundary, thirty miles from the bank of the Mississippi, and running parallel to the general course of the said river thirty miles west of the said river until the said line intersects a line drawn north and south one mile west of Shahkopa's village on Minnesota river, and by the said last mentioned line and the Mississippi and Crow-Wing rivers; On the north, by a line drawn easterly from a point one mile north of the Traders House on Hindahkea Lake (Lac Travers) to the said Crow-Wing river, and westerly from the said point to the head of the said Hindahkea Lake and thence to the first forks of the stream which enters Eahtonkah Lake near its head, and from the said forks to the western declivity of the Hray, or Coteau de Prairie; and on the west by the said western edge of the said Coteau de Prairie to the head of Eahn river (Rock river) where the boundary line of the said cession of 1830 passes the said river: But the right of hunting and fishing as heretofore on the tract above described is reserved to the said Bands until the same is disposed of by the government of the United States to other tribes or persons.

ARTICLE II. The preceding cession is made to the United States upon the following conditions, to wit:

First. That all that part of the country hereby ceded (or so much thereof as may be deemed to be necessary by the government of the United States) as lies north of latitude forty three degrees and thirty minutes, shall be set apart as an Indian Territory, and allotted to people of the Indian blood, for agricultural purposes, and within which no white man shall be allowed to settle or remain except by the permission of the President.

Second. That whenever the chiefs of any band, or persons of the Indian blood shall desire to have a settlement made for agricultural purposes the President shall cause a sufficient portion of the land which shall have been allotted to such tribe or persons to be surveyed into lots of one hundred acres each (as near as may be) and one quarter of a mile in width in front if the said lot shall be located on a river or a lake:

Third. That all persons within the said Territory shall be subject to such government, rules and regulations as shall be established by the Government of the United States therein; and a Governor or Superintendent shall be appointed therefor:

Fourth. That all such persons who shall become inhabitants of the said Territory and occupy and cultivate for two years such tract as may be allotted to them, shall be entitled to receive a patent from the President of the United States therefor, and shall hold the said tract in fee simple, but shall be incapable of selling, transferring, leasing or otherwise disposing of such tract to any person other than a person of the Indian blood and to such person only with the assent of the Governor or Superintendent of the said Territory. And the estates of all persons who shall decease within the said Territory (and until other provision shall be made) shall descend according to the rule of the civil law.

Fifth. That every person who shall become a settler and cultivator, as aforesaid on the terms aforesaid, and who in the opinion of the said Governor is civilized, shall be entitled to have his or her name, by making personal application therefor, recorded in a register to be kept by said officer, and on such record being so made, shall become a citizen of the United States:

Sixth. That there shall be allotted to the Lower Seeseeahto Band a tract of one hundred thousand acres of land, on the east bank of Minnesota river at Eminnezhadah, twenty four miles in front on said river and six miles in depth;

To the Upper Seeseeahto Band two hundred thousand acres on the east bank of Eahtonkah and Hindahkea Lakes, forty miles in front on said lakes, and eight miles in depth, for themselves and for such Wofpato and other Indians as choose to settle with them with their assent;

To the Upper Wofpato Band one hundred thousand acres on the east bank of Minnesota river and Eadah Lake, and adjoining the last mentioned tract;

To the Lower Wofpato Band fifty thousand acres on the west bank of the Minnesota river, commencing at the boundary line of the cession made by this treaty, and running up the said river to a point four miles above Eahchaahkah or Little rapids;

And to the Wofpakoota Band seventy thousand acres on the west bank of Minnesota river, at Oeyoowarha, having a front on two sides on said river and bounded in rear by a line commencing at Mahyahshkadah or White Rock, and running thence ten miles west and thence south to Minnesota river.

Seventh. That settlements shall be commenced at the following places, to wit: at Eahchaahkah, or Little rapids; at Oeyooworha, or Traverse des Sioux; at Mukahto, or the mouth of Blue Earth river; at Wauhahozhoo or the mouth of Cottonwood river; at Eminnezhadah, or Petit Rocher; at Eadah or Lac qui parle; and at Eahtonkah or Big Stone Lake. There shall be reserved at the mouth of Mukahto river a tract of land on either bank for the use and residence of the Governor or Superintendent. Grist and saw-mills, and such other machinery for manufacturing as shall be necessary, shall be erected at the expense of the United States at each of the said places as they shall be required, or at such places nearest to those named where sufficient water power can be obtained for the purposes of said mills, provided the cost of said mills and the dams shall not exceed the sum of thirty thousand dollars:

Eighth. The United States shall cause to be fenced and ploughed ten acres of land (if required) for every person who shall settle at either of the places above named, and furnish to each family such farming utensils, spinning wheels and looms as may be necessary, and seed wheat, corn, potatoes and garden seeds the first two years; and shall also furnish to each settler one yoke of oxen, one cow, five sheep and two swine and build a house, on the tract occupied by the settler, for his use, the cost of which shall not exceed one hundred dollars. And if any Indian shall kill or destroy any of said animals belonging to another person, the value thereof shall be deducted from his annuity and the agent shall purchase another like animal therewith and deliver the same to the person whose animal was destroyed.

Nineth. The United States shall also establish schools at each of the said places in which the children of the inhabitants of the said Territory shall be admitted when in the opinion of the Superintendent (and at the request of the chiefs) schools shall be required; and the sum of twenty thousand dollars shall be set apart for said purpose and invested in stock until it shall be so required, and the interest accruing thereon shall be reinvested annually. And the Superintendent (or Governor) shall appoint teachers for the said schools, and employ millers to tend the mills when erected, and the farmers and mechanics and workmen at each of said places to teach the said Indians how to cultivate the earth, and also the most useful mechanic arts. Female teachers shall likewise be employed at each of said stations, to teach the Indian women the arts of domestic life; and to each of said persons an adequate compensation for their services shall be paid by the United States not exceeding five hundred dollars to each person per annum, but the sum of one thousand dollars per annum may be allowed to the male and female Superintendents whenever they shall become necessary. A blacksmiths house and shop shall be built at each of said places and a blacksmith employed for each, and supplied with iron and steel, and the whole cost at each place shall not exceed one thousand dollars annually. And five thousand dollars shall be annually expended by the United States in the purchase of medicines and the support of physicians at each of said settlements if required.

Tenth. An agent for the Upper Seeseeahto band shall be appointed to reside at Eatonkah, who shall receive an annual salary of twelve hundred dollars and hold his office during good behavior and be removable by the President; and one at Eminnezhadah for the Lower Seeseeahto band; one at Eahchaahkah for the lower Wofpato band, one at Eadah for the Upper Wofpato band and one at Mukahto for the Wofpakoota band, with like salaries; and the said agents shall be the Interpreters for the said bands. It shall be the duty of said agents to take charge of the affairs and interests of the said bands as well as those of the government, and to see that the stipulations of this treaty are fulfilled by each of the parties thereto; and shall also perform such other duties as may be required of them by the government of the United States and said agents shall be in all respects under the orders and directions of the Governor of the said Territory. And all payments to be made by the United States to the said Bands shall be made at the said places last named. Houses shall be built for the said agents, the cost of which shall not exceed eight hundred dollars each. The Half breeds or persons of the Indian or mixed blood may settle at either of the above named places. The preceding stipulations for the employment of farmers, millers, mechanics, blacksmiths, teachers and agents shall continue in force for the term of twenty years.

Eleventh. The Superintendent or Governor of the said Territory shall appoint a trader for each band, for the term of four years (unless sooner removed by the President, for cause) who shall give such security as shall be required of him by the Governor that he will comply with all the laws for the regulation of trade with the Indians and for the government of said Territory, and will furnish to the said band such goods as shall be required of him by the chiefs and their agent, and keep a sufficient supply constantly on hand. And whenever a family or band shall require any article of merchandise, and desire to purchase it of the said trader, they shall first obtain the permission of their agent who shall keep an account of the articles he allows each person to purchase and his name. The trader shall also keep a similar account in which he shall also charge the price of the article; and such trader shall be allowed to sell to two thirds of the amount of the annuity due to each Indian and the same shall be paid to him by the agent at the time of the payment of the annuity if the Indian shall have traded to that amount with him, and the remaining third and the balance of the annuity if any which may be due to him shall be paid in specie to each Indian. The said trade shall only be permitted by the agent at such periods of the year when he shall be satisfied that the articles applied for by the Indians will be most useful to them; and the books of the trader shall be subject to the inspection of the Governor and agent or either of them. The trader and the agent shall annually in the month of December make an invoice of the goods which they shall deem necessary for the supply of the band the ensuing year, and the trader shall without delay take the proper steps to purchase them and have them at the establishment on or before the first day of July in each year. The said trader shall present his invoice of purchases to the Governor who shall fix the prices, at a reasonable rate per centum on the cost and charges, at which the goods shall be sold to the Indians, being first satisfied that the goods have been purchased at the usual rates. And the said trader shall sell the said goods to the Indians at such prices as shall be established by the Governor and receive his payment accordingly from the annuity.

The trader for the Lower Wofpato Band shall reside at Eahchaahkah (Little Rapids) on the Minnesota river; for the Upper Wofpato Band at Eadah (Lac qui parle); for the Wofpakoota Band at Oeyooworha (Traverse des Sioux); for the lower Seeseeahto Band at Eminnezhadah (Petit Rocher) and for the Upper Seeseeahto Band at such point as may be selected by the Governor on Eahtonkah Lake. The intent of this provision for traders is, to secure the goods, which the Indians require, at reasonable rates, and at those periods of the year when they are in the greatest need of them.

Twelfth. To prevent disturbances and to preserve peace among the nations to be settled in the said Territory, the United States agree to erect forts and garrison them so long as they may be necessary on Eahtonkah Lake and on the bank of the Minnesota river directly opposite the mouth of Mukahto river. The United States shall also construct a good wagon road from Mindota (or the mouth [of] St. Peters River) to the several places herein selected for the agricultural settlements; provided the said road shall not cost more than thirty thousand dollars; and shall also expend thirty thousand dollars in removing the obstructions to the navigation of the said Minnesota river.

Thirteenth. The United States shall invest the sum of one million of dollars in some safe stock and pay to the said Indian Bands on the first Monday in July annually forever an income of not less than five per cent thereon in specie; and the President is hereby authorized to reserve one third of the said income in any year, and as often as it shall be required, as a contingent fund to be expended for the benefit of the said Bands equally, if in his judgment such reservation shall be necessary; and the amount so reserved shall be expended accordingly or otherwise be paid to the said Bands in specie at the next annual payment; said annuity to be paid in equal proportions to each of said three Bands of Wofpatos, Wofpakootas, and Seeseeahtos, that is to say the one third of said annuity to each band annually.

Fourteenth. That the United States shall deliver to the said Bands for the term of ten years, by the said agents and at such seasons as the said agents shall deem most useful to them, one hundred and fifty barrels of pork, three hundred barrels of flour, four thousand pounds of tobacco, and and [*sic*] on the conclusion of this treaty there shall be delivered to the chiefs of the said bands at Oeyooworha to the amount of ten thousand dollars, in goods and provisions including those provisions which have been distributed at the making of this treaty. But the President may, whenever he shall be satisfied the said bands do not require the said pork and flour or at the request of the chiefs of said Bands discontinue the delivery of the same, and pay the value thereof to the said bands in specie as a part of their annuity. And five thousand dollars shall be expended by the United States in the purchase of horses to be delivered to the chiefs and principal men of the said bands within one year from the date of this Treaty as a present to them. And the United States will pay the said Bands eight thousand dollars in horses annually for ten years being in lieu of provisions which it was at first agreed should be delivered to the said Bands.

ART. III. Several claims of settlers and traders which are believed to be just having been presented to the Commissioner against the said Bands, at the special request of the said Bands it is agreed that all debts and claims against the said Bands shall be referred to the Governor of the Territory of Iowa, the Superintendent of Indian Affairs of Michigan and the said Commissioner, who are hereby authorized to adjudicate thereon, and such sum or sums, not exceeding one hundred and fifty thousand dollars, as shall be found by a majority of them to be equitably and justly due to the said claimants shall be paid by the United States as a part of the consideration of the cession aforesaid.

ART. IV. If either of the preceding articles or stipulations shall be rejected by the Senate of the United States, the whole of this treaty shall be null and void.

Done at Oeyooworha this thirty first day of July A. D. one thousand eight hundred and forty one.

[Signatures omitted.]

Letter from Doty to the Secretary of War

Mindota (St. Peters)
August 4, 1841

The Hon. John Bell
    Sec'y of War

SIR

I have the honour to transmit herewith a Treaty which was concluded on the 31st. July at Oeyoowora, with the chiefs and principal warriors of the Wofpakoota, Wofpato and Seeseeahto Bands of the Dakota nation, and which has also the signature of one of the Eyankto chiefs whose village is at Hindakeah Lake.

Maps are also enclosed, which present an imperfect sketch of the country, but which are the most accurate I could obtain after receiving your instructions. On the map of the Minnesota river, I have marked the tracts selected for the permanent occupation of these Bands of Agriculturalists. Two of the Bands were found divided into separate villages, far apart, and they could not be reunited at present. They were not pressed much upon this point, as settlements of other Indians must be made at the same places, on the opposite side of the river, and adjoining them, who will require the services of the agents who are to be appointed there. It will be perceived that they are all upon the *north* bank of the river, and the greatest number on the northern and least valuable part of the cession.

The Dakota nation occupies the entire territory which lies between the Mississippi & the Missouri rivers, north of the cession made to the United States in the year 1830. The nation is divided into five bands which occupy distinct portions of the territory, as much so as though they were independent tribes. Their names are Mindawaukanto, Wofpakoota, Wofpato, Seeseeahto & Eyankto. I do not find that the bands ever meet in general council as a nation, though they are regarded as one nation in all the wars which are prosecuted with them. They are now at war on their eastern border with the Chippeways, on their western with the Omahaws, and on their southern with the Saukees, Foxes & Pootowotomees. There is therefore no part of their country in which they can feel secure against an enemy.

This Treaty conveys to the United States about thirty millions of acres, of which less than one third is waste land. The consideration to be paid is a little less than thirteen hundred thousand dollars. A larger tract was treated for than was suggested in your instructions; but a tract of five millions of acres only, which should be of so good a quality that each one hundred acres would possess a sufficient quantity of prairie and timber, and an adequate supply of water for a farm, is not to be found in this region.

After a particular examination of that part of the Dakota country which lies upon, and in the vicinity of the Minnesota river, no doubt was entertained that the settlements to be made by the Indians, must be confined for many years to the borders of the streams. On leaving the banks of this river, the prairies north and west are extensive, & without running water. The "lakes" in its vicinity I find are generally ponds, filled with rushes and maynomin, and at this season of the year (altho it is said to be quite unusual) many of them are dry, so that there is great difficulty in obtaining water to drink. But the soil is every where rich, and the higher the prairie, the better the land seems to be— with the exception of the bottoms of the rivers, which are not surpassed for depth of soil or fertility, by any streams in the western states. This will certainly be a very good country for those tribes which have made little or no advance in husbandry, and who must have an opportunity to hunt occasionally. The Dakotas have many large fields of corn on the banks of the Minnesota, from its mouth to its source. I am informed that it is a perfectly safe crop, & that at Eadah Lake (or Lac qui parle) the yield is seldom less than fifty bushels to the acre. At Oeyoowora I found it was large enough to eat on the 13th of July—and it is now too hard to be eaten boiled.

The valley or bottoms of the Minnesota, are from one to three miles in width, and there is generally a prairie on one side of the stream, and timber on the opposite bank. Above the rapids (which are fifty miles from its mouth, & to which point the river may be navigated by steam boats) there is a district about twenty five miles long, which is known as the Free Wood district. The timber is cotton wood (very large) elm, ash, maple, black walnut, cherry & butternut, and the banks are cover'd with sumach, sweet elder & grape vines on which there are many clusters of grapes now ripe. In the beds of the small streams which enter the river in this district, I found several excellent specimens of *coal*, and in such quantities as to leave no doubt that the hills by which the valley is bounded in this distance [district], are filled with this min eral which will possess a great value in this country. From the hills on the margin above this district, I also obtained good specimens of copper & or iron ore; & there is no doubt that copper is abundant on Mukahto river. All of these specimens will be forwarded to the Department by first opportunity.

The country on the south of the Minnesota, as far as the boundary of the cession made by these Bands in 1830, from the mouth of Mukahto (Blue Earth) river, & extending east to the margin of the Mississippi is exceedingly rich and fertile, well watered by lakes & small streams, and with proportionate quantities of prairie & timber. Every mile square of it is good. I endeavoured to obtain a cession of a portion of this, with the western part of the Minnesota valley, but difficulties were inter- posed by other Bands which were insurmountable, & I found it was easier to obtain the *whole*, by treating with all of the Bands, than a *small portion.* And these were the only terms upon which they would consent to settle as agriculturalists north of the Minnesota, for as long as they retained any country south, they would remain there. They have been so well informed, & of late so well instructed by the advan- tages which other neighbouring Indians have derived from their treat- ing with the United States, that to obtain any portion of their land, liberal provisions were unavoidable. It therefore became necessary, in my opinion, to compensate the govt. for these provisions by the cession of the whole country, that after having placed the various bands in the north west in situations which will be acceptable to them—and without being cramped for territory in doing so—it may sell a portion of it to remunerate itself for the purchase. Besides, in treating with the Indians who are to settle there, the tract which is allotted to them may be made a part of the consideration which is given for the lands from which they are to remove. Also, many of the provisions of this Treaty are of such a nature that the government will be relieved from the necessity of making similar ones with other tribes on their removal to this country, but which would otherwise be required. They are of general benefit to all who may settle, and as much for the advantage of emigrants as that of these bands. And they are indispensable to the formation and prosperity of the settlement.

From the observations which I have made since my arrival here, I am satisfied that the best interests of the settlement will be promoted, by erecting in the first instance the whole of the country between the Mississippi & Missouri rivers, and north of latitude 43° 30′ to latitude 46 into an Indian Territory, but confining the settlements to the centre of the territory as far as practicable. This will prevent the Indians from having daily intercourse with the whiskey traders—a distinct class from the regular traders of the country. I now find them spread along the eastern bank of the Mississippi engaged in this trafic [*sic*] & buying the goods, corn, and other provisions which have been delivered to the Mississippi bands by the United States. At least four barrels of whiskey were bought of these traders & brought to the treaty ground at Oeyoowora by Indians the use of which was with the greatest difficulty restrained pending the negotiation. It seems that these men have enjoyed this illicit trafic so long, that it no longer attracts the attention of the agents of government in this quarter. I would therefore place the Indians so far from the borders of these rivers as practicable, and also from any land belonging to the United States upon which these people can squat.

This treaty provides for a radical change in the policy of the United States towards the Indians, & which I presume will mark the policy of this Administration hereafter.

It provides a mode by which persons of the Indian blood can become citizens of the United States. It is the fulfilment of the promise which the white man made the Indian, when he landed on this continent. It has often been renewed, with the assurance that so soon as the Indian became civilized he should be entitled to the civil and political privileges of our own citizens. This provision leaves it for the Indian to determine whether he will avail himself of this privilege or not.

It provides a mode by which an Indian may become the individual owner of the land he occupies, & hold it by patent from the President. This establishes the object of property *in the soil in individuals*, & with the assent of the Indian, establishes the law of descent.

It provides for a radical change in the system of Indian Trade, so far at least as that trade is dependent on the annuities. The Govt. will now be able to regulate and controul the trade, having the privilege to appoint and remove the trader and to fix his prices, without the danger which now exists from the competition of rival Traders, who are in no respect dependent upon the Government.

It provides for a change in the mode & place of payment of annuities, which by the present system are the bane of the Indians. They are not required to leave their villages to receive their goods or money, and are not therefore, at that period which is most dangerous, to their morals at least, brought into the white settlements. The whole amount is not to be paid to them at once, but they may receive to two thirds of the amount of their annuity of their trader, at such periods of the year, and in such articles, as in the opinion of their agent their circumstances demand. They will thus receive their annuity when it will be most useful to them.

In consequence of the failure of government to pay to Indians their annuities at the time appointed by the treaties with them, and at the seasons of the year when these necessities require, the supplies which they can only obtain on a *credit* from their traders, or with their annuities, the system of *credits* has been continued, and indeed been absolutely necessary in many instances to save the Indian from suffering. Nothing but punctuality on the part of Govt. can establish the relations which ought to exist between the Indians and the Govt.—that is, the Indians should feel dependent on the *Government*, and not on the *Trader*. Unless this dependence is established, it is in vain for the Govt. to attempt to exercise any influence over them, except that of force.

The provision in favour of an examination of the Traders claims was made, from the obligation which the Indians of this country acknowledge themselves to be under for the credits which they have given them for goods when they were in need, and the various benefits which they have bestow'd upon them at their establishments. The justice and validity of these claims they admitted, and desired that an allowance should be made, and also a stipulation for their immediate payment. This could not be done, because time would not permit, and because of the assurance which was felt that the Department would prefer to have the subject under its controul. One of the commissioners at least is intimately acquainted with the extent and character of the trade with these Bands for more than twenty year, & to this I may add my own knowledge of the persons engaged in the trade for about the same period. My own opinion is, that the just claims cannot exceed fifty thousand dollars.

This Treaty also provides a permanent home for the Half-Breeds, or persons of the Indian Blood, of the north west, who number about two thousand, and who are now floating between savage & civilized life, without being attached to either. In other Treaties, provision in money has been made for them, but this has been of no real advantage to them, as the money has either been immediately squandered, or given into the hands of white men who have been unable to return it.

Experience has shown that this class must be used in any attempt to civilize the Indians. They are the connecting link between the savage & civilized man, & ought to be employed by government as its agents, interpreters & teachers, where they possess, as they frequently do, the requisite qualifications. An opportunity will thus be given them to establish a character for themselves, to obtain a place in civilized life, I might say among human beings, for *Indian Blood*, and it will be for their interest to be faithful and give their best efforts in aid of the purposes of government—many of them are well educated, & the example of those who are farmers, and mechanics, as well as their teaching, will be most beneficial to the Indians.

I have the honour to be, with great respect

Your most obedient servant

J. D. Doty

Articles of a Treaty made and concluded at Mindota, in the Territory of Iowa, between James Duane Doty, Commissioner on the part of the United States, and the Minda Waukanto Bands of the Dakota Nation.

ARTICLE I. The chiefs and warriors of the said bands do hereby cede to the United States all of the right, title and claim of the said Bands to the country West of the Mississippi river.

ARTICLE II. The preceding cession is made and accepted upon the conditions contained in the first five and the eighth and eleventh sections or clauses of the second article of the Treaty concluded between the United States and the Wofpato, Wofpakoota and Seeseeahto Bands of the Dakota nation on the thirty-first day of July A.D. one thousand eight hundred and forty-one at Oeyoowora.

And the said Bands parties hereto, agree to remove to the north side of Minnesota river, at their own expense, and occupy as agriculturists such tracts as shall be allotted to them, allowing one hundred acres to each soul. The said Bands shall be at liberty to choose their places of residence either at Eachaahkah, opposite Mukahto, or below the Wofpakoota reservation; and the agents residing nearest to the places at which they shall become settled, shall perform the duties of agents for the said Bands.

ARTICLE III. The United States agree to invest in some safe stock the sum of sixty thousand dollars, for the benefit of the Shahkopa Band, and to pay to the said Band annually forever an interest thereof of not less than five per centum in the month of June, commencing with the month of June 1842. Also the sum of sixty-six thousand dollars for the benefit of the Waukea Tonka Band and to pay to the said Band annually forever an interest thereon of not less than five per centum. And also the sum of eighty thousand dollars for the benefit of the Waumunde Tonka, Mukapa Wichasta and Tahchunkah Washta Bands and to pay to the said Bands together annually forever an interest thereon of not less than five per centum.

And the United States agree to deliver to the said Bands, twenty-five hundred and twelve dollars worth of goods and provisions, the receipt of which the said Bands do hereby acknowledge to have received of the said Commissioner.

It is also agreed that the Shahkopee Band may settle next above the Wofpato Band at Eachaahkah; and the Waukea Tonka Band next below the Wofpakoota Band at Mahyashkadah.

ARTICLE IV. The United States agree to appoint three traders for the said Bands, according to the provisions of the said eleventh section of the said Treaty; and all payment to the said Bands either in money or goods shall be made at the three villages which may be established by them as aforesaid. And the United States also agree that all of the conditions and stipulations of the Treaty with the said Minda Waukanto Bands, concluded on the 29th day of September A.D. 1837, shall be and remain valid, and shall be executed and performed on its part, at the said villages; and the whole amount of the income provided for in the second article of the said Treaty, shall be paid to the said bands as aforesaid, in proportion to their numbers.

Done at Mindota, this eleventh day of August A.D. one thousand eight hundred and forty-one.

[No signatures on manuscript.]

From NARS, RG 75, LR, St. Peter's Agency, Roll 759 (1840–1844). The first treaty is also found in Thomas Hughes, *Old Traverse Des Sioux* (St. Peter, Minn.: Herald Publishing Co., 1929), pp. 166–170.

Treaty of Traverse des Sioux

Articles of a treaty made and concluded at Traverse des Sioux, upon the Min-
nesota River, in the Territory of Minnesota, on the twenty-third day of July,
eighteen hundred and fifty-one, between the United States of America, by Luke
Lea, Commissioner of Indian Affairs, and Alexander Ramsey governor and ex-
officio superintendent of Indian affairs in said Territory, commissioners duly
appointed for that purpose, and See-see-toan and Wah-pay-toan bands of
Dakota or Sioux Indians.

ARTICLE 1. It is stipulated and solemnly agreed that the peace and
friendship now so happily existing between the United States and the
aforesaid bands of Indians, shall be perpetual.

ARTICLE 2. The said See-see-toan and Wah-pay-toan bands of Dakota or Sioux Indians, agree to cede, and do hereby cede, sell, and relinquish to the United States, all of their lands in the State of Iowa;
and, also all their lands in the Territory of Minnesota, lying east of the
following line, to wit: Beginning at the junction of the Buffalo River
with the Red River of the North; thence along the western bank of said
Red River of the North, to the mouth of the Sioux Wood River; thence
along the western bank of said Sioux Wood River to Lake Traverse;
thence, along the western shore of said lake, to the southern extremity
thereof; thence in a direct line, to the junction of Kampeska Lake with
the Tchan-kas-an-data, or Sioux River; thence along the western bank
of said river to its point of intersection with the northern line of the
State of Iowa; including all the islands in said rivers and lake.

ARTICLE 3. [Stricken out.]

ARTICLE 4. In further and full consideration of said cession, the
United States agree to pay to said Indians the sum of one million six
hundred and sixty-five thousand dollars ($1,665,000) at the several
times, in the manner and for the purposes following, to wit:

1st. To the chiefs of the said bands, to enable them to settle their
affairs and comply with their present just engagement; and in consideration of their removing themselves to the country set apart for
them as above, which they agree to do within two years, or sooner, if
required by the President, without further cost or expense to the United
States, and in consideration of their subsisting themselves the first year
after their removal, which they agree to do without further cost or expense on the part of the United States, the sum of two hundred and

seventy-five thousand dollars, ($275,000): *Provided*, That said sum shall be paid to the chiefs in such manner as they, hereafter, in open council shall request, and as soon after the removal of said Indians to the home set apart for them, as the necessary appropriation therefor shall be made by Congress.

2d. To be laid out under the direction of the President for the establishment of manual-labor schools; the erection of mills and blacksmith shops, opening farms, fencing and breaking land, and for such other beneficial objects as may be deemed most conducive to the prosperity and happiness of said Indians, thirty thousand dollars, ($30,000).

The balance of said sum of one million six hundred and sixty-five thousand dollars, ($1,665,000,) to wit: one million three hundred and sixty thousand dollars ($1,360,000) to remain in trust with the United States, and five per cent. interest thereon to be paid, annually, to said Indians for the period of fifty years, commencing the first day of July, eighteen hundred and fifty-two (1852), which shall be in full payment of said balance, principal and interest, the said payment to be applied under the direction of the President, as follows, to wit:

3d. For a general agricultural improvement and civilization fund, the sum of twelve thousand dollars, ($12,000.)

4th. For educational purposes, the sum of six thousand dollars, ($6,000.)

5th. For the purchase of goods and provisions, the sum of ten thousand dollars, ($10,000).

6th. For money annuity, the sum of forty thousand dollars, ($40,000).

ARTICLE 5. The laws of the United States prohibiting the introduction and sale of spirituous liquors in the Indian country shall be in full force and effect throughout the territory hereby ceded and lying in Minnesota until otherwise directed by Congress or the President of the United States.

ARTICLE 6. Rules and regulations to protect the rights of persons and property among the Indians, parties to this treaty, and adapted to their condition and wants, may be prescribed and enforced in such manner as the President or the Congress of the United States, from time to time shall direct.

In testimony whereof, the said Commissioners, Luke Lea and Alexander Ramsey, and the undersigned Chiefs and Headmen of the aforesaid See-see-toan and Wah-pay-toan bands of Dakota or Sioux Indians, have hereunto subscribed their names and affixed their seals, in duplicate, at Traverse des Sioux, Territory of Minnesota, this twenty-third day of July, one thousand eight hundred and fifty-one.

[Signatures omitted.]

SUPPLEMENTAL ARTICLE.

1st. The United States do hereby stipulate to pay the Sioux bands of Indians, parties of this treaty, at the rate of ten cents per acre, for the lands included in the reservation provided for in the third article of the treaty as originally agreed upon in the following words:

"ARTICLE 3. In part consideration of the foregoing cession, the United States do hereby set apart for the future occupancy and home of the Dakota Indians, parties of this treaty, to be held by them as Indian lands are held, all that tract of country on either side of the Minnesota River, from the western boundary of the lands herein ceded, east, to the Tchay-tam-bay River on the north, and to Yellow Medicine River on the south side, to extend on each side, a distance of not less than ten miles from the general course of said river; the boundaries of said tract to be marked out by as straight lines as practicable, whenever deemed expedient by the President, and in such manner as he shall direct:" which article has been stricken out of the treaty by the Senate, the said payment to be in lieu of said reservation: the amount when ascertained under instructions from the Department of the Interior, to be added to the trust-fund provided for in the fourth article.

2d. It is further stipulated, that the President be authorized, with the assent of the said band of Indians, parties to this treaty, and as soon after they shall have given their assent to the foregoing *article*, as may be convenient, to cause to be set apart by appropriate landmarks and boundaries, such tracts of country without the limits of the cession made by the first [2d] article of the treaty as may be satisfactory for their future occupancy and home: *Provided,* That the President may, by the consent of these Indians, vary the conditions aforesaid if deemed expedient.

From Charles J. Kappler, comp. and ed., *Indian Affairs, Laws and Treaties,* II (Washington: Government Printing Office, 1904), 588–590.

The treaty of Mendota, signed August 5, 1851, is essentially the same as that of Traverse des Sioux, except for descriptions of lands ceded and lands held as a reservation, and amounts paid by the United States.

The following additional paragraph is included: "The entire annuity, provided for in the first section of the second article of the treaty of September twenty-ninth, eighteen hundred and thirty-seven, (1837), including an unexpended balance that may be in the Treasury on the first of July, eighteen hundred and fifty-two, (1852), shall thereafter be paid in money." See Kappler, *Indian Affairs, Laws and Treaties*, II 591–593.

Treaty of 1867

WHEREAS it is understood that a portion of the Sissiton and Warpeton bands of Santee Sioux Indians, numbering from twelve hundred to fifteen hundred persons, not only preserved their obligations to the Government of the United States, during and since the outbreak of the Medewakantons and other bands of Sioux in 1862, but freely perilled their lives during that outbreak to rescue the residents on the Sioux reservation, and to obtain possession of white women and children made captives by the hostile bands; and that another portion of said Sissiton and Warpeton bands, numbering from one thousand to twelve hundred persons, who did not participate in the massacre of the whites in 1862, fearing the indiscriminate vengeance of the whites, fled to the great prairies of the Northwest, where they still remain; and

WHEREAS Congress, in confiscating the Sioux annuities and reservations, made no provision for the support of these, the friendly portion of the Sissiton and Warpeton bands, and it is believed they have been suffered to remain homeless wanderers, frequently subject to intense sufferings from want of subsistence and clothing to protect them from the rigors of a high northern latitude, although at all times prompt in rendering service when called upon to repel hostile raids and to punish depredations committed by hostile Indians upon the persons and property of the whites; and

WHEREAS the several subdivisions of the friendly Sissitons and Warpetons bands ask, through their representatives, that their adherence to their former obligations of friendship to the Government and people of the United States be recognized, and that provision be made to enable them to return to an agricultural life and be relieved from a dependence upon the chase for a precarious subsistence: THEREFORE,

A treaty has been made and entered into, at Washington City, District of Columbia, this nineteenth day of February, A.D. 1867, by and between Lewis V. Bogy, Commissioner of Indian Affairs, and William H. Watson, commissioners, on the part of the United States, and the undersigned chiefs and head-men of the Sissiton and Warpeton bands of Dakota or Sioux Indians, as follows, to wit:

ARTICLE 1. The Sissiton and Warpeton bands of Dakota Sioux Indians, represented in council, will continue their friendly relations with the Government and people of the United States, and bind themselves individually and collectively to use their influence to the extent of their ability to prevent other bands of Dakota or other adjacent tribes from making hostile demonstrations against the Government or people of the United States.

ARTICLE 2. The said bands hereby cede to the United States the right to construct wagon-roads, railroads, mail stations, telegraph lines, and such other public improvements as the interest of the Government may require, over and across the lands claimed by said bands, (including their reservation as hereinafter designated) over any route or routes that *that* may be selected by the authority of the Government, said lands so claimed being bounded on the south and east by the treaty-line of 1851, and the Red River of the North to the mouth of Goose River; on the north by the Goose River and a line running from the source thereof by the most westerly point of Devil's Lake to the Chief's Bluff at the head of James River, and on the west by the James River to the mouth of Mocasin River, and thence to Kampeska Lake.

ARTICLE 3. For and in consideration of the cession above mentioned, and in consideration of the faithful and important services said to have been rendered by the friendly bands of Sissitons and Warpeton Sioux here represented, and also in consideration of the confiscation of all their annuities, reservations, and improvements, it is agreed that there shall be set apart for the members of said bands who have heretofore surrendered to the authorities of the Government, and were not sent to the Crow Creek reservation, and for the members of said bands who were released from prison in 1866, the following-described lands as a permanent reservation, viz:

Beginning at the head of Lake Travers[e], and thence along the treaty-line of the treaty of 1851 to Kampeska Lake; thence in a direct line to Reipan or the northeast point of the Coteau des Prairie[s], and thence passing north of Skunk Lake, on the most direct line to the foot of Lake Traverse, and thence along the treaty-line of 1851 to the place of beginning.

ARTICLE 4. It is further agreed that a reservation be set apart for all other members of said bands who were not sent to the Crow Creek reservation, and also for the Cut-Head bands of Yanktonais Sioux, a reservation bounded as follows, viz:

Beginning at the most easterly point of Devil's Lake; thence along the waters of said lake to the most westerly point of the same; thence on a direct line to the nearest point in the Cheyenne River; thence down said river to a point opposite the lower end of Aspen Island, and thence on a direct line to the place of beginning.

ARTICLE 5. The said reservations shall be apportioned in tracts of (160) one hundred and sixty acres to each head of a family or single person over the age of (21) twenty-one years, belonging to said bands and entitled to locate thereon, who may desire to locate permanently and cultivate the soil as a means of subsistence: each (160) one hundred and sixty acres so allotted to be made to conform to the legal subdivisions of the Government surveys when such surveys shall have been made; and every person to whom lands may be allotted under the provisions of this article, who shall occupy and cultivate a portion thereof for five consecutive years shall thereafter be entitled to receive a patent for the same so soon as he shall have fifty acres of said tract fenced, ploughed, and in crop: *Provided*, said patent shall not authorize any transfer of said lands, or portions thereof, except to the United States, but said lands and the improvements thereon shall descend to the proper heirs of the persons obtaining a patent.

ARTICLE 6. And, further, in consideration of the destitution of said bands of Sissiton and Warpeton Sioux, parties hereto, resulting from the confiscation of their annuities and improvements, it is agreed that Congress will, in its own discretion, from time to time make such appropriations as may be deemed requisite to enable said Indians to return to an agricultural life under the system in operation on the Sioux reservation in 1862; including, if thought advisable, the establishment and support of local and manual-labor schools; the employment of agricultural, mechanical, and other teachers; the opening and improvement of individual farms; and generally such objects as Congress in its wisdom shall deem necessary to promote the agricultural improvement and civilization of said bands.

ARTICLE 7. An agent shall be appointed for said bands, who shall be located at Lake Traverse; and whenever there shall be five hundred (500) persons of said bands permanently located upon the Devil's Lake reservation there shall be an agent or other competent person appointed to superintend at that place the agricultural, educational, and mechanical interests of said bands.

ARTICLE 8. All expenditures under the provisions of this treaty shall be made for the agricultural improvement and civilization of the members of said bands authorized to locate upon the respective reservations, as hereinbefore specified, in such manner as may be directed by law; but no goods, provisions, groceries, or other articles—except materials for the erection of houses and articles to facilitate the operations of agriculture—shall be issued to Indians or mixed-bloods on either reservation unless it be in payment for labor performed or for produce delivered: *Provided,* That when persons located on either reservation, by reason of age, sickness, or deformity, are unable to labor, the agent may issue clothing and subsistence to such persons from such supplies as may be provided for said bands.

ARTICLE 9. The withdrawal of the Indians from all dependence upon the chase as a means of subsistence being necessary to the adoption of civilized habits among them, it is desirable that no encouragement be afforded them to continue their hunting operations as a means of support, and, therefore, it is agreed that no person will be authorized to trade for furs or peltries within the limits of the land claimed by said bands, as specified in the second article of this treaty, it being contemplated that the Indians will rely solely upon agricultural and mechanical labor for subsistence, and that the agent will supply the Indians and mixed-bloods on the respective reservations with clothing, provisions, &c., as set forth in article eight, so soon as the same shall be provided for that purpose. And it is further agreed that no person not a member of said bands, parties hereto whether white, mixed-blood, or Indian, except persons in the employ of the Government or located under its authority, shall be permitted to locate upon said lands, either for hunting, trapping, or agricultural purposes.

ARTICLE 10. The chiefs and head-men located upon either of the reservations set apart for said bands are authorized to adopt such rules, regulations, or laws for the security of life and property, the advancement of civilization, and the agricultural prosperity of the members of said bands upon the respective reservations, and shall have authority, under the direction of the agent, and without expense to the Government, to organize a force sufficient to carry out all such rules, regulations, or laws, and all rules and regulations for the government of said Indians, as may be prescribed by the Interior Department: *Provided,* That all rules, regulations, or laws adopted or amended by the chiefs and head-men on either reservation shall receive the sanction of the agent.

In testimony whereof, we, the commissioners representing the United States, and the delegates representing the Sissiton and Warpeton bands of Sioux Indians, have hereunto set our hands and seals, at the place and on the day and year above written.

[Signatures omitted.]

From Charles J. Kappler, comp. and ed., *Indian Affairs, Laws and Treaties,* II (Washington: Government Printing Office, 1904), 956–959.

Letter from Bishop Whipple to President Lincoln

March 6, 1862

TO THE PRESIDENT OF THE UNITED STATES.

The sad condition of the Indians of this State, who are my heathen wards, compels me to address you on their behalf. I ask only justice for a wronged and neglected race. I write the more cheerfully because I believe that the intentions of the Government have always been kind; but they have been thwarted by dishonest servants, ill-conceived plans, and defective instructions.

Before their treaty with the United States, the Indians of Minnesota were as favorably situated as an uncivilized race could well be. Their lakes, forests, and prairies furnished abundant game, and their hunts supplied them with valuable furs for the purchase of all articles of traffic. The great argument to secure the sale of their lands is the promise of their civilization. . . . The sale is made, and after the dishonesty which accompanies it there is usually enough money left, if honestly expended, to foster the Indians' desires for civilization. Remember, the parties to this contract are a great Christian Nation and a poor heathen people.

From the day of the treaty a rapid deterioration takes place. The Indian has sold the hunting-grounds necessary for his comfort as a wild man; his tribal relations are weakened; his chief's power and influence circumscribed; and he will soon be left a helpless man without a government, a protector, or a friend, unless the solemn treaty is observed.

The Indian agents who are placed in trust of the honor and faith of the Government are generally selected without any reference to their fitness for the place. The Congressional delegation desires to award John Doe for party work, and John Doe desires the place because there is a tradition on the border than an Indian Agent with fifteen hundred dollars a year can retire upon an ample fortune in four years.

The Indian agent appoints his subordinates from the same motive, either to reward his friends' service, or to fulfill the bidding of his Congressional patron. They are often men without any fitness, sometimes a disgrace to a Christian nation; whiskey-sellers, bar-room loungers, debauchers, selected to guide a heathen people. Then follow all the evils of bad example, of inefficiency, and of dishonesty—the school a sham, the supplies wasted, the improvement fund squandered by negligence or curtailed by fraudulent contracts. The Indian, bewildered, conscious of wrong, but helpless, has no refuge but to sink into a depth of brutishness. There have been noble instances of men who have tried to do their duty; but they have generally been powerless for lack of hearty cooperation of others, or because no man could withstand the corruption which has pervaded every department of Indian affairs.

The United States has virtually left the Indian without protection. . . . I can count up more than a dozen murders which have taken place in the Chippewa Count[r]y within two years. . . . There is no law to protect the innocent or punish the guilty. The sale of whiskey, the open licentiousness, the neglect and want are fast dooming this people to death, and as sure as there is a God much of the guilt lies at the Nation's door.

The first question is, can these red men become civilized? I say, unhesitatingly, *yes*. The Indian is almost the only heathen man on earth who is not an idolater. In his wild state he is braver, more honest, and virtuous than most heathen races. He has warm home affections and strong love of kindred and country. The Government of England has, among Indians speaking the same language with our own, some marked instances of their capability of civilization. In Canada you will find there are hundreds of civilized and Christian Indians, while on this side of the line there is only degradation.

The first thing needed is *honesty*. There has been a marked deterioration in Indian affairs since the office has become one of mere political favoritism. Instructions are not worth the price of the ink with which they are written if they are to be carried out by corrupt agents. Every employee ought to be a man of purity, temperance, industry, and unquestioned integrity. Those selected to teach in any department must be men of peculiar fitness,—patient, with quick perceptions, enlarged ideas, and men who love their work. They must be something better than so many drudges fed at the public crib.

The second step is to frame instructions so that the Indian shall be the ward of the Government. They cannot live without law. We have broken up, in part, their tribal relations, and they must have something in their place.

Whenever the Indian desires to abandon his wild life, the Government ought to aid him in building a house, in opening his farm, in providing utensils and implements of labor. His home should be conveyed to him by a patent, and be inalienable. It is a bitter cause of complaint that the Government has not fulfilled its pledges in this respect. It robs the Indian of manhood and leaves him subject to the tyranny of wild Indians, who destroy his crops, burn his fences, and appropriate the rewards of his labor.

The schools should be ample to receive all children who desire to attend. As it is, with six thousand dollars appropriated for the Lower Sioux for some seven years past, I doubt whether there is a child at the lower agency who can read who has not been taught by our missionary. Our Mission School has fifty children, and the entire cost of the mission, with three faithful teachers, every dollar of which passes through my own hands, is less than seven hundred dollars a year.

In all future treaties it ought to be the object of the Government to pay the Indians in kind, supplying their wants at such times as they may require help. This valuable reform would only be a curse in the hands of a dishonest agent. If wisely and justly expended, the Indian would not be as he now is,—often on the verge of starvation.

There ought to be a concentration of the scattered bands of Chippewas upon one reservation, thus securing a more careful oversight, and also preventing the sale of fire-water and the corrupt influence of bad men. The Indian agent ought to be authorized to act as a United States Commissioner, to try all violations of Indian laws. It may be beyond my province to offer these suggestions; I have made them because my heart aches for this poor wronged people. The heads of the Department are too busy to visit the Indian country, and even if they did it would be to find the house swept and garnished for an official visitor. It seems to me that the surest plan to remedy these wrongs and to prevent them for the future, would be to appoint a commission of some three persons to examine the whole subject and to report to the Department a plan which should remedy the evils which have so long been a reproach to our nation. If such were appointed, it ought to be composed of men of inflexible integrity, of large heart, of clear head, of strong will, who fear God and love man. I should like to see it composed of men so high in character that they are above the reach of the political demagogues.

I have written to you freely with all the frankness with which a Christian bishop has the right to write to the Chief Ruler of a great Christian Nation. My design has not been to complain of individuals, nor to make accusations. Bad as I believe some of the appointments to be, they are the fault of a political system. When I came to Minnesota I was startled at the degradation at my door. I gave these men missions;

God has blessed me, and I would count every trial I have had as a way of roses if I could save this people.

May God guide you and give you grace to order all things, so that the Government shall deal righteously with the Indian nations in its charge.

Your servant for Christ's sake,

H. B. WHIPPLE,
Bishop of Minnesota.

From Henry B. Whipple, *Lights and Shadows of a Long Episcopate* (New York: Macmillan Co., 1899), pp. 510–514.

Bibliography

I. MANUSCRIPT MATERIAL

National Archives. All National Archives material cited in this book is from Record Group 75, Records of the Bureau of Indian Affairs. Until August, 1907, separate registers of "Letters Sent" and "Letters Received" were maintained. The Letters Sent, 1824–1881, have been reproduced as National Archives Microfilm Publication 21; Letters Received, 1824–1880, have been reproduced as Microfilm Publication 234. The following have been used:

Letters Sent, 1847–1870 (Rolls 40–95).

Letters Received:

St. Peter's Agency, 1824–1870 (Rolls 757–766).
Santee Sioux Agency, 1871–1876 (Rolls 768–769).
Flandreau Special Agency, 1873–1876 (Roll 285).
Nebraska Agencies, 1876–1880 (Rolls 519–529).
Sisseton Agency, 1867–1880 (Rolls 824–831).
Devils Lake Agency, 1871–1880 (Rolls 281–284).
Fort Berthold Agency, 1867–1870 (Roll 292).
Winnebago Agency, 1864 (Roll 937).

Bureau of Indian Affairs records since 1881 have not been microfilmed. The following files were searched at the National Archives building:

Santee Agency, 1881–1917.
Sisseton Agency, 1887–1891, 1907–1939.
Fort Totten Agency, 1907–1939.
Sioux in Minnesota, 1884–1906.
Pipestone School Agency, 1908–1939.
Yankton Agency, 1917–1933.
Winnebago Agency, 1933–1939.
Flandreau School Agency, 1901–1939.

Although Bureau of Indian Affairs records in the National Archives nominally end with 1939, the arrangement of the Central Classified Files is such that many files contain letters from the 1940's. Most records later than 1939, however, are located at the Federal Records Center, Alexandria, Virginia, or at the Bureau of Indian Affairs Central Office in Washington. Selected items from the following jurisdictions have been used at these depositories or at the Minneapolis Area Office:

Winnebago Agency
Sisseton Agency
Consolidated Turtle Mountain Agency
Flandreau School Agency
Pipestone School Agency
Minnesota Agency
Minneapolis Area Office
Aberdeen Area Office

Minnesota Historical Society. Relevant portions of the following manuscript collections have been searched:

Pond Papers, 1833–1891.
Riggs Papers, 1843–1870.
Taliaferro Papers, 1813–1868.
Whipple Papers, 1833–1908.
Williamson Papers, 1834–1878.

The Minnesota Historical Society also has a typewritten copy of "History Prairie Island Sioux, Begun by Thomas Rouillard—Related by Eliza Wells and translated by Grandson, Norman Richard Campbell," part of a family record kept in the Dakota language by a leading Prairie Island family.

Miscellaneous Manuscripts.
LEACH, DUANE M. "The Santee Sioux, 1866–1890." Master's thesis, University of South Dakota, 1959.
Untitled manuscript by A. A. Johnson, on the Prairie Island Sioux, in the Goodhue County Historical Society, Red Wing, Minn.

2. GOVERNMENT PUBLICATIONS

Federal Government.
BUREAU OF INDIAN AFFAIRS (Prairie Island Community Council). "Background Data Relating to the Sioux Indians in the Southern Part of Minnesota," MS.
CARTER, CLARENCE E., COMP. AND ED. *The Territorial Papers of the United States.* Washington: Government Printing Office, 1934–
COMMISSIONER OF INDIAN AFFAIRS. *Annual Reports.* 1849–1907.
Congressional Globe. 1866.
Congressional Record. 1949–1955.
Constitution and Bylaws for the Flandreau Santee Sioux Tribe, South Dakota. Washington: Government Printing Office, 1936.

Constitution and Bylaws of the Lower Sioux Indian Community in Minnesota. Washington: Government Printing Office, 1936.

Constitution and Bylaws of the Prairie Island Indian Community in Minnesota. Washington: Government Printing Office, 1936.

Constitution and Bylaws of the Santee Sioux Tribe of the Sioux Nation in the State of Nebraska. Washington: Government Printing Office, 1936.

Corporate Charter of the Flandreau Santee Sioux Tribe, South Dakota. Washington: Government Printing Office, 1937.

Corporate Charter of the Lower Sioux Indian Community in Minnesota. Washington: Government Printing Office, 1937.

Corporate Charter of the Prairie Island Indian Community in Minnesota. Washington: Government Printing Office, 1938.

Corporate Charter of the Santee Sioux Tribe of Nebraska. Washington: Government Printing Office, 1936.

DEPARTMENT OF THE INTERIOR. *Reports*, September 1960. *United States Indian Population and Land: 1960.*

DEPARTMENT OF HEALTH, EDUCATION, AND WELFARE, Public Health Service. *Indians on Federal Reservations in the United States: A Digest.* Part 3, 1959.

DEPARTMENT OF HEALTH, EDUCATION, AND WELFARE, Public Health Service, Division of Indian Health (Bemidji, Minn., Office). "Basic Data: Prairie Island Sioux Community," MS.

HODGE, FREDERICK W. *Handbook of the American Indians North of Mexico.* Bureau of American Ethnology Bulletins, No. 20. Washington, 1910.

KAPPLER, CHARLES J., COMP. *Indian Affairs, Laws and Treaties.* Vols. I and II. Washington: Government Printing Office, 1904.

ROYCE, CHARLES C. *Indian Land Cessions in the United States.* Bureau of American Ethnology, Annual Reports, No. 18, Pt. 1. Washington, 1899.

SECRETARY OF THE INTERIOR. *Annual Reports.* 1911–1938.

U. S. CENSUS. *Population.* 1930, 1940, 1950, 1960.

———. *Condition of the Indians, Minnesota.* 1890.

U. S. *Statutes at Large.*

The War of the Rebellion: A Compilation of the Official Records of the Union and Confederate Armies. 130 vols. Washington: Government Printing Office, 1886–1901.

25th Cong., 3rd Sess., *H. Ex. Doc. 103.*

26th Cong., 1st Sess., *S. Doc. 126.*

27th Cong., 2nd Sess., *S. Doc. 1.*

28th Cong., 1st Sess., *S. Doc. 1.*

29th Cong., 2nd Sess., *H. Ex. Doc. 4.*

30th Cong., 1st Sess., *H. Doc. 1.*

30th Cong., 1st Sess., *H. Ex. Doc. 8.*

30th Cong., 2nd Sess., *H. Ex. Doc. 1.*
31st Cong., 1st Sess., *S. Ex. Doc. 1.*
31st Cong., 2nd Sess., *S. Ex. Doc. 1.*
32nd Cong., 2nd Sess., *H. Ex. Doc. 1.*
33rd Cong., 1st Sess., *S. Ex. Doc. 1.*
33rd Cong., 1st Sess., *S. Ex. Doc. 61.*
34th Cong., 1st and 2nd Sess., *S. Ex. Doc. 1.*
35th Cong., 1st Sess., *H. Ex. Doc. 2.*
48th Cong., 1st Sess., *H. Ex. Doc. 71.*
50th Cong., 1st Sess., *H. Ex. Doc. 228.*
50th Cong., 2nd Sess., *H. Ex. Doc. 61.*
53rd Cong., 3rd Sess., *S. Ex. Doc. 79.*
54th Cong., 2nd Sess., *S. Rpt. 1362.*
82nd Cong., 2nd Sess., *H. Rpt. 2503.*
83rd Cong., 2nd Sess., *H. Rpt. 2680.*

State and County.

Minnesota in the Civil and Indian Wars 1861–1865. 2 vols. Comp., ed., and pub. under the supervision of the Board of Commissioners for the State. St. Paul: Pioneer Press Co., 1890 and 1893.

GOVERNOR'S INTERRACIAL COMMISSION OF MINNESOTA. *The Indian in Minnesota.* [St. Paul?], 1947, 1952.

MINNESOTA *Executive Documents.* 1862–1887.

Report of the 1958 Minnesota Interim Committee on Indian Affairs, 1959.

DAKOTA COUNTY (Minn.) Register of Deeds. Miscellaneous Records, Book "Q"; Abstract Book.

GOODHUE COUNTY (Minn.) Board of Commissioners. "Proceedings," 1888, 1935.

LIST OF INDIANS AT PRAIRIE ISLAND, filed October 21, 1890, in Goodhue County Auditor's Office.

REDWOOD COUNTY (Minn.) Register of Deeds. Deed Records 10 and 19.
Some information was also provided orally by the Registers of Deeds and Welfare officers of Scott and Yellow Medicine counties, Minnesota, and Knox County, Nebraska.

Canadian.

DOMINION OF CANADA. *Annual Report of the Department of Indian Affairs,* 1904.

Traditional Linguistic and Cultural Affiliations of Canadian Indian Bands. Ottawa: Indian Affairs Branch, Department of Citizenship and Immigration, 1964.

3. NEWSPAPERS

Cannon Falls (Minn.) *Beacon.*
Central Republican (Faribault, Minn.).

Faribault *Democrat.*
Faribault *Republican.*
Goodhue County Republican (Red Wing, Minn.).
Granite Falls *Tribune.*
Mankato (Minn.) *Independent.*
Mankato *Weekly Record* (published as *Semi-Weekly Record* July 1860–Nov. 1862).
Mankato *Weekly Union.*
Minnesota Pioneer (St. Paul), 1849–1855.
Minneapolis *Sunday Tribune.*
Moody County Enterprise (Flandreau, S. Dak.).
Morton (Minn.) *Enterprise.*
NCAI Sentinel.
New York *Times.*
Niobrara (Nebr.) *Pioneer.*
Niobrara *Tribune.*
Pioneer and Democrat (St. Paul), 1855–1862.
Red Wing *Argus.*
Red Wing *Daily Republican.*
Red Wing *Daily Republican Eagle.*
Red Wing *Sentinel.*
Redwood Falls *Sun.*
Redwood Reveille (Redwood Falls, Minn.).
St. Paul *Daily Times.*
St. Paul *Pioneer,* 1862–1875.
St. Paul *Pioneer Press,* 1875–
Scott County Argus (name changed to Shakopee *Argus* September 18, 1884).
Sisseton (S. Dak.) *Courier.*
Union and Dakotaian (Yankton, S. Dak.).
Word Carrier (Santee, Nebr.).

4. BOOKS

ADAMS, ARTHUR T., ED. *The Explorations of Pierre Esprit Radisson.* Minneapolis: Ross and Haines, 1961.
AMERICAN INDIAN CHICAGO CONFERENCE. *Declaration of Indian Purpose.* Chicago: American Indian Chicago Conference, 1961.
ANDREAS, A. T., ED. *An Illustrated Historical Atlas of the State of Minnesota.* Chicago: Lakeside Building, 1874.
ANDREWS, ALICE E., ED. *Recollections of Christopher C. Andrews: 1829–1922.* Cleveland: Arthur H. Clark Co., 1928.
BARTON, WINIFRED W. *John P. Williamson, a Brother to the Sioux.* Chicago: Fleming H. Revell Co., 1919.
BELTRAMI, J. C. [GIACOMO CONSTANTINO]. *A Pilgrimage in America.* Chicago: Quadrangle Books, 1962.

BISHOP, HARRIET E. *Floral Home; or First Years in Minnesota.* New York: Sheldon, Blakeman, and Co., 1857.

BLAIR, EMMA HELEN, ED. *The Indian Tribes of the Upper Mississippi Valley and Region of the Great Lakes.* 2 vols. Cleveland: Arthur H. Clark Co., 1911.

BRYANT, CHARLES S., AND ABEL B. MURCH. *A History of the Great Massacre by the Sioux Indians in Minnesota.* Cincinnati: Rickey and Carroll, 1864.

BUCK, DANIEL. *Indian Outbreaks.* Mankato: Pioneer Press Co., 1904.

CARVER, JONATHAN. *Three Years Travels Through the Interior Parts of North America.* Philadelphia: Key and Simpson, 1796.

CATLIN, GEORGE. *Letters and Notes on the Manners, Customs, and Conditions of the North American Indians.* Philadelphia: J. W. Bradley, 1869.

CHARLEVOIX, PIERRE F. X. *History and General Description of New France.* Trans. by John Gilmary Shea. 6 vols. New York: John Gilmary Shea, 1866–1872.

COLLIER, JOHN. *From Every Zenith.* Denver: Alan Swallow, 1963.

CONNOLLY, ALONZO P. *A Thrilling Narrative of the Minnesota Massacre and the Sioux War of 1862–63.* Chicago: A. P. Connolly, 1896.

COUES, ELLIOTT, ED. *The Expeditions of Zebulon Montgomery Pike.* 2 vols. New York: Francis P. Harper, 1895.

CROSS, MARION E., ED. *Father Louis Hennepin's Description of Louisiana.* Minneapolis: University of Minnesota Press, 1938.

CURTISS-WEDGE, FRANKLYN, ED. *History of Rice and Steele Counties.* 2 vols. Chicago: H. C. Cooper, Jr., and Co., 1910.

EASTMAN, CHARLES A. *From the Deep Woods to Civilization.* Boston: Little, Brown and Co., 1926.

———. *Indian Boyhood.* New York, McClure, 1902.

FEATHERSTONHAUGH, GEORGE W. *A Canoe Voyage up the Minnay Sotor.* London: R. Bentley, 1847.

FEY, HAROLD E., AND D'ARCY MCNICKLE. *Indians and Other Americans.* New York: Harper and Brothers, 1959.

FOLSOM, W. H. C. *Fifty Years in the Northwest.* St. Paul: Pioneer Press Co., 1888.

FOLWELL, WILLIAM W. *A History of Minnesota.* 2 vols. St. Paul: Minnesota Historical Society. Vol. I, 1956; Vol. II, 1961.

FOREMAN, GRANT. *The Last Trek of the Indians.* Chicago: University of Chicago Press, 1946.

FRIDLEY, RUSSELL W., LEOTA M. KELLETT, AND JUNE D. HOLMQUIST, EDS. *Charles E. Flandrau and the Defense of New Ulm.* New Ulm, Minn.: Brown County Historical Society, 1962.

FRITZ, HENRY E. *The Movement for Indian Assimilation, 1860–1890.* Philadelphia: University of Pennsylvania Press, 1963.

GRIDLEY, MARION E., ED. *Indians of Today.* 3d ed. Chicago: The Council Fire, 1960.

HAGAN, WILLIAM T. *The Sac and Fox Indians.* Norman: University of Oklahoma Press, 1958.

[Hancock, Joseph W.] *Goodhue County, Minnesota, Past and Present.* Red Wing: Red Wing Printing Co., 1893.

Hansen, Marcus L. *Old Fort Snelling, 1819–1858.* Minneapolis: Ross and Haines, 1958.

Harding, Walter, ed. *Thoreau's Minnesota Journey: Two Documents.* Geneseo, N.Y.: Thoreau Society, 1962.

Hassrick, Royal B. *The Sioux: Life and Customs of a Warrior Society.* Norman: University of Oklahoma Press, 1964.

Heard, Isaac V. D. *History of the Sioux War and Massacres of 1862 and 1863.* New York: Harper and Brothers, 1863.

Hennepin, Louis. *A Description of Louisiana.* Ed. by John Gilmary Shea. New York: John Gilmary Shea, 1880.

History of Goodhue County . . . . Red Wing: Wood, Alley and Co., 1878.

Hubbard, Lucius F., and Return I. Holcombe. *Minnesota in Three Centuries.* 4 vols. Mankato: Publishing Society of Minnesota, 1908.

Hughes, Thomas. *History of Blue Earth County.* Chicago: Middle West Publishing Co., [1901].

———. *Indian Chiefs of Southern Minnesota.* Mankato: Free Press Co., 1927.

———. *Old Traverse des Sioux.* St. Peter, Minn.: Herald Publishing Co., 1929.

Hyde, George E. *Spotted Tail's Folk: A History of the Brulé Sioux.* Norman: University of Oklahoma Press, 1961.

James, Harry C. *The Hopi Indians.* Caldwell, Idaho: Caxton Printers, 1956.

Jones, Robert Huhn. *The Civil War in the Northwest.* Norman: University of Oklahoma Press, 1960.

Keating, William H. *Narrative of an Expedition to the Sources of St. Peter's River* . . . . Minneapolis: Ross and Haines, 1959.

Kinzie, Juliette A. *Wau-bun, the Early Day in the Northwest.* Philadelphia: J. B. Lippincott Co., 1873.

Laviolette, Gontran, O. M. I. *The Sioux Indians in Canada.* Regina: Marian Press, 1944.

Le Duc, William G. *Minnesota Year Book for 1852.* St. Paul: W. G. Le Duc, 1852.

Lewis, Henry. *Making a Motion Picture in 1848.* Ed. by Bertha L. Heilbron. St. Paul: Minnesota Historical Society, 1936.

McConkey, Harriet E. Bishop. *Dakota War Whoop; or Indian Massacres and War in Minnesota, of 1862-'3.* St. Paul: D. D. Merrill, 1863.

McDermott, John Francis. *Seth Eastman: Pictorial Historian of the Indian.* Norman: University of Oklahoma Press, 1961.

Macgregor, Gordon. *Warriors Without Weapons.* Chicago: University of Chicago Press, 1946.

McKenney, Thomas L., and James Hall. *The Indian Tribes of North America.* Ed. by Frederick Webb Hodge. 3 vols. Edinburgh: J. Grant, 1933.

McLAUGHLIN, JAMES. *My Friend the Indian*. Boston: Houghton Mifflin Co., 1910.

McNICKLE, D'ARCY. *The Indian Tribes of the United States: Ethnic and Cultural Survival*. London: Oxford University Press, 1962.

MANYPENNY, GEORGE W. *Our Indian Wards*. Cincinnati: Robert Clarke and Co., 1880.

MAYER, FRANK BLACKWELL. *With Pen and Pencil on the Frontier in 1851*. Ed. by Bertha L. Heilbron. St. Paul: Minnesota Historical Society, 1932.

MERIAM, LEWIS, *et al. The Problem of Indian Administration*. Baltimore: Johns Hopkins Press, 1928.

NEILL, EDWARD D. *History of Dakota County and the City of Hastings*. Minneapolis: North Star Publishing Co., 1881.

——. *The History of Minnesota*. Philadelphia: J. B. Lippincott and Co., 1858.

——. *History of the Minnesota Valley, Including the Explorers and Pioneers of Minnesota*. Minneapolis: North Star Publishing Co., 1882.

——. *History of Rice County*. Minneapolis: Minnesota Historical Co., 1882.

NUTE, GRACE LEE. *Caesars of the Wilderness*. New York: D. Appleton-Century Co., 1943.

OEHLER, C. M. *The Great Sioux Uprising*. New York: Oxford University Press, 1959.

OLSON, JAMES C. *History of Nebraska*. Lincoln: University of Nebraska Press, 1955.

——. *Red Cloud and the Sioux Problem*. Lincoln: University of Nebraska Press, 1965.

PEARCE, ROY HARVEY. *The Savages of America: A Study of the Indian and the Idea of Civilization*. Baltimore: Johns Hopkins Press, 1953.

PETERSEN, WILLIAM J. *Steamboating on the Upper Mississippi*. Iowa City: State Historical Society of Iowa, 1937.

Plat Book of Scott County, Minnesota. [Philadelphia]: North West Publishing Co., 1898.

POND, SAMUEL W., JR. *Two Volunteer Missionaries Among the Dakotas*. Boston and Chicago: Congregational Sunday-School and Publishing Society, 1893.

PRESCOTT, PHILANDER. *The Recollections of Philander Prescott: Frontiersman of the Old Northwest*. Ed. by Donald Dean Parker. Lincoln: University of Nebraska Press, 1966.

PRUCHA, FRANCIS PAUL. *American Indian Policy in the Formative Years*. Cambridge: Harvard University Press, 1962.

RADISSON, PIERRE ESPRIT. *Voyages of Peter Esprit Radisson*. Ed. by Gideon Scull. New York: Peter Smith, 1943.

RIGGS, MARY BUEL. *Early Days at Santee*. Santee, Nebr.: Santee Normal Training School Press, 1928.

RIGGS, STEPHEN RETURN, ED. *Grammar and Dictionary of the Dakota Language.* Washington: Smithsonian Institution, 1852.

———. *Mary and I: Forty Years with the Sioux.* Boston: Congregational Sunday-School and Publishing Society, 1880.

———. *Tah-koo Wah-kan; or, the Gospel Among the Dakotas.* Boston: Congregational Publishing Society, 1869.

ROBINSON, DOANE. *A History of the Dakota or Sioux Indians.* Minneapolis: Ross and Haines, 1956. Originally published in 1904 as Vol. II of *South Dakota Historical Collections.*

RODDIS, LOUIS H. *The Indian Wars of Minnesota.* Cedar Rapids: Torch Press, 1956.

ROSE, ARTHUR P. *History of Jackson County, Minnesota.* Jackson: Northern Publishing Co., 1910.

RUSK, RALPH L., ED. *The Letters of Ralph Waldo Emerson.* 6 vols. New York: Columbia University Press, 1939.

SCHELL, HERBERT S. *History of South Dakota.* Lincoln: University of Nebraska Press, 1961.

SCHOOLCRAFT, HENRY ROWE. *Information Respecting the History, Condition and Prospects of the Indian Tribes of the United States.* 6 vols. Philadelphia: Lippincott, Grambo and Co., 1852–1857.

———. *Narrative Journal of Travels Through the Northwestern Regions of the United States ... in the Year 1820.* Ed. by Mentor L. Williams. East Lansing: Michigan State University Press, 1953.

SHARP, ABBIE GARDNER. *History of the Spirit Lake Massacre.* Des Moines: Mills and Co., 1885.

SMITH, ALICE ELIZABETH. *James Duane Doty: Frontier Promoter.* Madison: State Historical Society of Wisconsin, 1954.

SNELLING, WILLIAM J. *Tales of the Northwest.* Minneapolis: University of Minnesota Press, 1936.

TANNER, GEORGE C. *Fifty Years of Church Work in the Diocese of Minnesota 1857–1907.* St. Paul: Published by the Committee, 1909.

TEAKLE, THOMAS. *The Spirit Lake Massacre.* Iowa City: State Historical Society of Iowa, 1918.

THOMPSON, LAURA. *Culture in Crisis.* New York: Harper and Brothers, 1950.

THWAITES, REUBEN GOLD, ED. *The Jesuit Relations and Allied Documents.* 73 vols. New York: Pageant Book Co., 1959.

TURNER, KATHARINE C. *Red Men Calling on the Great White Father.* Norman: University of Oklahoma Press, 1951.

UTLEY, ROBERT M. *The Last Days of the Sioux Nation.* New Haven: Yale University Press, 1963.

WALL, OSCAR GARRETT. *Recollections of the Sioux Massacre.* Lake City, Minn.: Published by the Author, 1909.

WALLIS, WILSON D. *The Canadian Dakota.* Vol. XLI of Anthropological

Papers of the American Museum of Natural History. New York: American Museum of Natural History, 1947.

WELSH, WILLIAM, COMP. *Taopi and His Friends, or the Indians' Wrongs and Rights.* Philadelphia: Claxton, Remsen and Heffelfinger, 1869.

WEST, NATHANIEL. *The Ancestry, Life, and Times of Hon. Henry Hastings Sibley, LL.D.* St. Paul: Pioneer Press Publishing Co., 1889.

WHIPPLE, HENRY B. *Lights and Shadows of a Long Episcopate.* New York: Macmillan Co., 1899.

WINCHELL, NEWTON H. *The Aborigines of Minnesota.* St. Paul: Pioneer Co., 1911.

5. PERIODICALS

ACKERMAN, GERTRUDE W. "Joseph Renville of Lac qui Parle," *Minnesota History*, XII (1931), 231–246.

ADAMS, MRS. ANN. "Early Days at Red River Settlement and Fort Snelling," *Minnesota Historical Collections*, VI (1894), 75–115.

ADAMS, MOSES N. "The Sioux Outbreak in the Year 1862, with Notes of Missionary Work Among the Sioux," *Minnesota Historical Collections*, IX (1898–1900), 431–452.

ANDERSON, THOMAS G. "Narrative of Capt. Thomas G. Anderson," *Wisconsin Historical Collections*, IX (1882), 137–206. Reprinted 1909 by State Historical Society of Wisconsin, Madison.

BABCOCK, WILLOUGHBY M., JR. "Major Lawrence Taliaferro, Indian Agent," *Mississippi Valley Historical Review*, XI (December 1924), 358–375.

BLAKELEY, RUSSELL. "History of the Discovery of the Mississippi River and the Advent of Commerce in Minnesota," *Minnesota Historical Collections*, VIII (1895–1898), 303–414.

BLEGEN, THEODORE C. "The Pond Brothers," *Minnesota History*, XV (1934), 273–281.

———, ed. "Two Missionaries in the Sioux Country," *Minnesota History*, XXI (1940), 15–32, 158–175, 272–283.

"The British Regime in Wisconsin—1760–1800," *Wisconsin Historical Collections*, XVIII (1908), 223–468.

BRYMNER, DOUGLAS. "Capture of Fort McKay, Prairie du Chien, 1814," *Wisconsin Historical Collections*, XI (1888), 254–270.

BUELL, SALMON A. "Judge Flandrau in the Defense of New Ulm During the Sioux Outbreak of 1862," *Minnesota Historical Collections*, X (1900–1904), 783–818.

"The Bulger Papers," *Wisconsin Historical Collections*, XIII (1895), 10–153.

"Captivity Among the Sioux: The Story of Mary Schwandt," *Minnesota Historical Collections*, VI (1894), 461–474.

"Captivity Among the Sioux: The Story of Nancy McClure," *Minnesota Historical Collections*, VI (1894), 438–460.

CONNORS, JOSEPH. "The Elusive Hero of Redwood Ferry," *Minnesota History*, XXXIV (June 1955), 233–238.

CRUIKSHANK, ERNEST ALEXANDER. "Robert Dickson, the Indian Trader," *Wisconsin Historical Collections*, XII (1892), 133–153.

DANIELS, ASA W. "Reminiscences of Little Crow," *Minnesota Historical Collections*, XII (1905–1908), 513–530.

———. "Reminiscences of the Little Crow Uprising," *Minnesota Historical Collections*, XV (1909–1914), 323–336.

"Diary Kept by Lewis C. Paxson, Stockton, N.J.," *North Dakota Historical Collections*, II (1908), Pt. 2, 102–163.

"Dickson and Grignon Papers—1812–1815," *Wisconsin Historical Collections*, XI (1888), 271–315.

DOZIER, EDWARD P., GEORGE E. SIMPSON, AND J. MILTON YINGER. "The Integration of Americans of Indian Descent," American Academy of Political and Social Science *Annals*, CCCXI (1957), 158–165.

DURRIE, DANIEL STEELE. "Jonathan Carver, and 'Carver's Grant,'" *Wisconsin Historical Collections*, VI (1872), 220–270. Reprinted 1908 by State Historical Society of Wisconsin, Madison.

FORSYTH, THOMAS. "Journal of a Voyage from St. Louis to the Falls of St. Anthony, in 1819," *Wisconsin Historical Collections*, VI (1872), 188–219. Reprinted 1908 by State Historical Society of Wisconsin, Madison.

"The French Regime in Wisconsin 1634–1727," *Wisconsin Historical Collections*, XVI (1902), 1–477.

"The French Regime in Wisconsin, 1727–1748," *Wisconsin Historical Collections*, XVII (1906), 1–518.

"The French Regime in Wisconsin, 1743–1760," *Wisconsin Historical Collections*, XVIII (1908), 1–222.

GATES, CHARLES M. "The Lac qui Parle Indian Mission," *Minnesota History*, XVI (1935), 133–151.

GLUEK, ALVIN C., JR. "The Sioux Uprising: A Problem in International Relations," *Minnesota History*, XXXIV (Winter 1955), 317–324.

GRIGNON, AUGUSTIN. "Seventy-two Years of Recollections of Wisconsin," *Wisconsin Historical Collections*, III (1857), 197–295. Reprinted 1904 by State Historical Society of Wisconsin, Madison.

HANCOCK, JOSEPH W. "Missionary Work at Red Wing, 1849 to 1852," *Minnesota Historical Collections*, X (1900–1904), 165–178.

HOLCOMBE, RETURN I., ED. "A Sioux Story of the War," *Minnesota Historical Collections*, VI (1894), 382–400.

HOWARD, JAMES H. "Pan-Indian Culture of Oklahoma," *Scientific Monthly*, LXXXI (November 1955), 215–220.

HUGHES, THOMAS. "Causes and Results of the Inkpaduta Massacre," *Minnesota Historical Collections*, XII (1905–1908), 264–269.

HUMPHREY, JOHN AMES. "Boyhood Reminiscences of Life Among the Dakotas and the Massacre in 1862," *Minnesota Historical Collections*, XV (1909–1914), 337–348.

KANE, LUCILE M. "The Sioux Treaties and the Traders," *Minnesota History*, XXXII (June 1951), 65–80.

KELLOGG, LOUISE PHELPS. "Fort Beauharnois," *Minnesota History*, VIII (September 1927), 232–246.

KELSEY, CYNTHIA. "Changing Social Relationships in an Eastern Dakota Community," Minnesota Academy of Science *Proceedings*, XXIV (1956), 12–19.

KINGSBURY, DAVID L. "Sully's Expedition Against the Sioux, in 1864," *Minnesota Historical Collections*, VIII (1895–1898), 449–462.

LARPENTEUR, AUGUST L. "Recollections of the City and People of St. Paul, 1843–1898," *Minnesota Historical Collections*, IX (1898–1900), 363–394.

LASS, WILLIAM E. "The 'Moscow Expedition,'" *Minnesota History*, XXXIX (Summer 1965), 227–240.

———. "The Removal from Minnesota of the Sioux and Winnebago Indians," *Minnesota History*, XXXVIII (December 1963), 353–364.

"Le Sueur, The Explorer of the Minnesota River," *Minnesota Historical Collections*, I (1850–1856), 261–277.

"Lieut. James Gorrell's Journal," *Wisconsin Historical Collections*, I (1855), 24–48. Reprinted 1903 by State Historical Society of Wisconsin, Madison.

McNICKLE, D'ARCY. "Rescuing Sisseton," *The American Indian*, III (Spring 1946), 21–27.

"Memoir of the Sioux," trans. by John H. Ames and ed. by Edward D. Neill, *Macalester College Contributions*, First Series, No. 10 (1890), 223–238.

"Memorial Notices of Rev. Gideon H. Pond," *Minnesota Historical Collections*, III (1870–1880), 356–371.

MEYER, ROY W. "The Establishment of the Santee Reservation, 1866–1869," *Nebraska History*, XLV (March 1964), 59–97.

———. "The Prairie Island Community: A Remnant of Minnesota Sioux," *Minnesota History*, XXXVII (September 1961), 271–282.

"Narration of a Friendly Sioux, by Snana, the Rescuer of Mary Schwandt," *Minnesota Historical Collections*, IX (1898–1900), 427–430.

"Narrative of Paul Mazakootemane," trans. by Rev. S. R. Riggs, *Minnesota Historical Collections*, III (1870–1880), 82–90.

NEILL, EDWARD D. "Dakota Land and Dakota Life," *Minnesota Historical Collections*, I (1850–1856), 205–240.

———. "Relation of M. Penicaut," *Minnesota Historical Collections*, III (1870–1880), 1–12.

"Papers from the Canadian Archives, 1778–1783," *Wisconsin Historical Collections*, XI (1888), 97–212.

"Papers from the Canadian Archives, 1767–1814," *Wisconsin Historical Collections*, XII (1892), 23–132.

PETERSEN, WILLIAM J. "The 'Virginia,' the 'Clermont' of the Upper Mississippi," *Minnesota History*, IX (December 1928), 347–362.

PFALLER, LOUIS, O. S. B. "The Forging of an Indian Agent," *North Dakota History*, XXXIV (Winter 1967), 62–76.

POND, SAMUEL W. "The Dakotas or Sioux in Minnesota as They Were in 1834," *Minnesota Historical Collections*, XII (1905–1908), 319–501.

Pond, Samuel W., "Indian Warfare in Minnesota," *Minnesota Historical Collections*, III (1870–1880), 129–138.

Prescott, Philander. "Autobiography and Reminiscences of Philander Prescott," *Minnesota Historical Collections*, VI (1894), 475–491.

Provinse, John, et al. "The American Indian in Transition," *American Anthropologist*, LVI (June 1954), 387–394.

Relf, Frances H., ed. "Removal of the Sioux Indians from Minnesota" [letter from John P. Williamson, May 13, 1863], *Minnesota History Bulletin*, II (May 1918), 420–425.

Renville, Gabriel. "A Sioux Narrative of the Outbreak of 1862 and of Sibley's Expedition in 1863," *Minnesota Historical Collections*, X (1900–1904), 595–618.

Riggs, Stephen Return. "The Dakota Mission," *Minnesota Historical Collections*, III (1870–1880), 115–128.

———. "Dakota Portraits," ed. by Willoughby M. Babcock, Jr., *Minnesota History Bulletin*, II (November 1918), 481–568.

———. "Protestant Missions in the Northwest," *Minnesota Historical Collections*, VI (1894), 117–188.

Satterlee, Marion P. "Narratives of the Sioux War," *Minnesota Historical Collections*, XV (1909–1914), 349–370.

Sibley, Henry H. "Reminiscences, Historical and Personal," *Minnesota Historical Collections*, I (1850–1856), 374–396.

———. "Sketch of John Other Day," *Minnesota Historical Collections*, III (1870–1880), 99–102.

"Sioux Outbreak of 1862: Mrs. J. E. De Camp's Narrative of her Captivity," *Minnesota Historical Collections*, VI (1894), 354–380.

[Snelling, William Joseph?]. "Early Days at Prairie du Chien," *Wisconsin Historical Collections*, V (1868), 123–153. Reprinted 1907 by State Historical Society of Wisconsin, Madison.

[Snelling, William Joseph]. "Running the Gauntlet," *Minnesota Historical Collections*, I (1850–1856), 360–373.

Sterling, Everett W. "Moses N. Adams: A Missionary as Indian Agent," *Minnesota History*, XXXV (December 1956), 167–177.

Taliaferro, Lawrence. "Auto-Biography of Maj. Lawrence Taliaferro," *Minnesota Historical Collections*, VI (1894), 189–255.

"Taoyateduta Is Not a Coward," *Minnesota History*, XXXVIII (September 1962), 115.

Thompson, Hildegard. "Education Among American Indians: Institutional Aspects," *American Academy of Political and Social Science Annals*, CCCXI (May 1957), 95–104.

Trennery, Walter N. "The Shooting of Little Crow: Heroism or Murder?" *Minnesota History*, XXXVIII (September 1962), 150–153.

"Up the Mississippi in a Six-Oared Skiff in 1817," *Minnesota Historical Collections*, II (1860–1867), 9–88.

VAN CLEVE, CHARLOTTE OUISCONSIN. "A Reminiscence of Ft. Snelling," *Minnesota Historical Collections*, III (1870–1880), 76–81.

WARREN, WILLIAM W. "History of the Ojibway Nation," *Minnesota Historical Collections*, V (1885), 21–394.

WHITE, MRS. N. D. "Captivity Among the Sioux, August 18 to September 26, 1862," *Minnesota Historical Collections*, IX (1898–1900), 395–426.

WILFORD, LLOYD A. "The Prehistoric Indians of Minnesota," *Minnesota History*, XXV (June 1944), 153–157.

———. "The Prehistoric Indians of Minnesota: The Mille Lacs Aspect," *Minnesota History*, XXV (December 1944), 329–341.

WILLIAMS, J. FLETCHER. "A History of the City of St. Paul and of the County of Ramsey, Minnesota," *Minnesota Historical Collections*, IV (1876), 3–475.

WILSON, CHARLES C. "The Successive Chiefs Named Wabasha," *Minnesota Historical Collections*, XII (1905–1908), 504–512.

Index

Acton Township, Minn., 115, 122; massacre at, 114–115

Adams, Moses N., missionary at Traverse des Sioux, 91; agent at Sisseton, 204–208, 211, 214, 218, 231; conflict with scout party, 204–205; in charge of Flandreau colony, 247–249; influence on Sissetons, 328

Adams, Shubael P., 264–267

Afrahcootahs (Wahpekutes?), 16

Aid to Dependent Children (ADC), 312, 335

Aile Rouge, L', see Red Wing

Aiton, John F., 65

Aldrich, Cyrus, 140

Algonquins, 6, 16

Allen, S. E., 318

Allouez, Father Claude, 5

American Board of Commissioners for Foreign Missions, begin work with Sioux, 52, 65, 66; work with prisoners, 137; on Santee Reservation, 168, 175, 176, 178–179; succeeded by American Missionary Association, 190; on Sisseton Reservation, 204, 207, 214; at Flandreau, 247

American Fur Company, 36, 42, 59, 68, 70 n.

American Indian Chicago Conference, 357

American Missionary Association, 190, 312

American Revolution, 15, 18, 24, 28, 72

Anawangmani, Simon, 131

Apaches, 368 n.

Aquipaguetin, 7, 8

Arikaras, 232

Armstrong, Moses K., 250

Arrow, 34

Arthur, Chester A., 181, 182, 234

Ascension mission, 203, 206, 207

Assiniboins, viii, 16

Atkins, John D. C., 188, 189, 237, 285

Badlands, Battle of the, 136

Bailly, Alexis, 271 n.

Baird, Henry C., 185, 297

Baker, Fred A., 327, 328, 330

Balcombe, St. André Durand, 109, 149, 150, 151

Balmer, James W., 344–349, 351

Barton, Winifred W., 114 n.

Bazile Creek, 158–160, 164–165, 176, 178, 184

Beccasse, Le (Le Boucasse), 26

Beckwith, Paul, 231, 232, 233 n., 234

Bee, Bernard E., 98

Beeson, John, 144

Belknap, William W., 227

Bell, John, 73

Belland, Henry, Jr., 286

Beltrami, Giacomo Constantino, 44

Benedictine Order, 234

Bennett, Robert L., 296

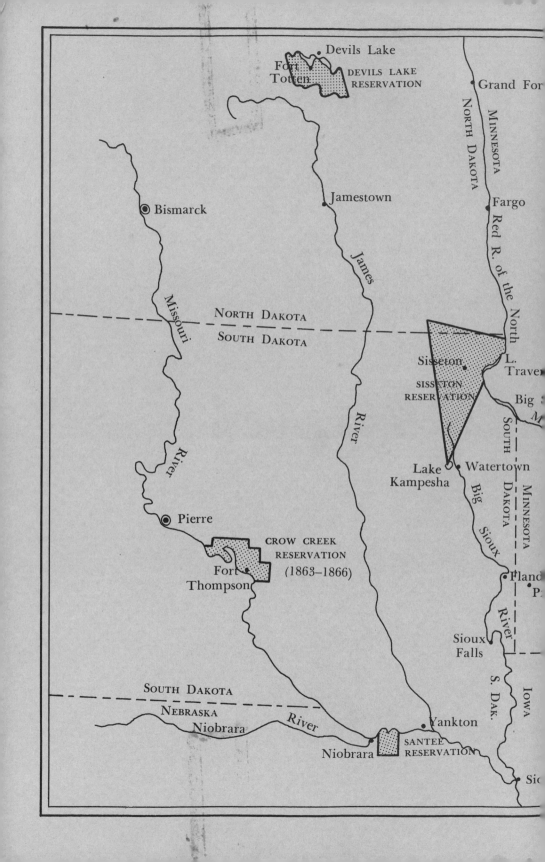